*Custom Edition for the University of New Mexico*

# MOSAICOS

## Spanish as a World Language

Matilde Olivella de Castells (Late)  /  Elizabeth E. Guzmán  /
Paloma Lapuerta  /  Judith E. Liskin-Gasparro

Taken from:

*Mosaicos: Spanish as a World Language*, Fifth Edition
by Matilde Olivella de Castells (Late), Elizabeth E. Guzmán, Paloma Lapuerta and Judith E.
Liskin-Gasparro

**Custom Publishing**

New York  Boston  San Francisco
London  Toronto  Sydney  Tokyo  Singapore  Madrid
Mexico City  Munich  Paris  Cape Town  Hong Kong  Montreal

**Pearson
Custom Publishing**
is a division of

www.pearsonhighered.com

ISBN 10: 0-558-37268-6
ISBN 13: 978-0-558-37268-2

# BRIEF CONTENTS

# SCOPE AND SEQUENCE

| Capítulo | Communicative objectives | A primera vista |
|---|---|---|

| Funciones y formas | Mosaicos | Enfoque cultural |
|---|---|---|

| Capítulo | Communicative objectives | A primera vista |
|---|---|---|

| Funciones y formas | Mosaicos | Enfoque cultural |
|---|---|---|

| Capítulo | Communicative objectives | A primera vista |
|---|---|---|

# PREFACE

## Welcome to the Fifth Edition of *Mosaicos*

Since the publication of its first edition more than a decade ago, *Mosaicos* has been widely acclaimed for its practical, communicative, culturally based approach to first-year Spanish. The approach has been refined over the course of several editions, and for this fifth edition we have been especially thorough in examining all aspects of the Student Text and all components of the *Mosaicos* program. The result is a fresh, twenty-first-century perspective on language teaching and learning in the context of a dynamic introduction to the Hispanic world and its people. We hope that both veteran users and those new to *Mosaicos* will discover a text that is richly contextualized, cognitively engaging, visually attractive, and readily accessible, accompanied by a wide array of resources that support student learning and make each class period valuable and enjoyable.

One of the hallmarks of the *Mosaicos* approach—and the rationale for the title—is the emphasis on the integration of the many different instructional strands that comprise a beginning Spanish course. We have made a special effort to ensure that this fifth edition effectively integrates elements that other programs often treat in isolation. We have gone farther than ever before in our effort to synthesize linguistic content with appropriate cultural contexts. We have refined and improved the open-ended *Situaciones* activities, in which students are asked to integrate their knowledge of grammatical structures and functions with thematically relevant vocabulary. Finally, we have made major revisions to the *Mosaicos* section of each chapter, in which students put linguistic and cultural knowledge together as they develop and practice their listening, speaking, reading, and writing skills.

*Mosaicos* reflects the wisdom and experience of the many expert language instructors who have used the program and have provided helpful suggestions over the years. But at a deeper level, it is grounded in current theories of language learning and in pedagogical principles embraced by most language instructors today. It presents vocabulary within communicative and cultural contexts. Its grammar sections move from meaning to form, providing an understanding of the language that is both functional and structural. It emphasizes the social aspects of language use by providing an abundance of carefully sequenced pair and group activities. It fosters awareness of the diversity of the Spanish-speaking world through photos, realia, maps, readings, and activities, as well as a new video program. By engaging students in the linguistic, cognitive, and social aspects of language learning, the distinctive *Mosaicos* approach draws on current knowledge about language learning to prepare first-year students to continue their study of Spanish language and culture at the intermediate level.

## Highlights of the Fifth Edition

While building on the strengths of earlier editions, the fifth edition of *Mosaicos* incorporates many new and remarkable features. With its focus on learning strategies and communicative functions, it provides students and instructors with more tools than ever before to enhance and enrich the learning experience.

### Vocabulary in Context

The *Mosaicos* program features a culturally and communicatively rich format for presenting and practicing new vocabulary. Through the two-page spread at the beginning of each chapter and in the *A primera vista* section that follows, students encounter new words in appropriate linguistic and cultural contexts.

The chapter-opening pages have been completely redesigned to provide a stimulating introduction both to the chapter theme and to the country or region that the chapter targets. New chapter titles highlight the text's active, functional approach to language learning, and abundant annotations on the chapter-opening pages guide instructors in introducing and recycling relevant vocabulary.

In the *A primera vista* section, new vocabulary is presented in contexts that reflect the chapter theme in various ways. Language samples, photos, line drawings, and realia are used to present new material, rather than word lists and translations. The activities that follow foster the use of new and previously learned vocabulary in natural, thematically relevant contexts. Special features include the following:

■ Boldface type is used within the language samples to highlight new words and phrases that students will need to learn to use actively. (A convenient list of these words and phrases is provided at the end of each chapter.)

■ Audio icons remind students that recorded versions of the language samples are available in the *Mosaicos* audio program.

■ *Cultura* boxes (many new to this edition) raise awareness of the cultural contexts in which the language is used and help students learn the skills of close observation and interpretation of cultural products.

■ *En otras palabras* boxes (all new to this edition) give examples of regional variations in the language.

## Grammar as Function and Meaning

In the newly renamed *Funciones y formas* section of each chapter, grammar is presented as a means to effective communication. The bulleted explanations—clear, concise, and easy to understand—are designed to be studied at home, although their integration into the main body of the text enables students to use them for quick reference as they practice communication in class.

■ Visuals and brief language samples are now used consistently to introduce new structures in meaningful contexts. The new structures are highlighted in boldface type.

■ Short comprehension-based activities (all new to this edition) draw students' attention to the connection between meaning and linguistic form, providing a bridge from *función* to *forma*. These *Piénselo* activities are designed to help students develop their ability to think about how each structure communicates meaning by means of particular forms.

■ A carefully designed sequence of communicative activities (many new or revised for this edition) follow the bulleted grammatical explanations. These activities focus attention on the communicative purpose of the linguistic structures while invoking culturally relevant contexts. All activities require students to process meaning as well as form so that they develop confidence in speaking and skill in using their linguistic knowledge to gather information, answer questions, and resolve problems.

■ A large number of open-ended *Situaciones* activities (many new or revised for this edition) prompt students to integrate relevant grammatical structures with contexts drawn from the chapter theme. Two *Situaciones* role-plays are now provided for each grammar topic, and the format of these activities has been standardized so that there are always two roles (Role A and Role B). *En directo* boxes introduce colloquial expressions and encourage students to use them in the *Situaciones* and other communicative activities.

■ Strategically placed *Lengua* boxes offer succinct grammatical information when it is needed to support self-expression.

■ The grammatical scope and sequence has been modified in order to meet the communicative needs of beginning students more effectively. The *Algo más* boxes used in the fourth edition to present new structures have been eliminated; all essential structures are now given the full range of explanation and activities. Major topics, such as the preterit and imperfect, **ser/estar**, and object pronouns, are recycled to enhance learning, and basic topics such as regular verbs and **gustar** are presented earlier to spread essential structures more evenly over the book's fifteen chapters.

## Integrated Culture

The fifth edition of *Mosaicos* builds on the successful integration of culture and language of previous editions. Each chapter focuses on a specific country or region, and numerous references to that country or region appear in the chapter's language samples, photos, maps, and realia. Related cultural content is interwoven throughout the activities and readings.

■ A newly designed two-page chapter opener highlights the country or region that is the focus of the chapter. It includes a relevant work of art as well as maps and photos. A new warm-up activity (called *A vista de pájaro*) encourages students to process the visually presented information while accessing relevant prior knowledge. Numerous annotations offer instructors factual, conversational, and linguistic suggestions to pique students' interest and ease them into the chapter.

■ The *Enfoque cultural* section of each chapter has new readings and accompanying activities. The first set of activities is available online as well as in the textbook. A final activity asks students to use the reading as a point of departure for expanding and sharing their knowledge. The standardized format of this section makes it possible for students to work with the readings independently so that class time may be devoted to the cultural content.

■ Brief *Cultura* boxes found throughout each chapter explain cultural products, practices, and perspectives, making the cultural contexts of the vocabulary and grammatical activities meaningful and accessible to students.

## Engaging New Video

A completely new video, entitled *Diarios de bicicleta*, has been scripted and filmed specifically to accompany the fifth edition of *Mosaicos*. Each episode of this engaging, often humorous video reflects the corresponding chapter's communicative objectives, recycling vocabulary and previewing functions and forms. The story line revolves around four recurring characters, but each episode is self-contained and independent of other episodes.

■ The video segment for each chapter includes short excerpts that highlight the language functions introduced in the *Funciones y formas* section of the text.

■ Pre-viewing, viewing, and post-viewing activities (all new to this edition) are provided in the Student Text in a special section of each chapter entitled *En acción*. Additional activities may be found in the Student Activities Manual.

## A Four-Skills Synthesis

Like its predecessors, the fifth edition devotes a prominent section of each chapter to the development and practice of communication skills. These newly streamlined *Mosaicos* sections provide students with a unique opportunity to bring together the chapter's thematic content and vocabulary with its linguistic structures and cultural focus. New features, texts, and activities enhance the effectiveness of this aspect of the program.

■ Specific strategies are now presented in each chapter for each of the four skills (listening, speaking, reading, and writing). The strategies build on each other within and across chapters. Activities are designed so that students systematically practice implementing the strategies presented.

■ New listening activities have been created for the *A escuchar* sections. The content and genre of the listening texts, as well as the accompanying strategies, consistently support the chapter theme.

■ In the *A conversar* sections, specific strategies are now provided for speaking as they are for other skill areas. The speaking activities that follow encourage structured pair interaction and help students develop interpersonal speaking skills.

■ The streamlined *A leer* sections now include only one reading each. The reading selections (many new to this edition) are drawn largely from authentic texts. They reflect a variety of discourse types, ranging from expository to journalistic to literary. Activities linked to the reading strategy boost students' comprehension and reading skills.

■ The process writing activities in the *A escribir* sections have been revised so that the pre- and post-writing activities now guide students through critical steps in the writing process. Where possible, these activities refer students back to the immediately preceding reading, deepening students' comprehension and awareness of text structure.

## Informed by National Standards

The *Standards for Foreign Language Learning: Preparing for the 21st Century*, whose five goal areas have served as an organizing principle for language instruction for more than a decade, inform the pedagogy of the fifth edition of *Mosaicos*. Marginal notes throughout the Annotated Instructor's Edition draw attention to the way specific activities or other elements of the program help students develop proficiency in the five goal areas. A number of general strategies have been followed.

**Communication.**    Students are prompted to engage in meaningful conversations throughout the text, providing and obtaining information, expressing their opinions and preferences, and sharing their experiences. Readings and listening activities invite them to interpret language on a variety of topics, while *presentaciones* and writing assignments call on them to present information and ideas in both written and oral modes.

**Cultures.**    Many features of the text, including the maps, photos, *Cultura* boxes, and the readings in the *Mosaicos* and *Enfoque cultural* sections of each chapter, give students an understanding of the relationship between culture and language throughout the Spanish-speaking world.

**Connections.**    Realia, readings, the *Enfoque cultural* application activities, and conversation activities throughout the text provide opportunities to make connections with other disciplines. Students gain information and insight into the distinctive viewpoints of Spanish speakers and their cultures.

Comparisons.   *Lengua* and *En otras palabras* boxes often provide students with points of comparison between English and Spanish (and among the varieties of Spanish spoken in different parts of the world). Readings and activities frequently juxtapose U.S. and Hispanic cultural products, practices, and perspectives.

Communities.   The text encourages students to extend their learning through guided research on the Internet and/or other sources, and many of the topics explored in *Mosaicos* can stimulate exploration, personal enjoyment, and enrichment beyond the confines of formal language instruction. Instructors are reminded to encourage students to become acquainted with Spanish-speaking communities in their areas.

## The Complete Program

*Mosaicos* is a complete teaching and learning program that includes a variety of resources for students and instructors, including an innovative offering of online resources.

## For the student

### Student Text
The *Mosaicos* Student Text is available in a complete, hardbound version, consisting of a preliminary chapter followed by Chapters 1 through 15. New to this edition is the option of three paperback volumes rather than the single hardcover version. Volume 1 of the paperback series contains the preliminary chapter plus Chapters 1 to 5; Volume 2, Chapters 5 to 10; and Volume 3, Chapters 10 to 15. All three volumes include the complete front and back matter.

### Student Activities Manual
The Student Activities Manual (SAM), thoroughly revised for this edition, includes workbook activities together with audio- and video-based activities, all designed to provide extensive practice of the vocabulary, grammar, culture, and skills introduced in each chapter. The organization of these materials now parallels that of the student text, with an *A primera vista* section followed by *En acción* video activities, *Funciones y formas*, *Mosaicos*, and *Enfoque cultural*. A new section in each chapter (entitled *Repaso*) provides additional activities designed to help students review the material of the chapter as well as to prepare for tests.

   The printed Student Activities Manual is available both in a single volume and in a series of separate volumes, paralleling the paperback volumes of the student text. The contents of the Student Activities Manual and MySpanishLab are also available online.

### Answer Key to Accompany Student Activities Manual
An Answer Key to the Student Activities Manual is available separately, giving instructors the option of allowing students to check their homework. The Answer Key now includes answers to all SAM activities.

### Supplementary Activities Book
Also available is a Supplementary Activities Book consisting of a range of fun, engaging activities that complement the vocabulary and grammar themes of each chapter. It offers instructors additional materials that can serve to energize and enrich their students' classroom experience.

### Audio CDs to Accompany Student Text
A set of audio CDs contains recordings of the *A primera vista* language samples and the end-of-chapter vocabulary lists. It also contains audio material for listening activities included in the student text. These recordings are also available online.

### Audio CDs to Accompany Student Activities Manual
A second set of audio CDs contains audio material for the listening activities in the Student Activities Manual. These recordings are also available online.

### Video on DVD
*Diarios de bicicleta* is an original video filmed to accompany the fifth edition of *Mosaicos*. Students see the vocabulary and grammar structures of each chapter in use in realistic situations while gaining a deeper understanding of Hispanic cultures. The video also includes segments highlighting the communicative functions of each chapter. Pre-viewing, viewing, and post-viewing activities are found in the *En acción* sections of the textbook and the Student Activities Manual. The video is available for student purchase on DVD, and it is also available within MySpanishLab.

## Meet the Cast

Here are the main characters of *Diarios de bicicleta*, who you will get to know when you watch the video:

| Javier | Luciana | Daniel | Gaby |

In addition to *Diarios de bicicleta*, two other videos are available for use in conjunction with the *Mosaicos* program. *Entrevistas* consists of interviews in which native speakers use authentic Spanish to address topics related to each chapter's theme. *Vistas culturales* contains nineteen 10–minute vignettes with footage from every Spanish-speaking country. Each of the accompanying narrations, which employ vocabulary and grammar designed for first-year language learners, was written by a native of the featured country or region. All three videos are also available online.

## For the instructor

### Annotated Instructor's Edition

The Annotated Instructor's Edition contains an abundance of marginal annotations (many newly written or revised for this edition) designed especially for novice instructors, instructors who are new to the *Mosaicos* program, or instructors who have limited time for class preparation. A new format allows ample space for annotations alongside full-size pages of the student text. Marginal annotations suggest warm-up and expansion exercises and activities and provide teaching tips, additional cultural information, and audioscripts for the in-text listening activities. Answers to discrete-point activities are printed in blue type for the instructor's convenience. *Resources* boxes (new to this edition) offer cross-references to related material in other components of the *Mosaicos* program, enabling instructors to see at a glance what material is available for student homework and additional practice, as well as for use in the classroom.

### Instructor's Resource Manual

The Instructor's Resource Manual (IRM) now contains complete lesson plans for all chapters, integrated syllabi for regular and hybrid courses, as well as helpful suggestions for new and experienced instructors alike. It also provides additional oral practice activities (similar to the *Situaciones* activities in the student text), videoscripts for all episodes of the *Diarios de bicicleta* video, audioscripts for listening activities in the Student Activities Manual, and a complete guide to all *Mosaicos* supplements. The Instructor's Resource Manual is available to instructors online at the *Mosaicos* Instructor Resource Center.

### Testing Program

The Testing Program has been thoroughly revised and expanded for this edition. The testing content correlates with the vocabulary, grammar, culture, and skills material presented in the student text. For each chapter of the text, a bank of testing activities is provided in modular form; instructors can select and combine modules to create customized tests tailored to the needs of their classes. Two complete, ready-to-use tests are also provided for each chapter. The tests and testing modules are available to instructors online at the *Mosaicos* Instructor Resource Center.

### Testing Audio CD

A special set of audio CDs, available to instructors only, contains recordings corresponding to the listening comprehension portions of the Testing Program.

### PowerPoint™ Presentations

A PowerPoint™ Presentation (new to this edition) is available for each chapter of the text. These dynamic, visually engaging presentations allow instructors to enliven class sessions and reinforce key concepts. The presentations are available to instructors online at the *Mosaicos* Instructor Resource Center.

### *Situaciones adicionales*

The *Situaciones adicionales* provide instructors with additional opportunities for reinforcing and assessing students' speaking skills.

### Instructor Resource Center

Several of the instructor supplements listed above—the Instructor's Resource Manual, the Testing Program, the Power-Point™ Presentations, and the *Situaciones adicionales* as well as the Supplementary Activities Book—are available for download at the access-protected *Mosaicos* Instructor Resource Center (www.pearsonhighered.com/educator). An access code will be provided at no charge to instructors once their faculty status has been verified.

## Online resources

### MySpanishLab™

MySpanishLab is a new, nationally hosted online learning system created for students in college-level language courses. It brings together—in one convenient, easily navigable site—a wide array of language-learning tools and resources, including an interactive version of the *Mosaicos* Student Activities Manual, an electronic version of the *Mosaicos* student text, and all materials from the *Mosaicos* audio and video programs. Readiness checks, chapter tests, and tutorials personalize instruction to meet the unique needs of individual students. Instructors can use the system to make assignments, set grading parameters, listen to student-created audio recordings, and provide feedback on student work. Instructor access is provided at no charge. Students can purchase access codes online or at their local bookstore.

### Companion Website

The open-access Companion Website (www.pearsonhighered.com/mosaicos) includes an array of activities and resources designed to reinforce the vocabulary, grammar, and cultural material introduced in each chapter. It also provides audio recordings for the student text and Student Activities Manual, links for Internet-based activites in the student text, and additional web exploration activities for each chapter. All contents of the Companion Website are also included in MySpanishLab.

## Acknowledgments

*Mosaicos* is the result of a collaborative effort among the authors, our publisher, and our colleagues. We are especially indebted to many members of the Spanish teaching community for their time, candor, and insightful suggestions as they reviewed the drafts of the fifth edition of *Mosaicos*. Their critiques and recommendations helped us to sharpen our pedagogical focus and improve the overall quality of the program. We gratefully acknowledge the contributions of the following reviewers:

Rafael Arias, *Los Angeles Valley College*
Alejandra Balestra, *University of New Mexico*
Aymará Boggiano, *University of Houston*
Amanda Boomershine, *University of North Carolina-Wilmington*
Talia Bugel, *Indiana University-Purdue University Fort Wayne*
José Carrasquel, *Florida International University*
Zoila Clark, *Florida International University*
Daria Cohen, *Rider University*
Alyce Cook, *Columbus State University*
Richard Curry, *Texas A&M University*
Marta de la Caridad Pérez, *Florida International University*
Beatrice DeAngelis, *University of Pittsburgh*
Marisol del Teso Craviotto, *Miami University of Ohio*
Angela Erickson-Grussing, *St. John's University/College of St. Benedict*
Juliet Falce-Robinson, *University of California-Los Angeles*
Gayle Fiedler-Vierma, *University of Southern California*
Óscar Flores, *State University of New York-Plattsburgh*
Ausenda Folch, *Florida International University*
Myriam García, *Florida International University*
Rosa María Gómez García-Bermejo, *Florida International University*

Frozina Goussak, *Collin County Community College*
Dawn Heston, *University of Missouri-Columbia*
Casilde Isabelli, *University of Nevada-Reno*
Keith Johnson, *California State University-Fresno*
Linda Keown, *University of Missouri-Columbia*
Ruth Konopka, *Grossmont College*
Lina Llerena Callahan, *Fullerton College*
Susana Liso, *University of Virginia-Wise*
Leticia López, *San Diego Mesa College*
Libardo Mitchell, *Portland Community College-Sylvania*
Dorothy Moore, *Gettysburg College*
Michelle Orecchio, *University of Michigan*
Teresa Pérez-Gamboa, *University of Georgia*
Ana María Pinzón, *Frederick Community College*
Mónica Prieto, *Florida International University*
Nuria Sagarra, *Pennsylvania State University*
Toni Trives, *Santa Monica College*
Clara Vega, *Almance Community College*
Celinés Villalba, *University of California-Berkeley*
Lisa Volle, *Central Texas College*
Sarah Williams, *University of Pittsburgh*
Loretta Zehngut, *Pennsylvania State University*

We are also grateful for the guidance of Elizabeth Lantz, development editor, for all of her work, suggestions, attention to detail, and dedication to the text. Her support and spirit helped us to achieve the final product. Special thanks are due to Celia Meana, development editor, for helping with the art program, with the final pages, and with many other editorial details. We would also like to thank the contributors who assisted us in the preparation of the fifth edition: Daria Cohen, Marisol del Teso Craviotto, Juliet Falce-Robinson, Linda Keown, Gustavo Mejía, Teresa Pérez-Gamboa, Anne Prucha, and Lilián Uribe. Special thanks to Ninon Larché and Debbie King for their assistance in the preparation of the manuscript. We are very grateful to other colleagues and friends at Prentice Hall: Meriel Martínez, Media Editor, for helping us produce such a great video, audio programs, and Companion Website; Melissa Marolla Brown, Development Editor for Assessment, for the diligent coordination among the text, Student Activities Manual, and Testing Program; Samantha Alducin, Senior Media Editor, for managing the creation of *Mosaicos* materials for My SpanishLab™; and Jenn Murphy, Assistant Editor/Editorial Coordinator, for her work in managing the preparation of the other supplements. Thanks to Katie Spiegel, Editorial Assistant, for her hard work and efficiency in obtaining reviews and attending to many administrative details.

We are very grateful to our marketing team, Kris Ellis-Levy, Denise Miller, and Bill Bliss, for their creativity and efforts in coordinating all marketing and promotion for this edition. Thanks, too, to our production team, Mary Rottino, Janice Stangel, and Manuel Echevarria, who guided *Mosaicos* through the many stages of production; to our partners at Macmillan Publishing Solutions, especially Jill Traut, for her careful and professional editing and production services. We also thank our art team, Gail Cocker, Peter Bull, and Andrew Lange, for their amazing creativity and beautiful maps and illustrations. Special thanks to Leslie Osher, John Christina, and Ximena Tamvakopoulos for the gorgeous interior and cover designs. Finally, we would like to express our sincere thanks to Phil Miller, Publisher, and Julia Caballero, Executive Editor, for their guidance and support through every aspect of this new edition.

## A Guide to *Mosaicos* Icons

| | | |
|---|---|---|
| | **A vista de pájaro** | This icon indicates a panoramic, quick overview. It accompanies the chapter opener activity and reminds students to activate background knowledge about the country or countries featured in the chapter, as well as to use the information presented in the map. |
| | **Text Audio Program** | This icon indicates that recorded material is available for students in the *Mosaicos* text audio program for students. The audio includes vocabulary and dialogues presented in *A primera vista*, as well as the listening activities presented in the text. |
| | **Pair Activity** | This icon indicates that the activity is designed to be done by students working in pairs. |
| | **Group Activity** | This icon indicates that the activity is designed to be done by students working in small groups. |
| | **Web Activity** | This icon indicates that the activity involves use of the World Wide Web. Helpful links and activities can be found on the *Mosaicos* Companion Website. |

# ABOUT THE AUTHORS

**Elizabeth E. Guzmán** is the Director of the Elementary and Intermediate Spanish Language Program at the University of Iowa. Previously, she served as Language Coordinator at St. John's University/College of St. Benedict, Director of the Spanish Program at Yale University, and Coordinator and Co-Director of the Elementary and Intermediate Language Program at The University of Michigan. In her native Chile, she supervised instructors of English as a Foreign Language. Ms. Guzmán received her B.A. in English from Universidad de Santiago (Chile) and her M.A. in English as a Second Language from West Virginia University, and then pursued doctoral studies at the University of Pittsburgh. She is a co-author of Prentice-Hall's *Identidades* and several earlier editions of *Mosaicos*.

**Paloma Lapuerta** holds the title of Professor of Spanish at Central Connecticut State University, where she teaches courses in Spanish language, culture, and literature. She has over twenty years of teaching experience at higher institutions around the world, including Spain, Switzerland, South Africa, and the United States, where she has taught at the University of Michigan, Dartmouth College, and the Middlebury College Spanish School. She completed her *Licenciatura* in Spanish Philology at the University of Salamanca, and she holds a Ph.D. in Spanish literature from the University of Geneva, Switzerland. She has published numerous articles and a book on Spanish culture and literature. She is a co-author of *Identidades*, *La escritura paso a paso*, and earlier editions of *Mosaicos*, all published by Prentice Hall.

**Judith E. Liskin-Gasparro** is a professor of Spanish at the University of Iowa, where she teaches courses in second language acquisition, pedagogy, and Spanish language. She is the co-director of FLARE (Foreign Language Acquisition Research and Education), which offers an interdisciplinary doctoral program in Second Language Acquisition, and she was formerly the Director of the Elementary and Intermediate Spanish Language Program. Previously, she taught at Middlebury College and worked as a test development consultant at Educational Testing Service. She received her B.A. in Spanish from Bryn Mawr College, her M.A. from Princeton University, and her Ph.D. in Foreign Language Education from the University of Texas at Austin. She has published articles and books on language learning and teaching and has led many workshops for language teachers. She is a co-author of *Identidades*, published by Prentice Hall.

# Preliminar

# *Bienvenidos*

El mundo hispano les da la bienvenida.

## In this chapter you will learn how to:

- introduce yourself, greet others, and say good-bye
- use expressions of courtesy
- spell in Spanish
- identify people and classroom objects
- locate people and things

- use numbers from 0–99
- express dates
- tell time
- use classroom expressions
- comment on the weather

### Personas que hablan español (en millones)

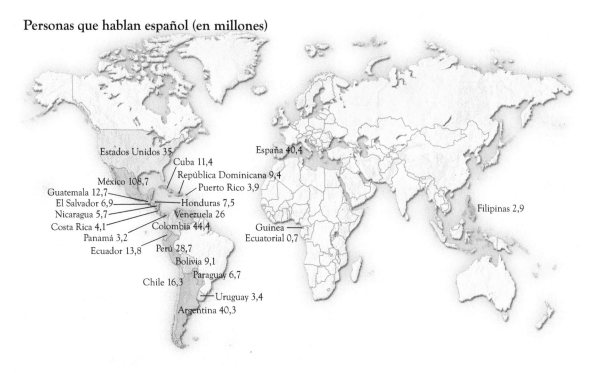

Estados Unidos 35
Cuba 11,4
República Dominicana 9,4
México 108,7
Puerto Rico 3,9
Guatemala 12,7
El Salvador 6,9 — Honduras 7,5
Nicaragua 5,7 — Venezuela 26
Costa Rica 4,1 — Colombia 44,4
Panamá 3,2
Ecuador 13,8 Perú 28,7
Bolivia 9,1
Paraguay 6,7
Chile 16,3
Uruguay 3,4
Argentina 40,3
España 40,4
Guinea Ecuatorial 0,7
Filipinas 2,9

**A vista de pájaro.** Relying on your knowledge of the world, look at the map and determine whether each statement is true (**Cierto**) or false (**Falso**).

1. ___F___ Más de (*More than*) 350 millones de personas hablan español en el mundo.
2. _____ En Filipinas no se habla español.
3. _____ En Estados Unidos hablan español más personas que (*more ... than*) en Chile.
4. _____ En Guinea Ecuatorial se habla español.
5. _____ En Brasil se habla portugués.
6. _____ El español se habla en 23 países.

# Las presentaciones

CD 1
Track 1

ANTONIO: **Me llamo** Antonio Mendoza.
**Y tú, ¿cómo te llamas?**

BENITO: Me llamo Benito Sánchez.

ANTONIO: **Mucho gusto.**

BENITO: **Igualmente.**

PROFESOR: **¿Cómo se llama usted?**

ISABEL: Me llamo Isabel Contreras.

PROFESOR: Mucho gusto.

LAURA: María, **mi amigo** José.

MARÍA: Mucho gusto.

JOSÉ: **Encantado.**

- Spanish has more than one word meaning *you*. Use **tú** when talking to someone on a first-name basis (a child, close friend, or relative).

  Use **usted** when talking to someone you address in a respectful or formal manner; for example, **doctor/doctora; profesor/profesora; señor/señora.** Also use **usted** to address individuals you do not know well.

- Young people normally use **tú** when speaking to each other.

- **Mucho gusto** is used by both men and women when they are meeting someone for the first time. A man may also say **encantado**, and a woman, **encantada**.

- You may respond to **mucho gusto** with either **encantado/a** or **igualmente.**

**P-1 Presentaciones.** PRIMERA FASE. Complete the following conversation with the appropriate expressions from the box on the right.

ALICIA: Me llamo Alicia. Y tú, ¿cómo te llamas?

ISABEL: Isabel Pérez. _____.

ALICIA: _____.

ALICIA: Isabel, _____.

ISABEL: Mucho gusto.

PEDRO: _____.

> Igualmente
> Mucho gusto
> Encantado
> mi amigo Pedro

SEGUNDA FASE. Move around the classroom, introducing yourself to several classmates and introducing classmates to each other.

4

# Los saludos y las despedidas

## Los saludos

CD 1
Track 2

SEÑOR: **Buenos días, señorita** Rivas.

SEÑORITA: Buenos días. **¿Cómo está usted, señor** Gómez?

SEÑOR: **Bien, gracias.** ¿Y usted?

SEÑORITA: **Muy** bien, gracias.

MARTA: **¡Hola, Inés! ¿Qué tal? ¿Cómo estás?**

INÉS: **Regular,** ¿y tú?

MARTA: **Bastante** bien, gracias.

SEÑORA: **Buenas tardes,** Felipe. ¿Cómo estás?

FELIPE: Bien, gracias. Y usted, ¿cómo está, **señora?**

SEÑORA: **Mal,** Felipe, mal.

FELIPE: **Lo siento.**

- Use **buenos días** until lunchtime.

- Use **buenas tardes** from noon until nightfall. After nightfall, use **buenas noches** (*good evening, good night*).

- **¿Qué tal?** is a more informal greeting. It is normally used with **tú,** but it may also be used with **usted.**

- Use **está** with **usted** and **estás** with **tú.**

**P-2 Saludos.** You work as a receptionist in a hotel. Which greeting (**buenos días, buenas tardes, buenas noches**) is appropriate at the following times?

1. 9:00 a.m.
2. 11:00 p.m.
3. 4:00 p.m.
4. 8:00 a.m.
5. 1:00 p.m.
6. 10:00 p.m.

## Las despedidas

CD 1
Track 3

| adiós | *good-bye* |
| hasta luego | *see you later* |
| hasta mañana | *see you tomorrow* |
| hasta pronto | *see you soon* |
| chao | *good-bye* |

### Cultura

When saying *hello* or *good-bye* and when being introduced, Spanish-speaking men and women almost always shake hands. When greeting each other, young girls and women often kiss each other on one cheek. This is also the custom for men and women who are close friends. In Spain they kiss on both cheeks. Men who are close friends normally embrace and pat each other on the back.

Native Spanish speakers also tend to stand physically closer to the person with whom they are talking than do English speakers.

■ **Adiós** is generally used when you do not expect to see the other person for a while. It is also used as a greeting when people pass each other but have no time to stop and talk.

■ **Chao** (also spelled **chau**) is an informal way of saying good-bye. It is popular in South America.

**P-3 Despedidas.** How would you say good-bye in these situations?
1. You'll see your friend tomorrow.
2. You arrange to meet your classmate at the library in 10 minutes.
3. Your roommate is leaving for a semester abroad.
4. You run into a good friend on campus.

## Expresiones de cortesía

CD 1
Track 4

| | |
|---|---|
| **por favor** | *please* |
| **gracias** | *thanks, thank you* |
| **de nada** | *you're welcome* |
| **lo siento** | *I'm sorry (to hear that)* |
| **con permiso** | *pardon me, excuse me* |
| **perdón** | *pardon me, excuse me* |

■ **Con permiso** and **perdón** may be used before the fact, as when asking a person to allow you to go by or when trying to get someone's attention. Only **perdón** is used after the fact, as when you have stepped on someone's foot or have interrupted a conversation.

**P-4 ¿Perdón o con permiso?** Would you use **perdón** or **con permiso** in these situations?

1.

2.

3.

4.

5.

**P-5 Despedidas y expresiones de cortesía.** Which expression(s) would you use in the following situations?

| | | |
|---|---|---|
| adiós | gracias | lo siento |
| de nada | hasta luego | por favor |

1. Someone thanks you.
2. You say good-bye to a friend you will see later this evening.
3. You ask if you can borrow a classmate's notes.
4. You hear that your friend is sick.
5. You receive a present from your cousin.
6. Your friend is leaving for a vacation in Costa Rica.

**P-6 Encuentros (*Encounters*).** You meet the following people on the street. Greet them, ask how they are, and then say good-bye. Switch roles and role play the encounters again.

1. su (*your*) amigo Miguel
2. su profesor/a

3. su amiga Isabel
4. su doctor/a

# ◄)) Distinguishing Registers

CD 1
Track 5

When you talk to different people, you use different registers, that is, you address them with various degrees of formality, depending on your level of intimacy and the context of the exchange. For example, when you talk to a professor, you probably use more formal language than when you talk to classmates or friends. In Spanish, one way to mark this difference is by using **tú** (informal) and **usted** (formal).

Now you will hear four brief conversations in which people greet each other. Before you listen, complete the following chart with the pronoun you think you would use in each case.

| WHEN TALKING TO YOUR ... | TÚ | USTED |
|---|---|---|
| 1. brother or sister | | |
| 2. doctor | | |
| 3. coach | | |
| 4. parents | | |

**P-7 Conversaciones.** As you listen to the four conversations, mark (✓) the appropriate column to indicate whether the greetings are formal (with **usted**) or informal (with **tú**). Do not worry if you do not understand every word.

FORMAL       INFORMAL

1. _____      _____
2. _____      _____
3. _____      _____
4. _____      _____

# ·)) El alfabeto

CD 1
Track 6

| | | | |
|---|---|---|---|
| a | a | o | o |
| b | be | p | pe |
| c | ce | q | cu |
| d | de | r | ere, erre |
| e | e | s | ese |
| f | efe | t | te |
| g | ge | u | u |
| h | hache | v | ve, uve |
| i | i | w | doble ve, doble uve |
| j | jota | | uve doble, ve doble |
| k | ka | x | equis |
| l | ele | y | i griega, ye |
| m | eme | z | zeta |
| n | ene | | |
| ñ | eñe | | |

### En otras palabras

Like English speakers, Spanish speakers have different accents that reflect their region or country of origin. For example, the letter **c** before vowels **e** and **i** and the letter **z** are pronounced like **s**, except in certain regions of Spain, where they are similar to the English *th*.

■ The Spanish alphabet includes **ñ**, a letter that does not exist in English. Its sound is similar to the pronunciation of *ni* and *ny* in the English words *onion* and *canyon*.

■ The letters **k** and **w** appear mainly in words of foreign origin.

 **P-8 ¿Cómo se escribe?** Ask your classmate how to spell these Spanish last names.

**MODELO:** Zamora
E1: *¿Cómo se escribe Zamora?*
E2: *Con zeta.*

1. Celaya
2. Montalvo
3. Salas
4. Bolaños
5. Henares
6. Velázquez

 **P-9 Los nombres.** You are at the admissions office of a university in a Spanish-speaking country. Spell out your first or last name for the clerk. Take turns.

**MODELO:** E1: *¿Cómo se llama usted?*
E2: *Me llamo David Robinson.*
E1: *¿Cómo se escribe Robinson?*
E2: *ere-o-be-i-ene-ese-o-ene.*

# Identificación y descripción de personas

**CD 1**
**Track 7**

CARLOS: **¿Quién es ese chico?**

SANDRA: **Es** Julio.

CARLOS: **¿Cómo es** Julio?

SANDRA: **Es** romántico y sentimental.

LUIS: ¿Quién es **esa chica**?

QUIQUE: Es Carmen.

LUIS: ¿Cómo es Carmen?

QUIQUE: Es activa y muy seria.

▪ The verb *ser* is used to identify and describe.

Esa chica **es** Carmen. Ella **es** activa y muy seria.

Rodolfo **es** su amigo. **Es** atractivo.

▪ Here are the forms of *ser* you will be using in this chapter.

| SER *(to be)* | | | |
|---|---|---|---|
| yo | **soy** | *I* | *am* |
| tú | **eres** | *you* | *are* |
| usted | **es** | *you* | *are* |
| él, ella | **es** | *he, she* | *is* |

■ To make a sentence negative, place **no** before the appropriate form of **ser**. When responding negatively to a question, say **no** twice.

Ella es inteligente.　　→　　Ella **no** es inteligente.

¿Es rebelde?　　→　　**No, no** es rebelde.

## Cognados

**Cognados** (*cognates*) are words from two languages that have the same origin and are similar in form and meaning. Since English and Spanish have many cognates, you will discover that you already recognize many Spanish words. Here are some cognates that you may use to describe people.

■ The following cognates use the same form to describe a man or a woman.

| | | | |
|---|---|---|---|
| arrogante | importante | optimista | popular |
| eficiente | independiente | paciente | responsable |
| elegante | inteligente | perfeccionista | sentimental |
| idealista | interesante | pesimista | tradicional |

■ The following cognates have two forms. The **-o** form is used to describe a male, and the **-a** form to describe a female.

| | | | |
|---|---|---|---|
| activo/a | creativo/a | introvertido/a | romántico/a |
| ambicioso/a | dinámico/a | moderno/a | serio/a |
| atlético/a | extrovertido/a | nervioso/a | sincero/a |
| atractivo/a | generoso/a | pasivo/a | tímido/a |
| cómico/a | impulsivo/a | religioso/a | tranquilo/a |

■ Some words appear to be cognates but do not have the same meaning in both languages. These are called false cognates. **Lectura** (*reading*) and **éxito** (*success*) are examples. You will find other examples in future chapters.

 **P-10 ¿Cómo es mi compañero/a?** Choose from the preceding lists of cognates to ask the person next to you about his/her personality.

**MODELO:**　E1:　*¿Eres pesimista?*
　　　　　　　E2:　*No, no soy pesimista. O Sí, soy (muy) pesimista.*

Then find out how your classmate describes himself/herself.

**MODELO:**　E1:　*¿Cómo eres (tú)?*
　　　　　　　E2:　*Soy activo, optimista y creativo.*

**P-11 Descripciones.** Ask each other about your classmates. Describe them by using cognates from the preceding lists.

**MODELO:**　E1:　*¿Cómo es... ?*
　　　　　　　E2:　*Es...*

# ¿Qué hay en el salón de clase?

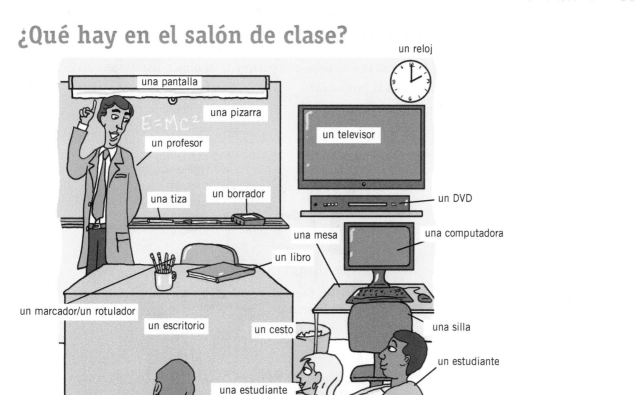

un reloj

una pantalla

una pizarra

un profesor

un televisor

una tiza

un borrador

un DVD

una mesa

una computadora

un libro

un marcador/un rotulador

un escritorio

un cesto

una silla

un estudiante

una estudiante

un cuaderno

una mochila

un bolígrafo

una calculadora

un lápiz

un pupitre

**P-12 Identificación.** With a partner, identify the items on this table.

**P-13 Para la clase de español.** Write down a list of the things you need for this class. Compare your list with that of your partner.

# ¿Dónde está?

■ To ask about the location of a person or an object, use **dónde + está**.

| | |
|---|---|
| **¿Dónde está** la profesora? | Está en la clase. |
| **¿Dónde está** el libro? | Está sobre el escritorio. |

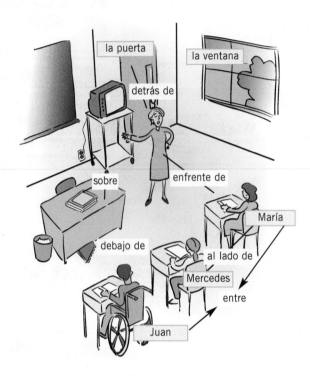

**P-14 Localización.** PRIMERA FASE. Indicate whether each statement is true (**Cierto**) or false (**Falso**), based on the relative position of people and objects in the drawing.

| | CIERTO | FALSO |
|---|---|---|
| 1. El televisor está detrás de la profesora. | _____ | _____ |
| 2. Juan está al lado de la profesora. | _____ | _____ |
| 3. El libro está sobre el escritorio. | _____ | _____ |
| 4. María está entre Mercedes y Juan. | _____ | _____ |
| 5. Mercedes está enfrente de la ventana. | _____ | _____ |
| 6. El cesto está debajo de un pupitre. | _____ | _____ |

SEGUNDA FASE. Now complete the following sentences, based on the relative position of people and objects in the drawing. Compare your answers.

1. La pizarra está _____ la profesora.
2. María está _____ la profesora.
3. Mercedes está _____ Juan y María.
4. Juan está _____ Mercedes.
5. El cesto está _____ Juan.
6. El televisor está _____ la pizarra y la puerta.

# ◄)) Listening with Visuals

CD 1
Track 8 When you are talking with someone, paying attention to the pictures or objects that the speaker points to or refers to can help you understand what is being said. These objects may be around you, or they may not, in which case you have only a mental representation of them. For example, when a friend describes his/her Spanish classroom, an image of a classroom comes to your mind based on your experience as a student.

In Spanish, make a list of the people and objects you expect to see in a classroom.

Now, as you listen to the statements about the location of people and objects, look at the drawing of the classroom on page 12 to help you understand what the speakers are saying.

Indicate (✓) whether each statement is true (**Cierto**) or false (**Falso**).

|    | CIERTO | FALSO |
|----|--------|-------|
| 1. | _____  | _____ |
| 2. | _____  | _____ |
| 3. | _____  | _____ |
| 4. | _____  | _____ |
| 5. | _____  | _____ |
| 6. | _____  | _____ |

**P-15 En la clase.** Look at the seating chart below, and then follow the instructions.

| María    | Juan     | Ester    | Susana  | Pedro |
|----------|----------|----------|---------|-------|
| Carlos   | Cristina | Ángeles  | Alberto | Anita |
| Mercedes | Victoria | Roberto  | Rocío   | Pablo |

| | |
|--|--|
| | El profesor Gallegos |

ESTUDIANTE 1:   Ask where Juan, Pedro, Cristina, Mercedes, Roberto, and Pablo are sitting.

ESTUDIANTE 2:   Ask where *María, Ester, Susana, Carlos, Ángeles, Alberto, Anita, Victoria, Rocío,* and *Profesor Gallegos* are sitting.

**P-16 ¿Dónde está?** Take turns asking where several items in your classroom are. Answer by giving their position in relation to a person or another object.

MODELO:   E1:   *¿Dónde está el libro?*
           E2:   *Está sobre el escritorio.*

**P-17 ¿Quién es?** Based on what your partner says regarding the location of another student, guess who he/she is.

MODELO:   E1:   *Está al lado de Juan. ¿Quién es?*
           E2:   *Es María.*

Los números 0 a 99

| | | | | | |
|---|---|---|---|---|---|
| 1 | un.. | | | | |
| 2 | dos | | | 30 | treinta |
| 3 | tres | 14 | catorce | 31 | treinta y uno |
| 4 | cuatro | 15 | quince | 40 | cuarenta |
| 5 | cinco | 16 | dieciséis | 50 | cincuenta |
| 6 | seis | 17 | diecisiete | 60 | sesenta |
| 7 | siete | 18 | dieciocho | 70 | setenta |
| 8 | ocho | 19 | diecinueve | 80 | ochenta |
| 9 | nueve | 20 | veinte | 90 | noventa |
| 10 | diez | 21 | veintiuno | | |

■ Numbers from sixteen through twenty-nine are usually written as one word. Note the spelling changes and the written accent on some forms.

18: **dieciocho**          22: **veintidós**

■ Beginning with thirty-one, numbers are written as three words.

31: **treinta y uno**          45: **cuarenta y cinco**

■ The number *one* has three forms in Spanish: **uno**, **un**, and **una**. Use **uno** when counting: **uno, dos, tres...** Use **un** or **una** before nouns: **un borrador, una mochila, veintiún libros, veintiuna mochilas.**

■ Use **hay** for both *there is* and *there are*.

| | |
|---|---|
| **Hay** un libro sobre la mesa. | *There is one book on the table.* |
| **Hay** dos libros sobre la mesa. | *There are two books on the table.* |

 **P-18 ¿Qué número es?** Your instructor will read a number from each group. Circle the number you hear. Then compare your responses with those of your partner.

| | | | | |
|---|---|---|---|---|
| **a.** | 8 | 4 | 3 | 5 |
| **b.** | 12 | 9 | 16 | 6 |
| **c.** | 37 | 59 | 41 | 26 |
| **d.** | 54 | 38 | 76 | 95 |
| **e.** | 83 | 62 | 72 | 49 |
| **f.** | 47 | 14 | 91 | 56 |

**P-19 Para la oficina.** You and your partner are student assistants in the Spanish department. You have to check a shipment of equipment and supplies that just arrived. Choose five items and tell your partner how many of each there are. He/She will take notes. Exchange roles.

MODELO:   4-7 mesas: *Hay cuatro mesas.*

a. 6-10 teléfonos
b. 8-12 escritorios
c. 1-2 silla(s)
d. 6-12 calculadoras
e. 10-20 cestos

f. 90-95 bolígrafos
g. 9-15 computadoras
h. 22-24 computadoras portátiles
i. 1-3 reloj(es)
j. ...

**P-20 Problemas.** Take turns solving the following arithmetic problems. Use **y** (+), **menos** (−), and **son** (=).

MODELO:   $2 + 4 =$          $12 - 5 =$
          Dos y cuatro son seis.          Doce menos cinco son siete.

a. $11 + 4 =$
b. $8 + 2 =$
c. $13 + 3 =$

d. $20 - 6 =$
e. $39 + 50 =$
f. $80 - 1 =$

g. $50 - 25 =$
h. $26 + 40 =$
i. $90 - 12 =$

**P-21 Los números de teléfono y las direcciones (*addresses*).** With your partner, take turns asking each other the phone numbers and addresses of the people listed in the chart below.

| | | |
|---|---|---|
| Cárdenas Alfaro, Joaquín | General Páez 40 | 423-4837 |
| Cárdenas Villanueva, Sara | Avenida Bolívar 7 | 956-1709 |
| Castelar Torres, Adelaida | Paseo del Prado 85 | 218-3642 |
| Castellanos Rey, Carlos | Colón 62 | 654-6416 |
| Castelli Rivero, Victoria | Chamberí 3 | 615-7359 |
| Castillo Montoya, Rafael | Santa Cruz 73 | 956-3382 |

MODELO:        Castellanos Rey, Carlos
        E1: *¿Cuál es la dirección de Carlos Castellanos Rey?*
        E2: *Calle Colón, número 62.*
        E1: *¿Cuál es su teléfono?*
        E2: *(Es el) 6-54-64-16*

---

### Cultura

In Spanish-speaking countries, the name of the street precedes the house or building number. Sometimes a comma is placed before the number.

**Calle Bolívar 132**
*132 Bolívar Street*

**Avenida de Gracia, 18**
*18 Gracia Avenue*

Telephone numbers are generally not stated as individual numbers, but in groups of two, depending on how the numbers are written or on the number of digits, which varies from country to country.

12-24-67:
**doce, veinticuatro, sesenta y siete**

243-89-07:
**dos cuarenta y tres, ochenta y nueve, cero siete**

## Los meses del año y los días de la semana

CD 1
Track 10

| | | | | | |
|---|---|---|---|---|---|
| **enero** | *January* | **mayo** | *May* | **septiembre** | *September* |
| **febrero** | *February* | **junio** | *June* | **octubre** | *October* |
| **marzo** | *March* | **julio** | *July* | **noviembre** | *November* |
| **abril** | *April* | **agosto** | *August* | **diciembre** | *December* |

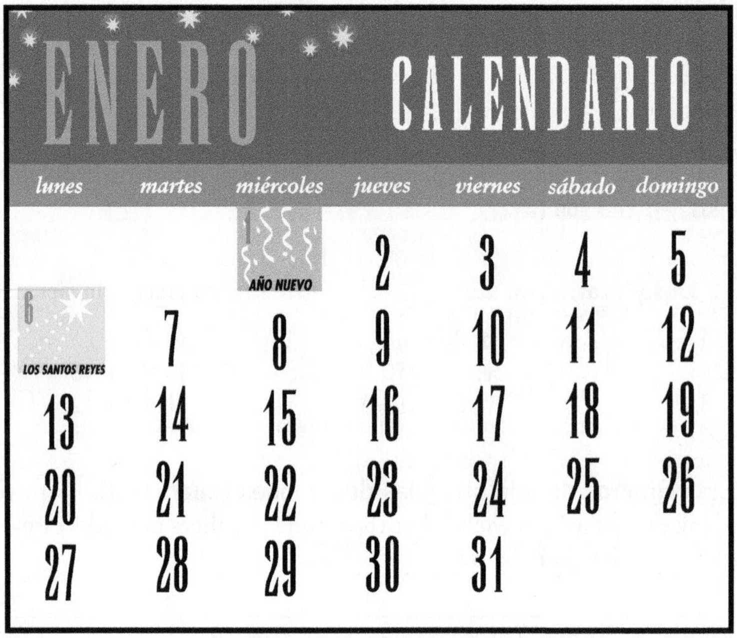
ENERO
CALENDARIO
lunes martes miércoles jueves viernes sábado domingo
1 AÑO NUEVO 2 3 4 5
6 LOS SANTOS REYES 7 8 9 10 11 12
13 14 15 16 17 18 19
20 21 22 23 24 25 26
27 28 29 30 31

Days of the week and months of the year are not generally capitalized in Spanish, but sometimes they are capitalized in advertisements and invitations.

- Monday (**lunes**) is normally considered the first day of the week.
- To ask what day it is, use **¿Qué día es hoy?** Answer with **Hoy es...**
- To ask about the date, use **¿Qué fecha es?** or **¿Cuál es la fecha?** Respond with **Es el (14) de (octubre).**
- Express *on + a day of the week* as follows:

| | |
|---|---|
| **el lunes** | *on Monday* |
| **los lunes** | *on Mondays* |
| **el domingo** | *on Sunday* |
| **los domingos** | *on Sundays* |

- Cardinal numbers are used with dates (e.g., **el dos, el tres**), except for the first day of the month, which is **el primero.** In Spain the first day is also referred to as **el uno.**

### Lengua

When dates are written using only numerals, the day normally precedes the month: *11/8* = **el 11 de agosto.**

**P-22 ¿Qué día de la semana es?** Using the preceding calendar, take turns asking *¿Qué día de la semana es... ?*

1. el 2
2. el 5
3. el 22
4. el 18
5. el 10
6. el 13
7. el 28
8. el...

**P-23 Preguntas.** Take turns asking and answering these questions.

1. ¿Qué día es hoy?
2. Hoy es... ¿Qué día es mañana?
3. Hoy es el... de... ¿Qué fecha es mañana?
4. ¿Hay clase de español los domingos? ¿Y los sábados?
5. ¿Qué días hay clase de español?

**P-24 Fechas importantes.** Working with a partner, tell each other the dates on which these events take place.

MODELO:    la reunión de estudiantes (10/9)
      E1: *¿Cuándo es la reunión de estudiantes?*
      E2: *(Es) el 10 de septiembre.*

1. el concierto de Marc Anthony (12/11)
2. el aniversario de Carlos y María (14/4)
3. el banquete (1/3)
4. la graduación (22/5)
5. la fiesta de bienvenida (24/8)

**P-25 El cumpleaños (*birthday*).** Find out when your classmates' birthdays are. Write their names and birthdays in the appropriate space in the chart.

MODELO:  E1: *¿Cuándo es tu cumpleaños?*
       E2: *(Es) el 3 de mayo.*

| CUMPLEAÑOS | | | |
|---|---|---|---|
| enero | febrero | marzo | abril |
| mayo | junio | julio | agosto |
| septiembre | octubre | noviembre | diciembre |

### Lengua

You may have noticed that the word **tú** (meaning *you*) has a written accent mark, and that the word **tu** (meaning *your*) does not. In *Mosaicos*, boxes similar to this one will help you focus on when to use accent marks. You will find a complete set of the rules for accentuation in the appendix.

# La hora

◼ Use **¿Qué hora es?** to inquire about the time. To tell time, use **Es la...** from one o'clock to one thirty and **Son las...** with the other hours.

| | |
|---|---|
| **Es la** una. | *It is one o'clock.* |
| **Son las** tres. | *It is three o'clock.* |

◼ To express the quarter hour, use **y cuarto** or **y quince**. To express the half hour, use **y media** or **y treinta**.

| | |
|---|---|
| Es la una **y media.**<br>Es la una **y treinta.** | *It is one thirty.* |
| Son las dos **y cuarto.**<br>Son las dos **y quince.** | *It is two fifteen.* |

◼ To express time after the half hour, subtract minutes from the next hour, using **menos**.

| | |
|---|---|
| Son las cuatro **menos** diez. | *It is ten to four.* |

◼ Add **en punto** for the exact time and **más o menos** for approximate time.

| | |
|---|---|
| Es la una **en punto.** | *It is one o'clock on the dot/sharp.* |
| Son las cinco menos cuarto,<br>    **más o menos.** | *It is about a quarter to five.* |

◼ For *a.m.* and *p.m.*, use the following:

**de la mañana**  (from midnight to noon)
**de la tarde**    (from noon to nightfall)
**de la noche**   (from nightfall to midnight)

**P-26 ¿Qué hora es en... ?**  What time is it in the following cities?

México, p.m.

San Juan, p.m.

Buenos Aires, p.m.

Madrid, p.m.

**P-27 El horario de María.**  Take turns asking and answering questions about María's schedule below. Then write down your own Monday schedule, omitting the time each class meets. Exchange schedules with your partner, and find out what time each of his/her classes starts.

MODELO:   E1:  *¿A qué hora es la clase de español?*
              E2:  *Es a las nueve.*

| LUNES | | | |
|---|---|---|---|
| 9:00 | la clase de español | 12:30 | el almuerzo |
| 10:00 | la clase de matemáticas | 1:00 | la clase de física |
| 11:00 | la clase de psicología | 5:00 | la clase de tenis |
| 12:00 | el laboratorio | | |

# El tiempo

Hoy hace sol. Hace buen tiempo.

Hoy llueve. Hace mal tiempo.

■ Use **¿Qué tiempo hace?** to inquire about the weather. To answer, you may use the following expressions that start with **hace**:

**Hace** buen tiempo.    *The weather is good.*
**Hace** mal tiempo.     *The weather is bad.*

■ To express that it is sunny or that it is raining use the following:

**Hace sol**.            *It is sunny.*
**Llueve./Está lloviendo**.  *It is raining.*

**P-28 ¿Qué tiempo hace hoy?** Take turns with your partner asking about the weather in these cities.

**MODELO:**        Miami: ☀
         E1:  *¿Qué tiempo hace en Miami?*
         E2:  *En Miami hace buen tiempo. Hace sol.*

1. Madrid: ☀
2. Quito: ☁
3. Lima: ☁
4. Ciudad de México: ☀
5. Bogotá: ☁
6. Nueva York: ☀

# ·)) Expresiones útiles en la clase

CD 1
Track 11

La tarea, por favor.

Vaya a la pizarra.

Conteste.

Repita.

Levante la mano.

Escriba.

Lea.

■ When asking two or more people to do something, the verb form ends in **-n**: **vaya → vayan, conteste → contesten, repita → repitan**.

■ Although you may not have to use all these expressions, it is useful to be able to recognize them and to respond accordingly. Other expressions that you may hear or say in the classroom include the following:

| | |
|---|---|
| **¿Comprende(n)?** | *Do you understand?* |
| **No comprendo.** | *I do not understand.* |
| **No sé.** | *I do not know.* |
| **Más despacio, por favor.** | *More slowly, please.* |
| **Más alto, por favor.** | *Louder, please.* |
| **Otra vez.** | *Again.* |
| **¿Tienen alguna pregunta?** | *Do you have any questions?* |
| **Tengo una pregunta…** | *I have a question.* |
| **¿En qué página?** | *On what page?* |
| **¿Cómo se dice… en español?** | *How do you say … in Spanish?* |
| **¿Cómo se escribe…?** | *How do you spell … ?* |
| **Vaya(n) a la pizarra.** | *Go to the board.* |
| **Conteste(n), por favor.** | *Please answer.* |
| **Presente.** | *Here (present).* |

# VOCABULARIO

## Las presentaciones — Introductions

| | |
|---|---|
| ¿Cómo se llama usted? | *What's your name?* (formal) |
| ¿Cómo te llamas? | *What's your name?* (familiar) |
| encantado/a | *pleased/nice to meet you* |
| igualmente | *likewise* |
| me llamo... | *my name is ...* |
| mucho gusto | *pleased/nice to meet you* |

## Los saludos — Greetings

| | |
|---|---|
| bastante | *rather* |
| bien | *well* |
| buenas tardes/buenas noches | *good afternoon/good evening, good night* |
| buenos días | *good morning* |
| ¿Cómo está? | *How are you (formal)?* |
| ¿Cómo estás? | *How are you (informal)?* |
| hola | *hi, hello* |
| mal | *bad* |
| muy | *very* |
| regular | *fair* |
| ¿Qué tal? | *What's up? What's new?* *(informal)* |

## En el salón de clase — In the classroom

| | |
|---|---|
| el bolígrafo | *ballpoint pen* |
| el borrador | *eraser* |
| la calculadora | *calculator* |
| el cesto | *wastebasket* |
| la computadora | *computer* |
| la computadora portátil | *laptop* |
| el cuaderno | *notebook* |
| el DVD | *DVD; DVD player* |
| el escritorio | *desk* |
| el lápiz | *pencil* |
| el libro | *book* |
| el mapa | *map* |
| el marcador/el rotulador | *marker* |
| la mesa | *table* |
| la mochila | *backpack* |
| la pantalla | *screen* |
| la pizarra | *chalkboard* |
| la puerta | *door* |
| el pupitre | *student desk* |
| el reloj | *clock* |
| la silla | *chair* |
| el televisor | *television set* |
| la tiza | *chalk* |
| la ventana | *window* |

## Las personas — People

| | |
|---|---|
| el amigo/la amiga | *friend* |
| el/chico/la chica | *boy/girl* |
| él | *he* |
| ella | *she* |
| el/la estudiante | *student* |
| el profesor/la profesora | *professor, teacher* |
| el señor (Sr.) | *Mr.* |
| la señora (Sra.) | *Ms., Mrs.* |
| la señorita (Srta.) | *Ms, Miss* |
| tú | *you* (familiar) |
| usted | *you* (formal) |
| yo | *I* |

## La posición — Position

| | |
|---|---|
| al lado (de) | *next to* |
| debajo (de) | *under* |
| detrás (de) | *behind* |
| enfrente (de) | *in front of* |
| entre | *between, among* |
| sobre | *on, above* |

## Verbos — Verbs

| | |
|---|---|
| eres | *you are* (familiar) |
| es | *you are* (formal), *he/she is* |
| está | *he/she is, you are* (formal) |
| estás | *you are* (familiar) |
| hay | *there is, there are* |
| soy | *I am* |

## Palabras y expresiones útiles — Useful words and expressions

| | |
|---|---|
| a | *at, to* |
| el año | *year* |
| ¿Cómo es? | *What is he/she/it like?* |
| el día | *day* |
| ¿Dónde está... ? | *Where is ... ?* |
| en | *in* |
| ese/a | *that* (adjective) |
| hoy | *today* |
| mañana | *tomorrow* |
| la mañana | *morning* |
| más o menos | *more or less* |
| el mes | *month* |
| mi(s) | *my* |
| ¿Quién es... ? | *Who is ... ?* |
| la semana | *week* |
| sí | *yes* |
| su(s) | *his/her/their* |
| tu(s) | *your* (familiar) |
| un/una | *a, an* |
| y | *and* |

See page 5 for expressions for leave-taking.
See page 6 for expressions of courtesy.
See page 10 for cognates.
See pages 14 and 16 for numbers, days of the week, and months.
See page 18 for telling time.
See page 19 for weather expressions.
See page 20 for classroom expressions.

# 1

# *En la universidad*

Un fresco del siglo XVI en la Universidad de Salamanca

## In this chapter you will learn how to:

- exchange information about classes
- identify locations at the university
- talk about academic life and daily occurrences
- ask and answer questions

**Cultural focus: España**

Museo Guggenheim

FRANCIA

Santiago de Compostela

Bilbao

Universidad de Salamanca

E S P A Ñ A

Barcelona

OCÉANO ATLÁNTICO

PORTUGAL

Salamanca    Segovia    Paella valenciana

Madrid ✹

Valencia

Plaza de toros

Córdoba

Mar Mediterráneo

Sevilla    Granada

La Alhambra

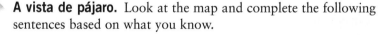 **A vista de pájaro.** Look at the map and complete the following sentences based on what you know.

1. ___ España está en...     a. América.     b. Europa.     c. Asia.
2. ___ La capital de España es...     a. Barcelona.     b. Madrid.     c. Sevilla.
3. ___ La paella es típica de...     a. Valencia.     b. Salamanca.     c. Madrid.
4. ___ En la universidad hay...     a. estudiantes.     b. catedrales.     c. toros.
5. ___ En la plaza de toros hay espectáculos (*shows*)...     a. religiosos.     b. cómicos.     c. populares.

# A PRIMERA VISTA

## Los estudiantes y los cursos

**CD 1 Track 19** Me llamo Rosa Pereda. **Estudio sociología** en la **Facultad de Humanidades** de la **Universidad** de Salamanca. Mis clases son muy temprano. **Llego** a la universidad a las ocho y media. Este semestre mis cursos son **economía, ciencias políticas, psicología, antropología** y **estadística.** La clase de economía es mi **favorita.** La clase de antropología es **difícil,** pero el profesor es muy **bueno.** La clase de psicología es **fácil** y muy **interesante.** Por las tardes **trabajo** en una **oficina.**

**CD 1 Track 20** Este chico es mi amigo. Se llama David Thomas. Es **norteamericano** y estudia español en mi universidad. También estudia **literatura, historia** y **geografía.** David es un chico muy responsable y **estudioso.** Generalmente llega a la universidad a las diez. **Habla** español y **practica todos los días** con sus **compañeros** de clase, sus profesores y sus amigos de la universidad. Por la tarde, **escribe** sus **tareas** en la computadora, estudia en el **laboratorio** con uno de sus **compañeros** y **escucha** música o **mira** programas en español en la televisión.

**1-1 ¿Qué sabe usted de Rosa?** Refer to the information about Rosa to match the information in the right column with the information on the left.

1. _e_ nombre completo          a. antropología
2. _c_ universidad              b. psicología
3. _d_ clase favorita           c. Salamanca
4. _a_ clase difícil            d. economía
5. _b_ clase fácil              e. Rosa Pereda

**1-2 ¿Y David?** Indicate whether each statement about David is true (**Cierto**) or false (**Falso**).

1. _C_ Es norteamericano.
2. _C_ Habla español.
3. _C_ Estudia literatura, historia y geografía.
4. _F_ Llega a la universidad a las nueve.
5. _C_ Practica español con sus amigos.
6. _F_ Escucha música por la mañana.

La Universidad de San Marcos, en Lima, Perú, se fundó en 1551.

# David y Carmen hablan de sus clases

**CD 1 Track 21**

DAVID: Hola, Carmen. ¿Cómo estás?

CARMEN: Hola, David. **¿Cómo te va?**

DAVID: Bueno…bastante bien, pero mi clase de historia es muy difícil.

CARMEN: ¿Quién es tu profesor?

DAVID: Se llama Pedro Hernández. Es inteligente y dedicado, pero la clase es **aburrida** y **saco malas notas.**

CARMEN: ¡Vaya! Lo siento. ¿Estudias lo suficiente?

DAVID: Estudio mucho.

CARMEN: **¡Qué lástima!** Mis cinco clases son excelentes. Y tú, **¿cuántas clases tienes?**

DAVID: **Tengo sólo** cuatro.

CARMEN: ¡Uy! Son las once. Tengo un **examen** de economía **ahora.** Hasta luego.

DAVID: Hasta pronto. **¡Buena suerte!**

**1-3 ¿En qué clase…?** Match the words on the left with the appropriate class on the right.

1. _c_ *Don Quijote* de Cervantes
2. _e_ números
3. _a_ mapa digital
4. _b_ animales
5. _f_ Freud
6. _d_ Napoleón

a. geografía
b. biología
c. literatura
d. historia
e. matemáticas
f. psicología

**1-4 Mis clases.** PRIMERA FASE. Make a list of your classes. Indicate the days and time each class meets and whether it is easy or difficult, interesting or boring. You will find some subjects in the list below.

economía – economics

bioquímica

física

artes plásticas

contabilidad

comunicaciones

sociología – sociology

cálculo – calculus

estadística

astronomía – astronomy

negocios

historia del arte – Art history

informática

seminario de…

filosofía – Philosophy

| CLASE | DÍAS | HORA | ¿CÓMO ES? |
|-------|------|------|-----------|
|       |      |      |           |
|       |      |      |           |
|       |      |      |           |
|       |      |      |           |
|       |      |      |           |

SEGUNDA FASE. Tell your partner about your classes. Take turns completing the following ideas.

1. Llego a la universidad a la(s)…
2. Mi clase favorita es…
3. El profesor/La profesora se llama…
4. La clase es muy…
5. Practico español en…
6. En mi clase de español hay…

**1-5 Las clases de mis compañeros/as.** PRIMERA FASE. Use the following questions to interview your partner. Take notes. Then switch roles.

1. ¿Qué estudias este semestre?
2. ¿Cuántas clases tienes?
3. ¿Cuál es tu clase favorita?
4. ¿Qué día y a qué hora es tu clase favorita?
5. Tu clase de español, ¿cómo es? ¿Es fácil o difícil? ¿Es interesante o aburrida?
6. ¿Trabajas con computadoras? ¿Dónde?
7. ¿Sacas buenas notas?
8. ¿Tienes muchos exámenes?

SEGUNDA FASE. Introduce your partner to another classmate and state one piece of interesting information about him/her. Your classmate will ask your partner about his/her classes.

MODELO:   USTED:   *Él es Pedro. Estudia ciencias políticas y tiene cuatro clases este semestre.*

SU COMPAÑERO/A:   *Mucho gusto. ¿_____?*

# ))) La universidad

CD 1
Track 22

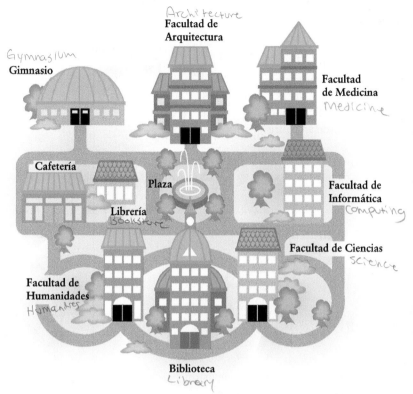

Gymnasium
**Gimnasio**

Architecture
**Facultad de Arquitectura**

**Facultad de Medicina**
Medicine

**Cafetería**

**Plaza**

**Librería**
Bookstore

**Facultad de Informática**
Computing

**Facultad de Ciencias**
Science

**Facultad de Humanidades**
Humanities

**Biblioteca**
Library

Carmen

Lorena

Álvaro

Juan

**1-6 ¿En qué facultad estudian?** PRIMERA FASE. Match the names of the university students pictured at the right with the school where they study.

1. _B_ Juan
2. _A_ Carmen
3. _D_ Lorena
4. _C_ Álvaro

a. Facultad de Medicina
b. Facultad de Arquitectura
c. Facultad de Humanidades
d. Facultad de Ciencias

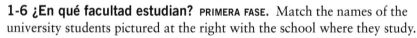

**SEGUNDA FASE.** Exchange the information with a classmate and indicate two classes that each student is probably taking.

MODELO:  E1:  *¿Dónde estudia Carmen?*
E2:  *Carmen estudia en la Facultad de... Probablemente tiene clase de... y de...*

**1-7 Mapa de la universidad.** Look at the map above and indicate if each statement is true (**Cierto**) or false (**Falso**). If it is **Falso,** correct the information.

1. _C_ La plaza está en el centro del campus.
2. _C_ La Facultad de Humanidades está junto a (*next to*) la biblioteca.
3. _F_ La cafetería está detrás del gimnasio. Enfrente
4. _C_ La Facultad de Ciencias está delante de (*in front of*) la Facultad de Informática.
5. _C_ La librería está al lado de la cafetería.
6. _F_ La Facultad de Medicina está al lado del gimnasio.

# Las actividades de los estudiantes

### En la biblioteca

CD 1
Track 23

Unos **alumnos** estudian en la biblioteca. **Toman apuntes** y trabajan en sus tareas. A veces **buscan** palabras en el **diccionario**. Frecuentemente **conversan** sobre sus clases.

### Los fines de semana

CD 1
Track 24

Los estudiantes **toman algo** en un **café**.

**Miran** televisión en **casa**.

**Bailan** en una **discoteca** con amigos.

**Caminan** en la **playa**.

**Montan** en bicicleta.

**1-8 Para escoger.** Look at the illustrations above. Then choose the word or phrase that completes the sentence logically.

1. Los estudiantes ___ en la biblioteca.
   a. toman café          b. estudian          c. hablan
2. Buscan palabras en ___ .
   a. el reloj          b. el diccionario          c. el laboratorio
3. Miran televisión en ___ .
   a. la biblioteca          b. la playa          c. casa
4. Montan en bicicleta ___ .
   a. los fines de semana          b. en el café          c. en una discoteca

## En la librería

CD 1
Track 25

ESTUDIANTE: **Necesito comprar** un diccionario para mi clase de literatura española.

DEPENDIENTE: **¿Grande** o **pequeño?**

ESTUDIANTE: Grande, y todo en español.

DEPENDIENTE: **Este** diccionario es muy bueno.

ESTUDIANTE: **¿Cuánto cuesta?**

DEPENDIENTE: Cuarenta y ocho **euros.**

**1-9 ¿Qué necesita?** Complete the following statements, based on the previous conversation.

1. El estudiante necesita...
2. Es un diccionario...
3. Es para su clase de...
4. El diccionario cuesta...

**1-10 ¿Cuánto cuesta?** During your semester abroad, you go to the university bookstore. Ask the salesclerk how much the following items cost.

### Cultura

Since 2002, the euro has been the official monetary unit of the so-called Eurozone, which includes (as of January 2008) Austria, Belgium, Cyprus, Finland, France, Germany, Greece, Ireland, Italy, Luxembourg, Malta, the Netherlands, Portugal, Slovenia, and Spain. In some other European countries and the United Kingdom, the euro, although not official, is accepted in stores. The euro currency sign is € and the banking code is EUR.

**MODELO:**

ESTUDIANTE: *¿Cuánto cuesta el mapa?*

DEPENDIENTE/A: *Cuesta cincuenta euros.*

**1-11 Entrevista (*Interview*).**  Ask where and when your classmate does each of the following activities.

MODELO:    practicar baloncesto (*basketball*)
E1:  *¿Dónde practicas baloncesto? ¿Y cuándo?*
E2:  *Practico baloncesto en la plaza por las tardes.*

| ACTIVIDAD | DÓNDE | CUÁNDO |
|---|---|---|
| 1. estudiar para un examen difícil | | |
| 2. mirar televisión | | |
| 3. tomar café/chocolate | | |
| 4. bailar salsa | | |
| 5. escuchar música | | |
| 6. comprar un diccionario/CDs/materiales para tus clases | | |

 **1-12 Las actividades de sus compañeros.**  PRIMERA FASE.  Go around the classroom and interview three people. Ask two different questions of each of them. Take notes to report later. Answer the questions of classmates who interview you.

1. ¿Qué haces (*do you do*) los fines de semana?
2. ¿Dónde miras televisión?
3. ¿Qué compras en la librería?
4. ¿Dónde estudias normalmente?
5. ¿Trabajas los fines de semana? ¿Dónde trabajas?

SEGUNDA FASE.  Now share your classmates' answers with the rest of the class.

MODELO:   *María estudia normalmente en casa. No trabaja los fines de semana.*

**1-13 ¿Qué hacen? (*What do they do?*)**  You will hear three people talking about their activities during the week and on weekends. Before you listen, list your own activities in the chart.

CD 1
Track 26

| MIS ACTIVIDADES DE TODOS LOS DÍAS | MIS ACTIVIDADES DEL FIN DE SEMANA |
|---|---|
| | |
| | |
| | |

Now pay attention to the general idea of what is said in the recording. As you listen, decide which activities each person is talking about. Then write the number of the speaker (1, 2, 3) next to the appropriate topic.

___ los estudios
___ el tiempo libre (*free time*)
___ el trabajo

# EN ACCIÓN

## Diarios de bicicleta: La chivita

### Antes de ver

**1-14** In this video segment, you will be introduced to four college students, some of whom do not know each other. Write down four expressions you think they may use to greet and introduce each other.

### Mientras ve

**1-15** As you watch, indicate whether the following statements refer to Javier (**J**), Daniel (**D**), Luciana (**L**), or Gabi (**G**).

1. ___ Son sus diarios de bicicleta.
2. ___ Es compañera de Gaby.
3. ___ Viaja en bicicleta.
4. ___ Es puntual, simpático y cómico.
5. ___ Olvida (*forgets*) su teléfono en la cafetería.

### Después de ver

**1-16** Check off the expressions you prepared in *Antes de ver* that were used in this segment.

# FUNCIONES Y FORMAS

## 1. Talking about academic life and daily occurrences: Present tense of regular *-ar* verbs

Sara    Marta

REPORTERO: Perdón. Soy Pablo Brito del canal 11 de televisión. ¿Su nombre, por favor?

SARA: Yo soy Sara y ella es Marta.

REPORTERO: ¿Tienen ustedes una vida muy activa?

MARTA: Sí, nosotras somos (*are*) atletas. **Practicamos** muchos deportes. Sara **participa** en maratones y **practica** el tenis. Yo **practico** el fútbol y el baloncesto.

SARA: Y los fines de semana **montamos** en bicicleta.

REPORTERO: ¡Qué interesante! Gracias, señoritas.

**Piénselo.** Check (✓) all the statements that are true, based on the reporter's interview with Sara and Marta.

1. _____ Pablo es un reportero de radio.
2. _____ Marta y Sara **practican** muchos deportes (*sports*).
3. _____ Marta **participa** en maratones.
4. _____ Marta **practica** el fútbol.
5. _____ Sara **practica** el baloncesto.
6. _____ Sara y Marta **montan** en bicicleta.

■ To talk about actions, feelings, and states of being, you need to use verbs. In both English and Spanish, the infinitive is the base form of the verb that appears in vocabulary lists and dictionaries. In English, infinitives are preceded by *to*: *to speak*. Infinitives in Spanish belong to one of three groups, depending on whether they end in **-ar**, **-er**, or **-ir**. Verbs ending in **-ar** are presented here, and verbs ending in **-er** and **-ir** are presented in the next section.

| HABLAR (*to speak*) | | | |
|---|---|---|---|
| yo | habl**o** | nosotros/as | habl**amos** |
| tú | habl**as** | vosotros/as | habl**áis** |
| él, ella, Ud. | habl**a** | ellos, ellas, Uds. | habl**an** |

*[Handwritten notes: AR verbs (us) / yo - o / tú - as / el, ella, Ud - a / nosotros - amos / vosotros - áis / ellos, ellas, uds - an (they)]*

■ Use the present tense to express what you and others generally or habitually do or do not do. You may also use the present tense to express an ongoing action. Context will tell you which meaning is intended.

Ana **trabaja** en la oficina.  { *Ana works in the office.*
{ *Ana is working in the office.*

Luis **practica** el piano todos los días.  *Luis practices the piano every day.*

■ Here are some expressions you may find useful when talking about the frequency of actions.

| | | | |
|---|---|---|---|
| **siempre** | *always* | **muchas veces** | *often* |
| **todos los días/meses** | *every day/month* | **a veces** | *sometimes* |
| **todas las semanas** | *every week* | **nunca** | *never* |

■ Some common **-ar** verbs are **bailar, buscar, caminar, comprar, conversar, escuchar, estudiar, llegar, mirar, montar, necesitar, participar, practicar, sacar, tomar,** and **trabajar.**

**1-17 Preferencias.** PRIMERA FASE. Rank these activities from 1 to 9, according to your preferences (1 = most interesting, 9 = least interesting).

_____ bailar en una discoteca
_____ mirar televisión en casa
_____ estudiar otras culturas
_____ comprar DVDs y CDs
_____ caminar en la playa

_____ montar en bicicleta cuando hace sol
_____ escuchar música rock
_____ conversar con los amigos con mensajes de texto
_____ bajar (*download*) música de Internet

SEGUNDA FASE. Now compare your answers with those of a classmate. Follow the model.

MODELO:  E1: *Para mí, bailar en una discoteca es número 1. ¿Y para ti?*
E2: *Para mí, caminar en la playa es número 1.*

**1-18 Mi rutina.** PRIMERA FASE. Indicate (✓) the activities that are part of your routine at school.

1. _____ Llego a la universidad a las nueve de la mañana.
2. _____ Converso con mis amigos por teléfono.
3. _____ Tomo notas en todas las clases.
4. _____ Hablo con mis compañeros en la cafetería.
5. _____ Estudio en la biblioteca por las mañanas.
6. _____ Trabajo en mis tareas todas las noches.
7. _____ Miro programas cómicos en la televisión.
8. _____ A veces practico un deporte con mis amigos/as.

SEGUNDA FASE. Now compare your answers with those of a classmate. The expressions in *En directo* will help you react as your classmate tells you about himself/herself. Report your findings to the class.

MODELO: *Daniel y yo somos (muy) similares. Él y yo miramos programas cómicos en la televisión./Daniel y yo somos (muy) diferentes. Yo estudio por las mañanas; él estudia por las tardes.*

---

**En directo**

To express disbelief:
**¡Qué increíble!**
To show surprise at a coincidence:
**¡Qué casualidad!**

---

**1-19 A preguntar.** PRIMERA FASE. Find four different classmates, each of whom does one of the following activities. Write each name on the appropriate line. The expressions in *En directo* will help you carry on the conversation.

MODELO: mirar televisión por la noche
E1: *¡Oye! ¿Miras televisión por la tarde?*
E2: *Sí, miro televisión por la tarde. O*
*No, no miro televisión por la tarde.*

| PERSONA | ACTIVIDAD |
|---|---|
| _____ | estudiar español todos los días |
| _____ | llegar a la universidad a las 9:30 a.m. |
| _____ | escuchar música clásica en casa por la noche |
| _____ | trabajar en una oficina por la tarde |

SEGUNDA FASE. Now report to the class your findings about your classmates' activities.

**1-20 Mis actividades.** PRIMERA FASE. Mark (✓) the space that indicates how often you do the following activities:

---

**En directo**

To get someone's attention:
**¡Oye!** (to someone your age or younger)
**Oiga, por favor.** (to someone unknown to you)
To interrupt to ask a question:
**Perdón, tengo una pregunta.**
To agree to answer:
**Con mucho gusto.**

---

| ACTIVIDADES | A VECES | MUCHAS VECES | SIEMPRE | NUNCA |
|---|---|---|---|---|
| estudiar con amigos | | | | |
| sacar buenas notas | | | | |
| montar en bicicleta los fines de semana | | | | |
| mirar televisión por la tarde | | | | |
| bailar los sábados | | | | |
| tomar café | | | | |

**SEGUNDA FASE.** Now tell each other how often you do these activities, and then ask where your partner does them.

**MODELO:** E1: *Yo estudio con amigos a veces, ¿y tú?*
E2: *Yo siempre estudio con amigos.*
E1: *¿Dónde estudian ustedes?*
E2: *Estudiamos en la biblioteca.*

**1-21 Un día típico en la vida de Luisa.** **PRIMERA FASE.** Describe what Luisa does on a typical day.

**MODELO:** *Luisa llega a la oficina a las nueve menos diez.*

1.

2.

3.

4.

**SEGUNDA FASE.** Now, based on a typical day in her life, describe Luisa's personality. Then explain what you normally do on a regular day.

Este bar de Madrid tiene una selección de tapas deliciosas.

## SITUACIONES

1. **Role A.** Your friend works in the afternoon. Ask a) where he/she works; b) the days of the week and the hours that he/she works; and c) if the job (**trabajo**) is interesting/boring/difficult/easy. Then answer your friend's questions about your job.

   **Role B.** Tell your friend that you work in the afternoon. Answer your friend's questions about your job. Then ask three questions about his/her job (**trabajo**).

2. **Role A.** You need to read *Don Quijote de la Mancha* by Miguel de Cervantes for your World Literature class, so you go to the university library. Tell the librarian that you need a book, and answer the librarian's questions about title (**título**) and author (**autor**).

   **Role B.** You are a librarian at the university library. A student tells you that he/she needs a book. Ask the title of the book (**¿cuál es el título?**) and the author (**autor**). Comment on the book.

## 2. Talking about academic life and daily occurrences: Present tense of regular -er and -ir verbs

REPORTERO: Y ustedes, ¿qué hacen durante el día?

PEDRO: Antonio estudia ciencias en la universidad. **Asiste** a sus clases y luego **corre** al laboratorio, donde trabaja todos los días. Habla con el profesor y **aprende** mucho. Los estudiantes de ciencias **leen** mucho, **escriben** trabajos de investigación y sacan buenas notas. Yo soy un estudiante de arquitectura, y mis compañeros y yo **leemos** y **escribimos** mucho también. Yo casi (*almost*) **vivo** en la biblioteca cuando estudio para los exámenes.

**Piénselo.** Check (✓) all the statements that are true, based on the reporter's interview with Pedro.

1. \_\_\_\_ Antonio estudia arquitectura.
2. \_\_\_\_ Antonio trabaja en el laboratorio y **aprende** (*learns*) mucho.
3. \_\_\_\_ Los estudiantes **leen** y **escriben** mucho.
4. \_\_\_\_ Antonio no **asiste** (*attends*) a sus clases.
5. \_\_\_\_ Los estudiantes de ciencias sacan buenas notas.
6. \_\_\_\_ Pedro estudia arquitectura.
7. \_\_\_\_ Pedro **vive** (*lives*) en el laboratorio.

■ You have learned in this chapter that the present tense is used to express activities and ongoing actions. You have also learned the present tense forms for verbs whose infinitives end in **-ar**. Now you will learn those forms for verbs whose infinitives end in **-er** and **-ir**.

■ Note that **-er** and **-ir** verbs have the same endings, except for the **nosotros/as** and **vosotros/as** forms.

| APRENDER (*to learn*) | | | |
|---|---|---|---|
| yo | aprend**o** | nosotros/as | aprend**emos** |
| tú | aprend**es** | vosotros/as | aprend**éis** |
| él, ella, Ud. | aprend**e** | ellos, ellas, Uds. | aprend**en** |

| VIVIR (*to live*) | | | |
|---|---|---|---|
| yo | viv**o** | nosotros/as | viv**imos** |
| tú | viv**es** | vosotros/as | viv**ís** |
| él, ella, Ud. | viv**e** | ellos, ellas, Uds. | viv**en** |

■ Other common **-er** and **-ir** verbs are **comer** (*to eat*), **comprender, correr, leer, responder** (*to respond*), **asistir,** and **escribir.**

■ The verb **ver** (*to see*) has an irregular **yo** form: **veo, ves, ve, vemos, veis, ven.**

**Veo** películas los fines de semana.     *I see movies on weekends.*

■ Use **deber** + *infinitive* to express that you should/must/ought to do something.

Los atletas **deben beber** mucha agua.     *Athletes should drink lots of water.*

**1-22 Mi profesor/a modelo.** PRIMERA FASE. Indicate which of the activities are part of the routine of an ideal instructor inside and outside the classroom.

|  | SÍ | NO |
|---|---|---|
| 1. Lee el periódico (*newspaper*) en clase. | _____ | _____ |
| 2. Escucha los problemas de los estudiantes. | _____ | _____ |
| 3. Bebe café y come en la clase. | _____ | _____ |
| 4. Escribe buenos ejemplos en la pizarra. | _____ | _____ |
| 5. Nunca prepara sus clases. | _____ | _____ |
| 6. Siempre asiste a clase. | _____ | _____ |
| 7. Responde a las preguntas de los estudiantes. | _____ | _____ |
| 8. Habla con los estudiantes en su oficina. | _____ | _____ |

SEGUNDA FASE. Compare your answers with those of a classmate. Together write two more activities typical of an ideal instructor and ask your instructor if they are part of his/her academic routine.

**1-23 Para pasarlo bien (*To have a good time*).** PRIMERA FASE. Indicate which of the following activities your classmates do to have a good time.

1. _____ Leen libros en español todas las semanas.
2. _____ Escriben mensajes de texto.
3. _____ Practican deportes con los amigos.
4. _____ Asisten a clase a las ocho de la mañana.
5. _____ Corren en el gimnasio y en el parque.
6. _____ Ven películas y programas de televisión en casa.
7. _____ Comen en restaurantes elegantes.
8. _____ Beben sólo Coca-Cola en las fiestas.

SEGUNDA FASE. Compare your answers with those of a classmate. Then exchange information with another pair (**pareja**) about the activities you all do to have a good time. Use the expressions in *En directo* to help you react naturally to your classmates' responses.

MODELO:   PAREJA 1:   *Nosotros bailamos en discotecas para pasarlo bien. ¿Y ustedes?*
          PAREJA 2:   *Bebemos café y conversamos con los amigos.*

| En directo |
|---|
| To react to what someone has said: |
| **¡Qué interesante!** |
| **¡Qué divertido!** *How funny!* |
| **¡Qué aburrido!** *How boring!* |

**1-24 Lugares y actividades.** Ask what your classmate does in the following places. He/She will respond with one of the activities listed. Then ask what your classmate does not do in those places.

MODELO:   en la clase
E1: *¿Qué haces en la clase?*
E2: *Veo películas en español.*
E1: *¿Qué no haces en la clase?*
E2: *No leo el periódico.*

| LUGARES | ACTIVIDADES |
|---|---|
| en la playa | beber cerveza |
| en un café | tomar el sol |
| en una discoteca | bailar salsa |
| en una fiesta | mirar televisión |
| en el cine | leer el periódico |
| en la casa | ver películas de horror |
| en un restaurante | escuchar música clásica |
| en la biblioteca | comer un sándwich y |
| | tomar un café |

**1-25 A preguntar.** PRIMERA FASE. Find four different classmates, each of whom does one of the following activities. Write each name in the chart below.

MODELO:   ver películas en casa
E1: *¿Ves películas en casa?*
E2: *Sí, veo películas en casa./ No, no veo películas en casa.*

| PERSONA | ACTIVIDAD |
|---|---|
| _____ | asistir a conciertos de música rock |
| _____ | beber café todos los días |
| _____ | vivir en casa con la familia |
| _____ | escribir mensajes de texto por la noche |

SEGUNDA FASE. Now report to the class your findings about your classmates' activities.

**1-26 ¿Qué deben hacer?** Read the situations in the column on the left and select the best advice from the column on the right.

1. ___ Maricela desea sacar buenas notas.
2. ___ Carlos corre en el parque.
3. ___ Luisa y Jorge están (*are*) muy nerviosos.
4. ___ Los estudiantes desean comer tapas.
5. ___ Óscar desea aprender a bailar.
6. ___ Carolina desea preparar tacos, burritos y enchiladas.

a. Debe trabajar en un restaurante mexicano.
b. Deben visitar España.
c. Debe estudiar todos los días.
d. Debe tomar clases de baile.
e. No deben beber café con cafeína.
f. Debe beber mucha agua.

## SITUACIONES

1. Role A. You see a classmate at a coffee shop with laptop and books spread out on the table. Ask if he/she a) drinks coffee every day; b) often studies in the coffee shop; c) reads the newspaper there; and d) writes on the computer in the coffee shop.

   Role B. You are sitting at a table with your laptop and books at your favorite coffee shop. A classmate comes in and walks over. Answer your classmate's questions about what you usually do there.

2. Role A. On the way to Spanish class you run into a classmate and ask how he/she is. Your classmate confides that he/she isn't getting good grades in Spanish. Suggest that he/she a) should always attend class; b) must read the chapter every week; c) should study in the library; and d) ought to look for a good dictionary.

   Role B. In the hallway you run into the person who sits next to you in Spanish class. When he/she asks how you are, say you're so-so. Explain that you are not getting good grades in Spanish and that you are not learning the vocabulary. Listen to your classmate's advice and thank him/her.

# 3. Specifying gender and number: Articles and nouns

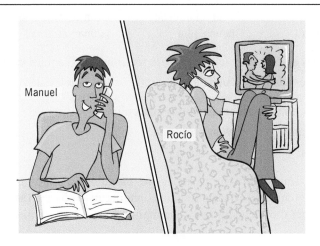

MANUEL: Hola, Rocío. Tengo **un** plan. ¿Estudiamos español en **la** universidad esta tarde? Necesito **un** diccionario para **la** tarea.

ROCÍO: ¡Buena idea! ¿En **la** biblioteca? **El** profesor de español es bueno, pero es **una** clase difícil. ¿Invitamos a mi amigo Marcos?

MANUEL: Fenomenal. Usamos **la** pizarra y **el** escritorio **del** salón 12 de **la** biblioteca.

**Piénselo.** Match the words on the right with those on the left. Use the dialogue and the endings of the nouns as clues.

1. ___ clase
2. ___ diccionario de español
3. ___ pizarra
4. ___ escritorio
5. ___ universidad

a. el
b. la
c. un
d. una

## Gender

■ Nouns are words that name a person, place, or thing. In English all nouns use the same definite article, *the*, and all singular nouns use the indefinite articles *a* and *an*. Spanish nouns, whether they refer to people or to things, have either masculine or feminine gender. Masculine singular nouns use **el** or **un** and feminine singular nouns use **la** or **una**.

The terms *masculine* and *feminine* are used in a grammatical sense and have nothing to do with biological gender.

|  | MASCULINE | FEMININE |  |
|---|---|---|---|
| SINGULAR DEFINITE ARTICLES | **el** | **la** | *the* |
| SINGULAR INDEFINITE ARTICLES | **un** | **una** | *a/an* |

■ Generally, nouns that end in **-o** are masculine and require **el** or **un**, and those that end in **-a** are feminine and require **la** or **una**.

| | | |
|---|---|---|
| **el/un** libro | **el/un** cuaderno | **el/un** diccionario |
| **la/una** mesa | **la/una** silla | **la/una** ventana |

■ Nouns that end in **-dad, -ción, -sión** are feminine and require **la** or **una**.

| | | |
|---|---|---|
| **la/una** universi**dad** | **la/una** lec**ción** | **la/una** televi**sión** |

■ Nouns that end in **-ma** are generally masculine.

| | |
|---|---|
| **el/un** progra**ma** | **el/un** proble**ma** |
| **el/un** dra**ma** | **el/un** poe**ma** |

■ In general, nouns that refer to males are masculine, and nouns that refer to females are feminine. Masculine nouns ending in **-o** change the **-o** to **-a** for the feminine; those ending in a consonant add **-a** for the feminine.

| | |
|---|---|
| **el/un** amig**o** | **la/una** amig**a** |
| **el/un** profesor | **la/una** profesor**a** |

■ Nouns ending in **-ante** and **-ente** may be feminine or masculine. Gender is signaled by the article (**el/la estudiante**).

■ Use definite articles with titles when you are talking about someone. Do not use definite articles when addressing someone directly.

**La** señorita Andrade es **la** secretaria en el Departamento de Lenguas Europeas. **El** profesor Campos es **el** director del departamento.

*Ms. Andrade is the secretary in the Department of European Languages. Professor Campos is the chair of the department.*

Todos los días, el profesor Campos dice "Buenos días, señorita Andrade". Ella contesta, "Buenos días, profesor Campos".

*Every day, Professor Campos says "Good morning, Ms. Andrade." She responds, "Good morning, Professor Campos."*

## Number

| | MASCULINE | FEMININE | |
|---|---|---|---|
| PLURAL DEFINITE ARTICLES | **los** | **las** | *the* |
| PLURAL INDEFINITE ARTICLES | **unos** | **unas** | *some* |

■ Add **-s** to form the plural of nouns that end in a vowel. Add **-es** to nouns ending in a consonant.

| | |
|---|---|
| la silla  →  las silla**s** | el cuaderno  →  los cuaderno**s** |
| la activi**dad**  →  las actividade**s** | el señor  →  los señor**es** |

■ Nouns that end in **-z** change the **z** to **c** before **-es**.

el lápi**z**  →  los lápi**ces**

■ To refer to a mixed group, use masculine plural forms.

los chic**os**     *the boys and girls*

**1-27 Conversaciones incompletas.** Complete the dialogues.

1. Supply the definite articles (**el, la, los, las**).
   E1: ¿Dónde está María?
   E2: Está en __ clase de __ profesora Sánchez.
   E1: ¡Qué lástima! Necesito hablar con ella. Es urgente.
   E2: Bueno, ella está en __ salón de clase hasta __ una, y por
   __ tarde trabaja en __ laboratorio.
   E1: ¿Y a qué hora llega?
   E2: Llega a ___ dos, más o menos.

2. Supply the indefinite articles (**un, una, unos, unas**).
   E1: Necesito comprar ___ calculadora y ___ lápices.
   E2: Y yo necesito ___ bolígrafo y ___ diccionario, pero ¿qué diccionario compro?
   E1: Para el curso de español, ___ profesores usan ___ diccionario pequeño y otros usan
   ___ diccionario grande. ¿Por qué (*Why*) no hablas con tu profesor?

3. Supply the definite or indefinite articles.
   E1: Tengo ___ examen de matemáticas mañana y necesito sacar ___ buena nota en esa clase.
   E2: ¿Quién es ___ profesor?
   E1: Es ___ doctora Solís.
   E2: ¡Ah! Es ___ profesora excelente.
   E1: Sí, pero ___ clase es muy difícil. Estudio y escribo ___ tareas todos
   ___ días, pero no saco buenas notas.
   E2: ¡Vaya! Lo siento mucho.

 **1-28 ¿Qué necesitan?** Take turns saying what these classmates need.

**MODELO:** Alicia tiene que buscar unas palabras. *Necesita un diccionario.*

1. Mónica tiene que tomar apuntes en la clase de historia.
2. Carlos y Ana deben hacer la tarea de matemáticas.
3. Alfredo tiene que estudiar para el examen de geografía.
4. Isabel tiene que escribir una composición para su clase de inglés.
5. Blanca y Lucía tienen que encontrar (*find*) dónde está Salamanca.
6. David tiene que escuchar una canción (*song*) para su clase de música.

## SITUACIONES

1. **Role A.** You have missed the first day of class. Ask a classmate a) at what time the class meets; b) who the professor is; and c) what you need for the class.

   **Role B.** Tell your classmate a) that the class is at 8:00 in the morning; b) the name of the professor and what he/she is like; and c) at least three items that your classmate needs for the class.

2. **Role A.** You work for the student newspaper at your college and have been asked to interview two students to find out how they typically spend their weekends. After introducing yourself, find out a) if they work, and where; b) what they study; and c) what they do (**hacen**) on Saturdays and Sundays.

   **Roles B, C.** Tell the interviewer a) if you work and, if so, where; b) the classes you take; and c) what you do on weekends, where, and with whom.

## 4. Expressing location and states of being: Present tense of *estar*

ELISA: ¿Humberto? Te habla Elisa.

HUMBERTO: ¡Elisa! ¡Qué sorpresa! ¿Dónde **estás**?

ELISA: **Estoy** en el aeropuerto de Barajas, en Madrid. ¿Y tú?

HUMBERTO: Mi padre y yo **estamos** de vacaciones en Nueva York. En este momento, mi padre **está** en la tienda *Best Buy*. ¿Y cómo **están** todos en tu familia?

ELISA: Todos **estamos** muy bien. ¡Qué bueno escucharte! Lo siento, Humberto, pero el vuelo (*flight*) sale (*leaves*) pronto. Hablamos más mañana. Adiós.

Elisa    Humberto

**Piénselo.** Indicate whether each statement is true (**Cierto**) or false (**Falso**), based on the conversation. If it is **Falso**, correct the information.

1. _____ Humberto **está** en el aeropuerto.
2. _____ Elisa **está** de vacaciones en Nueva York.
3. _____ Humberto **está** en una ciudad grande con una persona de su familia.
4. _____ La tienda *Best Buy* de esta conversación **está** en Madrid.
5. _____ Elisa y Humberto **están** contentos de hablar por teléfono.

■ You have already been using some forms of **estar**. Here are all the present tense forms of this verb.

| ESTAR (*to be*) | | | |
|---|---|---|---|
| yo | **estoy** | nosotros/as | **estamos** |
| tú | **estás** | vosotros/as | **estáis** |
| Ud., él, ella | **está** | Uds., ellos, ellas | **están** |

■ Use **estar** to express the location of persons or objects.

| | |
|---|---|
| ¿Dónde **está** Humberto? | *Where is Humberto?* |
| **Está** en Nueva York. | *He is in New York* |

■ Use **estar** to talk about states of health or being.

| | |
|---|---|
| ¿Cómo **está** la familia de Elisa? | *How is Elisa's family?* |
| **Está** muy bien. | *They are very well.* |

**1-29 En la cafetería.** In the cafeteria, you run across a former classmate. Complete the conversation, using the correct forms of **estar**. Then indicate in the parentheses if **estar** signals location (**L**) or a state of being (**S**).

ROBERTO: Hola, Carlos. ¿Qué tal? ¿Cómo _____?

CARLOS: _____ muy bien. ¿Y tú?

ROBERTO: Muy bien, muy bien. ¿Y cómo _____ tu hermana *(sister)* Ana?

CARLOS: Bien, gracias. Ella y mamá _____ en España ahora.

ROBERTO: ¡Qué suerte! Y nosotros _____ en la universidad, ¡y en la semana de exámenes!

**1-30 Horas y lugares favoritos.** PRIMERA FASE. Ask your classmate his/her favorite time of day or day of the week. Then ask where he/she usually is at that time or on that day.

MODELO: E1: *¿Cuál es tu hora favorita del día?*
E2: *Las 10:00 de la mañana.*
E1: *Generalmente, ¿dónde estás a las 10:00 de la mañana?*
E2: Estoy en... . ¿Y cuál es tu hora favorita?
E1: ... .
E2: ¿Y dónde estás?
E1: Estoy en... .

SEGUNDA FASE. Compare your responses with those of your partner. Identify any similarities and/or differences in your preferences.

**1-31 Conversación.** Ask a classmate where the people in these drawings are, how they feel, and what they are doing.

MODELO: E1: *¿Dónde está María Luisa?*
E2: *Está en la biblioteca.*
E1: *¿Cómo está?*
E2: *Está regular.*
E1: *¿Qué hace?*
E2: *Estudia.*

María Luisa

**1.** Berta   Lorena   **2.** Carlos   el Dr. Núñez   **3.** Marcelo   Eduardo

---

### SITUACIONES

1. Role A. As editor of the new student handbook, you must give the graphic designer directions for drawing the campus map. First draw a rough sketch of the map, including the places below. Then explain their location to the designer.

   la biblioteca

   la cafetería

   la Facultad de Ciencias

   la Facultad de Humanidades

   Role B. You are a graphic designer. Ask questions about the location of these buildings as you draw the new map. When you have finished, show the map to the editor to check if you have understood his/her explanations.

2. Role A. You are a new student at the university and you do not know where the gym is. Introduce yourself to a classmate. Explain that you want to run in the gym and ask where it is located. Thank your classmate for the help (**Gracias por la ayuda**).

   Role B. A new student will greet you and ask questions. Make your answers as complete and specific as possible.

## 5. Asking and answering questions: Interrogative words

Andrea Pérez conversa con su consejera (*advisor*) en la universidad. La consejera necesita rellenar (*fill out*) algunos formularios con información sobre Andrea. Aquí están algunas de las preguntas de la consejera y en la columna de la derecha, las respuestas de Andrea.

**CONSEJERA**

**¿Cómo** se llama la residencia estudiantil donde vives?
**¿Dónde** está?
**¿Cuándo** son tus clases?
**¿Cuánto** cuesta tu transporte por mes?
**¿Quién** es tu compañera de cuarto?
**¿Por qué** deseas (*want to*) estudiar psicología?

**ANDREA**

Se llama Casa Cervantes.
Está en la Avenida España.
Por la mañana y por la tarde.
Aproximadamente 35 euros.
Cristina Zapatero.
Para ayudar (*help*) a otras personas.

**Piénselo.** Match Andrea's responses in the left column with the questions her advisor asked her in the right column. **OJO:** You will be able to answer some of the advisor's questions with the information from the conversation above.

1. ___ Es el profesor Agustín Reyes-Torres.
2. ___ Se llama Cristina Zapatero.
3. ___ En la Casa Cervantes.
4. ___ 400 euros al mes.
5. ___ Por la tarde.

a. **¿Dónde** vives?
b. **¿Cuándo** es tu clase de psicología?
c. **¿Quién** es tu profesor favorito?
d. **¿Cómo** se llama tu compañera de cuarto?
e. **¿Cuánto** cuesta vivir en la residencia?

■ Interrogative words are used to ask questions or to obtain specific information. You have already been using many of these words.

| | | | |
|---|---|---|---|
| **¿cómo?** | *how/what?* | **¿cuál(es)?** | *which?* |
| **¿dónde?** | *where?* | **¿quién(es)?** | *who?* |
| **¿qué?** | *what?* | **¿cuánto/a?** | *how much?* |
| **¿cuándo?** | *when?* | **¿cuántos/as?** | *how many?* |
| **¿por qué?** | *why?* | **¿para qué?** | *why?/what for?* |

■ If a subject is used in a question, it normally follows the verb.

**¿Dónde trabaja Elsa?**      *Where does Elsa work?*

■ Use **por qué** to ask *why* and **porque** to answer *because*.

**¿Por qué** está Pepe en la biblioteca?    *Why is Pepe at the library?*
**Porque** necesita estudiar.      *Because he needs to study.*

■ Use **qué + ser** when you want to ask for a definition or an explanation.

**¿Qué es** la sardana?      *What is the sardana?*
Es un baile típico de Cataluña.    *It is a typical dance of Catalonia.*

### Lengua

All question words have a written accent over the stressed syllable: **cómo**, **dónde**.

When these words are used in a non-interrogative context, they do not have a written accent.

**¿Dónde está la biblioteca?**
*Where is the library?*

**Esta es la biblioteca donde estudio todos los días.**
*This is the library where I study everyday.*

■ Use **cuál(es) + ser** when you want to ask which one(s).

| | |
|---|---|
| **¿Cuál es** tu mochila? | *Which (one) is your backpack?* |
| **¿Cuáles son** tus papeles? | *Which (ones) are your papers?* |

■ Questions that may be answered with **sí** or **no** do not use a question word.

| | |
|---|---|
| ¿Trabajan ustedes los sábados? | *Do you work on Saturdays?* |
| No, no trabajamos. | *No, we do not.* |

■ Another way to ask a question is to place an interrogative tag after a declarative statement.

| | |
|---|---|
| Tú hablas inglés, **¿verdad?** | *You speak English, don't you?* |
| David es norteamericano, **¿no?** | *David is an American, isn't he?* |

**1-32 Preguntas.** First look at the cues in the right column and then complete the questions with **quién, cuándo, cuántos/as, cuál,** or **por qué,** as logical. Use your questions to interview two people as you walk around the room.

1. ¿ _____ clases tomas? — Tomo…
2. ¿ _____ son tus clases? — Por la…
3. ¿ _____ es tu clase favorita? — La clase de…
4. ¿ _____ es tu profesor/a favorito/a? — El profesor/La profesora…
5. ¿ _____ estudias español? — Porque…
6. ¿ _____ estudiantes hay en tu clase de español? — Hay…

> ### Lengua
>
> To request repetition or clarification of a statement, use **¿Cómo?** or **¿Perdón?** The use of **¿Qué?,** the equivalent of English *What?*, is generally considered rude by native speakers.

**1-33 Entrevista.** Ask your classmate questions to find out the following information. Use the appropriate expressions to show disbelief, coincidence, how interesting the answers are, and so on.

1. número de clases que toma este semestre
2. su clase favorita y razón (y por qué)
3. número de alumnos en la clase favorita
4. nombre del profesor favorito/de la profesora favorita
5. lugar donde estudia generalmente y cuántas horas estudia por (*per*) día
6. lugar donde trabaja

## SITUACIONES

1. **Role A.** You have just run across a friend you have not seen all year. Inquire about your friend's life in college including a) the location and size of his/her college/university; b) courses this semester; and c) his/her activities.

   **Role B.** You are talking with a friend you have not seen in a long time. Answer your friend's questions about your life in college. Then ask your friend some questions to get the same information.

2. **Role A.** It is the beginning of the term, and you need to add a psychology class. One of your friends is in a class that looks promising. Ask a) who the professor is; b) if there is a lot of homework; c) when the class meets; and d) if there is an exam soon. Then ask if you should know (**saber**) anything else (**algo más**) about the class.

   **Role B.** Your friend wants some information about your psychology class. Reply as specifically as possible to all of his/her questions. Then offer some additional information about the class.

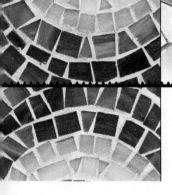

# MOSAICOS

## A escuchar

**ESTRATEGIA**

**Listen for the gist**

When you are having a conversation or are listening to other people talking in your native language, you may get the gist of what is said without understanding every word or paying attention to every detail. You do this by relying on what you do understand, your knowledge of the topic, and your subconscious expectations of what happens in a conversational exchange. You will find these techniques helpful when listening to Spanish.

### Antes de escuchar

**1-34 Preparación.** You will hear two students talking about their classes. Before listening to the recording, think about the topics they may talk about and make a list of the things you may expect to hear, based on your experience as a student.

### Escuchar

**1-35 ¿Comprende usted?** First read the following statements. Then listen to the conversation between Ana and Mario and indicate whether each statement is true (**Cierto**) or false (**Falso**).

CD 1
Track 27

1. _____ Mario y Ana estudian en la misma (*same*) universidad este semestre.
2. _____ Mario toma clases de ciencias y de humanidades.
3. _____ Ana lee en la biblioteca para sus clases.
4. _____ Ana toma clases por la tarde.
5. _____ Mario realmente visita otros países en una de sus clases.

### Después de escuchar

**1-36 Ahora usted.** Tell your classmate what you usually do on the following days and times. Your classmate will take notes. Then switch roles. Finally, verify with each other that the notes you took are correct.

| LUNES | MARTES | MIÉRCOLES | JUEVES | VIERNES |
|-------|--------|-----------|--------|---------|
| 8:00 a.m. | 3:00 p.m. | 5:00 p.m. | 9:00 p.m. | 1:00 p.m. |
| | | | | |

# A conversar

## Antes de conversar

**1-37 Preparación.** Write the questions answered by the clerk at your campus bookstore.

1. _____   La dirección de la librería es Calle Mayor, número 50.
2. _____   Sí, tengo libros de historia de España en español.
3. _____   Sí, tengo diccionarios en español.
4. _____   El diccionario bilingüe cuesta 40 euros.

## Conversar

**1-38 Entre nosotros.** You are a Spaniard studying in Malaga. Your American friend would like to purchase some gifts to take home: a fancy pen, a book on the history of Spain, a Spanish dictionary, and a map of Spain. Read the following ad and call the bookstore to find out if it has what your friend needs. Your classmate will play the role of the bookstore clerk. Remember to follow the formalities of phone conversations with someone you do not know.

**En directo**

To answer the phone in Spain:

**¿Diga?**

To greet someone formally:

**Buenos días./Buenas tardes.**

To ask if they have what you need:

**Necesito/Busco un/una...**

---

# LIBRERÍA CERVANTES

Papelería • Impresos • Artículos para escritorio

Libros de texto • Revistas

Casa especializada en estilógrafos y bolígrafos

**Plaza Constitución, 3**
**29005   Málaga**
**Teléfono  221 19 99**

---

## Después de conversar

**1-39 Un poco más.** Call your American friend to explain whether the bookstore has each item he/she needs and the price.

**Identify the format of a text**

Even before you start to read, you may draw on your experience with reading texts of different types to support your comprehension. Visual cues, photographs, type size, and the layout will help you make educated guesses about the content and meaning of the text.

# A leer

## Antes de leer

**1-40 Preparación.** Indicate which courses from the list students in the following majors (**carreras**) should take.

anatomía                   drogas tóxicas              medicinas alternativas
conflictos sociales        estructura del español     muralistas mexicanos
depresión                  fisiología
diseño gráfico             historia de la lengua

| MEDICINA | BELLAS ARTES | FARMACIA | PSICOLOGÍA | FILOLOGÍA |
|----------|--------------|----------|------------|-----------|
|          |              |          |            |           |
|          |              |          |            |           |

## Leer

**1-41 Primera mirada.** Circle the letter that completes each statement, based on the information in this web page.

1. Esta es una...                          **a.** página de un libro.   **b.** página web.
2. El logo indica que esta institución es... **a.** muy nueva.            **b.** muy antigua.
3. Esta página web presenta una lista de...  **a.** carreras.             **b.** clases.
4. La información de esta página web es...    **a.** muy específica.       **b.** muy general.
5. Esta institución tiene...                  **a.** un campus.            **b.** más de un campus.

**1-42 Segunda mirada.** Answer the following questions, according to the information in the text.

1. Al final (*the bottom*) de esta página web hay varias teclas (*keys*). ¿Qué tecla usan los estudiantes para conversar con personas que trabajan en la Universidad de Salamanca?
2. Imagínese que usted necesita información sobre su carrera en la Universidad de Salamanca. ¿Qué facultad tiene la información que usted necesita?

## Después de leer

**1-43 Ampliación.** Explore the **Servicio Central de Idiomas** page on the Universidad de Salamanca website by following the link on the *Mosaicos* web page and answer the questions that accompany the link. Be prepared to share your answers with the rest of the class.

# A escribir

## Antes de escribir

**1-44 Preparación.** As part of the course work in your Spanish class, you have been asked to correspond by e-mail with a university student in Spain. Think about and write down the information you would like to include in your first e-mail. Brainstorm...

1. some basic questions that this Spanish student may have about your college life.
2. some words and ideas that will help you answer those questions.
3. the order in which you will organize these ideas.

## Escribir

**1-45 Manos a la obra.** Now write the Spanish student an e-mail about life at your college or university. Use the information you gathered in *Preparación*. Consider including the following points, if you have not already listed them.

1. introducing yourself
2. telling how things are going for you
3. describing your school and your classes: class number and names, when you are taking them, how interesting (or not) your classes and professors are
4. describing your daily routine at school, what you do after classes and on weekends, where and with whom you do these activities, and so on

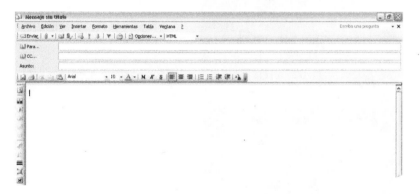

## Después de escribir

**1-46 Revisión.** After writing your e-mail, you may discuss it with a classmate. Then go over it carefully.

1. Make sure you have provided all the information your Spanish friend may need or any other you deem necessary. Pay attention to the content of your message and to the order in which you presented the information.
2. Revise any errors in language use, spelling, punctuation, accentuation, and so on.
3. Finally, make any changes that will help make your email clear and comprehensible to your e-mail pen pal.

---

**ESTRATEGIA**

### Brainstorm key ideas before writing

Brainstorming stimulates your creativity and helps you access your ideas. To brainstorm, make a note on a blank paper or computer screen of an idea or perspective you may want to emphasize. List words and ideas that will answer any questions that may arise.

Then organize them in the order in which you will use them in your text.

Thinking ahead and jotting down key words and ideas before you start to write your first draft is useful. It helps you think logically, focus on the topic, and put ideas in your own words.

# ENFOQUE CULTURAL

## Escuelas y universidades en España

El sistema escolar español es diferente del sistema de Estados Unidos y está dividido en cuatro partes: Educación Infantil, Educación Primaria, Educación Superior Obligatoria y, finalmente, el Bachillerato. En España, los niños y niñas hacen la Educación Infantil (que no es obligatoria sino voluntaria) hasta los seis años. Después empiezan la Educación Primaria, que es obligatoria y dura seis cursos, de los seis a los doce años de edad.

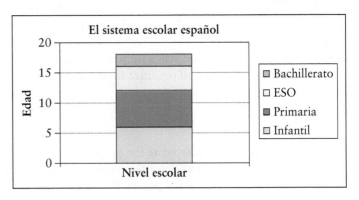

El sistema escolar español

- Bachillerato
- ESO
- Primaria
- Infantil

Entre los doce y los dieciséis años, los niños y niñas españoles cursan la Escuela Superior Obligatoria (ESO). La ESO completa la escolaridad obligatoria, pero muchos españoles continúan estudiando dos años más para terminar el Bachillerato, que los prepara para continuar con los estudios universitarios.

Rectorado de la Universidad Complutense

En España hay muchas universidades. La Universidad de Salamanca es una de las más antiguas del mundo y una de las más importantes de Europa. Esta universidad tiene un excelente programa de español para extranjeros y sus cursos de verano (durante junio, julio y agosto) tienen mucho prestigio.

De otra parte, la Universidad Complutense de Madrid es la más grande de España y también es muy antigua. Tiene un campus muy grande que se llama Ciudad Universitaria. Este nombre es muy apropiado, porque tiene más de 100.000 estudiantes.

El fútbol es un deporte muy popular en España.

En general, en las universidades españolas los estudiantes practican muchos deportes, pero la competencia entre universidades no es tan intensa como en Estados Unidos. Los deportes más populares entre los estudiantes universitarios españoles son el fútbol, el baloncesto y el atletismo, pero muchos estudiantes practican otros deportes también.

Los estudiantes universitarios españoles, como los de Estados Unidos, se divierten bailando en discotecas y clubes. Pero la música que escuchan no es necesariamente igual. A los jóvenes españoles les gusta escuchar música de rock en español. Hay muchos grupos de rock españoles. "El canto del loco" y "Fito y Fitipaldi" son dos grupos de rock español muy populares. A muchos jóvenes también les gusta bailar el flamenco, la música tradicional de Andalucía. En Sevilla, por ejemplo, hay clubes donde sólo tocan sevillanas, una música típica de esta ciudad. Finalmente, en su tiempo libre, muchos estudiantes españoles van de tapas y, por ejemplo, la Ciudad Universitaria está cerca de muchos bares de tapas.

**1-47 Comprensión.** PRIMERA FASE. **Reconocimiento de palabras clave.** Find in the text the Spanish word or phrase that best expresses the meaning of the following concepts:

preschool _____

middle school _____

high school _____

summer school _____

soccer _____

track _____

dance _____

SEGUNDA FASE. **Oraciones importantes.** Underline the statements that contain ideas found in the text. Then indicate where in the text those ideas appear.

1. Some Spanish students finish school at sixteen, while others continue with their education until they are eighteen.
2. Kindergarten is compulsory in Spain at the age of six.
3. Spanish universities are mostly private institutions.
4. The University of Salamanca has a long history.
5. The University of Madrid is so big that it is like a small city in itself.
6. Spanish universities offer their students the opportunity to practice sports.
7. Fito and Fitipaldi are two famous Spanish Formula drivers.
8. Many Spanish students enjoy dancing to traditional Spanish music.

TERCERA FASE. **Ideas principales.** Write a brief paragraph in English summarizing the main ideas expressed in the text.

**1-48 Use la información.** Prepare a poster to present to the class comparing what you have learned about the educational system of Spain to that of your own country. Use visuals to illustrate the different stages of the educational system, a few of the oldest and most important universities, and some of the activities that are popular with students in their free time.

# VOCABULARIO

### Las materias o asignaturas — *Subjects*

la antropología — *anthropology*
las ciencias políticas — *political science*
la economía — *economics*
el español — *Spanish*
la estadística — *statistics*
la geografía — *geography*
la historia — *history*
la informática/ — *computer*
  la computación — *science*
la literatura — *literature*
la psicología — *psychology*
la sociología — *sociology*

### Los lugares — *Places*

la biblioteca — *library*
el café — *cafe, coffee shop*
la cafetería — *cafeteria*
la casa — *house, home*
la discoteca — *dance club*
el gimnasio — *gymnasium*
el laboratorio — *laboratory*
la librería — *bookstore*
la oficina — *office*
la playa — *beach*
la plaza — *plaza, square*
la universidad — *university*

### Las Facultades — *Schools, departments*

de Arquitectura — *of Architecture*
de Ciencias — *of Sciences*
de Humanidades — *of Humanities*
de Informática — *of Computer Science*
de Medicina — *of Medicine*

### Las personas — *People*

el alumno/la alumna — *student*
el compañero/ — *partner,*
  la compañera — *classmate*
el dependiente/
  la dependienta — *salesperson*
ellos/ellas — *they*
nosotros/nosotras — *we*
ustedes — *you* (plural)

### Las descripciones — *Descriptions*

aburrido/a — *boring*
antiguo/a — *old*
bueno/a — *good*
difícil — *difficult*
estudioso/a — *studious*
excelente — *excellent*
fácil — *easy*
favorito/a — *favorite*
grande — *big*
interesante — *interesting*
malo/a — *bad*
norteamericano/a — *North American*
pequeño/a — *small*

### Verbos — *Verbs*

aprender — *to learn*
asistir — *to attend*
bailar — *to dance*
beber — *to drink*
buscar — *to look for*
caminar — *to walk*
comer — *to eat*
comprar — *to buy*
comprender — *to understand*
conversar — *to talk, to converse*
correr — *to run*
deber — *should*
escribir — *to write*
escuchar — *to listen (to)*
estar — *to be*
estudiar — *to study*
hablar — *to speak*
leer — *to read*
llegar — *to arrive*
mirar — *to look (at)*
montar (en bicicleta) — *to ride (a bicycle)*
necesitar — *to need*
participar — *to participate*
practicar — *to practice*
sacar buenas/malas notas — *to get good/bad grades*
tomar — *to take; to drink*
tomar apuntes/notas — *to take notes*
trabajar — *to work*
ver — *to see*
vivir — *to live*

### Palabras y expresiones útiles — *Useful words and expressions*

ahora — *now*
algo — *something*
¡Buena suerte! — *Good luck!*
¿Cómo te va? — *How is it going?*
con — *with*
¿Cuánto cuesta? — *How much is it?*
el diccionario — *dictionary*
este/a — *this*
el examen — *test*
el fin de semana — *weekend*
para — *for, to*
pero — *but*
¡Qué lástima! — *What a pity!*
sólo — *only* (adv.)
también — *also*
la tarea — *homework*
tengo/tienes — *I have/you have*
¿verdad? — *right?*

See page 33 for expressions of frequency.
See page 44 for question words.

# Mis amigos y yo

*Yo soy/Myself*, por Cristina Cárdenas, una pintora norteamericana de origen mexicano

## In this chapter you will learn how to:

- describe people, places, and things
- state where and when events take place
- express origin and possession
- express likes and dislikes

**Cultural focus:** **Estados Unidos**

Un rapero latino, Daddy Yankee

Los actores hispanos Antonio Banderas y Salma Hayek

CANADÁ

OCÉANO PACÍFICO

OCÉANO ATLÁNTICO

San Francisco

Chicago

New York
Philadelphia

E S T A D O S
U N I D O S

Los Angeles
Phoenix
Tucson

Santa Fe

Una margarita
con guacamole y chips

Houston

San Antonio

MÉXICO

Golfo de
México

Miami

Calle Ocho, Miami

El Álamo, San Antonio, Texas

**A vista de pájaro.** Using the map and photos, as well as what you may already know, provide the following facts about Hispanics.

1. Tres hispanos famosos
2. El grupo hispano más numeroso en Estados Unidos
3. La ciudad (city) en Estados Unidos con más puertorriqueños
4. El estado con más mexicanos
5. Un producto hispano
6. Un tipo de música latina

# A PRIMERA VISTA

## Mis amigos y yo

### ¿Quiénes somos?

CD 1
Track 35

Me llamo Mario Quintana. Soy de Puerto Rico y **tengo** veintidós **años. Me gusta** escuchar música y mirar televisión. Estudio en una universidad de Nueva York y **deseo** ser profesor de historia. Los chicos en estas fotografías son mis amigos. Ellos también son **hispanos** y estudian en la universidad. **Todos** somos **bilingües**.

Esta chica es Amanda Martone. Es **alta, delgada** y **morena**. Tiene los **ojos** de color café y el **pelo negro** y muy **largo**. Amanda es una chica muy **agradable**. Estudia **mucho** y desea ser economista. Su familia es dominicana, pero vive en Estados Unidos.

### Cultura

Puerto Rico was a Spanish colony for almost four centuries until it was ceded to the United States following the Spanish-American War in 1898. Puerto Rico is a freely associated commonwealth (*estado libre asociado*) of the United States, and its people have been U.S. citizens since 1917. Most Puerto Ricans on the mainland live in New York; New Jersey, Pennsylvania, and Illinois also have large Puerto Rican communities. However, Puerto Rico remains geographically and culturally part of Latin America and almost all of its residents speak Spanish as their primary language. English is also widely spoken. Being bilingual opens doors to better economic opportunities in Puerto Rico and on the mainland.

Esta chica se llama Ana Villegas. No es alta ni baja. Es de **estatura mediana** y usa **lentes de contacto**. Es **pelirroja** y tiene los ojos **oscuros**. Ana es **callada, trabajadora** y muy inteligente. Sus padres son cubanos.

Este chico se llama Ernesto Fernández. Ernesto es moreno y tiene los ojos **castaños** y el pelo **corto**. Es **bajo, fuerte,** muy **conversador** y **simpático. Le gusta usar** la computadora para conversar con sus amigos de aquí y de México.

Esta chica es Marta Chávez Conde. Es española y tiene veintiún años. Es **rubia,** tiene los ojos **azules** y es muy **divertida.** Este año está en Estados Unidos con su familia.

**2-1 Asociaciones.** To whom do the descriptions on the left refer?

1. _b_ Tiene el pelo largo.
2. ____ Tiene veintidós años.
3. ____ Es de España.
4. ____ Es bajo y fuerte.
5. ____ Usa lentes de contacto.
6. ____ Habla mucho.
7. ____ Tiene los ojos de color café.
8. ____ Tiene el pelo negro y es muy agradable.
9. ____ Tiene los ojos azules y el pelo rubio, es muy divertida.
10. ____ Desea ser profesor de historia.

a. Mario Quintana
b. Amanda Martone
c. Ernesto Fernández
d. Ana Villegas
e. Marta Chávez Conde

**2-2 ¿Quién es?** PRIMERA FASE. Read the texts on pages 56–57 again and write a list of at least eight expressions that you may use to describe people, including physical appearance (*apariencia*) and personality traits (*personalidad*).

SEGUNDA FASE. Now, without mentioning his/her name, describe a classmate in at least three sentences, using the vocabulary from the *Primera fase*, or any other that you may need. The rest of the group will try to guess who this person is. The group can ask questions if more information is needed to guess the student's identity.

MODELO: E1: *Es de estatura mediana y delgado. Tiene el pelo negro. Es fuerte y callado.*
E2: *¿Es... ?*

**2-3 ¿Qué me gusta?** Tell your classmate if you like each of the following activities. Then compare your responses.

comer en restaurantes italianos
escribir correos electrónicos
bailar los sábados por la noche

estudiar español
trabajar los fines de semana
tomar café por la noche

practicar tenis/fútbol/béisbol
tener animales en casa

MODELO: estar en casa por las noches
E1: *¿Te gusta estar en casa por las noches?*
E2: *Sí, me gusta. /No, no me gusta.*

## Cultura

According to the 2000 census, one of every seven people in the United States is of Hispanic origin. With a population of 44,252,278, Hispanics account for 14 percent of the country's inhabitants. The Foundation of the Americas predicts that, by 2015, Hispanics will be the largest minority in the United States, numbering about 62.7 million. Although Hispanics can be found everywhere in the United States, most live in Los Angeles, New York, Miami, San Francisco, and Chicago. Mexicans constitute the largest Hispanic group, followed by Puerto Ricans and Cubans.

## Lengua

Depending on the region or country, *moreno/a* or *negro/a* may be used to refer to African ancestry and skin color or to hair color. The word *trigueño/a* (from *trigo,* wheat) is used to describe light brown skin color. *Corto/a* generally refers to length (*pelo corto*), while *bajo/a* refers to height (*Ella es baja*).

# ▶))  Las descripciones

CD 1
Track 36 **¿Cómo son estas personas?**

fuerte          débil

joven     vieja/mayor

lista          tonto

trabajador       perezoso

simpático     antipático

triste       alegre

pobre        rica          casado        soltero

## ◀)) ¿Cómo son estos animales?

CD 1
Track 37  Este perro es **feo** y **gordo**.

Esta gata es **bonita** y **delgada**.

**2-4 Opuestos.** Complete the following statements about these famous people.

MODELO: *Shakira no es mayor, es joven.*

1. ____ Penélope Cruz no es gorda, es...
2. ____ El presidente de la compañía no es perezoso, es...
3. ____ Jennifer López no es antipática, es...
4. ____ Madonna no es tonta, es...
5. ____ Bill Gates no es pobre, es...
6. ____ Enrique Iglesias no es feo, es...

a. trabajador
b. lista
c. delgada
d. rico
e. guapo
f. simpática

## ◀)) ¿De qué color son estas cosas?

CD 1
Track 38

Este auto es **rojo** y es muy bueno.

Esta flor es **amarilla** y **blanca**. Es muy bonita.

La silla **azul** es alta.

La silla **verde** es baja.

## ◀)) Otros colores

CD 1
Track 39

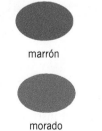

marrón

gris

rosado

morado

anaranjado

negro

**2-5 ¿De qué color son estas banderas (*flags*)?** PRIMERA FASE. Read each description and then write the name of the country under its flag.

1. La bandera de Bolivia es roja, amarilla y verde.
2. La bandera de Estados Unidos es roja, blanca y azul.
3. La bandera de España es roja y amarilla.
4. La bandera de México es verde, blanca y roja.
5. La bandera de Colombia es amarilla, azul y roja.

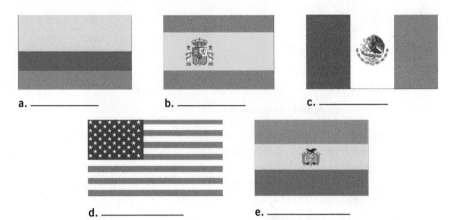

a. _____     b. _____     c. _____

d. _____     e. _____

SEGUNDA FASE. Take turns choosing a color and stating how many objects of that color are in the classroom. Your classmate will guess the color.

MODELO:   E1: *Hay dos mochilas y ocho pantalones vaqueros (jeans).*
         E2: *Es el azul.*

**2-6 Vamos a describir.** Describe the people in these photos.

Eva

Alicia y Raquel

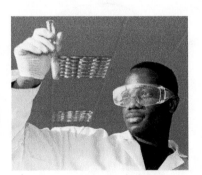

Alejandro

José Luis

**2-7 ¿Quién soy?** Write a brief description of yourself including at least three physical traits, two personality traits, and two activities that you like to do. Do not include your name on the paper. Give the paper to your instructor. He/She will ask each student to pick a description, read it, and try to guess who wrote it.

# El origen

### ¿De dónde son... ?

CD 1
Track 40

### Lengua

These are other examples of nationalities:

**alemán/alemana** (*German*), **canadiense, francés/francesa, japonés/japonesa, marroquí, nigeriano/a, polaco/a, portugués/ portuguesa.**

**2-8 Nacionalidades.** PRIMERA FASE. Indicate the nationalities of the following people.

MODELO: *Carolina Herrera es una diseñadora famosa de Venezuela.*
*Es venezolana.*

1. Albert Pujols es un jugador de béisbol de República Dominicana.
   Es _____ .
2. Salma Hayek es una actriz de México, protagonista de *Frida*. Es _____.
3. Rigoberta Menchú es una activista de Guatemala, Premio Nobel de la Paz, 1992. Es _____.
4. Julio Bocca es un bailarín de Argentina. Es _____.
5. Isabel Allende es escritora, originaria de Chile, autora de *La casa de los espíritus*. Es _____.
6. Oprah Winfrey es una presentadora de televisión de Estados Unidos.
   Es _____.
7. Gabriel García Márquez es un escritor de Colombia, autor de *Cien años de soledad*, Premio Nobel, 1982. Es _____.
8. Ricky Martin es un cantante de Puerto Rico. Es _____.

### En directo

To express some reasons why a person might interest you:

**Me gustan sus libros.**

**Escribe novelas fascinantes.**

**Trabaja por los pobres.**

**Es muy guapo/bonita/elegante.**

**Baila muy bien.**

**SEGUNDA FASE.** Which of the personalities in the *Primera fase* is interesting to you? Why?

**MODELO:** *Para mí, ...es interesante. Es un actor famoso/una actriz famosa.*

 **2-9 Adivinanzas (*Guesses*).** Think of a well-known person. A classmate will try to guess the identity by asking you questions.

**MODELO:** E1: *¿De dónde es?*
E2: *Es estadounidense./Es de Estados Unidos.*
E1: *¿Cómo es?*
E2: *Es de estatura mediana, rubio y muy rico.*
E1: *¿Qué es?/¿En qué trabaja?*
E2: *Es actor.*
E1: *¿Es Brad Pitt?*
E2: *¡Sí!*

 **2-10 Entrevista.** **PRIMERA FASE.** Interview a classmate to find out the following information:

1. his/her name
2. his/her age
3. what he/she is like
4. the things he/she likes to do
5. where he/she is from
6. ...

**SEGUNDA FASE.** Write an introduction to the interview and a description of this person, including physical traits. Then share it with the class.

**2-11 ¡Hola!** **PRIMERA FASE.** You will hear a student describe himself. Before you
CD 1 listen, mark (✓) in the *Antes de escuchar* column the information you think he
Track 41 may provide.

| | ANTES DE ESCUCHAR | DESPUÉS DE ESCUCHAR |
|---|---|---|
| 1. name | | |
| 2. age | | |
| 3. parents' names | | |
| 4. physical description | | |
| 5. country where he was born | | |
| 6. place where he intends to work | | |

**SEGUNDA FASE.** Now, listen and pay attention to the general idea of what is said. Then, in the *Después de escuchar* column, indicate which information the speaker provided.

# EN ACCIÓN

## Diarios de bicicleta: ¿Una cantante divina?

### Antes de ver

**2-12 PRIMERA FASE.** How well do you remember? Indicate whether the following statements refer to Javier (**J**) or to Daniel (**D**).

1. ___ Es mexicano.   2. ___ Es muy puntual.   3. ___ Es colombiano.

**SEGUNDA FASE.** In this segment a singer is scheduled to audition for a role in an up-coming musical. Guess what she looks like by underlining one sentence in each pair.

1. Es bonita. Es fea.
2. Es joven. Es vieja.
3. Tiene el pelo corto. Tiene el pelo largo.
4. Tiene los ojos verdes. Tiene los ojos negros.

### Mientras ve

**2-13** Indicate whether each statement is **cierto** (**C**) or **falso** (**F**) according to the video segment. Correct the statements that are false.

1. ___ Los amigos están en la cafetería.
2. ___ Luciana y Gabi necesitan escuchar audiciones para un nuevo musical.
3. ___ Beatriz Condes canta una canción tradicional mexicana.
4. ___ Beatriz Condes canta mal.

### Después de ver

**2-14** At the end of the video segment, a new character appears. Write five sentences in Spanish describing her.

# FUNCIONES Y FORMAS

## 1. Describing people, places, and things: Adjectives

Ana, Patricia y Teresa
estudian mucho. Son
inteligent**es** y trabajador**as**.

Eduardo
es alt**o** y
atlétic**o**.

Adriana
es baj**a** y
es muy
elegant**e**.

Carlos, Luis y Carmen son
sociabl**es** y activ**os**. Conversan y
bailan mucho en los clubes.

**Piénselo.** Complete the descriptions of the people in the drawings by supplying their names.

1. _____ es joven y delga**da**.
2. _____ , _____ y _____ son interesant**es** y estudios**as**.
3. _____ es moren**o** y guap**o**.
4. _____ , _____ y _____ son popular**es** y activ**os**.
5. _____ es colombian**o**.
6. _____ , _____ y _____ son español**as**.

- Adjectives are words that describe people, places, and things. Like articles (**el, la, los, las**) and nouns (**chica, chicas; libro, libros**), they generally have more than one form. In Spanish an adjective must agree in gender (masculine or feminine) and number (singular or plural) with the noun or pronoun it describes. Adjectives that describe characteristics usually follow the noun.
- Most masculine adjectives end in **-o**, and most feminine adjectives end in **-a**. To form the plural, these adjectives add **-s**.

|  | MASCULINE | FEMININE |
|---|---|---|
| SINGULAR | el chic**o** alt**o** | la chic**a** alt**a** |
| PLURAL | los chic**os** alt**os** | las chic**as** alt**as** |

■ Adjectives that end in **-e** and some adjectives that end in a consonant have the same form for both masculine and feminine. To form the plural, adjectives that end in **-e** add **-s**; those that end in a consonant add **-es**.

| | MASCULINE | FEMININE |
|---|---|---|
| SINGULAR | un lib**ro** interesant**e** | una revist**a** (*magazine*) interesant**e** |
| | un cuadern**o** azul | una mochil**a** azul |
| PLURAL | unos lib**ros** interesant**es** | unas revist**as** interesant**es** |
| | unos cuader**nos** azul**es** | unas mochil**as** azul**es** |

■ Other adjectives that end in a consonant add **-a** to form the feminine and **-es** or **-as** to form the plurals.

| | MASCULINE | FEMININE |
|---|---|---|
| SINGULAR | el alum**no** español | la alum**na** español**a** |
| | el alum**no** hablador | la alum**na** hablador**a** |
| PLURAL | los alum**nos** español**es** | las alum**nas** español**as** |
| | los alum**nos** hablador**es** | las alum**nas** hablador**as** |

■ Adjectives that end in **-ista** are both masculine and feminine. To form the plurals, add **-s**.

| | |
|---|---|
| Pedro es muy optim**ista**, pero Alicia es pesim**ista**. | *Pedro is very optimistic, but Alicia is pessimistic.* |
| Ellos no son material**istas**. | *They are not materialistic.* |

**2-15 ¿Cómo son estas personas?** Choose the correct completion to describe the following people. More than one answer may be possible.

1. Muchos alumnos de mi universidad son...
   a. latinoamericano.    b. hispanos.    c. norteamericanas.    d. mexicanos.

2. Mi profesora favorita es muy...
   a. joven.    b. activo.    c. inteligente.    d. delgado.

3. Mi amigo Nicolás es muy...
   a. tonta.    b. fuerte.    c. callado.    d. antipática.

4. Las dos chicas más inteligentes de la clase son...
   a. activos y sociables.    b. trabajadoras y estudiosas.    c. altos y morenos.    d. interesante y optimista.

**2-16 Cualidades necesarias.** Your school is hiring recent graduates to help recruit students interested in studying other languages and cultures. Mark (✓) the qualities you think these new employees should have and then describe them to a partner, making sure that adjectives agree with nouns. Your partner will mention additional qualities.

MODELO:    dos empleados bilingües en inglés y español
   E1: *Los empleados bilingües hablan bien inglés y español. Son activos y extrovertidos.*
   E2: *Sí. Son simpáticos, no son antipáticos. Hablan con los estudiantes y los padres de los estudiantes.*

1. dos especialistas en computadoras para el laboratorio de lenguas

   ____ activo    ____ bilingüe    ____ competente    ____ pasivo
   ____ agradable    ____ callado    ____ extrovertido    ____ trabajador

2. una recepcionista para la Oficina de Admisiones

   ____ eficiente    ____ imparcial    ____ perezoso    ____ simpático
   ____ hablador    ____ interesante    ____ perfeccionista    ____ tímido

**2-17 Personas importantes.** PRIMERA FASE. With your partner, take turns describing the people in the photos. Use at least three of the following descriptions: *atlético, cómico, extrovertido, guapo, inteligente, liberal, serio, simpático, tiene el pelo…, tiene los ojos…, trabajador, …*

Jimmy Smits es un actor famoso de cine (*movies*) y televisión.

Tish Hinojosa es una cantante mexicano-americana. Canta y escribe canciones también.

Julia Álvarez es una novelista y poeta dominicana. También es profesora.

Alex Rodríguez es un jugador de béisbol muy bueno.

SEGUNDA FASE. Now, take turns describing someone important in your life. Your partner will ask questions to get more information about that person.

## SITUACIONES

1. **Role A.** You have just rented an apartment near campus and are looking for a roommate (**compañero/a de apartamento**). You receive a call from an interested student. Verify the student's name and ask a) where he/she is from; b) what his/her personality traits are; c) if he/she works and, if so, where; and d) what he/she likes to do in his/her free time (**tiempo libre**).

   **Role B.** Through an ad (**anuncio**) on a campus bulletin board, you see that someone is looking for a roommate (**compañero/a de apartamento**). You call that person. Answer his/her questions in detail and ask any questions you may have.

2. **Role A.** Your friend calls to tell you that he/she has been dating someone new. Ask a) where your friend's new boyfriend/girlfriend (**novio/a**) is from; b) what he/she is like; c) what he/she studies; d) if he/she has a car and, if so, what it looks like (color, size); and e) at least one other question of your own invention.

   **Role B.** You call your friend to talk about your new boyfriend/girlfriend. Your friend asks a lot of questions. Answer in as much detail as possible.

## 2. Identifying and describing; expressing origin, possession, location of events, and time: Present tense of *ser*

Marc Anthony **es** un artista neoyorquino muy talentoso y versátil. **Es** cantante y actor. Sus padres **son** de Puerto Rico. También **es** compositor. Canta y escribe canciones de salsa, de pop y de pop latino, y **es** un actor muy bueno de cine y de teatro. Sus (*His*) conciertos **son** en Estados Unidos y en muchos países latinoamericanos.

**Piénselo.** Read the sentences about Marc Anthony on the left. Select the meaning expressed by **es** or **son** in each sentence from the list on the right.

1. \_\_\_ Marc Anthony **es** de ascendencia puertorriqueña.
2. \_\_\_ El próximo (*next*) concierto de Marc Anthony **es** en California.
3. \_\_\_ La esposa de Marc Anthony **es** Jennifer López.
4. \_\_\_ Las películas de Marc Antony **son** muy populares.
5. \_\_\_ Este álbum de Marc Antony **es** de Daniel. Es su álbum favorito.
6. \_\_\_ Marc Anthony **es** muy famoso como artista de salsa y de pop.

a. identificación
b. descripción
c. nacionalidad/origen
d. posesión
e. eventos (localización, hora)

■ You have practiced some forms of **ser** and have used them for identification (**Esta señora es la profesora de historia**) and to tell time (**Son las cuatro**). Here are other uses of this verb.

| SER (*to be*) | | | |
|---|---|---|---|
| yo | **soy** | nosotros/as | **somos** |
| tú | **eres** | vosotros/as | **sois** |
| Ud., él, ella | **es** | Uds., ellos/as | **son** |

■ As you have seen, **ser** is used with adjectives to describe an intrinsic feature of a person, place, or thing.

| | |
|---|---|
| ¿Cómo **es** ella? | *What is she like?* |
| **Es** atlética y extrovertida. | *She is athletic and outgoing.* |
| ¿Cómo **es** el apartamento? | *What is the apartment like?* |
| El apartamento **es** pequeño pero **es** muy cómodo. | *The house is small, but it is very comfortable.* |

## Lengua

Adjectives of nationality that end in a consonant form the feminine by adding **-a**.

**español → española**

Note that the feminine and plural forms do not have a written accent.

**portugués → portuguesa**
**portugueses → portuguesas**

**alemán → alemana**
**alemanes → alemanas**

Adjectives of nationality are not capitalized.

## Lengua

**De + el** contracts to **del**, but **de + la** and **de + los/las** do not contract.

El diccionario **es del** profesor, no **es de la** estudiante.
*The dictionary is the professor's, not the student's.*

■ **Ser** is used to express nationality; **ser + de** is used to express origin.

**NATIONALITY**

Gonzalo **es** chileno. — *Gonzalo is Chilean.*
Adriana **es** venezolana. — *Adriana is Venezuelan.*

**ORIGIN**

¿De dónde **son** Gonzalo y Adriana? — *Where are Gonzalo and Adriana from?*

Gonzalo **es** de Chile. — *Gonzalo is from Chile.*
Adriana **es** de Venezuela. — *Adriana is from Venezuela.*

■ **Ser + de** is used to express possession. The equivalent of the English word *whose?* is **¿de quién?**

**¿De quién es** el apartamento? — *Whose apartment is it?*
El apartamento **es de** Marta. — *The apartment is Marta's.*

■ **Ser + de** is also used to express the material of which something is made.

El reloj **es de** oro. — *The watch is (made of) gold.*
Las sillas **son de** madera. — *The chairs are made of wood/wooden.*

■ **Ser** is also used to express where an event takes place or time of an event.

El concierto **es** en el estadio. — *The concert is (takes place) in the stadium.*
La clase **es** a las nueve. — *The class is (takes place) at nine.*

**2-18 ¿Cómo somos?** PRIMERA FASE. Look at the following descriptions and write an X under the appropriate heading.

| | SÍ | NO |
|---|---|---|
| 1. Yo soy muy estudioso/a y trabajador/a. | ___ | ___ |
| 2. A veces soy callado/a. | ___ | ___ |
| 3. Soy norteamericano/a. | ___ | ___ |
| 4. Mis abuelos son de otro (*another*) país. | ___ | ___ |
| 5. Mi familia es muy religiosa y tradicional. | ___ | ___ |
| 6. Mi mejor amigo/a es extrovertido/a y conversador/a. | ___ | ___ |
| 7. Mis amigos y yo somos sociables y activos. | ___ | ___ |
| 8. Mis clases este semestre son interesantes. | ___ | ___ |

 SEGUNDA FASE. Now compare your answers with your partner's. Ask questions to get additional information.

**2-19 ¿Cómo y dónde?**  Ask what the following people, places, and objects are like. For your Spanish class, ask when and where it takes place, and for the computer lab, ask where it is located, as well as what the computers are like.

MODELO:  tu profesor/a de inglés

E1:  *¿Cómo es tu profesor de inglés?*

E2:  *Es alto, moreno y muy simpático.*

1. tus amigos
2. tu cuarto (*bedroom*)
3. tu compañero/a de cuarto (*roommate*)
4. el auto de tu mejor amigo/a
5. la clase de español
6. el laboratorio de computadoras

**2-20 ¿Qué es esto?**  Take turns to describe an object and its location in the classroom. Your partner will ask you questions and guess what it is.

MODELO:  E1:  *Es grande, es de plástico, está al lado de la ventana.*

E2:  *¿De qué color es?*

E1:  *Es roja.*

E2:  *¿Es la mochila de Juan?*

> ### Lengua
>
> **Madera** (*wood*), **plástico**, **tela** (*fabric*), **metal**, **oro** (*gold*), **vidrio** (*glass*) are some words used to describe what something is made of.

**2-21 Eventos y lugares.**  You are working at the university's information booth, and a visitor (your classmate) stops by. Answer his/her questions. Then switch roles.

MODELO:  la exposición del club de fotografía

VISITANTE:  *Perdón/Disculpe, ¿dónde es la exposición del club de fotografía?*

EMPLEADO/A:  *Es en la biblioteca.*

VISITANTE:  *¿Dónde está la biblioteca?*

EMPLEADO/A:  *Está en la calle Madison, enfrente del edificio* (building) *de biología.*

1. el concierto de música salsa
2. la conferencia (*lecture*) sobre el arte mexicano
3. el banquete para los estudiantes internacionales
4. la reunión de profesores
5. la fiesta del club de español
6. la ceremonia de graduación

## SITUACIONES

1. **Role A.** You meet a student from a Spanish-speaking country in one of your classes. Introduce yourself and find out a) the student's name; b) his/her city and country of origin; c) characteristics of his/her city; and d) what his/her friends are like.

   **Role B.** You are an international student from a Spanish-speaking country. Answer your classmate's questions and then ask questions to get the same information he/she obtained from you.

2. **Role A.** A friend has invited you to a party at his/her house on Saturday. Ask a) where the house is located; b) what it looks like (so you can find it easily); and c) what time the party is.

   **Role B.** You have invited a friend to a party at your house on Saturday. Answer your friend's questions. Then explain that the house belongs to your parents (**padres**), and tell your friend why your parents are not at home that weekend.

### 3. Expressing inherent qualities and changeable conditions: *Ser* and *estar* with adjectives

Todos los estudiantes **están** aburridos porque la profesora **es** aburrida.

**Piénselo.** Read the statements below and classify them as to whether they describe either a) a personality trait/physical characteristic or b) a feeling or perception that may change.

1. \_\_\_\_ La profesora **es** aburrida. Sus clases no son interesantes.
2. \_\_\_\_ Sofía **está** delgada en ese vestido (*dress*) negro.
3. \_\_\_\_ Los estudiantes **están** nerviosos. Tienen un examen difícil hoy.
4. \_\_\_\_ Normalmente, las modelos **son** altas y muy delgadas.
5. \_\_\_\_ Hoy los niños **están** contentos. Van (*They are going*) al parque.
6. \_\_\_\_ Roberto **es** estudioso y trabajador. Estudia mucho todos los días.

■ **Ser** and **estar** are often used with the same adjectives. However, the choice of verb determines the meaning of the sentence.

■ **Ser** + *adjective* states the norm—what someone or something is like.

| | |
|---|---|
| Jorge **es** delgado. | *Jorge is thin.* (He is a thin man.) |
| Sara **es** muy nerviosa. | *Sara is very nervous.* (She is a nervous person.) |
| El libro **es** nuevo. | *The book is new.* (It is a new book.) |

■ **Estar** + *adjective* expresses a change from the norm, a condition, or how one feels about the person or object being discussed.

| | |
|---|---|
| Jorge **está** delgado. | *Jorge is/looks thin.* (He lost weight recently, or he looks thin in a picture or because of the clothes he is wearing.) |
| Sara **está** muy nerviosa. | *Sara is very nervous.* (She is feeling nervous.) |
| El libro **está** nuevo. | *The book is/looks new.* (It is used, but it seems like a brand new book.) |

- The adjectives **contento/a, cansado/a, enojado/a** are always used with **estar**.

| | |
|---|---|
| Ella **está contenta** ahora. | *She is happy now.* |
| Los niños **están cansados.** | *The children are tired.* |
| Carlos **está enojado.** | *Carlos is angry.* |

- Some adjectives have one meaning with **ser** and another with **estar**.

| | |
|---|---|
| Ese señor **es** malo. | *That man is bad/evil.* |
| Ese señor **está** malo. | *That man is ill.* |
| La chica **es** lista. | *The girl is clever/smart.* |
| La chica **está** lista. | *The girl is ready.* |
| La manzana **es** verde. | *The apple is green.* |
| La manzana **está** verde. | *The apple is not ripe.* |
| La profesora **es** aburrida. | *The professor is boring.* |
| La profesora **está** aburrida. | *The professor is bored.* |

**2-22 ¿Qué pasa aquí?** Look at the drawings and then complete the descriptions about each one with the appropriate form of **ser** or **estar**.

1. Esteban _____ (1) un joven listo y estudioso. Este semestre saca buenas notas, excepto en la clase de economía. _____ (2) una clase muy difícil. Esteban _____ (3) nervioso porque mañana hay un examen sobre la Comunidad Económica Europea, pero él no _____ (4) listo. Debe estudiar toda la noche.

2. ¡Pobres niños! (*Poor children!*) La fruta _____ (5) buena y saludable (*healthful*), pero estas manzanas _____ (6) verdes, no _____ (7) buenas. Ahora los niños no _____ (8) contentos. Una niña _____ (9) mala porque le duele el estómago (*her stomach hurts*).

**2-23 Cambios (*Changes*).** Imagine that you and your partner know the people mentioned below. One of you will describe a person, using an adjective in the list. The other explains how the person has changed and why. Then switch roles.

**MODELO:**    Arturo/fuerte
       E1: *Arturo es fuerte.*
       E2: *Pero por su enfermedad (illness), ahora está muy débil.*

| PERSONAS | CARACTERÍSTICAS | RAZONES |
|---|---|---|
| 1. Ramón | alegre | por sus problemas |
| 2. Laura y Gustavo | callado/a | por la dieta |
| 3. Cristina | conversador/a | por el ejercicio |
| 4. Andrés | débil | por el exceso de estudio |
| 5. Ana y Sofía | extrovertido/a | por la falta (*lack*) de motivación |
| 6. Teresa | feliz | por su depresión |
| | fuerte | por sus buenas notas |
| | introvertido/a | |
| | optimista | |
| | perezoso/a | |
| | pesimista | |
| | trabajador/a | |
| | triste | |

¡Qué asco!

¡Horrible!

**2-24 Termómetro emocional.** PRIMERA FASE. Indicate (✓) how you feel in each situation. Then write two adjectives to further describe how you feel and how you think your classmate feels in these situations.

| LUGARES | ABURRIDO/A | CONTENTO/A | TRANQUILO/A | NERVIOSO/A | YO | MI COMPAÑERO/A |
|---|---|---|---|---|---|---|
| en la cafetería con mis compañeros | | | | | | |
| en los exámenes finales | | | | | | |
| en la oficina de un profesor/una profesora | | | | | | |
| en un concierto con mis amigos | | | | | | |
| en una fiesta formal | | | | | | |
| en mi casa por la noche | | | | | | |

SEGUNDA FASE. Now compare your responses with those of your partner and write down one similarity and one difference between the two of you. Report to the class.

MODELO:   en la clase de español
E1: *En la clase de español, yo estoy contento/a. Tú también estás contento/a en la clase de español, ¿verdad?*
E2: *Tienes razón. Yo estoy contento/a. O Estás equivocado/a. Yo estoy aburrido/a.*
E1: [a la clase] *Yo estoy contento/a en la clase de español, pero Amanda está aburrida.*

## SITUACIONES

1. **Role A.** You have traveled to another city for a job interview. A friend of a friend who lives in that city has offered to show you around. Make arrangements over the phone to meet this person, whom you do not know. Find out what the person looks like, so you will be able to spot him/her at your meeting place.

   **Role B.** You have offered to get together with a friend of a friend who has a job interview in your city. You do not know this person, so when you arrange over the phone to meet, you have to find out what the person looks like and something about his/her personality, so you can decide what to show him/her.

2. **Role A.** Show your classmate a photo. Identify the people and explain what they are like. Then respond to your friend's questions and comments about them.

   **Role B.** After your classmate tells you about the people in the photo, ask and comment about a) how they seem to be feeling, based on their facial expressions or what they are doing and b) where they appear to be.

## 4. Expressing ownership: Possessive adjectives

### Mis amigos y yo

Condorito—the main character of the comic strip magazine of the same name—introduces some of his closest friends. Look at the group portrait to follow what he says.

Condorito y sus amigos

**Mi** nombre es Condorito. Soy un cóndor simpático, listo y sincero.

Yayita y **su** pequeña Sobrina (*niece*) Yuyito son **mis** dos grandes amores (*sweethearts*). **La** sobrina **de** Yayita es muy atractiva, pero es muy dependiente de **su** tía (*aunt*)y de **su** abuelo Don Tremendón. **Nuestra** relación es especial. Nosotros pasamos mucho tiempo juntos.

**Mi** sobrino (*nephew*) Coné es amoroso, pero un poco llorón (*whiner*). **Su** mejor amiga es Yuyito. La actividad favorita **de ellos** es comer chocolate y jugar en el parque. Finalmente, Doña Tremebunda es la madre de **mi** novia Yayita. Honestamente no me gusta mucho hablar con ella porque es muy materialista. También es dominante y ambiciosa. Y **tu** familia y amigos, ¿cómo son?

**Piénselo.** Complete the following statements, using the information in Condorito's description.

1. Condorito tiene una novia. ____ nombre es _____ .
   **a.** Tu... Yayita      **b.** Mi... Doña Tremebunda      **c.** Su... Yayita

2. Condorito dice (*says*): *Nuestra relación es especial.* ¿A qué relación se refiere Condorito en esta afirmación?
   **a.** La relación de Condorito con Yayita y su familia.
   **b.** La relación de Yayita con la familia de ella.
   **c.** La relación entre Coné, Yayita, la familia de Yayita y él (Condorito).

3. Coné es ____ Condorito.
   **a.** la hija de      **b.** el sobrino de      **c.** el hijo (*son*) de

4. Condorito prefiere no pasar tiempo con Doña Tremebunda. ¿Por qué?
   **a.** por la apariencia física de ella      **b.** por la personalidad de ella
   **c.** por el hijo de ella

■ Possessive adjectives modify nouns to express possession. They always precede the noun they modify.

   **mi** amigo       **tu** familia

| POSSESSIVE ADJECTIVES | |
|---|---|
| mi(s) | *my* |
| tu(s) | *your* (familiar) |
| su(s) | *your* (formal), *his, her, its, their* |
| nuestro(s), nuestra(s) | *our* |
| vuestro(s), vuestra(s) | *your* (familiar plural) |

■ Possessive adjectives change number to agree with the thing possessed, not with the possessor.

   mi *clase*, mis *clases*

■ The **nosotros/as** and **vosotros/as** forms must agree also in gender.

   **nuestro** *profesor*, **nuestros** *amigos*; **nuestra** *profesora*, **nuestras** *amigas*

■ **Su** and **sus** have multiple meanings. To ensure clarity, you may use **de** + *the name of the possessor* or *the appropriate pronoun* instead of *su/sus*. For example, the multiple meanings of *su compañera* can be expressed as follows:

la compañera +
- **de ella** (la compañera de Elena)
- **de él** (la compañera de Jorge)
- **de usted**
- **de ustedes**
- **de ellos** (la compañera de Elena y Jorge)
- **de ellas** (la compañera de Elena y Olga)

## En otras palabras

The word for *car* in Spanish varies, depending on the country or region. The most widely accepted word is **el auto**, commonly used in the southern half of South America. In Mexico, Central America, the Caribbean, and the northern countries of South America, **el carro** is frequently used. **El coche** is used in Spain.

**2-25 Mi mundo (*world*). PRIMERA FASE.** Write down two things that you own (**pertenencias**) and two people whom you value very much. You may use the words in the box or choose others.

| Pertenencias: | un carro | una computadora portátil | un iPod |
|---|---|---|---|
| Personas: | un amigo/ una amiga | un profesor ideal/ una profesora ideal | un actor/ una actriz |

PERTENENCIAS

1. _____

2. _____

PERSONAS

1. _____

2. _____

**SEGUNDA FASE.** Take turns describing your selections. Take notes so that you can share with the class the similarities and differences between you and your classmate.

**Pertenencias**

E1: *Yo tengo un auto. Es rápido y moderno. Y tú, tienes un auto?*

E2: *Sí.*

E1: *¿Y cómo es tu auto?*

E2: *Mi auto es rojo y muy viejo.*

**Personas**

E1: *Mi madre es importante en mi vida (life). Es muy alegre y activa. Y tu mamá, ¿cómo es?*

E2: *Mi madre es tranquila y muy inteligente.*

**2-26 Mi familia.** Which of these statements apply to your family and friends? Mark (✓) your answers in the spaces under **Yo**. Then interview a classmate.

|  | YO | MI COMPAÑERO/A |
|---|---|---|
| 1. Mi familia es grande. | _____ | _____ |
| 2. Otros miembros de mi familia viven en nuestro barrio (*neighborhood*). | _____ | _____ |
| 3. A veces pasamos las vacaciones con mis abuelos (*grandparents*). | _____ | _____ |
| 4. Siempre conversamos sobre temas políticos. | _____ | _____ |
| 5. A veces no estamos de acuerdo y discutimos. | _____ | _____ |
| 6. Nuestros amigos visitan la casa frecuentemente. | _____ | _____ |

**2-27 Nuestra universidad.** PRIMERA FASE. In preparation for the *Segunda fase*, write some words that generally describe the following aspects of your university.

1. los profesores: _____

2. las clases: _____

3. los estudiantes: _____

4. los equipos (*teams*) de fútbol, baloncesto, béisbol, etc.: _____

5. el campus: _____

SEGUNDA FASE. Now write 1 or 2 sentences about each topic in the *Primera fase*. Be prepared to present your sentences to the class. The class will decide which sentences a) describe the school most accurately and b) present an appealing view of the school for prospective students.

## SITUACIONES

1. Role A. You are a Spanish professor. You inform a student about a lecture by another professor. Explain that a) the professor is visiting the university; b) there is a lecture by the professor (**una conferencia del profesor**) on Thursday; c) it will take place in the library.

   Role B. Your professor invites you to a lecture. Find out a) the time of the lecture; b) the speaker's name; and c) the topic (**tema**).

2. Role A. You are a student from Peru studying in the United States. You phone your parents and ask how they are. Tell about your host parents (**madre americana/padre americano**), brother (**hermano**), and sister (**hermana**). Describe their ages, appearance, personalities, and occupations.

   Role B. You live in Peru, and your child is studying in the United States. When he/she calls, ask about a) the host family schedule (**horario**) and b) activities of the host family.

### En directo

To initiate the conversation:

**Oye** (*Hey*)**, mi hermano americano es...**

**¿Sabes?** (*You know?*) **Mi hermano americano es...**

To acknowledge information by showing surprise:

**Ah, ¿sí?**

**¡No me digas!**
*Oh, really?, No way!, Wow!*

## 5. Expressing likes and dislikes: *Gustar*

The following is a transcript of a chat over the Internet between Marisa, a Mexican student living in Mexico City, and Carla, a Mexican American living in El Paso, Texas.

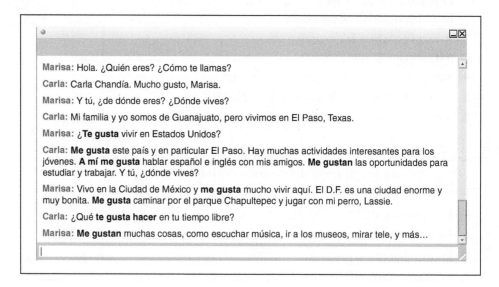

> **Marisa:** Hola. ¿Quién eres? ¿Cómo te llamas?
>
> **Carla:** Carla Chandía. Mucho gusto, Marisa.
>
> **Marisa:** Y tú, ¿de dónde eres? ¿Dónde vives?
>
> **Carla:** Mi familia y yo somos de Guanajuato, pero vivimos en El Paso, Texas.
>
> **Marisa:** **¿Te gusta** vivir en Estados Unidos?
>
> **Carla:** **Me gusta** este país y en particular El Paso. Hay muchas actividades interesantes para los jóvenes. **A mí me gusta** hablar español e inglés con mis amigos. **Me gustan** las oportunidades para estudiar y trabajar. Y tú, ¿dónde vives?
>
> **Marisa:** Vivo en la Ciudad de México y **me gusta** mucho vivir aquí. El D.F. es una ciudad enorme y muy bonita. **Me gusta** caminar por el parque Chapultepec y jugar con mi perro, Lassie.
>
> **Carla:** ¿Qué **te gusta hacer** en tu tiempo libre?
>
> **Marisa:** **Me gustan** muchas cosas, como escuchar música, ir a los museos, mirar tele, y más…

**Piénselo.** Indicate whether each paraphrase best refers to Marisa (**M**) or Carla (**C**).

1. \_\_\_\_ **Me gustan** las posibilidades académicas que ofrece Estados Unidos.
2. \_\_\_\_ **Me gusta** vivir en la capital de México.
3. \_\_\_\_ **Me gusta** ser bilingüe.
4. \_\_\_\_ **Me gustan** las actividades al aire libre (*open air*).
5. \_\_\_\_ **Me gusta** el arte.

■ To express what you like to do, use **me gusta** + *infinitive*. To express what you don't like to do, use **no me gusta** + *infinitive*.

| | |
|---|---|
| **Me gusta** hablar español. | *I like to speak Spanish.* |
| **No me gusta** mirar televisión. | *I don't like to watch television.* |
| **Me gusta** practicar deportes y salir con mis amigos. | *I like to play sports and go out with my friends.* |

■ To express that you like something or someone, use **me gusta** + *singular noun* or **me gustan** + *plural noun*.

| | |
|---|---|
| **Me gusta** la música clásica. | *I like classical music.* |
| **Me gustan** las personas alegres. | *I like happy people.* |

■ To ask a classmate what he/she likes, use **¿Te gusta(n)… ?** To ask your instructor, use **¿Le gusta(n)… ?**

| | |
|---|---|
| **¿Te gusta/Le gusta** tomar café? | *Do you like to drink coffee?* |
| **¿Te gustan/Le gustan** los chocolates? | *Do you like chocolates?* |

■ To state what another person likes, use **a** + *name of person* + **le gusta(n)…** When you are talking about the preferences of more than one person, use **a** + *name of person* + **les gusta(n)…**

**A Diego le gustan** las fiestas.          *Diego likes parties.*

**A Carlos le gusta** el fútbol.          *Carlos likes soccer.*

**A Diego y a Carlos les gusta** ir de vacaciones con sus padres.          *Diego and Carlos like to go on vacation with their parents.*

**2-28 Mis preferencias.** PRIMERA FASE. Mark (✓) your preferences in the following chart.

| ACTIVIDAD | ME GUSTA MUCHO | ME GUSTA UN POCO | NO ME GUSTA |
|---|---|---|---|
| escribir correos electrónicos en español | | | |
| comer en restaurantes de comida mexicana | | | |
| bailar salsa | | | |
| escuchar música rock en español | | | |
| aprender sobre la cultura de otros países | | | |
| visitar lugares históricos | | | |

SEGUNDA FASE. Now, compare your answers with those of a classmate. Share with the class one similarity and one difference between you and your partner in terms of your preferences.

**2-29 ¿Te gusta… ?** PRIMERA FASE. Ask if a classmate likes the following. Be sure to ask follow-up questions as appropriate.

1. el gimnasio de la universidad
2. los teléfonos celulares con conexión a Internet
3. la informática
4. los autos de este año
5. los animales
6. los conciertos de música clásica

SEGUNDA FASE. Write a brief note to another classmate in which you share two pieces of information about yourself and two pieces of information you discovered about your partner.

**2-30 ¿Qué te gusta hacer?** PRIMERA FASE. Write down some questions that you would ask a classmate to find out the following:

1. what he/she likes to do in his/her free time
2. in what restaurant he/she likes to eat with his/her family

SEGUNDA FASE. Interview two classmates and ask each of them the questions you prepared in the *Primera fase*. Compare their responses and be prepared to share with others your conclusions regarding how your classmates spend their time.

## SITUACIONES

1. **Role A:** You are at a park where you hear someone giving Spanish commands to a dog. Break the ice and introduce yourself. Ask a) the person's name; b) the dog's name and age; and c) if the dog is friendly (**manso**). Compliment the dog (smart, strong, very pretty, etc.). Tell the person that you like dogs very much and that you also like cats. Answer the questions this person asks.

   **Role B:** You are in the park training your dog and someone approaches. Answer this person's questions and ask if he/she has a dog, and if so, what it looks like. Say that you don't like cats because they are not active or fun. Finally, ask where this person is from and where he/she is studying Spanish.

2. **Role A:** You are at Panchero's, a Mexican restaurant. While you are waiting to be seated, you hear someone speaking Spanish to a child. Introduce yourself and ask the child's name and age. Compliment the parent on his/her beautiful child. Also ask the parent if he/she likes Panchero's and likes to eat at American restaurants like McDonald's.

   **Role B:** You and your two-year-old daughter are waiting to be seated at Panchero's, a Mexican restaurant. Someone asks you about your child. React to the person's comments and answer his/her questions.

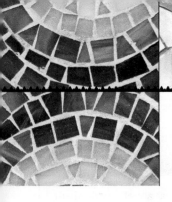

# MOSAICOS

## A escuchar

**ESTRATEGIAS**

**Listen for specific information**

When you ask a person specific questions, he/she may provide not only the answers you need, but also additional information. To listen efficiently, focus on the answers you requested. This will help you obtain the information you need.

### Antes de escuchar

**2-31 Preparación.** You will listen to a student telling her mother about how different her roommates are. Before listening to their conversation, write the name(s) of your own roommate(s) and a sentence that describes each of them.

### Escuchar

**2-32 ¿Comprende usted?** Listen to the conversation between a student and her mother. Mark (✓) the appropriate column(s) to indicate whether the following statements describe Rita, Marcela, or both.

CD 1
Track 42

|  | RITA | MARCELA |
|---|---|---|
| **1.** Estudia economía. |  |  |
| **2.** Le gusta bailar. |  |  |
| **3.** Es alta, morena y tiene los ojos negros. |  |  |
| **4.** Es muy seria, baja y delgada. |  |  |
| **5.** Estudia arte moderno. |  |  |

### Después de escuchar

**2-33 Ahora usted.** Complete the following sentences to say how you feel about your roommate(s).

1. Me gusta(n) mi(s) compañero/a(s) de cuarto porque…
2. A veces no me gusta(n) mi(s) compañero/a(s) de cuarto porque…
3. Mi(s) compañero/a(s) de cuarto y yo somos semejantes/diferentes porque…

# A conversar

**Describe a person**

Descriptions are most effective when they are well organized. When describing a person, you may want to include demographic information (e.g., age, nationality/origin), physical characteristics, and personality traits. A well-organized description presents information by category, beginning with an introductory phrase to prepare your listener.

## Antes de conversar

**2-34 Preparación.** *Mafalda*, like *Condorito*, featured earlier in this chapter, is a popular comic strip in the Spanish-speaking world. Go to the *Mosaicos* web page, choose one of the characters shown there, and read the description about him/her.

## Conversar

**2-35 Entre nosotros.** Describe the physical characteristics and personality traits of the *Mafalda* character you read about in **2-34**. Your partner will ask questions or comment as appropriate. Then switch roles.

## Después de conversar

**2-36 Un poco más.** Find out about another popular comic character, like those mentioned in the *Cultura* box below, and tell the class about him/her.

### Cultura

Mafalda is the name of a character in a comic strip of the same name created by the Argentinian cartoonist Quino. Extremely popular in the Spanish-speaking world, she is a six-year-old girl deeply concerned with political issues and world peace. Her naive yet sharp criticism of society has made her an icon for the defense of human rights. For more information go to the *Mosaicos* web page.

### En directo

To introduce information about physical characteristics:

**En cuanto a lo físico,... / Físicamente, es...**

To introduce information about personality:

**Es una persona... / Tiene un carácter...**

### Cultura

Many Hispanics who emigrate to other countries maintain connections to their culture by reading and listening to music in Spanish. In areas with large Hispanic populations, Spanish-language newspapers and magazines are available.

These carry some of the many comic strips popular in the Hispanic world, including *Mafalda* (Argentina), *Condorito* (Chile), and *Mortadelo y Filemón* (Spain). You will find information about these comic strips on the Internet.

# A leer

**Scan a text for specific information**

When you read in Spanish, your goal should be to read for ideas, not for the meaning of every word. One way to read for ideas is to search for particular pieces of information that you think will be in the text. Often the comprehension questions after the text will help you decide what information to search for as you read. This approach to reading, called *scanning*, works best if you a) focus on the information you are seeking and b) read the text through quickly at least twice, looking for specific information each time.

## Antes de leer

**2-37 Preparación.** PRIMERA FASE. Read the title of the text and examine its format. (This is the reading strategy you learned in *Capítulo 1*.) What type of text is it?

1. a series of e-mail messages
2. personal ads
3. ads for items for sale

**SEGUNDA FASE.** Scan the text and use your highlighter to mark the following information in each paragraph.

1. el nombre de la persona
2. la edad (*age*) de la persona
3. la dirección electrónica de la persona

## Leer

**2-38 Primera mirada.** Read the personal ads that follow and scan them for the information needed in the form. In some cases, it may not be possible to provide all the information requested.

| | PERSONA 1 | PERSONA 2 | PERSONA 3 | PERSONA 4 |
|---|---|---|---|---|
| nombre | | | | |
| edad | | | | |
| nacionalidad | | | | |
| estado civil | | | | |
| personalidad (1 ó 2 adjetivos) | | | | |
| le gusta... | | | | |

### Amigos sin fronteras

Soltera, sin hijos y sin compromiso. Me llamo Susana y tengo 24 años. Soy guatemalteca. Busco amigos extranjeros, solteros, separados o divorciados, jóvenes o mayores. Soy amable, cariñosa y muy trabajadora. Por mi trabajo, viajo mucho, pero me gusta la compañía de otras personas. Soy bilingüe. Hablo español e inglés. Escriban a sincompromiso@comcast.net.

Soy Ricardo Brown. 21 años, sincero, dedicado. Me gustan las fiestas. Soy soltero. Deseo conocer a una chica de unos 23 años, preferiblemente venezolana como yo. Prefiero una mujer activa e independiente. Me gusta practicar deportes y explorar lugares nuevos. Escríbanme a amigosincero@msn.com.

Me llamo Pablo Sosa, tengo 31 años, y soy chileno. Soy agradable y muy trabajador. Me gusta hacer mi trabajo a la perfección, pero soy tolerante. Los autos convertibles son mi pasión. Deseo mantener correspondencia por correo electrónico con jóvenes del extranjero para intercambiar información sobre los convertibles europeos o americanos. Mi dirección electrónica es locoporlosautos@yahoo.com.

Soy Xiomara Stravinsky, decoradora y fotógrafa argentina. Me gusta el arte, especialmente el impresionismo. Tengo 27 años y soy divorciada. Soy dinámica, agradable y generosa, pero tengo pocos amigos porque tengo dos trabajos y paso muchas horas con mis clientes. Necesito un cambio en mi vida. ¿Deseas ser mi amigo/a? Por favor, escríbeme a xiomarastravinsky@hotmail.com.

---

### Lengua

The letter **y** changes to **e** when it precedes a word beginning with **i** or **h**.

**inglés y español**, but **español e inglés**

**inteligente y agradable**, but **agradable e inteligente**

---

## Después de leer

**2-39 Ampliación.** PRIMERA FASE. What qualities do you associate with Susana (**S**), Ricardo (**R**), Pablo (**P**), and Xiomara (**X**)? Why? With a classmate, write the person's initial next to each quality, and support your opinions.

a. ____ sociable

b. ____ simpático/a

c. ____ divertido/a

d. ____ perfeccionista

e. ____ mayor

f. ____ flexible

g. ____ trabajador/a

h. ____ ocupado/a

SEGUNDA FASE. Find the best match for Susana, Ricardo, Pablo and Xiomara from the following responses received.

1. Tengo 22 años y me gustan todos los deportes. Mis padres viven en Caracas pero yo vivo en Miami.

2. Enseño arte en la escuela secundaria. Tengo tiempo para mis amigos los fines de semana.

3. Soy de Nicaragua. Soy muy sociable y deseo perfeccionar mi inglés.

4. Trabajo para *Autos de hoy*, una revista de Internet.

# A escribir

**Consider audience and purpose**

Writing is an act of communication between writer and reader. Writers usually have a purpose in mind, such as compiling information, informing the reader, describing something or someone, or expressing a point of view. Readers rely on their prior knowledge and on the quantity and quality of information presented to derive meaning from the text.

As you write, keep in mind your purpose and make the necessary adjustments to form and content to facilitate your audience's comprehension of the message.

## Antes de escribir

**2-40 Preparación. PRIMERA FASE.** Read the following ad written by a movie fan in your local Spanish-language newspaper.

> Fanático del cine necesita amigos para discutir películas los fines de semana. Tengo 24 años y estudio cinematografía. Me fascinan las películas de acción y también las románticas. Soy fuerte, activo, atlético y aventurero. Me gusta practicar deportes, especialmente el tenis y el esquí. Siempre estoy muy ocupado, pero tengo unas horas todas las semanas para conversar sobre películas y hacer deportes. Interesados, favor de enviar correo electrónico a fanaticodelcine@yahoo.com.

**SEGUNDA FASE.** You decide to respond to the ad. First, think about the following questions and mark (✓) your responses accordingly.

1. What is the purpose that **fanaticodelcine** has in mind when he writes the e-mail?
   a. ____ to find a girlfriend
   b. ____ to find someone (male or female) to talk with about movies

2. What would your purpose be if you responded to his personal ad?
   a. ____ to share your interest in movies with someone who is knowledgeable about the topic.
   b. ____ to date **fanaticodelcine**

**TERCERA FASE.** Now jot down information that will help you meet the goal of becoming the conversation partner of **fanaticodelcine.**

1. your age
2. your place of origin
3. words (adjectives) that describe you physically
4. expressions (adjectives) that describe your personality
5. activities (verbs) that you like to do that may match the needs of the person in the ad

# Escribir

**2-41 Manos a la obra.** Write an e-mail to *fanaticodelcine* using the information you prepared in the *Tercera fase* of **2-40**.

---

**Para:** [                                                    ]

**Asunto:** [ Anuncio                                          ]

---

Hola,_____

Respondo a tu anuncio del periódico. (*Provide your name.*)
_____

Primero, aquí tienes alguna información personal. (*Provide personal information.*)_____
_____
_____
_____

En segundo lugar, estas son algunas de las actividades que, al igual que tú, yo hago en mi tiempo libre. (*Provide activities that you, like fanaticodelcine, like to do in your free time.*)_____
_____
_____
_____

En tercer lugar, los fines de semana… (*Tell what you like to do.*)_____
_____
_____
_____

Finalmente, deseo ser tu amigo/a. Por favor, escríbeme un correo electrónico a mi dirección:_____
_____

Hasta pronto.
_____

---

# Después de escribir

**2-42 Revisión.** After writing your e-mail, read it again and check the following:

1. Did you include all the information *fanaticodelcine* needs? Do you think your information will be interesting to him?
2. Did you use punctuation correctly? Did you verify that there are no spelling or grammatical mistakes that may hinder comunication?
3. Make any necessary changes that will make your e-mail clear and comprehensible to *fanaticodelcine*.

# ENFOQUE CULTURAL

## Los hispanos y la expansión de Estados Unidos

Inicialmente, Estados Unidos está formado por trece colonias de Inglaterra. Estas trece colonias ocupan principalmente el noreste y la región del Atlántico. Las trece colonias se independizan de Inglaterra en la larga y violenta Guerra de Independencia. George Washington es un líder muy importante de esta guerra. El 4 de julio de 1776, el Congreso Continental firma la Declaración de Independencia en Filadelfia y George Washington es el primer presidente de la nueva república.

La expansión de Estados Unidos

Moneda de 25 centavos en honor de Luisiana, 2002

La primera expansión de las trece colonias hacia el oeste ocurre en 1803 durante la presidencia de Thomas Jefferson. En este año, el gobierno de Estados Unidos compra a Francia el inmenso territorio de Luisiana por 23 millones de dólares. Esta región ocupa unos 2.100.000 km². La compra de Luisiana incorpora todo el valle del Río Misisipi al territorio de Estados Unidos.

En 1810, el presidente James Madison anexa al territorio de Estados Unidos la región de Florida Occidental. Esta región está en la costa norte del Golfo de México y hoy pertenece a los estados de Luisiana, Misisipi, Alabama y Florida. Pero anteriormente, pertenece a España, Francia y también a Inglaterra. Durante un tiempo se llama la República Independiente de Florida Occidental. España disputa esta anexión, pero en 1819 acepta ceder todo el territorio de Florida, incluyendo la península de Florida.

*Bonnieblue*, la bandera de la República Independiente de Florida Occidental

Dinero de República Independiente de Texas

Entre 1845 y 1853, Estados Unidos anexa extensos territorios mexicanos. La anexión de Texas en 1845 causa la guerra entre México y Estados Unidos. En 1848, México cede otra parte muy grande de su territorio, incluyendo partes de Texas, Colorado, Arizona, Nuevo México y Wyoming, además de toda la extensión de California, Nevada y Utah. En 1853 Estados Unidos compra un área adicional en la frontera de México y el presidente Franklin Pierce paga diez millones de dólares. Los habitantes mexicanos de estas regiones son los ancestros de muchos latinos de Estados Unidos.

En 1898 Puerto Rico se convierte en un protectorado de Estados Unidos a causa de la guerra de Estados Unidos contra España. Los habitantes de Puerto Rico son ciudadanos de Estados Unidos desde 1917.

El escudo de Puerto Rico tiene el símbolo de San Juan y la inscripción en latín: "Su nombre es Juan".

**2-43 Comprensión.** PRIMERA FASE. **Reconocimiento de palabras clave.** Find in the text the Spanish word or phrase that best expresses the meaning of the following concepts:

1. war          _____
2. valley       _____
3. ancestors    _____
4. border       _____
5. coat of arms _____
6. citizen      _____

SEGUNDA FASE. **Oraciones importantes.** Underline the statements that contain ideas found in the text. Then indicate where in the text those words appear.

1. The colonies became independent after a long and violent war.
2. The Continental Congress signed the Declaration of Independence in Philadelphia.
3. George Washington was a good soldier, but a poor politician.
4. The purchase of the Mississippi Valley turned out to be a poor decision by President Jefferson.
5. Spain gave up its claim to Florida and West Florida without any resistance.
6. The United States and Mexico went to war over the annexation of Texas.
7. Puerto Ricans are citizens of the United States.

TERCERA FASE. **Ideas principales.** Write a brief paragraph in English summarizing the main ideas expressed in the text.

 **2-44 Use la información.** Prepare an oral presentation describing the current flag or a historic flag of one of the states that has a Hispanic heritage. Consult the *Mosaicos* web page where you will find a worksheet and relevant links to collect information about the flag.

## Las descripciones — Descriptions

| | |
|---|---|
| agradable | *nice* |
| alegre | *happy, glad* |
| alto/a | *tall* |
| antipático/a | *unpleasant* |
| bajo/a | *short* (in stature) |
| bilingüe | *bilingual* |
| bonito/a | *pretty* |
| callado/a | *quiet* |
| cansado/a | *tired* |
| casado/a | *married* |
| contento/a | *happy, glad* |
| conversador/a | *talkative* |
| corto/a | *short* (in length) |
| débil | *weak* |
| delgado/a | *thin* |
| divertido/a | *funny, amusing* |
| enojado/a | *angry* |
| estatura mediana | *average, medium* (height) |
| feo/a | *ugly* |
| fuerte | *strong* |
| gordo/a | *fat* |
| guapo/a | *good-looking, handsome* |
| joven | *young* |
| largo/a | *long* |
| listo/a | *smart; ready* |
| mayor | *old* |
| moreno/a | *brunette* |
| nervioso/a | *nervous* |
| nuevo/a | *new* |
| oscuro/a | *dark* |
| pelirrojo/a | *redhead* |
| perezoso/a | *lazy* |
| pobre | *poor* |
| rico/a | *rich, wealthy* |
| rubio/a | *blond* |
| simpático/a | *nice, charming* |
| soltero/a | *single* |
| tonto/a | *silly, foolish* |
| trabajador/a | *hardworking* |
| triste | *sad* |
| viejo/a | *old* |

## Las nacionalidades — Nationalities

| | |
|---|---|
| alemán/alemana | *German* |
| argentino/a | *Argentinian* |
| boliviano/a | *Bolivian* |
| canadiense | *Canadian* |
| chileno/a | *Chilean* |
| colombiano/a | *Colombian* |
| costarricense | *Costa Rican* |
| cubano/a | *Cuban* |
| dominicano/a | *Dominican* |
| ecuatoriano/a | *Ecuadorian* |
| español/a | *Spanish* |
| estadounidense | *U.S. citizen* |
| francés/francesa | *French* |
| guatemalteco/a | *Guatemalan* |
| hispano/a | *Hispanic* |
| hondureño/a | *Honduran* |
| japonés/japonesa | *Japanese* |
| marroquí | *Moroccan* |
| mexicano/a | *Mexican* |
| nicaragüense | *Nicaraguan* |
| nigeriano/a | *Nigerian* |
| panameño/a | *Panamanian* |
| paraguayo/a | *Paraguayan* |
| peruano/a | *Peruvian* |
| polaco/a | *Polish* |
| portugués/portuguesa | *Portuguese* |
| puertorriqueño/a | *Puerto Rican* |
| salvadoreño/a | *Salvadorian* |
| uruguayo/a | *Uruguayan* |
| venezolano/a | *Venezuelan* |

## Los colores — Colors

| | |
|---|---|
| amarillo/a | *yellow* |
| anaranjado/a | *orange* |
| azul | *blue* |
| blanco/a | *white* |
| marrón | *brown* |
| gris | *gray* |
| morado/a | *purple* |
| negro/a | *black* |
| rojo/a | *red* |
| rosado/a, rosa | *pink* |
| verde | *green; not ripe* |

## Verbos — Verbs

| | |
|---|---|
| desear | *to wish, to want* |
| ser | *to be* |
| usar | *to use* |

## Palabras y expresiones útiles — Useful words and expressions

| | |
|---|---|
| el auto, el coche, el carro | *car* |
| de | *of, from* |
| ¿de quién? | *whose?* |
| del | *of the* (contraction of *de + el*) |
| la flor | *flower* |
| le gusta(n) | *you* (formal) *like; he/she likes* |
| los lentes de contacto | *contact lenses* |
| me gusta(n) | *I like* |
| mucho *(adv.)* | *much, a lot* |
| mucho/a *(adj.)* | *many* |
| el ojo | *eye* |
| el pelo | *hair* |
| te gusta(n) | *you* (familiar) *like* |
| Tengo... años. | *I am . . . years old.* |
| tiene | *he/she has; you* (formal) *have* |
| todos/as | *everybody* |

See the English-Spanish and Spanish-English glossaries for other adjectives of nationality.
See page 74 for possessive adjectives.

3

# El tiempo libre

En este cuadro anónimo del siglo XVIII, vemos la boda de un hombre y una mujer. Ella es la princesa inca Ñusta Beatriz y él es un noble español, D. Martín de Loyola.

# In this chapter you will learn how to:

- discuss daily activities and leisure
- talk about food
- express where you are going
- make plans

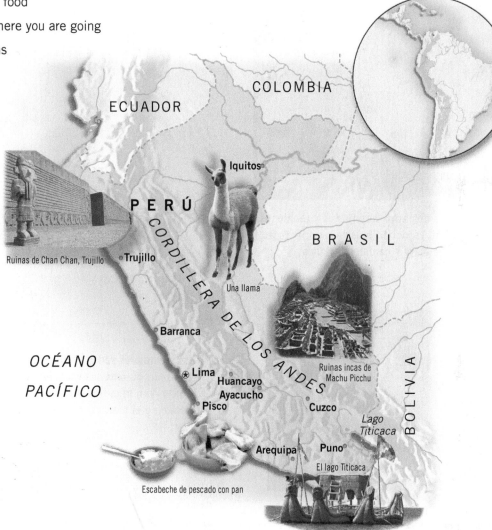

COLOMBIA

ECUADOR

PERÚ

CORDILLERA DE LOS ANDES

Iquitos

BRASIL

Ruinas de Chan Chan, Trujillo • Trujillo

Una llama

Barranca

Ruinas incas de Machu Picchu

OCÉANO

PACÍFICO

• Lima
Huancayo
Ayacucho
Pisco

Cuzco

BOLIVIA

Lago Titicaca

Arequipa    Puno

El lago Titicaca

Escabeche de pescado con pan

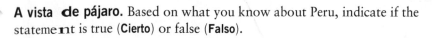

**A vista de pájaro.** Based on what you know about Peru, indicate if the statement is true (**Cierto**) or false (**Falso**).

1. _____ Perú está al sur de Colombia.
2. _____ La capital de Perú está en la costa del Atlántico.
3. _____ La comida de Perú es muy variada.
4. _____ Algunos peruanos son de origen inca y español.
5. _____ El Amazonas está entre Perú y Ecuador.
6. _____ La llama es un animal débil.

89

## ◀)) Las diversiones

CD 2
Track 1

En muchos **países** hispanos hay **fiestas** y **reuniones**.
Los **jóvenes** bailan, escuchan **música** o conversan.
A veces **tocan la guitarra** y **cantan canciones**
populares.

Estas **mujeres van** a la playa en su **tiempo libre** y
también **durante** las **vacaciones**. Allí, caminan y
conversan **mientras** otras personas **toman el sol**,
**nadan** en **el mar**, corren o **descansan**.

Este **hombre** lee el **periódico al aire libre** en un
parque de su **ciudad**. Y usted, ¿lee el
periódico? ¿Qué periódicos o **revistas** lee?

Muchos jóvenes van al **cine,**
especialmente los fines de
semana. También es común
**alquilar películas** para ver en
casa.

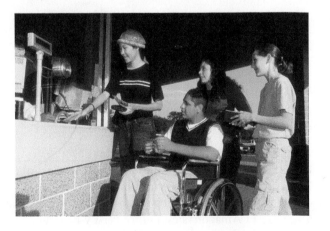

**3-5 ¿Adónde vamos?** PRIMERA FASE. You and your partner are in a study abroad program in Lima and are looking for something to do together over the weekend. Underline three activities in the cultural section of the newspaper that you find interesting. Then fill in the chart, including the day and time for each activity.

## AGENDA CULTURAL
## La guía de Lima

### Cine

El amor en los tiempos del cólera. Dir. Mike Newell. C.C. Británico. Calle Bellavista 531. Miraflores. 7:30 pm. Libre.

### Teatro

La casa de Bernarda Alba. Grupo de Teatro Lorca. C.C. Británico. Av. La Marina 2554. San Miguel. 7:30 pm. Libre.
Entre visillos. Basada en "La cantante calva", de Eugenio Ionesco. Auditorio Municipalidad de San Isidro. La República 455. El Olivar. 8 pm. Boletería.

### Música

Los andinos en concierto. Huainos, yaravíes, mulizas. ICPNA. Jr. Cuzco 446. Lima. 7 pm. S/. 10.00.
Noche flamenca. Ballet La flor de Sevilla. ICPNA. Av. Angamos Oeste 120. Miraflores. 7:30 p.m. S/. 25.00.
Amalia Sánchez en concierto. A beneficio del C.C. de Rehabilitación de Ciegos. C.C. Ricardo Palma. Larco 770. Miraflores. 8 pm. S/. 10.00.

### Exposición

Maestros en acción. Asociación de Docentes de la ENSABAP. Bellas Artes de La Molina. Av. Rinconada del Lago 1515. 7 pm.

### Libro

Lectura de poemas de Óscar Liria. Av. La Paz 646. 7:30 pm. Libre.

### Conferencia

La mujer en el arte. Con Lola Reyes. C. C. San Marcos. Parque Universitario. Lima. 6:30 pm. Libre.

### Literatura

Perú en la literatura francesa. Con Pierre Brillat. Alianza Francesa. Av. Arequipa 4595. Miraflores. 8 pm. S/.15.00, S/.10.00.

### Cultura

Huainos, yaravíes, and mulizas are Peruvian songs of pre-Columbian origin that are popular in the Andean region of the country. They are often performed and danced in the peñas, music clubs that promote traditional (Afro-Andean and Creole) music. In the peñas people dance all night long and enjoy excellent regional food.

| ¿ADÓNDE VAMOS? | ¿QUÉ VAMOS A VER/HACER/ESCUCHAR? | ¿CUÁNDO? |
|---|---|---|
| | | |
| | | |
| | | |

SEGUNDA FASE. Explain your plans to another pair. Decide if you can do some of the activities together.

# ◀)) La comida

CD 2
Track 3

**En el restaurante.** Ahora Lola y Manuel están en el restaurante El Jardín Limeño para **celebrar el cumpleaños** de Lola. Hablan con el **camarero**.

CAMARERO: Buenas noches. ¿Qué desean los señores?

MANUEL: Lola, ¿qué vas a comer?

LOLA: Para mí, una **ensalada** primero y después **pollo** con **verduras**.

MANUEL: Yo, para empezar, **ceviche** de **pescado**. Y luego un **bistec** con **papas**.

CAMARERO: ¿Y para beber?

LOLA: Vamos a beber **vino** blanco. Y también **agua** con gas, por favor.

CAMARERO: ¿Algo más?

MANUEL: Nada más, gracias.

## ESPECIALIDADES DE LA CASA

### ENTRADAS

| | |
|---|---|
| Ensalada de la casa | S/.10 |
| Ceviche de pescado | S/.15 |
| Papa a la huancaína | S/.10 |
| Causa a la limeña | S/.12 |

### PLATOS PRINCIPALES

| | |
|---|---|
| Chupe de camarones | S/.22 |
| Ají de gallina | S/.18 |
| Lomo saltado | S/.17 |
| Bistec con papas | S/.17 |
| Pollo con verduras | S/.16 |

### POSTRES

| | |
|---|---|
| Suspiro de limeña | S/.8 |
| Alfajor | S/.8 |
| Mazamorra morada | S/.6 |

### BEBIDAS

| | |
|---|---|
| Chicha morada | S/.4 |
| Jugo de maracuyá | S/.4 |
| Inca Kola | S/.3 |

## Cultura

Peruvian cooking mostly uses regional ingredients and follows preparation methods inherited from indigenous cultures. Ceviche is a typical dish of Peru and other countries in Latin America. It is generally made with seafood that is not cooked but rather marinated in lime juice and spices.

yuca frita · aceitunas · frijoles · ceviche de pescado · adobo de chancho · papas cocidas · tamales · rocotos rellenos

La comida peruana es muy variada. Sobre esta mesa hay ceviche de pescado, tamales, papas cocidas, rocotos (pimientos) rellenos, adobo de chancho (cerdo), yuca frita, frijoles y aceitunas.

## En directo

Expressions to take an order:

**¿Qué desean los señores?**

**¿Qué van a tomar/beber?**

Expressions to order food:

**Para mí, una ensalada, arroz con...**

**Me gustaría/Quisiera comer/tomar...**
*I would like to eat/ drink...*

**Yo quiero/deseo...**

## Cultura

The *Cultura* box above mentions one of the most typical dishes in Perú, *el ceviche.* Some other typical Peruvian dishes include *papa a la huancaína* (sliced boiled potatoes covered with a spicy creamy cheese sauce); *causa a la limeña* (seasoned mashed potato stuffed with tuna, egg, shrimp, or avocado); *chupe de camarones* (shrimp chowder); *ají de gallina* (shredded chicken casserole with walnuts, parmesan cheese, and Peruvian hot peppers); *suspiro de limeña* (a dessert made with milk and eggs); *alfajor* (two-layer cookies with *dulce de leche* between the layers; *mazamorra morada* (purple corn pudding).

## Más comidas y bebidas

CD 2
Track 4

el desayuno

el cereal
la leche
el té
el jugo de naranja
el café caliente
el pan tostado/las tostadas
los huevos fritos

el almuerzo

la ensalada de lechuga y tomate
el sándwich de jamón y queso
una cerveza fría
las papas fritas
el refresco
la fruta
la hamburguesa

la comida/la cena

el pescado
el arroz
el helado
el pollo
el agua
los vegetales/las verduras
la sopa
los espaguetis

**3-6 Calorías.** PRIMERA FASE. Which item in each group contains the most calories?

1. la sopa de tomate, una hamburguesa, la sopa de pollo
2. el pollo frito, el pescado, la ensalada
3. los vegetales, las frutas, las papas fritas
4. la cerveza, la leche desnatada (*skim*), el café
5. el helado de chocolate, el cereal, el arroz

**SEGUNDA FASE.** Mention items in the *Primera fase* that you eat or drink frequently. Do you both have the same preferences?

**MODELO:** E1: *Frecuentemente como ensaladas y bebo cerveza. ¿Y tú?*
E2: *Yo frecuentemente como hamburguesas con papas fritas y bebo refrescos.*

**3-7 Las comidas.** Tell a classmate what you usually have for breakfast, lunch, and dinner. Then find out what he/she usually eats for those meals.

**MODELO:** *En el desayuno, como tostadas y bebo café. ¿Y tú?*

**3-8 Dietas especiales.** Which is the best option from this menu for the following people?

1. Su amiga Luisa está un poco delgada y desea subir de peso (*gain weight*). ¿Qué va a comer de este menú?
2. Su mamá es alérgica a los mariscos (*seafood*). ¿Cuál de las ensaladas va a comer?
3. Su amigo José está un poco gordo y quiere bajar de peso (*lose weight*). ¿Cuál de los platos principales no debe comer?
4. El profesor/La profesora de español está enfermo/a (*sick*) del estómago hoy. ¿Qué debe comer?

---

### Cultura

Fast food is popular among young Hispanics, and American-style hamburger places may be found in Hispanic countries. They often adapt to local tastes, and it is not unusual to have hamburgers served with rice and black beans instead of fries. Beer and wine may also be sold in addition to soft drinks.

---

### MENÚ

**SOPAS**

| | |
|---|---|
| Sopa de pollo | S/. 9 |
| Sopa de tomate | S/. 7 |
| Sopa de vegetales | S/. 7 |
| Sopa de pescado | S/. 12 |

**ENSALADAS**

| | |
|---|---|
| Ensalada de lechuga y tomate | S/. 8 |
| Ensalada de pollo | S/. 14 |
| Ensalada de atún | S/. 12 |

**PLATOS PRINCIPALES**

| | |
|---|---|
| Bistec con papas y vegetales | S/. 20 |
| Hamburguesa con papas fritas | S/. 16 |
| Pescado con papas fritas | S/. 18 |
| Arroz con vegetales | S/. 15 |

**3-9 ¿Qué te gusta más?** Using the words below, ask what your partner prefers to drink **por las mañanas, para el almuerzo, por las noches.** Alternate asking questions and taking notes. Then explain your partner's preferences to the class.

MODELO:  E1:  *¿Qué te gusta beber por las mañanas, té o café?*
         E2:  *Me gusta más el café.*

| | | |
|---|---|---|
| el agua mineral con gas | una copa de vino | un refresco |
| el agua mineral sin gas | una cerveza | el té (helado) |
| un batido (*shake*) | un chocolate caliente | un vaso (*glass*) |
| de yogur y fruta | el jugo de naranja | de leche |

**3-10 En el café.** It is 9:00 on Saturday morning, and you and a friend are in a café in Lima. Ask what your friend wants to order. Then say what you are going to order.

MODELO:  E1:  *El desayuno es muy bueno aquí.*
              *¿Qué deseas comer?*
         E2:  _____ *¿Y tú?*
         E1:  _____ *¿Y qué vas a tomar?*
         E2:  _____

| DESAYUNOS | |
|---|---|
| café | S/.3 |
| té | S/.3 |
| café con leche | S/.5 |
| jugo de naranja | S/.5 |
| chocolate | S/.6 |
| tostadas | S/.5 |
| pan con mantequilla | S/.5 |
| pan dulce | S/.6 |
| cereal | S/.8 |
| huevos fritos | S/.10 |

**3-11 Un viaje (*trip*).** You are in Peru and are planning a day trip to Machu Picchu. Arrange to take some food and beverages with you.

1. Make a list of the food and beverages that you need to take.
2. Talk about the things that you are going to do.

**3-12 Nuestro menú.** You and your roommate want to have guests over for dinner tonight. Decide whom each of you is going to invite and what you are going to serve. Finally, compare your menu with that of another pair of classmates.

■ Vamos a invitar a _____ .

■ Vamos a servir _____ .

**3-13 ¿Qué hacen estos estudiantes?** PRIMERA FASE. You will listen to two students, Rafael and Miguel, talk about their activities and weekend plans. Before you listen, write down three activities you normally do during the week, and three that you plan for this weekend.

CD 2
Track 5

actividades de la semana: _____

planes para el fin de semana: _____

SEGUNDA FASE. Now, listen to Rafael and Miguel and pay attention to the general idea of what they say. Then check (✓) the activities they mention they will do during the weekend.

1. ___ estudiar para los exámenes
2. ___ comer en un restaurante
3. ___ descansar y tomar el sol
4. ___ trabajar en la librería
5. ___ celebrar el cumpleaños de Rafael

# EN ACCIÓN

## Diarios de bicicleta: La invitación

### Antes de ver

**3-14** In this video segment, Javier is at a restaurant. Based on your knowledge of Mexican restaurants in the United States, mark (✓) the sentences that you think describe restaurants in Mexico.

1. ___ Hay muchos colores.
2. ___ Hay música de mariachis.
3. ___ La comida cuesta mucho dinero.
4. ___ Muchos platos tienen chile.

### Mientras ve

**3-15** Mark (✓) the correct answer according to the information provided.

1. Javier va al restaurante para...
   - a. ___ desayunar
   - b. ___ almorzar
   - c. ___ cenar

2. Para comer, Javier pide...
   - a. ___ pollo con papas fritas y chile habanero.
   - b. ___ pollo con papas fritas y chile verde.
   - c. ___ sopa azteca.

3. Para beber, Javier pide...
   - a. ___ agua mineral bien fría.
   - b. ___ un té frío con limón.
   - c. ___ una limonada bien fría.

### Después de ver

**3-16 PRIMERA FASE.** Mark (✓) the statement that describes the problem that Javier has in this segment.

1. ___ Javier no tiene dinero para pagar la cuenta (*bill*).
2. ___ Gabi no puede almorzar con Javier.
3. ___ A Javier no le gusta la comida del restaurante.

**SEGUNDA FASE.** Write a sentence indicating how Javier's problem is solved.

# FUNCIONES Y FORMAS

## 1. Talking about daily activities: Present tense of *hacer, poner, salir, traer,* and *oír*

### Unos amigos nuevos conversan sobre sus actividades

CAROLINA: Bueno, para conocernos mejor, ¿por qué no jugamos a *Decir la verdad*? José Manuel, la primera pregunta es para ti. ¿Qué **haces** cuando estás aburrido?

JOSÉ MANUEL: **Pongo** la tele para ver películas. Ahora, Tomás, ¿adónde **sales** cuando tienes tiempo? ¿Y con quién?

TOMÁS: Bueno, **salgo a comer** con mi novia Pilar. Pero cuando tengo exámenes, debo **salir para** la biblioteca. Carolina, cuando **oyes** música salsa, ¿qué **haces**?

CAROLINA: Eso es muy fácil. Siempre bailo cuando **oigo** música salsa. Mi pregunta es para los dos. ¿Qué **hacen** ustedes en casa que no les gusta **hacer**?

TOMÁS: Yo **hago** mi cama porque me gusta el orden.

JOSÉ MANUEL: Mis hermanitos me **traen** su ropa y lavo ropa sucia (*dirty*) todo el fin de semana. La ropa sucia de ellos es repugnante. ¡Qué asco! ¿Y tú, Carolina?

CAROLINA: ¿Yo? Pues, **pongo la mesa** todos los días. ¡Qué lata!

José Manuel    Carolina    Tomás

**Piénselo.** Match each idea on the left with a logical ending on the right. More than one answer may be possible.

1. _____ **Pongo** la tele...
2. _____ **Pongo** la mesa...
3. _____ **Oigo** música...
4. _____ Debo **salir para** la biblioteca...
5. _____ **Hago** mi cama...
6. _____ Lavo la ropa que **traen** mis hermanos...

a. porque me gusta el orden.
b. cuando **salgo** con mis amigos.
c. para pasarlo bien (*have a good time*).
d. para ayudar (*help*) con el trabajo de casa.
e. porque me gusta ver películas.
f. porque deseo aprender mucho.

■ In the present tense, the verbs **hacer, poner, salir, traer,** and **oír** have irregular **yo** forms, but are regular in all other forms.

| HACER (*to make, to do*) | | | |
|---|---|---|---|
| yo | **hago** | nosotros/as | **hacemos** |
| tú | **haces** | vosotros/as | **hacéis** |
| Ud., él, ella | **hace** | Uds., ellos/as | **hacen** |

■ **Hacer** means *to do* or *to make*. It is used frequently in questions to ask in a general sense what someone does, is doing, or likes to do.

| | |
|---|---|
| ¿Qué **haces** para sacar buenas notas? | *What do you do to get good grades?* |
| **Hago** la tarea para mis clases todos los días. | *I do the homework for my classes every day.* |

| PONER (*to put*) | | | |
|---|---|---|---|
| yo | **pongo** | nosotros/as | **ponemos** |
| tú | **pones** | vosotros/as | **ponéis** |
| Ud., él, ella | **pone** | Uds., ellos/as | **ponen** |

■ **Poner** means *to put*. When used with some electrical appliances, **poner** means *to turn on*; **poner la mesa** means *to set the table*.

| | |
|---|---|
| Por la mañana **pongo** mis libros en mi mochila. | *In the morning I put my books in my backpack.* |
| Mi abuelo **pone** la televisión después de la cena. | *My grandfather turns on the TV after dinner.* |
| Yo **pongo** la mesa a la hora de la cena. | *I set the table at dinner time.* |

| SALIR (*to leave*) | | | |
|---|---|---|---|
| yo | **salgo** | nosotros/as | **salimos** |
| tú | **sales** | vosotros/as | **salís** |
| Ud., él, ella | **sale** | Uds., ellos/as | **salen** |

■ **Salir** can be used with several different prepositions. To express that you are leaving a place, use **salir de;** to express your destination, use **salir para;** to express with whom you go out or the person you date, use **salir con;** to express what you are going to do, use **salir a.**

| | |
|---|---|
| Yo **salgo de** mi cuarto a las 7:15 de la mañana. | *I leave my room at 7:15 in the morning.* |
| **Salgo para** la cafetería. | *I am leaving for the cafeteria.* |
| Mi mejor amiga **sale con** Mauricio. | *My best friend is dating Mauricio.* |
| Ellos **salen** a bailar los sábados. | *They go out dancing on Saturdays.* |

| TRAER (*to bring*) | | | |
|---|---|---|---|
| yo | **traigo** | nosotros/as | **traemos** |
| tú | **traes** | vosotros/as | **traéis** |
| Ud., él, ella | **trae** | Uds., ellos/as | **traen** |

| | |
|---|---|
| Yo siempre **traigo** un postre a estas fiestas. | *I always bring a dessert to these parties.* |

| OÍR (to hear) | | | |
|---|---|---|---|
| yo | **oigo** | nosotros/as | **oímos** |
| tú | **oyes** | vosotros/as | **oís** |
| Ud., él, ella | **oye** | Uds., ellos/as | **oyen** |

■ **Oír** means *to hear* in the sense of *to perceive sounds*. Note the spelling and the accent marks in the infinitive, **nosotros/as**, and **vosotros/as** forms.

Yo **oigo** música.
— ¿**Oyes** la alarma?
— No, no **oigo** nada.

*I hear music.*
— *Do you hear the alarm?*
— *No, I don't hear anything.*

### 3-17 La perfección andante (*Perfection in motion*). PRIMERA FASE. Are you organized, considerate, studious, and/or punctual? Check (✔) the statements that refer to things you do or don't do regularly.

1. _____ Yo **hago** mi cama temprano por la mañana.
2. _____ Cuando **oigo** que un amigo está triste, lo invito a salir.
3. _____ Siempre **pongo** música rock cuando estudio.
4. _____ Generalmente, **traigo** el periódico a la mesa para leer las noticias mientras desayuno.
5. _____ En general, no **traigo** el periódico a la mesa mientras desayuno porque prefiero conversar con mi familia.
6. _____ Por las mañanas, **hago** ejercicio y luego **salgo** para la universidad.

**SEGUNDA FASE.** Take turns talking about the activities you both do that show off your best qualities.

MODELO: E1: *Yo soy organizado. Siempre hago mi cama temprano. ¿Y tú?*
E2: *Pues, yo también... /No, yo no...*

### 3-18 ¿Usa usted bien su tiempo libre? PRIMERA FASE. Check (✔) the version of each activity that best describes your habits.

1. _____ Pongo la mesa para cenar.   _____ Como en cualquier lugar de la casa.
2. _____ Hago el desayuno.   _____ Salgo a desayunar fuera de casa.
3. _____ Hago la cama cada día.   _____ Hago la cama una vez por semana.
4. _____ Oigo las noticias en la radio.   _____ Veo las noticias en la televisión.
5. _____ Traigo el periódico a la casa.   _____ Leo el periódico en el cibercafé.
6. _____ Pongo la televisión para ver películas.   _____ Salgo al cine para ver películas.

**SEGUNDA FASE.** Working with a partner, compare your answers and determine which of you has more fun doing these things. Explain why.

**3-19 Mi rutina.** PRIMERA FASE. Talk about the activities that you routinely do. Then ask your classmate about his/her activities.

MODELO:     tener clases por la mañana/por la tarde
E1:  *Yo tengo clases por la mañana. ¿Y tú?*
E2:  *Yo tengo clases por la mañana y por la tarde./Yo también tengo clases por la mañana.*

1. normalmente salir de su casa temprano/tarde por la mañana
2. generalmente poner la radio/tele para escuchar su música favorita por la mañana
3. hacer la tarea en casa/en la biblioteca
4. frecuentemente salir a comer/ver películas con su familia por la noche
5. con frecuencia traer muchos libros a casa después de las clases

SEGUNDA FASE. Write a brief paragraph comparing your routine with that of your classmate. In your opinion, who has a more interesting routine, and why? Provide a few reasons.

**3-20 Para pasarlo bien.** PRIMERA FASE. Write a check (✓) next to the activities that, in your opinion, your classmates probably do to have fun.

1. _____ Ponen películas los fines de semana.
2. _____ Oyen música y bailan mientras estudian para los exámenes.
3. _____ Frecuentemente hacen fiestas con sus amigos.
4. _____ Asisten a conciertos y exposiciones de arte.
5. _____ Hacen ejercicio en el gimnasio o en el parque.
6. _____ Escuchan programas en la radio pública.
7. _____ Salen a comer en grupo.
8. _____ ...

SEGUNDA FASE. Using the activities you marked in the *Primera fase* as a starting point, ask if your instructor does the same activities to have fun. Refer to *En directo* to help you express your reactions to your instructor's responses.

MODELO:     PAREJA:  *Para pasarlo bien, nosotros asistimos a conciertos de música rock. ¿Asiste a conciertos de música rock para pasarlo bien?*
PROFESOR/A:  *No asisto a conciertos de música rock. Para pasarlo bien escucho conciertos de música clásica en la radio pública.*
PAREJA:  *¡Qué aburrido!*

---

**En directo**

To react to what someone has said:

**¡Qué interesante!**

**¡Qué divertido!**
*How funny!*

**¡Qué aburrido!**

---

**SITUACIONES**

1. **Role A.** You are interviewing a potential roommate for your two-bedroom apartment. Find out a) if he/she likes things to be neat (**si le gusta el orden**); b) what household chores he/she likes to do and does not like to do; and c) what he/she likes to do at home in his/her free time. Your interviewee will have questions for you also. At the end of the conversation, decide whether to accept this person as a roommate.

   Role B. You are new in town and are being interviewed by someone who has a room to rent in his/her apartment. Answer the questions in as much detail as possible and ask some questions of your own. At the end of the conversation, decide whether you are interested in the room.

2. **Role A.** You have just been hired to take care of a five-year-old boy for the summer. Ask what time the parent leaves the house in the morning and find out a) what the child eats and drinks for breakfast and lunch; b) whether he has to make his bed or set the table; and c) what his favorite activities are.

   Role B. You have just hired a college student to take care of your five-year-old son for the summer. Answer his/her questions. To get to know him/her better, ask a) what he/she studies at school and b) what he/she likes to do in his/her free time.

## 2. Expressing movement and plans: Present tense of *ir* and *ir a + infinitive*

### Elena, la chica en el centro, habla de sus amigos

Mis amigos y yo somos diferentes, pero somos muy unidos. Para mi cumpleaños, nosotros **vamos a** un restaurante todos los años. Los sábados, yo **voy a** la casa de mi amiga Estela, y luego ella **va** conmigo al gimnasio para hacer ejercicio. A veces Rafael, Humberto y Rodrigo también **van al** gimnasio con nosotras. Mi amiga Teresa, no sale mucho porque prefiere estudiar. Yo siempre bromeo (*joke*) con ella: "Tere, ¿**vas a** la biblioteca a pasarlo bien?" Fernando, es muy tranquilo y artístico y le fascina el silencio. Con frecuencia él y Estela **van a** la librería a comprar libros.

**Piénselo.** Read the following statements about Elena and her friends. Then indicate (✔) if the statement is **probable** or **improbable**, based on the information Elena provides.

|  | PROBABLE | IMPROBABLE |
|---|---|---|
| 1. Elena y sus amigos **van a** lugares juntos para celebrar su cumpleaños. | —— | —— |
| 2. Fernando **va a** los conciertos de música rock. | —— | —— |
| 3. Estela afirma: "Frecuentemente, yo **voy a** la librería a comprar libros". | —— | —— |
| 4. Teresa comenta: "Fernando y yo **vamos al** museo de arte esta tarde". | —— | —— |
| 5. Elena no **va a** las fiestas de cumpleaños de sus amigos. | —— | —— |

■ After the verb **ir**, use **a** to introduce a noun that refers to a place. When **a** is followed by the article **el**, the two words contract to form **al**.

| Voy **a la** fiesta de María. | *I am going to María's party.* |
| Vamos **al** gimnasio. | *We are going to the gym.* |

■ Use **¿adónde?** when asking *where (to)?* with the verb **ir**.

| **¿Adónde** vas ahora? | *Where are you going now?* |

| IR (*to go*) | | | |
|---|---|---|---|
| yo | **voy** | nosotros/as | **vamos** |
| tú | **vas** | vosotros/as | **vais** |
| Ud., él, ella | **va** | Uds., ellos/as | **van** |

■ To express a future action or condition, use the present tense of **ir a** + the infinitive form of the verb.

| Mis amigos **van a nadar** después. | *My friends are going to swim later.* |
| ¿**Vas a ir** a la fiesta? | *Are you going to go to the party?* |

■ The expression **vamos a** + *infinitive* can mean *let's*.

| **Vamos a cenar** en mi casa. | *Let's have dinner at my house.* |
| **Vamos a bailar** después. | *Let's go dancing afterward.* |

### Lengua

The following expressions denote future time:

**después, más tarde, esta noche, mañana, pasado mañana, la próxima semana, el próximo mes/año.**

**3-21 ¿Adónde van?** PRIMERA FASE. Josh and Steve are North American students visiting Peru for their summer vacation. Match the descriptions on the left with the places they plan to see on the right.

1. ____ Steve estudia historia. Por eso, desea ver la universidad prestigiosa y más antigua de América de Sur. Está en Lima. Él va a...

2. ____ Los dos amigos van a visitar uno de los lugares más misteriosos del planeta. Allí hay enormes figuras geométricas trazadas (*drawn*) en la tierra que son visibles solamente desde el aire. Ellos van a...

3. ____ Josh conoce (*meets*) a Susana en Perú. Ella lo invita a un evento folclórico donde las personas oyen poesía, música tradicional y comen y bailan también. Josh y Susana van a...

4. ____ Steve y Josh van a un lugar histórico imposible de ignorar. Es considerado el símbolo del imperio inca. Está cerca de Cuzco. Steve y Josh van a...

**a.** Machu Picchu

**b.** las líneas de Nazca

SEGUNDA FASE. Now indicate where you will go to do the following in Peru.

1. Para hacer amigos, conversar y bailar ritmos peruanos, yo voy a

_____ .

2. Voy a _____ para tomar fotos de los alumnos y el edificio de una universidad muy antigua.

3. Para escalar unas montañas altas de mucha importancia histórica, voy a

_____ .

**c.** la Universidad de San Marcos

**3-22 Intercambio.** PRIMERA FASE. Your classmate's friends are busy today. Find out when each friend is leaving the place listed and where he/she is going afterward.

MODELO: E1: *¿A qué hora sale del trabajo tu amigo Armando?*
E2: *(Sale) a las seis de la tarde.*
E1: *¿Adónde va después?*
E2: *Va al cine.*

**d.** una peña

| NOMBRE | HORA | LUGAR |
|--------|------|-------|
| Juan | 8:00 a.m. | gimnasio |
| Alicia | 9:30 a.m. | laboratorio de computadoras |
| Sofía | 8:30 p.m. | oficina |
| Tú | ... | ... |

SEGUNDA FASE. Exchange information with your partner about what each of you does at the times listed in the *Primera fase.*

MODELO: E1: *¿Qué haces a las 8:00 de la mañana?*
E2: *Salgo de mi casa para la universidad.*
E1: *¿Adónde vas cuando llegas a la universidad?*
E2: *Voy a mi clase de español. ¿Qué haces tú a las 8:00 de la mañana?*

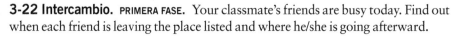

**3-23 ¡Qué lío! (What a mess!)** PRIMERA FASE. Cristina had a party at her house while her parents were out of town, and now her friends are helping her clean up. Match each situation on the left with its probable solution.

1. ____ Hay muchos platos sucios.
2. ____ Cristina ve mucha comida en la mesa.
3. ____ La casa está desordenada.
4. ____ Cristina y sus amigos necesitan energía para limpiar la casa.
5. ____ Los amigos de Cristina están cansados después de la fiesta.

a. Dos chicos van a ordenar todo.
b. Algunos amigos van a recoger (*pick up*) los platos.
c. Una amiga va a refrigerar la comida.
d. Una amiga va a preparar café.
e. Van a descansar.

SEGUNDA FASE. Brainstorm how Cristina's parents are going to react when they find out about her party. Some suggestions may include: *cancelar las tarjetas de crédito, prohibir fiestas/amigos, conversar seriamente,* ...

## SITUACIONES

1. **Role A.** Your friend has invited you to a concert. Call him/her to find out a) where and when the concert is going to be; b) who is going to sing; c) who is going to introduce (**presentar**) the group; and d) how much the ticket (**el boleto/el billete/la entrada**) costs.

   **Role B.** Your friend calls to find out about a concert you invited him/her to. Answer all the questions with as much information as possible.

2. **Role A.** You call to invite a friend to a café tonight where a mutual friend is going to sing. After your friend responds, ask about his/her plans for later in the evening: a) where he/she is going; b) with whom; and c) what time, etc.

   **Role B.** A friend calls to invite you to a café tonight where a mutual friend is going to sing. Inquire about the event to find out a) what time and where it will be and b) if other friends are going to go. Accept the invitation and mention your plans for later in the evening.

**3-24 Mi agenda para la semana.** Invite six classmates individually to do the following activities with you. Each will accept or reject your invitation according to his/her schedule for the week. Indicate the day, the activity and the name of the classmate who accepted your invitation.

MODELO: estudiar en la biblioteca el lunes
E1: *¿Vamos a estudiar en la biblioteca el lunes?*
E2: *Lo siento, Miguel, el lunes voy a ir al cine con David. Pero, ¿por qué no salimos a comer el martes?*
E3: *Buena idea. Vamos a salir el martes.*

1. ir a un concierto
2. mirar televisión en casa
3. tomar algo en un café
4. estudiar para un examen difícil
5. bailar en la discoteca
6. hacer ejercicio

| DÍA | ¿QUÉ VA A HACER? | ¿CON QUIÉN? |
|---|---|---|
| martes | comer en un restaurante peruano | Miguel |
| | | |

**3-25 Los planes de Maribel.** PRIMERA FASE. Take turns saying what Maribel is going to do at the times indicated.

SEGUNDA FASE. Tell your classmate what you are going to do at those times on Friday.

# 3. Talking about quantity: Numbers 100 to 2.000.000

**Piénselo.** Your instructor will say a number from each of the following series. Identify each number you hear. The numbers in the last row are dates.

| | | | |
|---|---|---|---|
| **1.** 114 | 360 | 850 | 524 |
| **2.** 213 | 330 | 490 | 919 |
| **3.** 818 | 625 | 723 | 513 |
| **4.** 667 | 777 | 984 | 534 |
| **5.** 1.310 | 1.420 | 3.640 | 6.860 |
| **6.** 10.467 | 50.312 | 100.000 | 2.000.000 |
| **7.** 1492 | 1776 | 1890 | 2001 |

■ You have already learned the numbers up to 99. In this section you will learn numbers to use to talk about larger quantities.

| | | | |
|---|---|---|---|
| 100 | cien/ciento | 1.000 | mil |
| 200 | doscientos/as | 1.100 | mil cien |
| 300 | trescientos/as | 2.000 | dos mil |
| 400 | cuatrocientos/as | 10.000 | diez mil |
| 500 | quinientos/as | 100.000 | cien mil |
| 600 | seiscientos/as | 150.000 | ciento cincuenta mil |
| 700 | setecientos/as | 500.000 | quinientos mil |
| 800 | ochocientos/as | 1.000.000 | un millón (de) |
| 900 | novecientos/as | 2.000.000 | dos millones (de) |

■ Use **cien** to say 100 when used alone or when followed by a noun. Use **ciento** for numbers from 101 to 199.

| | |
|---|---|
| 100 | **cien** |
| 100 chicos | **cien** chicos |
| 120 profesoras | **ciento** veinte profesoras |
| 177 libros | **ciento** setenta y siete libros |

■ Multiples of 100 agree in gender with the noun they modify.

| | |
|---|---|
| 200 periódicos | **doscientos** periódicos |
| 1.400 revistas | **mil cuatrocientas** revistas |

■ Use **mil** for *one thousand*. Multiples of 1,000 are also **mil**.

| | |
|---|---|
| 1.000 | **mil** alumnos, **mil** alumnas |
| 12.000 | **doce mil** residentes |

■ Use **un millón** to say *one million*. Use **un millón de** when a noun follows.

| | |
|---|---|
| 1.000.000 | **un millón** |
| 1.000.000 de personas | **un millón de personas** |
| 12.000.000 de dólares | **doce millones de dólares** |

■ In many Spanish-speaking countries, a period is used to separate thousands, and a comma is used to separate decimals.

| | |
|---|---|
| $1.000 | $19,50 |

 **3-26 ¿Cuándo va a ocurrir?** Exchange opinions with a classmate about when each of the following events will occur.

MODELO:  Todos los libros van a ser electrónicos.
E1: *En el año 2020.*
E2: *Estoy de acuerdo.* Or
*No estoy de acuerdo. Todos los libros van a ser electrónicos en 2050.*

1. Los adultos van a trabajar sólo 20 horas por semana.
2. Los estudiantes no van a ir a clases. Van a estudiar en universidades virtuales.
3. Todos los autos van a ser eléctricos y van a ser muy rápidos.
4. Los turistas van a ir de un país a otro sin pasaporte.
5. La contaminación va a ser muy grande, y las personas van a usar máscaras (*masks*) en los parques y en las calles.
6. Los robots, y no las personas, van a servir la comida en los restaurantes.
7. Las personas van a comunicarse por telepatía.
8. Muchas personas van a comer solamente la comida artificial.
9. Muchos turistas van a viajar (*travel*) al espacio interplanetario.
10. Los viajes en avión van a ser más rápidos y van a costar poco.

**3-27 Unas vacaciones. PRIMERA FASE.** Your classmate has chosen one of the destinations in the ad for an upcoming vacation. To find out where he/she is going, ask the following questions. Then switch roles.

1. ¿Adónde vas?
2. ¿Qué lugares vas a ver?
3. ¿Cuántos días vas a estar allí?
4. ¿Cuánto cuesta la excursión?

**SEGUNDA FASE.** Based on your classmate's answers, fill in the information and share it with the class.

1. planes que su compañero/a necesita hacer (sacar un pasaporte, obtener una visa, hacer reservaciones, etc.):

   _____

2. lugar(es) que va a visitar: _____

3. tiempo que va a estar allí: _____

4. costo de la excursión: _____

5. dinero extra que usted cree que su compañero/a va a necesitar: _____

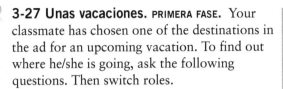

**AGENCIA MUNDIAL**

**A SU SERVICIO SIEMPRE** 20 años de experiencia, responsabilidad y profesionalidad.

TODOS LOS PRECIOS INCLUYEN PASAJES AÉREOS Y SERVICIOS TERRESTRES POR PERSONA

**PERÚ Y BOLIVIA**

**LIMA, AREQUIPA, CUZCO, MACHU PICCHU, PUNO, LA PAZ,** 15 días. La Ruta del Inca. Hoteles de 3 y 4 estrellas. Desayuno incluido.
**$2.760**

**PERÚ**

**LIMA, CUZCO, MACHU PICCHU, NAZCA,** 12 días. Visite fortalezas incas. Vea las misteriosas líneas de Nazca desde el aire. Hoteles de primera. Desayuno y cena incluidos.
**$3.150**

**LIMA, NAZCA, AREQUIPA, LAGO TITICACA,** 10 días. Admire la arquitectura colonial de Lima y Arequipa. Vea las líneas de Nazca desde el aire. Navegue en el lago más alto del mundo. Hoteles de primera.
**$2.620**

**ARGENTINA**

**BUENOS AIRES, BARILOCHE, MENDOZA,** 12 días. Disfrute de una gran metrópoli. Esquíe en uno de los lugares más bellos del mundo. Hoteles de 4 y 5 estrellas. Desayuno y cena.
**$3.590**

**CHILE Y ARGENTINA**

**SANTIAGO, PUERTO MONTT, BARILOCHE, BUENOS AIRES,** 12 días. Excursión a Viña del Mar y Valparaíso. Cruce de los Andes en minibús y barco. Hoteles de 3 y 4 estrellas.
**$4.075**

**CARIBE**

**JAMAICA,** 7 días. Happy Inn, todo incluido. Exclusivo para parejas.
**$2.480**

**PUERTO RICO**

**SAN JUAN,** 5 días. Hotel de 5 estrellas. Excursión a Ponce. Visita con guía al Viejo San Juan. Desayuno incluido.
**$1.995**

**MÉXICO**

**MÉXICO, TAXCO, ACAPULCO,** 7 días. Hoteles de 3 y 4 estrellas. Excursión a Teotihuacán. Desayuno bufet incluido.
**$1.800**

**CANCÚN,** 5 días. Hotel de 4 estrellas. Excursión a Cozumel. Visita a ruinas mayas. Las mejores playas.
**$1.510**

*Solicite los programas detallados con variantes de hoteles e itinerarios a su agente de viajes.*

Tel. 312-785-4455   Fax: 312-785-4456

## SITUACIONES

1. **Role A.** You have been saving up for a special trip (**viaje**) during the next school vacation, and you are now making plans. Call a friend to explain a) where you plan to go; b) who will travel with you; and c) what you plan to do.

   **Role B.** Your friend calls to tell you about his/her travel plans for the next school break. Ask a) with whom he/she is planning to go; and b) what places he/she is going to visit. You are curious about the cost of the trip (**viaje**), so you inquire about the cost of the flight (**el vuelo**), the hotel, and the activities your friend plans to do.

2. **Role A.** You have been working hard, and you would like to splurge on a weekend trip to do some special (but expensive) activities, like rent a car, go to a professional sports event or rock concert, eat in good restaurants, and shop (**ir de compras**). Call and invite your friend to go. Explain your plan and be prepared to answer questions about the cost of this weekend adventure.

   **Role B.** Your friend calls to invite you on an exciting (but expensive) weekend trip. After your friend explains the plan, ask questions to get an idea of the cost. Decide whether you can afford it, and either accept or decline the invitation.

### En directo

To call attention to an unusual fact:

**¡Fíjate qué noticia!**
*How about that!*

**¡Imagínate!**

To react to good news:

**¡Qué suerte!**

**¡Qué maravilla!**

**¡Qué bien!**

To convince someone:

**¡Ven/Anda, anímate!**
*Come on, cheer up!*

**Lo vamos a pasar muy bien.**
*We are going to have a good time.*

## 4. Stating what you know: *Saber* and *conocer*

ALFREDO: Me gustan mucho los músicos y ella **sabe** cantar muy bien.

ELENA: Sí, es una cantante fabulosa.

MARIO: Luisa, **conoces** a Liliana, ¿no?

LUISA: Sí, las dos estamos en la clase de arte de la profesora Ruiz.

**Piénselo.** Indicate (✓) in the appropriate box whether each sentence refers to knowing a fact, knowing how to do something, knowing a person, or being familiar with a place, an event, or a thing.

| | KNOWING A FACT | KNOWING HOW TO DO SOMETHING | KNOWING A PERSON | BEING FAMILIAR WITH A PLACE, EVENT, ETC. |
|---|---|---|---|---|
| 1. ¿**Conoces** la música afro-peruana? | —— | —— | —— | —— |
| 2. Me gusta mucho la música, pero no **sé** bailar. | —— | —— | —— | —— |
| 3. ¿**Sabes** los nombres de esos grupos musicales? | —— | —— | —— | —— |
| 4. ¿**Conoces** a Alfredo Roncal? Toca la guitarra. | —— | —— | —— | —— |
| 5. ¿**Sabes** si hay un club de música hispana en la ciudad? | —— | —— | —— | —— |
| 6. Alfredo **conoce** todos los clubes de música en la ciudad. | —— | —— | —— | —— |

■ Both *saber* and *conocer* mean *to know*, but they are not used interchangeably.

| | SABER | CONOCER |
|---|---|---|
| yo | sé | conozco |
| tú | sabes | conoces |
| Ud., él, ella | sabe | conoce |
| nosotros/as | sabemos | conocemos |
| vosotros/as | sabéis | conocéis |
| Uds., ellos/as | saben | conocen |

■ Use **saber** to express knowledge of facts or pieces of information.

Él **sabe** dónde está el club.    *He knows where the club is.*

■ Use **saber** + *infinitive* to express knowing how to do something.
  Yo **sé** tocar la guitarra.   *I know how to play the guitar.*

■ Use **conocer** to express familiarity with someone or something. **Conocer** also means *to meet*. Remember to use the *personal a* when referring to people.

| | |
|---|---|
| **Conozco a** los músicos. | *I know the musicians.* |
| **Conozco** bien ese club. | *I am very familiar with that club.* |
| Ella va a **conocer a** Luis. | *She is going to meet Luis.* |

> ## Lengua
>
> **Sé**, the **yo** form of the verb **saber**, has a written accent to distinguish it from the pronoun **se**.
>
> Yo **sé** que su hermano **se** llama José.

**3-28 Un encuentro entre dos estudiantes.** Raúl just arrived on campus, and he asks Sergio some questions. Select the correct words to complete their conversation.

| | | | |
|---|---|---|---|
| RAÚL: | Soy un estudiante nuevo y no (1) _____ dónde está la biblioteca. | **a.** sé | **b.** conozco |
| SERGIO: | Es muy fácil. Tú (2) _____ dónde está la cafetería, ¿no? Pues, está al lado. | **a.** sabes | **b.** conoces |
| RAÚL: | Gracias. ¿Y (3) _____ si hay un club de español? | **a.** sabes | **b.** conoces |
| SERGIO: | Sí, claro, y (4) _____ que esta noche tiene una reunión. | **a.** sé | **b.** conozco |
| RAÚL: | Magnífico. Sólo (5) _____ a dos o tres personas en la universidad. | **a.** sé | **b.** conozco |
| SERGIO: | Pues allí vas a (6) _____ a muchos estudiantes. | **a.** saber | **b.** conocer |

**3-29 ¿Sabes quién es...?** Ask your partner if he/she knows who is being referred to and if he/she knows that person. Take turns asking questions.

> MODELO:   el actor principal de *El ultimátum de Bourne*
> E1:  *¿Sabes quién es el actor principal de* El ultimátum de Bourne?
> E2:  *Sí, sé quién es. Es Matt Damon.*
> E1:  *¿Conoces a Matt Damon en persona?*
> E2:  *No, no conozco a Matt Damon./Sí, conozco a Matt Damon, pero solamente en fotografías.*

1. el/la representante de la Cámara de Representantes (*Congress*) de su distrito
2. el decano/la decana de la facultad
3. su profesor/a de español
4. el rey de España
5. el gobernador de su estado
6. el vicepresidente de Estados Unidos

**3-30 Adivina, adivinador.** In small groups, take turns reading the descriptions and guessing who is being described.

> MODELO:   E1:  *Es una chica muy pobre que va a un baile. Allí conoce a un príncipe, pero a las 12:00 de la noche ella debe volver a su casa.*
> E2:  *Sé quién es. Es Cenicienta* (Cinderella).

1. Es un gorila gigante con sentimientos (*feelings*) humanos. En una película aparece en el edificio Empire State de Nueva York.
2. Fue (*She was*) una mujer muy importante en Argentina. Su esposo gobernó (*governed*) ese país por varios años. Hay un musical con su nombre y también una película donde Madonna la representa.
3. Es una diseñadora de ropa y joyas, hija de un famoso pintor cubista español. Su perfume más famoso lleva su nombre.
4. Es un hombre de otro planeta con doble personalidad. Trabaja en un periódico, pero cuando se pone una ropa azul especial, puede volar (*fly*).

## SITUACIONES

1. **Role A.** If you have not already done so, make a list of five people, at least some of whom you think your partner knows personally. Choose three of them and ask a) if your partner knows them and b) what your partner knows about them. Be ready to answer similar questions.

   **Role B.** If you have not already done so, make a list of five people, at least some of whom you think your partner knows personally. Your partner will tell you the names of three people on his/her list and will ask a) if you know them and b) what you know about them. Answer and then ask your partner the same questions about three of the people on your list.

2. **Role A.** You are looking for a third roommate for your apartment. Your partner knows a student from Peru who is looking for a place to live. Ask your partner a) the Peruvian student's name; b) where in Peru he/she is from; and c) if your partner knows the Peruvian student well. Also find out if the Peruvian student knows how to cook Peruvian dishes and how to play soccer (**fútbol**).

   **Role B.** Your partner is looking for a third roommate for his/her apartment. Mention that you know a student from Peru who is looking for a place to live. Answer your partner's questions about that person.

**3-31 ¿Qué sabes hacer?** Ask your partner if he/she knows how to do the following things. If your partner says yes, ask more questions to get additional information.

MODELO:  bailar salsa y merengue
E1: *¿Sabes bailar salsa y merengue?*
E2: *Sí, sé bailar salsa y merengue./No, no sé bailar salsa y merengue. ¿Y tú?*

1. tocar un instrumento musical
2. cantar bien
3. preparar ceviche
4. manejar (*drive*) un autobús
5. cocinar platos muy elaborados
6. sacar (*take*) fotos con una cámara digital
7. hablar muchas lenguas
8. …

**3-32 Bingo.** To win this game of bingo, you have to fill in three boxes (horizontal, vertical, or diagonal) with the names of classmates who answer the answers correctly.

| ¿Quién sabe dónde está la ciudad de Cuzco? | ¿Quién sabe cuál es la capital de Perú? | ¿Quién sabe qué es Machu Picchu? Peter |
|---|---|---|
| ¿Quién conoce al presidente de Perú? | ¿Quién sabe cuál es la unidad monetaria de Perú? | ¿Quién sabe el nombre de un lago importante que está entre Perú y Bolivia? |
| ¿Quién conoce unos platos típicos de la cocina (*cuisine*) peruana? | ¿Quién conoce algún país hispanoamericano? | ¿Quién sabe cómo se llaman las montañas de Perú? |

**3-33 Saber y conocer.** Complete the conversation with the correct forms of **saber** and **conocer**. Review your answers with a partner.

PACO:  ¿ _____ (1) a esa chica?
AUGUSTO:  Sí, yo _____ (2) a todas las chicas aquí.
PACO:  Entonces, ¿ _____ (3) dónde vive?
AUGUSTO:  No, no _____ (4) dónde vive.
PACO:  ¿ _____ (5) cómo se llama?
AUGUSTO:  Lo siento, pero no _____ (6).
PACO:  Pero ¿cómo dices que _____ (7) a la chica? Tú no _____ (8) dónde vive y tú no _____ (9) su nombre.

# 5. Expressing intention, means, movement, and duration: Some uses of *por* and *para*

CARLOS: Papá, necesito tu auto **por** una semana. ¿Está bien?

PADRE: ¿**Por** una semana? ¿**Por** qué?

CARLOS: **Porque** mis amigos y yo vamos a ir la playa **para** las vacaciones de primavera.

PADRE: ¡%$#@!

Padre

Carlos

**Piénselo.** Indicate whether the following statements are true (**Cierto**) or false (**Falso**) according to the conversation.

1. ____ Carlos necesita el auto de su padre **por** una semana.
2. ____ El padre pregunta **por qué** Carlos desea el auto.
3. ____ Carlos desea ir a la playa **para** las vacaciones de primavera.
4. ____ Los amigos de Carlos necesitan el auto **para** trabajar.
5. ____ El padre está alegre **porque** Carlos necesita su auto.

■ **Por** and **para** have different meanings in Spanish, though sometimes they are both translated into English as *for*. The uses presented here include some you have already seen, as well as some new ones.

■ **Para** expresses *for* when you mean *intended for* or *to be used for*. It can refer to a person, an event, or a purpose.

| | |
|---|---|
| Necesito un diccionario **para** la clase. | *I need a dictionary for the class.* |
| Este diccionario es **para** David. | *This dictionary is for David.* |

■ **Para +** *infinitive* means *in order to*.

| | |
|---|---|
| Uso el autobús **para** ir a la universidad. | *I use the bus (in order) to go to the university.* |
| El restaurante hace publicidad **para** traer clientes. | *The restaurant does advertising (in order) to bring in customers.* |

■ **Por** appears in expressions such as **por favor, por teléfono,** and **por la mañana/tarde/noche.** Other expressions with **por** that you will find useful include the following:

| por ciento | *percent* | por fin | *finally, at last* |
|---|---|---|---|
| por ejemplo | *for example* | por lo menos | *at least* |
| por eso | *that is why* | por supuesto | *of course* |

■ **Por** and **para** can also be used to express movement in space and time.

**Para** indicates movement toward a destination.

| | |
|---|---|
| Caminan **para** la playa. | *They walk toward the beach.* |
| Vamos **para** el túnel. | *We are going toward the tunnel.* |

**Por** indicates movement through or by a place.

| | |
|---|---|
| Caminan **por** la playa. | *They walk along the beach.* |
| Vamos **por** el túnel. | *We are going through the tunnel.* |

You may also use **por** to indicate length of time or duration of an action.
Many Spanish speakers omit **por** in this case, or they use **durante**.

| | |
|---|---|
| Necesito el auto (**por**) tres días. | *I need the car for three days.* |

**3-34 ¿Por o para?** Match each use of **por** and **para** in the following text with the letter of its appropriate meaning from the list on the right.

Mis amigos y yo siempre estamos ocupados los fines de semana. Los viernes **por**[1] la noche, siempre vamos a un cine cerca de nuestro barrio. Cuando vamos **para**[2] el cine, caminamos **por**[3] el parque. Después del cine, a veces hacemos fiestas en casa. Yo compro una pizza y papas fritas **para**[4] comer con ellos. Si es una fiesta de cumpleaños, compro un regalo especial **para**[5] mi amigo. **Para**[6] celebrar, también invito a todos los miembros del grupo. A veces lo pasamos bien **por**[7] largas horas.

| | |
|---|---|
| 1. ____ | **a.** intended for (person) |
| 2. ____ | **b.** used for (purpose) |
| 3. ____ | **c.** in order to |
| 4. ____ | **d.** length of time |
| 5. ____ | **e.** movement toward a destination |
| 6. ____ | **f.** movement through or by a place |
| 7. ____ | |

**3-35 ¿Para dónde van?** Guess where these people are going, and compare your guesses with your classmate's. Then find out where your classmate is going after class, and why.

**MODELO:** Jorge busca su uniforme de fútbol.
*Va para el estadio.*

1. Es la una de la tarde y Pedro desea comer.
2. Sebastián lleva una mochila con sus libros de química y una calculadora.
3. Magdalena y Roberto van a consultar unos libros porque tienen un examen.
4. Gregorio va a comprar un libro para su clase de español.
5. Ana María va a ver una película de su actor favorito.
6. Amanda y Clara están muy elegantes y contentas. En este momento llegan Arturo y Felipe en su auto.

**3-36 Caminante.** Your classmate likes to walk. Ask him/her the following questions. Then switch roles.

1. ¿Te gusta caminar con amigos o solo/a? ¿Por qué?
2. ¿Por dónde caminas cuando quieres estar solo/a?
3. ¿Te gusta caminar por la playa o por un parque?
4. ¿Caminas por la mañana o por la tarde?
5. Cuando sales a caminar, ¿caminas por media hora o por más tiempo?

**3-37 ¿Para quiénes son los regalos (*gifts*)?** You are very generous and have bought the following gifts. Your partner asks whom they are for.

MODELO:        un disco compacto
        E1:   *¿Para quién es el disco compacto?*
        E2:   *Es para mi hermana.*

1. tres libros de español
2. dos billetes de avión
3. una revista de deportes
4. cuatro refrescos dietéticos
5. una guitarra española
6. un kilo de helado
7. una computadora portátil
8. un teléfono celular
9. un buen vino chileno
10. una colección de DVDs

## SITUACIONES

1. Role A. You run into a friend on the street who is carrying a large, gift-wrapped box. You are curious about the box, so you ask what it is and whom it is for.

   Role B. You are walking home from the store carrying a large, gift-wrapped package. You run into a friend on the way. Answer your friend's questions and explain why you are giving the gift.

2. Role A. You see your neighbor leaving his/her apartment, dragging a big suitcase. You are curious, so you ask a) where he/she is going; b) if the plane leaves in the afternoon or evening; c) how long he/she will be there; and d) why he/she is going.

   Role B. You are about to go on a long international trip, and as you are leaving your apartment with your suitcase you see your nosy neighbor. He/She asks a lot of questions. Answer in as much detail as possible.

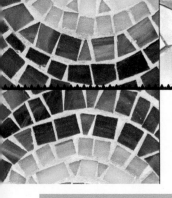

# MOSAICOS

## A escuchar

ESTRATEGIA

**Use background knowledge**

When you listen to a conversation, you can use your knowledge of the situation to understand what is being said. Relying on the experience and knowledge you bring to the listening experience will enhance your comprehension.

### Antes de escuchar

**3-38 Preparación.** You will listen to an ad for *ViajaMás*, a travel agency, which mentions several destinations in Latin America, the days of the flights, the flight numbers, and the price of a round-trip ticket from Miami. Before you listen, use your knowledge of Latin America and ticket prices to write down the name of one large city in each of the countries below that you think the ad may mention and the likely cost of each ticket.

| CIUDADES LATINOAMERICANAS | PRECIO DEL BOLETO DE IDA Y VUELTA DESDE MIAMI |
|---|---|
| Perú: | |
| Argentina: | |
| Venezuela: | |

### Escuchar

**3-39 ¿Comprende usted?** Now listen to the ad and complete the chart with the information you hear.

CD 2
Track 6

| CIUDAD | VUELO # | DÍAS | PRECIO DEL BOLETO |
|---|---|---|---|
| | | sábados y domingos | |
| Buenos Aires | 479 | | |
| | | | $250 |
| Bogotá | | | |

### Después de escuchar

**3-40 Ahora usted.** A friend who is studying Spanish wants to visit a capital city in Latin America but is unsure where to go. After listening to the ad, write an e-mail to your friend to suggest a city to visit.

**De:** _____

**Para:** _____

**Asunto:** Una ciudad interesante en América Latina

**Hola** _____

¡Tengo una información excelente para ti! Hay tarifas (*fares*) fantásticas para visitar _____! ¡Es una ciudad _____! Los vuelos salen los _____. Los boletos cuestan _____.

¿Por qué no hablamos por teléfono este fin de semana? _____

114

# A conversar

**Organize information for a presentation**

When preparing for an oral presentation, it is helpful to decide on a plan and then organize your information accordingly. In this section, you will make a presentation on students' food preferences. Organizing your information by meal (i.e., foods students would like to have available for breakfast, for lunch, etc.) is one approach; another is to start with categories of food that students like (e.g., **carnes**, **cereales**) and then list specific items in each category that students would like to see on the cafeteria menus. Both organizational plans will result in effective presentations.

## Antes de conversar

**3-41 Preparación.** A new cafeteria is going to open on campus. You have been hired to survey students' food preferences so that the cafeteria menu will feature the most popular foods. Find out what your classmates like to eat and drink. Write down the names of students who answer **Sí** or **No** in the appropriate column.

MODELO:  E1: *Susana, ¿comes cereal en el desayuno?*
E2: *Sí, como cereal en el desayuno./No, no como cereal.*

| | DESAYUNO | | ALMUERZO | | CENA | |
|---|---|---|---|---|---|---|
| | SÍ | NO | SÍ | NO | SÍ | NO |
| cereal con leche | | | | | | |
| café/chocolate caliente | | | | | | |
| jugo de naranja/tomate/manzana | | | | | | |
| hamburguesas | | | | | | |
| ensalada de frutas | | | | | | |
| vino | | | | | | |
| pan | | | | | | |
| ... | | | | | | |
| ... | | | | | | |

## Conversar

**3-42 Entre nosotros.** Analyze the information you collected and write down a proposed menu. Present it to the new cafeteria supervisor (your classmate). Explain what most students (**la mayor parte de los estudiantes**) eat and drink. Be prepared to answer the supervisor's questions.

## Después de conversar

**3-43 Un poco más.** Compare your menu with those of other classmates. Then vote on which menu is the most healthful and the most complete, and explain why.

*Cultura*

Despite differences from country to country, mealtimes in Hispanic countries generally differ from those in the United States. People typically eat breakfast at 7:00 or 8:00 a.m. It normally consists of **café**, **café con leche** (hot milk with strong coffee), **té**, or **chocolate caliente** with bread, a sweet roll, and sometimes juice or fruit. As this is a light breakfast, people sometimes have a snack in the late morning. Cereals are becoming more popular, especially among children and young adults.

In some countries, the main meal of the day is lunch (**el almuerzo** or **la comida**), eaten between 12:30 and 3:00 p.m. Supper (**la cena** or **la comida**) is served after 7:00 or 8:00 p.m., and sometimes as late as 10:00 p.m.

# A leer

**1.**

**NIÑOS**

CORPORACIÓN CULTURAL DE LIMA. Santa María y Gálvez. 2209451. A las 12 y 16 horas. Bagdhadas. S/. 12.

TEATRO INFANTIL A DOMICILIO. 2390176. El patito feo. Adaptación del cuento de Andersen. Compañía Arcoiris.

CENTRO LIMA. Av. Grau y Velásquez. A las 12, show especial de Navidad.

FANTASÍA DISNEY. Desde las 15. Niños, S/. 8; adultos, S/. 14. Parque de entretenimientos.

EL MUNDO FANTÁSTICO DE MAFALDA. Desde las 10. Entrada general a todos los juegos. Niños, S/. 12. Calle Domingo Sarmiento 358.

PLANETARIO DEL MORRO SOLAR. A las 12, 17 y 19. Gratis para niños; adultos, S/. 15. Circunvalación, Nuevo Perú. Tel. 5620841.

PARQUE DE LAS LEYENDAS (ZOO). De 9 a 19 hrs. Niños y 3ra edad, S/. 5; S/. 10, otro público. Cerro Tongoy, 3701725.

## Antes de leer

**3-44 Preparación.** PRIMERA FASE. The three ads in activity **3-45** come from a newspaper in Lima, Peru. Look them over quickly without reading them. Then mark which ad goes with each of the following descriptions.

1. ____ un restaurante de comida china
2. ____ actividades para niños
3. ____ un restaurante de comida tradicional peruana

SEGUNDA FASE. What word(s) in each ad helped you answer the questions in the *Primera fase*?

## Leer

**3-45 Primera mirada.** Read the ads and offer a solution for the following choices that have to be made. Be prepared to explain your solutions to the class.

1. El señor y la señora Molina tienen cuatro hijos entre tres y ocho años. A los niños les fascinan los animales. ¿Adónde van a ir probablemente? ¿Por qué?
2. Carlos está triste porque se fracturó una pierna y no puede (*he can't*) salir de la casa. Su mamá tiene una sorpresa para él. ¿Qué es?
3. Cuatro médicos franceses visitan el Hospital Central. El Dr. Moreira, director del hospital, desea invitar a sus colegas a cenar en un restaurante cómodo, con comida tradicional peruana. ¿A qué restaurante va a invitarlos? ¿Por qué?

**3-46 Segunda mirada.** Reread the ads **(3-45)** to answer the following questions.

**Anuncio 1:** ¿Qué palabras, indican que las actividades son para los niños? ¿Qué significa *3ra edad*? ¿Qué significa *otro público*?

**Anuncio 2:** Identifique qué expresión indica que este restaurante prepara comida nacional. ¿Cuánto cuesta el menú especial de los fines de semana?

**Anuncio 3:** ¿Qué expresiones se refieren a la buena calidad del restaurante? ¿Qué palabra significa *reservation*?

## Después de leer

**2.**

osta Verde

**Sabrosa comida tradicional peruana**
Menú especial los fines de semana

■ Aperitivo
■ Entrada
■ Segundo
■ Postre
■ Café y plus café (crema de café, crema de menta, anisado)

Valor: S/. 75

Carnes, pescados y mariscos preparados por los mejores cocineros del país

Avenida Arequipa 357
Reservas: 428 9654
Fax: 428 9655

**3-47 Ampliación.** With a classmate, answer the following questions about the four ads from Peru.

1. ¿Cuál de las siguientes actividades desean hacer ustedes en Lima: ir a un parque de entretenimiento (*amusement park*), comer comida tradicional peruana, ver teatro o comer comida china? ¿Por qué?
2. ¿Cuál de los dos restaurantes sirve comida que a ustedes les gusta más, Costa Verde o Chifa Lungfung?

**3.**

El Chifa Lungfung

La más exquisita, variada y exótica carta de comida cantonesa-peruana: finas carnes, pescados y todo tipo de mariscos.

**SÁBADOS Y DOMINGOS:**

**Almuerzos y cenas familiares**

...los esperamos

AIRE ACONDICIONADO
MÚSICA AMBIENTAL
CAMAREROS PROFESIONALES
AV. REPÚBLICA DE PANAMÁ 8720
RESERVAS 3817543, 3816532, 3814241

# A escribir

## Antes de escribir

**3-48 Preparación.** You are visiting a great vacation spot and want to write your friend a letter about it. To prepare to write the letter, do the following:

1. Write a tentative date for the letter: _____ (date) de _____ (month), 20____
2. Choose a salutation and a closing from the *En directo* box.
3. Prepare some information for the introduction. Mention the place where you are: Is it a beach, a park, a city, a historical landmark (**lugar histórico**)?
4. Decide on the information for the body of the letter:

   a. Make a list of words (adjectives) that describe the place: Is it small, big, beautiful, fun, interesting, historical?
   b. Write down some enjoyable activities (verbs) that people do there. Are they outdoor activities, sports (**deportes**), culturally oriented activities such as going to museums (**museos**), excursions (**excursiones**), fairs (**ferias**)?
   c. Indicate some of the activities that others do that you also like.

> **En directo**
>
> Salutations for casual correspondence:
>
> **Querido/a...**
>
> **Estimado/a...**
>
> **Hola...**
>
> Closings for casual correspondence:
>
> **Tu amigo/a,**
>
> **Hasta pronto,**
>
> **Cariños,**
>
> *Love*

## Escribir

**3-49 Manos a la obra.** Now write the letter to your friend, telling about your vacation. Use the information you prepared in activity **3-48** and any other that you think may be of interest to your friend.

## Después de escribir

**3-50 Revisión.** After completing your letter, read it at least twice with your friend in mind. Check the following:

1. Did you include the date in your letter?
2. Are your salutation and closing appropriate?
3. Did you include a brief introduction and enough information in the body of the letter to achieve your purpose?
4. Did you check for spelling or grammatical errors?
5. Finally, discuss your letter with one of your peers.

# ENFOQUE CULTURAL

## Breve perfil de Perú

Perú es un país extraordinario por su diversidad y riqueza histórica, geográfica y cultural. En efecto, Perú y México son las dos regiones más importantes durante la época colonial de América Latina. Pero antes de los españoles, en Perú ya existe uno de los imperios indígenas más interesantes del continente. Y, finalmente, en Perú encontramos ruinas espectaculares de las culturas indígenas y de la época colonial, y también ciudades modernas con una mezcla de razas y una diversidad étnica muy grande.

Antes de la llegada de los conquistadores españoles, el imperio de los incas es una de las principales civilizaciones nativas de América. Esta civilización es famosa por su compleja organización social, su avanzada arquitectura y sus sistemas de comunicación. Muchas ciudades conservan restos de esta cultura. Por ejemplo, en Cuzco, la capital del imperio inca, hay espectaculares construcciones, como la gran fortaleza de Sacsayhuamán. Y, naturalmente, una de las ciudades incas más prestigiosas es Machu Picchu.

El Conde de Nieva, virrey de Perú entre 1561 y 1584, depende del rey Felipe II.

Cuando los españoles conquistan América, dividen el territorio en tres tipos diferentes de administración. El tipo más importante de administración en el imperio español es el *virreinato*. Esta palabra "virreinato" se relaciona con "rey", porque la autoridad más importante es el virrey. El segundo tipo más importante de administración es la *gobernación*, bajo la autoridad del gobernador. Y el tercer tipo es la *capitanía general*, bajo la autoridad principal del capitán general. México, Perú y la Nueva Granada (la actual Colombia) son los tres virreinatos españoles en el continente americano durante la colonia.

La geografía de Perú es variada y compleja. Tiene una multitud de sistemas ecológicos que forman el hábitat de una infinidad de plantas y animales. Hay tres regiones

La fortaleza de Sacsayhuamán cerca de Cuzco

La geografía de Perú presenta tres regiones diferentes.

geográficas principales en Perú. La costa del Pacífico es muy rica en una gran variedad de peces y productos agrícolas. Una de las atracciones más famosas de esta región son las misteriosas líneas de Nazca. La segunda región es la sierra, que está formada por los Andes y que tiene algunas montañas muy altas, tales como el Nevado de Huascarán, el pico más alto de Perú, de aproximadamente 6.700 metros. La tercera región es la selva del Amazonas, al oriente de los Andes. Las grandes selvas tropicales de esta región son una de las fuentes principales de oxígeno en el planeta.

Finalmente, la cultura peruana es el resultado de la mezcla de la cultura indígena de los incas con la cultura española. Muchos peruanos, especialmente entre los habitantes de la sierra, hablan quechua, la lengua original de los incas. Pero Perú también tiene una gran influencia de culturas de origen africano y asiático. En resumen, la comida, el arte, la literatura, y todas las manifestaciones culturales peruanas son realmente únicas.

### En otras palabras

**Expresiones peruanas**

Me conseguí una **chamba**.
*I found a job.*

José y yo somos **patas**.
*José and I are buddies.*

¡Juanita es una **chancona**!
*Juanita is a nerd!*

**119**

**3-51 Comprensión.** PRIMERA FASE. **Reconocimiento de palabras clave.** Find in the text the Spanish word or phrase that best expresses the meaning of the following concepts:

1. profile _____
2. empire _____
3. rain forest _____
4. fort, fortress _____

5. fish, fishes _____
6. snow-capped peak _____
7. east _____

SEGUNDA FASE. **Oraciones importantes.** Underline the statements that contain ideas found in the text. Then indicate where in the text those ideas appear.

1. Before the arrival of the Spaniards, Cuzco was the capital of the Inca Empire.
2. The viceroyalties of Mexico and Peru were the most important colonies of Spain in the New World.
3. Colombia was one of the three viceroyalties in the Spanish Empire.
4. Peru has some beautiful modern cities, but they are all somewhat run down.
5. The mysterious Nazca drawings are located in the coastal region of Peru.
6. Some mountains, like Peru's highest peak, for example, are capped with snow.
7. A few mountains in the Peruvian Andes are very close to 8,000 meters high.
8. Spanish is not just the main language of Peru; it is the only language spoken there.

TERCERA FASE. **Ideas principales.** Write a brief paragraph in English summarizing the main ideas expressed in the text.

**3-52 Use la información.** You are visiting Peru, and you will spend tomorrow visiting Cuzco and its surroundings. Although it is late and you are tired, you take a few minutes to write a postcard to someone you really care about. Explain your plans for tomorrow: a) mention at least one place you plan to visit; b) if the place is in Cuzco or near/far (**cerca/lejos**); c) how you are going to get there; and d) what you are going to see. For help with this activity, go to the web page of *Mosaicos* and use the links provided there to write your postcard.

*De*.............................
.............................
.............................
.............................
.............................

*Para*...........................
.............................
.............................
.............................
.............................

# VOCABULARIO

CD 2
tracks 7–14

**Las diversiones y las celebraciones** — *Leisure activities and celebrations*

| | |
|---|---|
| la boda | *wedding* |
| la canción | *song* |
| el cumpleaños | *birthday* |
| la fiesta | *party* |
| la guitarra | *guitar* |
| la música | *music* |
| la película | *film* |
| la reunión | *meeting, gathering* |
| el tiempo libre | *free time* |
| las vacaciones | *vacation* |

**Las personas** — *People*

| | |
|---|---|
| el camarero/la camarera | *server, waiter/waitress (restaurant)* |
| el hombre | *man* |
| el/la joven | *young man/woman* |
| la mujer | *woman* |

**En un café o restaurante** — *In a coffee shop or restaurant*

| | |
|---|---|
| el agua | *water* |
| el almuerzo | *lunch* |
| el arroz | *rice* |
| la bebida | *drink* |
| el bistec | *steak* |
| el café | *coffee* |
| la cena | *dinner, supper* |
| el cereal | *cereal* |
| la cerveza | *beer* |
| el ceviche | *dish of marinated raw fish* |
| la comida | *food; meal; dinner, supper* |
| el desayuno | *breakfast* |
| la ensalada | *salad* |
| los espaguetis | *spaghetti* |
| el frijol | *bean* |
| la fruta | *fruit* |
| la hamburguesa | *hamburger* |
| el helado | *ice cream* |
| el huevo | *egg* |
| el jamón | *ham* |
| el jugo | *juice* |
| la leche | *milk* |
| la lechuga | *lettuce* |
| la naranja | *orange* |
| el pan | *bread* |
| el pan tostado/la tostada | *toast* |
| la papa | *potato* |
| las papas fritas | *French fries* |
| el pescado | *fish* |
| el pollo | *chicken* |
| el queso | *cheese* |
| el refresco | *soda, soft drink* |
| el sándwich | *sandwich* |
| la sopa | *soup* |

| | |
|---|---|
| el té | *tea* |
| el tomate | *tomato* |
| el vegetal/la verdura | *vegetable* |
| el vino | *wine* |

**La comunicación** — *Communication*

| | |
|---|---|
| el periódico | *newspaper* |
| la revista | *magazine* |
| el teléfono | *telephone* |

**Los lugares** — *Places*

| | |
|---|---|
| el cine | *movies* |
| la ciudad | *city* |
| el mar | *sea* |
| el país | *country, nation* |

**Las descripciones** — *Descriptions*

| | |
|---|---|
| caliente | *hot* |
| fabuloso/a | *fabulous, great* |
| frío/a | *cold* |
| frito/a | *fried* |
| rápido/a | *fast* |
| típico/a | *typical* |

**Verbos** — *Verbs*

| | |
|---|---|
| alquilar | *to rent* |
| cantar | *to sing* |
| celebrar | *to celebrate* |
| cenar | *to have dinner* |
| descansar | *to rest* |
| hacer la cama | *to make the bed* |
| nadar | *to swim* |
| poner la mesa | *to set the table* |
| tocar (un instrumento) | *to play (an instrument)* |
| tomar el sol | *to sunbathe* |

**Palabras y expresiones útiles** — *Useful words and expressions*

| | |
|---|---|
| ¿adónde? | *where (to)?* |
| al | *to the (contraction of a + el)* |
| al aire libre | *outdoors* |
| ¡claro! | *of course!* |
| cerca de | *close to, near* |
| después, luego | *after, later* |
| durante | *during* |
| ¡estupendo! | *fabulous!* |
| felicidades | *congratulations* |
| mientras | *while* |
| otro/a | *other, another* |
| ¿qué te parece? | *what do you think?* |
| si | *if* |

See *Lengua* box on page 102 for expressions that denote future time.
See page 106 for numbers from 100 to 2.000.000.
See page 111 for expressions with *por*.

# 4 En familia

**Fernando Botero, uno de los pintores contemporáneos más famosos de Colombia, pinta a unos padres con sus hijos en este cuadro titulado *En familia*.**

Source: © Fernando Botero, courtesy of Marlborough Gallery, New York.

# In this chapter you will learn how to:

- talk about family
- discuss what you have to do
- describe daily routines

Las calles
de Cartagena de Indias

*Mar Caribe*

Barranquilla

Cartagena de Indias

PANAMÁ

VENEZUELA

Medellín

Bucaramanga

Pereira

✦ Bogotá

Pieza antigua del Museo
del Oro de Bogotá

El Parque Nacional del café,
Departamento El Quindío

Cali

**COLOMBIA**

*Río Magdalena*

CORDILLERA DE LOS ANDES

Popayán

*OCÉANO*

*PACÍFICO*

ECUADOR

BRASIL

Arepas de queso

PERÚ

Cordillera de Los Andes

 **A vista de pájaro.** Complete las siguientes oraciones (*the following sentences*)
con la información correcta.

1. Ecuador, _____ y Brasil están al sur de Colombia.
2. _____ es la capital de Colombia.
3. El _____ es el mayor producto de exportación de Colombia.
4. Fernando Botero es un_____ colombiano.

123

# A PRIMERA VISTA

## 🔊 Los miembros de la familia

CD 2
Track 15

Una familia colombiana de tres generaciones: **abuelos, hijos** y **nietos**. ¿Cuántos **niños** hay? ¿Hay muchos niños en la familia de usted?

Estos tres niños son **hermanos**. A ellos les gusta **jugar** con el gato. El niño de la **izquierda** se llama Juan y es **el mayor**. La niña se llama Julia y es la segunda. El pequeño, a la **derecha**, se llama Roberto.

En esta foto vemos un **bautizo**. En estas ceremonias participan los **padres**, los **padrinos** y los **ahijados**. Para muchas familias hispanas, el bautizo es un día muy especial.

### El árbol familiar de Pablo

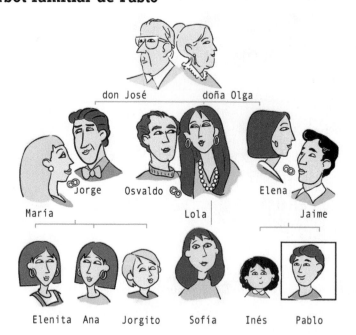

don José    doña Olga

María    Jorge    Osvaldo    Lola    Elena    Jaime

Elenita    Ana    Jorgito    Sofía    Inés    Pablo

---

### Lengua

Use your knowledge of gender and number in Spanish words to understand some variations that are not presented in *A primera vista*. If you know **esposa**, what do you think **esposo** means? If you know **padres**, what to you think **padre** means? Can you guess what **madrina** means? And **novia**?

# Pablo habla de su familia

CD 2
Track 16
Me llamo Pablo Méndez Sánchez y vivo con mis padres, mi **hermana** y mis **abuelos** en un apartamento en Bogotá, la capital de Colombia.

Mi **madre** tiene un **hermano**, mi **tío** Jorge. Su **esposa** es mi **tía** María. Tienen tres hijos y viven también en Bogotá. Mi **primo** Jorgito es el **menor**. Mis **primas** Elenita y Ana son **gemelas**. Mis primos son muy simpáticos y **pasamos** mucho tiempo **juntos**.

Mis tíos tienen sólo dos **sobrinos** en Bogotá, mi hermana Inés y yo. Su otra **sobrina**, la hija de mi tía Lola, vive en Cartagena, al norte del país.

La **nieta** favorita de mis abuelos es mi hermanita Inés. Tiene sólo tres años y es la menor de todos sus **nietos**.

**4-1 Asociación.** Asocie la descripción en la columna izquierda con la expresión correcta en la columna derecha.

1. ___ la esposa de mi padre
2. ___ el hermano de mi prima
3. ___ los padres de mi padre
4. ___ el hijo de mi hijo
5. ___ el hermano de mi madre

a. mi primo
b. mi nieto
c. mi madre
d. mis abuelos
e. mi tío

**4-2 La familia de Pablo.** Complete las siguientes oraciones (*following sentences*) de acuerdo con (*according to*) la información que usted tiene sobre la familia de Pablo.

1. La hermana de Pablo se llama _____ .
2. Don José y doña Olga son los _____ de Pablo.
3. Pablo es el _____ de Jaime.
4. Jaime es el _____ de Pablo, y Elena es su _____ .
5. Inés y Ana son _____ . Elenita y Ana son _____ .
6. Elena es la _____ de Jorgito, Elenita y Ana.
7. Lola es la _____ de Jorge y Elena.

# Otros miembros de la familia de Pablo

CD 2
Track 17

Paula   Sergio        Lola   Osvaldo

Roberto        Sofía

La única hermana de mi **mamá** es mi tía Lola. Lola y Sergio están **divorciados** y tienen una hija, mi prima Sofía. Ahora la tía Lola está casada con Osvaldo, el **padrastro** de Sofía. Sergio está casado con Paula y tienen un hijo, Roberto. Paula es la **madrastra** de Sofía, y Roberto es su **medio hermano**.

**Cultura**

The ending **-ito/a** (**Jorge** → **Jorgito**) is very common in Hispanic countries. It is frequently used to differentiate parents from children of the same name. It also expresses smallness (**hermanito/a, sillita**), affection, or intimacy (**mi primita**). Names that end in a consonant use the ending **-cito/a** (**Carmen** → **Carmencita**).

Hispanics are often given more than one name (**Carlos Alberto, María del Carmen**). These names are often combined (**Mariví,** from **María Victoria**). **María** may also be part of a man's name: **José María**.

**4-3 ¿Cierto o falso?** Marque (✓) la columna adecuada de acuerdo con la información sobre la familia de Lola.

|  | CIERTO | FALSO |
|---|---|---|
| 1. La tía Lola está casada con Sergio. | ___ | ___ |
| 2. Osvaldo es el papá de Roberto. | ___ | ___ |
| 3. Paula es la madrastra de Roberto. | ___ | ___ |
| 4. Lola es la madre de Sofía. | ___ | ___ |
| 5. Sofía tiene un medio hermano. | ___ | ___ |

 **4-4 ¿Quién es y cómo es?** PRIMERA FASE. Escojan (*Choose*) un miembro de una familia famosa (la familia real [*royal*] española, los Jackson, los Kennedy, los Bush, etc.). Preparen su árbol familiar.

SEGUNDA FASE. Túrnese (*Take turns*) con su compañero/a de clase (*classmate*) para describir el árbol familiar de esta persona.

MODELO: el príncipe Felipe
E1: *Su padre es el rey de España. Su madre es la reina Sofía. Felipe tiene dos hermanas. Está casado con la princesa Letizia.*
E2: *Tiene dos hijas y seis sobrinos. Su hermana Elena tiene un hijo y una hija. Su hermana Cristina tiene tres hijos y una hija.*

**4-5 El arte de preguntar.** PRIMERA FASE. Prepare las preguntas (*questions*) necesarias para obtener la siguiente información.

1. Tengo cuatro abuelos vivos (*alive*).
2. No, no soy hijo único/hija única.
3. Tengo dos hermanos.
4. Vivo con mi madre y mi padrastro.
5. Mis abuelos no viven con nosotros.
6. Tengo muchos primos.
7. Tengo una media hermana, pero no vive con nosotros.
8. Mi media hermana vive con su madre.

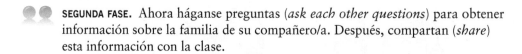 SEGUNDA FASE. Ahora háganse preguntas (*ask each other questions*) para obtener información sobre la familia de su compañero/a. Después, compartan (*share*) esta información con la clase.

 **4-6 Mi familia.** PRIMERA FASE. Preparen su árbol familiar individualmente. Luego, intercambien (*exchange*) su árbol.

SEGUNDA FASE. Háganse preguntas sobre su familia para obtener la siguiente información.

1. nombre de los abuelos vivos
2. nombre de los padres (padrastro/madrastra)
3. número y nombre de los hermanos (medios hermanos, hermanastros)
4. número y nombre de los primos
5. descripción de dos parientes (*relatives*)

# ·)) ¿Qué hacen los parientes?

CD 2
Track 18

Mis abuelos viven en una casa al lado del parque. Normalmente, ellos **pasean** por las mañanas y **almuerzan** muy temprano. Después, **duermen la siesta** y por la tarde **visitan** a sus **parientes**.

Jorgito es mi primo favorito. Es un poco menor que yo. Nosotros corremos y jugamos mucho **juntos**. También nos gusta ver el fútbol en la televisión y montar en bicicleta los domingos.

**Hace dos años que** mi prima Ana tiene **novio**, y **frecuentemente dice** que **quiere casarse** muy pronto. Elenita, su hermana gemela, **piensa** que Ana no debe casarse porque es muy joven.

Mi tío Jorge es un hombre muy **ocupado**. Sale de casa muy **temprano** y **vuelve tarde** todos los días. Mi tía María, su esposa, dice que él **prefiere** el trabajo a su familia. Pienso que en todas las familias hay problemas. En la mía también, pero me gusta mi familia.

> **Lengua**
>
> In Spanish, the direct object of a verb is normally introduced without a preposition. However, the preposition **a** is required when the direct object is a person or a specific animal: **los abuelos visitan a los parientes; la hija pasea al perro.**

**4-7 ¿Cierto o falso?** Conteste (*Answer*) de acuerdo con la información adicional sobre la familia de Pablo.

|  | CIERTO | FALSO |
|---|---|---|
| 1. Normalmente los abuelos están muy ocupados. | —— | —— |
| 2. Jorgito y Pablo montan en bicicleta frecuentemente. | —— | —— |
| 3. Elenita piensa que su hermana es muy joven para casarse. | —— | —— |
| 4. El tío Jorge cree que Elenita tiene problemas. | —— | —— |
| 5. El tío Jorge trabaja mucho. | —— | —— |
| 6. El tío Jorge llega temprano a su casa. | —— | —— |

**4-8 ¿Y qué hace su familia?** Hágale preguntas a su compañero/a para obtener más información sobre su familia. Use la siguiente guía (*guide*).

1. número de personas en la casa, edad (*age*) y relación de parentesco (*kinship*)
2. ocupación y descripción (física y de personalidad) de algunos (*some*) miembros de la familia
3. actividades de estas personas en su tiempo libre
4. nombre del pariente favorito, relación familiar y razón (*reason*) de su preferencia

# ◀)) Las rutinas familiares

CD 2
Track 19

En casa de Pablo hay mucha actividad por la mañana. Los niños **se despiertan** a las siete. **Se levantan, se lavan** y luego **desayunan** en la cocina con sus padres. Después salen para la escuela.

Poco después, la madre **se ducha, se seca, se viste** y **se maquilla.**

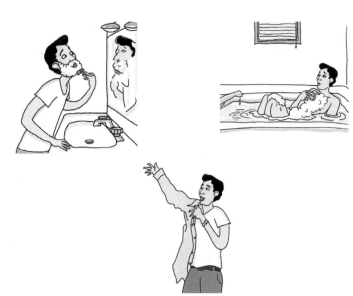

Más tarde, el padre **se afeita, se baña** y **se pone la ropa,** pero no sale de casa hasta las nueve.

**4-9 Cada cosa a su tiempo.** Ponga (*Put*) en orden cronológico las siguientes oraciones según (*according to*) las escenas.

____ La madre se maquilla.
____ Los niños se despiertan a las siete.
____ El padre se baña y luego se pone la ropa.
____ La madre se ducha.
____ El padre sale de casa a las nueve.
____ Los niños desayunan y después salen para la escuela.

### Lengua

The following are expressions to organize time sequentially: **Primero, luego, poco después, más tarde,** and **por último.**

**4-10 Las rutinas diarias.** Conteste las siguientes preguntas sobre la rutina diaria de la familia de Pablo:

1. ¿Con quién desayunan los niños?
2. ¿Quién se maquilla por las mañanas?
3. ¿A qué hora se despiertan los niños?
4. ¿Quién sale de casa a las nueve?
5. ¿Quién se afeita por las mañanas?
6. ¿Qué hace la madre después de ducharse?

**4-11 Mañanas ocupadas (*busy*).** Marque (✓) las acciones diarias de los miembros de su familia.

| | SE DESPIERTA TEMPRANO | SE DUCHA POR LA MAÑANA | SE PONE ROPA ELEGANTE | DESAYUNA CON LA FAMILIA |
|---|---|---|---|---|
| Mi padre (padrastro) | | | | |
| Mi madre (madrastra) | | | | |
| Mi hermano/a | | | | |
| Mi abuelo/a | | | | |
| Mi tío/a | | | | |

**4-12 ¿Y usted?** Complete el siguiente párrafo indicando el orden de las acciones en la rutina diaria de usted. Use las expresiones siguientes:

me ducho
me despierto
me levanto
salgo para la universidad
desayuno

Primero _____, luego _____ . Poco después _____, más tarde _____. Por último _____.

**4-13 ¿A qué hora?** Túrnense para hacerse las siguientes preguntas sobre la rutina diaria.

1. ¿A qué hora se levanta tu madre/padre/hermano?
2. ¿Te duchas por la mañana o por la noche?
3. ¿Quién se levanta temprano en tu familia?
4. ¿Te vistes antes o después de desayunar?
5. ¿Te pones ropa elegante o informal para ir a clase?
6. ¿A qué hora te acuestas durante la semana?
7. ¿A qué hora te acuestas durante los fines de semana?
8. ¿A qué hora te levantas durante los fines de semana?
9. ¿A qué hora tienes la clase de español?
10. ¿Quién se despierta antes los domingos en tu familia?

**4-14 Algunas familias hispanas.** You will listen to descriptions of four
CD 2
Track 20
Hispanic families. Before you listen, answer these questions: Is your family large or small? How many brothers and sisters, cousins, aunts, and uncles do you have?

Now pay attention to the general idea of what is said. As you hear each description, write a check mark (✓) in the corresponding column.

| | TIENE UNA FAMILIA GRANDE | TIENE HERMANOS | TIENE MUCHOS TÍOS | TIENE PRIMOS |
|---|---|---|---|---|
| Pedro | | | | |
| Alicia | | | | |
| Magdalena | | | | |
| Alberto | | | | |

# EN ACCIÓN

## Diarios de bicicleta: Nada de bromas

### Antes de ver

**4-15** En este segmento, Javier se encuentra con Luciana y su familia en el parque. Marque (✓) las actividades que las personas hacen normalmente cuando están en un parque.

1. ___ Juegan con una pelota (*ball*).
2. ___ Comen sándwiches y beben refrescos.
3. ___ Leen el periódico.
4. ___ Buscan trabajo.
5. ___ Escuchan música.

### Mientras ve

**4-16** Ponga en orden cronológico las acciones de Javier cuando la familia de Luciana le hace una broma (*plays a joke*).

___ Cierra los ojos.          ___ Se levanta y se va enojado.
___ Se pone el sombrero.      ___ Levanta los brazos y los mueve.
___ Se sienta.                ___ Abre los ojos.

### Después de ver

**4-17** ¿Qué ocurre después de esta escena? Marque (✓) todas las actividades que usted cree que son posibles.

1. ___ Javier come con la familia de Luciana.
2. ___ Javier sale del parque sin despedirse de (*without saying good-bye*) Luciana.
3. ___ La abuela habla con Javier.
4. ___ El padre de Luciana duerme una siesta después del almuerzo.
5. ___ Marcos está enojado y sale del parque.

# FUNCIONES Y FORMAS

**1. Expressing opinions, plans, preferences, and feelings: Present tense of stem-changing verbs:** $e \rightarrow ie$, $o \rightarrow ue$, **and** $e \rightarrow i$

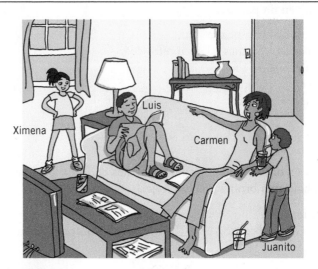

## Carmen habla

**Quiero** conversar seriamente con ustedes y les **pido** su ayuda. **Pienso** que mamá y papá **quieren** algunos cambios en casa. Ellos no **pueden** hacer todo. El día **empieza** muy temprano para ellos y **duermen** muy poco. Con frecuencia, **almuerzan** en la oficina, aunque **prefieren** comer en casa. Nosotros necesitamos ayudar. Luis y Ximena, ustedes **vuelven** a casa a las 2:00. Si ustedes le **sirven** el almuerzo a Juanito y **juegan** con él, nuestros padres van a estar muy contentos. **Cuesta** mucho dinero pagar los servicios de una niñera (*babysitter*). ¿**Piensan** ustedes que mis ideas son buenas o **tienen** otras?

**Piénselo.** Identifique a la(s) persona(s) que probablemente hace(n) estas actividades en la familia del texto anterior: Los padres (**P**), Luis y Ximena (**LX**), Juanito (**J**) o Carmen (**C**). A veces hay más de una respuesta correcta.

1. \_\_\_\_ **Almuerzan** fuera de casa.
2. \_\_\_\_ **Necesita** ayuda para almorzar.
3. \_\_\_\_ **Prefieren** almorzar en casa.
4. \_\_\_\_ **Vuelven** a casa a las 2:00.
5. \_\_\_\_ **Sirven** el almuerzo a su hermanito.
6. \_\_\_\_ **Pide** la colaboración de sus hermanos.

■ Some common verbs in Spanish undergo a vowel change in all forms of the present tense except **nosotros/as** and **vosotros/as**.

| PENSAR (e → ie) *(to think)* | | | |
|---|---|---|---|
| yo | pienso | nosotros/as | pensamos |
| tú | piensas | vosotros/as | pensáis |
| Ud., él, ella | piensa | Uds., ellos/as | piensan |

| VOLVER (o → ue) *(to return)* | | | |
|---|---|---|---|
| yo | vuelvo | nosotros/as | volvemos |
| tú | vuelves | vosotros/as | volvéis |
| Ud., él, ella | vuelve | Uds., ellos/as | vuelven |

| PEDIR (e → i) *(to ask for)* | | | |
|---|---|---|---|
| yo | pido | nosotros/as | pedimos |
| tú | pides | vosotros/as | pedís |
| Ud., él, ella | pide | Uds., ellos/as | piden |

■ Other common verbs that have vowel changes in the stem are:

| e → ie | o → ue | e → i |
|---|---|---|
| **cerrar** *(to close)* | **almorzar** *(to have lunch)* | **repetir** *(to repeat)* |
| **empezar** *(to begin)* | **costar** *(to cost)* | **servir** *(to serve)* |
| **entender** *(to understand)* | **dormir** *(to sleep)* | |
| **preferir** *(to prefer)* | **encontrar** *(to meet)* | |
| **querer** *(to want; to love)* | **poder** *(to be able to, can)* | |

■ Use **pensar +** *infinitive* to express what you or someone else is planning to do.

**Pienso estudiar** esta noche.     *I plan to study tonight.*

**Pensamos comer** a las ocho.     *We are planning to eat at 8:00.*

■ Note the irregular **yo** form in the following **e → ie** and **e → i** stem-changing verbs.

| **tener** *(to have)* | **tengo,** tienes, tiene, tenemos, tenéis, tienen |
|---|---|
| **venir** *(to come)* | **vengo,** vienes, viene, venimos, venís, vienen |
| **decir** *(to say, to tell)* | **digo,** dices, dice, decimos, decís, dicen |
| **seguir** *(to follow)* | **sigo,** sigues, sigue, seguimos, seguís, siguen |

■ In the verb *jugar* (to play a game or sport) **u** changes to **ue**.

Mario **juega** muy bien al tenis, pero     *Mário plays tennis very well, but we*
nosotros **jugamos** regular.         *play so-so.*

**4-18 Planes para la boda.** Beatriz y Miguel se casan en un mes. Complete la descripción de los planes para la boda con la forma correcta de un verbo apropiado.

| empezar | poder | querer | servir |
|---------|-------|--------|--------|
| entender | preferir | seguir | volver |

Beatriz y Miguel (1) _____ tener una boda pequeña, pero elegante. La ceremonia (2) _____ a las 7:00. Los sobrinos y primos jóvenes de los novios no asisten a la ceremonia. Ellos no (3) _____ la ceremonia, y (4) _____ jugar con una niñera en otra parte de la iglesia. Después de la ceremonia, todos van a un restaurante, donde los invitados (5) _____ bailar y cenar. Los camareros (6) _____ una cena italiana, porque los padres de Miguel son de Italia. Después de la cena, la familia (7) _____ a la casa de los padres de la novia. Los invitados (8) _____ en la celebración, pero Beatriz y Miguel salen para su luna de miel (*honeymoon*) a Colombia.

**4-19 ¿Qué piensan hacer?** Túrnense para decir qué piensa hacer cada (*each*) miembro de la familia en las situaciones siguientes.

MODELO:     Mi hermano quiere estar delgado.
E1: *Tu hermano probablemente piensa correr mucho.*
E2: *Él probablemente piensa empezar una dieta.*
E3: *Y probablemente piensa ir al gimnasio todos los días.*

1. Mi hermana tiene un examen de matemáticas mañana.
2. Mi hermana estudia bastante, pero no entiende muchos de los problemas.
3. Mi tía está enferma, por eso se siente muy débil y cansada.
4. Mis abuelos están de vacaciones en Colombia.
5. Mis primos quieren ir a Cartagena para visitar a los abuelos.
6. Mi tío lee y escucha comentarios contradictorios sobre Colombia, por eso, quiere aprender más sobre el país.

**4-20 ¿Qué pasa en las reuniones familiares?** PRIMERA FASE. Muchas familias se reúnen (*get together*) para las fiestas, los eventos especiales o sólo para reunirse. Describan las reuniones de su familia a su compañero/a. Tomen nota de las semejanzas (*similarities*) y las diferencias.

MODELO:     preparar la comida
E1: *En las reuniones de mi familia, mi abuela prepara mucha comida.*
E2: *En las reuniones de mi familia, tenemos mucha comida también. Pero mi madre y mi tía preparan la comida.*

1. venir
2. jugar con los niños
3. servir la comida
4. dormir en el sofá
5. preferir hablar de temas políticos
6. volver a casa

SEGUNDA FASE. Hablen de una semejanza y una diferencia entre las reuniones de su familia. Estén listos (*Be ready*) para compartir la información con la clase.

---

### Lengua

■ **Pensar en** is the Spanish equivalent of *to think of/about someone or something.*

**¿Piensas en** tu familia cuando estás fuera de casa?
*Do you think of/about your family when you are away from home?*

Sí, **pienso** mucho **en** ellos.
*Yes, I think of/about them a lot.*

■ **Pensar de** is used to ask for an opinion. **Pensar que** is normally used in the answer.

¿Qué **piensas de** los planes de ayuda familiar?
*What do you think of the plans to help families?*

**Pienso que** son excelentes.
*I think they are excellent.*

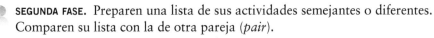

**4-21 Entrevista.** Túrnense para entrevistarse (*interview each other*). Hablen sobre los siguientes temas (*topics*) y después compartan la información con otro compañero/otra compañera.

1. la hora del almuerzo, qué prefiere comer y dónde
2. los deportes que prefiere practicar o mirar en la televisión
3. a qué hora empieza a hacer la tarea generalmente
4. si duerme una siesta durante el día
5. si vuelve a la casa de sus padres para las vacaciones
6. qué piensa hacer después de la universidad

**4-22 ¿Cuándo y con quién? PRIMERA FASE.** Háganse preguntas para obtener la siguiente información.

1. quiénes son sus amigos y qué actividades hacen juntos durante el año académico, durante la semana y los fines de semana
2. actividades de diversión (o deportivas) que hacen juntos, cuándo y dónde
3. actividades preferidas del fin de semana

**SEGUNDA FASE.** Preparen una lista de sus actividades semejantes o diferentes. Comparen su lista con la de otra pareja (*pair*).

MODELO: *Durante la semana, nosotros almorzamos en la cafetería de la universidad. ¿Y ustedes?*

**4-23 Una reunión.** En su universidad hay un fin de semana cuando los padres visitan a sus hijos en el campus. Ustedes quieren organizar una reunión para las familias de los miembros de su grupo. Decidan lo siguiente:

1. lugar y hora de la reunión
2. número de niños y adultos que van a participar (especifiquen la relación familiar)
3. comida y bebida que piensan servir
4. actividades y diversiones para los niños y para los adultos

---

### En directo

These expressions help maintain the flow of conversation:

**¡Cuánto me alegro!**
*I am so happy for you!*

**Claro, claro...**
*Of course . . .*

**¡Qué bien/bueno!**
*That's great!*

---

## SITUACIONES

1. **Role A.** You and a member of your family are planning to visit Latin America. Your friend has heard about your plans and calls with some questions. Answer your friend's questions in as much detail as possible.

   **Role B.** Your friend is planning to go to Latin America with a relative. Call to find out a) when he/she is planning to go; b) with whom; c) what country and cities he/she wants to visit and why; d) if his/her relative prefers to go to other places; and e) when they are returning.

2. **Role A.** The entire family has gathered for a party for the holidays. An elderly aunt/uncle is very curious about your life in college. After commenting on the party and several family members, answer her/his questions politely.

   **Role B.** You are at a family holiday gathering and you are very happy to see your young nephew/niece who is in college. After commenting on the party and several family members, ask about these aspects of college life: a) his/her classes; b) which class(es) he/she prefers; c) if the food is good; d) when vacation (**vacaciones**) starts; and e) what he/she plans to do after college.

## 2. Expressing obligation: *Tener que + infinitive*

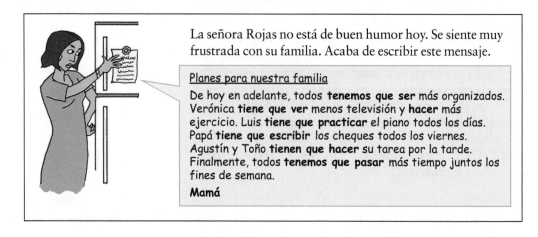

La señora Rojas no está de buen humor hoy. Se siente muy frustrada con su familia. Acaba de escribir este mensaje.

Planes para nuestra familia

De hoy en adelante, todos **tenemos que ser** más organizados. Verónica **tiene que ver** menos televisión y **hacer** más ejercicio. Luis **tiene que practicar** el piano todos los días. Papá **tiene que escribir** los cheques todos los viernes. Agustín y Toño **tienen que hacer** su tarea por la tarde. Finalmente, todos **tenemos que pasar** más tiempo juntos los fines de semana.

**Mamá**

**Piénselo.** Según el texto anterior, asocie la situación de la columna izquierda con la obligación de cada persona en la columna derecha.

1. \_\_\_ Verónica mira mucha televisión.
2. \_\_\_ La madre tiene planes para todos.
3. \_\_\_ El padre no se preocupa de los cheques.
4. \_\_\_ Luis no es muy constante con la música.
5. \_\_\_ Agustín y Toño probablemente prefieren practicar deportes y no estudian.
6. \_\_\_ Cada miembro de la familia hace sus actividades independientemente.

a. Todos **tienen que pensar** en la importancia de hacer actividades en familia.
b. **Tienen que dedicar** suficiente tiempo a sus estudios.
c. **Tiene que hacer** más actividades físicas.
d. **Tiene que colaborar** con su esposa.
e. **Tiene que practicar** regularmente.
f. La familia **tiene que organizar** sus actividades.

■ **Tener que +** *infinitive*. Use **tener que** to express what someone *has to, needs to,* or *must* do.

| | |
|---|---|
| Eliana, **tienes que estudiar** más. | *Eliana, you have to study more.* |
| **Tengo que visitar** a mis abuelos este fin de semana. | *I have to visit my grandparents this weekend.* |

**4-24 Mis obligaciones.** PRIMERA FASE. Marque (✓) las tareas que usted tiene que hacer regularmente. Luego compare sus obligaciones con las de otro compañero/otra compañera.

\_\_\_ sacar a caminar al perro
\_\_\_ hacer ejercicio
\_\_\_ comprar comida
\_\_\_ hacer la tarea para sus clases
\_\_\_ revisar el aceite (*oil*) del carro

\_\_\_ poner los platos sucios en el lavaplatos (*dishwasher*)
\_\_\_ escuchar los mensajes (*messages*) telefónicos
\_\_\_ ir a la universidad
\_\_\_ trabajar por las tardes
\_\_\_ visitar a mis parientes

SEGUNDA FASE. Ahora dígale (*tell*) a su compañero/a cuándo usted tiene que hacer cada tarea. Luego compare sus obligaciones con las de él/ella.

MODELO: E1: *Tengo que poner la mesa todos los días. ¿Y tú?*
E2: *Yo no tengo que poner la mesa, pero tengo que preparar la comida los domingos.*

**4-25 Un viaje (*trip*) a Colombia.** PRIMERA FASE. Su familia va a viajar a Colombia. Escoja la mejor recomendación para cada persona.

1. ____ Mariela quiere visitar un lugar interesante para una persona religiosa.
2. ____ A mis padres les gustaría ver el trabajo que se hace con metales preciosos en Colombia.
3. ____ Mi prima Mónica quiere escuchar música colombiana.
4. ____ Mis abuelitos prefieren las actividades al aire libre.

a. Tiene que asistir a un concierto de Los Príncipes del Vallenato.
b. Tiene que ir a la Catedral de Sal.
c. Tienen que ir al Museo del Oro.
d. Tienen que conocer el Parque Ecológico El Portal.

SEGUNDA FASE. Preparen una breve descripción de uno de los lugares o eventos mencionados en la *Primera fase*. Incluyan la localización y las actividades que las personas hacen allí. Luego, compartan la información con la clase.

1. los Príncipes de Vallenato
2. la Catedral de Sal
3. el Museo del Oro
4. el Parque Ecológico El Portal

**4-26 Sugerencias.** PRIMERA FASE. ¿Qué tienen que hacer (o no) las personas en estas circunstancias?

MODELO: Luis no tiene dinero (*money*).
E1: *¿Qué tiene que hacer Luis?*
E2: *Tiene que leer el periódico para encontrar trabajo.*

1. Mi amigo Juan tiene un examen el lunes.
2. Francisco siempre está cansado.
3. Manuel y Victoria no tienen una buena relación de pareja (*couple*).
4. Mi hermana Marta ve televisión todos los días y saca malas notas en sus clases.
5. Luis y Emilia quieren aprender español.
6. Isabel y Lucía desean visitar un país hispano, pero no hablan español.

SEGUNDA FASE. Escriban individualmente tres circunstancias. Cada persona explica sus circunstancias y su compañero/a dice qué tiene que hacer.

**SITUACIONES**

1. Role A. You run into your cousin downtown. Exchange greetings and explain that today is your father's birthday and that you have to buy a gift (**regalo**). You don't have much time because you have to return home at 5:00. Say that you are thinking of buying a DVD and ask what he/she thinks of the idea. Thank your cousin for the advice (**gracias por los consejos**).

Role B. You run into your cousin downtown. Exchange greetings. Your cousin needs some advice. Listen to his/her concerns and ask pertinent questions. Offer your opinion about whether a DVD is a good idea and, if so, what kind of DVD and where your cousin can find it.

2. Role A. You are worried about your bad relationship with your parents. They are angry because a) when you go out, you come home late; b) you do not study much; c) you prefer to spend a lot of time with your friends, but not with your family; d) you never play with your little sister; and e) when you are home you watch a lot of TV. Call a friend for advice. Answer your friend's questions in as much detail as possible.

Role B. A friend calls you to discuss family problems. Listen and ask appropriate questions. Say that he/she a) must return home early in the evenings; b) has to spend more time with family and play with his/her little sister; c) has to study every day to get good grades; and d) must not watch TV before studying.

### 3. Expressing when, where, or how an action occurs: Adverbs

Los senderistas (*hikers*) siguen una ruta difícil y tienen que caminar **lentamente**. Si van **rápidamente** van a estar cansados. Cruzan el riachuelo (*creek*) **cuidadosamente**. Hay animales peligrosos en la sierra, pero **afortunadamente** es otoño y **seguramente** no encuentran serpientes.

Sierra de Santa Marta, Colombia

**Piénselo.** Asocie la expresión en negrita (*bold*) en la columna izquierda con su significado (*meaning*) en la columna derecha.

1. ＿＿ Los senderistas piensan escalar **poco a poco**.
2. ＿＿ Si los senderistas suben la montaña **con rapidez**, ellos van a estar cansados.
3. ＿＿ **Por suerte**, ahora es otoño.
4. ＿＿ Los senderistas **saben que** no van a encontrar serpientes.
5. ＿＿ Cruzan el riachuelo **con mucha atención**.

a. rápidamente
b. afortunadamente
c. seguramente
d. cuidadosamente
e. lentamente

■ Adverbs are used to describe when, where, and how an action/event takes place. You may already be familiar with adverbs referring to time (**mañana, siempre, después**) and place (**allí, abajo, afuera**), and you have used adverbs to express how you feel (**bien, muy mal, regular**). These adverbs can also be used to express how things are done.

Diego nada **bien**, pero yo nado muy **mal**.          *Diego swims well, but I swim badly.*

■ Many Spanish adverbs end in **-mente,** an ending that corresponds to the English *-ly*. To form these adverbs, add **-mente** to the feminine singular form of the adjective. With adjectives that do not have a separate feminine form, simply add **-mente** to the singular form.

Abuelita camina **lentamente**.          *Grandma walks slowly.*

Mis tíos cantan **alegremente** en las fiestas.          *My aunts and uncles sing happily at parties.*

■ When two or more adverbs are used in a series, only the last one has the **-mente** ending. The other adverbs in the series have the same form as the feminine singular form of the adjective.

La profesora habla **clara** y **lentamente**.          *The professor speaks clearly and slowly.*

Siempre ganan **rápida** y **fácilmente** el partido.          *They always win the game quickly and easily.*

■ Some commonly used adverbs ending in **-mente** are:

| | | | |
|---|---|---|---|
| **básicamente** | **lógicamente** | **realmente** | **simplemente** |
| **frecuentemente** | **normalmente** | **regularmente** | **tradicionalmente** |
| **generalmente** | **perfectamente** | **relativamente** | **tranquilamente** |

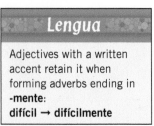

**Lengua**

Adjectives with a written accent retain it when forming adverbs ending in **-mente**:
**difícil → difícilmente**

**4-27 ¿Está de acuerdo o no? PRIMERA FASE.** Las características de la familia pueden variar entre una comunidad y otra. Indique si usted está de acuerdo (**Sí** o **No**) con las siguientes afirmaciones.

En mi comunidad...

1. \_\_\_\_ los padres frecuentemente hablan con los hijos adolescentes sobre temas importantes.
2. \_\_\_\_ los nietos regularmente visitan a sus abuelos.
3. \_\_\_\_ generalmente los hijos solteros viven con sus padres.
4. \_\_\_\_ los padres siempre hablan lentamente cuando están enojados con sus hijos.
5. \_\_\_\_ idealmente el padre trabaja fuera de casa y la madre trabaja en casa.
6. \_\_\_\_ los hijos adolescentes siempre tratan a sus padres cortésmente.

**SEGUNDA FASE.** Comparen sus respuestas y digan por qué están de acuerdo.

**MODELO:** E1: *Estoy de acuerdo con el número uno. Generalmente los padres hablan sobre temas importantes con sus hijos.*

E2: *No estoy de acuerdo. Los padres generalmente hablan sobre educación o dinero, pero no hablan de drogas.*

**4-28 ¿Lenta o rápidamente?** Escriba tres actividades de la siguiente lista que usted hace rápidamente y tres que hace lentamente. Indique el lugar y/o las circunstancias.

| | | | |
|---|---|---|---|
| almorzar | escribir composiciones | hablar español | pasear |
| beber | estudiar | leer el periódico | tomar apuntes |

**MODELO:** *Como rápidamente cuando tengo poco tiempo.*

**4-29 ¿Cómo lo hace usted?** Primero, individualmente escriba cómo o cuándo usted hace las siguientes actividades. Usando las palabras en la lista u otras, forme adverbios para escribir sus frases. Luego, comparen sus respuestas.

| | | | |
|---|---|---|---|
| difícil | frecuente | lógico | perfecto |
| fácil | lento | ocasional | rápido |

1. caminar cuando usted está muy cansado/a
2. pensar en la clase de matemáticas
3. respirar (*breathe*) después de una hora de ejercicio en el gimnasio
4. responder en un examen fácil

**4-30 Actividades frecuentes. PRIMERA FASE.** Hágale estas preguntas a su compañero/a. Después él/ella tiene que hacerle las mismas (*same*) preguntas a usted. Tome apuntes sobre las respuestas de su compañero/a.

1. ¿Qué haces normalmente con tu familia?
2. ¿A qué lugares vas regularmente con tu familia? ¿Y con tus amigos?
3. Generalmente, ¿sales por las noches? ¿Adónde vas y con quién?
4. ¿A quiénes llamas por teléfono más frecuentemente, a tus amigos o a tu familia?

**SEGUNDA FASE.** Ahora escriba una breve comparación entre usted y su compañero/a con respecto a cada pregunta en la *Primera fase*. ¿Hacen ustedes actividades semejantes o diferentes?

---

## En directo

To express surprise at what you hear:

**¡Qué increíble!**
*Incredible!*

**¡No me diga(s)!**
*Really!*

---

## SITUACIONES

1. **Role A.** Your class is conducting a survey regarding students' movie habits. Ask a classmate a) when and with whom he/she generally goes to the movies; b) the type of movies he/she normally prefers (**románticas, dramáticas, de ciencia ficción**, etc.); c) what he/she often eats or drinks at the movies; and d) the name of his/her favorite movie.

   **Role B.** Answer the questions a classmate will ask about your movie preferences.

2. **Role A.** In your Sociology and the Family course, you are helping to conduct a survey about family traditions and activities. Ask a classmate a) if the members of his/her immediate family generally eat together; b) if they visit other family members frequently; and c) which family member normally organizes family gatherings.

   **Role B.** First answer your classmate's questions about your family. Then ask him/her these questions for the survey: a) Who is generally more organized (**organizado/a**) at home, men or women?; b) Do family members frequently do activities together?; c) Who prepares dinner well in the family?; d) Who talks calmly when angry, your father or your mother?

## 4. Expressing how long something has been going on: *Hace* with expressions of time

PATRICIA: Señora, **¿cuánto tiempo hace que** practico esta sonata? ¡Estoy muy cansada!

SRA. ESCOBEDO: **Hace dos horas que** trabajas en ella. Pero una vez más, por favor, Patricia. El recital es en dos días.

Sra. Escobedo    Patricia

SRA. ESCOBEDO: Les presento a Patricia Suárez. Estudia el violín conmigo **hace cinco años.** Ahora va a tocar la Sonata N° 4 de Mozart.

**Piénselo.** Diga si las siguientes afirmaciones son lógicas (**L**) o ilógicas (**I**).

1. \_\_\_\_ **Hace mucho tiempo que** Patricia toca el violín perfectamente.
2. \_\_\_\_ **Hace cinco años que** Patricia no pasa mucho tiempo con sus amigos porque tiene que practicar la sonata.
3. \_\_\_\_ Patricia conoce a la profesora de violín **hace cinco años.**
4. \_\_\_\_ **Hace sólo un día que** Patricia trabaja en la sonata de Mozart.
5. \_\_\_\_ **Hace poco tiempo que** la señora Escobedo toca el violín.
6. \_\_\_\_ Los padres de Patricia no le pagan a la profesora por las clases de violín **hace un año.**

■ To say that an action/state began in the past and continues into the present, use **hace** + *length of time* + **que** + *present tense.*

**Hace dos horas que** juegan.    *They have been playing for two hours.*

■ If you begin the sentence with the present tense of the verb, do not use **que.**

Juegan **hace dos horas.**    *They've been playing for two hours.*

■ To find out how long an action/state has been taking place, use **cuánto tiempo** + **hace que** + *present tense.*

**¿Cuánto tiempo hace que** juegan?    *How long have they been playing?*

**¿Cuántas horas hace que** los niños juegan al fútbol?    *How many hours have the children been playing soccer?*

**4-31 Este soy yo.** PRIMERA FASE. Lea esta descripción y conteste las preguntas.

Me llamo Jaime Caicedo y soy de Cali, Colombia. Quiero aprender inglés para poder trabajar en una compañía internacional. Estudio inglés **hace dos años,** pero tengo que estudiar más para hablar correctamente. Siempre miro programas de televisión en inglés. Mis favoritos son *American Idol* y *Grey's Anatomy*. **Hace dos años que** miro estos programas y me gustan mucho. Tengo un auto **hace un año,** y salgo en él con mis amigos y también con mi novia. **Hace seis meses que** somos novios. Somos muy felices.

1. Jaime Caicedo es de...
   a. Estados Unidos.     b. Cali.     c. *Grey's Anatomy*.
2. Hace dos años que Jaime...
   a. tiene novia.   b. va al cine.    c. mira televisión en inglés.
3. Hace seis meses que Jaime...
   a. va a fiestas.    b. estudia inglés.    c. tiene novia.

SEGUNDA FASE. Ahora escriba su propia descripción, siguiendo el modelo en la *Primera fase*. Luego, comparta su descripción con un compañero/una compañera.

Me llamo (1) _____ . Soy de (2) _____ ,
(3) _____ (ciudad y país). Quiero aprender (4) _____
(lengua extranjera) porque (5) _____ . Estudio
(6) _____ (lengua extranjera) hace (7) _____ (período
de tiempo), pero tengo que estudiar más para hablar
correctamente. Miro (8) _____ películas como _____
(películas en español) y escucho la música de (9) _____
(cantante o grupo español) para aprender más.
Mi programa favorito es (10) _____ . Hace
(11) _____ (período de tiempo) que (12) _____
el programa y me gusta mucho. En mi tiempo libre,
(13) _____ . Tengo (14) _____ (vehículo/objeto o
animal) hace (15) _____ . Hace (16) _____ (período
de tiempo) que estudio en (17) _____ (nombre de la
universidad). Espero ser (18) _____ (profesión)
(19) _____ en el futuro.

**4-32 ¿Cuánto tiempo hace que...?** Túrnense para hacerse las siguientes preguntas. Después compartan la información con otra pareja.

1. ¿Dónde vive tu familia? ¿Cuánto tiempo hace que viven allí?
2. ¿Dónde trabajas? ¿Cuánto tiempo hace que trabajas allí?
3. ¿Cuánto tiempo hace que estudias en esta universidad?
   ¿Y por qué estudias español?
4. ¿Practicas algún deporte? ¿Cuánto tiempo hace que juegas al...?
   ¿Juegas bien?

## SITUACIONES

1. Role A. You live in Queens, New York, and a friend has come to visit. Explain that there are many Hispanic restaurants in this neighborhood (**barrio**). You suggest your favorite Colombian restaurant for dinner. When your friend asks about the Colombian food that they serve, you may want to mention **ajiaco de pollo** (a chicken stew made with potatoes, corn, and cream), **papas chorreadas** (potatoes covered with a sauce made with onions, tomatoes and milk), and **arroz con coco** (rice cooked in coconut milk).

   Role B. You are visiting a friend in Queens, New York. He/She suggests a Colombian restaurant for dinner. Ask a) how long he/she has been living in Queens; b) if he/she knows the restaurant well; c) what Colombian dishes they serve, and what they are like; and d) how much they cost.

2. Role A. You go to see your counselor (**consejero/a**) to talk about a personal problem (**un problema**). Greet the counselor and explain your problem. Answer the counselor's questions in as much detail as possible. When the session is over, thank the counselor.

   Role B. You are a student counselor (**consejero/a**). A student comes to you with a problem (**un problema**). Exchange greetings and ask a) how long the student has been at the university; b) how long he/she has been having the problem; and c) what he/she is doing to solve (**resolver**) the problem and for how long. Finally, suggest several things he/she has to do to improve (**mejorar**) the situation.

## 5. Talking about daily routine: Reflexive verbs and pronouns

Yo **me llamo** Óscar Torres. Mi esposa Rosa y yo tenemos una vida muy ocupada. Nosotros **nos levantamos** a las seis todos los días. Yo **me ducho** mientras Rosa se viste rápidamente. Después, Rosa **despierta** a Carlitos y a Roberto, nuestros hijos. Roberto **se viste**, y Rosa **viste** a Carlitos. Desayunamos y luego todos **nos lavamos** los dientes y a las siete salimos de la casa.

**Piénselo.** Para cada acción, indique si cada persona hace la acción a sí misma(s) (*him/her/themselves*) o a otra persona.

| ACCIÓN | A SÍ MISMO/A | A OTRA PERSONA |
|---|---|---|
| 1. Óscar **se ducha** por la mañana. | ____ | ____ |
| 2. Rosa **despierta** a Carlitos. | ____ | ____ |
| 3. La madre **viste** al niño porque es muy pequeño. | ____ | ____ |
| 4. Roberto **se viste** rápidamente. | ____ | ____ |
| 5. Nosotros **nos lavamos** los dientes después de desayunar. | ____ | ____ |
| 6. Rosa probablemente **se baña** por la noche, porque no tiene tiempo por la mañana. | ____ | ____ |

■ Reflexive verbs express what people do to or for themselves.

**REFLEXIVE:** Mi hermana **se lava**.     *My sister washes (herself).*
**NONREFLEXIVE:** Mi hermana **lava** el auto.     *My sister washes the car.*

| LAVARSE (*to wash oneself*) | | | |
|---|---|---|---|
| yo | **me lavo** | nosotros/as | **nos lavamos** |
| tú | **te lavas** | vosotros/as | **os laváis** |
| Ud., él, ella | **se lava** | Uds., ellos/as | **se lavan** |

■ A reflexive pronoun refers back to the subject of the sentence. English sometimes uses the pronouns ending in *-self/-selves* to express reflexive meaning. In many cases, Spanish uses reflexives where English does not.

Yo **me levanto, me ducho, me seco** y **me visto** rápidamente.     *I get up, take a shower, dry myself, and get dressed quickly.*

■ Place reflexive pronouns after the word **no** in negative constructions.

Rosa **no se ducha** por la mañana.     *Rosa does not take a shower in the morning.*

■ The pronoun **se** attached to the end of an infinitive indicates the verb is reflexive.

**vestir** — to dress (someone else)
**vestirse** — to get dressed (oneself)

■ With a conjugated verb followed by an infinitive, place the reflexive pronoun before the conjugated verb or attach it to the infinitive.

Yo **me** voy a levantar a las siete.
Yo voy a levantar**me** a las siete. } *I am going to get up at seven.*

■ When referring to parts of the body and articles of clothing, use definite articles rather than possessives with reflexive verbs.

Me lavo **los** dientes.          *I brush my teeth.*

Roberto se pone **la** chaqueta.          *Roberto puts on his jacket.*

■ Some verbs change meaning when used reflexively.

| | | | |
|---|---|---|---|
| **acostar** | to put to bed | **acostarse** | to go to bed, to lie down |
| **dormir** | to sleep | **dormirse** | to fall asleep |
| **levantar** | to raise, to lift | **levantarse** | to get up |
| **llamar** | to call | **llamarse** | to be called |
| **poner** | to put, to place | **ponerse** | to put on |
| **quitar** | to take away | **quitarse** | to take off |

**4-33 ¿Qué hacemos todos los días?** Ponga estas actividades en el orden más lógico.

____ Me duermo.   ____ Salgo para mis clases.   ____ Me lavo la cara *(face)*.
____ Me levanto.   ____ Me acuesto.                    ____ Desayuno.

**4-34 ¿Tenemos las mismas rutinas?** Hablen sobre sus actividades diarias.

**MODELO:**     despertarse
          E1:   *Yo me despierto a las siete. ¿Y tú?*
          E2:   *Generalmente, me despierto a las ocho.*

1. levantarse          3. vestirse          5. acostarse
2. ducharse            4. desayunar         6. dormirse

**4-35 Los horarios. PRIMERA FASE.** Usen la información en la tabla para escribir un párrafo sobre el horario de las hermanas gemelas *(twins)* Alicia y Blanca y su hermanito Carlitos.

| | CARLITOS | ALICIA Y BLANCA | YO |
|---|---|---|---|
| despertarse | 8:00 | 7:00 | |
| levantarse | 8:15 | 7:05 | |
| bañarse | 8:20 | 7:10 | |
| vestirse | 8:30 | 7:20 | |

**SEGUNDA FASE.** Ahora escriba individualmente sus actividades en la tabla. Luego, hablen de su horario y hagan comparaciones entre su horario y el de las personas de la *Primera fase.*

**SITUACIONES**

1. **Role A.** A young person in your family has to do a report for school based on an interview of a family member. That person is going to interview you. Exchange greetings and answer his/her questions as completely as possible.

   **Role B.** You are a middle school student who has to write a report about a family member (your classmate). Greet him/her and explain the purpose of the interview. Then find out a) where he/she lives and for how long he/she has lived there; b) what his/her daily routine is; and c) some differences between the routine of a college student and that of a middle school student.

2. **Role A.** You live in Bogota, and you would like your niece to attend a summer camp (**campamento de verano**) in the United States so she will learn English. Ask the camp director questions to find out a) how many children there are per counselor (**por consejero/a**); b) what time the children get up; c) what sports they play; d) what they eat; e) what they do in the evenings; and f) what time they go to bed.

   **Role B.** You are the director of the summer camp (**campamento de verano**). Answer the questions of the aunt/uncle of a prospective camper. Add as much information as possible.

# MOSAICOS

## A escuchar

### ESTRATEGIA

**Listen for a purpose**

Listening with a purpose in mind will help you focus your attention on what is important and relevant to meet your goal. As you focus your attention, you screen what you hear and select only the information you need, letting go of what seems irrelevant to your purpose.

### Antes de escuchar

**4-36 Preparación.** Usted va a escuchar el mensaje de Pedro para Julio sobre una fiesta sorpresa (*surprise*) que está organizando Pedro. Antes de escuchar, escriba el propósito (*purpose*) posible de un mensaje como este. ¿A qué información específica es importante poner atención?

propósito posible: _____

información específica: _____

### Escuchar

CD 2
Track 21

**4-37 ¿Comprende usted?** First read the information you will need to have in order to attend the party Pedro is organizing. Then, as you listen, complete the sentences with the rest of the information. Don't worry if you do not understand every word.

1. La fiesta es para...
2. La fiesta va a ser en la casa de...
3. El día de la fiesta es...
4. Julio debe llevar (*take*)...
5. Julio tiene que llegar a la casa a las...
6. La dirección es...

### Después de escuchar

**4-38 Ahora usted.** Usted va a dar una fiesta sorpresa para un amigo/una amiga en la clase de español y desea invitar a su profesor/a de español. Complete la nota que usted va a poner en el buzón (*mailbox*) de su profesor/a.

Estimado/a profesor/a _____:

Este fin de semana, pienso dar una fiesta sorpresa para _____.

¿Le gustaría venir? Vamos a comer _____ y _____. Vamos a tener refrescos para todos.

La fiesta va a ser el _____ en mi casa a las _____ de la noche.
Mi dirección es _____.

Lo/La espero el _____.

Hasta pronto.

_____

144

# A conversar

## Antes de conversar

**4-39 Preparación.** Complete las siguientes afirmaciones con los nombres de sus parientes, la relación de parentesco y sus actividades.

MODELO: *Mi primo David come* en restaurantes los fines de semana.

1. ... cerveza frecuentemente cuando mira(n) fútbol en la televisión.
2. ... mucho y con frecuencia está(n) cansado/a(s).
3. ... a conciertos de música popular.
4. ... en casa los fines de semana. Descansan, leen, escuchan música, etc.
5. ... ejercicio físico tres o cuatro veces por semana.
6. ... con amigos o con la familia en casa el día de su cumpleaños.
7. ... música romántica a todas horas.
8. ... por el teléfono celular. Llama(n) a sus amigos día y noche.

## Conversar

**4-40 Entre nosotros.** Conteste las preguntas de sus compañeros/as con los nombres de los miembros de su familia para comparar las dos categorías.

MODELO: E1: *¿Quiénes son las personas artísticas en tu familia, las mujeres o los hombres?*

E2: *En mi familia, las mujeres son muy artísticas. Por ejemplo, mi hermana Carlota pinta y escribe poemas. En contraste con las mujeres, los hombres son deportistas. Mi primo Alberto, por ejemplo, practica tenis y fútbol.*

1. ¿Quiénes son las personas activas en tu familia, las mujeres o los hombres?
2. ¿Qué miembros de la familia pasan mucho tiempo en casa, los jóvenes o los mayores?
3. ¿Quiénes son muy sociables, las mujeres o los hombres, los jóvenes o los mayores? ¿Por qué?

## Después de conversar

**4-41 Un poco más.** Completen un pequeño informe (*report*) con la información de su grupo de la actividad **4-40**. Luego compartan la información con el resto de la clase.

1. En nuestras familias (los hombres/las mujeres) _____ son muy activos/as. Por ejemplo, _____. Por otro lado, _____ no son muy activos. Por ejemplo, _____.
2. (Los jóvenes/Los mayores) _____ pasan mucho tiempo en casa porque _____. Por ejemplo, _____ . En cambio, _____ no pasan mucho tiempo en casa porque _____. Por ejemplo, _____ .
3. (Las mujeres/Los hombres/Los jóvenes/Los mayores) _____ son muy sociables. Por ejemplo, _____ . En contraste, _____ no son muy sociables. Por ejemplo, _____ .

**Use title and illustrations to anticipate content**

Before you start to read, it is important to gather as much information about the text as possible. The title, section headings, and illustrations can help you anticipate content, so pay special attention to them before you start to read. Verbalize to yourself (aloud or by writing notes) what you think the text is about, and refer to your notes as you are reading, correcting them as necessary. This will help you focus on understanding each section of the text as you read it.

# A leer

## Antes de leer

**4-42 Preparación.** Lea el título y los subtítulos del artículo a continuación y observe las fotos. Luego, use la información del título, los subtítulos y las fotos para contestar las siguientes preguntas.

1. Basándose en el título del artículo, los subtítulos, las fotos y sus leyendas (*captions*), adivine el tema del artículo.
   a. la comunicación entre amigos
   b. la comunicación entre los miembros de una familia
   c. la comunicación con los colegas en el trabajo

2. En su opinión, ¿cuáles de las siguientes ideas va a incluir el artículo? (Hay más de una respuesta correcta.)
   a. Hoy en día la comunicación entre padres e hijos es mejor que (*better than*) en el pasado.
   b. Los jóvenes no hablan con sus padres sobre sus problemas porque los padres siempre están ocupados.
   c. La vida moderna afecta la comunicación entre padres e hijos.
   d. La tecnología tiende a reducir la comunicación sobre temas importantes.

3. Marque (✓) las actividades de la siguiente lista que usted asocia usted con una buena relación entre padres e hijos.

   a. ____ conversar
   b. ____ pasar tiempo juntos
   c. ____ hablar por teléfono
   d. ____ pelear (*argue*)
   e. ____ escribir correos electrónicos a un miembro de la familia que vive lejos (*far*)

   f. ____ comprar regalos con frecuencia
   g. ____ expresar cariño (*affection*) verbalmente
   h. ____ no hablar de sus problemas con los padres

## Leer

**4-43 Primera mirada.** Lea los dos primeros párrafos del texto y siga las instrucciones.

Subraye (*Underline*)...

1. las palabras en el título que probablemente indican el tema del artículo.
2. una palabra que describe la condición de la familia de hoy.
3. una palabra que indica la importancia de la comunicación dentro de la familia.

Escriba...

4. una causa de los problemas de comunicación en la familia.
5. dos necesidades de los hijos que tienen padres que trabajan fuera de casa.
6. dos efectos de la ausencia de los padres de la casa.

## La importancia de la comunicación familiar

### La familia en crisis

Los expertos afirman que la familia de hoy está en crisis por la falta[1] de comunicación entre sus miembros o por la mala comunicación que existe entre ellos. También dicen que la comunicación es vital en todas las relaciones, especialmente en las relaciones familiares.

### Ausencia de los padres

¿Por qué hay problemas de comunicación en las familias? Hay varias razones. Una razón es que la madre y el padre trabajan largas horas fuera de casa y los hijos están solos mucho tiempo, sin la compañía y la supervisión de sus mayores. La ausencia casi todos los días de los padres puede crear cierta independencia en los hijos y una distancia emocional que causa dificultades en la comunicación entre padres e hijos.

La comunicación entre padres e hijos sobre temas importantes forma relaciones familiares fuertes y cariñosas.

### La tecnología

Un segundo factor es la tecnología. Nuestro mundo está controlado por la tecnología en casa, en el trabajo, etc. Evidentemente la tecnología facilita muchas cosas, pero su uso excesivo puede complicar la vida. Un gran número de hogares[2] están conectados a Internet, así que muchos jóvenes tienen acceso ilimitado al correo electrónico y a la Red, sobre todo a los sitios web de comunicación social y entretenimiento, como MySpace y YouTube. Idealmente, el bajo costo de la conexión debería afectar positivamente la comunicación en la familia, pero la realidad indica que la comunicación moderna (e.g., correo electrónico, mensajes de texto) tiende a ser más breve y más superficial. Los hijos prefieren no discutir sus problemas por correo electrónico o mensajes de texto. Prefieren hablar directamente con sus padres, si es que sus padres tienen el tiempo. Lo mismo ocurre con el teléfono celular. Es cierto que muchos jóvenes usan celulares para llamar a sus padres, pero no muchos usan el celular para conversar largamente con sus padres sobre temas personales importantes. ¡Muy pocos!

La tecnología puede facilitar la comunicación familiar.

### Conclusión

En conclusión, el tiempo limitado que los padres pueden dar a sus hijos y la tendencia a usar la tecnología para comunicaciones muy breves pueden afectar negativamente las relaciones familiares. Por eso es importante crear oportunidades para una comunicación real y profunda dentro de la familia. Si usted usa la tecnología de manera positiva para pasar tiempo con sus familiares y para expresar el amor y el cariño que siente por ellos, su familia va a ser más fuerte y unida.

[1]lack  [2]homes

**4-44 Segunda mirada.** Ahora lea el resto del artículo y siga las indicaciones.

En el párrafo sobre la tecnología, el artículo presenta otra razón de la mala comunicación entre padres e hijos.

Indique…

1. una palabra asociada con los problemas de comunicación familiares.
2. por qué la tecnología probablemente afecta las relaciones de la familia.
3. dos ejemplos de cómo la tecnología puede causar problemas en la familia.
4. dos palabras que indican la calidad de la comunicación cuando usamos el correo electrónico o los mensajes de texto.
5. dos formas de usar la tecnología positivamente en la comunicación con la familia.

## Después de leer

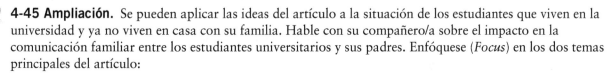

**4-45 Ampliación.** Se pueden aplicar las ideas del artículo a la situación de los estudiantes que viven en la universidad y ya no viven en casa con su familia. Hable con su compañero/a sobre el impacto en la comunicación familiar entre los estudiantes universitarios y sus padres. Enfóquese (*Focus*) en los dos temas principales del artículo:

■ la separación física entre los padres y los hijos
■ el uso de la tecnología como medio de comunicación

# A escribir

## ESTRATEGIA

**Choose between informal and formal language to express the desired tone**

Choosing the appropriate level of formality when you write to someone depends on your relationship to that person. When writing to elders in your family, such as parents or grandparents, a more formal tone may be needed than when writing to friends. The abbreviated format and casual language of computer-based communication may not be the best choice to show your elders love and respect. When you write to them, either in letters or on the computer, choose your language more carefully and write about issues more seriously than you would when corresponding with friends.

The salutation, closing, and forms of address used in letter writing also reflect your degree of closeness and formality. The expressions in *En directo* include some common salutations and forms of address that are appropriate to use when you write to elders in your family.

## Antes de escribir

**4-46 Preparación.** PRIMERA FASE. La madre de Julián, un alumno universitario colombiano, está triste y preocupada porque su hijo estudia en la Universidad de los Andes y vive lejos de casa. Ella le escribe la siguiente carta a su hijo. Lea la carta.

Querido Julián:

¿Qué tal estás? ¿Cómo van tus clases? Hace un mes que no tenemos información sobre ti. ¡No escribes correos electrónicos, no llamas por teléfono! ¿Qué ocurre?

Bueno, es el fin del semestre y debes tener mucho trabajo. ¿Estás muy estresado? ¿Duermes suficiente? ¿Comes bien en la universidad? En tu próxima visita, pienso preparar tus platos favoritos. Tu hermana Mariela, tus abuelos y tíos van a estar con nosotros y vamos a conversar largas horas.

Tengo una sorpresa para ti. Gustavo tiene novia. Se llama Alicia. Pasan mucho tiempo juntos; van al cine, salen a comer por las noches, etc. La semana próxima ambos tienen vacaciones y, para conocerla un poco más, Gustavo piensa ir a Cartagena con ella. Las temperaturas allí están perfectas para nadar y descansar un poco.

Tengo que confesarte que tu padre y yo pensamos mucho en ti. ¿Por qué no escribes? ¿Tienes problemas en tus clases? ¿Trabajas mucho? ¿Estás desconectado de Internet? Por favor, escribe o llama pronto.

Un beso de papá, Mariela y toda la familia.

Abrazos,

Tu madre

**SEGUNDA FASE.** Usted es Julián. Prepárese para responder a la carta de su madre. Haga lo siguiente:

1. Identifique las preguntas de su madre que usted quiere contestar y escriba algunas ideas que piensa incluir. Seleccione las palabras adecuadas para lograr (*achieve*) el tono adecuado.
2. Escriba algunas preguntas que usted quiere hacerle a su madre: sobre su padre, sus hermanos, sus abuelos, su perro o gato, etc.

## Escribir

**4-47 Manos a la obra.** Ahora responda a la carta de su madre. Use la información de la *Segunda fase* de la actividad **4-46**. Seleccione cuidadosamente las palabras para mostrar respeto a su madre. Recuerde incluir la fecha, un saludo y una despedida (*closing*) apropiados.

Querida madre:

## Después de escribir

**4-48 Revisión.** Revise los siguientes aspectos de su carta.

1. Primero, el grado de intimidad (*intimacy*) y formalidad para comunicarse con su madre. ¿Incluye usted un saludo y una despedida apropiados en la carta? ¿Usa usted el vocabulario adecuado para dirigirse (*address*) a su madre?
2. La coherencia de sus ideas y la cantidad de información que su madre probablemente desea
3. Luego, la precisión gramatical: la estructura de las oraciones, la concordancia, etc.
4. Finalmente, la ortografía, la acentuación

# ENFOQUE CULTURAL

## La riqueza de Colombia

**N**ormalmente asociamos a Colombia con el café de Juan Valdez, un personaje inventado por las agencias de publicidad, como el representante de Colombia ante el mundo. En realidad, Colombia se conoce en todas partes por la calidad suave de su café y el símbolo de Juan Valdez es una de las imágenes corporativas más famosas del mundo. Sin embargo, Colombia es mucho más que su café. Su diversidad geográfica y climática, y la variedad natural, étnica y cultural de sus regiones hacen de Colombia un país con un inmenso potencial.

Para empezar, Colombia es el único país de América del Sur que tiene costas en los dos mares. La costa Atlántica, que es la región caribeña, tiene playas espectaculares, montañas impresionantes en la Sierra Nevada de Santa Marta, selvas tropicales en el Urabá y un desierto en La Guajira. Los habitantes de la costa Atlántica tienen fama de tener un carácter alegre y festivo. La costa Pacífica es la región con mayor biodiversidad del mundo y es la región más lluviosa del planeta. Una gran parte de la población afro-colombiana habita en las dos costas.

Las cinco regiones de Colombia continental

En contraste, la Amazonía colombiana forma parte de la zona de selvas tropicales que se extienden a Perú, Brasil y Venezuela para formar el "pulmón del mundo". Se llama así porque es la zona donde se produce la mayor cantidad del oxígeno que respiramos. En esta región se hablan más de cien idiomas indígenas, y hay una gran variedad de animales y plantas. Los indígenas de la región usan muchas de estas plantas como medicinas y muchos científicos investigan los beneficios de estas plantas para la medicina. En la Amazonía, por ejemplo, hay una estación científica para el estudio de la malaria, donde el Dr. Manuel Patarroyo hace investigación para encontrar una vacuna contra esta enfermedad.

La región de los Llanos Orientales está formada por grandes praderas que se extienden a Venezuela. Colombia y Venezuela son dos países hermanos que están unidos por su historia y geografía. La ganadería y la agricultura son las actividades más importantes de esta región. En efecto, los llaneros o habitantes de esta región, son muy aficionados a los caballos y en las fiestas populares practican un deporte similar al rodeo para demostrar sus destrezas. Además, los Llanos Orientales son el hábitat de una gran variedad de aves, reptiles, mamíferos y peces. Esta es la única región de Colombia donde habita el oso hormiguero, un bello animal que come hormigas.

El oso hormiguero habita en los Llanos Orientales de Colombia.

Medellín, conocida como "la capital de la montaña"

La región andina de Colombia es la zona central del país. Precisamente en esta región, cerca de la ciudad de Armenia, se produce el mejor café de Colombia. Está formada por la Cordillera de los Andes y es el lugar donde vive la gran mayoría de los colombianos. Aquí están las ciudades más grandes del país: Bogotá, la capital; Medellín, la ciudad más industrial; Cali, la tercera ciudad más grande de Colombia. La mayoría de la clase media de Colombia vive en las ciudades de la zona central y aquí se encuentran también las universidades más importantes del país, que atraen a jóvenes de todas las regiones colombianas.

Además de las cinco regiones continentales, Colombia tiene una región insular. Las Islas de San Andrés y Providencia están en el Caribe y son un verdadero paraíso tropical. Sus playas blancas, las aguas cristalinas y tranquilas del mar, sus bellas palmeras y sus excelentes restaurantes hacen de estas islas un lugar ideal para el turismo. Las otras islas colombianas están en el Océano Pacífico y son una reserva natural y ecológica. Cerca de la Isla Gorgona se pueden ver ballenas durante gran parte del año.

### En otras palabras

Expresiones colombianas

Sacar una A en español es difícil. Eso no es como **soplar y hacer botellas**.
*To get an A in Spanish is hard. It is not as easy as it looks.*

No puedo ir al cine. Tengo mucho **camello**.
*I can't go to the movies. I have a lot of work.*

Te llamo más tarde. Ahora **estoy de afán**.
*I'll call you later. I'm in a hurry now.*

**4-49 Comprensión.** PRIMERA FASE. **Reconocimiento de palabras clave.** Encuentre en el texto la palabra o expresión que mejor expresa el significado de las siguientes ideas.

1. mild, soft      _____
2. to begin with      _____
3. rainy      _____
4. lung      _____
5. research      _____
6. vaccine      _____
7. ant      _____

SEGUNDA FASE. **Oraciones importantes.** Subraye las afirmaciones que contienen ideas que se encuentran en el texto. Luego indique en qué parte del texto están.

1. Juan Valdez was created by a marketing agency.
2. The Pacific coast of Colombia is the rainiest region in the world.
3. Most of the oxygen in the Earth's atmosphere is produced in the Amazon region.
4. Manuel Patarroyo is a Colombian who is searching for a cure for HIV.
5. Spanish is the only language spoken in the Amazonian region of Colombia.
6. The Eastern Prairies (*Llanos Orientales*) of Colombia extend into Venezuela, giving these sister countries a common geography.
7. Different varieties of anteaters can be found all over Colombia.
8. Most Colombians live in the Andean region.

TERCERA FASE. **Ideas principales.** Escriba un párrafo breve en inglés resumiendo (*summarizing*) las ideas principales expresadas en el texto.

 **4-50 Use la información.** Prepare un afiche (*poster*) para hacer una presentación sobre dos colombianos famosos. Elija personas que representen áreas diferentes de la vida colombiana, como la política, las artes, la música, los deportes, etc. Incluya fotos y la siguiente información: lugar donde viven, el trabajo que hacen y otra información de interés. Para preparar esta actividad visite la página web de *Mosaicos* y siga los enlaces útiles.

# VOCABULARIO

| **La familia** | **The family** |
|---|---|
| la abuela | grandmother |
| el abuelo | grandfather |
| el ahijado/la ahijada | godchild |
| la esposa | wife |
| el esposo | husband |
| la hermana | sister |
| el hermano | brother |
| el hermanastro | stepbrother |
| la hermanastra | stepsister |
| la hija | daughter |
| el hijo | son |
| el hijo único/la hija única | only child |
| la madrastra | stepmother |
| la madre | mother |
| la madrina | godmother |
| la mamá | mom |
| la media hermana | half-sister |
| el medio hermano | half-brother |
| la nieta | granddaughter |
| el nieto | grandson |
| el niño/la niña | child |
| la novia | fiancée, girlfriend |
| el novio | fiancé, boyfriend |
| el padrastro | stepfather |
| el padre | father |
| los padres | parents |
| el padrino | godfather |
| el papá | dad |
| el pariente | relative |
| el primo/la prima | cousin |
| la sobrina | niece |
| el sobrino | nephew |
| la tía | aunt |
| el tío | uncle |

| **Verbos** | **Verbs** |
|---|---|
| acostar(se) (ue) | to put to bed; to go to bed |
| afeitar(se) | to shave; to shave (oneself) |
| almorzar (ue) | to have lunch |
| bañar(se) | to bathe; to take a bath |
| casar(se) | to get married |
| cerrar(ie) | to close |
| costar (ue) | to cost |
| decir (g, i) | to say, to tell |
| desayunar | to have breakfast |
| despertar(se) (ie) | to wake (someone up); to wake up |
| dormir(se) (ue) | to sleep; to fall asleep |
| dormir (ue) la siesta | to take a nap |
| duchar(se) | to give a shower to; to take a shower |
| empezar (ie) | to begin, to start |

| | |
|---|---|
| entender (ie) | to understand |
| jugar (ue) | to play (a game, sport) |
| lavar(se) | to wash (oneself) |
| levantar(se) | to raise; to get up |
| maquillar(se) | to put makeup on (someone); to put makeup on (oneself) |
| pasar | to spend (time) |
| pasear | to take a walk, to stroll |
| pedir (i) | to ask for; to order |
| peinar(se) | to comb (someone's hair); to comb (one's hair) |
| pensar (ie) | to think |
| pensar (ie) + infinitive | to plan to + verb |
| poder (ue) | to be able to, can |
| poner(se) (g) la ropa | to put one's clothes on |
| preferir (ie) | to prefer |
| querer (ie) | to want |
| quitar(se) | to take away; to take off |
| secar(se) | to dry (oneself) |
| seguir (i) | to follow, to go on |
| sentarse (ie) | to sit down |
| sentir(se) (ie) | to feel |
| servir (i) | to serve |
| tener (g, ie) | to have |
| venir (g, ie) | to come |
| vestir(se) (i) | to dress; to get dressed |
| visitar | to visit |
| volver (ue) | to return |

| **Las descripciones** | **Descriptions** |
|---|---|
| divorciado/a | divorced |
| gemelo/a | twin |
| ocupado/a | busy |

| **Palabras y expresiones útiles** | **Useful words and expressions** |
|---|---|
| el bautizo | baptism, christening |
| la derecha | right |
| la foto(grafía) | photo(graph) |
| la izquierda | left |
| juntos/as | together |
| el/la mayor | the oldest |
| el/la menor | the youngest |
| la noticia | news |
| tarde | late |
| temprano | early |
| un poco | a little |

See *Lengua* box on page 129 for time expressions.
See *Lengua* box on page 134 for other expressions with *pensar*.
See page 138 for a list of adverbs.
See page 140 for time expressions with *hacer*.

# Mi casa es su casa

*Cuadro de un pueblo hondureño*, Jorge Fermán, pintor de Honduras

# In this chapter you will learn how to:

- discuss housing, furnishings, and architecture
- talk about daily chores and household activities
- talk about activities in progress
- describe physical and emotional states

**Cultural focus: Nicaragua, El Salvador, Honduras**

Mar Caribe

BELICE

MÉXICO

Ruinas mayas

GUATEMALA

HONDURAS

Copán    Tegucigalpa

El café

EL SALVADOR
San Salvador

NICARAGUA

Mango verde
con limón y sal

León

Un edificio de arquitectura colonial

Managua

Granada

El Volcán de Izalco

COSTA
RICA

OCÉANO PACÍFICO

PANAMÁ

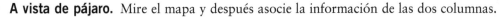

**A vista de pájaro.** Mire el mapa y después asocie la información de las dos columnas.

1. ___ Tegucigalpa...
2. ___ El mango verde con limón y sal...
3. ___ Al oeste de El Salvador...
4. ___ Las ruinas de Copán...
5. ___ El café...
6. ___ Granada y otras ciudades de Nicaragua...

a. es un plato típico de El Salvador.
b. es un producto de exportación de los tres países.
c. es la capital de Honduras.
d. tienen arquitectura colonial.
e. son de la civilización maya.
f. está el volcán de Izalco.

155

# A PRIMERA VISTA

## En casa

CD 2
Track 26
or CD 3
Track 1

En las ciudades de Nicaragua, El Salvador y Honduras, hay **viviendas** de diferentes **estilos**. La ciudad de Granada, en Nicaragua, tiene **calles** y plazas como esta, con casas coloniales de colores alegres. En Tegucigalpa, la capital de Honduras, hay **edificios** de **apartamentos**. Algunas personas prefieren vivir **cerca** del **centro**. **Creen** que los **barrios** de las **afueras** están muy **lejos** del **trabajo** y de los centros de diversión.

| Alquileres | |
|---|---|
| **Categoría:** | Alquiler Apartamentos |
| **Ciudad:** | Tegucigalpa |
| **Ubicación:** | Palmira |
| **Descripción:** | PALMIRA ALQUILER DE APARTAMENTO MUY AMPLIO, CÉNTRICO Y ACCESIBLE, 2 HABITACIONES, SALA–COMEDOR, COCINA, 1 BAÑO, ÁREA DE LAVANDERÍA, ESTACIONAMIENTO, TELÉFONO. |
| **Precio:** | $ 450,00 |

### En otras palabras

Some words for the parts of a house vary from one region to another in the Spanish-speaking world. Here are some examples:

**habitación, dormitorio, cuarto, alcoba, recámara**

**sala, salón, living**

**planta, piso**

**piscina, pileta, alberca**

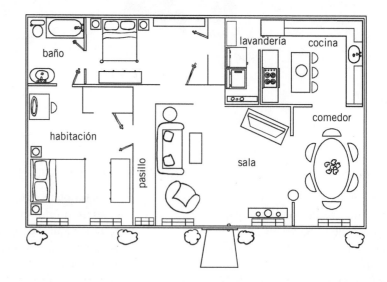

# El apartamento del anuncio

CD 2
Track 27
and
CD 3
Track 2

MARTA DÍAZ: Hola, buenos días. Me llamo Marta Díaz. ¿Es posible visitar el apartamento del anuncio?

DIEGO LÓPEZ: Sí, claro. Mucho gusto, señorita Díaz. Yo soy Diego López. Pase, pase. Como usted puede ver, el apartamento es muy alegre.

MARTA DÍAZ: ¡Ah, sí! Tiene muchas ventanas.

DIEGO LÓPEZ: Esta es la **sala**. Es muy grande. Junto a la sala hay un **comedor** pequeño y al lado está la **cocina**.

MARTA DÍAZ: ¡La cocina es lindísima!

DIEGO LÓPEZ: Sí, todos los **electrodomésticos** son nuevos. A la izquierda del **pasillo** hay dos **habitaciones** y un **baño**.

MARTA DÍAZ: Esta habitación tiene muy buena **vista** al **jardín**. Además, los **muebles** son de buena calidad. Me gusta el apartamento. ¿Cuánto es el **alquiler**?

DIEGO LÓPEZ: 8.000 lempiras al mes.

MARTA DÍAZ: Pues, señor López, me encantan el apartamento y esta **zona** céntrica. Y el precio es muy bueno. Voy a decidir esta noche y lo llamo mañana.

DIEGO LÓPEZ: Perfecto, señorita Díaz. Hasta mañana.

> ### En otras palabras
>
> The Spanish word for *apartment* varies according to the country. **El apartamento** is used in Central America, Colombia, and Venezuela, while **el departamento** is common in Mexico, Argentina, Peru and Chile. The word used in Spain is **el piso**.

> ### En otras palabras
>
> The expressions **Pase(n)** and **Adelante** invite people to enter a room or a house in many Spanish-speaking countries. In others, like Colombia, the expression **Siga(n)** is preferred.

**5-1 Asociación.** Indique si las siguientes afirmaciones son ciertas (**C**) o falsas (**F**), según el diálogo anterior.

1. ___ Marta Díaz quiere comprar el apartamento.
2. ___ La sala es pequeña.
3. ___ El apartamento tiene dos baños.
4. ___ Los electrodomésticos son nuevos.
5. ___ Los muebles son de buena calidad.
6. ___ A Marta no le gusta la zona céntrica.

**5-2 ¿En qué piso viven?** Pregúntele a su compañero/a dónde viven las diferentes personas. Su compañero/a debe contestarle de acuerdo con el dibujo (*drawing*).

MODELO: E1: *¿Dónde viven los Girondo?*
E2: *Viven en el cuarto piso, en el apartamento 4-A.*

> ### Lengua
>
> Ordinal numbers are adjectives and agree in gender and number with the noun they modify (e.g., **la segunda casa, el cuarto edificio**). **Primero** and **tercero** drop the final **-o** when used before a masculine singular noun.
>
> el **primer** apartamento
> el **tercer** piso

> ### Cultura
>
> Notice that the first floor is normally called **la planta baja** in most Hispanic countries. The second floor is called **el primer piso**.

décimo: Rodríguez
noveno: Peralta
octavo: Elizondo
séptimo: Díaz
sexto: Gómez
quinto: Lizaur
cuarto: Sánchez
tercero: Carreras
segundo: Iglesias
primer piso: Olmos
planta baja

| 5-A López | 5-B Alemán |
| 4-A Girondo | 4-B Mujica |
| 3-A Ozollo | 3-B Ponce |
| 2-A Cárdenas | 2-B García-Gil |
| 1-A Jiménez | 1-B Valbuena |
| PB-A Martínez | PB-B Casal |

**5-3 Un hotel de lujo.** Ustedes van a gastar los millones que ganaron (*won*) en la lotería para construir un hotel de lujo en la Bahía de Jiquilisco, cerca de San Salvador. Decidan cómo distribuir los siguientes espacios del hotel.

MODELO:    el restaurante
E1:  *¿En qué piso vamos a poner el restaurante?*
E2:  *Debe estar en la planta baja.*

1. la discoteca
2. la recepción
3. el gimnasio
4. la oficina de seguridad

5. las habitaciones
6. la piscina
7. la cafetería con vista a la playa
8. el salón de computadoras

**5-4 Agentes de bienes raíces (*real estate*).** PRIMERA FASE. Los fines de semana ustedes trabajan en una agencia de bienes raíces. Para vender o alquilar la casa del dibujo escriban un anuncio similar al anuncio de la página 156.

Incluyan la siguiente información en su anuncio:

1. número de habitaciones
2. número de baños
3. distribución (*layout*) de los cuartos
4. color de la sala
5. otras características (garaje, jardín, sótano [*basement*], ático, etc.)

6. localización de la casa en relación al centro de la ciudad
7. localización de la casa en relación a la universidad
8. precio de la casa

SEGUNDA FASE. Presenten su anuncio al resto de la clase y contesten las preguntas de sus compañeros sobre la casa que quieren vender o alquilar.

**5-5 Ventajas y desventajas.** Discutan los aspectos positivos y negativos de los siguientes temas relacionados con la vivienda. Escriban una ventaja y una desventaja para cada uno de los siguientes puntos. Después compartan sus opiniones con el resto de la clase.

|  | VENTAJAS | DESVENTAJAS |
|---|---|---|
| 1. vivir en un apartamento<br>2. vivir en una casa<br>3. tener una piscina<br>4. vivir con un compañero/una compañera de cuarto/casa |  |  |

# La casa, los muebles y los electrodomésticos

CD 2
Track 28
or CD 3
Track 3

## 5-6 ¿Aparatos eléctricos, muebles o accesorios? PRIMERA FASE. Escriba cada una de las siguientes palabras en la columna apropiada.

la alfombra    el cuadro      el/la radio
el armario     la butaca      el refrigerador
la cómoda      el horno       las sábanas
las cortinas   el lavaplatos  la silla

### En otras palabras

Words for household items often vary from one region to another, for example:

**manta, cobija, frazada**

**armario, clóset**

**bañera, bañadera, tina**

**refrigerador, nevera**

**estufa, cocina**

| APARATOS ELÉCTRICOS | MUEBLES | ACCESORIOS |
|---|---|---|
|  |  |  |
|  |  |  |
|  |  |  |
|  |  |  |

SEGUNDA FASE. Respondan a las siguientes preguntas relacionadas con la *Primera fase*.

1. Según ustedes, ¿qué aparato eléctrico cuesta más dinero?
2. ¿Qué muebles necesita todos los días un/a estudiante? ¿Necesita un aparato electrónico también? ¿Cuál?
3. ¿Qué accesorios tienen ustedes en su cuarto?
4. ¿En qué parte de la casa generalmente están estos objetos?

**5-7 El curioso.** Intercambien preguntas para describir los cuartos de la casa/el apartamento de cada uno/a. Traten (*Try*) de obtener la mayor información posible.

MODELO:  E1:  *¿Cómo es la sala de tu casa?*
E2:  *Es pequeña. Hay una alfombra verde y un sofá grande. También hay dos sillas modernas y una mesa con una lámpara. ¿Y cómo es tu dormitorio?*

**5-8 Preparativos.** PRIMERA FASE. Usted va a mudarse (*move*) a una casa muy grande y tiene que comprar muchas cosas. Organice su lista de compras según las siguientes categorías.

|  | MUEBLES | ACCESORIOS | ELECTRODOMÉSTICOS/ APARATOS ELECTRÓNICOS |
|---|---|---|---|
| para el dormitorio |  |  |  |
| para la sala |  |  |  |
| para el comedor |  |  |  |
| para la cocina |  |  |  |

SEGUNDA FASE. Comparta la lista con su compañero/a. Él/Ella le va recordar (*remind you about*) otras cosas que probablemente va a necesitar.

MODELO:  E1:  *Voy a comprar una cama nueva para el dormitorio.*
E2:  *¿No vas a comprar sábanas y mantas?/¿Y no necesitas un sofá?*

**5-9 Por catálogo.** Miren las fotos del catálogo y elijan (*choose*) un producto de cada categoría. Intercambien sus preferencias y expliquen en qué lugar de la casa van a poner estos accesorios. Las palabras de la lista los/las pueden ayudar.

barato/a     caro/a          de buena calidad     grande     pequeño/a
bonito/a     confortable     de color...          lindo/a

MODELO:  E1:  *Me gusta la primera toalla porque no es cara y es muy linda. Es para el cuarto de baño.*
E2:  *Yo prefiero la tercera porque es más grande.*

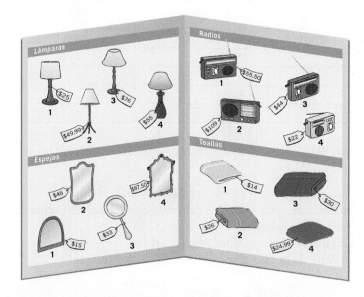

# Las tareas domésticas

CD 2
Track 29
or CD 3
Track 4

Gustavo **lava** los **platos**.

Beatriz **seca** los platos.

Beatriz **cocina**. Ella usa mucho los electrodomésticos.

Gustavo **limpia** el baño y **pasa** la **aspiradora**.

Gustavo **saca** la **basura**.

Gustavo **barre** la terraza.

Beatriz **tiende** la **ropa**.

la lavadora    la secadora

Después la **dobla** cuando está **seca**.

Beatriz **plancha** la ropa.

**5-10 Por la mañana.** ¿En qué orden hace usted estas actividades por la mañana? Use las siguientes expresiones para indicar el orden: **primero, luego, más tarde, después, finalmente.** Compare sus respuestas con las de su compañero/a.

___ lavar los platos        ___ desayunar
___ preparar el café        ___ secar los platos
___ salir para la universidad        ___ hacer la cama

**5-11 Actividades en la casa.** Pregúntele a su compañero/a dónde hace estas cosas normalmente cuando está en casa.

MODELO:    E1:   *¿Dónde ves televisión?*
            E2:   *Veo televisión en mi cuarto. ¿Y tú?* O
                 *No veo televisión. ¿Y tú?*

1. dormir la siesta
2. escuchar música
3. planchar
4. lavar la ropa

5. pasar la aspiradora
6. estudiar para un examen
7. tender la ropa
8. hablar por teléfono con amigos/as

**5-12 ¡A compartir las tareas!** PRIMERA FASE. Ustedes van a compartir una casa el próximo año académico. Preparen una lista de todas las tareas domésticas que van a hacer.

**SEGUNDA FASE.** Discutan qué tareas va a hacer cada uno/a de ustedes según sus gustos. Finalmente, hagan un calendario de tareas y compártanlo con el resto de la clase.

MODELO: *A mí me gusta planchar la ropa pero a mi compañero/a no le gusta. Por eso, yo voy a planchar la ropa los lunes por la tarde.*

CD 2
Track 30
or CD 3
Track 5

**5-13 El agente de bienes raíces.** PRIMERA FASE. Mr. and Mrs. Mena and their two children live in San Salvador. They have decided to move to a larger place and they are talking to a real estate agent. Before you listen, write down the kind of dwelling and the characteristics of the neighborhood they may be looking for.

**SEGUNDA FASE.** Now, as you listen, circle the letter next to the correct information.

1. Los señores Mena quieren comprar...
   a. una casa.
   b. un apartamento.

2. El señor y la señora Mena prefieren vivir...
   a. en una buena zona.
   b. lejos de un parque.

3. El agente de bienes raíces...
   a. no sabe cómo ayudarlos.
   b. tiene una casa buena para ellos.

4. El agente dice que la casa del barrio La Mascota...
   a. cuesta mucho.
   b. tiene un buen precio.

5. El señor Mena dice que...
   a. los niños necesitan estar al aire libre para jugar.
   b. los niños no necesitan jugar al aire libre.

# EN ACCIÓN

## Diarios de bicicleta: El apartamento

### Antes de ver

**5-14 PRIMERA FASE.** En este segmento, Javier está buscando un lugar para vivir. Escriba cuatro muebles o accesorios que probablemente va a necesitar para su habitación o apartamento.

**SEGUNDA FASE.** ¿Qué características le parecen a usted más importantes cuando busca un apartamento o una habitación? Marque (✓) sus respuestas.

1. ___ Está cerca de la universidad o del trabajo.
2. ___ Es barato/a.
3. ___ Tiene mucha luz natural.
4. ___ Es grande.
5. ___ Está amueblado/a.

### Mientras ve

**5-15** Marque (✓) lo que Javier menciona cuando le describe un apartamento a Daniel.

En la sala:
___ la mesa
___ el sofá
___ la silla
___ el televisor
___ la lámpara

En la cocina:
___ el microondas
___ la estufa
___ el lavaplatos
___ el fregadero
___ el refrigerador

En el baño:
___ el inodoro
___ la ducha
___ la bañera
___ el lavabo
___ el jacuzzi

En el cuarto:
___ el clóset
___ la mesa de noche
___ la lámpara
___ la cama
___ la alfombra

### Después de ver

**5-16** Al final de este segmento, Javier decide compartir casa con Daniel. Imagine cómo es esta casa y escriba cinco oraciones para describirla.

163

# FUNCIONES Y FORMAS

## 1. Expressing ongoing actions: Present progressive

ÓSCAR: ¿Aló?

CATALINA: Hola, Óscar. Te habla Catalina. ¿Qué **estás haciendo**?

ÓSCAR: Hola, Catalina. **¡Estoy trabajando** mucho!

CATALINA: ¿Por qué?

ÓSCAR: Mis padres **están pasando** sus vacaciones en la playa y vuelven mañana. ¡La casa es un desastre total!

CATALINA: ¿Así que **estás limpiando**?

ÓSCAR: ¡Claro! **Estoy barriendo** el piso, **ordenando** la sala, **recogiendo** la ropa de mi cuarto…. Y tú, ¿qué **estás haciendo**?

CATALINA: ¿Yo?… Nada. **Estoy leyendo** el periódico y **tomando** un café.

**Piénselo.** Indique las oraciones que son **ciertas** (**C**) o **falsas** (**F**), de acuerdo con la conversación entre Catalina y Óscar.

1. ___ Catalina y Óscar **están trabajando** juntos.
2. ___ Óscar **está descansando**.
3. ___ Óscar **está pasando** sus vacaciones con sus padres en la playa.
4. ___ Óscar **está limpiando** la casa de sus padres.
5. ___ Óscar no está contento porque él **está trabajando** mucho en casa.

■ Use the present progressive to emphasize that an action or event is in progress at the moment of speaking, rather than a habitual action.

| | |
|---|---|
| Óscar **está limpiando** la casa. | *Oscar is cleaning the house.* (at this moment) |
| Óscar **limpia** la casa. | *Oscar cleans the house.* (habitually) |

■ Form the present progressive with the present tense of **estar** + *present participle*. To form the present participle, add **-ando** to the stem of **-ar** verbs and **-iendo** to the stem of **-er** and **-ir** verbs.

| ESTAR | | PRESENT PARTICIPLE |
|---|---|---|
| yo | **estoy** | |
| tú | **estás** | hablando |
| Ud., él, ella | **está** | comiendo |
| nosotros/as | **estamos** | escribiendo |
| vosotros/as | **estáis** | |
| Uds., ellos/as | **están** | |

■ When the verb stem of an **-er** or an **-ir** verb ends in a vowel, add **-yendo**.

| leer | → | le**yendo** |
|---|---|---|
| oír | → | o**yendo** |

■ Stem-changing **-ir** verbs (**o → ue, e → ie, e → i**) change **o → u** and **e → i** in the present participle.

| dormir (ue) | (**o → u**) | d<u>u</u>rmiendo |
|---|---|---|
| sentir (ie) | (**e → i**) | s<u>i</u>ntiendo |
| pedir (ie) | (**e → i**) | p<u>i</u>diendo |

■ Spanish does not use the present progressive to express future time, as English does; Spanish uses the present tense instead.

| **Salgo** mañana. | *I am leaving tomorrow.* |
|---|---|
| ¿**Te levantas** temprano mañana? | *Are you getting up early tomorrow?* |

**5-17 Un día ocupado.** Hoy es un día muy ocupado para la familia Villa. Asocie las acciones de la columna de la izquierda con las explicaciones de la columna de la derecha para averiguar (*find out*) por qué.

1. ___ La Sra. Villa está preparando una cena deliciosa y un pastel (*cake*) especial.
2. ___ Su hijo Marcelo está barriendo la terraza.
3. ___ Su hija Ana está lavando los platos en el fregadero.
4. ___ Alicia está decorando la mesa.
5. ___ Pedro está hablando por teléfono.

a. Está llamando a su mejor amigo para invitarlo a la fiesta.
b. El lavaplatos no está funcionando.
c. Es una ocasión especial.
d. Es el cumpleaños de su esposo.
e. Está muy sucia (*dirty*) y unos amigos vienen a celebrar el cumpleaños.

Rodrigo      Soledad

**5-18 La vida activa.** Túrnense para describir lo que está haciendo cada persona en estas escenas. Indiquen en qué lugar de la casa está cada uno de ellos. Luego, imaginen lo que, según ustedes, cada persona va a hacer más tarde.

**MODELO:** E1: *Rodrigo y Soledad están cantando en una fiesta. Están en la terraza.*
E2: *Después van a bailar y conversar con sus amigos.*

Pepe         Catalina      Arturo        Gonzalo       Carlos

**5-19 Lugares y actividades.** PRIMERA FASE. Miren las siguientes fotografías de celebraciones y hagan lo siguiente:

## SITUACIONES

1. **Role A.** Your best friend calls to invite you to go out. Respond that you and your housemates are busy cleaning the apartment. Explain the chores that each of you is doing.

   **Role B.** Call your best friend to invite her/him to go out with you. Ask what your friend and her/his roommates are doing. Ask if your friend can go out later (**más tarde**).

2. **Role A.** There is a big family gathering at your aunt's house today, but you are away at school. Call and greet the family member who answers the phone. Explain that you will not be attending, and excuse yourself for not being there. Ask how everyone is and what each family member is doing at the moment.

   **Role B.** You are at a big family gathering today. A family member calls to say he/she can't attend. Answer the phone. Greet the caller and answer his/her questions. Finally, mention that everyone says hello (**todos te mandan saludos**) and say good-bye.

1.

3.

2.

Asocien las fotos con el país/los países en que probablemente se realiza cada una: Foto **1.** \_\_\_, **2.** \_\_\_, **3.** \_\_\_
a. España          c. México          e. Uruguay
b. Estados Unidos  d. Ecuador         f. en muchos países

SEGUNDA FASE. Descríbanle a otra pareja dos o tres actividades que las personas están haciendo en la escena de una de las fotos. La otra pareja debe adivinar el nombre del lugar. Luego, entre todos, escriban una descripción completa de una de las fotos. Incluyan el nombre de la fiesta o celebración, su significado cultural y las actividades de las personas en la foto.

## 2. Describing physical and emotional states: Expressions with *tener*

Hoy es un día de verano y los Robledo se mudan. **Tienen prisa** porque ya son las tres de la tarde. El señor Robledo y su hija Isabel **tienen calor** porque hace cuatro horas que trabajan bajo (*under*) el sol. Ella **tiene mucha sed** y está bebiendo agua. El bebé, Nicolás, llora porque **tiene hambre**. La señora Robledo le da de comer mientras la abuelita Rosa duerme la siesta. Después de empacar su ropa y todas sus fotografías, libros y plantas, Rosa **tiene mucho sueño**. ¡Qué día para los Robledo!

**Piénselo.** Asocie la descripción del estado físico con la(s) persona(s) del dibujo. Escriba el nombre de la(s) persona(s) al lado de la descripción.

_____ 1. Va a comer porque **tiene hambre**.
_____ 2. Está tomando agua porque **tiene sed**.
_____ 3. No **tienen frío** porque es verano y hace calor.
_____ 4. Está cansada y **tiene sueño**.
_____ 5. **Tienen calor** porque están trabajando bajo el sol.
_____ 6. **Tienen prisa** porque quieren salir pronto.

■ Spanish uses **tener** + *noun* for many conditions and states where English uses *to be* + *adjective*. You have already seen the expression **tener... años: Eduardo tiene veinte años.** Here are some other useful expressions.

| TENER + *NOUN* | | | |
|---|---|---|---|
| | hambre | | *hungry* |
| | sed | | *thirsty* |
| | sueño | | *sleepy* |
| | miedo | | *afraid* |
| tener | calor | to be | *hot* |
| | cuidado | | *careful* |
| | frío | | *cold* |
| | suerte | | *lucky* |
| | prisa | | *in a hurry/rush* |
| | razón | | *right, correct* |

■ With these expressions, use **mucho/a** to indicate *very*.

Tengo **mucho** calor (frío, miedo, sueño, cuidado).

*I am very hot (cold, afraid, sleepy, careful).*

Tienen **mucha** hambre (sed, suerte).

*They are very hungry (thirsty, lucky).*

**5-20 Asociaciones.** Lea las situaciones en que están usted y algunos miembros de su familia. Luego asocie las situaciones con las expresiones de la derecha.

1. Mi hermano siempre tiene _____ y, por eso, está comiendo ahora.
2. Mi hermana duerme a todas horas porque siempre tiene _____ .
3. En este momento mis primos están visitando la Antártida; probablemente tienen _____ .
4. Mis abuelos están bebiendo agua en la cocina porque tienen _____ .
5. Mi mamá tiene _____ ; siempre gana (*wins*) cuando juega a la lotería.
6. ¡Uf! Todavía estoy planchando mi blusa y mis amigos van a llegar en cinco minutos. Yo tengo _____ .

a. sed
b. prisa
c. suerte
d. sueño
e. mucho frío
f. hambre

**5-21 ¿Qué están haciendo, dónde están y cómo se sienten?** PRIMERA FASE. Observen a las personas en los dibujos y hagan lo siguiente.

1. Digan qué está(n) haciendo la(s) persona(s) y dónde está(n).
2. Describan su estado físico.

MODELO: *El padre y su hijo están durmiendo en el sofá. Tienen sueño.*

1.

2.

3.

4.

**SEGUNDA FASE.** Respondan a las siguientes preguntas sobre las escenas de la *Primera fase*. Expliquen.

1. ¿Cuál de los dibujos describe mejor cómo se sienten ustedes en este momento?
2. ¿Qué dibujo refleja (*reflects*) el clima de su región en diciembre?
3. ¿A qué hora se sienten ustedes como las personas del dibujo del modelo?

**5-22 ¿Estados de ánimo (*moods*) semejantes o diferentes?** PRIMERA FASE. Primero, termine las siguientes ideas y, luego, compare sus respuestas con las de su compañero/a. Tome apuntes de las respuestas de su compañero/a. Use expresiones con **tener.**

1. En las mañanas de invierno, yo siempre _____ .
2. Cuando mi madre pasa mucho tiempo limpiando nuestra casa, ella

   _____ .
3. Generalmente, cuando mis hermanos y yo hacemos barbacoa, nosotros

   _____ .
4. Cuando yo leo un libro aburrido, siempre _____ .
5. Inmediatamente yo _____ cuando llego a casa y mi esposo está preparando mi plato favorito.

**SEGUNDA FASE.** Usando sus apuntes de la *Primera fase*, escriba una semejanza y una diferencia entre usted y su compañero/a.

## SITUACIONES

1. **Role A.** You share an apartment with a messy friend. Complain to him/her that a) his/her books, backpack, etc., are always all over the living room; b) he/she uses a lot of dishes, but never washes them; c) his/her bottles of soft drinks (**botellas de refrescos**) are always on the table; and d) he/she makes a lot of noise (**ruido**) during the night and you can't sleep.

   **Role B.** The friend with whom you share an apartment has some complaints about you. Apologize and explain that you a) don't pick up your books or wash the dishes because you are always in a rush to do homework; b) drink a lot of soft drinks because you are always thirsty; and c) go to bed late because you're not sleepy before midnight or later and also because you're scared at night. Say as convincingly as you can that you are going to be more careful in the future.

2. **Role A.** You are a young child. It is a busy Saturday morning at your house, and nobody is paying any attention to you. Go to your parent and say the following: a) You are hungry and want to eat; b) you are thirsty and want some juice; and c) you are bored and want to play outside. What you really want is your parent's attention, so you react negatively to suggestions that you entertain yourself.

   **Role B.** You are the parent of a young child. You are really busy, and you think your child is old enough to take care himself/herself for awhile. When your child makes demands, say that if he/she a) is hungry, there is fruit in the kitchen; b) is thirsty, there is orange juice in the refrigerator; c) is bored, he/she has a lot of toys (**juguetes**) in his/her room. Explain that you are in a hurry and cannot play outside. Suggest things your child can do while you are busy with your household tasks.

## 3. Avoiding repetition in speaking and writing: Direct object nouns and pronouns

**A.**

**¿Qué hacen estas personas?**

**B.**

**C.**

La abuela cuida (*takes care of*) a la niña. **La** cuida todos los días.

El padre lava los platos y los niños **los** secan.

Las señoras preparan la comida en la cocina del restaurante y después **la** sirven.

**Piénselo.** Ponga la letra de la foto correcta al lado de la descripción.

1. ___ La niña está contenta porque su abuela **la** cuida.
2. ___ El padre trabaja y los niños **lo** ayudan.
3. ___ Las señoras tienen una parrilla (*grill*) enorme. Ellas **la** usan todos los días.
4. ___ Las cocineras (*cooks*) están preparando mucha carne en la parrilla. Después, los clientes van a comer**la**.
5. ___ La abuela está cuidando a la niña. La abuela **la** quiere mucho.
6. ___ El padre está en la cocina con sus hijos. Él **los** mira con cariño y habla con ellos mientras trabajan.

■ Direct objects answer the question *what?* or *whom?* in relation to the verb.

| | |
|---|---|
| ¿Qué dobla Pedro? | *What does Pedro fold?* |
| (Pedro dobla) **las toallas.** | *(Pedro folds) the towels.* |

■ Direct objects may be nouns or pronouns. When direct object nouns refer to a specific person, a group of persons, or a pet, the word **a** precedes the direct object. This **a** is called the *personal a* and has no equivalent in English. The personal **a** followed by **el** contracts to **al**.

| | |
|---|---|
| Amanda seca **los platos.** | *Amanda dries the dishes.* |
| Amanda seca **al perro.** | *Amanda dries off the dog.* |
| ¿Ves la piscina? | *Do you see the swimming pool?* |
| ¿Ves **al** niño en la piscina? | *Do you see the child in the swimming pool?* |

■ With the verb *tener* the personal **a** is not needed.

María tiene un hijo.        *María has a child.*

■ Direct object pronouns replace direct object nouns and are used to avoid repeating the noun while speaking or writing. These pronouns may refer to people, animals, or things already mentioned.

| DIRECT OBJECT PRONOUNS | | | |
|---|---|---|---|
| **me** | *me* | **nos** | *us* |
| **te** | *you* (familiar, singular) | **os** | *you* (familiar plural, Spain) |
| **lo** | *you* (formal, singular), *him, it* (masculine) | **los** | *you* (formal and familiar, plural), *them* (masculine) |
| **la** | *you* (formal, singular), *her, it* (feminine) | **las** | *you* (formal and familiar plural), *them* (feminine) |

■ Place the direct object pronoun before the conjugated verb form.

¿Barre **la cocina** Mirta?      *Does Mirta sweep the kitchen?*

No, no **la** barre.          *No, she does not sweep it.*

¿Cuidas **a tu hermanito**?      *Do you take care of your little brother?*

Sí, **lo** cuido.           *Yes, I take care of him.*

■ With compound verb forms (a conjugated verb and an infinitive or present participle), a direct object pronoun may be placed before the conjugated verb, or may be attached to the accompanying infinitive or present participle.

¿Vas a ver **a Rafael**?       *Are you going to see Rafael?*

Sí, **lo** voy a ver mañana. ⎱
Sí, voy a ver**lo** mañana. ⎰   *Yes, I am going to see him tomorrow.*

¿Están limpiando **la casa**?    *Are they cleaning the house?*

Sí, **la** están limpiando. ⎱
Sí, están limpiándo**la**. ⎰    *Yes, they are cleaning it.*

■ Since the question word **quién(es)** refers to people, use the *personal a* when **quién(es)** is used as a direct object.

¿**A quién** vas a ayudar?      *Whom are you going to help?*

Voy a ayudar **a Pedro**.      *I am going to help Pedro.*

**5-23 La división del trabajo.** Sus compañeros Martín, Pedro y Julio comparten un apartamento y usted le hace las siguientes preguntas a Julio para saber cómo dividen las tareas domésticas entre ellos. Escriba la letra de la respuesta más apropiada de Julio.

1. ¿Quién limpia la nevera?
   **a.** Yo lo limpio.      **b.** Pedro la limpia.   **c.** Nosotros las limpiamos.
2. ¿Quién hace las camas?
   **a.** Pedro la hace.      **b.** Yo los hago.      **c.** Martín las hace.
3. ¿Quién tiende la ropa?
   **a.** Los tres lo tendemos.   **b.** Pedro los tiende.   **c.** Martín la tiende.
4. ¿Quién saca la basura?
   **a.** Martín lo saca.      **b.** Pedro las saca.   **c.** Yo la saco.
5. ¿Quién pasa la aspiradora?
   **a.** Martín y yo las pasamos.   **b.** Pedro la pasa.   **c.** Ellos lo pasan.

**5-24 ¿Qué es lógico hacer?** PRIMERA FASE. Las afirmaciones de la columna de la izquierda describen la situación doméstica de esta familia. Léalas y, luego, asocie cada afirmación con una acción lógica.

1. ___ Las camas están sin hacer.
2. ___ La ropa está seca.
3. ___ Los dormitorios están desordenados.
4. ___ El aire acondicionado no funciona.
5. ___ Las ventanas están sucias.
6. ___ No pueden poner el auto en el garaje porque hay muchos muebles viejos y cajas con libros.

**a.** Los hijos los van a ordenar.
**b.** La madre las hace después de leer el periódico.
**c.** El padre las va a limpiar.
**d.** La hija va a plancharla.
**e.** Los hijos lo van a organizar y limpiar.
**f.** El hijo mayor lo va a reparar (*fix*).

 **SEGUNDA FASE.** Dígale a su compañero/a cuál(es) de las afirmaciones de la *Primera fase* describe(n) mejor su apartamento o casa en este momento. Luego, explíquele qué va a hacer usted y cuándo.

**5-25 Mis responsabilidades en casa.** PRIMERA FASE. Averigüe (*Find out*) si su compañero/a es responsable de las siguientes tareas domésticas en su casa.

MODELO:     sacar la basura
                      E1:  *¿Sacas la basura?*
                      E2:  *Sí, la saco. O No, no la saco. ¿Y tú?*

1. lavar los platos
2. ordenar el garaje
3. tender las cortinas después de lavarlas
4. limpiar la ducha y la bañera
5. lavar las sábanas
6. cortar el césped

SEGUNDA FASE. Ahora, comparen sus respuestas. Después díganle a otra pareja cuáles son las tareas domésticas que ustedes dos hacen y averigüen si ellos las hacen también.

MODELO:   E1:  *Nosotros no lavamos los platos en casa porque tenemos lavaplatos. ¿Y ustedes los lavan?*
                   E2:  *Sí, nosotros los lavamos y hacemos las camas también.*

**5-26 El apartamento de mi compañero/a.** Usted va a cuidar el apartamento de su compañero/a por una semana, y quiere saber lo que debe hacer y lo que puede hacer allí.

MODELO:   E1:  *¿Debo sacar la basura?*
                   E2:  *Sí, la debes sacar/debes sacarla todos los días.*

| ¿DEBO O NO DEBO? | SÍ | NO | ¿PUEDO O NO PUEDO? | SÍ | NO |
|---|---|---|---|---|---|
| regar (*water*) las plantas | _____ | _____ | leer los libros | _____ | _____ |
| pasear al perro | _____ | _____ | usar los electrodomésticos | _____ | _____ |
| limpiar el apartamento | _____ | _____ | invitar a un amigo/una amiga | _____ | _____ |
| poner la alarma | _____ | _____ | hacer la tarea en la computadora | _____ | _____ |
| … | _____ | _____ | … | _____ | _____ |

**5-27 Los preparativos para la visita.** La familia Granados está muy ocupada porque espera la visita de unos parientes. Conteste las preguntas de su compañero/a sobre lo que está haciendo cada miembro de la familia.

MODELO:   E1:  *¿Quién está preparando la comida?*
                   E2:  *La abuela la está preparando/está preparándola.*

**5-28 Una mano amiga. PRIMERA FASE.** Su compañero/a le va a hacer preguntas sobre sus relaciones con otras personas. Conteste, escogiendo a una de las personas de la lista.

| | |
|---|---|
| mi madre | mi novio/a   ¿...? |
| mi mejor amigo/a | mi padre |

MODELO:     ayudar económicamente
E1: *¿Quién te ayuda económicamente?*
E2: *Mis padres me ayudan económicamente.*

1. querer mucho
2. escuchar en todo momento
3. llamar por teléfono con frecuencia
4. ayudar con los problemas
5. aconsejar (*advise*) cuando estás indeciso/a
6. entender siempre

**SEGUNDA FASE.** Dígale a su compañero/a lo que usted hace por las siguientes personas. Indique en qué circunstancias lo hace.

MODELO:     su esposo/a
E1: *Lo/La ayudo cuando está cansado/a.*
E2: *Y yo lo/la escucho cuando tiene problemas en el trabajo.*

1. su papá
2. su mamá
3. su mejor amigo/a
4. su novio/a
5. sus vecinos (*neighbors*)
6. su compañero/a de cuarto

## SITUACIONES

### En directo

To assist a customer in a store:

**¿Qué desea?**
*What would you like?*
(lit., *What do you desire?*)

**¿En qué puedo ayudarlo/a?**
*How can I help you?*

To request a product:

**Quisiera...**
*I would like . . .*

**¿Podría ver...?**
*Could I see . . .?*

**¿Podría mostrarme...?**
*Could you show me . . .?*

1. **Role A.** You are at a furniture store buying a sofa. Tell the salesperson which sofa you want and ask when they can deliver (**entregar**) it. Explain that you are not going to be home at that time, but that you can be home in the afternoon. Agree to the time and thank the salesperson.

   **Role B.** You are a salesperson at a furniture store. Tell the customer that the sofa he/she wants is a very good one and that you can deliver (**entregar**) it next Monday morning. Mention that you can deliver it between three and five o'clock in the afternoon if the customer prefers.

2. **Role A.** You and your little brother/sister have to do some chores at home. Since you are older, you tell your sibling three or four things that he/she has to do. Be prepared to respond to complaints and questions.

   **Role B.** You and your older brother/sister have to do some chores at home. Because you are younger, you get some orders from your sibling about what you have to do. You do not feel like working, and you especially do not like being bossed around, so respond to everything you hear with a complaint or a question.

## 4. Pointing out and identifying people and things: Demonstrative adjectives and pronouns

AGENTE: **Esta** casa blanca es muy moderna y el precio es bueno.

CLIENTE: Pero **esa** tiene jardín y **esta** no tiene, ¿verdad?

AGENTE: No, **esta** casa y **aquella** no tienen jardín. Por eso, la casa amarilla es más cara.

**Piénselo.** En su presentación, el señor Mendoza describe algunos tipos de vivienda para un grupo de salvadoreños que desean comprar una casa. Indique si cada una de las siguientes descripciones se refiere a la vivienda que está cerca (**C**), un poco lejos (**P**) o lejos (**L**) del señor Mendoza.

1. ___ **Esta** casa de dos pisos está en una ciudad. Tiene muchas ventanas en cada piso, pero no tiene jardín.
2. ___ **Aquella** casa donde están la madre y su hija es de material sólido y de un color alegre.
3. ___ **Esa** casa es de construcción sólida y tiene dos pisos y un garaje. Tiene una pequeña área verde enfrente.

## Demonstrative Adjectives

■ Demonstrative adjectives agree in gender and number with the noun they modify. English has two sets of demonstratives (*this, these* and *that, those*), but Spanish has three sets.

| | | | |
|---|---|---|---|
| *this* | **este** cuadro<br>**esta** butaca | *these* | **estos** cuadros<br>**estas** butacas |
| *that* | **ese** horno<br>**esa** casa | *those* | **esos** hornos<br>**esas** casas |
| *that (over there)* | **aquel** camión<br>**aquella** casa | *those (over there)* | **aquellos** camiones<br>**aquellas** casas |

■ Use **este, esta, estos,** and **estas** when referring to people or things that are close to you in space or time.

**Este** escritorio es nuevo.      *This desk is new.*

Traen el sofá **esta** tarde.      *They will bring the sofa this afternoon.*

■ Use **ese**, **esa**, **esos**, and **esas** when referring to events, people, or things that are not relatively close to you. Sometimes they are close to the person you are addressing.

| | |
|---|---|
| **Esa** lámpara es muy bonita. | *That lamp is very pretty.* |
| **Ese** amigo de Lola vende su auto, ¿verdad? | *That friend of Lola's is selling his car, isn't he?* |

■ Use **aquel**, **aquella**, **aquellos**, and **aquellas** when referring to people or things that are more distant, or to events that are distant in time.

| | |
|---|---|
| **Aquel** edificio es muy alto. | *That building (over there) is very tall.* |
| En **aquella** visita los niños jugaron en el parque. | *During that (long ago) visit, the children played in the park.* |

## Demonstrative pronouns

■ Demonstratives can be used as pronouns to mean *this one/these* or *that one/those*, thus avoiding repetition when speaking or writing.

| | |
|---|---|
| Compran este espejo y **ese**. | *They are buying this mirror and that one.* |
| Estas lámparas y **aquellas** son mis favoritas. | *These lamps and those over there are my favorites.* |

■ To refer to a general idea or concept, or to ask for the identification of an object, use **esto**, **eso**, or **aquello**. These forms are invariable.

| | |
|---|---|
| Trabajan mucho y **eso** es muy bueno. | *They work a lot, and that is very good.* |
| ¿Qué es **esto**? | *What is this?* |
| Es un espejo. | *It is a mirror.* |
| **Aquello** es un edificio de la universidad. | *That (over there) is a university building.* |

**5-29 Cerca, relativamente cerca o lejos.** Decida qué adjetivo demostrativo debe usar de acuerdo con el lugar donde se encuentran los siguientes objetos.

### Cerca de usted

1. ___ mesa es de Honduras.    **a.** Esta **b.** Esa **c.** Aquella
2. ___ cuadros también son de Honduras.    **a.** Estos **b.** Esos **c.** Aquellos

### Relativamente cerca de usted

3. ___ sofá es muy grande.    **a.** Este **b.** Ese **c.** Aquel
4. ___ alfombra tiene unos colores muy alegres.    **a.** Esta **b.** Esa **c.** Aquella

### Lejos de usted

5. ___ espejo es nuevo.    **a.** Este **b.** Ese **c.** Aquel
6. ___ lámparas son antiguas.    **a.** Estas **b.** Esas **c.** Aquellas

**5-30 ¿Quién es?** Coloque (*Place*) sus fotos en la clase de acuerdo con las instrucciones del profesor/de la profesora. Luego pregunte a un compañero/una compañera quién es el sujeto de cada foto.

**MODELO:** E1: *¿Quién es este/ese/aquel hombre?* (según la distancia de la foto de E1)

E2: *Este/Ese/Aquel hombre es Antonio Banderas.* (según la distancia de la foto de E2)

**5-31 En una mueblería en Managua.** Usted y su compañero/a van a hacer los papeles de dos amigos/as nicaragüenses que deciden vivir juntos/as. Van a una mueblería para comprar muebles y accesorios. Usen las palabras y frases para hablar sobre lo que ven. Sigan el modelo.

| | | |
|---|---|---|
| bonito/a | feo/a | (no) me gusta(n) |
| caro/a | me encanta(n) | |

**MODELO:** E1: *¿Te gusta el sofá?*
E2: *¿Cuál? ¿Aquel sofá verde?*
E1: *No, ese sofá azul.*
E2: *Sí, me encanta.* O *No, es muy feo.*

**5-32 Descripciones.** Cada uno de ustedes va a pensar en tres objetos o muebles y va a decir en qué parte de la casa están. Su compañero/a va a hacerle preguntas para adivinar qué mueble u objeto es.

**MODELO:** E1: *Este mueble está generalmente en el comedor.*
E2: *¿Es grande?*
E1: *Puede ser grande o pequeño.*
E2: *¿Lo usamos para comer?*
E1: *Sí.*
E2: *Es la mesa.*

---

### SITUACIONES

1. **Role A.** You have a good job and want to move to a nicer apartment. The property manager of several apartment complexes has already shown you pictures of one apartment (**ese apartamento**) and is now showing you pictures of a second one (**este apartamento**). Discuss with the property manager a) the rent (**el alquiler**); b) the number of rooms; and c) the facilities, such as laundry room (**lavandería**), garage, and pool, of both apartments. Say which of the two apartments you want to see and explain why.

   **Role B.** You are the property manager of several apartment complexes. You have already shown your client pictures of one apartment (**ese apartamento**) and now are showing pictures of a second one (**este apartamento**). Answer his/her questions by saying that a) the rent of the first apartment is $900 dollars per month and the second one is $1,100; b) both apartments have two bedrooms; and c) the first apartment comes with a one-car garage, while this one has a two-car garage. Also tell him/her the advantages of each of the two apartments.

2. **Role A.** You are in a car with a real estate agent, who is showing you some houses for sale in the neighborhood where you hope to live. You are interested in knowing more about one house on the side of the street closer to you (**esta casa**), another house on other side of the street (**esa casa**), and a third house (**aquella casa**) a couple of blocks away.

   **Role B.** You are a real estate agent driving with a client who is interested in three houses. Answer the client's questions about the three houses.

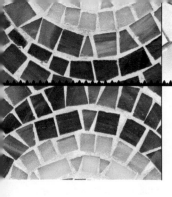

# MOSAICOS

## A escuchar

### Antes de escuchar

**5-33 Preparación.** Usted va a escuchar la descripción de una casa. Antes de escuchar, piense en las casas que conoce y haga una lista de cuatro cuartos y de tres objetos (muebles, aparatos eléctricos o accesorios) que usted espera encontrar en cada uno de los cuartos.

### Escuchar

**5-34 ¿Comprende usted?** Now, look at the following drawing, and as you hear the different statements about the location of pieces of furniture and objects, mark (✓) the appropriate column to indicate whether each of the statements is true (**Cierto**) or false (**Falso**).

CD 2
Track 31
or CD 3
Track 6

| | CIERTO | FALSO |
|---|---|---|
| 1. | —— | —— |
| 2. | —— | —— |
| 3. | —— | —— |
| 4. | —— | —— |
| 5. | —— | —— |
| 6. | —— | —— |
| 7. | —— | —— |
| 8. | —— | —— |

### Después de escuchar

**5-35 Ahora usted.** Describa su vivienda (número de cuartos, colores, muebles, etc.) a un compañero/una compañera. Él/Ella va a tomar notas para describirle su casa a otra persona de la clase. Verifique si la información es correcta. Luego, intercambien roles.

178

# A conversar

## Antes de conversar

**5-36 Preparación.** Usted necesita alquilar un apartamento. Escriba algunas características esenciales y algunas secundarias del apartamento que usted necesita.

## Conversar

**5-37 Entre nosotros.** Usted y su mejor amigo/a estudian en San Salvador este año y quieren alquilar un apartamento. Van a conversar por teléfono sobre unos apartamentos que se anuncian en el periódico.

**PRIMERA FASE.** Trabajando individualmente, piense en las características esenciales y secundarias de un buen apartamento. Lea los anuncios y decida qué apartamento prefiere. Organice mentalmente lo que va a decir. Luego, piense en el lenguaje que va a usar para expresarse y para negociar con su amigo/a, por ejemplo, *en mi opinión...*, *entiendo tu punto de vista pero...*, *(no) estoy de acuerdo porque...*

### ALQUILERES

1. Se alquila condominio residencial privado, 3er nivel, 2 dormitorios, 1 baño, cuarto y baño empleada, cocina con despensa, sala y comedor separados, garaje 2 carros, área recreación niños. SVC 4.500 vigilancia incluida. 22 24 46 30.

2. Alquilo apartamento cerca de centro comercial. Transporte público a la puerta. Ideal para profesionales. 1 dormitorio, 1 baño con jacuzzi, con muebles y electrodomésticos, terraza, sistema de seguridad, garaje doble. SVC 7.500. Tfno. 22 65 16 92.

3. Alquilo apartamento, cerca zona universitaria. 3 dormitorios. 1ra planta. Ideal para estudiantes. (SVC 1.800) Contactar al 22 35 37 83.

4. Alquilo preciosa habitación en casa particular. Semi-amueblada. Amplia, enorme clóset, cable gratis. Alimentación opcional. Información al teléfono 22 63 28 07.

**SEGUNDA FASE.** Hable con su amigo/a por teléfono para llegar a un acuerdo sobre el apartamento que los/las dos quieren alquilar. En su conversación, pueden referirse a algunos de los siguientes temas: el alquiler, la localización, el número de habitaciones y baños, si tiene muebles o no, si tiene aire acondicionado/calefacción.

## Después de conversar

**5-38 Un poco más.** Ya que usted y su compañero/a saben qué apartamento les gusta más, tienen que dar el próximo paso (*next step*). Conversen para decidir lo siguiente:

1. ¿Por qué es este apartamento el favorito de ustedes?
2. ¿Qué preguntas quieren hacerle al dueño del apartamento para obtener más información?

Tomen apuntes, porque van a presentar sus ideas a la clase.

**ESTRATEGIA**

**Plan what you want to say**

Speaking consists of more than knowing the words and structures you need. You also have to know what you want to say. Planning what you want to say—both the information you want to ask for or convey and the language you will need to express yourself—before you start to speak will make your speech more accurate and also more coherent.

**En directo**

To find out who is answering your call:

**¿Con quién hablo?** *With whom am I speaking?*

To request to talk with someone specific:

**¿Está... [nombre de la persona], por favor?** *Is . . . [person's name] there, please?*

**Deseo hablar con... [nombre de la persona].** *I would like to speak with . . . [person's name].*

# A leer

## Antes de leer

**5-39 Preparación.** Muchas casas modernas tienen los aparatos que aparecen en la siguiente lista. Para cada función, escriba el/los aparato(s) correspondiente(s).

| | |
|---|---|
| aire acondicionado central | red (*network*) inalámbrica |
| música ambiental en todos los cuartos | reproductor de DVD |
| computadora | sensor de temperatura |
| fotocopiadora | teléfono |
| lámpara | televisor |
| microondas | ventilador |

**FUNCIÓN**                                                                 **APARATOS**

1. para trabajar desde (*from*) casa                    _____
2. para hacer trabajos domésticos                     _____
3. para controlar la temperatura de la casa     _____
4. para comunicarse con otras personas           _____
5. para entretenerse (*have fun*) en casa           _____

## Leer

**5-40 Primera mirada.** El siguiente artículo describe la casa del futuro. Léalo y pase un marcador (*highlighter*) por las palabras en cada párrafo que se asocian con tecnología.

**Segunda mirada.** Lea el artículo otra vez y haga lo siguiente.

1. En el primer párrafo, el autor del artículo da una definición de una casa inteligente. Escriba la definición.
2. El segundo párrafo contrasta la casa inteligente con la casa tradicional. ¿Cuál es la diferencia? Escríbala.
3. El segundo párrafo también indica algunas formas en que la casa inteligente ayuda a las personas que viven en ella. Indique una función útil para una persona de su familia. ¿Por qué es útil?
4. En el tercer párrafo, se mencionan algunas de las funciones múltiples de los aparatos eléctricos y electrónicos. ¿Cuál de estas funciones múltiples es más beneficiosa para un/a estudiante? ¿Por qué?
5. En el cuarto párrafo se explica cómo la tecnología ayuda a los miembros de la familia a mantenerse en contacto (to *stay in touch*). ¿A su familia le gustaría (*would like*) usar esta tecnología?
6. En el quinto párrafo se mencionan algunos beneficios de la tecnología para divertirse en casa. ¿Cuál de las opciones le gusta más?
7. En el último párrafo, el autor introduce una duda sobre los beneficios de la casa del futuro. Subraye la frase donde se introduce la duda.

# La casa inteligente del futuro

Las casas inteligentes o automatizadas ya existen en el presente. Tienen un gran número de aparatos eléctricos y electrónicos, controlados por una computadora, que se comunican entre ellos. Pero, ¿cuáles son las diferencias entre una casa tradicional y una inteligente?

Básicamente, la casa inteligente incorpora los últimos avances tecnológicos en beneficio de las personas que viven en ella. A través de complejos dispositivos[1] y sensores, estas casas facilitan el trabajo doméstico de sus dueños: abren y cierran cortinas y puertas, hacen funcionar electrodomésticos (microondas, ventiladores, etc.), el aire acondicionado y la calefacción central, por ejemplo. Los sensores también controlan el movimiento de unos robots móviles que limpian las alfombras y los pisos y, en el patio, limpian la piscina y cortan el césped.

Además, la casa inteligente ofrece un uso más eficiente y múltiple de los aparatos eléctricos y electrónicos en su interior. Un microondas se puede usar para calentar comida y también para ver televisión. De la misma manera, un refrigerador puede conectarse a Internet y permitir a una persona navegar por la Red o enviar mensajes electrónicos.

La casa inteligente del futuro facilita también las relaciones entre los miembros de la familia. Por ejemplo, cuando los miembros de la familia no están juntos, pueden reunirse para cenar o para pasar tiempo juntos, gracias a las tecnologías de videoconferencia en Internet. Con el video y la voz sobre IP, los miembros de la familia en todo el mundo pueden conversar, interactuar y cenar juntos de forma virtual.

La sala en la casa inteligente es el centro de entretenimiento, donde todos los dispositivos están conectados a la red inalámbrica central. Los juegos bajo demanda están disponibles[2] a través de la televisión de banda ancha[3] y satélite. Las películas de alta definición, la televisión sin anuncios y el contenido digital a petición[4] son normales. También es normal distribuir música y películas a cada habitación de la casa desde el servidor central.

En resumen, la casa del futuro es una versión técnicamente más sofisticada de la casa del presente. Es difícil predecir con exactitud cómo vamos a vivir dentro de 50 años. Sin embargo, muchos se preguntan si esta abundancia de tecnología va a afectar nuestra vida positiva o negativamente.

---

[1]*devices*  [2]*available*  [3]*broadband*  [4]*on demand*

## Después de leer

**5-41 Ampliación.** PRIMERA FASE. Lea la siguiente nota que el arquitecto de una casa inteligente le escribe a uno de sus colegas. Complete los espacios en blanco con la palabra adecuada.

| | | |
|---|---|---|
| funcionar | juegos bajo demanda | tecnológicos |
| funciones | películas de alta definición | urgentemente |
| inteligente | sensores | ventanas |

---

Manolo,

¡Te tengo una gran sorpresa! El diseñador (*designer*) Óscar de la Renta necesita (1) _____ construir una casa (2) _____ en Managua. Como sabes, de la Renta es muy rico y quiere los últimos avances (3) _____ en ella. Desea una casa con dispositivos para abrir y cerrar puertas y (4) _____ . También quiere incorporar electrodomésticos con (5) _____ múltiples. Quiere calefacción controlada por (6) _____ . Desde luego (*Of course*) quiere un centro de entretenimiento que le permita mirar (7) _____ y recibir programación digital y (8) _____ . Tú sabes mucho de sistemas automatizados y yo de construcción, y pienso que eres la persona ideal para ayudarme en este proyecto. Vamos a darle una casa espectacular. Todo va a (9) _____ perfectamente.

Debemos responder pronto. Llámame.

Ricardo

---

 **SEGUNDA FASE.** Ahora comparen sus propias viviendas con la casa inteligente de la lectura. Hablen de la tecnología, los electrodomésticos y los aparatos electrónicos.

# A escribir

## Antes de escribir

**5-42 Preparación.** PRIMERA FASE. El periódico *La Prensa* de Tegucigalpa, Honduras, invita al público a participar en el concurso (*contest*) *La casa automatizada del futuro.* Uno de los requisitos del concurso es escribir un panfleto, según se explica en el anuncio del periódico.

---

El diario *La Prensa* invita al público a participar en el concurso *La casa automatizada del futuro.*

**Bases del concurso:**

Los participantes deben enviar la siguiente información por correo electrónico al Comité de Selección de *La casa automatizada del futuro*:

1. información personal: nombre completo, dirección, teléfono y dirección de correo electrónico
2. un panfleto descriptivo de la casa automatizada con la siguiente información:
   a. tamaño de la casa en pies (*feet*) o metros cuadrados (*square meters*)
   b. número y nombre de las habitaciones
   c. aparatos eléctricos y electrónicos de la casa y sus funciones
   d. dispositivos y sensores y su(s) función(es)
3. si es posible, un dibujo o foto digital de la casa automatizada

Fecha límite: el 30 de marzo

Premio: Una computadora portátil de último modelo y alta resolución, con programas de alta capacidad y funcionalidad.

---

SEGUNDA FASE. Usted decide participar en el concurso con un proyecto excepcional. Para preparar su proyecto para el comité que selecciona a los ganadores (*winners*), tenga en cuenta las bases del concurso y tome notas de los puntos 1, 2 y 3 que aparecen en el anuncio.

## Escribir

**5-43 Manos a la obra.** Ahora prepare su panfleto. Para hacer la descripción de *La casa automatizada del futuro*, use sus ideas de la *Segunda fase* de la actividad **5-42**. Recuerde incluir toda la información que pide el concurso. Considere la cantidad de información necesaria y el tono apropiado para sus lectores, los miembros del Comité de Selección. ¡Buena suerte!

## Después de escribir

**5-44 Revisión.** Antes de presentar su panfleto, revise:

1. primero, la claridad de sus ideas
2. la cantidad y la sofisticación de la información dada
3. lo apropiado del tono (impersonal, serio) para un comité de periodistas
4. la precisión gramatical (el vocabulario común y corriente y el vocabulario más técnico, las estructuras que utiliza para describir, la concordancia, etc.)
5. finalmente, la ortografía y la acentuación

**Select the appropriate content and tone for a formal description**

To write a description using a formal tone, you will need to do the following:

- Anticipate what your audience may know about the topic, including relevant details.
- Adapt the language of your text to the level of your readership. For example, if you are writing about technology for computer experts, you do not have to explain basic terms like *servidor* or *voz sobre IP*. Focus on the amount and kind of information your readers will need.
- Use an impersonal and formal tone. If you wish to address your reader(s) directly, use **usted/ustedes**.

# ENFOQUE CULTURAL

## La geografía espectacular de Nicaragua, El Salvador y Honduras

Una característica de la geografía de Nicaragua, El Salvador y Honduras es la gran cantidad de volcanes que hay en estos países. En realidad, toda la región centroamericana del Pacífico es rica en volcanes. Algunos son grandes montañas de una belleza impresionante; algunos están activos y producen explosiones de lava o ceniza; otros, en cambio, no tienen actividad volcánica notable. Algunos son muy viejos, otros, en cambio, como el Volcán de Cerro Negro, que nació en 1850, son relativamente jóvenes.

Muchos volcanes tienen una actividad constante que consiste en pequeñas explosiones internas, expulsión de gases y temblores de tierra que los humanos no perciben, pero que se pueden medir usando instrumentos científicos. Algunas veces, esa actividad normal aumenta sin presentar un peligro inmediato. Sin embargo, los científicos y el gobierno se preocupan cuando esto ocurre. El volcán de San Cristóbal, por ejemplo, tuvo un aumento importante (pero no peligroso) de su actividad normal en mayo de 2006.

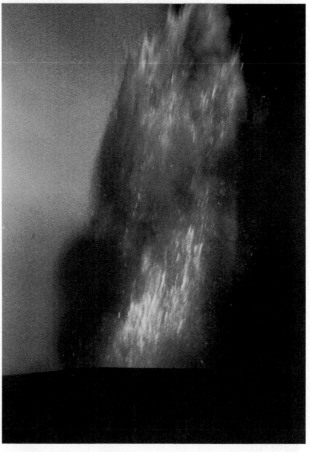

El volcán Cerro Negro de Nicaragua durante una explosión en 1995

Otra característica importante de toda la región centroamericana es la propensión a producir terremotos. Managua, la capital de Nicaragua, constantemente se ve afectada por grandes terremotos. En 1931, por ejemplo, un terremoto destruyó muchos edificios y causó la muerte de más de mil personas. También en 1972, un terremoto destruyó una gran parte del centro de esta ciudad, como muestra la foto. El 13 de enero de 2001, un violento terremoto mató a más de 700 personas y dejó a más de medio millón de personas sin casa en El Salvador. Y el 13 de febrero de 2001, un terremoto de 6,6 de intensidad destruyó en El Salvador más de 30.000 casas y dejó más de 300 muertos.

El terremoto de 1972 destruyó muchas casas del centro de Managua.

Finalmente, esta región también se caracteriza por ser muy montañosa y por tener selvas y playas espectaculares. El Salvador, por ejemplo, aunque es el país más densamente poblado de las Américas, tiene montañas, selvas y playas naturales de gran belleza. Las playas salvadoreñas del Pacífico son bellísimas y son un paraíso para los aficionados al surfing. Más del 80% del terreno de Honduras consiste de montañas, pero tiene también selvas. Honduras es uno de los países con mayor biodiversidad, porque tiene muchas especies diferentes de plantas y animales.

Gustavo Estrasser en una competencia en La Libertad, El Salvador

**En otras palabras**

Expresiones nicaragüenses

Él es **ñeque**.
*He is strong/vigorous.*

Ella **está jalando** con Luis.
*She is Luis's girlfriend.*

Ese **chavalo** es terrible.
*That kid is terrible.*

**En otras palabras**

Expresiones salvadoreñas

María **chinea** a su hijo.
*María holds her child in her arms continuously.*

Sólo es un **cipote**.
*He is only a child.*

—¿Vas a la playa mañana?
*—Are you going to the beach tomorrow?*

—**Primero** Dios.
*—God willing.*

**En otras palabras**

Expresiones hondureñas

Parece que José **me agarró de ojo de gallo**.
*It looks like José has ill will towards me.*

¿Qué está haciendo ese **güirro**?
*What is that child doing?*

**5-45 Comprensión.** PRIMERA FASE. **Reconocimiento de palabras clave.** Encuentre en el texto la palabra o expresión que mejor expresa el significado de las siguientes ideas.

1. ash                    _____
2. increases              _____
3. danger                 _____
4. earthquakes            _____
5. mountainous            _____
6. jungles                _____
7. paradise               _____

SEGUNDA FASE. **Oraciones importantes.** Subraye las afirmaciones que contienen ideas que se encuentran en el texto. Luego indique en qué parte del texto están.

1. Many volcanoes in this region are located near the Pacific Ocean.
2. Some volcanoes are amazingly beautiful.
3. One can find some young volcanoes in this region.
4. Volcanoes are dangerous, and people are afraid of them.
5. Most volcanoes are always active, although people may not be able to feel it.
6. Although small increments in volcano activity are not dangerous, scientists usually worry about them.
7. Central America is prone to earthquakes.
8. Earthquakes and volcanoes have destroyed the biodiversity of the surrounding area.

TERCERA FASE. **Ideas principales.** Escriba un párrafo breve en inglés resumiendo las ideas principales expresadas en el texto.

 **5-46 Use la información.** Usted tiene $300.000 dólares y quiere comprar una casa en Nicaragua, Honduras o El Salvador. Siguiendo los enlaces, busque la mejor casa, apartamento o propiedad rural que puede comprar con ese dinero. Prepare un afiche (*poster*) para mostrar en la clase. Debe incluir: localización, tipo de propiedad, características más importantes de la propiedad y su precio. Incluya también información adicional de interés para usted. Para preparar esta actividad, visite la página web de *Mosaicos* y siga los enlaces útiles.

# VOCABULARIO

**La arquitectura** — *Architecture*

| | |
|---|---|
| el alquiler | *rent* |
| el apartamento | *apartment* |
| el edificio | *building* |
| el estilo | *style* |
| las ruinas | *ruins* |
| la vivienda | *housing* |

**En una casa** — *In a home*

| | |
|---|---|
| el aire acondicionado | *air conditioning* |
| el armario | *closet, armoire* |
| el baño | *bathroom* |
| la basura | *garbage, trash* |
| la calefacción | *heating* |
| la chimenea | *fireplace* |
| la cocina | *kitchen* |
| el comedor | *dining room* |
| el cuarto | *room; bedroom* |
| la escalera | *stairs* |
| el garaje | *garage* |
| la habitación | *bedroom* |
| la lavandería | *laundry room* |
| el pasillo | *corridor, hall* |
| la piscina | *swimming pool* |
| el piso | *floor; apartment* |
| la planta baja | *first floor, ground floor* |
| la sala | *living room* |
| la terraza | *terrace* |

**Los muebles y accesorios** — *Furniture and accessories*

| | |
|---|---|
| la alfombra | *carpet, rug* |
| la butaca | *armchair* |
| la cama | *bed* |
| la cómoda | *dresser* |
| la cortina | *curtain* |
| el cuadro | *picture, painting* |
| el espejo | *mirror* |
| la lámpara | *lamp* |
| el sofá | *sofa* |

**Los electrodomésticos** — *Appliances*

| | |
|---|---|
| la aspiradora | *vacuum cleaner* |
| la lavadora | *washer* |
| el lavaplatos | *dishwasher* |
| el (horno) microondas | *microwave (oven)* |
| el/la radio | *radio* |
| el refrigerador | *refrigerator* |
| la secadora | *dryer* |
| el ventilador | *fan* |

**Para la cama** — *For the bed*

| | |
|---|---|
| la almohada | *pillow* |
| la manta | *blanket* |
| la sábana | *sheet* |

**En el baño** — *In the bathroom*

| | |
|---|---|
| la bañera | *bathtub* |
| la ducha | *shower* |
| el inodoro | *toilet* |
| el jabón | *soap* |
| el lavabo | *bathroom sink* |
| la toalla | *towel* |

**En la cocina** — *In the kitchen*

| | |
|---|---|
| la estufa | *stove* |
| el fregadero | *kitchen sink* |
| el plato | *dish, plate* |

**En el jardín** — *In the garden*

| | |
|---|---|
| la barbacoa | *barbecue pit; barbecue (event)* |
| el césped | *lawn* |
| la hoja | *leaf* |

**Los lugares** — *Places*

| | |
|---|---|
| las afueras | *outskirts* |
| el barrio | *neighborhood* |
| la calle | *street* |
| el centro | *downtown, center* |
| cerca (de) | *near, close (to)* |
| lejos (de) | *far (from)* |
| el pueblo | *village* |
| la zona | *area* |

**Las descripciones** — *Descriptions*

| | |
|---|---|
| limpio/a | *clean* |
| ordenado/a | *tidy* |
| seco/a | *dry* |
| sucio/a | *dirty* |

**Verbos** — *Verbs*

| | |
|---|---|
| ayudar | *to help* |
| barrer | *to sweep* |
| cocinar | *to cook* |
| cortar | *to cut; to mow (lawn)* |
| creer | *to believe* |
| doblar | *to fold* |
| limpiar | *to clean* |
| ordenar | *to tidy up* |
| pasar la aspiradora | *to vacuum* |
| planchar | *to iron* |
| preparar | *to prepare* |
| recoger (j) | *to pick up* |
| regar (ie) | *to water* |
| sacar | *to take out* |
| tender (ie) | *to hang (clothes)* |

**Palabras útiles** — *Useful words*

| | |
|---|---|
| la desventaja | *disadvantage* |
| el trabajo | *work* |
| la ventaja | *advantage* |
| la vista | *view* |

See page 157 for ordinal numbers.
See *Lengua* box on page 160 for more electronic items.
See page 167 for expressions with **tener**.
See page 171 for direct object pronouns.
See pages 175–176 for demonstrative adjectives and pronouns.

# De compras

Simón Bolívar (1783-1830), nacido en Caracas, Venezuela, es un héroe de la independencia latinoamericana.

# In this chapter you will learn how to:

- talk about clothing, prices, and shopping
- talk about past events
- express likes and dislikes

## Cultural focus: **Venezuela**

Mar Caribe

Islas
Los Roques

Isla
Margarita

OCÉANO
ATLÁNTICO

La industria del petróleo

Maracaibo
Barquisimeto

Valencia

Caracas
✳

Barcelona

Maturín

Lago
Maracaibo

CORDILLERA DE MÉRIDA

Mérida

Río Orinoco

Ciudad
Bolívar

Ciudad
Guayana

La moderna ciudad de Caracas

**VENEZUELA**

Las hayacas,
un plato típico venezolano

Puerto
Ayachucho

Salto Ángel

GUYANA

COLOMBIA

El pájaro turpial,
símbolo de Venezuela

Salto Ángel

BRASIL

 **A vista de pájaro.** Piense en lo que sabe de Venezuela e indique si la afirmación es cierta (**C**) o falsa (**F**).

1. ___ Venezuela es una república independiente.
2. ___ La fauna de Venezuela es muy variada.
3. ___ El río Amazonas pasa por Venezuela.
4. ___ El petróleo es la industria más importante de Venezuela.
5. ___ Caracas está cerca del océano Pacífico.
6. ___ Panamá está al sur de Venezuela.

## ◀)) Las compras

CD 3
Track 19

En este **centro comercial venden** de todo. Hay **tiendas** de **ropa** y de **zapatos**. También hay **tiendas** de muebles y accesorios para la casa, hay librerías, tiendas de **juguetes** para los niños e incluso hay un **supermercado**.

Muchas personas **van de compras** a los **mercados** al aire libre. Este es un mercado de la calle en Sabana Grande, Venezuela. En los mercados tradicionales venden **telas**, objetos de **artesanía, joyas, bolsos**, etc., pero a veces también hay discos, aparatos electrónicos y otras **cosas** para la casa.

En los mercados tradicionales los turistas a veces compran **regalos** para su familia y sus amigos. A esta señora le gustan las joyas artesanales. Ella compra un **collar** de **plata** para su mejor amiga, una **pulsera** para su hermana, unos **aretes** para su hija y un **anillo** de **oro** para sí misma (*herself*).

## De compras

CD 3
Track 20 José Manuel va a un **almacén** a comprar un regalo para su novia. Él necesita la ayuda de la dependienta.

DEPENDIENTA: **¿En qué puedo servirle?**

JOSÉ MANUEL: **Quisiera** comprar un regalo para mi novia. Un bolso o una **billetera**, por ejemplo.

DEPENDIENTA: Hay unos bolsos de **cuero** preciosos y no son muy **caros**. **Enseguida** le **muestro** los que tenemos.

[La dependienta trae unos bolsos.]

JOSÉ MANUEL: No sé. M**e gustaría** comprar este bolso, pero no puedo **gastar** mucho. ¿Cuánto cuesta?

DEPENDIENTA: Sólo **vale** 80 bolívares. Es bastante **barato**.

JOSÉ MANUEL: Sí, no es mucho **dinero**. Es un buen **precio**.

DEPENDIENTA: Y **están** muy **de moda**. Las chicas jóvenes los **llevan** mucho.

JOSÉ MANUEL: Bueno, lo voy a comprar.

DEPENDIENTA: Muy bien, señor. ¿Va a **pagar** con **tarjeta de crédito** o **en efectivo**?

JOSÉ MANUEL: En efectivo.

**6-1 ¿Adónde van?** Las siguientes personas necesitan comprar algunas cosas. Indique a qué tienda deben ir.

1. ___ María necesita unos libros para su clase de literatura.
2. ___ Juan quisiera cocinar comida venezolana para sus amigos.
3. ___ Rosa piensa comprar unos regalos para sus sobrinos.
4. ___ Felipe necesita una cómoda para su cuarto.
5. ___ Olga necesita unos zapatos nuevos para una entrevista de trabajo.
6. ___ Catalina va a comprar un collar elegante para ir a una fiesta.

a. mueblería
b. juguetería
c. zapatería
d. supermercado
e. joyería
f. librería

---

### Lengua

To soften requests, Spanish uses the forms **me gustaría** (instead of **me gusta**) and **quisiera** (instead of **quiero**). English does this with the phrase *would like*.

**Me gustaría/Quisiera** ir a ese almacén.
*I would like to go to that department store.*

---

**6-2 ¿Qué tienen que hacer?** Ustedes tienen que hacer muchas cosas esta semana. Hablen de lo que necesitan comprar y decidan a qué tiendas van a ir.

MODELO: planear nuestro viaje a Venezuela
*Necesitamos comprar un billete de avión para Caracas. Vamos a ir a una agencia de viajes.*

1. preparar un postre para la fiesta de Jaime
2. hacer un regalo para mi novio/a por su cumpleaños
3. entretener a mi sobrino de cinco años
4. comprar zapatos para mi viaje
5. amueblar el comedor de mi apartamento
6. leer una novela divertida

**6-3 En el mercado tradicional.** PRIMERA FASE. Túrnense para comprar unos recuerdos (*souvenirs*) en un mercado tradicional en Caracas. Pregunten el precio de los siguientes productos. Regateen (*haggle*) para obtener un precio más barato.

cuadros de Venezuela · bolsas de cuero · platos de artesanía · aretes · collares · anillos · casas en miniatura · joyas · pulseras

MODELO:  E1:  *Quisiera comprar este cuadro ¿Cuánto cuesta?*
E2:  *Cuesta 50 bolívares.*
E1:  *¡Uy, es muy caro! Lo compro por 38.*
E2:  *Pero, es muy bonito. Tiene colores muy alegres.*
E1:  *Sí, es muy bonito, pero no tengo suficiente dinero.*
E2:  *Bueno, está bien. Lo vendo por 40.*

SEGUNDA FASE. Ahora está con su mejor amigo/a (otro compañero/otra compañera). Muéstrele sus compras y explique:

1. qué es
2. para quién lo compra
3. cuánto cuesta

MODELO:  *Esto es un collar de plata para mi prima Isabel. Cuesta 35 bolívares.*

# La ropa

CD 3
Track 21

**La ropa formal**  **La ropa informal**  **La ropa interior y de estar en casa**

la sudadera
la blusa
la camiseta
la bata
las pantimedias
el traje de chaqueta
la camisa
la corbata
el camisón
el saco
el/la piyama
el pañuelo
el cinturón
los pantalones
el sostén
el impermeable
la falda
los calzoncillos
los zapatos
las medias/los calcetines
las zapatillas
**Roberto**  **Marisa**  **Miguel**  **Sonia**  los vaqueros/los jeans
el paraguas  las zapatillas  las sandalias
los zapatos de tacón  de deporte

## 6-4 ¿Cuándo se usa? Indique qué prenda(s) (*article[s]*) de vestir se usa(n) en cada situación.

1. Para ir a correr o al gimnasio nos ponemos (*put on*) _____.
2. Para ir a dormir llevamos (*wear*) _____.
3. Para ir a una fiesta nos ponemos _____.
4. Después de bañarnos y antes de vestirnos nos ponemos _____.

# Telas y diseño

CD 3
Track 22

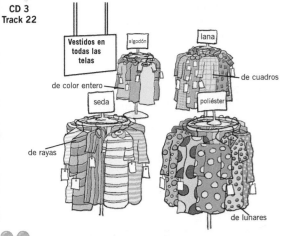

Vestidos en todas las telas
algodón
lana
de color entero
de cuadros
seda
poliéster
de rayas
de lunares

## 6-5 ¿Qué ropa llevan? PRIMERA FASE. Túrnense para describir la ropa que llevan algunas personas de la clase y adivinen (*guess*) quiénes son.

**SEGUNDA FASE.** Cuenten (*Count*) cuántas personas de la clase llevan los siguientes accesorios y prendas de vestir. Después comparen sus números.

1. aretes en las orejas _____
2. anillos en las manos _____
3. zapatillas de deporte _____
4. camisas de cuadros _____
5. camisas de color entero _____
6. vestidos o faldas _____

---

### En otras palabras

Some words referring to clothing differ from one region to another. For example, in Spain **el/la piyama** is **el pijama**, **medias** means *stockings*, but in some countries of Latin America it also means *socks*. Depending on the country, the words **aros**, **aretes**, **pendientes**, **pantallas**, or **zarcillos** are used for *earrings*. In Argentina and Uruguay **pollera** is used instead of **falda**.

### Lengua

Here is some useful vocabulary for the body (**el cuerpo**): **la cabeza** (*head*), **las orejas** (*ears*), **la nariz** (*nose*), **los brazos** (*arms*), **las manos** (*hands*), **las piernas** (*legs*), **los pies** (*feet*). You will learn more words related to parts of the body in *Capítulo 11*.

## Las rebajas

CD 3
Track 23

MARTA: Las **rebajas** son **magníficas**. Mira esa falda de rayas. Está **rebajada** de 60 bolívares a 50. ¿Por qué no vemos si tienen tu **talla**?

ANA: Sí, y **me pruebo** la falda para ver si **me queda** bien. Uso la talla 38 y a veces es difícil **encontrarla**. Esta falda es de algodón y es **preciosa**.

MARTA: O te pruebas la falda en casa y si te queda mal, la **cambias**.

[**Entran en** la tienda.]

ANA: Buenos días, señorita, **quisiera** probarme la falda que está en **el escaparate** en la talla 38.

DEPENDIENTA: Lo siento, pero las únicas tallas que **nos quedan** son más grandes, la 42 y la 44.

ANA: ¡Qué lástima! Gracias.

Le queda **estrecha**.   Le queda **ancha**.

La chaqueta y la falda están **rebajadas**.

**6-6 La falda de rayas.** Describa la experiencia de Ana, buscando la afirmación de la derecha que lógicamente se asocia con la afirmación de la izquierda.

1. ___ Ana necesita una falda en la talla 38.
2. ___ La falda no es de color entero.
3. ___ Ana prefiere las telas naturales.
4. ___ Ana entra en la tienda, pero no se prueba la falda.
5. ___ La falda no es muy cara.
6. ___ Marta dice que Ana debe cambiar la falda.

a. La dependienta dice que no tienen su talla.
b. Está rebajada.
c. Sabe que la talla 42 le va a quedar ancha.
d. Como no la va a comprar, no la va a cambiar.
e. Es de rayas.
f. Le gusta la falda porque es de algodón.

**6-7 El cumpleaños de Nuria.** Ustedes van a una tienda para comprarle un regalo a una buena amiga, pero cada artículo que ven presenta un problema. Piensen en la solución.

| ARTÍCULO | PROBLEMA | SOLUCIÓN |
|---|---|---|
| collar | Es muy caro. | *Debemos buscar uno más barato.* |
| impermeable | Le queda ancho. | |
| vaqueros | Son de poliéster. | |
| sudadera | Es pequeña. | |
| blusa | Las rayas son muy anchas. | |
| bolso | No es de cuero. | |

# ◀)) ¿Qué debo llevar?

CD 3
Track 24 En el **invierno** hace frío. ¿Qué ropa llevamos?

Cuando hace calor en el **verano,** ¿qué nos ponemos para ir a la playa?

Y cuando llueve en la **primavera** y en el **otoño,** usamos impermeable y paraguas.

**6-8 ¿Frío o calor?** Indique cuándo se usa la siguiente ropa, asociando las palabras de la izquierda con la oración más lógica de la derecha.

1. ___ los guantes
2. ___ el traje de baño
3. ___ las botas
4. ___ el suéter
5. ___ los pantalones cortos
6. ___ el sombrero

**a.** Sirve para protegernos del sol.
**b.** Los llevamos en las manos cuando hace frío.
**c.** Son más cómodos cuando hace buen tiempo.
**d.** Nos lo ponemos para ir a la playa.
**e.** Es de lana, para llevar cuando hace frío.
**f.** Las llevamos en los pies en invierno.

**6-9 Vacaciones en Venezuela.** PRIMERA FASE. Usted y su amigo/a van a pasar sus vacaciones en Venezuela. Primero escojan el plan que más les interesa de las siguientes opciones.

1. Quince días en Isla Margarita. Por el día: ir a la playa; por la noche: ir a las discotecas.
2. Tomar un curso de verano en la Universidad Central de Venezuela en Caracas. Por la mañana: clases de español; por las tardes: lugares de interés turístico.
3. Explorar la fauna y flora de la región de Canaima. Por el día: caminar mucho; por las noches: estar en un campamento.

**SEGUNDA FASE.** Ahora, preparen una lista de la ropa y accesorios que van a necesitar para su plan de vacaciones.

| PLAN #____ | YO | MI COMPAÑERO/A |
|---|---|---|
| por la mañana | | |
| por la tarde | | |
| por la noche | | |

**TERCERA FASE.** Informen a la clase sobre sus planes y la ropa y accesorios que van a necesitar.

**MODELO:** *Vamos a ir a la ciudad venezolana de Mérida. Yo necesito unos zapatos de tenis para caminar por la ciudad. Mi compañero/a necesita unos pantalones cortos. También necesitamos suéteres porque Mérida está en las montañas.*

**6-10 Comprando ropa para todos.** Cada uno/a de ustedes debe comprar ropa para hacer unos regalos a tres personas diferentes de la lista. Expliquen para quiénes son los regalos. Su compañero/a le va a dar algunas ideas de qué comprar y el lugar donde puede comprar, según la información de los anuncios.

1. su sobrinita de 6 años
2. su mamá para el Día de la Madre
3. un amigo/una amiga que necesita ropa informal
4. un hermano que va a pasar unos días en el Caribe
5. su padre para su cumpleaños
6. su novio/a para el Día de los Enamorados

**6-11 Ropa para cada ocasión.** You will listen to a brief conversation regarding the clothes people will wear for an event. Before you listen, list what you would wear on the following occasions.

**CD 3 Track 25**

fiesta elegante _____.

fiesta informal _____

Now as you listen, indicate [✓] the clothes and event mentioned.

| ROPA | EVENTO |
|---|---|
| —— ropa elegante | —— entrevista de trabajo |
| —— falda y chaqueta | —— reunión de jóvenes |
| —— traje pantalón y blusa | —— excursión de fin de semana |
| —— pantalones cortos y camiseta | —— fiesta formal |

# EN ACCIÓN

## Diarios de bicicleta: Una camisa de moda

### Antes de ver

**6-12** En este segmento, Luciana y Gabi están preparándose para su musical. Marque (✓) los accesorios o ropa que probablemente van a llevar.

Accesorios:

___ un anillo
___ aretes
___ una bufanda
___ un collar
___ gafas de sol
___ una gorra

Ropa:

___ una falda y una blusa
___ pantalones cortos
___ una bata
___ un vestido
___ zapatos de tacón
___ una sudadera

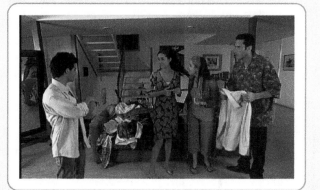

### Mientras ve

**6-13** Indique si las siguientes afirmaciones son ciertas (**C**) o falsas (**F**) según este segmento. Si son falsas (**F**), corrija la información.

1. ___ Luciana y Gabi se están probando ropa para ir a una fiesta de graduación.
2. ___ Javier va a tener una cita (*date*) con Carmen.
3. ___ Luciana y Gabi creen que Javier debe probarse ropa distinta.
4. ___ Javier necesita comprar una nueva camisa.
5. ___ Marcos cree que está muy guapo con la camisa que le da Luciana.
6. ___Gabi dice que es muy torpe (*clumsy*).

### Después de ver

**6-14** ¿Qué puede recomendar usted para resolver los siguientes problemas?

1. La falda que le gusta a Gabi es muy formal.
2. La camisa que compró Javier no está de moda.
3. Los pantalones que se prueba Javier le quedan muy anchos.

# FUNCIONES Y FORMAS

## 1. Talking about the past: Preterit tense of regular verbs

Querido diario,

Esta mañana Álvaro y yo **gastamos** mucho dinero en ropa para vernos bien en la fiesta de boda de mi cuñada Gabriela esta tarde. Yo **compré** un hermoso vestido de fiesta y un chal de encaje (*lace shawl*). Álvaro **compró** un traje, una camisa y una corbata.

A las 7:00 de la tarde, **empezó** la ceremonia religiosa. La fiesta con familia y amigos **comenzó** a las 9:00 y **terminó** a las 4:00 de la mañana. Todos **comimos**, **bailamos** y **cantamos** mucho. Vamos a recordar este día especial por mucho tiempo. Gabriela y Gonzalo son una pareja perfecta.

Ahora voy a dormir. Estoy muy cansada.
Camila

**Piénselo.** ¿Qué pasó el día de la boda? Ordene cronológicamente la siguiente información (1 = primer evento, etc.), según lo que Camila escribe en su diario.

___ La fiesta con familia y amigos **comenzó** a las 9:00.

___ Camila **compró** un hermoso vestido de fiesta y un chal de encaje.

___ La fiesta **terminó** a las 4:00 de la mañana.

___ Todos **comieron**, **bailaron** y **cantaron** mucho.

---

■ Spanish has two simple tenses to express the past: the preterit and the imperfect (**el pretérito** y **el imperfecto**). Use the preterit to talk about past events, actions, and conditions that are viewed as completed or ended.

|  | | HABLAR | COMER | VIVIR |
|---|---|---|---|---|
| | yo | habl**é** | com**í** | viv**í** |
| | tú | habl**aste** | com**iste** | viv**iste** |
| Ud., él, ella | | habl**ó** | com**ió** | viv**ió** |
| nosotros/as | | habl**amos** | com**imos** | viv**imos** |
| vosotros/as | | habl**asteis** | com**isteis** | viv**isteis** |
| Uds., ellos/as | | habl**aron** | com**ieron** | viv**ieron** |

■ Note that the **nosotros/as** forms of the preterit of **-ar** and **-ir** verbs are the same as their present tense forms. Context will help you determine if a **nosotros/as** verb form is present or past.

**Llegamos** a la tienda a las tres.
$\left\{\begin{array}{l}\textit{We arrive at the store at three.}\\\textit{We arrived at the store at three.}\end{array}\right.$

Salí de la universidad a las dos y **llegamos** a casa a las tres.
*I left the university at two and we arrived home at three.*

■ Stem-changing verbs ending in **-ar** and **-er** do not have a stem change in the preterit.

| | |
|---|---|
| **pensar:** | pensé, pensaste, pensó, pensamos, pensasteis, pensaron |
| **volver:** | volví, volviste, volvió, volvimos, volvisteis, volvieron |

■ Verbs ending in **-car** and **-gar** have a spelling change in the **yo** form of the preterit that reflects how the word is pronounced. Verbs ending in **-zar** have a spelling change in the **yo** form because Spanish rarely uses a **z** before **e** or **i**.

| | |
|---|---|
| **sacar:** | sa**qué**, sacaste, sacó… |
| **llegar:** | lle**gué**, llegaste, llegó… |
| **empezar:** | empe**cé**, empezaste, empezó… |

> ### Lengua
>
> The **yo** and the **usted/él/ella** preterit verb forms are stressed on the last syllable and end in a vowel. Therefore, they carry a written accent: **hablé, comí, viví; habló, comió, vivió.**

■ There are some expressions you can use with the preterit to denote past time.

| | | | |
|---|---|---|---|
| anoche | *last night* | la semana pasada | *last week* |
| anteayer | *day before yesterday* | una semana atrás | *a week ago* |
| ante(a)noche | *night before last* | hace un día/mes/año (que) | *it has been a day/month/ year since* |
| ayer | *yesterday* | | |
| el año/mes pasado | *last year/month* | | |

**6-15 Ayer yo…** PRIMERA FASE. Marque (✓) sus actividades de ayer y añada una actividad en cada grupo.

| POR LA MAÑANA | POR LA TARDE | POR LA NOCHE |
|---|---|---|
| ____ Desayuné. | ____ Almorcé en la cafetería. | ____ Preparé la cena. |
| ____ Llegué a tiempo a mis clases. | ____ Saqué libros de la biblioteca. | ____ Miré televisión. |
| ____ Estudié varias horas. | ____ Lavé la ropa. | ____ Planché mi ropa. |
| ____ Llamé por teléfono a un amigo/una amiga. | ____ Compré comida para toda la semana. | ____ Salí con mis amigos. |

SEGUNDA FASE. Comparen sus respuestas. ¿Tienen actividades semejantes o diferentes? Expliquen.

**6-16 El sábado pasado. PRIMERA FASE.** Miren las siguientes escenas y expliquen cómo pasaron el sábado Carmen y Rafael.

El sábado por la mañana          El sábado por la tarde

El sábado por la noche

 **SEGUNDA FASE.** Escriban un párrafo para compartir oralmente con la clase sobre el sábado pasado de Carmen y Rafael.

 **6-17 ¿Cómo pasaron el fin de semana? PRIMERA FASE.** Conversen sobre el fin de semana de ustedes.

1. ¿Cuáles fueron (*were*) las actividades de cada uno/a de ustedes?
2. ¿Dónde y con quién?
3. ¿A qué hora?
4. ¿Gastó mucho dinero? ¿Cómo lo gastó?

**SEGUNDA FASE.** Decidan qué persona de su grupo pasó el mejor fin de semana. Describan las actividades de esta persona en una presentación oral a la clase.

## SITUACIONES

1. **Role A.** You run into a classmate whose parents visited campus the previous weekend. Ask a) what day and time his/her parents arrived; b) where they ate breakfast and lunch; c) what places on campus they visited; and d) what time his/her parents left. Express your reactions to the information.

   **Role B.** Your classmate wants to know about your parents' visit to campus last weekend. Answer his/her questions in as much detail as possible. Ask if your classmate's parents are going to visit soon.

2. **Role A.** Your classmate and his/her significant other (**pareja**) went on a shopping spree last weekend. Ask a) what store(s) they shopped in; b) what each of them bought; c) what time they returned home; and d) what his/her plans are for wearing or using the items he/she bought.

   **Role B.** Answer your classmate's questions about your shopping spree with your significant other (**pareja**) over the weekend. Then find out if your classmate went shopping over the weekend, played a sport, or watched a lot of TV.

## 2. Talking about the past: Preterit of *ir* and *ser*

CLIENTA: Compré este vestido aquí el sábado pasado. Pero ahora me queda estrecho.

SUPERVISORA: ¿Quién **fue** el vendedor que le vendió el vestido, señorita?

CLIENTA: No sé su nombre, pero **fue** su compañero, un señor alto y delgado.

SUPERVISORA: ¿Qué pasó? ¿Lavó el vestido en casa?

CLIENTA: Claro que no. Hay que lavar este vestido en seco (*dry clean*). **Fui** a una lavandería (*dry cleaner*).

SUPERVISORA: Los irresponsables **fueron** los empleados de la lavandería. No limpiaron en seco su vestido. Lo lavaron.

Una semana después...

**Piénselo.** Indique si las siguientes afirmaciones son ciertas (**C**) o falsas (**F**), según la conversación entre la clienta y la supervisora.

1. ___ El vendedor **fue** el compañero de la supervisora.
2. ___ La clienta **fue** a una tienda especializada para limpiar el vestido.
3. ___ Lavar el vestido **fue** un error por parte de los empleados de la lavandería.
4. ___ La supervisora **fue** amable con la clienta porque trató de comprender el problema.
5. ___ Los vendedores de la tienda de ropa **fueron** las personas responsables del problema con el vestido.

■ The verbs **ir** and **ser** have identical forms in the preterit. They are used often in speaking and writing, and the context will help you to determine the meaning.

| IR and SER | | | |
|---|---|---|---|
| yo | **fui** | nosotros/as | **fuimos** |
| tú | **fuiste** | vosotros/as | **fuisteis** |
| Ud., él, ella | **fue** | Uds., ellos/as | **fueron** |

■ You will also be able to differentiate between **ir** and **ser** in the preterit because **ir** is often followed by the preposition **a**.

| | |
|---|---|
| Ernesto **fue** a la tienda. | *Ernesto went to the store.* |
| **Fue** vendedor en esa tienda por dos años. | *He was a salesman at that store for two years.* |

**6-18 ¿Quién fue a este lugar?** Las siguientes personas fueron a Venezuela para conocer algunos lugares, según sus intereses personales. Primero, lea cada situación y luego, relacione las fotos con cada una de ellas.

**A.** Salto Ángel

**B.** Isla Margarita

**C.** Maracaibo

**D.** El puente Angostura sobre el río Orinoco

1. ___ Andrés visitó un lugar con agua para navegar. Le fascinan los deportes acuáticos, pero no le gusta el mar.
2. ___ Alguien habló sobre este lugar espectacular y único en el mundo. Dice que es semejante a las cataratas de Niágara. Usted decidió ir para ver el lugar.
3. ___ Los estudiantes del primer año de español de su universidad fueron de viaje a una playa exótica. Allí conocieron a otros turistas de muchas partes del mundo. Hablaron mucho español y un poco de inglés.
4. ___ Los ingenieros Roberto y Angélica decidieron ir a un lugar para investigar las últimas tecnologías en el procesamiento del petróleo. Por eso, fueron a este lugar con una población de más de dos millones y medio de personas.

**6-19 ¿Quiénes fueron estas personas?** Investiguen la siguiente información sobre uno de estos famosos y hagan una breve presentación en clase.

| | | | |
|---|---|---|---|
| Alfonso X | Atahualpa | Roberto Clemente | Frida Kahlo |
| Doroteo Arango Arámbula | Simón Bolívar | Ernesto Guevara | Mario Molina |
| | Pablo Casals | Nicolás Guillén | Pablo Luis Picasso |

1. ¿Quién fue él/ella?
2. ¿Dónde nació, vivió y murió (*died*) esta persona?
3. ¿Por qué fue famoso/a? Indiquen como mínimo dos o tres hechos (*facts*) sobre su vida.

## SITUACIONES

1. **Role A.** A classmate tells you that he/she went to a concert last weekend. Ask a) where the concert was; b) what time it started; c) with whom he/she went; d) what time the concert ended; and e) where he/she went afterward. Express your reactions to the information.

   **Role B.** Your classmate wants to know about the concert you went to last weekend. Answer your classmates questions to find out if he/she went to a party or concert over the weekend, if he/she went out with friends, and so on. Ask for details about where, when, and with whom he/she went.

2. **Role A.** As part of your coursework in Spanish, you have been asked to interview a classmate to find out about the role some people may have had in his/her life. Ask a) who was an important authority figure (*figura de autoridad*) in his/her childhood (**infancia**); b) who was his/her best childhood friend; and c) who was his/her favorite teacher in elementary school (**escuela primera**). Express your reactions and ask additional questions.

   **Role B.** Your classmate will interview you to find out about some important people in your childhood (**infancia**). Answer the questions in as much detail as possible.

# 3. Indicating to whom or for whom an action takes place: Indirect object nouns and pronouns

LUCY: Oye, Panchito, ¿qué **te** compran tus padres para tu cumpleaños, ropa, chocolates o qué?

PANCHITO: No **me** dan ni ropa ni chocolates. Siempre **me** compran libros súper interesantes. Y tus padres, ¿qué **te** compran a ti, Lucy?

LUCY: Mi mamá siempre **nos** compra ropa a mi hermano y a mí. A mí **me** gusta mucho la ropa nueva.

PANCHITO: ¿Y qué **les** das tú a tus padres para sus cumpleaños?

LUCY: ¡A mi mamá **le** doy muchos besitos y a mi papá **le** doy muchos problemas porque no hago mi tarea!

**Piénselo.** Primero, identifique **quién hace** la acción: Lucy, Panchito, Lucy y su hermano, los padres de Panchito, la mamá o el papá de Lucy. Luego, en la línea de la derecha, indique **quién recibe** el beneficio de la acción.

1. _____ **le** compran libros a _____ .
2. _____ **les** compra ropa a _____ .
3. _____ **le** da muchos besos a _____ .
4. _____ **le** causa problemas a _____ porque no hace la tarea.

■ Indirect object nouns and pronouns tell *to whom* or *for whom* an action is done, in other words, who is affected by an action.

| INDIRECT OBJECT PRONOUNS | | | |
|---|---|---|---|
| **me** | *to/for me* | **nos** | *to/for us* |
| **te** | *to/for you* (familiar) | **os** | *to/for you* (familiar) |
| **le** | *to/for you* (formal), *him, her, it* | **les** | *to/for you* (formal), *them* |

■ Indirect object pronouns have the same form as direct object pronouns except in the third person: **le** and **les**.

| | |
|---|---|
| Mi madre **me** compró ropa la semana pasada. | *My mother bought me clothes last week. [My mother bought clothes for me last week.]* |
| Yo **te** presto mis zapatos para la fiesta. | *I will lend you my shoes for the party. [I will lend my shoes to you for the party.]* |
| ¿El dependiente? Ella **lo** ve todas las mañanas. (*direct object*) | *The salesperson? She sees him every morning.* |
| ¿El dependiente? Ella **le** da los recibos por la mañana. (*indirect object*) | *She gives him the receipts in the morning.* |

■ Place the indirect object pronoun before a conjugated verb form. It may be attached to a present participle, in which case an accent mark is added, or to an infinitive.

**Les** voy a vender mi carro. }
Voy a vender**les** mi carro. } *I am going to sell them my car.*

Juan **nos** está preparando la cena. }
Juan está preparándo**nos** la cena. } *Juan is preparing dinner for us.*

■ Use indirect object pronouns even when the indirect object noun is stated explicitly.

Yo **le** presté mi libro a **Victoria**.     *I lent my notes to Victoria.*

■ To eliminate ambiguity, **le** and **les** are often used with the preposition **a +** *pronoun.*

**Le** hablo **a usted**.     *I am talking to you.* (not to *him/her*)

Siempre **les** cuento mis secretos     *I always tell my secrets to them.*
  **a ellos**.     (not to *you/ustedes*)

■ For emphasis, use **a mí, a ti, a nosotros/as**, and **a vosotros/as** with indirect object pronouns.

Pedro **te** habla a **ti**.     *Pedro is talking to you.* (not to someone else)

■ **Dar** is almost always used with indirect object pronouns. Notice the difference in meaning between **dar** (*to give*) and **regalar** (*to give as a gift*). Other verbs of transmission (of things, ideas, words) that are generally used with indirect object pronouns include **decir, describir, escribir, explicar, mostrar, prestar**, and **vender**.

Ella le **da** el cinturón a Pedro.     *She gives (hands) Pedro the belt.*
Ella le **regala** el cinturón a Pedro.     *She gives Pedro the belt (as a gift).*

---

### Lengua

**Dar** uses the same endings as **-er** and **-ir** verbs in the preterit:

**di, diste, dio, dimos, disteis, dieron**

Jorge le **dio** a Elena una copia de sus apuntes. *Jorge gave Elena a copy of his notes.*

Mis padres me **dieron** dinero para la matrícula. *My parents gave me money for tuition.*

---

**6-20 La Academia de la Moda.** Ustedes están tomando una clase (Elegancia con Poco Dinero) en La Academia de la Moda. Marquen (✔) las sugerencias que su profesor les da a ustedes.

1. _____ Nos da nombres de tiendas de ropa buena y barata.
2. _____ A mí me recomienda artículos sobre la moda actual.
3. _____ Nos muestra telas que son elegantes y que no son muy caras.
4. _____ A mí me da ejemplos de cómo combinar ropa y accesorios.

**6-21 Para estar a la última moda.** Cada uno/a de ustedes desea o necesita lo que se indica en la lista a continuación. Explíquense (*to each other*) la situación. Después pidan y den una recomendación.

MODELO:   E1:  *Quiero llevar zapatos muy cómodos. ¿Qué me recomiendas?*
          E2:  *Te recomiendo unas sandalias de la marca Teva.*

1. Quiero llevar pantalones de moda (*in style*).
2. Deseo protegerme del sol.
3. Quiero ropa buena y barata.
4. Quiero verme (*look*) más delgado/a.
5. Me gustaría llevar ropa elegante y fina a la entrevista de trabajo.

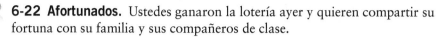

**6-22 Afortunados.** Ustedes ganaron la lotería ayer y quieren compartir su fortuna con su familia y sus compañeros de clase.

1. Hagan una lista de dos o tres miembros de su familia a quienes desean regalarles algo.
2. Indiquen el regalo que piensan hacerle a cada uno/a.

MODELO:  E1:  *A nuestros padres les vamos a regalar un crucero por el Caribe.*
      E2:  *A Sara vamos a comprarle una mochila.*

**6-23 Entrevista.** PRIMERA FASE. Basándose en la siguiente lista, pregúntense sobre sus hábitos de compras y los regalos que ustedes hacen y reciben de otras personas.

1. ir de compras: ¿Qué? ¿Tienda(s) favoritas?
2. comprar regalos caros: ¿A quién(es)? ¿Cuándo?
3. le compran regalos a usted: ¿Quién(es)?

SEGUNDA FASE. Escriba una comparación entre sus hábitos y los de su compañero/a en la *Primera fase.* Use las siguientes preguntas como guía (*as a guide*). Prepárese para compartir su texto con otro compañero/otra compañera.

1. ¿Tienen ustedes hábitos de compras semejantes o diferentes?
2. ¿Compran en las mismas tiendas? ¿Compran regalos semejantes o diferentes?
3. ¿A quién(es) le(s) dan regalos? ¿Quiénes les dan regalos a ustedes? ¿Qué tipos de regalos reciben?

## SITUACIONES

1. **Role A.** You are a customer at a department store. Tell the salesperson a) you are looking for a present for a friend (specify male or female); b) you are not sure what you should buy for him/her; and c) the amount that you can spend.

   **Role B.** You are a salesperson. A customer asks for your advice. Inquire about the friend's age, taste, size, favorite color, and any other pertinent information. Make suggestions and offer information about the quality of the products, prices, sales, and so forth.

2. **Role A.** You are shopping for clothes for your new job. Tell the salesperson that you like a garment (specify) in the window and inquire if they have your size. Answer the salesperson's questions and decide what you want to try on.

   **Role B.** You are a salesperson. First ask the customer for more details to identify the garment the customer is referring to. Then explain that: a) you have it in brown, blue, gray, and black; b) you also have some new items that you can show him/her (describe the styles); and c) ask if he/she would like to see them.

## 4. Expressing likes and dislikes: *Gustar* and similar verbs

DEPENDIENTE: **¿Le gustan** estas camisas?

JORGE: No, no **me gustan**, pero **me gusta** esta chaqueta.

DEPENDIENTE: Es una buena chaqueta para el otoño. **¿Le interesan** los deportes, señor?

JORGE: **Me encanta** practicar deportes, pero no **me gusta** mirar los partidos en televisión. **Me fascinan** el tenis, el béisbol y el fútbol.

**Piénselo.** Indique si las siguientes afirmaciones son ciertas (**C**) o falsas (**F**), según la información en esta escena. Si no hay información suficiente para contestar, indique que usted no sabe (**NS**).

1. ___ A Jorge **le gusta** una de las camisas que le muestra el dependiente.
2. ___ A Jorge **le interesa** comprar una chaqueta.
3. ___ A Jorge **le queda** poco dinero, porque la chaqueta es muy cara.
4. ___ A Jorge **le encantan** varios deportes.
5. ___ A Jorge **le gusta** mirar los partidos de fútbol en la televisión.
6. ___ A los amigos de Jorge **les interesa** jugar al fútbol con él.

---

▪ In previous chapters you have used the verb **gustar** to express likes and dislikes. As you have seen, **gustar** is not used the same way as the English verb *to like*. **Gustar** is similar to the expression *to be pleasing (to someone)*.

**Me gusta** esta chaqueta.  *I like this jacket.* (lit. *This jacket is pleasing to me.*)

▪ The subject of **gustar** is the person or thing that is liked. The indirect object pronoun shows to whom the person or thing is pleasing.

| | | | |
|---|---|---|---|
| me | | *I* | |
| te | | *you* (familiar) | |
| le | gusta el traje. | *you* (formal), *he/she* | *like(s) the suit.* |
| nos | | *we* | |
| os | | *you* (familiar) | |
| les | | *they, you* (formal and familiar) | |

- The most frequently used forms of **gustar** in the present tense are **gusta** and **gustan** and for the preterit **gustó** and **gustaron**. If one thing is liked, use **gusta/gustó**. If two or more things are liked, use **gustan/gustaron**.

| | |
|---|---|
| Me **gusta** ese **collar**. | *I like that necklace.* |
| No me **gustaron** los anillos. | *I did not like the rings.* |

- To express what people like or do not like to do, use **gusta** followed by one or more infinitives.

| | |
|---|---|
| Nos **gusta caminar** por la mañana. | *We like to walk in the morning.* |
| ¿No te **gusta correr** y **nadar**? | *Don't you like to run and swim?* |

- Some other Spanish verbs that follow the pattern of **gustar** are **encantar** and **fascinar** (*to like a lot, to love*), **interesar** (*to interest; to matter*), **parecer** (*to seem*), and **quedar** (*to fit; to have something left*).

| | |
|---|---|
| No te **interesan** las humanidades. | *You are not interested in the humanities.* |
| Leí la novela y me **encantó**. | *I read the novel and I loved it.* |
| El curso me **parece** muy difícil. | *The course seems very difficult to me.* |
| No me **queda** mucho dinero. | *I don't have much money left.* |
| No le **quedan** bien los pantalones. | *His/her pants don't fit well.* |
| Nos **fascina** la moda europea. | *We love European fashion.* |

- To express that you like or dislike a person, use **caer bien** or **caer mal**, which follow the pattern of **gustar**.

| | |
|---|---|
| **Les cae bien** Miriam. | *They like Miriam.* |
| Esa dependienta **me cae mal**. | *I do not like that salesclerk.* |

- To emphasize or clarify to whom something is pleasing, use **a + mí, a + ti, a + él/ella, a + usted**(es), etc. or **a +** *noun*.

| | |
|---|---|
| **A mí** me gustaron los zapatos, pero **a Pedro** no le gustaron. | *I liked the shoes, but Pedro did not like them.* |

**6-24 Mis preferencias en la ropa.** PRIMERA FASE. Indique si le encanta(n), le gusta(n) o no le gusta(n) la ropa que sigue.

| | | |
|---|---|---|
| la ropa deportiva | los suéteres de lana | los vaqueros |
| las chaquetas de cuero | las gorras | los pantalones cortos |

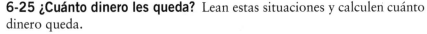

SEGUNDA FASE. Comparen sus preferencias, y luego, explíquenle al resto de la clase si ustedes coinciden en sus gustos.

MODELO: E1: *A dos de nosotros nos gusta la ropa deportiva.*
E2: *Y a todos nos encantan los vaqueros.*

**6-25 ¿Cuánto dinero les queda?** Lean estas situaciones y calculen cuánto dinero queda.

MODELO: Pilar tiene 50 bolívares. Paga 25 bolívares por un vestido y 10 por unos aretes. ¿Cuánto dinero le queda?
*Le quedan 15 bolívares.*

1. Ernesto tiene 75 bolívares. Le da 15 a su hermano. ¿Cuánto dinero le queda?
2. Érica tiene 25 bolívares. Va al cine y a cenar con una amiga. El cine cuesta 5 y la cena 12. ¿Cuántos bolívares le quedan?
3. Gilberto tiene 40 bolívares. Compra un suéter por 39. ¿Cuánto dinero le queda?
4. Mis amigos tienen 30 bolívares. Van a la playa y almuerzan en un restaurante por 25 bolívares. ¿Cuántos les quedan?

**6-26 ¿Qué les parece a ustedes?** Los famosos en las siguientes fotos asisten a eventos públicos. Den su opinión sobre su ropa y accesorios.

**MODELO:** E1: *No me gusta el traje de... No es apropiado llevar un traje blanco en el invierno.*

E2: *Me gusta la combinación de colores del hombre, pero la corbata no va bien con la camisa.*

La jugadora de tenis Serena Williams llega a una recepción formal.

La Reina Isabel II de Inglaterra con Ricky Martin, Paul McCartney y otros cantantes

El Dalai Lama de Tibet y la actriz Penélope Cruz en una exposición de arte en Barcelona

## SITUACIONES

1. **Role A.** You are shopping at an outdoor market where haggling is the norm. You select an item that you plan to give as a gift. In your interaction with the vendor a) say how much you like what the vendor is selling; b) ask the price of the item you are interested in; c) react to what you hear and offer a lower price; d) comment on the item, saying whom you plan to give it to; and e) come to an agreement on the price.

   **Role B.** You are a vendor at an outdoor market. A customer is interested in an item of yours. In your interaction with the customer a) respond to his/her compliments; b) give the price of the item; c) explain why you cannot accept the customer's offer of a lower price; d) respond to his/her comments on the item; and e) come to an agreement on the price.

2. **Role A.** You are at the store where you bought a pair of shorts last week. Tell the clerk that a) you tried them on at home and they didn't fit well; b) you don't like the color; and c) you want to return (**devolver**) them.

   **Role B.** You are the clerk at a clothing store. A customer wants to return (**devolver**) a pair of shorts. Listen to his/her case, and a) ask why the customer bought them if they didn't fit well and he/she didn't like the color; b) explain that the he/she can exchange the shorts for something else (**otra cosa**), but cannot return them; and c) show the person some other shorts and ask if he/she likes them.

## 5. Describing people, objects, and events: More about *ser* and *estar*

ABUELA: Cuidado, Susana, el café **está** muy caliente. [*A la madre*] ¡La niña **está** muy grande!

MADRE: Claro, tiene cinco años. **Es** muy alta para su edad.

SUSANA: Abuelita, ¿qué **es** ese cuadro?

ABUELA: **Son** montañas de la cordillera de los Andes en Chile.

**Piénselo.** Clasifique las frases a continuación de acuerdo con la función de **ser** o **estar**.

| | CONDICIÓN | CARACTERÍSTICA |
|---|---|---|
| 1. El café **está** caliente. | ___ | ___ |
| 2. ¡La niña **está** muy grande! | ___ | ___ |
| 3. **Es** muy alta para su edad. | ___ | ___ |
| 4. **Son** montañas de los Andes. | ___ | ___ |
| 5. La nieve (*snow*) en las montañas **es** fría. | ___ | ___ |

■ In *Capítulo 2*, you learned to use **ser** to identify, describe, and express nationality, ownership, and origin. You also learned to use **ser** to talk about dates and time and to tell where an event takes place.

| Víctor **es** de Venezuela. | *Victor is from Venezuela.* (nationality) |
|---|---|
| **Es** un bailarín profesional. | *He is a professional dancer.* (profession) |
| **Es** alto y delgado y **es** muy fuerte. | *He is tall and thin, and he is very strong.* (distinguishing characteristics) |
| Estas figuras pintadas **son** de Víctor, tiene una colección grande. | *These painted figures belong to Víctor; he has a big collection.* (possession) |
| El próximo espectáculo de su compañía de baile **es** mañana a las ocho. **Va a ser** en el Centro de Bellas Artes. | *The next performance of his dance company is tomorrow at eight o'clock. It is going to take place in the Fine Arts Center.* (time/location of event) |

■ **Ser** is also used to talk about what something is made of.

| El reloj **es** de oro. | *The watch is (made of) gold.* |

■ You also learned in *Capítulo 2* that **estar** is used to indicate location, to talk about health and similar conditions, and to describe changes in feelings or perceptions. It is also used to express ongoing actions, presented in *Capítulo 4*.

| | |
|---|---|
| El Centro de Bellas Artes **está** en el centro. | *The Fine Arts Center is downtown.* (location) |
| Víctor **estaba** (*was*) enfermo la semana pasada, pero ahora **está** bien. | *Victor was sick last week, but now he is fine.* (health) |
| Víctor **está** nervioso antes del espectáculo, pero siempre **está** contento después. | *Victor is nervous before the performance, but he is always happy afterward.* (feelings, condition) |
| Algunos bailarines **están** ensayando ahora. | *Some dancers are rehearsing now.* (ongoing action) |

■ When describing people or objects, use **ser** to convey an intrinsic characteristic. Use **estar** to convey a feeling or perception. The difference in meaning is sometimes so pronounced that the adjectives have different English translations.

| ADJECTIVE | WITH SER | WITH ESTAR |
|---|---|---|
| **aburrido/a** | *boring* | *bored* |
| **bueno/a** | *good* (character) | *well* (health); *physically attractive* |
| **grave** | *serious* (situation) | *seriously ill* |
| **listo/a** | *clever* | *ready* |
| **malo/a** | *bad* (character) | *ill* |
| **muerto/a** | *dead* (atmosphere) | *deceased* |
| **rico/a** | *rich, wealthy* | *delicious* (food) |
| **verde** | *green* | *unripe* |
| **vivo/a** | *lively* (personality) | *alive* |

| | |
|---|---|
| Javier **es** malo, les roba dinero a sus compañeros y dice mentiras. | *Javier is bad; he steals money from his classmates and tells lies.* |
| Roberto Tovares **es** rico. Tiene una casa en California, un rancho en México y un apartamento en París. | *Roberto Tovares is wealthy. He has a house in California, a ranch in Mexico, and an apartment in Paris.* |
| ¡Esta sopa **está** riquísima! ¿Usaste una receta diferente? | *This soup is delicious! Did you use a different recipe?* |

 **6-27 Una familia va de compras.** Observen la foto de una familia venezolana que sale de un centro comercial en Caracas. Describan a las personas que ven, e incluyan la información de las preguntas. Si es necesario, usen su imaginación.

1. ¿Quiénes son las personas?
2. ¿Cómo son?
3. ¿Dónde están?
4. ¿Cómo están?
5. ¿Qué están haciendo?

**6-28 La mañana horrible de Javier.** Lea el cuento sobre la mañana de Javier y complételo con la forma apropiada de **ser** o **estar**.

Javier se despierta temprano. (1) _____ las seis de la mañana. La casa (2) _____ muy fría, y el agua en la ducha (3) _____ fría también. ¡Javier no (4) _____ nada contento! Su reunión con la profesora de historia (5) _____ a las 10:00 y él no (6) _____ listo. Necesita leer un artículo antes de la reunión, pero no sabe dónde (7) _____. Tiene hambre, pero no hay pan, los plátanos (8) _____ verdes y (9) _____ demasiado tarde para hacer café. La situación (10) _____ grave, piensa Javier.

Javier entra en la oficina de la profesora Guzmán a las 10:00. Ella (11) _____ normalmente relajada, pero hoy (12) _____ tensa. Le dice a Javier que su borrador (*draft*) no (13) _____ bueno y que tiene que trabajar mucho más. Cuando sale de la reunión, Javier (14) _____ muy preocupado.

**6-29 ¿Quiénes son y cómo están?** Mire las siguientes fotos y explique quiénes son estas personas, cómo son y cómo están en estas situaciones.

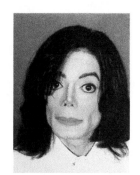

1. **Role A.** Your classmate asks about the photo of your family (or friends). Explain a) who the people are; b) where they are; c) what they are like; and d) how they are feeling in the photo.

   **Role B.** Ask your classmate to see the photo he/she is holding. Ask as many questions as you can about the people in the photo, their activities, and the setting.

2. **Role A.** You have lost your favorite sweater. You think you may have left it in your Spanish class, so you go to the department office, where they have a lost-and-found box (**una caja de objetos perdidos**). Explain to the secretary a) what you lost (**perder**); b) where your Spanish class is held; and c) what your sweater is made of and what it looks like. Answer the secretary's questions.

   **Role B.** You are the department secretary, and the lost-and-found box (**la caja de objetos perdidos**) is in your office. A student comes to ask about a lost sweater. Ask the student a) to identify himself/herself; b) what the sweater looks like; and c) where and when the student lost (**perder**) it.

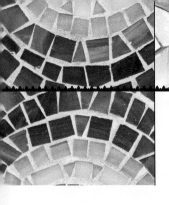

# MOSAICOS

## A escuchar

**Take notes to recall information**

When you want to remember something that you are listening to, like an academic lecture, you benefit from taking notes. Taking notes in other situations is helpful also. For example, when you ask for directions, you will remember them better if you take notes.

### Antes de escuchar

**6-30 Preparación.** Usted va a escuchar una conversación entre Andrea, una adolescente, y sus padres. Andrea habla con ellos sobre la ropa que va a necesitar durante el año escolar. Antes de escuchar, prepare una lista de las cosas que usted tuvo que comprar para el invierno antes del comienzo de las clases este año.

accesorios de invierno: _____

ropa de invierno: _____

### Escuchar

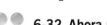

CD 3
Track 26

**6-31 ¿Comprende usted?** Now listen to the conversation between Andrea and her parents. As you listen, take notes on what she needs. Write at least three items per category that Andrea mentions.

1. Para ir a clases Andrea necesita. . .
2. Para practicar deportes Andrea tiene que comprar. . .
3. Para salir con sus amigos Andrea quiere. . .

### Después de escuchar

**6-32 Ahora usted.** Responda oralmente a las siguientes preguntas. Su compañero/a debe tomar apuntes. Luego, intercambien papeles. Finalmente, cada uno debe verificar si su compañero/a tiene la información correcta.

1. ¿Qué ropa, muebles para su cuarto y/o aparatos electrónicos compró cada uno/a de ustedes antes de comenzar sus clases en la universidad este semestre?
2. ¿Qué accesorios compró cada uno/a de ustedes? ¿Dónde los compró?
3. ¿Fueron ustedes a las rebajas? ¿Gastó cada uno/a mucho dinero?

# A conversar

**ESTRATEGIA**

**Negotiate a price**

In Hispanic cultures, negotiating the price of an item in an open-air market or other location in which the price is not fixed is an activity that has both linguistic and cultural rules. You should haggle over a price only if you intend to buy the item. Your initial offer, while lower than the selling price given by the vendor, should be reasonable, because an excessively low price may be insulting. In your negotiation, which may last several turns, you may include a brief comment about the desirability of the item and a reaction to the price suggested by the vendor.

### En directo

To haggle:
CLIENTE/A
**Me gusta este/a _____, pero no tengo tanto dinero.**

**Sólo puedo pagar…**

**¡Es muy caro/a!**

**¿Qué le parece(n)… bolívares/dólares (etc.)?**

**Le doy… bolívares/dólares (etc.).**

VENDEDOR/A
**¡Imposible!**

**Me cuesta(n) más…**

**El material es importado/de primera calidad.**

**Lo siento, pero no puedo darle… por ese precio.**

## Antes de conversar

**6-33 Preparación.** Usted quiere comprar unos regalos o algunas cosas para su cuarto/apartamento en un mercado al aire libre. Complete la tabla con la información.

| ¿QUÉ QUIERE COMPRAR? | ¿PARA QUIÉN(ES)? | DESCRIPCIÓN DEL PRODUCTO |
|---|---|---|
| | | |
| | | |
| | | |
| | | |

## Conversar

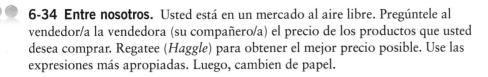

**6-34 Entre nosotros.** Usted está en un mercado al aire libre. Pregúntele al vendedor/a la vendedora (su compañero/a) el precio de los productos que usted desea comprar. Regatee (*Haggle*) para obtener el mejor precio posible. Use las expresiones más apropiadas. Luego, cambien de papel.

## Después de conversar

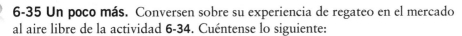

**6-35 Un poco más.** Conversen sobre su experiencia de regateo en el mercado al aire libre de la actividad **6-34**. Cuéntense lo siguiente:

1. qué productos compró y para quién los compró
2. qué precio le dio el vendedor/la vendedora por cada producto
3. cuánto dinero le ofreció usted
4. cuánto pagó finalmente

# A leer

**ESTRATEGIA**

**Use context to figure out the meaning of unfamiliar words**

All readers encounter unknown words and phrases, even in their native language. In our native language we automatically use the surrounding context and our overall comprehension of the text to figure out the meaning of these unknown words and phrases, and we can learn to use the same strategy in the second language. As you read, think about what each sentence or paragraph means. When you come to a word you don't know, reread the last line or two, focusing on the overall meaning. In many cases, this strategy will enable you to understand the unknown word without using a dictionary.

## Antes de leer

**6-36 Preparación.** PRIMERA FASE. Mire rápidamente el texto en la actividad **6-37** y use su conocimiento del tema para responder a las preguntas. Hay más de una respuesta correcta.

1. ¿Qué tipo de texto es?
   a. sugerencias para comprar en Internet
   b. publicidad (*advertising*) para una tienda virtual
   c. una lista de tiendas que venden sus productos por Internet
2. ¿Qué información lo/la ayudó a responder a la pregunta 1?
   a. el título
   b. los gráficos
   c. unas palabras clave (*key*) en el texto
3. Según su experiencia, ¿qué información sobre las compras espera encontrar en el texto?
   a. productos que están a la venta (*for sale*) y los precios
   b. formas de pago
   c. precios especiales para algunos productos

 **SEGUNDA FASE.** Converse con su compañero/a sobre lo siguiente:

1. ¿Les gusta comprar en Internet, o prefieren ir a las tiendas? ¿Por qué?
2. ¿Conocen algunas megatiendas en Internet? ¿Cuál(es)?
3. ¿Qué cosas compran en las megatiendas en Internet?
4. ¿Qué cosas no compran en Internet? ¿Por qué?

# Leer

**6-37 Primera mirada.** Lea la página web de CompreenInternet.net que aparece a continuación.

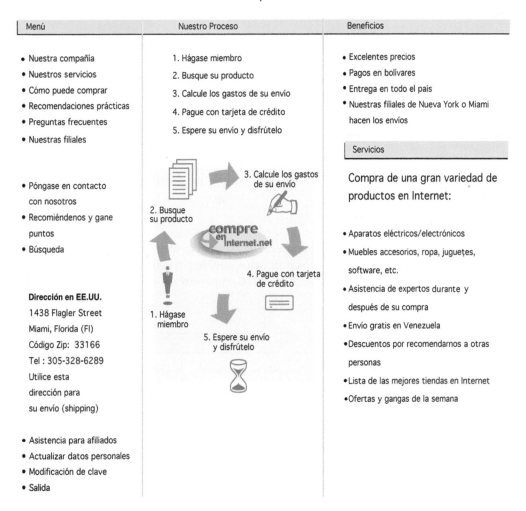

**Bienvenido a CompreenInternet.net**

| Menú | Nuestro Proceso | Beneficios |
|---|---|---|

**Menú**
- Nuestra compañía
- Nuestros servicios
- Cómo puede comprar
- Recomendaciones prácticas
- Preguntas frecuentes
- Nuestras filiales

- Póngase en contacto con nosotros
- Recomiéndenos y gane puntos
- Búsqueda

**Dirección en EE.UU.**
1438 Flagler Street
Miami, Florida (Fl)
Código Zip: 33166
Tel : 305-328-6289
Utilice esta dirección para su envío (shipping)

- Asistencia para afiliados
- Actualizar datos personales
- Modificación de clave
- Salida

**Nuestro Proceso**
1. Hágase miembro
2. Busque su producto
3. Calcule los gastos de su envío
4. Pague con tarjeta de crédito
5. Espere su envío y disfrútelo

3. Calcule los gastos de su envío
2. Busque su producto
4. Pague con tarjeta de crédito
1. Hágase miembro
5. Espere su envío y disfrútelo

**Beneficios**
- Excelentes precios
- Pagos en bolívares
- Entrega en todo el país
- Nuestras filiales de Nueva York o Miami hacen los envíos

**Servicios**

Compra de una gran variedad de productos en Internet:

- Aparatos eléctricos/electrónicos
- Muebles accesorios, ropa, juguetes, software, etc.
- Asistencia de expertos durante y después de su compra
- Envío gratis en Venezuela
- Descuentos por recomendarnos a otras personas
- Lista de las mejores tiendas en Internet
- Ofertas y gangas de la semana

Ahora, indique si las siguientes afirmaciones son correctas (**C**) o incorrectas (**I**). Si son incorrectas (**I**), corrija la información.

1. ___ Los productos y servicios que CompreenInternet.com ofrece son principalmente para personas que viven fuera de Venezuela.
2. ___ La sección **Nuestro proceso** de la página web les indica a los clientes las fases de una compra en Internet.
3. ___ Las tiendas que promociona (*advertises*) CompreenInternet.com incluyen sólo tiendas que están en Venezuela.
4. ___ CompreenInternet.com tiene su oficina central en Venezuela.
5. ___ Los clientes pueden comprar ropa solamente.
6. ___ Los clientes pueden ahorrar (*save*) dinero si compran en Internet.

**6-38 Segunda mirada.** Lea otra vez la página web de CompreenInternet.net y seleccione la alternativa correcta.

1. En el **Menú** de CompreenInternet.net, la frase **Nuestras filiales** significa...
   a. los clientes de CompreenInternet.net.
   b. las tiendas asociadas con CompreenInternet.net.
   c. un producto que vende CompreenInternet.net.
2. Los clientes que compran en CompreenInternet.net pagan en...
   a. dólares
   b. bolívares
   c. dólares y bolívares
3. La expresión **Hágase miembro** en la sección **Nuestro proceso** probablemente significa que para comprar, las personas deben...
   a. subscribirse a una lista de clientes de la tienda en Internet.
   b. trabajar para la compañía para comprar a precios especiales.
   c. comprar un mínimo al año.
4. La expresión **envío gratis** significa que los clientes...
   a. van a un almacén (*warehouse*) para recoger sus compras.
   b. no pagan por recibir los productos en su casa.
   c. pagan un precio reducido por algunos productos.

## Después de leer

 **6-39 Ampliación.** Lean una vez más la página web de CompreenInternet.net y completen la tabla con los productos que, según ustedes, las chicas, los chicos o ambos visitan con más frecuencia. Compartan sus respuestas con las de otra pareja.

| LAS CHICAS | LOS CHICOS | AMBOS |
|---|---|---|
|  |  |  |
|  |  |  |
|  |  |  |
|  |  |  |

# A escribir

**Sequence events**

In our interactions with others, we all talk about or write about experiences and events that occur over time in a sequence. That sequence can serve as the basis of the step-by-step chronological organization of the piece we are writing. Using the correct connectors to indicate the succession of events or transitions will help you make your writing clearer and easier for readers to follow.

## Antes de escribir

**6-40 Preparación.** Usted compró un producto en Internet (ropa, un mueble, un accesorio, etc.), pero el producto resultó ser diferente de sus expectativas. Usted está muy decepcionado/a (*disapppointed*) y decide escribirle una carta a alguien de su familia para contarle su experiencia. Haga lo siguiente:

1. Escriba el nombre de la tienda donde usted compró el producto.
2. Indique qué producto compró en Internet y si compró más de uno.
3. Prepare una lista de nombres y adjetivos para describir lo que usted compró, por ejemplo, un vestido negro largo, una camisa blanca ancha, un plato decorativo de cerámica.
4. Narre lo que ocurrió en orden cronológico. ¿Cuándo hizo (*did you make*) la compra en Internet? ¿Qué ocurrió después de hacer la compra? ¿Qué hizo usted primero, después, más tarde, etc.? ¿Cuánto costó y cómo pagó usted, con una tarjeta de crédito?
5. Escriba la razón de su insatisfacción con el producto.

## Escribir

**6-41 Manos a la obra.** Ahora escríbale la carta a alguien de su familia para contarle qué le ocurrió. Use la información que preparó en la actividad **6-40**. Incluya la fecha, el saludo, el cierre de la carta y la despedida.

## Después de escribir

**6-42 Revisión.** Ahora lea su carta por lo menos dos veces. Piense en la persona que la va a leer. Verifique lo siguiente:

1. ¿Incluyó usted toda la información necesaria?
2. ¿Escribió en su carta la fecha, el saludo, el cierre de la carta y la despedida?
3. ¿Organizó los eventos cronológicamente para contar paso a paso lo que ocurrió? ¿Usó algunas expresiones que indican transición temporal para hacer más comprensible su narración?
4. ¿Revisó la gramática de su texto: el vocabulario correcto, la concordancia (*agreement*), el tiempo (presente, pasado)?
5. ¿Usó la puntuación y ortografía correctas?

---

### En directo

To indicate the succession of events or temporal transitions, you may use the following connectors: **primero, luego, más tarde, antes de eso, después (de eso), finalmente**

---

### Cultura

Although big department stores are increasingly popular in Spanish-speaking countries, people still enjoy shopping at local neighborhood stores. For example, instead of buying bread from a large supermarket, some prefer to go to the neighborhood bakery (**panadería**), where they probably have a long-standing relationship with the bakery owner and employees.

# ENFOQUE CULTURAL

## El mundo fascinante de Simón Bolívar

El nombre completo de Bolívar es Simón José Antonio de la Santísima Trinidad Bolívar y Ponte Palacios y Blanco. Nace en Caracas en 1783 en una familia aristocrática y muy rica. Cuando Bolívar tiene siete años de edad, su padre muere y dos años después también muere su madre. El joven Simón vive entonces con un tío y es educado por dos de los más importantes intelectuales de la época, Simón Rodríguez y Andrés Bello. A los catorce años es un oficial en el ejército español y a los quince, viaja por primera vez a Europa. Allí se casa con una mujer española y regresa a Venezuela. Ocho meses después, su joven esposa muere, posiblemente de una enfermedad tropical, y a los 20 años, Bolívar regresa a Europa, se une a los movimientos revolucionarios de esa época y promete ganar la independencia de los países americanos.

Estatua de Simón Bolívar, el Libertador, en París

Manuela Sáenz

Su vida es muy apasionada y romántica, llena de aventuras, amor y heroísmo. Las guerras de la independencia son muy violentas y demandan mucho esfuerzo e inteligencia política. Bolívar viaja a caballo por Venezuela, Colombia, Ecuador, Perú y Bolivia en condiciones muy difíciles. Varias veces casi lo asesinan sus adversarios y sólo milagrosamente salva su vida. Durante muchos años mantiene una relación amorosa con Manuela Sáenz, una mujer de carácter fuerte y muy valiente, reconocida como una de las primeras feministas de la América hispana.

Durante más de veinte años, hasta su muerte en 1830, Bolívar es el líder político y militar más importante de la América española. Consigue la independencia de Venezuela en 1813; la de Colombia y Panamá en 1820; la de Ecuador en 1823; y la de Perú y Bolivia en 1825. Durante once años, Bolívar unifica estos cinco países, bajo el nombre de la Gran Colombia, pero después de su muerte, la Gran Colombia se divide nuevamente.

Estos países tienen mucho en común. En primer lugar, frecuentemente se llaman *países bolivarianos* porque Bolívar los liberó. Para ellos Bolívar es tan importante como George Washington para los estadounidenses. Muchos latinoamericanos recuerdan el ideal de Bolívar de hacer un país grande y fuerte de las antiguas colonias españolas. Y este ideal está presente en los Juegos Bolivarianos que se celebran cada cuatro años en distintas ciudades de estos países (en Armenia y Pereira, Colombia, en 2005 y en Sucre, Bolivia, en 2009).

Jugadoras de baloncesto en los juegos bolivarianos

**6-43 Comprensión.** PRIMERA FASE. **Reconocimiento de palabras clave.** Encuentre en el texto la palabra o expresión que mejor expresa el significado de las siguientes ideas.

1. at age fourteen _____
2. officer _____
3. disease _____
4. wars _____
5. travels by horse _____
6. several times _____
7. feminists _____
8. unifies _____

SEGUNDA FASE. **Oraciones importantes.** Subraye las afirmaciones que contienen ideas que se encuentran en el texto. Luego indique en qué parte del texto están.

1. There was a difference of fifteen years in the ages of Bolivar's parents.
2. After both of his parents died, Bolivar lived with an uncle.
3. Bolívar had a long and happy marriage to a Spanish woman.
4. Many times Bolívar came close to being assassinated, but managed to escape with his life.
5. He had a long love affair with a woman known as an early Latin American feminist.
6. Bolivar's ideal was to create one large, strong country out of all of the old Spanish colonies.
7. The games in honor of Bolívar are played regularly in Caracas.
8. Venezuela won the most gold medals in the most recent games.

TERCERA FASE. **Ideas principales.** Escriba un párrafo breve en inglés resumiendo las ideas principales expresadas en el texto.

**6-44 Use la información.** Prepare una presentación oral sobre algo relacionado con el nombre de Bolívar. Puede ser un país, una región de un país, una ciudad, dinero, una universidad, etc. Explique cuál es el objeto de su presentación, en qué país está y otras características interesantes. Para preparar esta actividad, visite la página web de *Mosaicos* y siga los enlaces útiles.

# VOCABULARIO

| Los accesorios | Accessories |
|---|---|
| el anillo | ring |
| el arete | earring |
| la billetera | wallet |
| la bolsa/el bolso | purse |
| la bufanda | scarf |
| el cinturón | belt |
| el collar | necklace |
| las gafas de sol | sunglasses |
| la gorra | cap |
| el guante | glove |
| la joya | piece of jewelry |
| el pañuelo | handkerchief |
| el paraguas | umbrella |
| la pulsera | bracelet |
| el sombrero | hat |

| Las compras | Shopping |
|---|---|
| el almacén | department store; warehouse |
| el centro comercial | shopping center |
| el escaparate | store window |
| el mercado | market |
| el precio | price |
| la rebaja | sale |
| el regalo | present |
| el supermercado | supermarket |
| la tarjeta de crédito | credit card |
| la tienda | store |

| La ropa | Clothes |
|---|---|
| el abrigo | coat |
| la bata | robe |
| la blusa | blouse |
| las botas | boots |
| los calcetíns | socks |
| los calzoncillos | boxer shorts |
| la camisa | shirt |
| la camiseta | T-shirt |
| el camisón | nightgown |
| la chaqueta | jacket |
| la corbata | tie |
| la falda | skirt |
| el impermeable | raincoat |
| las medias | stockings, socks |
| los pantalones | pants |
| los pantalones cortos | shorts |
| las pantimedias | pantyhose |
| el/la piyama | pajamas |
| la ropa interior | underwear |
| el saco | blazer, jacket |
| las sandalias | sandals |
| el sostén | bra |
| la sudadera | sweatshirt; jogging suit |
| el suéter | sweater |
| el traje | suit |
| el traje de baño | bathing suit |
| el traje de chaqueta | suit |
| el traje pantalón | pantsuit |
| los vaqueros/los jeans | jeans |
| el vestido | dress |

| | |
|---|---|
| las zapatillas | slippers |
| las zapatillas de deporte | tennis shoes |
| los zapatos | shoes |
| los zapatos de tacón | high-heeled shoes |

| Verbos | Verbs |
|---|---|
| cambiar | to change, to exchange |
| dar | to give, to hand |
| encantar | to delight, to love |
| encontrar (ue) | to find |
| entrar (en) | to go in, to enter |
| fascinar | to fascinate, to be pleasing to |
| gastar | to spend |
| gustar | to be pleasing to, to like |
| interesar | to interest |
| llevar | to wear, to take |
| mostrar (ue) | to show |
| pagar | to pay (for) |
| parecer (zc) | to seem |
| ponerse | to put on |
| probarse (ue) | to try on |
| quedar | to fit; to be left over |
| regalar | to give (a present) |
| valer | to be worth |
| vender | to sell |

| Las descripciones | Descriptions |
|---|---|
| ancho/a | wide |
| barato/a | inexpensive, cheap |
| caro/a | expensive |
| estrecho/a | narrow, tight |
| magnífico/a | great |
| precioso/a | beautiful |
| rebajado/a | marked down |

| Palabras y expresiones útiles | Useful Words and Expressions |
|---|---|
| la artesanía | handicrafts |
| la cosa | thing |
| el cuero | leather |
| el dinero | money |
| en efectivo | in cash |
| ¿En qué puedo servirle(s)? | How may I help you? |
| enseguida | immediately |
| estar de moda | to be fashionable |
| ir de compras | to go shopping |
| el juguete | toy |
| Me gustaría... | I would like . . . |
| el oro | gold |
| Quisiera... | I would like . . . |
| la plata | silver |
| la talla | size (clothes) |

See *Lengua* box on p. 193 for body parts.
See p. 193 for a list of **telas** and **diseños**.
See *Lengua* box on page 194 for expressions relating to clothing size and footwear.
See p. 195 for the seasons of the year.
See p. 199 for a list of expressions denoting past time.

# Los deportes

*Jefa* (1923), de Xul Solar, pintor argentino (1887-1963)
Source: The Museum of Fine Arts, Houston.

# In this chapter you will learn how to:

- talk about sports and physical activities
- ask and answer questions about weather
- discuss past events

**Cultural focus: Argentina, Uruguay**

Una parrillada de carne

PARAGUAY

BRASIL

Tucumán

**ARGENTINA**

Córdoba

**URUGUAY**

Mendoza

Paysandú

Distrito de La Boca

Colonia

Punta del Este

Las playas
de Punta del Este

**Buenos Aires**

Montevideo

*LA PAMPA*

Mar del Plata

Bahía Blanca

*OCÉANO*

*ATLÁNTICO*

Bariloche

Un gaucho dirigiendo el ganado

Río Gallegos

Ushuaia

Glaciar Perito Moreno

*OCÉANO PACÍFICO*

CHILE

CORDILLERA DE LOS ANDES

LA PATAGONIA

**A vista de pájaro.** Piense en lo que sabe de estos países y conteste las preguntas.

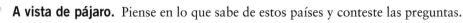

1. ___ Argentina está en...              **a.** Centroamérica.    **b.** el Cono Sur de América.    **c.** el Caribe.
2. ___ La capital de Uruguay es...        **a.** Montevideo.      **b.** Buenos Aires.               **c.** Santiago.
3. ___ La parrillada argentina            **a.** pescado.         **b.** pollo.                      **c.** carne de vaca o res.
   típica se hace con...
4. ___ El deporte favorito de la          **a.** el esquí.        **b.** el fútbol.                  **c.** la natación.
   mayoría de los uruguayos es...
5. ___ En la Patagonia hay...             **a.** playas famosas.  **b.** glaciares.                  **c.** pistas de esquí.

223

# A PRIMERA VISTA

## 🔊 Los deportes

CD 3
Track 33

El **fútbol** es el **deporte** número uno en los países hispanos.

Hay excelentes **equipos** de fútbol en Argentina, Uruguay, Colombia, México y otros países hispanos. Los mejores **jugadores** de los equipos locales forman un equipo nacional. Esta selección representa al país en los **juegos** de los **campeonatos** internacionales y participa, **cada** cuatro años, en la Copa **Mundial**.

En la zona del Caribe, el **béisbol** es el deporte más popular y muchos jugadores, como Alex Rodríguez "A-Rod" y Carlos Beltrán, son originarios de allí y juegan en los mejores equipos de Estados Unidos.

El **esquí** es un deporte que practican muchas personas en Argentina, Chile y España. Aquí vemos a unos jóvenes que van a **esquiar** en las **pistas** de Bariloche, Argentina, uno de los centros de esquí más importantes de la América del Sur.

El **ciclismo**, el **tenis** y el **golf** son otros deportes que cuentan con figuras renombradas en Hispanoamérica y España. Los españoles Miguel Indurain, Roberto Heras y Alberto Contador fueron **campeones** del Tour de France. En esta **carrera**, que **dura** más de 20 días, los **ciclistas recorren** a veces unos 200 kilómetros, el equivalente de 120 millas, en un solo día. Por otro lado, el jugador Sergio García, conocido como "El Niño", es la promesa del golf español.

En cuanto al tenis, David Nalbandian, argentino, y Fernando González, chileno, son actualmente dos de los **tenistas** más conocidos del Cono Sur. Pero la figura más importante del tenis hispano en la actualidad es el español Rafael Nadal.

### En otras palabras

While the majority of Spanish speakers use **jugar + al + deporte**, as does *Mosaicos*, some omit **al** (**jugar tenis**, **jugar golf**, etc.).

Some speakers say **básquetbol**, with the stress on the first syllable, rather than **baloncesto**. **Vóleibol** has several variants, including **volibol**, with the stress on the last syllable.

**7-1 Deportes: ¿Quién es?** PRIMERA FASE. Asocie los deportes de la columna de la izquierda con los jugadores hispanos a la derecha.

1. ____ ciclismo
2. ____ tenis
3. ____ béisbol
4. ____ golf

   a. Sergio García
   b. Alex Rodríguez
   c. Rafael Nadal
   d. Alberto Contador
   e. David Nalbandian

SEGUNDA FASE. Ahora hablen entre ustedes de dos de sus jugadores favoritos/jugadoras favoritas. Expliquen quiénes son y a qué deporte juegan, dónde juegan, qué campeonatos ganaron y por qué son sus jugadores favoritos/jugadoras favoritas.

## Deportes y equipos deportivos

CD 3
Track 34

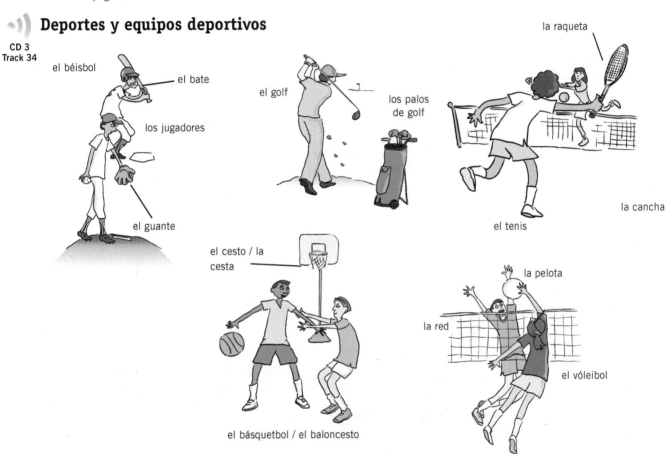

el béisbol
el bate
los jugadores
el guante

el golf
los palos de golf

la raqueta
el tenis
la cancha

el cesto / la cesta
el básquetbol / el baloncesto

la pelota
la red
el vóleibol

**7-2 ¿Qué necesitamos para jugar?** PRIMERA FASE. Escriba el equipo que se necesita para practicar cada deporte.

| DEPORTE | EQUIPO |
|---|---|
| béisbol | |
| golf | |
| vóleibol | |
| baloncesto | |
| tenis | |

**SEGUNDA FASE.** Entreviste a su compañero/a para conversar sobre el equipo que necesita para practicar deportes.

1. ¿Qué deporte(s) practicas? ¿Por qué?
2. ¿Qué equipo necesitas para practicarlo(s)?
3. ¿Dónde compras el equipo y la ropa que necesitas?

 **7-3 ¿Qué deporte es?** Túrnense para identificar los siguientes deportes.

1. Hay nueve jugadores en cada equipo y usan un bate y una pelota.
2. Es un juego para dos o cuatro jugadores; necesitan raquetas y una pelota.
3. En este deporte los jugadores no deben usar las manos.
4. Para practicar este deporte necesitamos tener una bicicleta.
5. En cada equipo hay cinco jugadores que lanzan (*throw*) el balón a un cesto.
6. Para este deporte necesitamos una red y una pelota. Mucha gente lo juega en la playa.

 **7-4 Su deporte favorito.** Háganse las preguntas necesarias para averiguar lo siguiente.

1. el deporte favorito para practicar
2. el lugar donde lo practica, con quién y cuándo
3. el deporte favorito para ver
4. el lugar y las personas con quienes ve su deporte favorito
5. los nombres de sus equipos favoritos/as
6. la marca (*brand*) de ropa deportiva que más le gusta

 **7-5 Concurso.** Ustedes van a organizar un concurso sobre deportes. En grupos de tres o cuatro, elijan a uno/a de los/las deportistas en las fotos y hagan lo siguiente en tres minutos:

1. Identifiquen al/a la atleta y su deporte. (5 pts)
2. Digan algún campeonato/torneo (*tournament*) que este/a atleta ganó. (5 pts)
3. Digan el equipo que necesita para practicar su deporte. (5 pts)
4. Cuenten algún dato personal o profesional de esta persona. (5 pts)

**SEGUNDA FASE.** Compartan con la clase la información sobre este/a atleta. El grupo con la información más completa es campeón.

---

## En otras palabras

Different words are used in Spanish for *ball*, depending on the context. The ball in basketball and volleyball is usually called a **balón**. Both **pelota** and **balón** are used for the soccer ball. **Pelota** is also used in golf and tennis. **Bola** or **bolo** is used in bowling.

# ◀)) El tiempo y las estaciones

CD 3
Track 35 ## Verano

¿Qué tiempo hace? Hace buen tiempo y hace calor. Es un día perfecto para jugar al vóleibol en la playa. El cielo **está despejado** y **hace mucho sol.**

## Otoño

**Hace fresco** y mucho **viento.** No es fácil jugar al golf cuando hace viento. Pero el otoño es muy bonito porque muchos **árboles** cambian de color antes de **perder** las hojas.

## Invierno

Hoy hace mal tiempo. Anoche **nevó** y hoy hace frío. Hay mucha **nieve** y **hielo** en las calles. Los **lagos** también **se congelaron** y algunas personas **aprovechan** para **patinar sobre el hielo.**

## Primavera

Hoy **está nublado** y **está lloviendo.** Por eso, estos chicos no pueden jugar al fútbol y están **jugando a los bolos.** Pero **la lluvia** es muy buena para las plantas y las flores, y además limpia la **atmósfera contaminada.**

> ### En otras palabras
>
> In some Spanish-speaking countries the expressions **jugar (al) boliche** or **ir de bowling** are preferred to **jugar a los bolos.**

**7-6 Condiciones meteorológicas.** Asocie la situación de la columna de la izquierda con la oración más lógica de la derecha.

1. ___ Las calles están blancas.
2. ___ Las personas llevan impermeable y paraguas.
3. ___ La casa es un horno y vamos a ir a la playa.
4. ___ Los árboles se mueven (*move*) mucho.
5. ___ Vamos a celebrar mi cumpleaños en el parque porque el clima está perfecto.
6. ___ El cielo (*sky*) está cubierto (*overcast*) y parece que va a llover.

a. Hace muy buen tiempo.
b. Hace mucho viento.
c. Está lloviendo.
d. Hace mucho calor.
e. Está nevando.
f. Está nublado.

**7-7 ¿Qué tiempo hace?** Un amigo/Una amiga lo/la llama por teléfono desde otra ciudad. Pregúntele qué tiempo hace allí y averigüe cuáles son sus planes. Su amigo/a debe hacerle preguntas a usted también.

MODELO: E1: *¡Qué sorpresa! ¿Dónde estás?*
E2: _____
E1: *¿Qué tiempo hace allí?*
E2: _____

> ### En directo
>
> To thank a friend for calling:
>
> **Mil gracias por llamar. ¡Fue un gusto escucharte!**
> *Many thanks for calling. It was a pleasure to hear your voice!*
>
> **Gracias por llamar. ¡Qué placer escucharte!**
> *Thanks for calling. What a pleasure to hear from you!*

**7-8 El tiempo y las actividades.** PRIMERA FASE. Túrnense para explicar qué les gusta hacer a usted y a sus amigos en las siguientes condiciones.

1. Cuando llueve yo…
2. Cuando hace mucho calor me gusta…
3. A veces cuando nieva…
4. Mis amigos y yo… cuando hace mal tiempo.
5. En invierno…
6. Los estudiantes… cuando hace buen tiempo.
7. Cuando está nublado…
8. Hoy hace viento pero…

SEGUNDA FASE. Preparen un breve diálogo que incluya al menos (*at least*) los siguientes elementos:

1. una pregunta
2. tres expresiones de tiempo
3. un deporte

MODELO: E1: *Hola, Carmen. ¿Vamos a la playa esta tarde? Hace mucho calor.*
E2: *Sí, pero en la televisión dicen que esta tarde va a llover.*
E1: *Está nublado pero pienso que no va a llover.*
E2: *Bueno, pues vamos. Es mejor jugar al vóleibol cuando está nublado.*

**7-9 Las temperaturas.** PRIMERA FASE. Escojan una ciudad de este mapa de Uruguay y túrnense para completar la siguiente conversación.

E1: *¿Qué temperatura hace en _____?*
E2: *_____ grados. Su equivalente en Fahrenheit es _____.*
E1: *¿Y qué tiempo hace allí?*
E2: *_____. ¿Y qué temperatura hace en _____?*

SEGUNDA FASE. Siguiendo el modelo de la *Primera fase*, preparen un pronóstico del tiempo (*weather report*) de su región para presentar por televisión. Indiquen:

1. la temperatura de tres ciudades
2. el tiempo que hace hoy
3. el tiempo que va a hacer mañana

## Cultura

In Hispanic countries the Celsius system is used. To convert degrees Fahrenheit to the Celsius system, subtract 32, multiply by 5, and divide by 9.

86°F – 32 = 54

54 x 5 = 270

270/9 = 30°C

---

**Sol y Luna de Hoy**

**Sol**
sale .........06:30 hs
se pone...17:29 hs
**Luna**
sale .........23:42 hs
se pone...11:03 hs

**Fases de la luna**

menguante
Jul. 24

nueva
Jul. 30

creciente
Ago. 6

llena
Ago. 15

---

ARTIGAS 17°c

RIVERA 18°c

SALTO 14°c

TACUAREMBÓ 15°c

PAYSANDÚ 16°c

FRAY BENTOS 12°c

DURAZNO 9°c

MONTEVIDEO 14°c

cielo claro — algo nuboso — nuboso — inestable — lluvioso — tormenta eléctrica

# ¿Qué pasó ayer?

CD 3
Track 36 **Un partido importante**

Ayer fue el juego decisivo del campeonato de fútbol.

Rigoberto **se despertó** temprano.

**Se levantó.**

**Se vistió.**

**Se sentó** a comer un buen desayuno. Después **se fue** para el **campo** de fútbol.

Durante el partido el árbitro **pitó** un **penalti.**

Un jugador del equipo **contrario se enfadó** y **discutió** con el **árbitro,** pero el equipo de Rigoberto **metió un gol** y **ganó.**

Después del partido Rigoberto **se quitó** el uniforme, **se bañó** y **se puso** la ropa.

Luego fue a una fiesta para celebrar el triunfo.

**Volvió** a casa muy tarde, **se acostó** y **se durmió** enseguida.

**7-10 ¿Qué significa?** Busque la definición de estas palabras relacionadas con los deportes.

1. ___ ganar
2. ___ equipo
3. ___ gol
4. ___ partido
5. ___ árbitro
6. ___ campeón/campeona

a. jugador/a número 1 en un deporte
b. persona que mantiene el orden en un partido
c. tener más puntos al terminar un juego
d. juego entre dos equipos o individuos
e. punto en un partido de fútbol
f. un grupo de jugadores

**7-11 El partido de Rigoberto.** Contesten las preguntas sobre las actividades de Rigoberto el día del partido.

1. ¿Qué hizo (*did*) Rigoberto primero?
2. ¿Qué hizo después de levantarse?
3. ¿Qué desayunó Rigoberto?
4. ¿Por qué se enfadó un jugador del equipo contrario?
5. ¿Quién ganó el partido?
6. ¿Adónde fue Rigoberto después del partido?

**7-12 ¿Las actividades de ayer?** PRIMERA FASE. Háganse preguntas para obtener la siguiente información sobre las actividades de cada uno/a de ustedes ayer.

1. hora de despertarse y de levantarse ayer
2. desayuno que tomó
3. número de horas de estudio
4. deporte(s) que practicó y por cuánto tiempo
5. hora de acostarse

SEGUNDA FASE. Después, comparen sus actividades, contestando las siguientes preguntas:

1. ¿Quién de ustedes se levantó más temprano ayer?
2. ¿Quién tomó un desayuno más nutritivo?
3. ¿Quién estudió más?
4. ¿Quién practicó deportes por más tiempo?
5. ¿Quién se acostó más tarde?

**7-13 El clima en Hispanoamérica.** You will listen to the weather forecast for four cities in Latin America. Before you listen, write down the information that you might hear in a weather forecast in each season.

CD 3
Track 37

primavera _____
verano _____
otoño _____
invierno _____

Now, focus on the general idea of what is said. As you listen, indicate (✓) whether each forecast predicts good or bad weather.

| | BUEN TIEMPO | MAL TIEMPO |
|---|---|---|
| Montevideo | _____ | _____ |
| Buenos Aires | _____ | _____ |
| Caracas | _____ | _____ |
| Ciudad de México | _____ | _____ |

# EN ACCIÓN

## Diarios de bicicleta: Aficionados al fútbol

### Antes de ver

**7-14** Los deportes juegan un papel importante en el mundo hispano. Escriba los nombres de algunos atletas españoles y latinoamericanos que usted asocia con los siguientes deportes: tenis, béisbol, fútbol y boxeo.

### Mientras ve

**7-15** Ponga en orden cronólogico las siguientes acciones de Javier, según lo que le dice a Daniel.

\_\_\_ Me desperté.

\_\_\_ Fui al parque.

\_\_\_ Me invitaron a jugar al fútbol.

\_\_\_ Me senté junto a un árbol.

\_\_\_ Me encontré con un señor y me dijo cómo llegar al parque.

\_\_\_ Me dormí por unos minutos.

\_\_\_ Me encontré con Martín y Claudia.

\_\_\_ Dejé la bicicleta junto al árbol.

\_\_\_ Ahora necesito encontrar mi bicicleta.

\_\_\_ No usé el candado de mi bicicleta.

### Después de ver

**7-16** Cuéntele a su compañero/a una experiencia en la que usted perdió algo. Incluya el mayor número de detalles posible.

# FUNCIONES Y FORMAS

## 1. Talking about the past: Preterit of reflexive verbs and pronouns

Rodolfo

REPORTERO: ¡Felicitaciones por el triunfo! ¡Jugaron como campeones!

RODOLFO: Gracias. El triunfo es de todo el equipo. Fue un partido difícil, pero **nos preparamos** bien.

REPORTERO: ¿Y cómo empezó este día de victoria para ti, Rodolfo?

RODOLFO: Bueno, anoche **me acosté** temprano. Hoy, yo **me levanté** a las 5:30, **me duché** muy rápido para el entrenamiento, **me vestí** y **me fui** a la cancha.

REPORTERO: ¿Y cómo **se prepararon** ustedes para enfrentar al equipo rival?

RODOLFO: Eh... Primero, es fundamental **sentirse** ganador y también es importante tener un buen entrenador como el nuestro.

**Piénselo.** Indique si las siguientes afirmaciones son probables (**P**) o improbables (**I**), según la conversación entre Rodolfo y el reportero.

1. ___ Todos los jugadores del equipo **se acostaron** tarde la noche antes del partido.
2. ___ Rodolfo **se levantó** temprano el día del partido.
3. ___ Rodolfo **se duchó** rápidamente para llegar a tiempo a la cancha.
4. ___ El equipo no **se preparó** bien para el partido, por eso, ganó.
5. ___ Según Rodolfo, lo más importante para ganar es **sentirse** nervioso.

■ In *Capítulo 4* you learned about reflexive verbs. Now you will use these verbs in the preterit. The rules that apply to reflexive verbs are the same in the past tense as in the present.

■ As you have seen, reflexive verbs express what people do *to* or *for themselves.*

Los jugadores **se levantaron** a las cinco.     *The players got up at five o'clock.*

Yo **me preparé** rápidamente.     *I got ready quickly.*

| LEVANTARSE | | | |
|---|---|---|---|
| yo | **me levanté** | nosotros/as | **nos levantamos** |
| tú | **te levantaste** | vosotros/as | **os levantasteis** |
| Ud., él, ella | **se levantó** | Uds., ellos/as | **se levantaron** |

■ With a conjugated verb followed by an infinitive, place the reflexive pronoun before the conjugated verb or attach it to the infinitive.

Yo **me** empecé a preparar a las cinco.
Yo empecé a preparar**me** a las cinco. } *I started to get ready at five.*

■ With the present progressive (**estar + -ndo**), place the reflexive pronoun before the conjugated form of **estar** or attach it to the present participle. When attaching a pronoun to the present participle, add a written accent mark to the stressed vowel (the vowel preceding **-ndo**).

Amelia **se** está duchando ahora.
Amelia está duch**á**ndo**se** ahora. } *Amelia is taking a shower now.*

Nosotros **nos** estamos lavando los dientes.
Nosotros estamos lav**á**ndo**nos** los dientes. } *We are brushing our teeth.*

■ Remember that when referring to parts of the body and clothing, the definite articles are used with reflexive verbs.

Me lavé **el** pelo.          *I washed my hair.*

Alicia se quitó **la** sudadera.          *Alicia took off her sweatshirt.*

■ Some verbs that use reflexive pronouns do not necessarily convey the idea of doing something to or for oneself. These verbs normally convey the idea of mental or physical states.

María **se enfermó** gravemente la semana pasada.          *María got seriously sick last week.*

**Nos preocupamos** mucho cuando fue al hospital.          *We got very worried when she went to the hospital.*

■ Reflexive verbs that convey the idea of mental or physical states do not take an object. The following verbs are in that category.

| | | | |
|---|---|---|---|
| **arrepentirse (ie)** | *to regret* | **enfadarse** | *to get upset, angry* |
| **atreverse** | *to dare* | **quejarse** | *to complain* |
| **divertirse (ie)** | *to have fun* | **sentirse (ie)** | *to feel* |
| **disculparse** | *to apologize* | | |

La entrenadora **se disculpó** de no asistir a la práctica del viernes pasado.          *The coach apologized for not attending last Friday's practice.*

El público **se quejó** del pobre desempeño de los jugadores.          *The public complained about the poor performance of the players.*

> ### Lengua
> Do you know why the verb forms **duchándose** and **lavándonos** have an accent mark?

**7-17 ¿Cómo fue su día ayer?** Ponga estas actividades en el orden más lógico.

___ Me preparé para un examen.     ___ Me desperté temprano.
___ Me dormí.     ___ Me senté a desayunar.
___ Me levanté.     ___ Me bañé.
___ Me fui a la universidad.     ___ Al final del día, me sentí
___ Me acosté.                      cansado/a.

**7-18 ¿Cómo reaccionan?** PRIMERA FASE. Cuando ustedes tienen un partido importante, ¿hacen actividades semejantes o diferentes? ¿Reaccionan bien o mal?

MODELO:    E1:   *Yo me acuesto temprano la noche anterior.*
              E2:   *Yo no. Yo me acuesto a la hora de siempre.*

1. Yo me despierto...
2. A veces yo me enfado si...
3. Nuestro entrenador se queja cuando nosotros...
4. Cuando el entrenador está enfadado, yo no me atrevo a...
5. Cuando los jugadores cometen un error en la cancha, ellos...
6. Cuando esperamos el comienzo de un partido importante, nosotros siempre...
7. Cuando jugamos muy bien, nosotros...
8. Después de un partido difícil, siempre...

SEGUNDA FASE. Comparen la información de la *Primera fase* con la de otra pareja. ¿Son semejantes o diferentes sus actividades? ¿Reaccionan igual o de una manera diferente?

MODELO:    E1:   *Juan y yo nos despertamos muy temprano el día de un partido*
                     *importante. ¿Y ustedes?*
              E2:   *Yo me despierto temprano también, pero Susana se levanta tarde.*
                     *Dice que no está nerviosa antes de los partidos.*

**7-19 Mis actividades de ayer.** Haga una lista de por lo menos tres actividades físicas que usted hizo ayer para cuidar de su salud.

**7-20 ¿Qué les ocurrió a estas personas?** Lean las siguientes situaciones y hablen de lo que hicieron (*did*) estas personas después. Usen los verbos de la lista u otros propios. Después, comparen sus opiniones con las de otros compañeros/otras compañeras.

| afeitarse | despertarse | lavarse | mirarse | perfumarse | quitarse |
| bañarse | enfadarse | maquillarse | peinarse | probarse | secarse |

MODELO:          Bernardo se despertó cuando sonó el despertador.
              E1:   *Luego se levantó lentamente. En tu opinión, ¿qué pasó después?*
              E2:   *Probablemente se afeitó.*

1. Teresa se miró en el espejo.
2. Juan y Tomás entraron en el vestuario (*locker room*) del gimnasio después del partido.
3. Marisa y Erica salieron de una tienda deportiva.
4. Ramón salió de la ducha.
5. Marta no está contenta. Habló con la capitana del equipo de unos temas personales y luego la capitana les contó todo a otras jugadoras.
6. Pablo llegó tarde a la cancha.

**7-21 Nuestra preparación para el campeonato.** El mes pasado ustedes representaron a su universidad en un campeonato de tenis en Montevideo. Digan lo que hicieron (*you did*)...

1. para prepararse físicamente.
2. para prepararse mentalmente.
3. para cumplir (*to fulfill*) con las responsabilidades académicas.

**7-22 Loreta se levantó con el pie izquierdo (*got up on the wrong side of the bed*).** PRIMERA FASE. Observen las siguientes escenas y cuenten lo que ocurrió. Usen su imaginación y los verbos de la lista u otros, si es necesario.

| | | | |
|---|---|---|---|
| acostarse | ducharse | explicar | practicar |
| despertarse | enfadarse | golpear (*to knock*) | sentarse |
| disculparse | enojarse | levantarse | sonar |

SEGUNDA FASE. Cuenten lo que ocurrió entre las 8:00 y las 9:00 de la mañana.

## SITUACIONES

1. **Role A.** You are a well-known athlete who is greatly admired by young people in your country. A television reporter will interview you to prepare a special feature about your life. Answer the reporter's questions as fully as possible. Remember that you are considered a role model by young people.

   **Role B.** You are a television reporter. Today you are interviewing a highly respected and admired sports figure. After introducing yourself and greeting the athlete, find out a) what school he/she went to; b) when he/she started to play; c) what his/her daily routine is to keep in shape (**estar en forma**); and d) what sports he/she practiced yesterday.

2. **Role A.** You are visiting a friend who is preparing for the Olympics (**Olimpiadas**) at a training resort (**centro de entrenamiento**). Ask a) how many athletes are there; b) what time the athletes went to bed last night; c) what time they got up today; d) when they started practice today; e) what they ate for breakfast and where they ate; and d) if these activities are similar to his/her usual routine.

   **Role B.** A friend is visiting you today at the training resort (**centro de entrenamiento**) where you are preparing for the Olympics. Answer your friend's questions and add any information of interest.

## 2. Talking about the past: Preterit of *-er* and *-ir* verbs whose stem ends in a vowel

VICTOR: Federico, ¿miraste el partido entre la selección de Argentina y la de Colombia?

FEDERICO: No, Víctor. Pero **oí** las noticias por la radio, y mi hermano **leyó** la crónica del partido en el periódico. La selección colombiana ganó dos a uno. Los argentinos no jugaron bien ¿Y tú? ¿Viste el partido?

VICTOR: Desafortunadamente no, pero **leí** en Internet que los jugadores argentinos no **oyeron** las instrucciones de su entrenador y cometieron muchos errores. Por eso, el árbitro les marcó un penalti.

FEDERICO: Tienes razón, yo **oí** que el plan estratégico de defensa que **construyeron** no fue bueno. Ellos **creyeron** que ganarles a los colombianos es fácil, pero es un equipo muy bueno.

**Piénselo.** ¿Quién lo hizo (*Who did it*): Federico (**F**), Víctor (**V**), el hermano de Federico (**HF**), los jugadores argentinos (**JA**)?

1. ___ **Oyó** las noticias del partido por la radio.
2. ___ **Leyó** la crónica en el periódico.
3. ___ **Leyó** en Internet comentarios sobre el partido.
4. ___ No **oyeron** las instrucciones.
5. ___ **Creyeron** que ganar es fácil.
6. ___ **Construyeron** (*They built*) una mala estrategia de defensa.

■ You have already learned the preterit forms of regular **-er** and **-ir** verbs. For verbs whose stem ends in a vowel, the preterit ending for the **usted/él/ella** form is **-yó** and for the **ustedes/ellos/ellas** form, the ending is **-yeron**.

| LEER | | | |
|---|---|---|---|
| yo | leí | nosotros/as | leímos |
| tú | leíste | vosotros/as | leísteis |
| Ud., él, ella | leyó | Uds., ellos/as | le**yeron** |

| OÍR | | | |
|---|---|---|---|
| yo | oí | nosotros/as | oímos |
| tú | oíste | vosotros/as | oísteis |
| Ud., él, ella | o**yó** | Uds., ellos/as | o**yeron** |

Los jugadores **oyeron** los comentarios negativos de los reporteros deportivos.

Cuando el entrenador **oyó** el pitazo final, abrazó a los jugadores.

Los miembros del equipo **construyeron** una casa con la organización Hábitat para la Humanidad.

*The players heard the negative comments of the sports commentators.*

*When the coach heard the final whistle, he hugged the players.*

*The members of the team built a house with Habitat for Humanity.*

---

**Lengua**

Note that **-er** and **-ir** verbs whose stems end in a vowel (**creer**, **leer**, **oír**) have an accent mark on the **i** in the infinitive and in the preterit endings that begin with **i**.

No la **oí** llegar anoche.
*I didn't hear her arrive last night.*

---

**7-23 ¿Cómo se enteraron (*found out*) de los resultados?** El fin de semana pasado se jugó la Copa Davis. Las siguientes personas son fanáticas del tenis. Indique cómo se enteró cada uno de ellos de los resultados de los partidos. Use los verbos creer, leer, mirar y oír.

1. Paula y su novio pasaron el fin de semana en las montañas y _____ los resultados en la radio durante su viaje de regreso a la ciudad.
2. Mercedes trabajó en la biblioteca todo el fin de semana. Cuando su hermano le contó los resultados, ella no lo _____.
3. Ricardo participó en un partido de fútbol entre su universidad y una universidad rival. Él _____ los resultados en el periódico.
4. Los Belmar salieron a hacer ejercicio a la hora del partido. Prefieren el aire libre a mirar televisión y _____ los resultados en el periódico al día siguiente.

**7-24 La semana pasada.** Miren la lista de actividades e indiquen en cuáles participaron todos ustedes la semana pasada.

concluir un proyecto importante

construir algo

contribuir con su tiempo a una organización sin fines de lucro (*non-profit*)

ir a la biblioteca

leer el periódico de la universidad

mirar una película para una clase

oír música en español

---

**SITUACIONES**

1. **Role A.** You have just written a book on Hispanics in professional sports in the United States. A reporter for your local newspaper is interviewing you. Respond to the reporter's questions about your work.

   **Role B.** You are a newspaper reporter interviewing the author of a new book on professional Hispanic athletes in the United States. After introducing yourself, ask a) what sports he/she wrote about; b) whether he/she read newspapers from Latin America to write the book; c) what contributions the first Hispanic players made to professional sports in the United States; and d) what he/she concluded from the research (**investigación**).

2. **Role A.** Call a friend to invite him/her to go to a sports event with you. Mention a) what the event is; b) that you read about it in the newspaper; and c) that you want to see the city's new stadium (**estadio**).

   **Role B.** Your friend calls to invite you to a sports event. Respond to the invitation with questions and comments. Then decide if you want to go and either accept or decline the invitation.

## 3. Talking about the past: Preterit of stem-changing *-ir* verbs

**Mensaje sin título**

Archivo   Edición   Ver   Insertar   Formato   Herramientas   Tabla   Ventana   ?                                  Escriba una pregunta   ▾ ✕

Enviar | 📎 ▾ | 🔲 ⚒ | 🖨 ! | ↓ | ▼ | ✍ | 📋 Opciones... ▾ | HTML ▾

| Para... | Alberto López |
| CC... | |
| Asunto: | Noticias del equipo |

Arial   ▾ 10 ▾ A ▾ N K S | 📋 ▤ ▥ ▦ | ⋮≡ ≔ ⊑ ⊒ | 🔧

Querido Sr. López,

¡Nos encanta Argentina! Anoche salimos a bailar, excepto Raquel y Estela, que no **durmieron** en el avión. Ellas no **se divirtieron** anoche, ¡pero nosotras sí!

Esta mañana desayunamos en un café cerca del hotel. Todas nosotras **pedimos** desayunos enormes excepto Laura, que **pidió** sólo café. Rafael, el camarero que nos **sirvió**, se **rió** de lo mucho que comimos. Pero como somos atletas, tenemos que comer bastante.

Esta mañana comenzamos su plan de entrenamiento bajo la dirección del Sr. Lucero. Marcela tiene problemas en su pierna derecha, por eso **prefirió** no caminar mucho. María Jesús y Paulina **se sintieron** cansadas después de bailar toda la noche, pero **siguieron** las instrucciones y se quejaron solamente un poco.

Mañana se celebra el Carnaval de Primavera en Buenos Aires. Le vamos a escribir en un par de días.

Muchos saludos de su equipo.

Dibujar ▾ | Autoformas ▾ | ╲ ╲ □ ○ ▨ ◁ ⬡ ▨ 🖼 | ◇ ▾ ✎ ▾ A ▾ ≡ ▦ ⇌ 🔲 🗐

🏁 Inicio | 🔲 🔲 🔲 » | 🔲 Messenger ▾ | 🔲 Bandeja de entrad... | 🔲 Mensaje sin título | ► ■ ◄◄ ❚❚ ► ◄ ►► ⟨ 🔲 🔲 🔲 🔲 🔲 🔲 22:39

**Piénselo.** Después de cada oración, escriba a qué persona(s) se refiere, según la breve nota anterior.

1. No **durmieron** en el avión. _____ y _____
2. No desayunó esta mañana; **pidió** un café solamente. _____
3. Se **rió** de lo mucho que comieron las jugadoras. _____
4. **Prefirió** no caminar mucho. _____
5. No **se divirtieron** anoche porque no salieron con sus amigas. _____ y _____
6. **Se sintieron** cansadas, pero **siguieron** el plan de entrenamiento. _____ y _____

■ In the preterit, stem-changing **-ir** verbs change **e → i** and **o → u** in the **usted, él, ella** and **ustedes, ellos/as** forms. The endings are the same as those of regular **-ir** verbs.

Marta **prefirió** salir temprano.              *Marta preferred to leave early.*

Las jugadoras **durmieron** tranquilamente.     *The players slept calmly.*

| PREFERIR (e → i) | | | |
|---|---|---|---|
| yo | preferí | nosotros/as | preferimos |
| tú | preferiste | vosotros/as | preferisteis |
| Ud., él, ella | prefirió | Uds., ellos/as | prefirieron |

| DORMIR (o → u) | | | |
|---|---|---|---|
| yo | dormí | nosotros/as | dormimos |
| tú | dormiste | vosotros/as | dormisteis |
| Ud., él, ella | durmió | Uds., ellos/as | durmieron |

■ The following are other stem-changing **-ir** verbs:

| | | |
|---|---|---|
| **despedirse** | *to say goodbye* | Los hinchas se despidieron de su equipo. *The fans said goodbye to their team.* |
| **divertirse** | *to have fun* | Todos se divirtieron con la presentación de las barras paralelas. *Everyone had fun with the performance of the parallel bars.* |
| **morir** | *to die* | Un hincha murió de un ataque al corazón cuando su equipo perdió. *A fan died of a heart attack when his team lost.* |
| **pedir** | *to ask for/order* | El entrenador pidió agua para los jugadores. *The coach asked for water for the players.* |
| **reír** | *to laugh* | El árbitro se rió cuando un perro cruzó la cancha. *The referee laughed when a dog crossed the field.* |
| **repetir** | *to repeat* | El reportero repitió el nombre del jugador que marcó el gol. *The reporter repeated the name of the player who scored the goal.* |
| **seguir** | *to follow* | Los jugadores siguieron las instrucciones de su entrenador. *The players followed the instructions of their coach.* |
| **sentirse** | *to feel* | Todos se sintieron felices con el triunfo. *Everyone felt happy about the victory.* |
| **servir** | *to serve* | Los hinchas le sirvieron perros calientes gratis al público. *Fans served free hot dogs to the public.* |
| **vestirse** | *to get dressed* | Los jugadores se vistieron para ir a celebrar. *The players got dressed to go out and celebrate.* |

**7-25 Carrera de un campeón.** Un famoso deportista recibió muchas medallas durante su carrera. ¿Cómo lo logró (*accomplished*)? Marque (✓) la alternativa más apropiada, según usted.

1. ___ **a.** Durmió poco antes de cada partido.
   ___ **b.** Siempre durmió por lo menos ocho horas.

2. ___ **a.** Prefirió evitar el alcohol.
   ___ **b.** Prefirió beber alcohol moderadamente.

3. ___ **a.** Se preparó solo.
   ___ **b.** Prefirió prepararse con un entrenador.

4. ___ **a.** Prefirió comer poco, pero bien.
   ___ **b.** Comió mucho durante toda su vida, pero hizo mucho ejercicio físico.

5. ___ **a.** Practicó sólo antes de los partidos importantes.
   ___ **b.** Practicó constantemente.

6. ___ **a.** Repitió sus victorias con frecuencia.
   ___ **b.** Raras veces repitió sus victorias.

7. ___ **a.** Cuando no ganó un partido, se sintió deprimido y no continuó tratando.
   ___ **b.** Se sintió triste cuando no ganó un partido, pero pidió ayuda para mejorar.

**7-26 Momentos cruciales.** Indique lo que hicieron las siguientes jugadoras del equipo femenino de básquetbol unos minutos antes del partido.

1. Marta (vestirse) _____ con la camiseta número 3.
2. Ana y Luisa Fernanda (seguir) _____ con atención los pasos del calentamiento (*warm-up*).
3. Carmen (preferir) _____ no beber agua antes del partido.
4. Las jugadoras del equipo contrario (reírse) _____ cuando su entrenador les hizo una broma (*joke*).
5. La entrenadora les (repetir) _____ las instrucciones a todas las jugadoras.
6. El equipo (sentirse) _____ animado (*encouraged*) con los aplausos del público.

**7-27 Celebrando la victoria.** Uno de los equipos de su universidad ganó un campeonato importante y ustedes organizaron una fiesta en su honor. Explíquenle a otra pareja los siguientes detalles de la fiesta. Usen los verbos de la lista.

| | | | |
|---|---|---|---|
| despedirse | pedir | repetir | servir |
| divertirse | reír | sentirse | vestirse |

1. hora y lugar de la fiesta
2. número de personas que asistieron y cómo se vistieron para la fiesta
3. tipo de cooperación que ustedes pidieron para los gastos de la fiesta
4. cómo se divirtieron en la fiesta
5. comida y bebida que sirvieron en la fiesta y tipo de música que escucharon
6. reconocimiento (*recognition*) que les dieron a los jugadores
7. sentimientos de los jugadores durante la fiesta
8. a qué hora los invitados se despidieron y se fueron de la fiesta

## SITUACIONES

1. **Role A.** You had to work late last night and missed an important basketball game at your school. Call a friend who went to the game. After greeting your friend, a) explain why you did not go; b) ask questions about the game; c) answer your friend's questions; and d) accept your friend's invitation to go to another game next Saturday.

   **Role B.** A friend calls to find out about last night's basketball game. Answer your friend's questions and then a) say that there is another game on Saturday; b) find out if your friend is free that evening; and c) if free, invite him/her to go with you.

2. **Role A.** You read in today's newspaper that your favorite football (**fútbol americano**) player was interviewed on TV last night. Call your friend, who watched the interview, to find out a) on which channel (**canal**) he/she watched the interview; b) the time of the interview; c) who interviewed (**entrevistar**) the football player; and d) what they talked about.

   **Role B.** Your friend calls to get the details of a TV interview of his/her favorite football (**fútbol americano**) player. Answer all of your friend's questions in as much detail as possible.

## 4. Emphasizing or clarifying information: Pronouns after prepositions

ROBERTO: Estas flores son **para ti**, Cristina.

CRISTINA: ¿**Para mí**? Gracias, Roberto.

\*\*\*

ROBERTO: Oye, Cristina. El partido es mañana. ¿Quieres ir **conmigo**?

CRISTINA: No puedo ir **contigo**, Roberto. Mis primos están aquí, y voy al partido **con ellos**.

**Piénselo.** Indique quién dice cada oración, Roberto (**R**) o Cristina (**C**).

1. ___ ¿Quieres ir **conmigo**?
2. ___ Estas flores son **para ti**.
3. ___ No puedo ir **contigo**.
4. ___ ¿**Para mí**?
5. ___ Voy **con ellos**.

▪ In *Capítulo 6* you used **a + mí, a + ti**, and so on, to clarify or emphasize the indirect object pronoun: **Le di el suéter a él.** These same pronouns are used after other prepositions, such as **de, para**, and **sin**.

| a | | mí |
|------|---|------------------|
| de | | ti |
| para | + | usted, él, ella |
| por | | nosotros/as |
| sin | | vosotros/as |
| sobre | | ustedes, ellos/as |

| | |
|---|---|
| Siempre habla **de ti**. | *He is always talking about you.* |
| Las raquetas son **para mí**. | *The racquets are for me.* |
| No quieren ir **sin nosotros**. | *They do not want to go without us.* |

■ In a few cases, Spanish does not use **mí** and **ti** after prepositions. After **con**, use **conmigo** and **contigo**. After **entre**, use **tú y yo**.

| | |
|---|---|
| ¿Vas al partido **conmigo**? | Are you going to the game with me? |
| Sí, voy **contigo**. | Yes, I am going with you. |
| **Entre tú** y **yo**, ella tiene unos problemas serios. | Between you and me, she has some serious problems. |

**7-28 Un amigo preguntón.** Un amigo de Rosario le hace muchas preguntas. Conecte sus preguntas en la columna de la izquierda con un comentario lógico de Rosario en la columna de la derecha.

1. ¿Con quién vas a ir al partido de tenis, Rosario?
2. ¿Por qué no vemos las finales del campeonato con Sofía?
3. Rosario, ¿para quién es esta raqueta de tenis?
4. ¿Pueden mis amigos ir a la cancha con nosotros?
5. Después del partido de ayer encontramos una sudadera. ¿Es de Carlos?
6. ¿De quién van a recibir el trofeo los ganadores?

a. La compré para ti. ¿Te gusta?
b. Imposible. No podemos ir con ellos. Tengo sólo dos billetes.
c. Contigo, ¡por supuesto!
d. Sí, es de él.
e. De nosotros. De ti y de mí. ¡Qué emocionante!
f. Prefiero verlas sin ella. Habla mucho y no puedo concentrarme.

**7-29 Haciendo planes.** ¿Cuándo van a hacer las siguientes actividades? Escojan individualmente una opción en cada número y, luego pregúntense entre ustedes.

**MODELO:**  E1:  ¿Cuándo puedes ir al cine conmigo?
  E2:  Puedo ir contigo el sábado.

1. estudiar español/historia/biología
2. ir al parque/al partido de béisbol/al concierto
3. jugar al golf/al tenis/al vóleibol

**7-30 ¿Con quién va?** Completen el siguiente diálogo, usando pronombres.

JULIA: Yo salgo ahora. ¿Vienes conmigo?
CELIA: No, no puedo ir _____. Tengo que trabajar media hora más en la tienda.
JULIA: ¡Cuánto lo siento! Entonces, ¿vas a ir con Roberto?
CELIA: Sí, voy a ir con _____ más tarde.
JULIA: Seguro que él no quiere ir sin _____ . Tú eres su mejor amigo/a.
CELIA: Sí, somos muy buenos amigos. ¿Y sabes dónde te vas a sentar?
JULIA: Sí, voy a sentarme entre _____ y _____ .

## 5. Talking about the past: Some irregular preterits

ABUELA: ¡Bienvenidos! Pasen, por favor. ¿No **vino** Carmencita? ¿Está enferma?

MADRE: Está trabajando. **Estuvo** en la biblioteca hasta muy tarde anoche, pero no **pudo** terminar su proyecto. Nos **dijo** que es largo y difícil.

\* \* \*

CARMENCITA: ¿Mis padres? **Tuvieron** que ir a la casa de mi abuela, pero no **quise** ir a otra cena aburrida. Les **dije** una pequeña mentira sobre un proyecto...

**Piénselo.** Marque (✓) si las afirmaciones en la columna de la izquierda probablemente expresan la **verdad**, una **mentira** (*lie*) o si **no se sabe**, según la información en las conversaciones.

|  | VERDAD | MENTIRA | NO SE SABE |
|---|---|---|---|
| 1. Carmencita **tuvo** que terminar un proyecto. | — | — | — |
| 2. Los padres de Carmencita **tuvieron** que ir a la casa de la abuela. | — | — | — |
| 3. Carmencita no **quiso** ir a la casa de su abuela. | — | — | — |
| 4. Carmencita **estuvo** en la biblioteca por muchas horas. | — | — | — |
| 5. Carmencita **hizo** un proyecto para una clase. | — | — | — |
| 6. Carmencita les **dijo** la verdad a sus padres. | — | — | — |

■ Some verbs have irregular forms in the preterit because they use different stems than in the present tense. The preterit endings are added to those stems. Note that the **yo, usted, él,** and **ella** preterit endings of these verbs are unstressed and therefore do not have written accents.

■ The verbs **hacer, querer,** and **venir** have an **i** in the preterit stem.

| INFINITIVE | NEW STEM | PRETERIT FORMS |
|---|---|---|
| hacer | hic- | hice, hiciste, hizo, hicimos, hicisteis, hicieron |
| querer[1] | quis- | quise, quisiste, quiso, quisimos, quisisteis, quisieron |
| venir | vin- | vine, viniste, vino, vinimos, vinisteis, vinieron |

---

[1]The verb **querer** in the preterit followed by an infinitive normally means to *try (but fail) to do something.*
  **Quise hacerlo** ayer.          *I tried to do it yesterday.*

■ The verbs **estar, tener, poder, poner,** and **saber** have a **u** in the preterit stem.

| INFINITIVE | NEW STEM | PRETERIT FORMS |
|---|---|---|
| estar | estuv- | estuve, estuviste, estuvo, estuvimos, estuvisteis, estuvieron |
| tener | tuv- | tuve, tuviste, tuvo, tuvimos, tuvisteis, tuvieron |
| poder[2] | pud- | pude, pudiste, pudo, pudimos, pudisteis, pudieron |
| poner | pus- | puse, pusiste, puso, pusimos, pusisteis, pusieron |
| saber[3] | sup- | supe, supiste, supo, supimos, supisteis, supieron |

■ The verbs **decir, traer,** and all verbs ending in **-ducir** (e.g., **traducir,** *to translate*) have a **j** in the stem and use the ending **-eron** instead of **-ieron. Decir** also has an **i** in the stem.

| INFINITIVE | NEW STEM | PRETERIT FORMS |
|---|---|---|
| decir | dij- | dije, dijiste, dijo, dijimos, dijisteis, dijeron |
| traer | traj- | traje, trajiste, trajo, trajimos, trajisteis, trajeron |
| traducir | traduj- | traduje, tradujiste, tradujo, tradujimos, tradujisteis, tradujeron |

 **7-31 ¿Qué hizo usted ayer? PRIMERA FASE.** De la siguiente lista de quehaceres (*chores*), usted sólo pudo hacer dos o tres. Marque (✓) lo que hizo y lo que no pudo hacer.

| | SÍ | NO |
|---|---|---|
| 1. lavar la ropa | _____ | _____ |
| 2. comprar los zapatos de tenis | _____ | _____ |
| 3. probarse el uniforme nuevo | _____ | _____ |
| 4. conocer al nuevo entrenador | _____ | _____ |
| 5. mirar el video del último partido | _____ | _____ |
| 6. comentar las estrategias del próximo partido | _____ | _____ |

 **SEGUNDA FASE.** Hágale preguntas a su compañero/a para averiguar qué pudo hacer ayer.

**MODELO:**  comprar el trofeo para el campeonato
E1: *¿Compraste el trofeo para el campeonato?*
E2: *Quise comprarlo, pero no pude.*
E1: *¿Por qué no pudiste comprarlo?*
E2: *Porque tuve que regresar al laboratorio.*

---

[2]**Poder** used in the preterit usually means *to manage to do something.*
  **Pude hacerlo** esta mañana.          *I managed to do it this morning.*
[3]**Saber** in the preterit normally means *to learn* in the sense of *to find out.*
  **Supe** que llegó anoche.          *I learned that he arrived last night.*

**7-32 ¿Qué ocurrió?** Expliquen qué le ocurrió a Javier el día de su cumpleaños. Den la mayor cantidad de información posible.

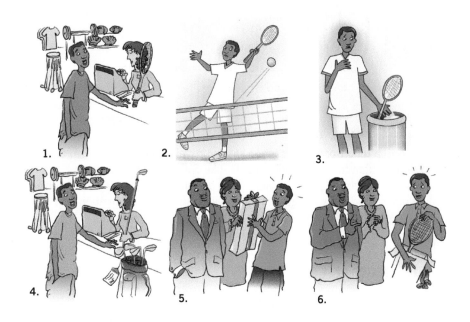

1.  2.  3.

4.  5.  6.

**7-33 Unos días de descanso.** Su compañero/a estuvo unos días en Argentina. Hágale preguntas sobre los siguientes puntos para saber más de su viaje.

1. lugares adonde fue
2. tiempo que estuvo en Argentina
3. cosas interesantes que hizo
4. los lugares que le gustaron más
5. si pudo hablar español y con quién(es)

## SITUACIONES

1. **Role A.** Congratulations! You won a contest (**concurso**) to attend the World Cup. Tell your classmate that you won the contest and that you went to the World Cup. Answer all of his/her questions in detail.

   **Role B.** Your classmate won a contest and tells you about it. Ask a) how he/she found out about the contest; b) how long he/she was away; c) how many games he/she attended; d) with whom he/she went; and e) details about the last game.

2. **Role A.** Imagine that yesterday you went to a sports event and had the opportunity to meet your favorite sports star. Explain to a friend a) where you went; b) what happened and where; c) what you did when you saw this person; d) what he/she said to you; and d) what happened finally.

   **Role B.** Your friend tells you that he/she met a very famous sports star yesterday. Ask about what happened and what they talked about.

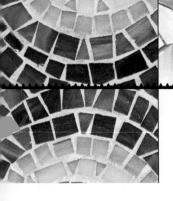

# MOSAICOS

## A escuchar

**ESTRATEGIA**

**Differentiate fact from opinion**

When you listen to a report or a newscast on the radio, television, or the Internet, you need to differentiate facts from opinions. Unlike opinions, which express personal attitudes, beliefs, or points of view, facts are provable. You may distinguish facts from opinions by identifying fact indicators, which include information that refers to data, statistics, numbers, and other verifiable evidence.

### Antes de escuchar

**7-34 Preparación.** Usted va a escuchar una conversación entre un reportero y Nicolás, un esquiador argentino que habla sobre su viaje al centro de esquí en Bariloche, Argentina. Antes de escuchar la conversación, escriba una oración con información concreta sobre el tiempo o sobre las pendientes (*slopes*) en las pistas de esquí. Después escriba una opinión sobre la gente del lugar que, según usted, Nicolás probablemente va a conocer.

### Escuchar

**7-35 ¿Comprende usted?** Now listen to the conversation and write down in Spanish three pieces of factual information and three opinions Nicolás offered about the place and/or the people.

CD 3
Track 38

información concreta:

1. _____
2. _____
3. _____

opinión personal:

1. _____
2. _____
3. _____

### Después de escuchar

**7-36 Ahora usted.** Hágale preguntas a su compañero/a para averiguar la siguiente información.

1. un deporte que practica y dónde lo practica
2. el tiempo que hace cuando lo practica
3. su atleta favorito/a en ese deporte y por qué

# A conversar

## Antes de conversar

**7-37 Preparación.** PRIMERA FASE. Hagan una lista de los deportes que se practican en Argentina y/o Uruguay, según su conocimiento de la región.

SEGUNDA FASE. En la página web de *Mosaicos*, busquen los deportes que escribieron en la *Primera fase*. Elijan uno que se practica en Argentina o Uruguay, busquen la siguiente información sobre ese deporte y tomen apuntes.

1. el nombre del deporte
2. dos o tres datos históricos básicos sobre el deporte: a) cuándo empezó a practicarse; b) dónde empezó; c) algo interesante sobre los comienzos (*beginnings*) del deporte
3. una persona argentina o uruguaya famosa en la historia de este deporte: a) nombre, fecha y lugar de nacimiento y b) datos sobre su carrera deportiva

## Conversar

**7-38 Entre nosotros.** Hagan una presentación de no más de un minuto sobre el deporte que investigaron, usando la información que aprendieron. Divídanse el trabajo de preparar y hacer su presentación entre ustedes. Pueden usar *PowerPoint* e imágenes de Internet para crear una presentación interesante.

## Después de conversar

**7-39 Un poco más.** Elija un deporte y un/a atleta de las presentaciones que hicieron sus compañeros/as de clase. Usando sus apuntes, prepare dos informes breves (de no más de un minuto). Incluya la información indicada en las fichas (*note cards*) a continuación.

| Deporte |
| --- |
| Nombre: |
| Dónde y cuándo empezó a practicarse: |
| Dónde se practica ahora: |
| Su popularidad: |

| Atleta |
| --- |
| Nombre y nacionalidad: |
| Fecha de nacimiento: |
| Campeonatos que ganó: |
| Su reputación nacional e internacional: |

# A leer

**Predict and guess content**

You may enhance your comprehension of a text by predicting and guessing its content before you start to read. Begin by brainstorming the information you are likely to find in the text and identifying the text format. Try this with a magazine article in English and think consciously about how you rely on your own knowledge and reading experiences, as well as textual information, to anticipate what you will read. When you read in Spanish, try to use the strategies that you deploy automatically when you read in your native language.

## Antes de leer

**7-40 Preparación.** PRIMERA FASE. Mire el texto "Los deportes: Una pasión uruguaya". Lea el título y examine las fotos. Tome un minuto máximo para escanear el texto, buscando nombres de lugares y deportes conocidos. Luego responda a las preguntas.

1. Después de examinar el texto, seleccione su tema entre las posibilidades a continuación.
   a. los lugares en Uruguay dónde se practican los deportes
   b. los atletas más famosos de Uruguay
   c. el amor de los uruguayos por los deportes

2. Marque (✓) las ideas que usted anticipa encontrar en el texto.
   a. ___ los deportes más populares de Uruguay
   b. ___ el origen de los deportes de Uruguay
   c. ___ los lugares donde se practican algunos deportes en Uruguay
   d. ___ los campeonatos que ganaron los equipos de fútbol uruguayo
   e. ___ los deportes favoritos de los uruguayos en comparación con los de otros países latinoamericanos

SEGUNDA FASE. Ahora, respondan a estas preguntas.

1. ¿Les gustan los deportes individuales o prefieren los de equipo? ¿Por qué?
2. ¿Saben esquiar? ¿Esquían en la nieve o en el agua? ¿Esquían bien o regular?
3. ¿Qué tipos de surf conocen? ¿Han oído hablar (*Have you heard about*) del surf en la arena? ¿Qué saben acerca del deporte?
4. ¿Conocen el fútbol de salón? ¿Se practica en su país? ¿Dónde?

# Leer

## Los deportes: Una pasión uruguaya

Uruguay es un país pequeño donde los deportes forman una parte integral de la vida de la mayor parte de sus habitantes.

Entre las grandes pasiones nacionales, desde luego, está el fútbol. Desde su infancia, muchos uruguayos acompañan fielmente a sus equipos predilectos. En varias ocasiones, la selección nacional uruguaya ganó títulos y campeonatos importantes.

Pero los uruguayos son un pueblo inquieto, de una personalidad versátil que no limita su interés a un solo deporte. El básquetbol, el ciclismo, el fútbol de salón, el rugby, el boxeo y la pelota de mano son otros deportes que tienen muchos aficionados.

Las hermosas y privilegiadas playas del Uruguay también favorecen los deportes acuáticos, como el surf, que, según los expertos, cuenta hoy con un gran número de aficionados. En 1993 en Uruguay se formó la Unión de Surf del Uruguay (USU). Ese mismo año, el país envió a sus representantes a competir internacionalmente en el Primer Campeonato Panamericano de Surf en Isla Margarita, Venezuela. Hoy en día la USU promueve el surf, arbitra las competencias clasificatorias a nivel nacional, apoya a los competidores nacionales, representa a Uruguay en competencias internacionales y compite en los Juegos Olímpicos con la Selección Uruguaya de Surf.

Sin duda, uno de los lugares predilectos de los uruguayos y turistas extranjeros para practicar el surf es Punta del Este. Ubicada al sureste del Uruguay, a 140 kilometros de Montevideo, Punta Este es una hermosa península de enormes playas, con arenas finas y gruesas, rocas y un entorno de bosques y médanos[1].

Precisamente en estos médanos nació, en el siglo pasado, una variante del surf que está despertando grandes polémicas en el país: el surf en la arena o sandsurf. Los brasileños inventaron este deporte en los años ochenta para no aburrirse cuando no había olas. La agradable temperatura de las playas uruguayas, la escasez de olas que a veces impide practicar el surf en el agua y la formación arenosa de algunas playas aumentaron considerablemente el número de personas que practican el surf en la arena. Por ejemplo, los médanos de Valizas son los más grandes de Sudamérica y los terceros más grandes del mundo, algunos con 30 metros de altura y una longitud de bajada[2] de aproximadamente 125 metros. Sin embargo, las autoridades uruguayas están controlando e incluso prohibiendo la práctica de este deporte por el posible deterioro ecológico que ocasiona. No hay duda de que la prohibición del surf en la arena no va a detener el espíritu activo de los uruguayos. Su creatividad los incentivará a buscar o inventar otras opciones para entretenerse.

[1]*dunes*   [2]*slope*

**7-41 Primera mirada.** Diga si las siguientes citas textuales (*quotations*) representan información concreta (**C**) o una opinión (**O**) del autor.

1. ___ Desde su infancia, muchos uruguayos acompañan fielmente a sus equipos predilectos.
2. ___ Pero los uruguayos son un pueblo inquieto, de una personalidad versátil que no limita su interés a un solo deporte.
3. ___ En 1993 en Uruguay se formó la Unión de Surf del Uruguay (USU).
4. ___ Punta del Este es una hermosa península de enormes playas, con arenas finas y gruesas, rocas y un entorno de bosques y médanos.
5. ___ La agradable temperatura de las playas uruguayas, la escasez de olas que a veces impide practicar el surf en el agua y la formación arenosa de algunas playas aumentaron considerablemente el número de personas que practican el surf en la arena.
6. ___ No hay duda de que la prohibición del surf en la arena no va a detener el espíritu activo de los uruguayos.

Ahora, marque (✓) la estrategia que lo/la ayudó a predecir el contenido del texto.

a. ___ Hice una lluvia de ideas (*brainstorming*) antes de leer el texto.
b. ___ Usé mi experiencia personal con los deportes.
c. ___ Analicé el formato del texto.
d. ___ Observé los elementos visuales del texto como las fotos.

**7-42 Segunda mirada.** Lea el artículo otra vez y, según la información que aparece en él, haga lo siguiente:

1. Indique dos razones que explican la popularidad del fútbol en Uruguay.
2. Diga por qué los uruguayos tienen un carácter inquieto.
3. Nombre tres deportes que se juegan en equipo, dos que son principalmente deportes individuales y uno que no requiere una pelota.
4. Dé dos razones para explicar por qué Punta del Este es un lugar ideal para practicar el surf acuático.
5. Explique dos hechos que provocaron el nacimiento del surf en la arena.
6. En su opinión, ¿deben prohibir el surf en la arena? ¿Por qué?

## Después de leer

**7-43 Ampliación.** Determinen cuál es el deporte favorito del grupo. Luego preparen una hoja descriptiva sobre ese deporte sin mencionar el nombre. Incluyan la siguiente información e intercambien su hoja con otro grupo que debe adivinar cuál es el deporte.

1. lugar donde se practica
2. deporte individual o en grupo (número de personas en el equipo)
3. clima ideal para practicarlo: Se practica en invierno… /cuando hace…
4. un jugador famoso/una jugadora famosa de este deporte
5. su opinión sobre ese jugador/esa jugadora

# A escribir

## Antes de escribir

**7-44 Preparación.** PRIMERA FASE. Los expertos afirman que el ejercicio físico beneficia a las personas. Respondan a las siguientes preguntas:

1. ¿Qué tipos de actividad física puede hacer una persona? Hagan una lista de posibles actividades físicas (ejercicio o deportes).
2. ¿Es la edad de la persona un factor importante en el tipo de actividad física que hace? ¿Por qué? Escriban una o dos razones, según los expertos.
3. ¿Son la frecuencia y la cantidad de actividad factores importantes en el ejercicio físico? ¿Por qué? Indiquen la frecuencia y la cantidad de actividad física que puede beneficiar a una persona joven y a una persona mayor, según los expertos.
4. ¿Cuáles son dos o tres beneficios del ejercicio físico, según los expertos? Escriban por lo menos una palabra (detalle) que apoye (*supports*) cada uno de los beneficios. ¿Conocen ustedes a alguna persona que se benefició con la actividad física? ¿Qué comenzó a hacer esta persona? ¿Cómo se benefició con el ejercicio?

## Escribir

**7-45 Manos a la obra.** Como proyecto final en su clase *Ejercicio y longevidad*, usted debe escribir un artículo electrónico para los jóvenes hispanos de la escuela secundaria que no hacen actividad física. Usando la información que recogió en **7-44**, escriba su artículo. Incluya lo siguiente:

1. Los beneficios del ejercicio físico, según los expertos. Escriba detalles lógicos que apoyen cada uno de los beneficios.
2. Tipos de actividad física que pueden beneficiar a una persona joven. Escriba una o dos razones, según los expertos.
3. Indique cómo la frecuencia y la cantidad de actividad física benefician a una persona, según los expertos. Dé detalles.

## Después de escribir

**7-46 Revisión.** Antes de presentar su proyecto, revise:

1. la organización y la cantidad de información: ¿Es lógica y clara la organización? ¿Hay suficientes detalles que apoyan la idea central de cada párrafo?
2. el vocabulario general y vocabulario especializado, las estructuras que utilizó para presentar la información, la concordancia, etc.
3. las expresiones para presentar la información factual o la opinión de los expertos
4. la división de los párrafos, la ortografía y la acentuación, etc.

---

### ESTRATEGIA

**Add supporting details**

Supporting details are sentences, facts, examples, and ideas that follow the topic sentence or main idea and make up the body of a paragraph. Details should be sequenced logically and support the main idea of the paragraph. Paragraph structure may be visualized as follows:

Main idea
    Supporting detail #1
    Supporting detail #2
    Supporting detail #3
Closing sentence

As you write, think of how you will organize the supporting details to develop the main idea of each paragraph. Anticipate and use details that your reader can expect to see after reading the topic sentence.

---

### En directo

To express facts:

**Los expertos afirman/dicen/aseguran que...**

**La investigación indica que...**

**Los estudios muestran que...**

To express an opinion:

**A mí me parece que...**

# ENFOQUE CULTURAL

## El arte del asado y la tradición ganadera en Argentina y Uruguay

Si le preguntamos a una persona de Argentina o de Uruguay cuál es su comida favorita, probablemente va a responder que es la carne. En efecto, en estos dos países la carne es más que un producto para la exportación. Es, también, el núcleo de muchas tradiciones y está unida a celebraciones, fiestas familiares y, en general, a la cultura de la región. En otras palabras, la ganadería y todo lo relacionado con el ganado contribuyen no solamente a la economía de los dos países, sino también al modo de vida y a las costumbres de sus habitantes.

Un asado argentino con carne de vaca

Indiscutiblemente, en Argentina y Uruguay el asado es un verdadero arte. Algunas personas comparan el asado de Argentina y Uruguay con la parrillada o *cook-out* de Estados Unidos, pero en realidad, son muy diferentes. Aunque la parrillada tradicional en Estados Unidos se compone principalmente de hamburguesas hechas de carne molida, también incluye pollo, costillas (*ribs*) y otros cortes de carne. Inclusive, en los últimos tiempos se han empezado a usar verduras y frutas, por consideraciones de salud. Por otra parte, el asado de Argentina y Uruguay incluye diferentes tipos de carne, además de algunos órganos internos de la vaca. La salsa típica que acompaña el asado argentino es el *chimichurri*, una salsa de aceite y una variedad de hierbas, mientras que en Estados Unidos frecuentemente se prepara una mezcla de salsa de tomate con salsa *Worcestershire* y azúcar.

La contribución de la ganadería a la economía es impresionante. En Uruguay, por ejemplo, la ganadería constituye cerca del 20% de la economía. Este porcentaje tan alto no lo produce solamente la carne, sino también el cuero y la lana que se usan para fabricar ropa, zapatos y otros artículos de vestir. El valor de las exportaciones de carne uruguaya supera los 500 millones de dólares, pero es necesario sumar unos 150 millones que valen las exportaciones de lana de ovejas y aproximadamente 300 millones por la venta de cueros. Estos resultados son todavía más impresionantes en el caso de Argentina, donde hay unos 40 millones de vacas y aproximadamente 25 millones de ovejas, en un país que tiene unos 40 millones de personas.

Los vaqueros que trabajan en la ganadería se llaman *gauchos*. Es cierto que el modo de vida de los gauchos está unido al arte, la literatura y la cultura de estos países. En la foto se puede ver a un gaucho en su traje típico. Las imágenes de estos vaqueros y su vida romántica y aventurera pertenecen a la literatura y el arte desde el siglo XIX. Por ejemplo, *Facundo* es uno de los más famosos libros latinoamericanos del siglo XIX. En él, Domingo Sarmiento describió con detalle la vida y las costumbres de los gauchos. José Hernández inventó otro de los grandes estereotipos gauchos en un largo poema en el que cuenta la vida, las aventuras y los sufrimientos de *Martín Fierro*, un gaucho argentino. De otra parte, Ricardo Güiraldes publicó *Don Segundo Sombra*, otro ejemplo de la representación literaria del gaucho, a principios del siglo XX.

El traje típico del gaucho argentino

(sombrero, pañuelo, poncho, camisa, boleadora, cinturón, bombachas, botas de cuero)

Domingo Faustino Sarmiento (1811-1888), escritor, fue el primer presidente civil de República Argentina, desde 1868 a 1874.

---

### En otras palabras

Expresiones argentinas

**Che**, **vos**, ¿dónde está la pelota?
*Hey, you, where is the ball?*

**¡No te mandes la parte!**
*Don't brag!*

---

### En otras palabras

Expresiones uruguayas

Tengo un **gurí** y dos **gurisas**.
*I have a boy and two girls.*

**¡Qué bárbaro!**
*Great!*

**7-47 Comprensión.** PRIMERA FASE. **Reconocimiento de palabras clave.** Encuentre en el texto la palabra o expresión que mejor expresa el significado de las siguientes ideas.

1. meat or beef        _____
2. cattle ranching     _____
3. barbecue            _____
4. on the other hand   _____
5. leather             _____
6. sheep               _____
7. baggy trousers      _____

SEGUNDA FASE. **Oraciones importantes.** Subraye las afirmaciones que contienen ideas que se encuentran en el texto. Luego indique en qué parte del texto están.

1. Argentinians value meat only as a commodity for export.
2. Cattle and cattle ranching are deeply embedded in the culture of Argentina and Uruguay.
3. Besides meat, some internal organs of the cow are used in a typical Argentinian *asado*.
4. There are more cows and sheep in Uruguay than there are in Argentina.
5. About one-fifth of the economy of Uruguay depends on cattle farming.
6. The combined exports of meat, wool and leather from Uruguay are worth close to one billion dollars.
7. Argentinian cowboys love to dance the tango.
8. Many authors have portrayed the life of Argentinian cowboys in their literature since the nineteenth century.

TERCERA FASE. **Ideas principales.** Escriba un párrafo breve en inglés resumiendo las ideas principales expresadas en el texto.

 **7-48 Use la información.** Haga un afiche para comparar tres de las más importantes regiones ganaderas del continente americano: Texas, los Llanos de Colombia y Venezuela, y la pampa argentina. Para preparar esta actividad, visite la página web de *Mosaicos* y siga los enlaces útiles. Incluya lo siguiente:

1. una foto de cada una de las regiones y una explicación breve para cada una de ellas
2. una descripción de tres características de cada una de las regiones, por ejemplo, el clima, la naturaleza, las personas, las costumbres, la ropa, la comida, etc.

# ))) VOCABULARIO

## Los deportes — *Sports*

| | |
|---|---|
| el baloncesto/el básquetbol | *basketball* |
| el béisbol | *baseball* |
| el ciclismo | *cycling* |
| el esquí | *skiing, ski* |
| el fútbol | *soccer* |
| el golf | *golf* |
| el tenis | *tennis* |
| el vóleibol | *volleyball* |

## El equipo deportivo — *Sports equipment*

| | |
|---|---|
| el bate | *bat* |
| el balón/la pelota | *ball* |
| el cesto/la cesta | *basket, hoop* |
| el gol | *goal* |
| los palos | *golf clubs* |
| la raqueta | *racquet* |
| la red | *net* |

## Los eventos — *Events*

| | |
|---|---|
| el campeonato | *championship* |
| la carrera | *race* |
| el juego/el partido | *game* |

## Los lugares — *Places*

| | |
|---|---|
| el campo | *field* |
| la cancha | *court, golf course* |
| la pista | *slope; court; track* |

## Las personas — *People*

| | |
|---|---|
| el árbitro | *umpire, referee* |
| el campeón/la campeona | *champion* |
| el/la ciclista | *cyclist* |
| el entrenador/la entrenadora | *coach* |
| el equipo | *team; equipment* |
| el jugador/la jugadora | *player* |
| el/la tenista | *tennis player* |

## La naturaleza — *Nature*

| | |
|---|---|
| el árbol | *tree* |
| la atmósfera | *atmosphere* |
| el lago | *lake* |

## El tiempo — *Weather*

| | |
|---|---|
| está despejado | *it's clear* |
| está nublado | *it's cloudy* |
| hace fresco | *it's cool* |
| hace sol | *it's sunny* |
| el hielo | *ice* |
| la lluvia | *rain* |
| la nieve | *snow* |
| el viento | *wind* |

## Las descripciones — *Descriptions*

| | |
|---|---|
| contaminado/a | *polluted, contaminated* |
| contrario/a | *opposing* |
| mundial | *world, worldwide* |

## Verbos — *Verbs*

| | |
|---|---|
| aprovechar | *to take advantage* |
| congelar(se) | *to freeze* |
| discutir | *to argue* |
| durar | *to last* |
| enfadarse | *to get angry* |
| esquiar | *to ski* |
| ganar | *to win* |
| ir(se) | *to go away, to leave* |
| jugar (ue) a los bolos | *to bowl* |
| llover (ue) | *to rain* |
| meter un gol | *to score a goal* |
| nevar (ie) | *to snow* |
| patinar | *to skate* |
| perder (ie) | *to lose* |
| pitar | *to whistle* |
| recorrer | *to travel, to cover (distance)* |
| traducir (zc) | *to translate* |

## Palabras y expresiones útiles — *Useful Words and Expressions*

| | |
|---|---|
| cada | *each* |
| conmigo | *with me* |
| contigo | *with you (familiar)* |
| el penalti | *penalty (in sports)* |

> See page 233 for other reflexive verbs.
> See page 239 for other stem-changing -ir verbs.

# Nuestras tradiciones

La pintora mexicana Frida Kahlo pintó este cuadro en 1932. Su título es *Autorretrato entre México y Estados Unidos*.

# In this chapter you will learn how to:

- talk about holidays, traditions, and celebrations
- express ongoing actions in the past
- narrate past events
- make comparisons

## Cultural focus: **México**

Tijuana

Una banda de mariachis

La Paz

Chihuahua

Monterrey

ESTADOS UNIDOS

Río Grande

Golfo de México

Las ruinas prehispánicas de Teotihuacán

Golfo de California

MÉXICO

Zacatecas

El Zócalo en Ciudad de México

Guadalajara

Morelia

Ciudad de México

Puebla

Oaxaca

Bahía de Campeche

Cancún

Mérida

Las ruinas de Tulum

BELICE

GUATEMALA

OCÉANO PACÍFICO

El mole poblano, una de las especialidades de la comida mexicana

**A vista de pájaro.** Complete las siguientes oraciones con sus propias palabras.

1. Los mariachis son...
2. La Catedral Metropolitana está en...
3. La playa de Cancún está en...
4. Algunos platos típicos de la comida mexicana son...
5. Frida Kahlo es...
6. Los mayas y los aztecas construyeron...

# A PRIMERA VISTA

## Las fiestas y las tradiciones

CD 4
Track 1

Estas **carretas adornadas** y sus dueños hicieron el **camino** para llegar a El Rocío, un pequeño pueblo de la provincia de Huelva, en el suroeste de España, donde está la Ermita (*Hermitage*) de la Virgen del Rocío. En el pueblo **se reúnen** cada año cerca de un millón de personas para celebrar la fiesta de la Virgen del Rocío.

El Día de los **Muertos**, también conocido como el Día de los **Difuntos**, se conmemora el 2 de noviembre. Mucha **gente** va al **cementerio** ese día o el día anterior para **recordar** y llevarles flores a sus familiares o amigos difuntos. Especialmente en México, los **preparativos** para el Día de los Muertos **comienzan** con mucha anterioridad y hay familias que pasan la noche del primero al 2 de noviembre **acompañando** a sus muertos en el cementerio, como se ve en esta foto tomada en Pátzcuaro.

Las fiestas y los bailes que se celebran en diversas partes del mundo ayudan a **mantener** las **costumbres** de los **antepasados**. La Diablada es uno de los **festivales** folclóricos con más colorido en Hispanoamérica. Se celebra durante el **carnaval** de Oruro en Bolivia y también en el norte de Chile y en otros países, entre ellos, Perú.

La música, el baile y la **alegría** reinan en los carnavales. Hay **desfiles** de **carrozas** y **comparsas** que bailan en las calles, muchas personas **se disfrazan** y todo el mundo **se divierte**. El **último** día de Carnaval es el martes antes del **comienzo** de la Cuaresma (*Lent*).

Esta es una de las **procesiones** de Semana Santa en Antigua, Guatemala. Esta ciudad fue la antigua capital de Guatemala y es famosa por su arquitectura colonial y las **maravillosas** alfombras que se hacen con flores, **semillas** y **aserrín** para el paso de las procesiones.

El Día de San Fermín, el 7 de julio, se inicia la **celebración** de los sanfermines en Pamplona, España. Esta celebración, que dura del 7 al 14 de julio, es famosa mundialmente por los encierros. Los jóvenes corren por las calles seguidos de los **toros**, hasta llegar a la plaza donde **encierran** a los toros y más tarde tienen lugar las **corridas**.

**8-1 Definiciones.** Asocie el nombre de la festividad en la columna de la izquierda con su descripción en la columna de la derecha.

1. ____ San Fermín
2. ____ La Diablada
3. ____ El Rocío
4. ____ Carnaval
5. ____ El Día de los Muertos
6. ____ Semana Santa

a. Se celebra durante el carnaval de Oruro en Bolivia. personas bailan en las calles disfrazadas de demonios.

b. Muchas personas se disfrazan y bailan en comparsas por las calles.

c. Todos van al cementerio a hacer ofrendas a los seres queridos que están muertos.

d. Hay procesiones por las calles y en Antigua, Guatemala, se hacen unas alfombras de aserrín, flores y semillas.

e. Los jóvenes corren por las calles delante de los toros.

f. Es una fiesta en el sur de España. La gente va en carretas hasta una ermita.

**8-2 Describir las imágenes.** PRIMERA FASE. Describan las fotos anteriores detalladamente contestando las siguientes preguntas.

1. ¿Qué están haciendo las personas en las fotos?
2. ¿Qué ropa llevan las personas? ¿Qué colores hay en las fotos?
3. ¿Qué objetos hay en las fotos? ¿Para qué sirven?
4. ¿Hay animales? ¿Qué hacen estos animales?
5. ¿Piensan que la festividad de la foto es religiosa? ¿Por qué?
6. Según ustedes, ¿es la festividad divertida? ¿Por qué?

SEGUNDA FASE. Elijan una de las fotos y descríbanla en un párrafo. Incluyan las ideas sobre las que conversaron en la *Primera fase*.

**8-3 Contextos.** PRIMERA FASE. Hablen sobre las ideas, sentimientos o costumbres que evocan las siguientes palabras.

MODELO: el carnaval
*La palabra carnaval me hace pensar en música, baile, alegría, carrozas, desfiles, calles.*

1. los cementerios
2. los toros
3. las flores
4. los disfraces
5. las alfombras de aserrín
6. el baile

SEGUNDA FASE. Elijan una de las palabras de la *Primera fase* y escriban una oración en la que la palabra aparezca en un contexto familiar para ustedes. Compartan esta oración con la clase.

MODELO: *Cuando visitamos a los amigos llevamos flores.*

## Cultura

El Día de Acción de Gracias (*Thanksgiving*) no se celebra en los países hispanos y tampoco es tradicional el Día de las Brujas (*Halloween*), aunque empieza a celebrarse en algunas ciudades de Hispanoamérica y de España. Por otro lado, debido a la importancia e influencia de la religión católica en los países hispanos, algunas fiestas católicas se consideran también fiestas oficiales y son días feriados. Pero lo más importante es la gran diversidad de fiestas locales. Muchas personas trabajan todo el año para garantizar el éxito de estas celebraciones en las que la gente baila y se divierte durante días enteros.

## ))) Otras celebraciones

CD 4
Track 2

la Nochebuena

la Navidad

la Nochevieja

el Año Nuevo

el Día de la Independencia de México

la Pascua

el Día de la Madre

el Día del Padre

el Día de Acción de Gracias

el Día de las Brujas

el Día de los Enamorados/del Amor y la Amistad

**8-4 Asociaciones. PRIMERA FASE.** Asocie las fechas de la izquierda con los días festivos de la derecha.

1. ___ el 25 de diciembre
2. ___ el 2 de noviembre
3. ___ el 6 de enero
4. ___ el 4 de julio
5. ___ el 24 de diciembre
6. ___ el 31 de diciembre
7. ___ el 14 de febrero
8. ___ el 31 de octubre

a. el Día de la Independencia de Estados Unidos
b. el Día de las Brujas
c. la Nochebuena
d. la Nochevieja/el Fin de Año
e. el Día de los Enamorados/del Amor y la Amistad
f. el Día de los Reyes Magos
g. el Día de los Muertos
h. la Navidad

**SEGUNDA FASE.** Comenten entre ustedes las respuestas a las siguientes preguntas.

1. ¿Cuál(es) de estas fiestas celebra cada uno/a de ustedes?
2. ¿Cuál es la fiesta favorita de la mayoría de las personas del grupo, y por qué?
3. ¿En cuál de estas fiestas reciben regalos? ¿Qué tipo de regalos?
4. ¿En cuál de estas fiestas hay una comida especial?

 **8-5 Festivales o desfiles.** Piense en algunos festivales o desfiles importantes y complete el cuadro. Su compañero/a va a hacerle preguntas sobre ellos.

MODELO:   E1:   *¿En qué fiesta o desfile importante estás pensando?*
          E2:   *En el Cinco de Mayo.*
          E1:   *¿Dónde lo celebran?*
          E2:   *En México y en algunas ciudades de Estados Unidos, como Austin, Texas.*

El Cinco de Mayo es una fiesta que celebra la victoria de México contra Francia en la Batalla de Puebla en 1862. Ese día hay desfiles y los mexicanos visten sus trajes típicos.

| FESTIVAL O DESFILE | FECHA | LUGAR | DESCRIPCIÓN | OPINIÓN |
|---|---|---|---|---|
|  |  |  |  |  |
|  |  |  |  |  |
|  |  |  |  |  |
|  |  |  |  |  |

 **8-6 Unos días festivos.** Hablen sobre cómo celebran ustedes estas fechas.

MODELO:   E1:   *¿Cómo celebras tu cumpleaños?*
          E2:   *Lo celebro con mi familia y mis amigos. Recibo regalos, y mi madre prepara mi comida favorita con pastel de chocolate de postre. Después escuchamos música, conversamos y a veces bailamos.*

1. la Nochevieja/el Fin de Año
2. el Día de las Brujas
3. el Día de Acción de Gracias
4. el Día de la Independencia
5. el Año Nuevo
6. el Día de la Madre

 **8-7 Una celebración importante.** PRIMERA FASE. Escojan una celebración importante del mundo hispano (Carnaval, Semana Santa, Año Nuevo, Las Posadas, La Diablada, Día de la Independencia, etc.) y busquen información en Internet sobre:

1. el lugar donde se celebra
2. la época del año
3. las actividades
4. los vestidos o disfraces
5. la comida

 **SEGUNDA FASE.** Imagínese que usted y su compañero/a estuvieron en un país hispano durante la celebración que investigaron en la *Primera fase*. Explíquenles a otros/as dos compañeros/as cómo celebraron y qué pasó. Ellos les van a hacer preguntas para obtener más información.

## Lengua

The words **fiesta**, **festividad**, and **festival** are often used interchangeably. **Fiesta** may mean a holiday or a party or celebration. **Festividad** normally refers to a public festivity or a holiday. **Festival** often involves a series of events or celebrations of a public nature. Another term for holiday is **día festivo**. **Día feriado** is a legal holiday.

## ◀)) Las invitaciones

### ¿Quieres salir conmigo?

LUISA: Hola, Arturo, ¿cómo estás?

ARTURO: Bien, Luisa, ¿y tú?

LUISA: Estupendamente. Mira, me gustaría **invitarte** a cenar conmigo el sábado. Es la ocasión perfecta para hablar de tu viaje a México.

ARTURO: La verdad es que me gustaría mucho, pero mañana no puedo porque tengo un partido de fútbol.

LUISA: ¡Qué lástima! ¿Y el domingo, día 15?

ARTURO: El domingo está bien. Si quieres, podemos **quedar** antes para **dar un paseo** por la ciudad. Las calles están adornadas para las fiestas, y la ciudad está muy **animada**.

LUISA: ¡Qué buena idea! Nos vemos en la plaza a las seis.

ARTURO: Bueno, pues nos vemos allí y luego decidimos adónde vamos a cenar.

LUISA: Gracias, Arturo, hasta el domingo.

ARTURO: Hasta el domingo.

---

### En directo

To accept an invitation:

**Gracias. Me encanta la idea.**

**Con mucho gusto.**

**Encantado/a.**

**Será un placer.**
*It will be a pleasure.*

To apologize:

**Me gustaría ir, pero...**

**¡Qué lástima/pena! Ese día tengo que...**

**No puedo, tengo un compromiso.**
*I can't, I have a prior engagement.*

---

**8-8 Una invitación. PRIMERA FASE.** Completen el siguiente cuadro según la conversación de Luisa y Arturo.

| FECHAS DE LAS INVITACIONES | EXPRESIONES QUE USA ARTURO |
|---|---|
| primera invitación: | para disculparse por no aceptar: |
| segunda invitación: | para aceptar la invitación: |

**SEGUNDA FASE.** Ahora invite a su compañero/a a cenar, o a ir al teatro o a un partido importante. Después, su compañero/a va a invitarlo/la a usted. Pueden usar las expresiones del diálogo y de *En directo*.

## Celebraciones personales

CD 4
Track 4

La boda del príncipe Felipe en mayo de 2004 fue un gran acontecimiento histórico y social en España y millones de hispanos pudieron ver por televisión. En los países hispanos, el padrino de la boda es la persona que acompaña a la novia al altar y generalmente es su padre. La madrina está en el altar con el novio y normalmente es su madre.

**8-9 Una invitación de boda.** Lean la invitación de boda y la de la recepción, y contesten las preguntas. Luego preparen una lista con las diferencias que encuentran ustedes entre estas invitaciones y las de su país.

Agradecemos su presencia
después de la ceremonia religiosa
en el Club de Golf Chapultepec
Av. Conscripto N° 425, Lomas
Hipódromo

Pedro Martín Salda
Juana Montoya de Martín

Eduardo Calderón Solís
Elisa Noriega de Calderón

R.S.V.P.
529-99-43
520-16-85

Personal

participan el matrimonio de sus hijos

Estelita
y
Alberto

y tienen el honor de invitarle a la ceremonia
religiosa que se celebrará el viernes 9 de febrero,
a las diecinueve treinta horas en el Convento de
San Joaquín, Santa Cruz Cocalco N° 15,
Legaria, dignándose impartir la
bendición nupcial
el R.P. José Ortuno S.J.
Ciudad de México

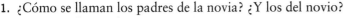

1. ¿Cómo se llaman los padres de la novia? ¿Y los del novio?
2. ¿Cómo se llaman los novios?
3. ¿Qué día es la boda?
4. ¿A qué hora es?
5. ¿En qué país se celebra esta boda?
6. ¿Adónde van a ir los invitados después de la ceremonia?

**8-10 Una ocasión memorable.** Lean la invitación y contesten las preguntas.

Nuestro querido hijo

## David

será llamado a la lectura de la Tora
con motivo de su Bar Mitzvah
el jueves 18 de noviembre
a las ocho de la mañana en la Sinagoga
Centro Hebreo, Avenida 13-15 Zona 9.

Nos sentiremos muy honrados en compartir
con ustedes tan memorable ocasión
y será un placer recibirles en el desayuno
que seguidamente ofreceremos en el
salón de fiestas de la sinagoga.

**David y Ruth Bauman**
Fax: (502) 238-2042
Ciudad de Guatemala, Guatemala

1. ¿Cuál es el motivo de la celebración?
2. ¿Qué día es la celebración? ¿A qué hora?
3. ¿Hay otra actividad, además de la celebración religiosa?
4. ¿Quiénes son David y Ruth Bauman?
5. ¿En qué país tiene lugar esta celebración?

**8-11 Una fiesta especial.** PRIMERA FASE. Piense en una celebración o fiesta en la que usted participó recientemente. Escriba algunas notas sobre lo siguiente:

1. ¿Cuál es el nombre de la fiesta?
2. ¿Dónde se celebró? ¿Cuántos invitados asistieron?
3. Describa la comida que sirvieron.
4. ¿Cómo se divirtió la gente? ¿Tocaron música?
5. ¿Gastaron mucho los anfitriones (*hosts*)?

 SEGUNDA FASE. Ahora explíquense los detalles de esta fiesta. Incluyan detalles de la *Primera fase*.

 **8-12 Identificar la fiesta.** You will listen to four short dialogues about different holidays celebrated in the Hispanic world. Before you listen, write down the names of two holidays that you have studied or read about in this chapter.

CD 4
Track 5

Pay attention to the general idea of what is said. As you listen, identify the holiday each conversation refers to by writing the appropriate conversation number next to it.

____ el Día del Amor y la Amistad/Día de los Enamorados
____ el Día de los Muertos
____ el Día de los Reyes Magos
____ el Día de las Brujas

# EN ACCIÓN

## Diarios de bicicleta: La ponchera

### Antes de ver

**8-13** En este segmento, Marcos, Luciana y Javier están organizando una fiesta de cumpleaños para Gabi. Escriba cinco preguntas para averiguar si todo está listo para la fiesta.

**MODELO:** *¿Hicieron el pastel de cumpleaños?*

### Mientras ve

**8-14** Indique si las siguientes afirmaciones se refieren a Marcos (**M**), a Luciana (**L**) o a Javier (**J**).

1. ____ Quería hacer un pastel de cumpleaños.
2. ____ Invitó a toda la gente.
3. ____ Pusieron la mesa.
4. ____ Dejó caer (*dropped*) la ponchera.

### Después de ver

**8-15** Responda a las siguientes preguntas.

1. ¿Cuándo recibió la ponchera la mamá de Luciana y Marcos?
2. Según Marcos, ¿quién rompió la ponchera?
3. Según su hermana, ¿de quién fue la culpa?
4. ¿Quién le dijo la verdad a la mamá?

# FUNCIONES Y FORMAS

## 1. Expressing ongoing actions and descriptions in the past: The imperfect

ABUELA: **Antes** la música **era** suave y romántica. **Tenía** más melodía y las orquestas **eran** magníficas. **Hoy en día** no **hay** música, sólo ruido, y a la gente **no le interesa** bailar.

NANCY: **Antes** las familias **cenaban** juntas. **Conversaban** mientras **comían**, y los hijos **se aburrían** (*got bored*) mucho. **¡Era** una tortura! **Ahora** es mucho mejor. Cuando **tengo** hambre, **preparo** algo para comer. Además, los padres no **controlan** tanto la vida de sus hijos.

**Piénselo.** Indique (✔) a qué función se refiere cada afirmación.

| ACTIVIDAD | DESCRIPCIÓN EN EL PASADO | ACCIÓN O DESCRIPCIÓN HABITUAL EN EL PASADO | ACCIÓN EN EL PRESENTE |
|---|---|---|---|
| 1. La música del pasado **tenía** más melodía. | _____ | _____ | _____ |
| 2. Hoy en día no **hay** música. | _____ | _____ | _____ |
| 3. Antes las familias **cenaban** juntas. | _____ | _____ | _____ |
| 4. Los hijos **se aburrían** mucho. | _____ | _____ | _____ |
| 5. Cuando **tengo** hambre, **preparo** algo para comer. | _____ | _____ | _____ |
| 6. Los padres no **controlan** tanto la vida de sus hijos. | _____ | _____ | _____ |

- You have already learned to use the preterit to talk about actions in the past. In these scenes, the grandmother and granddaughter use a different past tense, the **imperfect**, because they are focusing on how things used to be and what usually took place 50 or 60 years ago. If they were talking about a specific completed action, like something they did yesterday, they would use the preterit. Generally, the imperfect is used to:

- express habitual or repeated actions in the past (without focus on the completion of the action).

Nosotros **íbamos** a casa para cenar todos los días a las seis.

*We used to go home to eat dinner every day at six o'clock.*

■ express an action or state that was in progress in the past (not whether the action or state was completed).

| | |
|---|---|
| Todos los invitados **hablaban** y **bailaban**. **Estaban** muy contentos. | *All the guests were talking and dancing. They were very happy.* |

■ describe characteristics and conditions in the past.

| | |
|---|---|
| El desfile **era** muy largo y **había** muchos espectadores. | *The parade was very long and there were many spectators.* |

■ tell time in the past.

| | |
|---|---|
| **Era** la una de la tarde; no **eran** las dos. | *It was one in the afternoon; it was not two.* |

■ express a person's age in the past.

| | |
|---|---|
| Ella **tenía** quince años entonces. | *She was fifteen years old then.* |

■ Some expressions of time and frequency that often accompany the imperfect to express ongoing or repeated actions or states in the past are **mientras, a veces, siempre, generalmente,** and **frecuentemente**.

| IMPERFECT | | | |
|---|---|---|---|
| | **HABLAR** | **COMER** | **VIVIR** |
| yo | habl**aba** | com**ía** | viv**ía** |
| tú | habl**abas** | com**ías** | viv**ías** |
| Ud., él, ella | habl**aba** | com**ía** | viv**ía** |
| nosotros/as | habl**ábamos** | com**íamos** | viv**íamos** |
| vosotros/as | habl**abais** | com**íais** | viv**íais** |
| Uds., ellos/as | habl**aban** | com**ían** | viv**ían** |

■ Note that the endings for **-er** and **-ir** verbs are the same and have a written accent over the **í** of the ending.

■ The Spanish imperfect has several English equivalents.

| | |
|---|---|
| Mis amigos **bailaban** mucho. | *My friends danced a lot.* |
| | *My friends were dancing a lot.* |
| | *My friends used to dance a lot.* |
| | *My friends would dance a lot.* |
| | (implying a repeated action) |

■ There are no stem changes in the imperfect.

| | |
|---|---|
| Ella no duerme bien ahora, pero antes d**o**rmía muy bien. | *She does not sleep well now, but she used to sleep very well before.* |

■ Only three verbs are irregular in the imperfect.

**ir**  iba, ibas, iba, íbamos, ibais, iban

**ser**  era, eras, era, éramos, erais, eran

**ver**  veía, veías, veía, veíamos, veíais, veían

■ The imperfect form of **hay** is **había** (*there was, there were, there used to be*). It is invariable.

| | |
|---|---|
| **Había** una invitación en el correo. | *There was an invitation in the mail.* |
| **Había** muchas personas en la fiesta. | *There were many people at the party.* |

### 8-16 Cuando tenía cinco años. Marque (✓) cuáles eran sus actividades cuando usted tenía cinco años.

1. \_\_\_\_ Jugaba en el parque con mi perro.
2. \_\_\_\_ Ayudaba a mi mamá en la casa, especialmente cuando teníamos invitados.
3. \_\_\_\_ Salía con mis padres los fines de semana.
4. \_\_\_\_ Iba a la playa en el verano.
5. \_\_\_\_ Veía televisión hasta muy tarde.
6. \_\_\_\_ Celebraba el Año Nuevo con mis amigos.
7. \_\_\_\_ Asistía a las fiestas de la familia.
8. ...

### 8-17 En mi escuela secundaria. PRIMERA FASE. Marque (✓) la frecuencia con que usted y sus amigos/as hacían estas cosas. Luego compare sus respuestas con las de su compañero/a.

MODELO: decorar los salones de clase
*Frecuentemente decorábamos los salones de clase.*

| ACTIVIDADES | SIEMPRE | FRECUENTEMENTE | A VECES | NUNCA |
|---|---|---|---|---|
| hablar sobre las competencias deportivas en las clases | | | | |
| organizar reuniones para aumentar el espíritu de la escuela (*pep rallies*) | | | | |
| ir a los partidos de fútbol y otros deportes | | | | |
| asistir a conciertos y obras de teatro | | | | |
| participar en un equipo, en la banda, etc. | | | | |
| otra actividad | | | | |

SEGUNDA FASE. Hablen de los siguientes temas.

1. ¿Cuáles eran las tradiciones en su escuela para celebrar y aumentar el espíritu de equipo (*team spirit*) que realizaban con más frecuencia?
2. ¿Cuáles eran sus actividades favoritas?

**8-18 El apagón (*blackout*).** El sábado pasado los señores Herrera organizaron una fiesta en su casa. Desafortunadamente durante la fiesta hubo un apagón en su barrio. Basándose en el dibujo escriba un párrafo para explicar lo que hacían las personas cuando se fue la luz.

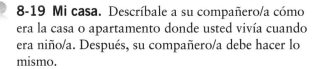 **8-19 Mi casa.** Descríbale a su compañero/a cómo era la casa o apartamento donde usted vivía cuando era niño/a. Después, su compañero/a debe hacer lo mismo.

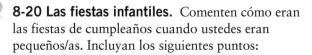 **8-20 Las fiestas infantiles.** Comenten cómo eran las fiestas de cumpleaños cuando ustedes eran pequeños/as. Incluyan los siguientes puntos:

1. lugar de la celebración
2. horas (comienzo y final)
3. dos o tres actividades que hacían
4. personas que participaban
5. comida y bebida que servían
6. ropa que llevaban

**8-21 Antes y ahora.** Expliquen cómo era la vida antes y cómo es ahora con respecto a los siguientes temas:

1. la familia (tamaño, grado de movilidad, porcentaje de divorcios)
2. la mujer en la sociedad (participación en el mundo del trabajo/de la política, su independencia económica)
3. las ciudades (tamaño, los problemas ambientales (*environmental*) como la contaminación, la delincuencia, el crimen)

---

**En directo**

To talk about how things used to be:

**Entonces…**

**Por aquel entonces…**

**En aquellos tiempos…**

---

## SITUACIONES

1. **Role A.** You are a famous public figure (a singer, professor, scientist, athlete, etc.) being interviewed by a television reporter. Offer as many details about your background as possible.

   **Role B.** You are interviewing a famous person for a television program. Ask a) what his/her family life and hometown were like when he/she was young; b) the type of music he/she used to listen to; c) the books he/she used to read; d) the holidays he/she celebrated most.

2. **Role A.** You are an exchange student and would like to find out about your host's weekend and summer activities when he/she was in high school. Ask a) what activites there were for high school students in his/her community, b) what he/she generally did on Saturday evenings and with whom; and c) what he/she usually did in the summer.

   **Role B.** You are the host of an exchange student. Answer his/her questions about your weekend and summer activities when you were in high school. Describe a summer trip to a friend's house in Guadalajara, Mexico, and say that you a) spoke Spanish every day; b) went to the outdoor markets often; c) listened to the mariachis very often; and d) used to eat excellent Mexican food every day.

## 2. Narrating in the past: The preterit and the imperfect

**Había** una vez una chica que **vivía** con su padre, porque su madre **estaba** muerta. La chica **se llamaba** Cenicienta. **Era** muy bella y muy buena, y todos los vecinos la **querían** mucho. Pero un día, su vida **cambió**. Su padre **se casó** con una mujer muy mala que **tenía** dos hijas. La mujer y sus hijas **vinieron** a vivir a la casa de Cenicienta. Las hijas **eran** muy crueles y **odiaban** (*hated*) a Cenicienta, su hermanastra...

**Piénselo.** Lea las afirmaciones y marque (✔) su función en el cuento: contar los eventos, o dar información de fondo (*background information*) sobre el contexto o los personajes.

|  | CONTAR LOS EVENTOS | DAR INFORMACIÓN DE FONDO |
|---|---|---|
| **1.** La chica **se llamaba** Cenicienta. | _____ | _____ |
| **2. Era** muy bella y muy buena. | _____ | _____ |
| **3.** Todos los vecinos la **querían** mucho. | _____ | _____ |
| **4.** Pero un día, su vida **cambió**. | _____ | _____ |
| **5.** Su padre **se casó** con una mujer muy mala. | _____ | _____ |
| **6.** La mujer y sus hijas **vinieron** a vivir a la casa de Cenicienta. | _____ | _____ |

■ The preterit and the imperfect are not interchangeable. They fulfill different functions when telling a story or talking about an event in the past.

■ Use the preterit:

**1.** to express a sequence of actions completed in the past (note that there is a forward movement of narrative time).

> **Oyeron** un ruido, se **levantaron**, y **bajaron** las escaleras.    *They heard a noise, got up, and went downstairs.*

**2.** to talk about the beginning or end of an event, action, or condition.

> Pepito **leyó** a los cinco años.    *Pepito read (began to read) at age five.*
>
> El niño **se enfermó** el sábado.    *The child got sick (became sick) on Saturday.*
>
> Pepito **leyó** el cuento.    *Pepito read (finished) the story.*
>
> El niño **estuvo** enfermo ayer.    *The child was sick yesterday (and is no longer sick).*

**3.** to talk about an event, action, or condition that occurred over a specified period of time.

> **Vivieron** en México por diez años.    *They lived in Mexico for ten years.*

■ Use the imperfect:

1. to talk about customary or habitual actions, events, or conditions in the past.

Todos los días **llovía** y por eso **leíamos** mucho.

*It used to rain every day, and that's why we read a lot.*

2. to express an ongoing part of an event, action, or condition.

En ese momento **llovía** mucho y los niños **estaban** muy tristes.

*At that moment it was raining a lot, and the children were very sad.*

■ In a story, the imperfect provides the background information, whereas the preterit tells what happened. Frequently an action or situation (expressed with the imperfect) is ongoing when something else (expressed with the preterit) suddenly happens.

**Era** Navidad. Todos **dormíamos** cuando los niños **oyeron** un ruido en el techo.

*It was Christmas. All of us were sleeping when the children heard a noise on the roof.*

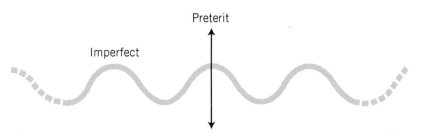

**8-22 ¡Qué día más malo!** Ayer iba a ser un día especial para Pedro, pero sus planes terminaron mal. Marque (✓) las tres cosas más graves que le ocurrieron a Pedro mientras trataba de realizar sus planes.

1. _____ Mientras se bañaba temprano por la mañana, se cayó en el baño.
2. _____ Mientras desayunaba tranquilamente, el teléfono sonó y no pudo terminar de comer.
3. _____ Iba a la tienda para comprarle un anillo a su novia cuando alguien le robó el dinero.
4. _____ Mientras llamaba por teléfono a un restaurante para reservar una mesa, el restaurante se incendió.
5. _____ Iba a proponerle matrimonio a su novia cuando su ex-novia lo llamó por teléfono.
6. _____ Mientras preparaba una cena deliciosa para celebrar el cumpleaños de su novia, el perro se comió el pastel.

**8-23 La última vez.** Túrnense para preguntarse cuándo fue la última vez que cada uno de ustedes hizo estas cosas y cómo se sentía mientras las hacía.

MODELO:      ver un partido de béisbol
   E1: *¿Cuándo fue la última vez que viste un partido de béisbol?*
   E2: *Vi un partido de béisbol la semana pasada.*
   E1: *¿Y cómo te sentías mientras veías el partido?*
   E2: *Estaba aburrido/a, porque no me gusta mucho el béisbol.*

1. participar en un campeonato
2. ganar un premio
3. estar en un desfile
4. disfrazarse
5. bailar en un carnaval
6. ...

Compradores en un mercado de Mérida.

**8-24 Una visita al mercado.** Imagínese que usted fue de compras a un mercado al aire libre de Mérida y ahora le cuenta a un amigo/una amiga lo que pasó. Complete las oraciones usando el imperfecto del verbo en la primera columna y el pretérito del verbo en la segunda columna.

**MODELO:** Ser las once cuando…
*Eran las once cuando llegué al mercado.*

1. Caminar al mercado cuando…       ver unas botellas bonitas
2. Mirar las botellas cuando…       hablarme la vendedora
3. Probarse un cinturón de cuero cuando…   empezar a llover
4. Ser las dos de la tarde cuando…   ver a mi amigo José
5. Tomar un café para escapar de la lluvia cuando…   (nosotros) volver al mercado para hacer nuestras compras

 **8-25 Un cuento.** Completen esta narración usando el pretérito o el imperfecto.

En el mes de abril del año pasado mi familia y yo (1) _____ (ir) a México de vacaciones. Primero nosotros (2) _____ (estar) en Ciudad de México por dos días. Allí (3) _____ (ver) a unos parientes y (4) _____ (visitar) lugares muy interesantes, como el Museo Nacional de Antropología, donde (5) _____ (poder) admirar una excelente colección de objetos de la cultura azteca, y a las tiendas de la Zona Rosa, donde mi mamá (6) _____ (comprar) unas blusas preciosas.

En la mañana del tercer día, nosotros (7) _____ (irse) a Iztapalapa, que está bastante cerca de la capital. (8) _____ (Hacer) un tiempo fabuloso. Como (9) _____ (ser) primavera, muchos árboles y plantas (10) _____ (tener) flores, y todo (11) _____ (estar) muy verde. Nosotros (12) _____ (salir) del hotel cerca de las cinco de la tarde y poco después (13) _____ (llegar) a una plaza donde (14) _____ (haber) mucha gente. Allí (15) _____ (ver) las procesiones de la Semana Santa. El ambiente (16) _____ (ser) impresionante; las personas (17) _____ (llevar) túnicas largas y (18) _____ (caminar) lentamente por la calle. ¡Nunca vamos a olvidar esa experiencia!

**8-26 Un evento inolvidable.** Cuéntele a su compañero/a algo inesperado que le ocurrió el año pasado. Indique qué pasó, dónde y cuándo. Describa la escena y los personajes.

## 3. Comparing people and things: Comparisons of inequality

| Número de días del Carnaval de la Primavera | 3 | 2 |
|---|---|---|
| Asistencia del público | 25.390 | 18.864 |
| Mujeres | 6.000 | 2.000 |
| Hombres | 4.000 | 5.000 |
| Niños | 25.000 | 27.000 |
| puesto (Budget) | 150.000.,000 | 180.000.,000 |

Para planificar el Carnaval de la Primavera debemos mirar las estadísticas de los años recientes. ¿Vamos a celebrar el carnaval **más de** dos días? En el año 2008, la asistencia fue **mayor que** la del 2009. En el 2008, había **más** mujeres **que** hombres, pero en el 2009 participaron **menos** mujeres **que** en el año anterior. Para tener un **mejor** carnaval **que** en años anteriores, vamos a necesitar **más** dinero **que** en los años pasados.

**Piénselo.** Indique si las siguientes afirmaciones son ciertas (**C**), falsas (**F**) o posibles (**P**), según las estadísticas.

1. \_\_\_\_ En el año 2009 había **menos** participación del público **que** en el 2008.
2. \_\_\_\_ En el año 2009 participaron **menos** niños **que** adultos en el carnaval.
3. \_\_\_\_ Los organizadores probablemente gastaron **más** dinero en el año 2009 **que** en el 2008.
4. \_\_\_\_ En el futuro el carnaval va a durar **más de** dos días.
5. \_\_\_\_ En el futuro, los carnavales van a ser **mejores que** los del pasado.

■ Use **más... que** or **menos... que** to express comparisons of inequality with nouns, adjectives, and adverbs.

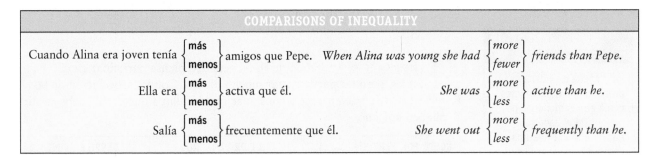

| COMPARISONS OF INEQUALITY | | | |
|---|---|---|---|
| Cuando Alina era joven tenía {**más** / **menos**} amigos que Pepe. | | When Alina was young she had {more / fewer} friends than Pepe. | |
| Ella era {**más** / **menos**} activa que él. | | She was {more / less} active than he. | |
| Salía {**más** / **menos**} frecuentemente que él. | | She went out {more / less} frequently than he. | |

■ Use **de** instead of **que** before numbers.

En el año 2008, había **más de** diez carrozas en el desfile.

*In 2008, there were **more than** ten floats in the parade.*

El año pasado había **menos de** diez carrozas.

*Last year there were **fewer than** ten floats.*

■ The following adjectives have both regular and irregular comparative forms.

| bueno/a | más bueno/a o mejor | *better* |
|---|---|---|
| malo/a | más malo/a o peor[1] | *worse* |
| pequeño/a | más pequeño/a o menor | *smaller* |
| joven | más joven o menor | *younger* |
| grande | más grande o mayor | *bigger* |
| viejo/a | más viejo/a o mayor[2] | *older* |

Esta banda es { mejor / peor } que aquella. *This band is* { *better* / *worse* } *than that one.*

■ **Bien** and **mal** are adverbs. They have the same irregular comparative forms as the adjectives **bueno** and **malo**.

bien → mejor    Yo canto **mejor** que Héctor.    *I sing better than Héctor.*

mal → peor    Héctor canta **peor** que yo.    *Héctor sings worse than I.*

## 8-27 Comparación de dos desfiles. PRIMERA FASE. Lea la siguiente información sobre dos desfiles mexicanos, uno de Veracruz y el otro de Mérida. Complete las frases con **más que, menos que, más de** o **menos de**, según la información en la tabla.

|  | **VERACRUZ** | **MÉRIDA** |
|---|---|---|
| habitantes | 444.438 | 649.770 |
| promedio (*average*) de público que participa | 14.000 personas | 12.000 personas |
| número de bandas | 8 | 6 |
| número de policías | 200 | 175 |

1. Mérida tiene _____ habitantes _____ Veracruz.
2. _____ personas asisten al desfile de Veracruz _____ al desfile de Mérida.
3. Los dos desfiles tienen _____ _____ cinco bandas.
4. Mérida gasta _____ dinero en seguridad (*security*) _____ Veracruz.
5. _____ _____ medio millón de personas viven en Veracruz.
6. Probablemente el público de Mérida es _____ entusiasta _____ el de Veracruz.

**SEGUNDA FASE.** La banda de su universidad piensa participar en uno de estos desfiles, pero no puede gastar mucho dinero. Con la información de la *Primera fase* y la que aparece a continuación, decidan a qué desfile debe asistir. Expliquen por qué.

| COSTO POR PERSONA | DESFILE DE VERACRUZ | DESFILE DE MERIDA |
|---|---|---|
| transporte | 5.824,50 pesos | 6.552,60 pesos |
| hotel por día | 880,50 pesos | 915,25 pesos |
| comidas por día | 450,00 pesos | 348,00 pesos |

---

[1]**Más bueno/a** and **más malo/a** are not used interchangeably with **mejor** and **peor**. **Más bueno/a** and **más malo/a** refer to a person's moral qualities. **Mejor** and **peor** refer to skills and abilities.

[2]Use **mayor** to refer to a person's age. **Más viejo/a** is generally used with nouns other than people.

**8-28 Las alfombras de aserrín.** Los artesanos de Guatemala hacen alfombras de aserrín para celebrar la Semana Santa. Comparen las dos alfombras según los siguientes criterios. Pueden usar estas expresiones u otras.

| | | | |
|---|---|---|---|
| colores fuertes | corto | figuras | rectangular |
| colores suaves | diseño | imágenes | simple |
| colorido | elaborado | largo | sofisticado |

1. el tamaño
2. los colores

3. el estilo
4. su preferencia por una de las alfombras

**A.**

**B.**

**8-29 Personas famosas.** Compare a las siguientes personas. Considere lo siguiente.

1. su aspecto físico
2. su edad
3. el tipo de trabajo que hacen
4. el dinero o popularidad que tienen

Brad Pitt

Salma Hayek en el papel de Frida Kahlo en la película *Frida*

## SITUACIONES

1. **Role A.** You and your fiancé/fiancée disagree about wedding plans. You prefer small weddings. Try to persuade your groom/bride by comparing small and large weddings with regard to: a) expenses (**gastos**); b) stress (**estrés**); c) work involved; and d) possible problems.

   **Role B.** You and your fiancé/fiancée are planning your wedding. You prefer big weddings. Listen to the opinions of your fiancé/fiancée and try to come to an agreement.

2. **Role A.** You are a student government representative presenting a proposal to the dean to change the graduation ceremony. Compare the ceremony at your school with one at a rival institution. Say that the other ceremony is better because it is smaller, better organized, less expensive, and usually has better music and speeches (**discursos**).

   **Role B.** You are the dean. A student government representative is proposing changes in the graduation ceremony. Listen to the presentation and ask questions to compare the advantages of both types of ceremonies.

## 4. Comparing people and things: Comparisons of equality

**PRESIDENTA DEL COMITÉ ORGANIZADOR:** Este año tuvimos un Carnaval de Primavera **tan** espectacular **como** el de 2008, que hasta este año era nuestro carnaval más grande. En los tres días del carnaval asistió **tanto** público **como** en el año 2008, un total de 25.400 personas. Además, los grupos musicales tocaron música **tan** buena **como** la música del carnaval de 2008. También el número de bailarines se mantuvo igual. Hubo **tantos** bailarines **como** en el 2008. Estoy muy agradecida de ustedes porque colaboraron **tanto como** en otros años. Vamos a planificar el carnaval del próximo año **tan bien como** el de este año.

**Piénselo.** Indique si las siguientes afirmaciones interpretan correcta (**C**) o incorrectamente (**I**) la información que dio la Presidenta del Comité Organizador.

1. ____ En 2008 asistieron unas 25.400 personas al carnaval y este año asistió el mismo número de personas.
2. ____ Este año los grupos musicales tocaron música que al público le gustó **menos que** en otros años.
3. ____ Este año el Comité Organizador hizo un trabajo **tan bueno como** el trabajo de otros años.
4. ____ La planificación del carnaval fue buena este año y la del próximo año va a ser buena también.

■ In the previous section you learned to express comparisons of inequality. In this section you will learn how to indicate that two people, things, or activities are equal in some way.

| COMPARISONS OF EQUALITY | |
|---|---|
| tan... como | *as ... as* |
| tanto/a... como | *as much ... as* |
| tantos/as... como | *as many ... as* |
| tanto como | *as much as* |

■ Use **tan... como** to express comparisons of equality with adjectives and adverbs.

| | |
|---|---|
| La boda fue **tan** elegante **como** la fiesta. | *The wedding was as elegant as the party.* |
| El padre bailó **tan** bien **como** su hija. | *The father danced as well as his daughter.* |

■ Use **tanto/a... como** and **tantos/as... como** to express comparisons of equality with nouns.

| | |
|---|---|
| Había **tanta** alegría **como** en el Carnaval. | *There was as much joy as at Mardi Gras.* |
| Había **tantos** invitados **como** en mi fiesta de graduación. | *There were as many guests as at my graduation party.* |

■ Use **tanto como** to express comparisons of equality with verbs.

| | |
|---|---|
| Los invitados bailaron **tanto como** nosotros. | *The guests danced as much as we did.* |

**8-30 Cuatro estudiantes afortunados.** Lean algunos datos personales sobre cuatro estudiantes. Luego, indiquen si las afirmaciones a continuación son ciertas (**C**) o falsas (**F**). Si son falsas (**F**), corrijan la información.

| | PEDRO | VILMA | MARTA | RICARDO |
|---|---|---|---|---|
| hermanos | 2 | 3 | 3 | 2 |
| clases | 5 | 5 | 4 | 6 |
| dinero para gastos personales cada mes | 5.000 pesos | 8.500 pesos | 5.000 pesos | 8.500 pesos |
| películas en DVD | 200 | 180 | 180 | 215 |
| viajes a otros países | 3 | 8 | 3 | 8 |

1. ____ Pedro tiene **tantos** hermanos **como** Vilma.
2. ____ Vilma tomó **tantas** clases este semestre **como** Ricardo.
3. ____ La familia de Marta es **tan** grande **como** la familia de Vilma.
4. ____ Cada mes, Ricardo recibe **tanto** dinero de sus padres **como** Vilma.
5. ____ Marta probablemente gasta **más** dinero en películas **que** Vilma.
6. ____ La familia de Pedro viaja **tanto como** la familia de Ricardo.

**8-31 Sus opiniones.** PRIMERA FASE. Haga lo siguiente.

1. Escriba los nombres de dos celebridades en su cultura.
2. Escriba los nombres de dos festividades o desfiles que se realizan en su ciudad, región o país.
3. Escriba dos programas cómicos de la televisión.

SEGUNDA FASE. Ahora, expresen su opinión y comparen los nombres que escribieron en la *Primera fase*. Usen la información dada y modifiquen los adjetivos cuando sea necesario.

MODELO: 　*Tom Cruise y Johnny Depp*: calidad de su trabajo (bueno/a, mediocre, malo/a)
　　　E1: *Tom Cruise es tan buen actor como Johnny Depp.*
　　　E2: *Sí, estoy de acuerdo.* O: *No, Johnny Depp es mejor actor que Tom Cruise.*

1. Dos celebridades: apariencia física, calidad de su trabajo (atractivo, alto, famoso, bueno...)
2. Dos desfiles o celebraciones locales o nacionales: número de personas, carrozas (divertido, colorido, numeroso, alegre)
3. Dos programas cómicos de la televisión: calidad, grado de interés para el público (bueno, malo, mediocre, cómico, loco, divertido)

**SITUACIONES**

1. **Role A.** You are reminiscing about Independence Day celebrations when you were a child. Tell your son/daughter (your classmate) that you think that a) in the past Americans were more patriotic (**patrióticos**); b) the celebrations were less expensive; and c) the celebrations were more family oriented (**se celebraban en familia**) than today.

   **Role B.** Your dad/mom (your classmate) argues that today's Independence Day celebrations are less family oriented than in the past. You disagree. State that a) today Americans are as patriotic as they were in the past; b) people used to spend less money because they made less money; and c) today families celebrate Independence Day together as much as in the past.

2. **Role A.** Your next-door neighbors are three students, two of whom are identical twins (**gemelos/as**). Even though you have lived there for a year, you cannot tell them apart. When you run into the third roommate on campus, you mention all the ways in which the twins seem absolutely alike to you. Ask your neighbor's help in telling them apart.

   **Role B.** You and your long-time friends, who are identical twins (**gemelos/as**), share an apartment. When your neighbor asks you for help in telling them apart, describe a) two ways in which they are exactly alike in appearance, abilities, and preferences and b) two ways in which they are different that allow you to tell them apart.

## 5. Comparing people and things: The superlative

PERLA: Lupita, ¿tienes algún plan especial para el Día de los Muertos?

LUPITA: Claro que sí. En mi comunidad, visitamos a familiares y amigos muertos en el cementerio. Les llevamos **la mejor** música mexicana y su comida preferida. Es **el** día **más importante del** año para recordarlos. Creemos que ellos vuelven a su tumba el 1 y 2 de noviembre para disfrutar de **la mejor** compañía, la de su familia y amigos.

PERLA: ¡Qué interesante! Para mi familia **el** acto **más** importante es recordarlos con **las** flores **más** hermosas **de** la estación.

**Piénselo.** Complete las siguientes oraciones con el nombre de la persona que expresa la información.

1. _____ lleva al cementerio **la mejor** música mexicana.
2. Según _____, el Día de los Muertos es **el** día **más importante del** año para recordar a los familiares y amigos muertos.
3. _____ dice que **la** compañía **más** agradable para los muertos es la de sus familiares y amigos.
4. _____ dice que su familia lleva la comida que les gustaba **más** a sus familiares muertos.
5. _____ dice que para su familia, **la** manera **más** apropiada **de** recordar a los muertos es llevarles flores.

■ Use superlatives to express *most* and *least* as degrees of comparison among three or more entities. To form the superlative, use *definite article* + *noun* + **más/menos** + *adjective*. To express *in* or *at* with the superlative, use **de**.

| | |
|---|---|
| Es **el** disfraz **menos** creativo (**de** la fiesta). | *It is the least creative costume (at the party).* |
| México es **el** país con **más** fiestas **de** América del Norte. | *Mexico is the country with the most holidays in North America.* |

■ Do not use **más** or **menos** with **mejor, peor, mayor,** or **menor**.

| | |
|---|---|
| ¿Esos desfiles? Son **los mejores** desfiles **del** país. | *Those parades? They are the best parades in the country.* |
| Ivonne es **la mejor** bailarina **del** grupo. | *Ivonne is the best dancer of the group.* |

■ You may delete the noun when it is clear to whom or to what you refer.

| | |
|---|---|
| Son **los mejores del** país. | *They are the best (ones) in the country.* |

■ To express the idea of *extremely*, add the ending **-ísimo** (**-a, -os, -as**) to the adjective. If the adjective ends in a consonant, add **-ísimo** directly to the singular form of the adjective. If it ends in a vowel, drop the vowel before adding **-ísimo**.

| | | |
|---|---|---|
| **fácil** | Este baile es **facilísimo**. | *This dance is extremely easy.* |
| **grande** | La carroza es **grandísima**. | *The float is extremely big.* |
| **bueno** | Las orquestas son **buenísimas**. | *The orchestras are extremely good.* |

> **Lengua**
>
> A Spanish word can have only one written accent. Therefore, an adjective with a written accent loses the accent when **-ísimo/a** is added.
>
> **fácil > facilísimo/a**
> **rápido > rapidísimo/a**

**8-32 Estadísticas demográficas.** Lea la información de la tabla. Luego indique a qué país de la columna B se refiere cada oración de la columna A.

| | MÉXICO | GUATEMALA | ESTADOS UNIDOS |
|---|---|---|---|
| población (aprox.) del país | 104.700.000 habitantes | 12.728.000 habitantes | 302.688.000 habitantes |
| población de la capital | México, DF: 19.232.000 | Ciudad de Guatemala: 3.942.000 | Washington, DC: 588.292 |
| número de lenguas indígenas | 62 | 24 | aprox. 150 familias de lenguas |
| religión predominante | 89% son católicos (aprox. 93.180.000) | 49% son católicos (aprox. 6.237.000) | 52% son protestantes (aprox. 157.398.000) |
| número de estados o departamentos | 32 estados | 22 departamentos | 50 estados |

**A**

1. ____ Este país tiene **el mayor número** de habitantes.
2. ____ Esta ciudad capital es **la más** grande.
3. ____ Es el país donde existe **el mayor** número de lenguas indígenas.
4. ____ Este es el país con **menos** lenguas indígenas.
5. ____ Este país tiene **el menor** porcentaje de personas que profesan el catolicismo.
6. ____ Este país tiene **el mayor** número de gobiernos estatales o departmentales.

**B**

a. Guatemala
b. México
c. Estados Unidos

**8-33 ¿En qué pueblo o ciudad?** Respondan a las siguientes preguntas y, luego, comparen sus respuestas con las de otra pareja. ¿Están de acuerdo o tienen opiniones diferentes?

¿En qué pueblo o ciudad de su país...

1. sirven la mejor comida étnica?
2. se come la comida más picante (*spicy*)?
3. se vende el café cubano más fuerte?
4. celebran las mejores fiestas de Año Nuevo?
5. hay el mayor número de desfiles hermosos?
6. tocan la mejor música folclórica estadounidense?

## SITUACIONES

1. **Role A.** You are interviewing a well-known film critic about American movies. Ask a) which is the best American film and why; b) who is the best actor/actress; c) which is the worst film of the year; and d) what he/she thinks of Hispanic films.

   **Role B.** You are a well-known film critic. Answer the questions according to your own opinions regarding the best/worst American films and actors. Mention that a) there are some excellent Mexican, Argentinian, and Spanish films and b) several of them won Oscars in the last ten years.

2. **Role A.** You travelled to Mexico for Spring Break and liked the country very much. Tell your classmate the five things you liked best about Mexico and if there was something you found extremely interesting. Provide examples.

   **Role B.** Ask questions about your classmate's trip. Then tell where you went during Spring Break. Share five of the best things you liked about the place you visited.

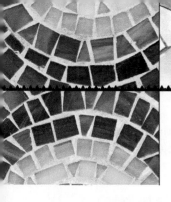

# MOSAICOS

## A escuchar

**Draw conclusions based on what you know**

Understanding what someone says involves comprehending the literal meaning of the words you hear. It also may involve using the context and the information the speaker provides in order to draw conclusions that go beyond literal comprehension. This process is called inferencing, or making inferences.

When you talk to someone or overhear a conversation, you can understand what is said even when the speaker does not express the meaning explicitly. For example, if you are driving with a friend and get lost, you may say, "There is a gas station up there on the right." Your friend will probably infer that you want to stop to ask for directions.

### Antes de escuchar

**8-34 Preparación.** Es el fin de año y dos amigos conversan sobre el feriado que se aproxima. Antes de escuchar la conversación, escriba el nombre de una festividad de la cual probablemente ellos van a hablar. Luego, escriba dos preguntas que en su opinión alguien va a hacer sobre este feriado.

### Escuchar

**CD 4
Track 6**

**8-35 ¿Comprende usted?** First, read the statements below, and then listen as two friends talk about a Mexican holiday. After listening, mark (✓) the statements that provide information you can infer from what you heard.

1. ___ Daniel es mexicano.
2. ___ Sandra es una persona muy tímida.
3. ___ Sandra no es estadounidense.
4. ___ Daniel está triste porque no va a celebrar la Navidad con su familia.
5. ___ Pedir posada es una costumbre en que participa solamente la familia.
6. ___ Daniel no conoce algunas costumbres mexicanas.

### Después de escuchar

**8-36 Ahora usted.** Comparta sus respuestas a estas preguntas con su compañero/a.

1. ¿Qué fiesta o tradición religiosa le gustaría celebrar en un país hispano? ¿Por qué?
2. ¿Celebran esa fiesta en su ciudad o país? ¿Cómo la celebran?
3. ¿Qué fiesta o tradición celebra usted solamente con sus amigos?

# A conversar

**Conduct an interview**

To conduct an interview, you need to ask two types of questions: (a) questions to open up a topic and (b) follow-up questions to get additional information. Open-ended questions that function as invitations to speak—such as **¿Podría hablar de los deportes que practicaba de niño/a?**—will elicit longer and more detailed responses than direct, closed-ended questions like **¿Qué deportes practicaba cuando era niño/a?** Questions that can be answered with **Sí** or **No** are not likely to elicit much information, unless you follow up with **¿Por qué?** Listen carefully to what your interviewee says so that you can ask relevant follow-up questions.

## Antes de conversar

**8-37 Preparación.** ¿Tuvieron usted y uno/a de sus compañeros/as una infancia y adolescencia semejantes? Escriban preguntas que los/las ayuden a obtener información en las siguientes áreas, u otras áreas de interés para ustedes.

1. deportes que su compañero/a practicaba y miraba en la televisión entre los siete y los doce años de edad
2. la(s) fiesta(s) más importantes para la familia de su compañero/a y cómo la(s) celebraba
3. una o dos costumbres de la familia que a él/ella le gustaba(n) y otras que no le gustaban y por qué
4. ...

## Conversar

**8-38 Entre nosotros.** Entreviste a su compañero/a usando las preguntas de la actividad **8-37** y tome notas de sus respuestas.

## Después de conversar

**8-39 Un poco más.** Anónimamente, escriban un breve informe comparativo de la infancia y adolescencia de ustedes. Sus compañeros van a leer su informe y van a tratar de averiguar quiénes son ustedes. Sigan los modelos y frases a continuación o combínenlos, de acuerdo con sus experiencias. Mantengan su identidad en secreto.

**MODELO:**

**ALMAS GEMELAS**

*Somos dos almas gemelas. Tanto mi compañero/a como yo nacimos en...*

**MUNDOS APARTES**

*Somos dos mundos apartes. Mi compañero/a nació en.... Yo nací en...*

1. Durante la infancia/adolescencia...
2. Con respecto a los deportes/las fiestas...
3. La persona A y la persona B tuvieron una niñez/adolescencia semejante/diferente porque...

### En directo

To ask someone to talk about a topic:

**¿Me podría(s) hablar sobre... ?**
*Can you talk to me more about . . . ?*

**¿Qué me puede(s) decir usted sobre/de... ?**
*What can you tell me about . . . ?*

**Me gustaría saber...**
*I would like to know . . .*

To ask someone to expand on a topic:

**¿Podría(s) hablar más sobre... ?**

**¿Qué más me puede(s) decir sobre... ?**

### En directo

To show empathy:

**¡Oh! ¡Qué lástima! ¡Cuánto lo siento!**
*How sad! I'm so sorry.*

To share someone's happiness:

**¡Qué fabuloso/bueno!**
*How fabulous/great!*

**¡Cuánto me alegro!**
*I'm so happy to hear that!*

To express interest in what someone said:

**¡Qué interesante!**
*How interesting!*

# A leer

## Antes de leer

**8-40 Preparación.** Las creencias sobre la muerte varían de una cultura a otra. Indiquen si creen que las siguientes prácticas se asocian con la cultura egipcia (**E**), con alguna cultura indígena americana (**I**) o con ambas (**A**).

1. \_\_\_\_ Creían que había vida después de la muerte.
2. \_\_\_\_ Construían pirámides para honrar a los muertos.
3. \_\_\_\_ Vestían a los muertos con ropa funeraria especial.
4. \_\_\_\_ Ponían una máscara sobre la cara del muerto.
5. \_\_\_\_ Enterraban (*They buried*) al muerto en las pirámides, en tumbas o sepulcros, de acuerdo al estatus social de la persona muerta.
6. \_\_\_\_ La familia de la persona muerta depositaba joyas y objetos de valor en la tumba o pirámide.
7. \_\_\_\_ Rociaban (*They sprayed*) el cadáver con un polvo de color rojo para simbolizar el renacimiento (*rebirth*).

## Leer

### Creencias y costumbres mayas sobre la muerte

El origen de los mayas es incierto. Sin embargo, se sabe que esta civilización ocupó y se desarrolló[1] en los actuales territorios de Guatemala, México, Belice, Honduras y El Salvador. Durante su período de mayor esplendor, los mayas construyeron ciudades y pirámides, donde enterraban a sus gobernantes y los veneraban después de muertos.

Los mayas compartían con otras culturas mesoamericanas algunas creencias y costumbres. Entre otras cosas, creían en la vida después de la muerte y en la interacción entre el mundo humano y el mundo espiritual. Creían que el destino de una persona después de la muerte dependía de la forma en que moría y no de su conducta mientras vivía. Las tumbas y los vestuarios funerarios confirman que los mayas creían que el espíritu se prolongaba más allá de la muerte. La mayoría de los muertos iba a Xibalbá, un lugar en el mundo de abajo.

Para llegar a Xibalbá había que superar numerosos peligros. El espíritu debía comer bien y cuidarse. Por eso, los mayas

dejaban en la tumba una vestimenta funeraria. También colocaban comida, agua y amuletos protectores, de acuerdo con el estatus social del muerto.

Los mayas rociaban el cadáver con un polvo rojo que simbolizaba el renacimiento. También lo adornaban con joyas, collares, pulseras y anillos de jade, hueso[2] o concha[3] y un cinturón ceremonial. En muchas tumbas ponían una máscara sobre la cara del muerto para ocultar su identidad. En la boca le ponían una cuenta[4] de jade, símbolo de lo precioso y lo perenne, para preservar su espíritu inmortal.

Algunas de estas creencias y costumbres todavía se conservan, con ciertas variaciones, en algunas comunidades de Guatemala, México y El Salvador.

[1]*developed*   [2]*bone*   [3]*shell*   [4]*bead*

**8-41 Primera mirada.** Determine si las siguientes afirmaciones representan información explícita (**E**) en el texto o si son inferencias (**I**) basadas en el contenido. Si es una inferencia, indique la oración o las oraciones en el texto en que se basa(n).

1. ____ Los expertos no saben de dónde vinieron los mayas.
2. ____ Los mayas crearon una gran civilización.
3. ____ Las comunidades mayas tenían autoridades que los gobernaban.
4. ____ Como los egipcios, los mayas construyeron edificios magníficos para honrar la memoria de personas de alto estatus en su comunidad.
5. ____ Los mayas, como otros grupos indígenas, pensaban que la vida continuaba después de la muerte.
6. ____ Para los mayas, el tipo de muerte determinaba el destino de una persona.
7. ____ No todos los mayas iban al mismo destino después de la muerte.
8. ____ La comida, el agua y los amuletos ayudaban al espíritu del muerto a llegar a su destino final.

**8-42 Segunda mirada.** Complete las siguientes ideas con información explícita en el texto.

1. Los mayas, como otras culturas indígenas de Mesoamérica, creían en...
2. Dos costumbres que demuestran que los mayas tenían estas creencias son...
3. Para llegar a su destino final, el espíritu de los muertos tenía que...
4. Para indicar que el espíritu del muerto nacía otra vez, los mayas...
5. Para simbolizar la importancia y la inmortalidad del espíritu, los mayas...

## Después de leer

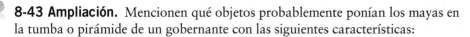

**8-43 Ampliación.** Mencionen qué objetos probablemente ponían los mayas en la tumba o pirámide de un gobernante con las siguientes características:

1. Era físicamente activo.
2. Le gustaba mucho el arte.
3. Estudiaba astronomía.
4. Le fascinaba la guerra.
5. Tenía ocho hijas, todas muy bellas.

# A escribir

**Select and sequence details to write effective narratives**

A successful narrative is characterized by a logical, clear, and believable sequence of events, and a good description of setting and characters.

Use organizational strategies such as a graphic organizer or a story map to visualize the order of events in and the time frame (present, past). Use dialogue to make your story more believable.

To describe the main characters, select feelings and traits that will make them stand out. Place the characters in the appropriate setting (rural, mysterious, etc.).

Structure your narration:

■ Introduce the character(s), describe the setting, and begin the action.

■ Present the unfolding of the action. Describe the characters and the tensions caused by their actions or by the events around them.

■ Present a closure to the actions/tensions, or leave it open for your reader to imagine the ending.

## Antes de escribir

**8-44 Preparación. PRIMERA FASE.** Lea la siguiente narración y siga las instrucciones.

Eran alrededor de las siete de la tarde del 24 de mayo cuando ocurrió algo totalmente inesperado. Era una noche de otoño y hacía viento. Empezaba a oscurecer.

Era el cumpleaños de nuestra gran amiga Guadalupe Martínez. Aunque tenía sólo veinte años, Guadalupe era una chica excepcional. Estudiaba en la UNAM[1] y también trabajaba para ayudar a su familia de ocho hermanos. Todos sus amigos la admirábamos por su generosidad, optimismo y alegría. Guadalupe era la hermana y amiga que todos soñábamos[2] tener.

El día de su cumpleaños por la mañana, Francisco y yo rompimos nuestra rutina. Pensábamos darle una sorpresa para su cumpleaños. Después de todo, ¡sólo se cumplen veintiún años una vez en la vida! Primero, fuimos a un centro comercial y le buscamos un regalo especial. Encontramos un plato decorativo guatemalteco y un CD. Francisco también le compró un perfume, y yo agregué un libro al cesto de regalos. Más tarde, volvimos a casa y envolvimos los regalos.

A las seis de la tarde Francisco y yo caminábamos a casa de Guadalupe. Estábamos a unos 80 metros de su casa cuando la ambulancia pasó a gran velocidad. Francisco y yo intuitivamente nos miramos y empezamos a caminar con más rapidez, pero en silencio. A sólo unos metros de su casa, supimos que algo pasaba en casa de Guadalupe. Corrimos. Cuando llegamos a la puerta, un enfermero nos dijo: "La señorita Martínez tuvo un accidente. Se quebró una pierna y dos costillas. La llevamos al hospital".

Inmediatamente, Francisco y yo llamamos al resto de nuestros amigos. Esa noche, todos los amigos de Guadalupe fuimos a saludarla al hospital. Fue un cumpleaños diferente a todos los anteriores, porque lo celebramos en el hospital, al lado de la cama de nuestra gran amiga Guadalupe.

[1]Universidad Nacional Autónoma de México
[2]*dreamed*

**SEGUNDA FASE.** Conteste las siguientes preguntas basadas en la historia que acaba de leer.

1. ¿Cuál es el propósito de la historia? Márquelo (✓).
   a. ___ describir un evento emocional e inesperado
   b. ___ entretener a los lectores
   c. ___ informar a los lectores sobre una experiencia triste
   d. ___ enseñar algo
2. ¿Son efectivos la selección de los personajes y los detalles de ellos, el entorno (*setting*) y la trama (*plot*)? ___ Sí ___ No
3. ¿Cuáles son las razones posibles para su respuesta a la pregunta 2? Márquelas (✓).
   a. ___ La protagonista se describe de una manera interesante.
   b. ___ La historia es ágil: la acción ocurre rápidamente y hay suficiente descripción.
   c. ___ Hay demasiada descripción y la historia es lenta.
   d. ___ Hay suficiente información sobre el entorno.
   e. ___ La historia sigue un orden cronológico.
   f. ___ La narración tiene una organización clara: una introducción, un desarrollo y un fin.
   g. ___ La historia es realista para el lector.

## Escribir

**8-45 Manos a la obra. PRIMERA FASE.** Usted va a narrar una historia personal, real o imaginaria. Primero, determine lo siguiente:

1. ¿Cuál es el objetivo de su narración, informar, relatar, entretener o enseñar?
2. ¿Cuántos protagonistas hay? ¿Qué características físicas y de personalidad tienen?
3. ¿Va a relatar usted en el pasado o en el presente? ¿Va a organizar los hechos en orden cronológico?
4. Escriba una lista de verbos que lo/la ayuden a describir el ambiente (*setting*), y otros que cuenten la acción.
5. ¿Qué información va a presentar en la introducción? ¿Cuál va a ser el conflicto? ¿Usted va a resolverlo o el lector va a imaginar el final de la historia?

> **En directo**
>
> To indicate chronological order:
>
> Primero,...
>
> Después,.../Después de (un tiempo),...
>
> Luego,...
>
> Más tarde,...
>
> Finalmente,.../Por fin,...

**SEGUNDA FASE.** Ahora, use la información de la *Primera fase* para escribir su narración, empezando del presente al pasado. Las siguientes expresiones en *En directo* pueden ser muy útiles.

## Después de escribir

**8-46 Revisión.** Lea su narración, pensando en su lector. Verifique lo siguiente:

1. ¿Incluyó la información que su lector necesita? ¿Es la trama creíble? ¿Describió suficientemente a los personajes y el ambiente?
2. ¿Tiene su narración una introducción, un conflicto y una conclusión?
3. ¿Usó expresiones apropiadas para indicar el orden cronológico, concordancia de tiempos (presente, pasado), etc.?
4. ¿Revisó la gramática, vocabulario, puntuación y ortografía?

Ahora, comparta su narración con un/a compañero/a. Converse con él/ella sobre las áreas débiles de su narración, si los hay.

# ENFOQUE CULTURAL

## Cultura y tradiciones mexicanas

La cultura popular de México es una de las más ricas y variadas de toda América Latina. En México se conservan muchas tradiciones y celebraciones nacionales, regionales, religiosas, políticas y familiares. Además, existe una gran riqueza en otros aspectos de la cultura, tales como la comida, la música e inclusive el idioma. En gran parte, esta riqueza cultural se debe a la mezcla de las antiguas culturas indígenas que existían en México y la europea, en particular la española. Esta mezcla resultó en una cultura popular tradicional y original a la vez.

Aunque México es hoy un país industrializado y moderno, su cultura popular es rica en tradiciones.

Aunque en México existe una separación de la iglesia y el estado, la religión es, ciertamente, uno de los aspectos más sobresalientes de la cultura popular. Son muchas las tradiciones y celebraciones que tienen relación con aspectos de la cultura religiosa en México. Indudablemente una de las tradiciones religiosas más importantes es la veneración a la Virgen de Guadalupe. Según la tradición, la virgen María se le apareció a un indígena pobre llamado Juan Diego y le habló en náhuatl, el idioma de los aztecas. La virgen le pidió construir una iglesia en el Tepeyac, al norte de la actual Ciudad de México. Más tarde, una imagen de la virgen apareció milagrosamente en la camisa de Juan Diego. Esta imagen se convirtió en un símbolo de la identidad de México. Así la iglesia del Tepeyac es uno de los lugares religiosos más visitados en todo el continente americano.

La Virgen de Guadalupe es uno de los íconos más representativos de la identidad mexicana.

La celebración del Día de los Muertos también tiene sus orígenes en la cultura azteca. Los aztecas daban mucha importancia a la muerte y muchos de sus ritos se centraban en la muerte. La unión de esa tradición azteca con las tradiciones cristianas españolas produjo en México un culto muy especial de la muerte. Un aspecto interesante de este culto es el tratamiento a veces humorístico de la muerte, muy diferente del tratamiento solemne de la muerte en Estados Unidos o en otros países. En efecto, símbolos de la muerte como los esqueletos y las calaveras se representan en galletas, dulces y todo tipo de juguetes para niños. Las familias construyen altares en

Los Voladores de Papantla descienden girando alrededor de un poste de 30 metros de alto en una ceremonia relacionada con el calendario maya.

sus casas para ofrecer a los muertos las comidas y bebidas que disfrutaban en vida. Resulta interesante comparar la fiesta de *Halloween* en Estados Unidos y el Día de los Muertos, porque existen muchas diferencias entre ellas, a pesar de algunas semejanzas superficiales. En primer lugar, el origen celta de *Halloween* contrasta con el origen cristiano-azteca de la fiesta mexicana. En segundo lugar, mientras en Estados Unidos se trata de una fiesta principalmente para los niños que recorren las calles con disfraces macabros pidiendo dulces, la fiesta mexicana es principalmente una fiesta familiar dedicada a honrar a los muertos de cada familia.

Otra tradición muy espectacular de origen indígena es la de los Voladores de Papantla. Cuatro hombres de origen totonaca, uno de los muchos pueblos indígenas de México, se suben a un poste de 30 metros de altura que representa el árbol de la vida. Atados por la cintura, se lanzan dando círculos alrededor del poste, mientras otro hombre toca instrumentos prehispánicos y baila en lo alto del poste. Esta ceremonia se realiza en honor del Sol y tiene sus raíces en el calendario maya. Los voladores representan los cuatro elementos y los cuatro puntos cardinales.

Finalmente, la comida mexicana popular incluye muchos productos autóctonos, poco utilizados en la cocina europea, o en otras regiones americanas, tales como diferentes especies de hongos, cactus y flores. Por otra parte, la música y danza mexicanas también se unen a las tradiciones indígenas, como en el caso de la Mazoyiwua o Danza del Venado, que es una de las formas de más pura tradición prehispánica. La artesanía mexicana, con raíces en la cultura tradicional, es una de las más interesantes, coloridas y variadas de todo el mundo hispano. Y desde luego, la riqueza lingüística de México incluye más de 60 lenguas indígenas, además de innumerables variaciones del castellano.

### En otras palabras

Expresiones mexicanas

¿Cómo estás, mi **cuate?**
*How are you, my friend?*

Pablo es **chaparro**, pero su abuelo era alto.
*Pablo is short, but his grandfather was tall.*

Mi amiga Stephanie es **güera** y tiene los ojos azules.
*My friend Stephanie is blonde and has blue eyes.*

Mi **recámara** tiene una ventana grande.
*My bedroom has a large window.*

**8-47 Comprensión.** PRIMERA FASE. **Reconocimiento de palabras clave.** Encuentre en el texto la palabra o expresión que mejor expresa el significado de las siguientes ideas.

1. at the same time    _____
2. outstanding          _____
3. undoubtedly          _____
4. skulls               _____
5. cookies              _____
6. pole                 _____
7. roots                _____
8. mushrooms            _____

SEGUNDA FASE. **Oraciones importantes.** Subraye las afirmaciones que contienen ideas que se encuentran en el texto. Luego indique en qué parte del texto están.

1. Native cultures of Mexico mixed with Spanish traditions to produce an original culture.
2. Religion is probably not a major component of Mexican popular culture.
3. Decorations for the All Souls' Day celebration sometimes include humorous images of Death.
4. The Tree of Life is represented by a 30–meter pole in the **Flyers of Papantla** ceremony.
5. The **Flyers of Papantla** ceremony is rooted in the Mayan calendar.
6. Flowers are used as ingredients in some Mexican dishes.
7. Traditional Mexican dances are very similar to (or are modeled on) traditional Spanish dances.
8. Many native languages, as well as variations of Spanish, are regularly spoken in Mexico.

TERCERA FASE. **Ideas principales.** Escriba un párrafo breve en inglés resumiendo las ideas principales expresadas en el texto.

**8-48 Use la información.** Usted fue a México y asistió a una de las siguientes celebraciones. Escríbale un correo electrónico a su profesor/a y cuéntele cuál de las siguientes celebraciones vio y dónde las vio. Incluya al menos cuatro datos sobre ella. Para preparar esta actividad, visite la página web de *Mosaicos* y siga los enlaces útiles.

a. el Cinco de Mayo
b. el Día de los Muertos
c. el Baile de los Viejitos
d. la Danza del Venado
e. el Día de la Virgen de Guadalupe

CD 4
cks 7–13

# VOCABULARIO

**Las fiestas y las celebraciones** — *Holidays and celebrations*

| | |
|---|---|
| la alegría | *joy* |
| el aserrín | *sawdust* |
| el carnaval | *carnival* |
| la carreta | *cart, wagon* |
| la carroza | *float (in a parade)* |
| la celebración | *celebration* |
| la comparsa | *group dressed in similar costumes* |
| la corrida (de toros) | *bullfight* |
| la costumbre | *custom* |
| el desfile | *parade* |
| el día feriado | *legal holiday* |
| el día festivo | *holiday* |
| el festival | *festival* |
| la festividad, la fiesta | *festivity; holiday; celebration* |
| la invitación | *invitation* |
| el preparativo | *preparation* |
| la procesión | *procession* |
| la semilla | *seed* |
| el toro | *bull* |
| la tradición | *tradition* |

**Las personas** — *People*

| | |
|---|---|
| el antepasado | *ancestor* |
| la gente | *people* |
| el rey/la reina | *king/queen* |

**La música** — *Music*

| | |
|---|---|
| la melodía | *melody* |
| la orquesta | *orchestra* |
| el ruido | *noise* |

**Los lugares** — *Places*

| | |
|---|---|
| el camino | *road; way* |
| el cementerio | *cemetery* |
| la iglesia | *church* |
| el teatro | *theater* |

**El tiempo** — *Time*

| | |
|---|---|
| antes | *before* |
| el comienzo | *beginning* |
| entonces | *then* |
| hoy en día | *nowadays* |
| mientras | *while* |

**Las descripciones** — *Descriptions*

| | |
|---|---|
| adornado/a | *decorated* |
| animado/a | *lively* |
| difunto/a, muerto/a | *dead* |
| maravilloso/a | *marvelous* |
| suave | *soft* |
| último/a | *last* |

**Verbos** — *Verbs*

| | |
|---|---|
| acompañar | *to accompany* |
| comenzar (ie) | *to begin* |
| dar un paseo | *to take a walk* |
| disfrazarse (c) | *to wear a costume* |
| divertirse (ie, i) | *to have a good time* |
| encerrar (ie) | *to lock up, shut in* |
| invitar | *to invite* |
| mantener (g, ie) | *to maintain* |
| quedar | *to arrange to meet* |
| recordar (ue) | *to remember* |
| reunirse | *to get together* |

See page 260 for the names of popular celebrations.
See page 267 for expressions of time and frequency.
See pages 273, 274, and 276 for expressions to use to make comparisons.

CAPÍTULO

9

# Hay que trabajar

Tapices de lana en un mercado de Antigua, Guatemala. Se elaboran a mano en la región de Momostenango, que está al oeste de la capital.

# In this chapter you will learn how to:

- talk about the workplace and professions
- talk about the past
- give instructions

Las ruinas mayas de Tikal
**Tikal**

**BELICE**

*Lago Petén Itzá*
**Flores**

*Mar*

*Caribe*

**MÉXICO**

Plátanos fritos

**GUATEMALA**

*Lago de Izabal*

**Río Dulce**

*SIERRA DE LOS CUCHUMATANES*

**Chichicastenango**

**Quetzaltenango**

*Lago Atitlán*

Palacio presidencial

★ **Guatemala**

**HONDURAS**

**Antigua**

**Escuintla**

El lago Atitlán

Un mercado al aire libre en Antigua

**EL SALVADOR**

*OCÉANO PACÍFICO*

 **A vista de pájaro.** Piense en lo que sabe de Guatemala y conteste las siguientes preguntas.

1. ¿Cómo se llaman los habitantes de Guatemala?
2. ¿Cuál era la antigua capital de Guatemala?
3. ¿Qué país está al este de Guatemala?
4. ¿Qué civilización fue muy importante en Guatemala?
5. ¿Qué idiomas habla la gente (*people*)?
6. ¿Cuáles son probablemente algunos recursos económicos importantes?

291

# A PRIMERA VISTA

## ◀)) El trabajo

En muchos lugares de Latinoamérica la **agricultura** es un sector significativo de la economía nacional. En estos cuadros del pintor guatemalteco Pedro Rafael González Chavajay vemos a algunos **agricultores cosechando** el café y los plátanos.

Los productos del **campo** se venden después en los mercados locales junto con las telas y las joyas que **elaboran** los **artesanos**.

Este **carpintero** está trabajando la **madera** en su **taller** para hacer una silla. Otras personas que trabajan con materias primas son los **herreros**, los **peleteros**, los **ceramistas** y los **joyeros**. Desafortunadamente, para muchas personas es difícil encontrar un buen trabajo para **sobrevivir** y tienen que **emigrar** a las grandes ciudades o a otros países.

**9-1 ¿A qué se dedican?** Diga si las siguientes afirmaciones son ciertas (**C**) o falsas (**F**). Si la respuesta es falsa (**F**), corrija la información.

1. ___ Los peleteros hacen zapatos, bolsas y chaquetas.
2. ___ Los ceramistas trabajan con el hierro.
3. ___ Los herreros trabajan los metales.
4. ___ Los carpinteros hacen los trabajos del campo.
5. ___ Los joyeros trabajan la plata y el oro para hacer pulseras y collares, por ejemplo.
6. ___ Los agricultores plantan y cosechan productos naturales.

**9-2 Las preparaciones.** Varios estudiantes planeaban una fiesta para celebrar su graduación. Indique adónde fueron y con quiénes hablaron para conseguir lo que necesitaban para la fiesta.

MODELO: María quería comprar un kilo de carne para hacer una parrillada en el jardín.
*Fue a la carnicería y habló con el carnicero/la carnicera.*

1. Juan necesitaba pescado para preparar un ceviche.
2. Paula tenía que comprar unos zapatos.
3. Carlos y Laura querían regalarle un collar elegante a Felicia.
4. Elisa quería encargar (*order*) una mesa de madera pequeña para poner los aperitivos.
5. Sofía pensaba regalarle un libro a Diego.
6. Martín y Luis necesitaban unos pantalones formales nuevos para ir a la fiesta.
7. Lorenzo quería comprar algo de fruta para hacer el postre.
8. Pilar quería adornar la casa con flores.

**9-3 Descripciones.** Miren los cuadros en la p. 292 y descríbanse las escenas con el mayor detalle posible. Tengan en cuenta las siguientes ideas:

1. lugar donde están estas personas
2. rasgos físicos
3. edad aproximada
4. ropa que llevan
5. lo que están haciendo
6. lo que están pensando algunas de las personas en la escena
7. cómo se sienten

---

### Lengua

The suffix **-ero/-era** is often used in Spanish to designate trades and professions, e.g., **camarero/a** (*server*), **plomero/a** (*plumber*), **peluquero/a** (*hairdresser*). Another common suffix is **-ista**, e.g., **electricista** (*electrician*); **contratista** (*contractor*).

# Los oficios y las profesiones

CD 4
Track 15

Una **chef** muestra algunas de sus **especialidades**.

Dra. Alicia Gonica de Pérez
CARDIÓLOGA

Consultorio
La Concepción 81
Calle 18, 402, Ciudad de Guatemala
Teléfono: (502) 23622001
Fax: (502) 23670721

Una **médica** le inyecta antibióticos a una paciente en su **consultorio**.

Unos **bomberos apagan** un **incendio** en Ciudad de Guatemala.

Una **ejecutiva** llama por teléfono a un **cliente**.

Una **locutora espera** la **señal** para comenzar un programa de noticias en una estación de radio.

Un **técnico** revisa los controles de una **compañía** petrolera.

## Cultura

Un importante cambio social en los países hispanos en las últimas décadas es el ingreso masivo de las mujeres al mercado laboral. Sin embargo, aún existen desigualdades: el desempleo entre las mujeres es mayor; su representación en las empresas de alta productividad es mucho menor; y los salarios de las mujeres son más bajos de los que reciben los hombres por el mismo tipo de trabajo.

Además, el trabajo doméstico no remunerado todavía se considera una obligación asociada con las mujeres y las niñas. No obstante, en muchos países hispanos ya se ofrecen programas educativos para combatir la discriminación. Algunos países, como Perú y Chile, tienen Ministerios de la Mujer para proteger y atender las necesidades de las mujeres.

Un **peluquero** le corta el pelo a una **clienta**.

# Otras ocupaciones

CD 4
Track 16

la juez

el abogado

el actor

el ama de casa

el policía

la bibliotecaria

la cajera

el chofer

la científica

el contador

la electricista

la enfermera

la mujer de negocios

el ingeniero

el intérprete

el obrero

el psicólogo

la periodista

el plomero

la arquitecta

### 9-4 ¿Qué profesión debe tener?

Lean las siguientes descripciones y digan qué profesión u oficio de la lista deben tener las personas con estas características. **OJO:** A veces, más de una respuesta es posible.

| | | |
|---|---|---|
| abogado/a | científico/a | médico/a |
| actor/actriz | ingeniero/a | plomero/a |
| artista | mecánico/a | psicólogo/a |

1. A Pablo le gusta observar y analizar el comportamiento (*behavior*) de las personas.
2. Los hermanos Pedraza siempre resuelven los problemas del auto de su padre. Lo examinan y lo reparan a la perfección.
3. Eva y Ana tienen facilidad para resolver los problemas de otras personas. También tienen la habilidad de exponer oralmente.
4. A Jaime le fascina desarmar (*disassemble*) aparatos electrónicos para estudiar cómo funcionan.
5. Daniela es una chica muy sensible y una gran observadora. Le fascina expresar sus sentimientos y experiencias de manera artística.
6. Adela siempre lee libros sobre anatomía. Ella sabe el nombre de cada parte del cuerpo humano.

### 9-5 Las profesiones y la personalidad.

**PRIMERA FASE.** Digan cómo deben ser estos/as profesionales. Seleccionen las palabras de la lista para describir las características deseadas.

**MODELO:** un bombero
*Debe ser valiente, serio y responsable. No debe ser descuidado (careless).*

| | | | | | |
|---|---|---|---|---|---|
| autoritario | dedicado | detallista | inteligente | perezoso | serio |
| calculador | delgado | estudioso | irónico | responsable | simpático |
| cuidadoso | descuidado | guapo | paciente | romántico | valiente |

1. un médico/una médica
2. un actor/una actriz
3. un hombre/una mujer de negocios
4. un peluquero/una peluquera
5. un locutor/una locutora
6. un ama de casa
7. un ejecutivo/una ejecutiva
8. un mecánico/una mecánica
9. un cocinero/una cocinera
10. un abogado/una abogada

**SEGUNDA FASE.** Intercambien ideas sobre lo siguiente.

1. ¿Conoce a algún/a... (*nombre de la profesión*)? ¿Cómo se llama? ¿Dónde trabaja?
2. ¿Qué características personales o especiales, en su opinión, lo/la ayudan en su profesión?

**9-6 Asociaciones.** Asocien una o más profesiones con los siguientes lugares de trabajo, y digan lo que hacen estas personas.

| LUGAR | PROFESIÓN | ¿QUÉ HACE? |
|---|---|---|
| **1.** el hospital | enfermero/a, médico/a | Atiende a los pacientes. |
| **2.** el restaurante | | |
| **3.** la clase | | |
| **4.** la estación de radio | | |
| **5.** la tienda de ropa | | |
| **6.** el consultorio médico | | |
| **7.** la peluquería | | |

**9-7 ¿Cuál es la profesión?** Primero identifiquen la ocupación o profesión, según la descripción. Luego, digan dos ventajas y una desventaja de esta ocupación o profesión.

MODELO:   Trabaja en una biblioteca haciendo catálogos de libros.
   E1:   *Es un bibliotecario/una bibliotecaria.*
   E2:   *Dos ventajas de ser bibliotecario/a son estar en contacto con muchos libros y trabajar en un lugar tranquilo.*
   E3:   *Una desventaja es la falta de ejercicio físico.*

| | PROFESIÓN | 2 VENTAJAS | 1 DESVENTAJA |
|---|---|---|---|
| **1.** Escribe artículos para el periódico. | | | |
| **2.** Presenta programas de televisión. | | | |
| **3.** Traduce simultáneamente. | | | |
| **4.** Mantiene el orden público. | | | |
| **5.** Apaga incendios. | | | |
| **6.** Defiende o acusa a personas delante de un/a juez. | | | |

**9-8 Mi ocupación ideal para el futuro. PRIMERA FASE.** Piense en su ocupación o profesión ideal. Su compañero/a le va a hacer preguntas para adivinar la ocupación o profesión en que piensa.

MODELO:   E1:   *En tu profesión ideal, ¿las personas deben viajar mucho?*
   E2:   *Sí.*
   E1:   *¿Y deben hablar con clientes para hacer negocios?*
   E2:   *Sí.*
   E1:   *¡Ah! ¡Tú quieres ser hombre/mujer de negocios!*

**SEGUNDA FASE.** Haga una lista de tres requisitos de su trabajo ideal y compruebe si usted los tiene. Intercambie esta información con su compañero/a.

MODELO:   *Me gustaría ser actor/actriz. Un actor/una actriz debe leer mucho; debe saber representar emociones y sentimientos y debe ser flexible para trabajar muchas horas. A mí me gusta leer y soy flexible, pero no puedo representar muy bien las emociones.*

# ◄)) Buscando trabajo

### CD 4
### Track 17 La entrevista de trabajo

SRA. ARCE: Buenos días, Sr. Solano. Soy Marcela Arce, presidenta de la compañía.

SR. SOLANO: Mucho gusto, señora.

SRA. ARCE: Siéntese, por favor. Usted **solicitó** el **puesto** de **gerente de ventas**, ¿verdad?

SR. SOLANO: Sí, señora. Leí en *El Diario de Centro América* que había una **vacante**. Después pedí y **llené** una **solicitud**.

SRA. ARCE: Sí, aquí la tengo, y también su **currículum**. **Por cierto**, es excelente.

SR. SOLANO: Muchas gracias.

SRA. ARCE: **Actualmente** usted trabaja en la empresa Badosa. ¿Por qué quiere **dejar** su puesto?

SR. SOLANO: Bueno, **en realidad** yo estoy muy contento allí, pero a mí me gustaría trabajar en una compañía internacional y poder usar otras lenguas. Como usted ve en mi currículum, yo hablo español, inglés y francés.

SRA. ARCE: En su solicitud, usted indica que desea un **sueldo** de 30.000 quetzales al mes. **Sin embargo,** para el puesto que tenemos, el sueldo que **se ofrece** es de 25.500 quetzales.

SR. SOLANO: Sí, lo sé, pero la diferencia no es tan importante. **Lo importante** es que aquí puedo tener la oportunidad de comunicarme con los clientes en su **propia** lengua. Yo creo que esto puede mejorar las ventas de Computel notablemente.

SRA. ARCE: Pues si le parece bien el sueldo, ¿por qué no pasamos a la oficina del director general para seguir hablando?

SR. SOLANO: ¡Cómo no!

**9-9 Los datos de la entrevista.** Busquen los siguientes datos en el diálogo anterior.

1. nombre de la presidenta de la compañía
2. puesto que solicita el Sr. Solano
3. nombre de la compañía donde el Sr. Solano trabaja actualmente
4. nombre de la compañía donde desea trabajar
5. lenguas que habla
6. sueldo que desea el Sr. Solano
7. sueldo que se ofrece en el nuevo puesto
8. motivo para cambiar de puesto

**9-10 ¿En qué orden?** Cuando alguien busca un trabajo, normalmente ¿en qué orden ocurren las siguientes actividades? Ordénelas de 1 a 8.

\_\_\_ Me llaman de la Compañía Rosell para una entrevista.

\_\_\_ Les contesto que no, que se cerró el almacén.

\_\_\_ Leo los anuncios del periódico.

\_\_\_ Envío la solicitud a la Compañía Rosell.

\_\_\_ Voy a la compañía para la entrevista.

\_\_\_ Me preguntan si me despidieron (*fired*) del trabajo anterior.

\_\_\_ Preparo mi currículum y lleno la solicitud para la Compañía Rosell.

\_\_\_ Me ofrecen el puesto de vendedor/a.

**9-11 El arte de entrevistarse.** PRIMERA FASE. Escoja el anuncio más interesante del periódico *La Hora* e imagínese que solicita ese puesto. Su compañero/a, en el papel de jefe/a de personal, lo/la entrevista a usted y toma notas para obtener la siguiente información. Luego cambien de papel.

1. nombre de la persona que solicita el puesto
2. estudios que tiene
3. lenguas que habla
4. lugar donde trabaja y responsabilidades
5. experiencia anterior
6. razones para querer trabajar en esta compañía

---

## INSTITUTO DE CIRUGÍA PLÁSTICA: CLÍNICA CÁRDENAS
### Necesita enfermera

**Prótesis:**
implantes faciales (Botox, silicona)
liposucción papada
abdomen
muslos

**Informes:**
Clínica Centro, Zona 10
**Tel: (502) 2534147**

*Llamar a secretaria: Marta*

---

## Hotel VILLA ANTIGUA
Necesita

**RECEPCIONISTA**
• Experiencia
• Bilingüe español-inglés

**CAMARERA**
• Mín. 2 años de experiencia
• Disponible trabajar por las mañanas y tardes

**Dirigirse al Hotel VILLA ANTIGUA**
Jefe de Personal
9a. Calle Poniente, Carretera a
Ciudad Vieja, Antigua, Guatemala
**Teléfono:** +(502) 78323956 ó +(502) 78323955

---

EMPRESA EXPORTADORA
DE ARTESANÍAS
Requiere

## CONTADOR

**Requisitos:**
• Experiencia mínima de 5 años
• Graduado del Colegio de Contadores Públicos
• Para cita llamar al Sr. López al (502) 2764532

---

## EMPRESA MINERA

*Requiere*
### 3 Ingenieros de sistemas

REQUISITOS:
1. Mayor de 25 años
2. Experiencia en minas de cobre
3. Flexibilidad horaria (incluidos fines de semana)

OFRECEMOS:
1. Ingreso superior a 20.000 quetzales
2. Capacitación profesional
3. Bonos de participación

*Interesados enviar currículum a:*
*Minas de Guatemala S.A.*

**Oficina de Personal**
Diagonal 19, 29-78, Zona 11
Ciudad de Guatemala, Guatemala
Teléfono: (502) 2762147
Fax: (502) 2763482

---

SEGUNDA FASE. Ahora informe al presidente de la empresa (otro compañero/otra compañera) sobre las calificaciones del candidato/de la candidata.

**9-12 ¿Comportamiento apropiado?** Preparen una lista de cinco acciones que se deben hacer antes de una entrevista y cinco que no se deben hacer durante una entrevista. Después comparen su lista con la de otros compañeros/otras compañeras.

| LO QUE SE DEBE HACER ANTES DE UNA ENTREVISTA | LO QUE NO SE DEBE HACER DURANTE UNA ENTREVISTA |
|---|---|
| | |
| | |
| | |
| | |
| | |

**9-13 Mi profesión.** You will listen to Julieta Odriozola talk about her profession. Before you listen, write down the names of four professions that have traditionally been associated with women.

CD 4
Track 18

Now, pay attention to the general idea of what is said. As you listen mark (✓) the appropriate ending to each statement.

1. Julieta Odriozola es…
   ___ artista.
   ___ política.
   ___ periodista.

2. Julieta tiene un horario…
   ___ de 9 a 5.
   ___ variable.
   ___ de lunes a sábado.

3. Julieta hace casi todo su trabajo en…
   ___ su auto.
   ___ su casa.
   ___ diferentes lugares.

4. Julieta trabaja básicamente con…
   ___ artistas jóvenes.
   ___ personas importantes.
   ___ empleados de la comunidad.

# EN ACCIÓN

## Diarios de bicicleta: ¿Qué quieres ser?

### Antes de ver

**9-14** Asocie cada una de las profesiones de la izquierda con una palabra relacionada en la columna derecha.

1. ____ ingeniero/a
2. ____ bombero/a
3. ____ médico/a
4. ____ chef
5. ____ abogado/a
6. ____ actor/actriz

**a.** salud
**b.** cine
**c.** comida
**d.** documentos legales
**e.** máquinas y computadoras
**f.** incendios

### Mientras ve

**9-15** Escriba todas las profesiones que se mencionan en este segmento.

### Después de ver

**9-16** Exprese su opinión sobre los siguientes temas:

- la profesión en que es posible ayudar a más gente
- la profesión más difícil
- la profesión más lucrativa
- la profesión más peligrosa (*dangerous*)

# FUNCIONES Y FORMAS

### 1. Avoiding repetition: Review of direct and indirect object pronouns

| | |
|---|---|
| BÁRBARA: | Carlota, ¿por qué llevas chanclas (*flip-flops*)? |
| CARLOTA: | **Le** di mis zapatos al zapatero porque se rompieron. |
| BÁRBARA: | ¿Y no tienes frío? |
| CARLOTA: | Sí, pero no tengo otra opción. El zapatero va a arreglarlos en una hora. Y tú, Bárbara, ¿por qué no tienes chaqueta? Hace frío. |
| BÁRBARA: | **La** dejé en casa. |
| CARLOTA: | Bueno, yo **te** presto mi suéter. |

Bárbara       Carlota

**Piénselo.** Para cada oración, escriba las palabras en negrita (*boldface*) en la columna apropiada. **OJO:** En algunas oraciones hay más de un objeto directo u objeto indirecto.

| | OBJETO DIRECTO | OBJETO INDIRECTO |
|---|---|---|
| **1. Le** di mis **zapatos** al **zapatero.** | ———— | ———— |
| **2.** El zapatero va a arreglar los **zapatos** de Carlota. | ———— | ———— |
| **3.** El zapatero va a arreglar**los.** | ———— | ———— |
| **4.** ¿Por qué no tienes **chaqueta?** | ———— | ———— |
| **5. La** dejé en casa. | ———— | ———— |
| **6. Te** presto mi **suéter.** | ———— | ———— |

■ In *Capítulo 5* you learned that direct objects answer the question *what?* or *whom?* in relation to the verb. They can refer to people, animals, or objects. When a direct object noun refers to a specific person, a group of people, or a pet, the *personal* **a** precedes the direct object. To avoid repetition in speaking or writing, direct object pronouns can replace direct object nouns if the noun has already been mentioned.

| | |
|---|---|
| ¿Ves **al chef**? | *Do you see the **chef**?* |
| Sí, **lo** veo. Está al lado de la cocina. | *Yes, I see **him**. He is next to the kitchen.* |
| La Dra. Martín recibe **a sus pacientes** en la clínica. | *Dr. Martín sees **her patients** in the clinic.* |
| **Los** recibe todos los días. | *She sees **them** every day.* |

■ In *Capítulo 6* you learned that indirect object nouns and pronouns tell *to whom* or *for whom* an action is done. They most often occur in the context of transferring information or objects, such as giving someone a gift, telling someone a story, or asking someone for something.

| | |
|---|---|
| La maestra siempre **les** dice la verdad a los niños. | *The teacher always tells the children the truth.* |
| El camarero no **nos** trajo la sopa. | *The waiter did not bring us the soup.* |

■ Direct and indirect object pronouns are placed before conjugated verbs. When a conjugated verb is followed by an infinitive or present participle, the pronouns can either precede the conjugated verb or be attached to the infinitive or present participle.

¿Las fotos de la casa?
La arquitecta está compilándo**las**.

¿Las fotos de la casa?
La arquitecta **las** está compilando.

*The photos of the house?*
*The architect is compiling them.*

Su asistente va a mandar**nos** todos los documentos.

Su asistente **nos** va a mandar todos los documentos.

*Her assistent is going to send us all the documents.*

■ Direct and indirect object pronouns have the same form, except in the third person. Note that **le/les** refer to either males or females.

| DIRECT OBJECT PRONOUNS | | INDIRECT OBJECT PRONOUNS | |
|---|---|---|---|
| me | nos | me | nos |
| te | os | te | os |
| lo | los | le | les |
| la | las | | |

## 9-17 Los preparativos para la evaluación. PRIMERA FASE.

Usted trabaja en la oficina de una arquitecta y mañana empieza la evaluación anual. Indique qué empleado/a está haciendo cada uno de los preparativos para la visita de los evaluadores: la arquitecta (**A**) o el asistente administrativo (**AA**).

1. \_\_\_\_ Está terminando el último informe.
2. \_\_\_\_ Está examinando los materiales para ver si hay errores.
3. \_\_\_\_ Está sacando las fotocopias.
4. \_\_\_\_ Está organizando el horario.

 **SEGUNDA FASE.** Compare sus respuestas con las de su compañero/a, siguiendo el modelo.

MODELO: E1: *¿Quién está examinando el presupuesto (*budget*)?*
E2: *El asistente administrativo está examinándolo.*

**9-18 Comunicaciones y transacciones.** Mire los dibujos y explique dónde ocurre la escena y lo que pasa en cada una.

Pancho • dependienta

MODELO: enviar/flores
*Pancho está en la floristería. Le va a enviar flores a su esposa porque es el Día de los Enamorados.*

Juan • María

jefa • asistente

artesana • turistas

1. mandar/mensaje de texto   2. dar/documentos   3. vender/telas tradicionales

**9-19 Gerentes y empleados. PRIMERA FASE.** La compañía Hipertermo fabrica casas modulares que utilizan la energía solar y es famosa por la buena relación entre sus empleados. Escriban los factores que, según ustedes, contribuyen a la buena comunicación entre los gerentes y los empleados.

1. sugerir formas más eficientes de hacer el trabajo
2. dar las gracias por la alta calidad de su trabajo
3. explicar los beneficios de usar la energía solar
4. ofrecer ayuda para resolver conflictos
5. comunicar inmediatamente problemas con las máquinas
6. pedir ayuda cuando tienen dudas

| LOS GERENTES... | LOS EMPLEADOS... |
|---|---|
| les explican a los empleados claramente sus responsabilidades. | les dan buenas ideas a los gerentes. |
| | |
| | |
| | |

**SEGUNDA FASE.** Los gerentes quieren premiar (*reward*) a los empleados al final del año. ¿Qué van a hacer los gerentes para los empleados?

MODELO: escribir una carta de agradecimiento
*Los gerentes van a escribirles una carta de agradecimiento.*

1. subir el salario
2. dar una fiesta
3. escribir evaluaciones negativas de su trabajo
4. comprar regalos
5. decir que están muy contentos con su trabajo
6. pedir más horas de trabajo por semana

### SITUACIONES

1. **Role A.** You meet with a career counselor (**consejero/a vocacional**) for tips on how to look for a job. Explain the type of job you are looking for, and answer the counselor's questions about your past experience. Ask the counselor questions of your own.

   **Role B.** You are a career counselor (**consejero/a vocacional**) who is meeting with a new client. After listening to the client, ask whether he/she a) prepared a résumé; b) looked for job ads (and where); c) applied for a job (which one); and d) prepared questions to ask in an interview. Be ready to answer the client's questions.

2. **Role A.** You are at an outdoor market in Antigua, Guatemala. You are at a stand that has blouses, tapestries, and jewelry. Tell the vendor that a) you want to give your sister a blouse for her birthday; b) you would like to take your parents a tapestry; and c) you want to buy a necklace for a good friend. Respond to the vendor's questions and ask an additional question about each item.

   **Role B.** You are a Guatemalan artisan selling your goods at a market in Antigua. An American student is interested in buying some gifts. Ask questions to help the customer make appropriate choices, and answer his/her questions about the items.

## 2. Avoiding repetition: Use of direct and indirect object pronouns together

| | |
|---|---|
| CONSEJERA: | ¿Ya **le** mandó su currículum al director? |
| CLIENTE: | Sí, **se lo** mandé la semana pasada. |
| CONSEJERA: | ¿Recibió alguna confirmación? |
| CLIENTE: | Sí, ellos **me la** mandaron rápidamente. **La** recibí hoy. |

**Piénselo.** Lea las oraciones y escriba en la columna apropiada los objetos directos y los indirectos, tanto los pronombres como los sustantivos (*nouns*).

| | OBJETO INDIRECTO | OBJETO DIRECTO |
|---|---|---|
| **MODELO:** La secretaria **me** dio una cita para el lunes. | me | cita |
| 1. ¿Ya **le** mandó su currículum al director? | _____ | _____ |
| 2. **Se lo** mandé la semana pasada. | _____ | _____ |
| 3. Ellos **me la** mandaron rápidamente. | _____ | _____ |
| 4. **La** recibí hoy. | _____ | _____ |

■ You have already learned how to use indirect object pronouns or direct object pronouns in sentences. In this section you will learn how to use both types of pronouns in the same sentence.

| INDIRECT OBJECT PRONOUNS | | DIRECT OBJECT PRONOUNS | |
|---|---|---|---|
| me | nos | me | nos |
| te | os | te | os |
| le (se) | les (se) | lo | los |
| | | la | las |

■ When direct and indirect object pronouns are used in the same sentence, the indirect object pronoun precedes the direct object pronoun. Place double object pronouns before conjugated verbs.

Ella **me** dio **la solicitud**.
   i.o.      d.o.

*She gave me the application.*

Ella **me la** dio.
   i.o. d.o.

*She gave it to me.*

### Lengua

You have learned that when the stress falls on the third syllable from the end of a word, a written accent is required. Therefore, you need to add one on the verb when double object pronouns are attached to an infinitive.

**¿Va a darme la solicitud?**
**→ ¿Va a dármela?**

When double object pronouns are attached to a present participle, the stress falls on the fourth syllable from the end, and a written accent is also required:

**Se la está dando. →**

**Está dándosela.**
     4   3 2 1

■ In compound verb constructions, you may place double object pronouns before the conjugated verb or attach them to the accompanying infinitive or present participle.

| | |
|---|---|
| Él quiere dar**me el contrato**.<br>       i.o.    d.o. | *He wants to give me the contract.* |
| Él quiere dár**melo**.<br>       i.o.d.o. | |
| Él **me lo** quiere dar.<br>  i.o. d.o. | *He wants to give it to me.* |
| Ella **te** está diciendo **la verdad**.<br>     i.o.            d.o. | *She is telling you the truth.* |
| Ella **te la** está diciendo.<br>    i.o. d.o. | |
| Ella está diciéndo**tela**.<br>           i.o.d.o. | *She is telling it to you.* |

■ The indirect object pronouns **le** and **les** change to **se** before **lo, los, la,** or **las.**

| | |
|---|---|
| **Le** dio **el puesto** a Verónica.<br> i.o.      d.o. | *He gave the job to Veronica.* |
| **Se lo** dio.<br>i.o. d.o. | *He gave it to her.* |
| **Les** va a mostrar **el anuncio**.<br> i.o.           d.o. | *She is going to show them/you<br>(ustedes) the ad.* |
| **Se lo** va a mostrar.<br>i.o. d.o. | *She is going to show it to<br>them/you (ustedes).* |

■ When a direct object pronoun and a reflexive pronoun are used together, the reflexive pronoun precedes the direct object pronoun.

| | |
|---|---|
| Siempre **me** envío **correos electrónicos**<br>        i.o.             d.o.<br>    para recordar lo que debo hacer. | *I always send myself e-mails to<br>remember what I have to do.* |
| Siempre **me los** envío.<br>      i.o. d.o. | *I always send them to myself.* |

**9-20 ¿Qué hizo el supervisor?** Usted es el dueño/la dueña de una compañía. Habla con un empleado nuevo/una empleada nueva para saber si el supervisor hizo todo lo que tenía que hacer para explicarle cómo funciona su departamento.

MODELO:     darle el manual de la compañía
        E1:  *¿Le dio el manual de la compañía?*
        E2:  *Sí, me lo dio.*

1. explicarle la campaña de publicidad
2. mostrarle los anuncios
3. traerle las revistas
4. pedirle un documento que faltaba
5. dejarle las fotos
6. describirle los modelos que se necesitan.

**9-21 ¿Qué hace usted? PRIMERA FASE.** La imparcialidad, la amabilidad y la confidencialidad son fundamentales en el trabajo. Lea las siguientes situaciones y seleccione lo que usted haría (*would do*) en cada una.

1. Un cliente le pide a usted el teléfono de la oficina del presidente de la compañía.
   a. ____ Usted se lo da.         b. ____ Usted no se lo da.
2. Alguien quiere leer un documento confidencial.
   a. ____ Usted se lo muestra.    b. ____ Usted no se lo muestra.

3. La nueva jefa de personal viene a una reunión de su departamento. Alguien tiene que presentarla a los empleados.
   a. ___ Usted se la presenta.          b. ___ Usted no se la presenta.
4. Una empleada nueva le dice a usted que quiere dos semanas de vacaciones después de trabajar sólo tres meses.
   a. ___ Usted se las da.               b. ___ Usted decide no dárselas.

**SEGUNDA FASE.** ¿Están de acuerdo usted y su compañero/a? Justifiquen su respuesta entre ustedes.

**MODELO:**     Un cliente le pide a usted información personal sobre las finanzas de otro cliente. Los dos clientes son hermanos.

   E1:  *No se la doy porque no le gustaría al segundo cliente.*
   E2:  *Yo se la doy porque los dos clientes son hermanos.*

**9-22 ¡El cliente siempre tiene razón! PRIMERA FASE.** Ustedes se entrevistan sobre el servicio en un restaurante donde cada uno de ustedes comió recientemente. Tomen notas sobre las respuestas de su compañero/a para compartir con la clase.

1. ¿Cuándo les sirvieron el agua?
2. ¿Les trajeron pan a la mesa?
3. ¿Les dijo el camarero cuáles eran los platos especiales del día?
4. ¿Se los describió?
5. ¿Les ofreció postres y café?
6. ¿Cómo fue el servicio en general?

**SEGUNDA FASE.** Presenten a la clase un breve resumen del servicio en sus respectivos restaurantes.

## SITUACIONES

1. **Role A.** You are a reporter for *El Quetzalteco*, a regional newspaper en Quetzaltenango, and you have just arrived in Guatemala City to cover a story. You were in such a rush to leave Quetzaltenango that you left your laptop and camera (**cámara**) in the taxi. Call a fellow reporter in the capital city and a) explain what happened; b) ask if he/she can lend you a laptop and camera; and c) say that you need them right away.

   **Role B.** You are a reporter for *El Súper Canal 3* in Guatemala City. A reporter from Quetzaltenango calls to tell you about an urgent problem. Ask a) when he/she left the laptop and computer in the taxi and b) if he/she called the taxi company. When the reporter asks you for a favor, say that he/she can come to your office to pick them up right away.

2. **Role A.** As manager of a large bank, you asked an employee to deliver (**entregar**) an important package (**un paquete**) to another bank. When he/she returns, ask a) if he/she delivered it; b) at what time he/she delivered it; c) to whom he/she gave it.

   **Role B.** You work at a large bank. You have just returned from delivering (**entregar**) an important package (**un paquete**) to another bank. The manager is anxious about whether the package reached its destination. Answer the manager's questions to ease his/her concerns.

## 3. Talking about the past: More on the imperfect and preterit

PERIODISTA: Sr. Mario Parada, usted estaba en el Bancafé cuando entraron los ladrones (*robbers*), ¿verdad? ¿Qué **estaba haciendo**?

SR. PARADA: Yo **estaba hablando** con la cajera. **Iba a** hacer un depósito, pero claro, no **pude** realizar la transacción.

PERIODISTA: ¿Qué hicieron los empleados cuando **supieron** que había ladrones en el banco?

SR. PARADA: Todo pasó muy rápido. En el momento del robo, los cajeros **estaban respondiendo** a las preguntas de los clientes. Los oficiales de seguridad vieron a los ladrones y **quisieron** detenerlos (*stop them*) pero no **pudieron**.

Periodista        Mario Parada

**Piénselo.** Indique quién(es) estaba(n) haciendo las siguientes actividades cuando ocurrió el asalto: Mario Parada (**M**), los cajeros de Bancafé (**CA**), los clientes (**CL**) o los oficiales de seguridad (**O**).

1. _____ **Estaban trabajando** en Bancafé.
2. _____ **Estaba poniendo** dinero en su cuenta de Bancafé.
3. _____ **Estaban haciendo** alguna transacción en Bancafé.
4. _____ **Estaban ayudando** a los clientes que tenían preguntas.

---

■ You have used the imperfect to express an action or event that was in progress in the past. You may also use the imperfect progressive to emphasize the ongoing nature of the activity in the past. Form the imperfect progressive with the imperfect of **estar** and the present participle (**-ndo**).

| | |
|---|---|
| Mario **estaba hablando** con la cajera cuando entraron los ladrones. | *Mario was talking to the teller when the robbers came in.* |
| Los vicepresidentes del banco **estaban trabajando** en el segundo piso cuando oyeron los gritos. | *The vice presidents of the bank were working on the second floor when they heard the shouts.* |

■ To express intentions in the past, use the imperfect of **ir + a +** *infinitive*.

| | |
|---|---|
| **Iba a salir**, pero era muy tarde. | *I was going to go out, but it was very late.* |

■ In *Capítulo 7* you practiced the preterit of **saber** with the meaning of finding out about something. You also practiced the preterit of **querer** with the meaning of wanting or trying to do something, but failing to accomplish it.

| | |
|---|---|
| **Supe** que Jorge consiguió trabajo. | *I found out that Jorge got a job.* |
| **Quise** entrevistarme con el gerente, pero fue imposible. | *I wanted (and tried) to get an interview with the manager, but it was impossible.* |

In the negative, the preterit of **querer** conveys the meaning of refusing to do something.

| | |
|---|---|
| **No quise** ir. | *I refused to go.* |

■ Other verbs that convey a different meaning in English when the preterit is used are **conocer** and **poder**.

| IMPERFECT | | PRETERIT | |
|---|---|---|---|
| Yo **conocía** a Ana. | *I knew Ana.* | **Conocí** a Ana. | *I met Ana.* |
| **Podía** hacerlo. | *I could (was able to) do it.* | **Pude** hacerlo. | *I accomplished (managed to do) it.* |
| **No podía** hacerlo. | *I couldn't (wasn't able to) do it.* | **No pude** hacerlo. | *I couldn't do it. (I tried and failed.)* |

**9-23 Una oficina muy ocupada.** Ustedes visitaron la oficina que aparece en la siguiente escena. Túrnense para preguntar qué estaban haciendo las personas cuando cada uno/a de ustedes llegó.

MODELO:  E1:  *¿Qué estaba haciendo Alicia cuando tú llegaste a la oficina?*
E2:  *Estaba conversando con un cliente.*

**9-24 Una explicación lógica.** Ayer ustedes tuvieron una reunión en su compañía para mostrarles unos productos nuevos a unas empresas extranjeras. Den una explicación lógica de todo lo que salió mal.

> **MODELO:** La secretaria no contestaba el teléfono.
> E1: *Estaba buscando un intérprete para la reunión.*
> E2: *No, estaba buscando un salón más grande.*

1. Varios empleados llegaron tarde.
2. El técnico no pudo arreglar una computadora que se necesitaba para la presentación.
3. Los periodistas no podían comprender lo que decía un director extranjero.
4. No les sirvieron café ni refrescos a los invitados.
5. Uno de los vendedores no quiso mostrar los productos nuevos.
6. No se pusieron anuncios en los periódicos.

**9-25 ¡A usar la imaginación!** Estas descripciones indican lo que estaban haciendo varias personas ayer. Identifiquen cuál era el oficio o profesión de ellos y qué iban a hacer después.

> **MODELO:** Esta persona llevaba un traje espacial, guantes, botas muy grandes y un plástico transparente frente a los ojos para poder ver.
> E1: *Era un astronauta.*
> E2: *Iba a caminar en la Luna.*

1. Un señor tenía un secador en la mano y le arreglaba el pelo a una señora que estaba sentada enfrente de él.
2. Unos señores iban en un camión rojo con una sirena. El camión iba muy rápido y los autos paraban al lado derecho de la calle.
3. Una joven que llevaba un vestido similar a los que se llevaban en la época de Cleopatra hablaba frente a una cámara. Estaba muy maquillada y tenía una línea negra alrededor de los ojos.
4. Un señor estudiaba los planos de un edificio y decía que ciertas cosas no estaban bien.

**9-26 El diario de vida de Arturo.** Lea una página del diario de Arturo, un estudiante de antropología enamorado de Guatemala. Escriba en el espacio la forma apropiada del verbo entre paréntesis, según el contexto.

En el ano 2007, yo (1) _____ (conocí/conocía) a mi novia Elizabeth en mi segundo viaje a Guatemala. En ese momento, yo ya (2) _____ (conocí/conocía) Antigua y un par de lugares de interés para los turistas. Después de nuestro encuentro, yo inmediatamente (3) _____ (supe/sabía) que mis visitas a Guatemala (4) _____ (fueron/iban) a ser más frecuentes. Ese año nosotros no (5) _____ (pudimos/podíamos) viajar juntos por el país, pero el año siguiente lo hicimos. Su familia, ella y yo (6) _____ (pudimos/podíamos) explorar juntos la reserva ecológica Calahuar. Caminamos todo el día por el bosque (*forest*). Después de caminar tantas horas, yo no (7) _____ (pude/podía) dar un paso más, pero al día siguiente (8) _____ (pudimos/podíamos) continuar el viaje a San Pedro La Laguna en Atlitán.

**9-27 ¡Malas sorpresas!** Lean las siguientes situaciones y digan cuáles eran los planes probables de estas personas.

MODELO: Martín está enfadado porque su bicicleta se descompuso (*broke*).
    E1: *Martín no pudo ir al parque con sus amigos.*
    E2: *Él quiso arreglar la bicicleta, pero fue imposible.*

1. Lorena está molesta porque la fotocopiadora de la oficina no funciona.
2. Usted y su pareja caminaron a su restaurante favorito, pero el restaurante estaba cerrado.
3. El jefe de producción llamó a una reunión urgente ayer. Anoche comenzó a nevar y muchos empleados no llegaron a su trabajo porque los caminos estaban en malas condiciones.
4. Al carro de Marta y Francisco se le acabó (*ran out of*) la gasolina cerca de la playa. Tuvieron que dejarlo en la carretera.
5. Esteban tenía una entrevista con el jefe de personal a las 9 pero no llegó a tiempo.

## SITUACIONES

1. **Role A.** One of your employees did not come to an important meeting, so you call him/her to your office. Greet your employee and ask why he/she was not present. After listening to the explanation, say that a) this is the second time this happened and b) he/she has to attend all meetings in the future.

   **Role B.** You were expected to attend an important meeting at work, but you could not make it. After greeting your boss, apologize and explain the circumstances. As you were driving to work, your spouse called to say that a) there was a fire in the kitchen; b) the firefighters were there; and c) the children were fine but scared. Explain that you had to go home.

2. **Role A.** You are the caterer (**proveedor/a de comida**) hired for a large wedding party. While the party was taking place, the deck (**terraza**) of the house collapsed (**colapsar**), resulting in several injured people (**heridos**). An investigator (your classmate) interviews you about the accident.

   **Role B.** You are a police officer investigating the accident. Ask the caterer a) approximately how many guests and servers were on the deck (**terraza**) when it collapsed (**colapsar**); b) what the guests were doing there; and c) what the caterer was doing when the deck collapsed. Then thank the caterer for the information.

## 4. Giving instructions or suggestions: Formal commands

RICARDO: Buenos días, señorita. Me llamo Ricardo Roldán Díaz. ¿Podría darme una solicitud para el puesto de asistente de contador?

SECRETARIA: Claro que sí, Sr. Roldán. Por favor, **llene** la solicitud y **mándenosla** pronto.

RICARDO: ¿Puedo mandársela por correo electrónico?

SECRETARIA: Sí, **envíela** por correo electrónico, pero también por correo postal.

**Piénselo.** Ricardo llega a casa con la solicitud que le dio la secretaria. Lea las sugerencias que Ricardo leyó en un manual sobre cómo buscar puestos profesionales y marque (✓) las que le parecen apropiadas en la cultura de usted.

1. ___ Llene la solicitud inmediatamente.
2. ___ Escriba con letra clara.
3. ___ Mándele flores a la secretaria.
4. ___ No se olvide de incluir su currículum.
5. ___ Firme la solicitud.
6. ___ No deje ningún espacio en blanco.

■ Commands (**los mandatos**) are the verb forms used to tell others to do something. Use formal commands with people you address as **usted** or **ustedes**. To form these commands, drop the final **-o** of the **yo** form of the present tense and add **-e(n)** for **-ar** verbs and **-a(n)** for **-er** and **-ir** verbs.

■ Verbs that are irregular in the **yo** form of the present tense maintain the same irregularity in the command form.

|        |    |        | USTED  | USTEDES |         |
|--------|----|--------|--------|---------|---------|
| pensar | →  | pienso | piense | piensen | *think* |
| dormir | →  | duermo | duerma | duerman | *sleep* |
| repetir| →  | repito | repita | repitan | *repeat*|
| poner  | →  | pongo  | ponga  | pongan  | *put*   |

■ The use of **usted** and **ustedes** with command forms is optional. When used, they normally follow the command.

Pase/Pase **usted.**                    *Come in.*

■ To make a formal command negative, place **no** before the affirmative command.

**No salga** ahora.                     *Do not leave now.*

■ Object pronouns and reflexive pronouns are attached to the end of affirmative commands. (Note the written accent over the stressed vowel). Object pronouns and reflexive pronouns precede negative commands and are not attached.

**Cómpre**la.                           *Buy it.*

**No** la **compre.**                   *Do not buy it.*

**Háblen**le.                           *Talk to him/her.*

**No** le **hablen.**                   *Do not talk to him/her.*

**Siénte**se.                           *Sit down.*

**No** se **siente.**                   *Do not sit down.*

■ The verbs **dar, ir, ser,** and **saber** have irregular command forms.

dar: **dé, den** ir: **vaya, vayan** ser: **sea, sean** saber: **sepa, sepan**

■ Verbs ending in **-car, -gar, -zar, -ger,** and **-guir** have spelling changes in command forms.

| sacar | sac**o** | → | sa**que**, sa**quen** |
|---|---|---|---|
| jugar | jue**go** | → | jue**gue**, jue**guen** |
| almorzar | almuer**zo** | → | almuer**ce**, almuer**cen** |
| recoger | reco**jo** | → | reco**ja**, reco**jan** |
| seguir | si**go** | → | si**ga**, si**gan** |

**9-28 Preguntas de un/a estudiante.** Usted no asistió a clase durante la semana dedicada a Guatemala y quiere saber qué tiene que hacer para ponerse al día. Su compañero/a, en el papel de profesor/a, va a contestar afirmativamente a sus preguntas. Después, cambien de papel.

MODELO:     estudiar el Capítulo 9
        E1:  *¿Estudio el Capítulo 9?*
        E2:  *Sí, estúdielo.*

1. contestar las preguntas sobre los lugares turísticos en Guatemala
2. mirar los DVDs de bailes folklóricos de Guatemala
3. escribir algunas expresiones populares entre los jóvenes guatemaltecos
4. leer el *Enfoque cultural* sobre Guatemala
5. hacer la tarea sobre las culturas indígenas de Guatemala

**9-29 En el hospital.** Un enfermero/Una enfermera entra en la habitación y le hace las siguientes preguntas al/a la paciente. Túrnense para hacer los papeles de enfermero/a y paciente.

**MODELO:** E1: *¿Le abro las cortinas?*
E2: *Sí, ábramelas, por favor. Quisiera leer.*

1. ¿Le pongo la televisión?
2. ¿Le traigo un jugo?
3. ¿Le pongo otra almohada?
4. ¿Me llevo estas flores?
5. ¿Le traigo el teléfono?
6. ...

**9-30 Mandatos del entrenador de un equipo.** Preparen una lista de sugerencias que el entrenador/la entrenadora puede darles a los miembros de su equipo para lograr los objetivos siguientes. Comparen su lista con la de otra pareja.

**MODELO:** para mantenerse en buen estado físico
*Practiquen todos los días. No se acuesten tarde.*

1. para tener mejor rendimiento (*performance*)
2. para prepararse mentalmente para un partido difícil
3. para evitar problemas con el árbitro
4. para dormir bien cuando tienen mucho estrés
5. para ser buenos alumnos y buenos deportistas también

 **9-31 ¿Qué deben hacer estas personas?** Busquen una solución a los siguientes problemas y díganle a cada persona lo que debe hacer.

**MODELO:** El Sr. Álvarez dice: "No estoy contento en mi trabajo".
E1: *Sr. Álvarez, busque otro trabajo inmediatamente.*
E2: *Hable con su jefe y explíquele la situación.*

1. La Sra. Jiménez dice: "Necesito más vendedores en mi compañía".
2. El Sr. Jiménez se queja (*complains*): "Tengo que terminar un informe económico mensual pero mi computadora no funciona".
3. Unos hombres de negocios van a ir a Ciudad de Guatemala, pero no saben hablar español.
4. La Sra. Peña tuvo un accidente serio con su auto; el chofer que provocó el accidente no quiere darle la información que ella necesita para informar a su seguro.
5. La Sra. Hurtado entra en su apartamento y ve que hay agua en el piso de la cocina.
6. Su esposa quiere ir al Festival Folclórico Nacional de Cobán, pero el Sr. Fernández no se siente bien.

## Cultura

En la ciudad de Cobán, en el centro de Guatemala, se celebra anualmente un festival de personas nativas de Guatemala, La Fiesta Nacional Indígena de Guatemala (Festival Folclórico). Incluye un certamen (*contest*) de belleza para mujeres indígenas de Guatemala. Participan aproximadamente 100 señoritas que expresan sus ideales en su idioma materno y en español. La ganadora es coronada con el título de *Rabin Ajau*, que significa Hija del Rey en Q'eqchi', un idioma maya.

## SITUACIONES

1. **Role A.** Tell your neighbor that you are leaving for three days for job interviews. Ask if your neighbor can do a few things for you. After he/she agrees, tell him/her to a) feed (**dar de comer a**) the cat and play with her every day; b) water the plants; c) pick up the mail (**correspondencia**); and d) any other things that you may need. Thank him/her for helping out.

   **Role B.** Your neighbor tells you that he/she is going to be away. Agree to help him/her out. After you find out what you will have to do, ask: a) whom should you call if there is an emergency (**emergencia**) and b) get the telephone number of the vet (**veterinario/a**).

2. **Role A.** You have moved to Quetzaltenango, Guatemala, and want to open a checking account (**cuenta corriente**) at Bancafé. Since you are not familiar with their system, ask an employee for help. After the employee gives you all the details, thank him/her, and say that you are very happy with the service the bank provides the customers.

   **Role B.** You are an employee at Bancafé in Quetzaltenango, Guatemala. Explain to a new customer a) how to write a check in Spanish (see example below); b) how to write the date in Spanish; c) where to put the name of the person to whom he/she is writing the check; d) how to write the amount (**cantidad**) in numbers; e) how to write the amount in words; and f) where to sign the check (**firmar el cheque**).

| | |
|---|---|
| **Serie AD**  **6703690** | **$** _____ |
| | $\dfrac{012\text{-}0587}{446}$ |
| **12 Av. 5-50** **Zona 1** | |
| _____ . _____ DE _____ AÑO _ _ _ _ _ | |
| PÁGUESE A LA ORDEN DE _____ | O AL PORTADOR |
| LA CANTIDAD DE _____ | |
| _____ PESOS M/L | |
| **BANCO DE CAFÉ, S.A.** _____ | |

06703690   0190587446004210 2   01

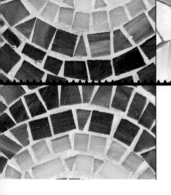

# MOSAICOS

## A escuchar

**ESTRATEGIA**

**Use contextual guessing**

When you have a conversation in a second language, it is very possible that you may not understand everything the other person says. You can figure out the overall message by using contextual cues; that is, by paying attention to the topic or to the words that precede or follow what you did not understand.

### Antes de escuchar

**9-32 Preparación.** En la siguiente conversación, dos amigas hablan sobre las ventajas y desventajas de su trabajo. Antes de escuchar, escriba el nombre de una profesión relacionada con los negocios y otra con la salud. Luego, escriba una ventaja y una desventaja para cada una de las profesiones.

| PROFESIÓN | VENTAJA | DESVENTAJA |
|-----------|---------|------------|
| _____ | _____ | _____ |
| _____ | _____ | _____ |

### Escuchar

**9-33 ¿Comprende usted?** First, read the words in the left column and listen to the conversation between Estela and Susana. Then state the probable meaning of each word in English based on the contextual cues you heard in the conversation. Finally, write down the cue words that helped you understand.

CD 4
Track 19

| ESCUCHÉ... | POSIBLE SIGNIFICADO | ADIVINÉ EL SIGNIFICADO PORQUE... |
|------------|---------------------|----------------------------------|
| **1.** neuróloga | | |
| **2.** primordial | | |
| **3.** guardias | | |

### Después de escuchar

**9-34 Ahora usted.** Compartan las respuestas a las siguientes preguntas.

1. ¿Cuáles son las ventajas y desventajas de la profesión que le gusta a usted?
2. En general, ¿qué profesión u ocupación le parece a usted que es menos estresante?
3. ¿Qué profesión u ocupación, según usted, da más satisfacciones personales? ¿Por qué?

# A conversar

## Antes de conversar

**9-35 Preparación.** Lea los siguientes anuncios con ofertas de trabajo, escoja un anuncio para un puesto que a usted le interese y prepare una lista de requisitos que, en su opinión, usted cumple (*meet*). Comparta su lista con su compañero/a.

INSTITUTO PRIVADO
*necesita*

# DIRECTOR/A

**Lugar de residencia, Región de los Lagos**

Empresa de Hotelería necesita
Director/a

Requisitos: Estudios universitarios avanzados. Experiencia mínima de 1 a 2 años en ventas directas, preferiblemente en el área de servicios. Edad 26 a 32 años. Excelente presentación. Poseer vehículo propio. Buenas relaciones interpersonales.

Ofrecemos: Salario a convenir según experiencia, gasolina, comisiones sobre ventas. Excelente ambiente de trabajo. Oportunidades de crecimiento.

*Sueldo compatible con calificaciones*

**Interesados,** enviar currículum a
gruporecursoshumanos@hotmail.com

---

**EMPRESA DE EXPORTACIONES**
necesita para Chile y el extranjero

# VENDEDORES/AS REPRESENTANTES

**Sueldo inicial 1,000.000**
**Comisión de ventas**

Casa Tadeo necesita
Asistente de Ventas y Mercadeo
Requisitos: Estudios universitarios de administración de empresas o mercadeo. De preferencia con experiencia en puesto similar de 1 año, no indispensable. Proactivo, extrovertido, dinámico, con autoridad, con iniciativa, organizado, colaborador. Habilidad para trabajar independientemente. Excelente manejo de equipos de cómputo. Buen dominio del inglés. Filosofía de servicio al cliente.
Ofrecemos: Salario competitivo. Oportunidades de capacitación. Excelente oportunidad de desarrollo en una empresa de alto crecimiento. Ambiente agradable de trabajo.

**Interesados,** llamar al teléfono
2533-2459
Lunes a viernes de 8:30 a 15:00 hrs.

---

# JEFE DE SERVICIO
necesita importante empresa
**MANUFACTURERA DE PLÁSTICOS**

Nos urge un buen diseñador gráfico
Requisitos: Conocer al 100% PhotoShop y Freehand. Manejar ambiente Mac y PC. De preferencia estudiante de diseño en la U, con ideas frescas. Dispuesto a trabajar bajo presión.
Ofrecemos: Salario a convenir. Capacitación constante. Desarrollo dentro de la organización. Horario flexible. Seguro de vida y médico.
**Interesados,** enviar currículum y fotografía reciente, especificando pretensiones de sueldo, a Casilla 2568, Correo Guatemala, zona 1, Guatemala

---

**BANCO AZTECA**
*necesita*
# 10 CONTADORES AUDITORES
**Lugar de trabajo ideal: Viña del Mar**

- Título universitario
- Mínimo dos años de experiencia
- Flexibilidad horaria
- Deseo de viajar a otras regiones del país
- Capacidad de organización y trabajo

*Sueldo atractivo*
**Interesados,** enviar currículum, con fotografía a:
Bco. Azteca, 7 Av. 19-28, zona 5

### En directo

To welcome someone to your office:

**Pase/Adelante, por favor./Tenga la amabilidad de pasar.** *Please come in.*

**Por favor, tome asiento.** *Please have a seat.*

**Siéntese aquí, por favor.** *Sit here, please.*

To put someone at ease:

**Por favor, póngase cómodo/a.** *Please, make yourself comfortable.*

To say good-bye at the end of an interview:

**Fue un placer conocerlo/la.** *It was a pleasure to meet you.*

## Conversar

**9-36 Entre nosotros.** Ahora escojan un papel. Uno/a de ustedes es el jefe/la jefa de personal de una compañía representada en los anuncios y dos son personas que solicitan el mismo trabajo en esa compañía. Sigan las siguientes instrucciones para cada papel.

**Jefe/a de personal:** Entreviste separadamente a dos personas que están interesadas en el mismo puesto. Pregúnteles sobre su experiencia, sus estudios, sus preferencias de sueldo, etc. y decida cuál es la persona indicada para el puesto.

**Personas que buscan trabajo:** Escojan el anuncio con el trabajo que los dos necesitan. Respondan a las preguntas del jefe/de la jefa de personal y háganle preguntas para saber más acerca del puesto.

## Después de conversar

**9-37 Un poco más. PRIMERA FASE.** Los jefes de personal y las personas que buscaban trabajo deben informar a la clase sobre lo siguiente:

---

**Informe de las personas que buscaban trabajo:**

1. ¿Qué puesto buscaba usted? ¿Qué requisitos para el puesto cumple usted?
2. ¿Qué aspecto de la oferta de trabajo le pareció más atractivo?
3. ¿Cree usted que va a recibir la oferta de trabajo? ¿Por qué?

---

**Informe de los jefes de personal:**

1. ¿Qué puesto ofrecía su compañía en el anuncio?
2. ¿Qué requisitos debía tener el candidato/la candidata que buscaba su compañía?
3. ¿A qué candidato/a(s) va a contratar usted? ¿Por qué?

---

**SEGUNDA FASE.** Presenten la entrevista ideal entre el jefe de personal y el candidato más apropiado para cada anuncio de trabajo.

# A leer

### Organize textual information into categories

To understand what you are reading, you need to focus on what is being conveyed by the text. By *focus* we mean organizing the information into meaningful categories, which helps you connect the information to what you already know. As you read, focus on the main points in each of the three sections. Use the subtitles to help you anticipate the content.

## Antes de leer

**9-38 Preparación.** Lea el título y los subtítulos del texto y mire la foto. Basándose en esta información y en lo que usted sabe sobre la inmigración, marque (✓) las ideas que piensa encontrar en el texto.

1. \_\_\_\_ Muchas mujeres guatemaltecas en Estados Unidos se casan con hombres mexicanos.
2. \_\_\_\_ El término "guatemexicoestadounidense" se refiere a familias cuyos (*whose*) miembros pertenecen a estas tres culturas.
3. \_\_\_\_ La concentración más grande de guatemaltecos en Estados Unidos está en Los Ángeles.
4. \_\_\_\_ La inmigración de guatemaltecos a Estados Unidos tiene un impacto económico positivo en Guatemala.

## Leer

### Los guatemaltecos en Estados Unidos

**Matrimonios entre guatemaltecos y mexicanos**

Gustavo Rivera conoció a Marta Rodríguez en un club hispano de Los Ángeles y la invitó a bailar.

"¿De dónde eres?", preguntó Marta. "De México", respondió Gustavo.

Después de esa noche, los dos empezaron a conversar por teléfono y a salir juntos. Marta, que era de Ciudad de México, se dio cuenta que Gustavo hablaba español con un acento diferente y usaba unas palabras diferentes también. Después de un tiempo, ella le preguntó: "¿De dónde eres realmente, Gustavo?" Esta vez, Gustavo le dijo la verdad: "Soy de Guatemala". Pasaron dos años y Gustavo y Marta se casaron. Ahora tienen tres hijos: Martita, de tres años, Gustavo, de dos y la bebé Rosita, de seis meses. Esta familia representa una tendencia demográfica que está aumentando en Los Ángeles y en otras ciudades del suroeste: más inmigrantes guatemaltecos y mexicanos se casan entre sí y tienen hijos, creando familias hispanas mixtas que tienen conexiones con tres países al mismo tiempo. Esa mezcla es ahora tan común que dio lugar al nombre de "guatemexicoestadounidenses" para describir a esas familias.

**Nuevas tendencias demográficas**

Hay varias razones que explican esta nueva tendencia demográfica. Primero, el número de personas de ascendencia guatemalteca en Estados Unidos está creciendo. Según la Organización Internacional para las Migraciones (OIM), en 2006 había 1.178.000 guatemaltecos en Estados Unidos. La mayoría de ellos son jóvenes, entre 15 y 44 años, y hay muchos más hombres que mujeres. Se estima que el 72% son hombres y el 28% mujeres. Es evidente que, por esta razón, cuando los guatemaltecos en Estados Unidos se casan, muchos se casan con mujeres no guatemaltecas.

Segundo, cuando llegan a Estados Unidos, los inmigrantes guatemaltecos buscan vivienda en comunidades hispanas establecidas, donde viven principalmente inmigrantes mexicanos, el grupo hispano más grande del país. La constante interacción de hombres guatemaltecos y mujeres mexicanas inevitablemente resulta en más matrimonios entre los dos grupos.

Esta mezcla de culturas hispanas no se limita a guatemaltecos y mexicanos. Los hispanos son, como los estadounidenses, de diversas nacionalidades. Una persona puede decir, por ejemplo, "la madre de mi madre es de Irlanda, y los padres de mi padre eran alemanes". Lo mismo está ocurriendo con los hispanos.

**Impacto económico en Guatemala**

En muchos sentidos, Gustavo Rivera es un inmigrante guatemalteco típico. Como el 88% de los guatemaltecos que viven en Estados Unidos, Gustavo se mantiene activo económicamente, trabaja en una fábrica que manufactura materiales para tejados (*roofs*). Como el 33% de los guatemaltecos en Estados Unidos, vive en Los Ángeles. Y como el 93% de los emigrantes guatemaltecos, mantiene contacto con su familia en Guatemala. Llama a sus padres todas las semanas y les envía remesas todos los meses. Según la OIM, más de 600.000 familias en Guatemala reciben remesas de familiares que viven en el extranjero.

El impacto económico de las remesas en Guatemala es considerable. Se estima que las remesas estimulan la economía de Guatemala, igual que la de otros países centroamericanos. También ayudan a estos países a evitar la recesión.

**9-39 Primera mirada.** Indique a qué categoría pertenecen las siguientes afirmaciones, según el contenido del artículo: información personal sobre una familia (**P**), información general sobre los inmigrantes guatemaltecos en Estados Unidos (**EU**) o información sobre Guatemala (**G**).

1. ____ Viven en comunidades donde el grupo predominante son los mexicanos.
2. ____ Se conocieron en un club de baile.
3. ____ Reciben dinero de sus familiares que viven en el extranjero.
4. ____ Se casan con personas de otras culturas.
5. ____ El dinero que viene del exterior estimula la economía.
6. ____ No dijo la verdad sobre su país de origen.
7. ____ Hay más hombres que mujeres.
8. ____ Muchas veces sus hijos nacen en un país diferente de donde nacieron los padres.

**9-40 Segunda mirada.** El artículo explica algunos fenómenos de causa y efecto. Conecte cada fenómeno en la columna de la izquierda con su resultado lógico en la columna de la derecha.

1. ____ La mayoría de los inmigrantes son jóvenes.
2. ____ Hay más hombres que mujeres entre los inmigrantes guatemaltecos.
3. ____ Los mexicanos son el grupo hispano más numeroso en Estados Unidos.
4. ____ La gran mayoría de los inmigrantes guatemaltecos tienen trabajo.
5. ____ Hay una tendencia en Estados Unidos a casarse con personas de diferentes ascendencias culturales.

a. Hay muchas parejas en las que una persona es mexicana y la otra es de otra cultura hispana.
b. Mandan remesas a sus familiares en Guatemala.
c. Se casan en su nuevo país.
d. Se casan con mujeres no guatemaltecas.
e. Hay cada vez más familias hispanas compuestas de (*composed of*) personas de diferentes países.

## Después de leer

 **9-41 Ampliación.** Con su compañero/a, escriban una lista de la información nueva que aprendieron del artículo. Luego, indiquen qué información les parece más interesante.

# A escribir

> **Focus on purpose, content, and audience**
>
> Getting the job you want may be a challenge in today's competitive labor market. Responding effectively to an employment ad is an important first step. Answering an ad takes as much skill as being interviewed.
>
> To get the job that is right for you, whether during college or after graduation, consider the following when responding to an ad in any language:
>
> ▪ Your purpose: What kind of job do you want (management or entry level; full- or part-time; permanent or temporary, etc.)?
>
> ▪ Your response: What academic degree do you need for the job (high school, college, other)? What general abilities and job-specific skills should you possess?
>
> ▪ Your audience: What experience does the employer require? What personality characteristics will you need to be considered a serious candidate?

## Antes de escribir

**9-42 Preparación.** Usted ve un anuncio de trabajo en Internet de la señora Álvarez de Colón de Guatemala. La familia va a mudarse a Estados Unidos y quiere contratar a dos estudiantes en Estados Unidos para el verano, uno/a para cuidar a sus dos hijos (de 4 y 6 años) y enseñarles inglés y el otro/la otra para preparar comidas típicamente americanas. Planee un correo electrónico para solicitar uno de los trabajos. Haga una lista de las categorías de información sobre su experiencia y sus talentos que piensa mencionar.

## Escribir

**9-43 Manos a la obra.** Ahora escríbale un correo electrónico a la señora Álvarez de Colón. En un mensaje breve, organizado y convincente, preséntese y explique cómo su experiencia, su conocimiento y sus talentos lo/la preparan para el puesto.

## Después de escribir

**9-44 Revisión.** Lea lo que escribió, pensando en su lectora. Verifique lo siguiente:

1. ¿Qué categorías de información incluyó? ¿Falta alguna categoría importante?
2. Como usted no conoce a esta persona, ¿se dirigió a ella usando la forma *usted*?
3. ¿Tiene su correo electrónico una organización clara, es decir, una introducción, un cuerpo y un cierre?
4. ¿Revisó el vocabulario, expresiones de cortesía y de despedida, la concordancia, el tiempo (presente, pasado), el uso de los mandatos, etc.?

Comparta su mensaje electrónico con un compañero/una compañera. Esto puede darle la perspectiva de un lector/una lectora sobre la claridad de su texto y sobre la cantidad de información que usted incluyó.

# ENFOQUE CULTURAL

## Historia y trabajo en Guatemala

Los restos de la gran civilización maya sobreviven hoy día en sitios como Tikal, Yaxha y Naachtun en Guatemala. Las ruinas que se conservan nos permiten imaginar cómo fueron esas ciudades en sus momentos de esplendor. Cuando las visitamos, frecuentemente pensamos en la complejidad y el simbolismo religioso de muchas de esas construcciones, o en el lujo de los palacios, o en la avanzada técnica de construcción. Y sin embargo, un aspecto muy importante que con

Gran Plaza de Tikal

frecuencia olvidamos es la diversidad de profesiones, trabajos y artes que tuvieron que desarrollar los mayas para construir dichas ciudades. En efecto, fue necesario especializar a los trabajadores, de manera que surgieron profesiones independientes para realizar actividades específicas. Pintores, escultores, cortadores de piedra, carpinteros, ceramistas, astrónomos, todos contribuyeron con su trabajo especializado.

Mientras estas personas trabajaban en la construcción de las ciudades, los agricultores tenían que cultivar la comida para alimentar a todos estos trabajadores urbanos que no tenían tiempo para producir su propia alimentación. Y como es lógico, cuando el centro de producción es diferente del centro de consumo, los comerciantes se ocupan de llevar los productos del campo y venderlos en los mercados de la ciudad. Pero los comerciantes mayas hicieron más que eso, pues desarrollaron unas rutas comerciales que los llevaron más allá de las fronteras locales. Efectivamente, la red de caminos de los comerciantes mayas cubría una inmensa parte de México y Centroamérica.

Xaman-ek, considerado el dios de los comerciantes, según está representado en el Códice Dresden

El mercado indígena de Antigua, un ejemplo del llamado "capitalismo del centavo"

Cuando vemos la sofisticación y la complejidad de la antigua civilización maya, nos preguntamos por qué es hoy Guatemala uno de los países más pobres del continente. Aunque la respuesta a esta pregunta es demasiado compleja para contestarla en pocas palabras, sí podemos decir que la sociedad creada a partir de la colonia española marginó a la población indígena y limitó su posibilidad de participar en la economía. Y, puesto que más del 60% de la población guatemalteca hoy día se considera indígena, un porcentaje muy elevado de la población tiene que encontrar su subsistencia en una economía limitada, a la que Sol Tax, un famoso antropólogo de la Universidad de Chicago, llamó "capitalismo del centavo". Lo más interesante, sin embargo, es que a pesar de tantos años de marginalización, el espíritu comerciante de los indígenas no ha desaparecido y continúa muy visible hoy día en los mercados indígenas.

Desafortunadamente, en la actualidad, los más emprendedores entre los marginados de Guatemala buscan en la emigración mejores condiciones de trabajo y formas para participar en la economía. Esta necesidad de buscar oportunidades económicas fuera de Guatemala se ve reforzada por las periódicas catástrofes naturales que ocurren en la región, tales como terremotos y huracanes. Otro factor que afecta a la ola migratoria son los acontecimientos de carácter político, tales como las guerras civiles o las dictaduras militares que persiguen a los indígenas. En la actualidad, más de una cuarta parte de los inmigrantes centroamericanos en Estados Unidos son de Guatemala, y se calculan en cerca del millón.

**9-45 Comprensión.** PRIMERA FASE. **Reconocimiento de palabras clave.** Encuentre en el texto la palabra o expresión que mejor expresa el significado de las siguientes ideas.

1. remnants     _____
2. stonecutters _____
3. to feed      _____
4. merchants    _____
5. trade routes _____
6. complexity   _____
7. civil wars   _____

SEGUNDA FASE. **Oraciones importantes.** Subraye las afirmaciones que contienen ideas que se encuentran en el texto. Luego indique en qué parte del texto están.

1. For all their complexity, Mayan cities lacked religious symbolism.
2. We often fail to see the variety of trades that were required to build a Mayan city.
3. Mayan farmers were forced to stop growing food crops to work on the construction of the great Mayan cities.
4. Mayan merchants traded their products well beyond the borders of the Maya Empire.
5. Guatemala is one of the poorest countries in the continent today.
6. Well over half of the population of Guatemala is considered to be indigenous.
7. Military dictatorships have been successful in curbing emigration.
8. Natural disasters are one of the factors that motivate Guatemalans to emigrate.

TERCERA FASE. **Ideas principales.** Escriba un párrafo breve en inglés resumiendo las ideas principales expresadas en el texto.

 **9-46 Use la información.** Escriba una carta contestando a un anuncio de trabajo en Guatemala. Su carta debe incluir lo siguiente:

1. qué trabajo solicita usted
2. dónde trabaja actualmente y por cuánto tiempo
3. qué experiencia tiene usted en ese tipo de trabajo
4. cuándo puede empezar a trabajar

Para preparar esta actividad, visite la página web de *Mosaicos* y siga los enlaces útiles.

# VOCABULARIO

CD 4
cks 20–24

| | |
|---|---|
| **Las profesiones, oficios y ocupaciones** | **Professions, trades, and occupations** |
| el/la abogado/a | lawyer |
| el actor/la actriz | actor/actress |
| el/la agricultor/a | farmer |
| el ama/o de casa | housewife, homemaker |
| el/la arquitecto/a | architect |
| el/la artesano/a | craftsman/woman, craftsperson |
| el/la bibliotecario/a | librarian |
| el/la bombero/a | firefighter |
| el/la cajero/a | cashier |
| el/la carpintero/a | carpenter |
| el/la ceramista | potter |
| el/la chef | chef |
| el/la chofer | driver |
| el/la científico/a | scientist |
| el/la contador/a | accountant |
| el/la contratista | contractor |
| el/la ejecutivo/a | executive |
| el/la electricista | electrician |
| el/la empleado/a | employee |
| el/la enfermero/a | nurse |
| el/la gerente (de ventas) | (sales) manager |
| el herrero | blacksmith; ironworker |
| el hombre/la mujer de negocios | businessman/woman |
| el/la ingeniero/a | engineer |
| el/la intérprete | interpreter |
| el jefe/la jefa | boss |
| el/la joyero/a | jeweller |
| el/la juez | judge |
| el/la locutor/a | radio announcer |
| el/la médico/a | medical doctor |
| el/la obrero/a | worker |
| el/la peletero/a | furrier |
| el/la peluquero/a | hairdresser |
| el/la periodista | journalist |
| el/la plomero/a | plumber |
| el/la policía | policeman/woman |
| el/la (p)sicólogo/a | psychologist |
| el/la técnico/a | technician |
| el/la vendedor/a | salesman, saleswoman |

| | |
|---|---|
| **Los lugares** | **Places** |
| el banco | bank |
| el campo | countryside |

| | |
|---|---|
| la compañía/la empresa | company |
| el consultorio | office (of doctor, dentist, etc.) |
| la peluquería | beauty salon, barbershop |
| el taller | workshop |

| | |
|---|---|
| **El trabajo** | **Work** |
| la agricultura | farming |
| el anuncio | ad, advertisement |
| el cliente/la clienta | client |
| el currículum | résumé |
| la entrevista | interview |
| la especialidad | specialty |
| la experiencia | experience |
| el incendio | fire |
| la madera | wood |
| el puesto | position |
| la solicitud | application |
| el sueldo | salary |
| la vacante | opening |
| las ventas | sales |

| | |
|---|---|
| **Verbos** | **Verbs** |
| apagar | to extinguish, to turn off |
| cosechar | to harvest |
| dejar | to leave |
| elaborar | to produce |
| emigrar | to emigrate |
| enviar | to send |
| esperar | to wait for |
| llenar | to fill (out) |
| mandar | to send |
| ofrecer (zc) | to offer |
| sobrevivir | to survive |
| solicitar | to apply (for) |

| | |
|---|---|
| **Palabras y expresiones útiles** | **Useful words and expressions** |
| actualmente | at the present time |
| ¡Cómo no! | Of course! |
| en realidad/realmente | in fact, really |
| lo importante | the important thing |
| por cierto | by the way |
| propio/a | own |
| la señal | signal |
| sin embargo | nevertheless |

# ¡A comer!

Este cuadro del siglo XVIII presenta a un indígena yumbo cerca de Quito, Ecuador. Junto a él hay árboles y frutas típicas de su país.

# In this chapter you will learn how to:

- discuss food, menus, diets, and shopping for food
- state impersonal information
- give instructions
- talk about the recent past and the future

Cultural focus: **Ecuador**

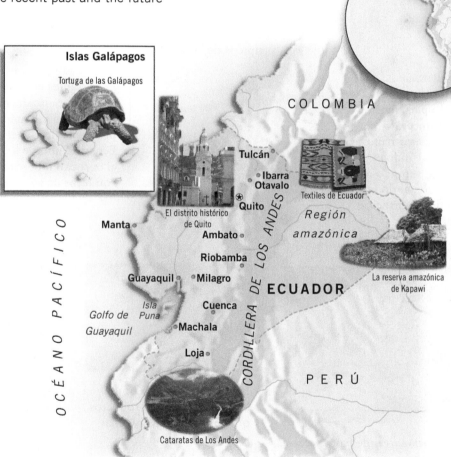

Islas Galápagos

Tortuga de las Galápagos

COLOMBIA

Tulcán

Ibarra
Otavalo

Textiles de Ecuador

Quito

El distrito histórico
de Quito

Región
amazónica

Manta

Ambato

Riobamba

La reserva amazónica
de Kapawi

Guayaquil • Milagro

ECUADOR

Isla
Puna

Cuenca

CORDILLERA DE LOS ANDES

Golfo de
Guayaquil

Machala

Loja

PERÚ

OCÉANO PACÍFICO

Cataratas de Los Andes

 **A vista de pájaro.** Mire los siguientes grupos de palabras y ponga un círculo alrededor de la palabra que no corresponde.

1. pescado, comida, lima, tomate, papaya, volcán
2. tela, diseño, artesanía, bombero, mercado, joyas
3. catedral, toro, casa, calle, iglesia, ciudad
4. selva, río, plato, planta, árbol, calor
5. montaña, tortilla, catarata, agua, nube, verde
6. tortuga, isla, naturaleza, textil, animal, roca

## Los productos y las recetas

CD 4
Track 25
or CD 5
Track 1

En Ecuador se cultiva mucha fruta, sobre todo **piña, limón, melón, papaya, maracuyá** y **plátano.** Mucha de esta fruta se exporta a Estados Unidos y otros países. Aquí vemos a unas personas trabajando en una compañía de exportación de plátanos cerca de Guayaquil.

En los mercados ecuatorianos, como en los de otros países hispanoamericanos, hay buenos puestos de **pasteles** donde se venden los **dulces** típicos de la región.

El pescado y los **mariscos** son muy importantes en la dieta de algunos países hispanoamericanos como Chile, Perú y Ecuador. En la provincia de Esmeraldas, en Ecuador, uno de los platos típicos es el encocado, pescado que se cocina con **leche de coco.**

Esta mujer ecuatoriana vende frutos secos mientras cuida las **ovejas.** De las ovejas se aprovechan la carne en comida y la lana en suéteres, mantas, etc. Además, los **campesinos** usan la leche para hacer queso y yogur. Junto a la carne de **cordero,** la de **res** y la de cerdo son las que más se usan en la comida de Ecuador y se venden en los mercados y en las carnicerías.

En el mercado de Zumbahua se encuentran los productos que se usan en las muchas **recetas** de la comida de Ecuador. La forma de combinar estos productos con el cilantro y otras **hierbas** y **especias** dan fama a la gastronomía ecuatoriana.

### En otras palabras

The words for some vegetables and spices vary from region to region. **Aguacate** is known as **palta** in some South American countries; **maíz** is known as **elote** in Mexico and in some Central American countries and as **choclo** in parts of South America. Other examples are **cilantro/culantro,** **achiote/pimentón** (paprika), and **frijoles/porotos.**
Names of fruits also vary: **plátano** in Spain becomes **cambur** in Venezuela; in other places, like Colombia, **banano** is used, and elsewhere (in Uruguay, for example) it is **banana.** Other examples include **melocotón** (Spain)/**durazno** (Latin America); **fruto de la pasión** (Spain)/**maracuyá** (Colombia)/**parchita** (Venezuela, Mexico).

**10-1 Definiciones.** Asocie las definiciones a continuación con las palabras que aparecen en los textos y fotos anteriores.

1. una lista de ingredientes y de instrucciones para elaborar una comida
2. un animal del que se aprovecha la lana, la leche y la carne
3. una fruta alargada que se pela y que les gusta mucho a los monos
4. un plato ecuatoriano que se cocina con pescado y leche de coco
5. una tienda donde se vende pescado
6. las personas que cultivan productos del campo
7. dulces que se venden en las pastelerías y en los mercados
8. la carne de una oveja pequeña

**10-2 Una receta ecuatoriana.** Lea la siguiente receta y clasifique sus ingredientes según las siguientes categorías.

a. carnes o pescados:
b. vegetales:
c. condimentos:
d. frutas:

### Pescado encocado

Ingredientes:
1 coco
1 libra de camarones
2 libras de pescado crudo

1 un tomate grande rojo, pelado y picado
un poquito de achiote
sal, pimienta, comino al gusto

Refrito:
1 cebolla paiteña finamente picada
¼ taza de cebolla blanca finamente picada
1 pimiento picado
4 cucharadas de cilantro picado
4 cucharadas de perejil picado
2 dientes de ajo machacados
4 cucharadas de aceite

Elaboración:
Haga un refrito con los ingredientes. Agréguele una libra de camarones crudos, pelados y limpios y dos libras de pescado crudo, cortado en trozos. Refríalos durante un rato y luego agregue la mitad de la leche del coco. Tape la olla y deje cocinar durante 20 ó 30 minutos. Después, añada la otra mitad de la leche del coco. Sirva inmediatamente, acompañado de arroz blanco y plátano verde asado.

> **Lengua**
>
> These are some useful words that appear in the recipe: **almejas** (*clams*), **perejil** (*parsley*), **paiteña** (*a type of onion*), **diente de ajo** (*clove of garlic*), **picado** (*chopped*), and **comino** (*cumin*). Other cooking expressions include **picar** (*chop*), **pelar** (*peel*), **machacar** (*crush*), **tapar** (*cover*), **agregar/añadir** (*add*), **taza** (*cup*), and **cucharada** (*spoonful*).

> **Lengua**
>
> To give instructions on how to prepare a recipe, the following grammatical constructions may be used: 1. commands (**cocine el arroz, añada la sal**); 2. se + verb (**se cocina el arroz, se añade la sal**); 3. the infinitive (**cocinar el arroz, añadir la sal**).

**10-3 Mi receta favorita.** Escojan una receta simple. Escriban los ingredientes y después explíquenle a otra pareja cómo se prepara el plato. Las siguientes palabras pueden facilitarles la explicación:

**batir** (*to beat*)     **cortar** (*to cut*)     **freír** (**i**) (*to fry*)     **hervir** (**ie**) (*to boil*)

## ◄)) En el supermercado

CD 4
Tracks 26–30
or CD 5
Tracks 2–6

### Las frutas y las verduras

el ajo | los pimientos verdes | las zanahorias
los pepinos | las espinacas | el maíz el elote el choclo
las cebollas | los plátanos/ las bananas | las peras
las manzanas | las toronjas/ los pomelos | las uvas
los aguacates | las cerezas | las fresas

### Los productos lácteos

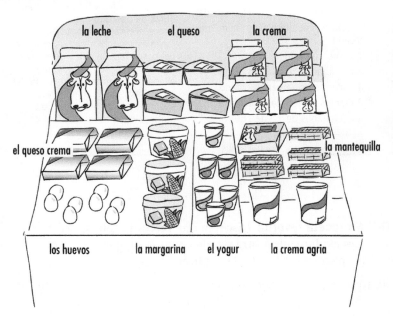

la leche | el queso | la crema
el queso crema | | la mantequilla
los huevos | la margarina | el yogur | la crema agria

## El pescado y la carne

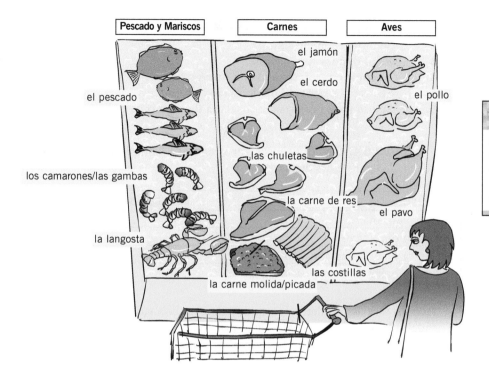

**Pescado y Mariscos** | **Carnes** | **Aves**

el pescado
los camarones/las gambas
la langosta
la carne molida/picada

el jamón
el cerdo
las chuletas
la carne de res
las costillas

el pollo
el pavo

## Los condimentos y las legumbres

la sal
la pimienta
la mostaza
la vainilla
la harina
el/la azúcar
el aderezo
el vinagre    el aceite
la manteca    la salsa de tomate    la mayonesa
los frijoles    las lentejas    los garbanzos

## El pan y las bebidas

el pan
los churros
las galletas
el pan dulce
los refrescos    el vino tinto    el vino blanco

**10-4 Asociaciones.** Después de asociar cada explicación con la palabra adecuada, comenten si les gustan o no estos alimentos.

1. ____ Se toma mucho en el verano, cuando hace calor.
2. ____ Se pone en la ensalada.
3. ____ Se usan para hacer vino.
4. ____ Se come en el desayuno con huevos fritos.
5. ____ Se prepara para el Día de Acción de Gracias.
6. ____ Se usa para preparar la ensalada de atún o de pollo.

a. el jamón
b. las uvas
c. la mayonesa
d. el helado
e. el aderezo
f. el pavo

**10-5 Dietas diferentes.** PRIMERA FASE. Completen la tabla con comidas adecuadas para estas dietas.

| DIETA | SE DEBE COMER | NO SE DEBE COMER |
|---|---|---|
| vegetariana | | |
| para diabéticos | | |
| para desarrollar músculos | | |
| para bajar de peso (*lose weight*) | | |

SEGUNDA FASE. Completen las siguientes ideas con sus recomendaciones para cada una de estas personas. Digan por qué.

1. Laura, que es vegetariana, debe comer…
2. Mi padre, que es diabético,…
3. Luis, que levanta pesas (*weights*),…
4. Joaquín y Amalia quieren bajar de peso. Por lo tanto…

**10-6 ¿Qué necesitamos?** PRIMERA FASE. Ustedes son estudiantes de intercambio en Ecuador. Le quieren preparar una cena a su familia ecuatoriana. Hagan lo siguiente.

1. Describan el menú: ¿Qué plato principal van a servir? ¿Van a hacer ensaladas? ¿Van a servir bebidas? ¿Qué bebidas?
2. Hagan una lista de los ingredientes que necesitarán. ¿Van a necesitar verduras, vegetales, legumbres, especias, frutas?

SEGUNDA FASE. Ahora compartan sus planes con otra pareja.

**10-7 Los estudiantes y la comida.** PRIMERA FASE. Hablen de las comidas típicas de los estudiantes de su universidad. Respondan a las siguientes preguntas.

1. ¿Qué comieron hoy?
2. ¿Cuándo y dónde comieron?
3. ¿Cuánto gastaron en comida?

SEGUNDA FASE. Hagan una lista de recomendaciones para una dieta estudiantil más saludable (*healthy*) y compártanla con el resto de la clase. Piensen en el desayuno, el almuerzo, la cena y las meriendas (*snacks*).

# ·)) La mesa

CD 4
Track 31
or CD 5
Track 7

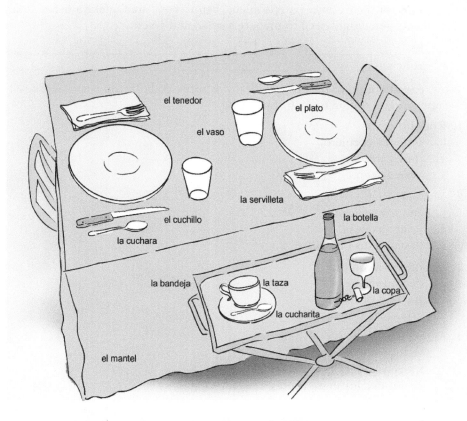

el tenedor
el plato
el vaso
la servilleta
el cuchillo
la botella
la cuchara
la bandeja · la taza
la copa
la cucharita
el mantel

**10-8 Entrenamiento de un camarero/una camarera.** Ustedes son camareros en un restaurante pero uno/a de ustedes es nuevo/a en el puesto. Dígale a al camarero nuevo/a la camarera nueva dónde debe poner cada cosa de acuerdo con el dibujo. Después cambien de papel.

MODELO:  E1:  *Ponga el cuchillo a la derecha del plato.*
E2:  *Muy bien. ¿Y dónde pongo la copa?*
E1:  _____

**10-9 Los preparativos de un banquete.** Ustedes trabajan en el servicio de comidas de la universidad y tienen que organizar un banquete para sus profesores. Primero preparen un menú, una lista de lo que tienen que comprar para el banquete y un presupuesto (*budget*). Luego deben dividirse el trabajo. Cada uno/a de ustedes es responsable de dar instrucciones a los otros/las otras sobre lo siguiente:

1. cómo elaborar el menú
2. cómo preparar la mesa
3. cómo decorar la sala

CD 4
Track 32
or CD 5
Track 8

---

### En directo

To express that you had a good time:

**Lo pasé muy bien./Lo pasamos muy bien.**

**Fue estupendo.**

**Estuvo muy divertido.**

---

**10-10 Una cena.** Usted estuvo muy ocupado/a ayer porque tuvo invitados a cenar. Dígale a su compañero/a todas las cosas que hizo. Él/Ella le va a preguntar dónde hizo las compras, a quién invitó, qué sirvió, y si lo pasaron bien. Después cambien de papel.

**10-11 Una cena perfecta.** You will listen to a married couple talk about their plans for their dinner party tonight. Before you listen, make a list of four ingredients you would need to prepare a salad and an entrée.

ensalada _____

plato principal _____

Now, pay attention to the general idea of what is said. As you listen, mark (✓) the appropriate ending to each statement.

1. Rodolfo es...
   —— un buen cocinero.
   —— muy perezoso.
   —— vegetariano.

2. Manuela va a...
   —— cocinar ceviche.
   —— poner la mesa.
   —— llamar a los invitados.

3. Rodolfo va a comprar...
   —— pescado y maíz.
   —— limón y camarones.
   —— espinacas y aguacates.

4. Manuela tiene...
   —— todos los ingredientes.
   —— muchos vegetales y frutas.
   —— casi todos los ingredientes.

---

## Cultura

La comida de los países hispanoamericanos es muy variada. En Ecuador, al igual que en Perú, el ceviche de pescado o de camarón es muy popular. Otro plato muy popular es la fritada, un combinado de diversas carnes con plátano (*plantain*) maduro, plátano tostado y maíz. Y entre los postres, además de la pastelería, es muy sabroso el dulce de higos (*candied figs*).

# EN ACCIÓN

## Diarios de bicicleta: Lección de cocina

### Antes de ver

**10-12** Prepare una lista de algunos problemas inesperados que pueden ocurrir antes de una fiesta o de una cena importante.

### Mientras ve

**10-13** Muchas recetas para pozole incluyen los siguientes ingredientes. Marque (✓) los que menciona Luciana.

1. ___ carne de cerdo
2. ___ chiles
3. ___ ajos
4. ___ cebollas

5. ___ tomates
6. ___ cilantro
7. ___ maíz
8. ___ aceite

### Después de ver

**10-14** Ponga en el orden apropiado los siguientes pasos para hacer pozole.

___ Se quitan las semillas de los chiles y se cocinan con el tomate.

___ Se licuan los chiles, los tomates y el cilantro.

___ Se pone a cocinar la carne con las cebollas y ajos.

___ Se unen la carne, los chiles y tomates y el maíz.

___ Se corta la carne ya cocinada en trocitos muy pequeños.

___ Se sirve en platos hondos y se adorna con tostadas.

___ Se agrega sal y se deja sazonar unos minutos.

# FUNCIONES Y FORMAS

## 1. Stating impersonal information: *Se* + verb constructions

**PROFESOR:** **Se consumen** muchos carbohidratos y mucha grasa. ¿Sabían ustedes que en Estados Unidos **se comen** 23 libras de pizza por persona al año?

**RICARDO:** [piensa] ¿Cuánta cerveza **se bebe** con 23 pizzas?

**PROFESOR:** **Se comen** sólo 16 libras de manzanas, bla bla bla...

**RICARDO:** [piensa] En esta clase **se duerme** mucho.

**Piénselo.** ¿Cuánto más sabe usted sobre la dieta estadounidense? Indique si las siguientes afirmaciones son ciertas (**C**) o falsas (**F**), según la información del profesor y lo que usted sabe.

1. ____ **Se consumen** muchas grasas (*fats*).
2. ____ **Se compra** más fruta en el supermercado ahora que en el pasado.
3. ____ **Se dice** que los niños comen más y hacen menos actividad física.
4. ____ **Se bebe** mucho café, especialmente en las universidades.
5. ____ **Se consume** más pizza que manzanas.
6. ____ **Se recomienda** desayunar todos los días.

■ Spanish uses the **se +** *verb* construction to emphasize the occurrence of an action rather than the person(s) responsible for that action. The noun (what is bought, sold, offered, etc.) usually follows the verb. The person(s) who buy(s), sell(s), offer(s), and so on, is not mentioned. This is normally expressed in English with the passive voice (is/are **+** *past participle*).

**Se habla** español en este restaurante.   *Spanish is spoken in this restaurant.*

■ Use a singular verb with singular nouns and a plural verb with plural nouns.

**Se necesita** un horno para hacer galletas.   *An oven is needed to make cookies.*

**Se venden** vegetales allí.   *Vegetables are sold there.*

■ Use a singular verb when the **se +** *verb* construction is followed not by a noun, but rather by an adverb, an infinitive, or a clause. This is expressed in English with indefinite subjects such as *they, you, one,* and *people.*

| | |
|---|---|
| **Se trabaja** mucho en ese manzanal. | *They work a lot in that apple orchard.* |
| **Se puede** encontrar muchos tipos de manzanas allí. | *You can find many different types of apples there.* |
| **Se dice** que venden sidra excelente también. | *People say they sell excellent cider too.* |

**10-15 Asociaciones. PRIMERA FASE.** Asocie las actividades con los lugares donde ocurren.

1. ____ Se cambian cheques en…       **a.** un almacén.
2. ____ Se vende ropa en…            **b.** un restaurante.
3. ____ Se toma el sol y se nada en… **c.** un banco.
4. ____ Se sirven comidas en…        **d.** una playa.

**SEGUNDA FASE.** Piense en un edificio o lugar público que le gusta mucho. Luego dígale a su compañero/a qué se hace allí.

**MODELO:** *Me gusta mucho la zona peatonal* (pedestrian area) *de mi ciudad. Allí se camina mucho y en el verano se escucha la música de conjuntos locales.*

**10-16 El supermercado y las tiendas de conveniencia.** Indique (✓) los productos y/o servicios que se encuentran en los supermercados solamente y los que se encuentran comúnmente en las tiendas de conveniencia también. Compare sus respuestas con las de su compañero/a.

| PRODUCTOS/SERVICIOS | SUPERMERCADO SOLAMENTE | SUPERMERCADO Y TIENDA DE CONVENIENCIA |
|---|---|---|
| productos lácteos | | |
| carnes orgánicas | | |
| frutas de América del Sur | | |
| detergente para lavadoras | | |
| alimentos enlatados (*canned*) | | |
| pescado fresco | | |
| DVDs para alquilar | | |

### En otras palabras

The concept of *convenience stores* is expressed differently according to the country. In Mexico they are **tiendas de conveniencia,** translated directly from English. In Costa Rica the term **tiendas de gasolinera** is used because of where such stores are usually located. In Spain they are **tiendas de 24h** to convey the convenience of being always open.

**10-17 Recetas creativas. PRIMERA FASE.** Lean estas recetas originales. Luego, intercambien opiniones sobre cuáles les gustaría probar y cuáles no.

1. Plátano derretido (*melted*): Se corta un plátano en rebanadas (*slices*) no muy finas. Se echa azúcar. Se calienta en el microondas por uno o dos minutos.
2. Batido de tarta de manzana (*apple pie smoothie*): Se ponen en la licuadora (*blender*): media taza de jugo de manzana, tres cucharadas de helado de vainilla y media cucharadita de canela (*cinnamon*). Se bate por un minuto.
3. Hamburguesa y salsa con queso (*nacho cheese sauce*): Se calienta la parrilla. Se pone la hamburguesa en la parrilla. Se pone la salsa con queso en el panecillo y se calienta. Se pone la hamburguesa en el panecillo.
4. Ensalada de pollo: Se abre una bolsa de lechuga prelavada. Se cortan en rebanadas dos pechugas de pollo (*chicken breasts*) cocidas, y se corta media libra de queso en cubos pequeños. Se combinan los ingredientes en una fuente (*bowl*). Se agrega un aliño de vinagre balsámico.

**SEGUNDA FASE.** Preparen juntos una receta para compartir con la clase.

**10-18 ¿Cómo se prepara este plato?** PRIMERA FASE. Usted y su compañero/a quieren darle una sorpresa a otra persona. Por eso, deciden prepararle su plato favorito. Primero, seleccionen uno de estos platos:

Luego, escriban en la caja una lista de los ingredientes que se necesitan para hacer el plato.

| CARNES | VERDURAS/VEGETALES | ESPECIAS | OTROS |
|--------|--------------------|----------|-------|
|        |                    |          |       |
|        |                    |          |       |
|        |                    |          |       |

**SEGUNDA FASE.** Usted sabe cocinar, pero su amigo/a no. Responda a sus preguntas mientras ustedes preparan el plato. Los siguientes verbos pueden ser útiles.

asar         dorar (*brown*)      rallar (*grate*)

cocinar      hervir               (so)freír

cortar       hornear              tostar

MODELO:  E1:  *Vamos a preparar pollo asado. ¿Qué se hace con el pollo?*

E2:  *Primero se lava bien el pollo. Luego se ponen sal y pimienta.*

E1:  *¿Y después?*

E2:  *Se asa en el horno por dos horas y se dora.*

## SITUACIONES

1. Role A. You are an international student who has just arrived in town. A student has offered to help with your orientation. You are not familiar with shopping in the United States, so you ask a) where one buys personal items like vitamins and toothpaste (**pasta de dientes**); b) where on campus one can find a decent meal; c) where one goes to buy fresh fruit; and d) where one can get good American pizza. Ask follow-up questions to be sure you understand the answers.

   Role B. You have offered to show a new international student around campus. Answer his/her questions about where one goes to buy different things. Offer several options, and be prepared to answer your new friend's questions.

2. Role A. You have just moved into your own apartment, and you are living away from home for the first time. You have never done your own food shopping and are not sure how to go about it. Ask a friend for help and ask questions so he/she will expand on the explanation.

   Role B. A friend has just told you that he/she does not know how to go food shopping. Explain the process step by step, starting with the shopping list (**se hace una lista...**). Provide additional explanation or clarification in response to your friend's questions.

## 2. Talking about the recent past: Present perfect and participles used as adjectives

ALICIA: Hola, César, ¿qué tal?

CÉSAR: Hola, Alicia. **¿Has visto** a Javier? ¡Estoy muy molesto!

ALICIA: ¿Por qué? ¿Qué te pasa?

CÉSAR: Como sabes, el examen de historia es pasado mañana y yo no **he leído** el libro todavía. ¿Lo **has leído** tú? ¿Lo **ha leído** Javier? ¿Javier te **ha dado** sus notas? No sé qué voy a hacer sin sus notas. ¡Las necesito para estudiar!

ALICIA: Cálmate, César. Yo **he leído** el libro y **he escrito** unas notas. **He hablado** con Javi. No **ha terminado** el libro todavía, pero va a llamarte esta tarde.

**Piénselo.** Lea las afirmaciones e indique a quién(es) se aplica cada una: a Alicia (**A**), a César (**C**) y/o a Javier (**J**).

1. \_\_\_\_ **Ha hablado** con Javier.
2. \_\_\_\_ **Ha escrito** unas notas.
3. \_\_\_\_ **Ha leído** una parte del libro.
4. \_\_\_\_ No **ha hecho** mucho en su curso de historia.
5. \_\_\_\_ No **han visto** a Javier.
6. \_\_\_\_ No **ha abierto** el libro.

■ Both Spanish and English have perfect tenses that are used to refer to past actions, events, and conditions. Both languages use an auxiliary verb (**haber** in Spanish, *to have* in English) followed by a past participle.

■ Use the present perfect to refer to a past event, action, or condition that has some relation to the present.

| | |
|---|---|
| Lucho, ¿ya **has leído** la receta de paella? | *Lucho, have you read the recipe for paella yet?* |
| No, no **he leído** la receta todavía. | *No, I have not read the recipe yet.* |

| PRESENT TENSE OF HABER | + | PAST PARTICIPLE |
|---|---|---|
| yo | he | |
| tú | has | |
| Ud., él, ella | ha | hablado |
| nosotros/as | hemos | comido |
| vosotros/as | habéis | vivido |
| Uds., ellos/as | han | |

■ Form the present perfect by using the present tense of **haber** as an auxiliary verb with the past participle of the main verb. **Tener** is never used as the auxiliary verb to form the perfect tense.

| | |
|---|---|
| Los cocineros **han trabajado** mucho en el banquete. | *The cooks have worked a lot on the banquet.* |
| Unos miembros de la organización ya **han traído** los manteles. | *Some members of the organization have already brought the tablecloths.* |

■ All past participles of **-ar** verbs end in **-ado**, whereas past participles of **-er** and **-ir** verbs generally end in **-ido**. If the stem of an **-er** verb ends in a vowel, use a written accent on the **i** of **-ido** (leer → leído). In English, past participles are often formed with the endings *-ed* and *-en*, as in *finished* and *eaten*.

■ Some **-er** and **-ir** verbs have irregular past participles. Here are some of the more common ones:

| IRREGULAR PAST PARTICIPLES | | | |
|---|---|---|---|
| hacer | **hecho** | abrir | **abierto** |
| poner | **puesto** | escribir | **escrito** |
| romper | **roto** | cubrir | **cubierto** |
| ver | **visto** | decir | **dicho** |
| volver | **vuelto** | morir | **muerto** |

■ Place object and reflexive pronouns before the auxiliary **haber**. Do not place any word between **haber** and the past participle.

| | |
|---|---|
| ¿**Le** has dado las servilletas a César? | *Have you given César the napkins?* |
| No, todavía no **se las** he dado. | *No, I have not given them to him yet.* |

■ The present perfect of **hay** is **ha habido** with both singular and plural nouns.

| | |
|---|---|
| **Ha habido** más trabajo últimamente. | *There has been more work lately.* |
| **Ha habido** varios banquetes y otros eventos. | *There have been several banquets and other events.* |

■ **OJO:** To state that something has just happened use the present tense of **acabar + de +** *infinitive*, not the present perfect.

| | |
|---|---|
| **Acabamos de volver** del supermercado. | *We have just returned from the supermarket.* |
| **Acabo de probar** la sopa y está deliciosa. | *I have just tasted the soup, and it is delicious.* |

■ Spanish uses **estar +** *past participle* to express a state or condition resulting from a prior action.

| ACTION | RESULT |
|---|---|
| Ella preparó la sopa. | La sopa **está preparada**. |
| Luego cerró las ventanas. | Las ventanas **están cerradas**. |

■ When a past participle is used as an adjective, it agrees with the noun it modifies.

| una puerta **cerrada** | *a closed door* |
| los restaurantes **abiertos** | *the open restaurants* |
| unas botellas **lavadas** | *some washed bottles* |

**10-19 Lo que no he hecho.** Usted y su compañero/a deben decir las cosas de cada lista que no han hecho. Después, comparen sus respuestas con las de otros estudiantes.

1. Yo nunca he estado en…
   **a.** Paraguay.      **b.** Guatemala.      **c.** Ecuador.
2. Yo nunca he visto…
   **a.** las Islas Galápagos.      **b.** un volcán activo.      **c.** un huracán.
3. Yo nunca he comido…
   **a.** aguacate.      **b.** un postre con leche de coco.      **c.** langosta.
4. Yo nunca he escrito…
   **a.** una receta.
   **b.** una lista de compras (*shopping list*) en español.
   **c.** el menú para una cena formal.
5. Yo nunca he roto…
   **a.** una taza.      **b.** un vaso.      **c.** un plato.
6. Yo nunca he dicho…
   **a.** "no" a una invitación a cenar.
   **b.** una broma (*joke*) de mal gusto durante una comida formal.
   **c.** una palabra en español en un resturante hispano en este país.

**10-20 Hispanos famosos/Hispanas famosas. PRIMERA FASE.** Piensen en un hispano famoso/una hispana famosa y preparen una lista de cinco cosas que ustedes creen que ha hecho para tener éxito (*to be successful*). Después compartan su lista con la de otra pareja y háganse preguntas.

**MODELO:** *Cameron Díaz es una actriz famosa.*
*Ha actuado en más de treinta películas.*

| HISPANO FAMOSO/HISPANA FAMOSA | LO QUE HA HECHO PARA TENER ÉXITO |
|---|---|
| _____ | _____ |
|  | _____ |
|  | _____ |
|  | _____ |

**SEGUNDA FASE.** Digan tres cosas que ustedes han hecho que los/las ha ayudado a tener éxito en su vida personal, académica o profesional.

**10-21 Para hacer una cena importante.** Usted y su compañero/a van a preparar una cena para la visita de una persona importante a su universidad. Háganse preguntas para ver qué preparativos ha hecho cada uno/a para la cena.

**MODELO:**      comprar la carne
      E1: *¿Has comprado la carne?*
      E2: *No, no la he comprado todavía.*

1. determinar el número de invitados
2. leer las recetas
3. cortar los vegetales
4. hacer el postre
5. decidir qué música se va a tocar
6. poner la mesa
7. asignar los asientos
8. decorar el lugar de la cena

**10-22 Justo ahora.** Con su compañero/a, digan qué acaban de hacer estas personas. Den la mayor información posible.

**MODELO:**      Juan y Ramiro salen del estadio.
      E1: *Acaban de ver un partido de béisbol muy importante.*
      E2: *Fueron a ver a los Calcetines Rojos porque es su equipo favorito.*

1. Maricarmen y sus amigos ya no tienen hambre.
2. Pedro y Alina salen de una tienda donde se alquilan películas.
3. Mercedes y Paula traen palomitas de maíz (*popcorn*) para todo el grupo.
4. Un hombre sale corriendo de un banco.
5. Jorge y Rubén salen de un supermercado.
6. Frente a todos sus amigos, Rubén le da una sorpresa a su novia.

**10-23 Robo (*Robbery*) en un restaurante.** El siguiente párrafo cuenta algo que ocurrió en el restaurante del chef Marco Tovares. Para saber lo que pasó, llene los espacios en blanco con la forma correcta del participio pasado de los verbos entre paréntesis.

El chef Marco Tovares salió de la cocina de su restaurante en Nueva York para asegurarse de que todo iba bien en el comedor esa noche. Vio que el locutor de televisión Jorge Ramos y otras tres personas estaban (1) _____ (sentar) en una mesa. De repente Marco vio que la bolsa de una de las mujeres estaba (2) _____ (abrir) y que un hombre en otra mesa la estaba mirando. Como la mujer estaba (3) _____ (distraer), el ladrón aprovechó el momento (4) _____ (esperar). Sacó la billetera de la bolsa de ella. La mujer no se dio cuenta, pero Marco lo vio todo. Se acercó a la mesa y le dijo al hombre: —¿Cómo está la comida esta noche? ¿Todo bien? El hombre parecía muy nervioso, y curiosamente tenía las manos (5) _____ (cerrar). Marco le dijo: —¿Podría acompañarme un momento, por favor? El hombre fue con Marco al fondo del restaurante, le dio la billetera (6) _____ (robar) y salió. Marco se acercó a la mesa de Jorge Ramos y les explicó lo ocurrido. Todos estaban muy (7) _____ (sorprender). La mujer víctima del robo dijo: —Hace diez años que vivo en Nueva York, y ¡nunca he (8) _____ (ser) víctima de un robo hasta esta noche! Muchísimas gracias por su ayuda.

**10-24 ¿Qué ha pasado? PRIMERA FASE.** Su compañero/a y usted han ordenado su apartamento esta mañana. Pero acaban de entrar por la tarde, y ven que todo está muy desordenado. Túrnense para describirle al/a la policía lo que han hecho para ordenar el apartamento y lo que ven ahora, usando las palabras entre paréntesis. Añadan más información donde sea posible.

MODELO:   las ventanas (cerrar, abrir)
POLICÍA:   *¿Qué ha pasado con las ventanas?*
E1:   *Las he cerrado esta mañana…*
E2:   *pero ahora están abiertas.*

1. el espejo del baño (usar, romper)
2. la cama (tender, desordenar)
3. el televisor (apagar, encender)
4. las camisas (colgar, tirar al piso)
5. la puerta del apartamento (cerrar, abrir)
6. la comida en el refrigerador (cubrir, descubrir [*to uncover*])

**SEGUNDA FASE.** Después de escuchar el relato de ustedes, el/la policía hace lo siguiente:

1. Les hace preguntas para conseguir más información.
2. Les dice tres cosas que hay que hacer ahora.

## SITUACIONES

1. **Role A.** You are a reporter who has been assigned to interview the new chef of a restaurant in your community. Ask about a) other restaurants where he/she has worked; b) prizes (*premios*) he/she has won; c) some examples of dishes he/she has developed; and d) changes he/she has already made in the restaurant.

   **Role B.** You are the new chef of one of the nicest restaurants in town, and a reporter is interviewing you for the local newspaper. Answer the reporter's questions, adding as many details possible.

2. **Role A.** You are in charge of discipline at a strict boarding school. Call one of the students to your office to ask about his/her activities. Explain that the teachers have just told you that a) he/she has not attended classes for four days; b) he/she has not done homework for two weeks; and c) he/she has not eaten in the cafeteria all week. Say that the teachers are worried. You want to track his/her every movement to determine the problem. Start with **¿A qué hora te has levantado hoy?** and continue from there.

   **Role B.** You are a student at a strict boarding school. You have been acting strangely, and you don't want to explain why. The teacher in charge of discipline has asked to speak to you. Answer the teacher's questions with enough detail to fool him/her into thinking you are telling the truth.

## 3. Giving instructions in informal settings: Informal commands

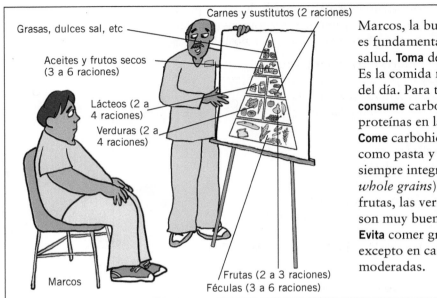

Grasas, dulces sal, etc

Aceites y frutos secos
(3 a 6 raciones)

Lácteos (2 a
4 raciones)

Verduras (2 a
4 raciones)

Carnes y sustitutos (2 raciones)

Frutas (2 a 3 raciones)

Féculas (3 a 6 raciones)

Marcos

Marcos, la buena alimentación es fundamental para la buena salud. **Toma** desayuno siempre. Es la comida más importante del día. Para tener energía, **consume** carbohidratos y proteínas en las tres comidas. **Come** carbohidratos complejos, como pasta y pan, pero siempre integrales (*made from whole grains*). **No olvides** las frutas, las verduras y la leche, son muy buenas para la salud. **Evita** comer grasas y azúcares, excepto en cantidades moderadas.

**Piénselo.** Según las sugerencias del enfermero, escoja los alimentos o bebidas que Marcos debe consumir o evitar para alimentarse bien.

1. _____ Come…
2. _____ Evita…
3. _____ Bebe…

a. helado todos los días.
b. pan blanco.
c. manzanas, peras, plátanos, uvas.

d. suficiente leche.
e. pollo y pescado.
f. refrescos.

■ To ask a friend to do or not to do something, use an informal command. Use that form with anyone else you address as **tú**, such as someone your own age or someone with whom you have a close relationship.

■ To form the affirmative **tú** command, use the present indicative **tú** form without the final **-s**.

| | PRESENT INDICATIVE | AFFIRMATIVE *TÚ* COMMAND |
|---|---|---|
| cocinar | cocinas | **cocina** |
| beber | bebes | **bebe** |
| consumir | consumes | **consume** |

■ For the negative **tú** command, use the negative **usted** command form and add the final **-s**.

| | NEGATIVE *USTED* COMMAND | NEGATIVE *TÚ* COMMAND |
|---|---|---|
| preparar | no prepar**e** | no prepar**es** |
| comer | no com**a** | no com**as** |
| subir | no sub**a** | no sub**as** |

■ Placement of object and reflexive pronouns with **tú** commands is the same as with **usted** commands.

| AFFIRMATIVE COMMAND | NEGATIVE COMMAND |
|---|---|
| Prepárelo (usted). | No **lo** prepare (usted). |
| Bébela (tú). | No **la** bebas (tú). |

■ The plural of **tú** commands in Spanish-speaking America is the **ustedes** command.

| | |
|---|---|
| **Cocina (tú).** | **Cocinen (ustedes).** |
| **Bebe (tú).** | **Beban (ustedes).** |
| **Sube (tú).** | **Suban (ustedes).** |

■ Some **-er** and **-ir** verbs have shortened affirmative **tú** commands, but their negative command is regular.

| | AFFIRMATIVE | NEGATIVE |
|---|---|---|
| poner | **pon** | **no pongas** |
| salir | **sal** | **no salgas** |
| tener | **ten** | **no tengas** |
| venir | **ven** | **no vengas** |
| hacer | **haz** | **no hagas** |
| decir | **di** | **no digas** |
| ir | **ve** | **no vayas** |
| ser | **sé** | **no seas** |

| | |
|---|---|
| **Sal** a las tres si quieres llegar a las cuatro. | *Leave at 3:00 if you want to arrive at 4:00.* |
| **No salgas** sin paraguas; va a llover. | *Don't leave without an umbrella; it is going to rain.* |
| **Sé** generoso con tus amigos. | *Be generous with your friends.* |
| No **seas** impaciente. | *Don't be impatient.* |
| **Dime** la verdad. | *Tell me the truth.* |
| **No nos digas** mentiras. | *Don't tell us any lies.* |

**10-25 Consejos.** Escoja los consejos más adecuados, según cada situación.

1. Su compañero/a comió demasiado en una fiesta de cumpleaños y ahora le duele mucho el estómago.
   a. Come más para recuperarte.
   b. Llama al médico.
   c. Ve a la farmacia y compra medicamentos.
   d. Camina una hora esta tarde.
   e. Practica deportes para olvidarte del dolor de estómago.
   f. No te acuestes.

2. Su hermana está enferma. Está congestionada y tiene fiebre.
   a. Toma sopa de pollo.
   b. Come una hamburguesa.
   c. No duermas mucho.
   d. Bebe jugos y agua.
   e. No bebas vino ni cerveza.
   f. No consumas mucha cafeína.

3. A su hijo le fascina la comida chatarra (*junk food*), por eso, subió diez libras en un mes.
   a. Ve a los restaurantes de comida rápida.
   b. Bebe muchas gaseosas.
   c. Come en casa, no en restaurantes.
   d. No tomes alcohol.
   e. Evita los batidos de McDonald's.
   f. No pidas ensaladas.

4. Su mamá quiere alimentarse mejor para tener más energía y bajar de peso.
   a. Evita la grasa.
   b. Toma muchos helados.
   c. Come huevos moderadamente.
   d. Compra papas fritas.
   e. Acuéstate y descansa.
   f. Si no tienes energía, consume mucha cafeína.

5. Su mejor amigo quiere preparar una cena espectacular para su novia.
   a. Compra pizza.
   b. Haz un plato sofisticado.
   c. No olvides de comprar un buen vino.
   d. Prepara la mesa el día anterior.
   e. No le pongas chile picante al plato. Ella detesta la comida picante.
   f. Ponle mucha sal a la comida.

**10-26 Una cura de reposo.** Su amigo/a estuvo muy enfermo/a y su médico le recomendó pasar dos semanas de descanso en las Termas de Papallacta o en la reserva natural Playa de Oro en Ecuador. Como usted ha visitado los dos lugares, dígale a su amigo/a qué debe hacer allí. Después cambien de papel.

MODELO: visitar la reserva/no pensar en los negocios
*Visita la reserva Playa de Oro./No pienses en los negocios.*

1. disfrutar del sol
2. respirar aire puro y descansar
3. no hacer tarea
4. tomar fotos y hacer videos
5. probar un plato típico ecuatoriano
6. salir por las noches y conversar con las personas del lugar
7. tomar baños termales a diario
8. asistir a un concierto de música andina

**10-27 Buenos hábitos alimenticios.** PRIMERA FASE. Ustedes están preocupados por los hábitos de comida de uno/a de sus amigos/as. Lean lo que esta persona come y bebe en un día típico e identifiquen los problemas que tiene.

Se levanta al mediodía todos los días. Tan pronto se levanta, toma varias tazas de café. Una hora más tarde, come tres huevos fritos con tocino y tostadas. Toma dos tazas de café cubano con bastante azúcar. Luego lee el periódico en su dormitorio, mira televisión y come chocolate mientras habla por teléfono con sus amigos. Por la tarde, llama por teléfono al restaurante de la esquina y pide una hamburguesa con papas fritas y toma unas cervezas. Después, duerme una siesta larga. Por la noche, tiene problemas para dormir, por eso, toma un batido.

SEGUNDA FASE. Hagan una lista con cinco recomendaciones o instrucciones que su amigo/a debe seguir. Comparen su lista con las de otros grupos.

**10-28 Cocina paso a paso (*step by step*).** PRIMERA FASE. Busquen una receta para el sancocho, una sopa que se come en Ecuador. Escriban la lista de los ingredientes y estén listos/as para describirlos.

SEGUNDA FASE. En el papel de dos chefs de televisión, presenten la preparación del sancocho. Sigan los siguientes pasos: a) describan el plato; b) presenten sus ingredientes; y c) expliquen cómo se prepara el plato.

## SITUACIONES

1. **Role A.** You are not feeling well, so you call your friend to ask for the recipe to make chicken soup. Take notes as your friend gives you the recipe. Ask questions as necessary.

   **Role B.** Your friend is not feeling well and calls to ask for the recipe for chicken soup. Tell him/her to a) buy skinless chicken (**pollo sin piel**); b) wash and cut garlic, onions, carrots, and celery (**apio**); c) sauté (**saltear**) the chicken and vegetables with a little olive oil; and d) add water, salt, and pepper and cook for 30 minutes.

2. **Role A.** To improve your health, you visit a nutritionist. Explain what you generally eat for breakfast, lunch, and dinner. Ask questions and answer the nutritionist's questions.

   **Role B.** A client comes to you for help with eating habits. Ask what he/she eats for breakfast, lunch, and dinner. Advise your client a) to eat fruits, vegetables, fish, and chicken; b) not to drink soft drinks or alcohol; c) to consume foods with lots of fiber; and d) to do physical activity daily. Answer your client's questions.

## 4. Talking about the future: The future tense

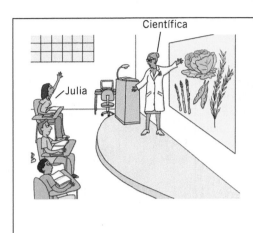

CIENTÍFICA: Según los expertos, para el año 2030 la población geriátrica **se duplicará** en comparación con la del presente. La gente **comerá** mejor y **vivirá** más años porque **tendrá** buena salud.

JULIA: ¿Y nuestra dieta **será** semejante a la de hoy? ¿Qué **comeremos**?

CIENTÍFICA: Se piensa que **consumiremos** más alimentos naturales, porque más gente **comprenderá** sus beneficios. Al mismo tiempo, muchos alimentos **serán** modificados genéticamente. Los individuos **tratarán** de protegerse de ciertas condiciones y enfermedades, como la diabetes y el cáncer.

**Piénselo.** Indique si las siguientes afirmaciones son ciertas (**C**) o falsas (**F**), según la científica. Si la respuesta es falsa (**F**), corrija la información.

1. \_\_\_\_ **Habrá** menos personas mayores en el futuro.
2. \_\_\_\_ Las personas **tendrán** una vida más larga.
3. \_\_\_\_ Más personas **comprenderán** el beneficio de los alimentos naturales.
4. \_\_\_\_ La gente **podrá** comer grasas y dulces porque la ciencia los protegerá contra las enfermedades.

■ You have been using the present tense and **ir a** + *infinitive* to express future plans. Spanish also has a future tense. Although you have these other ways to express a future action, event, or state, it is important to be able to recognize the future tense in reading and in listening.

■ The future tense is formed by adding the endings **-é, -ás, -á, -emos, -éis**, and **-án** to the infinitive. All verbs, **-ar, -er, -ir**, regular or irregular, use these endings.

| FUTURE TENSE | | | |
|---|---|---|---|
| | **HABLAR** | **COMER** | **VIVIR** |
| yo | hablar**é** | comer**é** | vivir**é** |
| tú | hablar**ás** | comer**ás** | vivir**ás** |
| Ud., él, ella | hablar**á** | comer**á** | vivir**á** |
| nosotros/as | hablar**emos** | comer**emos** | vivir**emos** |
| vosotros/as | hablar**éis** | comer**éis** | vivir**éis** |
| Uds., ellos/as | hablar**án** | comer**án** | vivir**án** |

| Rafael **visitará** Ecuador el mes próximo. | *Rafael will visit Ecuador next month.* |
|---|---|
| Él y sus colegas **volverán** después de dos semanas. | *He and his colleagues will return after two weeks.* |
| **Se reunirán** con los dueños de unas haciendas de café. | *They will meet with the owners of some coffee plantations.* |

■ Some verbs have irregular stems in the future tense and can be grouped into three categories according to the irregularity. The first group drops the **-e** from the infinitive ending.

| IRREGULAR FUTURE—GROUP 1 | | |
|---|---|---|
| **INFINITIVE** | **NEW STEM** | **FUTURE FORMS** |
| poder | **podr-** | podré, podrás, podrá, podremos, podréis, podrán |
| querer | **querr-** | querré, querrás, querrá, querremos, querréis, querrán |
| saber | **sabr-** | sabré, sabrás, sabrá, sabremos, sabréis, sabrán |

■ The second group replaces the **e** or **i** of the infinitive ending with a **-d**.

| IRREGULAR FUTURE—GROUP 2 | | |
|---|---|---|
| poner | **pondr-** | pondré, pondrás, pondrá, pondremos, pondréis, pondrán |
| salir | **saldr-** | saldré, saldrás, saldrá, saldremos, saldréis, saldrán |
| tener | **tendr-** | tendré, tendrás, tendrá, tendremos, tendréis, tendrán |
| venir | **vendr-** | vendré, vendrás, vendrá, vendremos, vendréis, vendrán |

■ The third group consists of two verbs that have completely different stems in the future tense.

| IRREGULAR FUTURE—GROUP 3 | | |
|---|---|---|
| decir | **dir-** | diré, dirás, dirá, diremos, diréis, dirán |
| hacer | **har-** | haré, harás, hará, haremos, haréis, harán |

| Los estudiantes **sabrán** más sobre la nutrición después de tomar el curso. | *The students will know more about nutrition after taking the course.* |
|---|---|
| **Tendrán** que leer mucho. | *They will have to read a lot.* |
| También **harán** un proyecto de investigación. | *They will also do a research project.* |
| ¿A qué hora vendrán a cenar? | *What time will they be coming for dinner?* |
| Querrán probar un poco de todo. | *They will want to try a little of everything.* |

*Cultura*

Ecuador tiene muchos parques nacionales y reservas ecológicas cuyo propósito es conservar la riqueza natural de las cuatro regiones del país: las Islas Galápagos, la costa, la sierra y la selva amazónica. En las reservas se encuentran muchas especies de flora y fauna. Para los visitantes, hay muchas maneras de explorar las reservas y gozar de la naturaleza.

**10-29 ¿Qué lugares de Ecuador visitarán estas personas?** Complete las oraciones de la izquierda con la forma correcta del verbo en la columna de la derecha.

1. A Carlos y Eugenia les gusta comer bien. Ellos ____ al restaurante especializado en la cocina de Guayaquil.
2. A doña Lourdes y a su hija les fascinan la zoología y la botánica. Ellas ____ un viaje a las Islas Galápagos para ver la gran variedad de especies animales.
3. Don Jorge y yo ____ el mercado indígena de Cuenca para comprar artesanía ecuatoriana.
4. A ti te gusta disfrutar del aire libre, ver la arquitectura colonial y las montañas. Tú ____ por la Plaza San Blas en Quito.
5. A mí me interesa la protección de los animales y la flora. Yo ____ a la Reserva Cuyabeno que está a 500 kilómetros de Quito.

a. viajaré
b. caminarás
c. irán
d. visitaremos
e. harán

**10-30 Intercambio: Un viaje a Guayaquil.** PRIMERA FASE. Ramiro va a Guayaquil a visitar a su familia. Háganse preguntas y contesten de acuerdo con la agenda que Ramiro preparó.

MODELO:  E1:  *¿Qué hará Ramiro el miércoles por la noche?*
         E2:  *Cenará con unos amigos.*
         E1:  *¿Cuándo irá al cine con los primos?*
         E2:  *Irán al cine el martes.*

| LUNES | MARTES | MIÉRCOLES | JUEVES | VIERNES |
|---|---|---|---|---|
| salir para Guayaquil | visitar el Parque de las Iguanas | salir de compras al Mercado Artesanal | viajar al Parque Nacional El Cajas | empacar las maletas |
| cenar con los tíos | conocer a otros familiares | ir a un museo | caminar en la reserva, sacar fotos | almorzar con toda la familia |
| acostarse temprano | ir al cine con los primos | cenar con unos amigos | dormir en el parque | regresar a Estados Unidos |

SEGUNDA FASE. Hagan una lista de cinco actividades que Ramiro probablemente hará al regresar a Estados Unidos. Expliquen por qué.

**10-31 Planes para una fiesta para celebrar un matrimonio.** PRIMERA FASE. Sus amigos José y Silvia se casaron durante sus vacaciones en Ecuador. Regresarán a Estados Unidos en dos semanas y ustedes van a organizar una fiesta para celebrar su matrimonio. Planifiquen la fiesta considerando lo siguiente: número de invitados, lugar de la fiesta, menú que ofrecerán (comida y bebida), música, baile y otras actividades en la fiesta.

SEGUNDA FASE. Compartan sus planes con otra pareja. Hagan una lista de tres semejanzas y tres diferencias entre las fiestas que las dos parejas organizarán.

**10-32 ¿Qué recomendaciones seguirá?** Maricela sufre de estrés, insomnio y anemia. Por eso les pide sugerencias a su mejor amiga y a su nutricionista. A continuación aparecen sus recomendaciones. Discutan qué recomendaciones probablemente seguirá Maricela y expliquen por qué.

| RECOMENDACIONES DE LA NUTRICIONISTA | RECOMENDACIONES DE SU MEJOR AMIGA |
|---|---|
| 1. Coma en pequeñas cantidades por lo menos cuatro veces al día. | 1. Come cuando quieras. Si subes de peso puedes seguir una dieta. |
| 2. No consuma cafeína para tener energía. Consuma proteínas para obtener energía. | 2. Para tener energía, come mucho chocolate y, luego, haz ejercicio. |
| 3. Consuma calcio. Beba leche y coma frutas. | 3. Toma helado todos los días porque la leche tiene mucho calcio. |
| 4. Para eliminar la tensión y relajarse, haga yoga. | 4. Escucha música suave y no contestes el teléfono de la oficina. |
| 5. Compre verduras y carnes orgánicas en supermercados especializados en productos naturales. | 5. Pide ensalada con pollo en los restaurantes de comida rápida y un refresco de dieta. |

## SITUACIONES

1. **Role A.** You are organizing a picnic and some of the guests are vegetarians. Call your nutritionist friend (your classmate) to discuss what food to serve. Say that a) you will prepare vegetarian and non-vegetarian food; b) for the vegetarians, you will make salads and a Spanish tortilla; c) for the meat eaters, you will serve a chicken salad and want to have hamburgers; and d) you will serve beer, soft drinks, and juice. Ask your friend for advice.

   **Role B.** A friend is calling to ask for advice regarding the menu for a picnic that will include both vegetarian and non-vegetarian guests. Give your friend feedback on the proposed menu and offer additional advice.

2. **Role A.** You and a friend are concerned about people's quality of life and the food they eat. Tell your friend that you think in ten years from now people will eat a) more healthful foods; b) fewer fats and sugars; and c) less junk food (**comida chatarra**). Add that you think food will be more expensive but of better quality and that people will live longer because they will be healthier.

   **Role B.** You don't agree with your friend's opinions about what people will eat ten years from now. In your view, a) people will continue to eat unhealthful food; b) people will continue to eat fats and sugar; c) children will have more opportunities to eat junk food (**comida chatarra**) because parents will be very busy; d) food will cost less, so people will eat more; and e) people will die younger but happier.

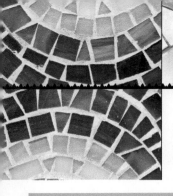

# MOSAICOS

## A escuchar

Note-taking is a useful strategy for recording what you hear. To take useful notes, you need to sort out and prioritize the information as you listen, writing down what is relevant to your purpose. For example, you may want to write down the directions for making a new dish that you hear on a cooking show. As you listen, you need to jot down important details to prepare the dish yourself. The details the chef chats about may be fun to listen to but may not be essential to the recipe.

### Lengua

**Pimienta** refers to the spice (*ground pepper*) and **pimiento** refers to the vegetable. Therefore, **pimienta roja** is the red (*cayenne*) pepper that one sprinkles on pizza, and **pimiento rojo** is a red bell pepper. Chili pepper has its own word—**un chile** or **ají**, as in **chile habanero**, **chile jalapeño**, and so forth.

### Antes de escuchar

**10-33 Preparación.** Usted escuchará una lista de productos que compraron Andrea, Carolina, Roberto y Darío. Antes de escuchar, prepare una lista de productos que usted compra regularmente y otra de aquellos que usted compra en ocasiones especiales.

### Escuchar

CD 4
Track 33
or CD 5
Track 9

**10-34 ¿Comprende usted?** Andrea, Carolina, Roberto, and Darío have each offered to contribute a dish for their friend Óscar's birthday party. Each has bought some kind of vegetable and meat or seafood to prepare his/her dish. As you listen, mark (✓) the foods that each of them bought.

| ANDREA | CAROLINA | ROBERTO | DARÍO |
|---|---|---|---|
| ___ sal | ___ ajos | ___ mermelada | ___ huevos |
| ___ pollo | ___ cerdo | ___ pepinos | ___ ajos |
| ___ carne molida | ___ espinacas | ___ pimienta | ___ fruta |
| ___ azúcar | ___ jamón | ___ aceite | ___ jamón |
| ___ zanahorias | ___ langosta | ___ pavo | ___ aderezo |
| ___ aguacates | ___ maíz | ___ aguacates | ___ pimientos verdes |
| ___ camarones | ___ pollo | ___ zanahorias | ___ pasta |

### Después de escuchar

**10-35 Ahora usted.** Compartan las respuestas a las siguientes preguntas.

1. ¿Cuál es su plato favorito?
2. ¿Qué productos o ingredientes compra usted para prepararlo?
3. ¿Con quién comparte generalmente su plato favorito? ¿Por qué?
4. ¿Qué dice esta persona cuando usted prepara este plato?

# A conversar

## Antes de conversar

**10-36 Preparación.** PRIMERA FASE. Marque cuáles de los siguientes alimentos son más saludables (**+**) o menos saludables (**–**).

____ los camarones     ____ las espinacas     ____ el jamón     ____ el pollo

____ la carne de res     ____ la fruta     ____ las legumbres     ____ el queso

____ la cerveza     ____ las galletas     ____ el pan blanco     ____ los refrescos

____ los dulces     ____ el helado     ____ las papas     ____ el vino

**SEGUNDA FASE.** Escriban en la tabla los productos o alimentos de la *Primera fase* que en general producen los siguientes efectos. Prepárense para explicar por qué. **OJO:** Algunos se pueden poner en más de una categoría.

| ENGORDAN | ADELGAZAN (*ARE SLIMMING*) | DAN ENERGÍA | AUMENTAN EL COLESTEROL |
|---|---|---|---|
|  |  |  |  |
|  |  |  |  |

## Conversar

**10-37 Entre nosotros.** Averigüen las preferencias de comida de los miembros del grupo en las siguientes categorías. Después, sumen los números en las columnas para saber qué comida les gusta más y cuál les gusta menos.

**MODELO:**     los mariscos
      E1:   *¿Te gustan los mariscos?*
      E2:   *Me encantan. ¿Y a ti?*
      E1:   *A mí no me gustan.*

| ALIMENTO | ENCANTAR | GUSTAR MUCHO | GUSTAR | NO GUSTAR |
|---|---|---|---|---|
| la fruta |  |  |  |  |
| las verduras |  |  |  |  |
| la carne |  |  |  |  |
| los mariscos |  |  |  |  |
| los productos lácteos |  |  |  |  |
| los dulces |  |  |  |  |

## Después de conversar

**10-38 Un poco más.** Comparen los resultados de **10-37** para determinar las categorías de alimentos que se consumen más en la clase. Luego, respondan a estas preguntas.

1. ¿Qué tipos de comida se comen más en la clase?
2. En general, ¿ustedes se alimentan bien o mal? ¿Por qué?
3. ¿Deben ustedes mejorar su dieta? ¿Qué deben hacer?

# A leer

**Learn new words by analyzing their connections with known words**

All readers of a second language encounter words that are unfamiliar to them. In some cases it is possible to skip over the word and still understand the overall meaning of the sentence or paragraph. In other cases, it is better to focus on the unfamiliar word and guess its meaning. You may find you can guess the meaning of the unfamiliar word by mentally linking it to words you know that are related to it in meaning or in grammatical form. Figuring out word meanings in this way can help you expand your vocabulary.

## Antes de leer

**10-39 Preparación.** Lea el título y los subtítulos de la lectura en la p. 355, mire las fotos y lea sus leyendas. Luego, conteste las preguntas, usando esos elementos y también su conocimiento general.

1. ¿Qué información espera encontrar en el artículo?
   a. una definición del término *fusión culinaria*
      Sí   No
   b. una dieta para bajar de peso
      Sí   No
   c. recetas para platos de cocina fusión
      Sí   No
   d. información sobre la influencia china en la cocina de un país
      Sí   No
   e. información sobre la cocina Tex-Mex
      Sí   No

2. Marque (✔) los elementos que lo/la ayudaron a responder a la pregunta 1.
   a. ＿＿ el título y los subtítulos
   b. ＿＿ las fotos junto con sus leyendas
   c. ＿＿ mi conocimiento de cocina

3. ¿Qué es la fusión culinaria? Marque (✔) la definición más lógica, según su conocimiento general.
   a. ＿＿ La combinación de la cocina con otras artes, como la decoración de interiores
   b. ＿＿ Una cocina que combina la influencia de dos tradiciones culinarias
   c. ＿＿ Una manera tradicional de preparar la comida que la gente conserva por muchas generaciones

4. Prepare una lista de comidas Tex-Mex que usted conoce. ¿Cuáles le gustan más? Luego, indique si aparecieron en el artículo.

## Leer

### La fusión culinaria: una tendencia nueva con una historia larga

Tortilla española envuelta en una tortilla mexicana

#### La fusión en la cocina contemporánea

Todos hemos comido platos que combinan la cocina de dos países o culturas. El llamado *California roll*—el sushi japonés con un relleno[1] de cangrejo[2], queso crema y aguacate—es un ejemplo; la *taco pizza*, que se hace con la masa de una pizza cubierta de los ingredientes típicos del taco—carne molida, frijoles refritos, salsa, queso amarillo y especias picantes—es otro. La fusión culinaria, o cocina fusión, es un concepto que señala la mezcla de ingredientes y estilos culinarios de diferentes culturas en el menú de un restaurante o aun en un mismo plato. El término *cocina fusión* fue inventado en California en la década de los 1960s por unos chefs que combinaban los estilos de las cocinas de Asia (china, japonesa, tailandesa) con las legumbres frescas y naturales de California y las salsas hechas de frutas cítricas y tropicales. Hoy en día es común encontrar restaurantes en Estados Unidos con nombres como *Roy's Hawaiian Fusion Cuisine* o *Fusion Restaurant and Lounge*. Hay muchas posibles combinaciones, limitadas solamente por la creatividad del chef y los gustos de los clientes.

#### La fusión en la historia culinaria

A pesar de la creciente popularidad de estas combinaciones gastronómicas, sería un error pensar que la cocina fusión es un fenómeno nuevo. Siempre donde conviven grupos de personas de dos culturas nace una fusión de sus tradiciones culinarias. Dos ejemplos de este antiguo fenómeno en las Américas son la cocina chino-peruana y la cocina mexicano-norteamericana, o Tex-Mex.

#### El Chifa: La cocina fusión de Perú

La cocina peruana es una mezcla de muchas influencias: indígena, española, africana, china y japonesa. El Chifa, o cocina chino-peruana, es el resultado de la mezcla de la comida criolla de Lima con la cocina traída por los inmigrantes chinos desde mediados del siglo XIX. El término *el Chifa* se refiere tanto a la comida como a los restaurantes donde se sirve.

Los chinos que fueron a Perú se adaptaron a la sociedad y sus costumbres, pero siempre mantuvieron sus tradiciones culinarias. Con el progreso económico, luego pudieron importar de China unas especias y otros productos esenciales para su comida, pero por lo general tenían que cultivar las verduras que necesitaban o sustituirlas por ingredientes locales.

No es una exageración decir que la cultura chino-peruana de los inmigrantes chinos asimilados a la sociedad peruana revolucionó la gastronomía. Algunos platos considerados típicamente peruanos, como el arroz chaufa (preparado con carne picada, cebollitas, pimentón, huevos y salsa de soja) y el tacu-tacu (una tortilla hecha de un puré de frijoles, arroz, ajo, ají y cebolla) reflejan la influencia de la cocina china.

#### La comida Tex-Mex: La cocina mexicana en Estados Unidos

Un ejemplo de la cocina fusión que se conoce en todas partes de Estados Unidos es la cocina Tex-Mex. Se trata de una fusión de dos estilos, el de México y el de Texas. La cocina que conocemos hoy en día como Tex-Mex se originó en una mezcla de la comida del pueblo nativo de Texas y la cocina española. Los indígenas contribuyeron con ingredientes como los frijoles pintos, los nopales (las hojas de un cacto), las cebollas silvestres[3] y el mesquite. La influencia española empezó con la llegada del ganado[4] a la región, traído por los colonizadores al final del siglo XVI. También hay influencias del norte de África en la comida Tex-Mex. Un grupo de colonizadores de las Islas Canarias y de Marruecos inmigraron a lo que es ahora San Antonio, Texas en el siglo XVIII. De ellos vinieron combinaciones nuevas de especias (sobre todo el comino), cilantro y chiles en la comida Tex-Mex. El chili con carne de San Antonio todavía retiene los sabores de la cocina marroquí.

Nachos, un plato popular de la cocina Tex-Mex

En los últimos treinta años ha habido esfuerzos de separar lo que se considera *la cocina mexicana* de lo que conocemos como *la cocina mexicana americanizada*, o Tex-Mex. En comparación con la cocina mexicana, la Tex-Mex utiliza más carne y usa las tortillas para envolver una mayor variedad de rellenos. Los nachos, los tacos fritos, las chalupas, el chile con queso y el chile con carne son invenciones Tex-Mex que no se encuentran en la cocina mexicana tradicional. La costumbre universal en los restaurantes Tex-Mex de servir las *tortilla chips* con salsa picante como aperitivo tampoco existe en la cocina mexicana tradicional.

---

[1]*filling*   [2]*crab*   [3]*wild*   [4]*cattle*

**10-40 Primera mirada.** Según el contenido del artículo, ¿son las siguientes afirmaciones ciertas (**C**) o falsas (**F**)? Si la afirmación es falsa, corrija la información.

1. ___ El término *cocina fusión* fue inventado por unos chefs en Estados Unidos.
2. ___ El artículo afirma que la cocina fusión se limita a la combinación de influencias asiáticas en la cocina del Oeste.
3. ___ La cocina peruana incorpora influencias culinarias de muchos países.
4. ___ Llegaron inmigrantes chinos a Perú en el siglo XVIII.
5. ___ Los chinos en el Perú han mantenido su tradición culinaria sin cambios.
6. ___ El Chifa es un término que se refiere a la cocina chino-peruana.
7. ___ La cocina Tex-Mex es igual a la cocina mexicana.
8. ___ Se usa menos carne y menos queso en la cocina Tex-Mex que en la cocina mexicana tradicional.
9. ___ Los nachos y las fajitas son invenciones de la cocina Tex-Mex.
10. ___ El chile con carne que se come en San Antonio, Texas usa especias similares a las que se usan en Marruecos, en el norte de África.

**10-41 Segunda mirada.** Busque en el artículo palabras que se asocien con lo siguiente.

1. dos sinónimos de *fusión culinaria*: _____

2. carnes: _____

3. Asia: _____

4. platos de la cocina Chifa: _____

5. platos de la cocina Tex-Mex: _____

6. referencias a países: _____

## Después de leer

 **10-42 Ampliación.** PRIMERA FASE. Preparen una lista de platos que ustedes comen o que han visto en restaurantes que, en la opinión del grupo, son ejemplos de la cocina fusión. Luego, seleccionen uno de estos platos.

SEGUNDA FASE. Preparen una presentación sobre el plato y sus antecedentes culinarios y preséntenla a la clase. Recuerden de dirigirse a su público cuando hacen la presentación.

# A escribir

**Summarize information**

We often face the need to report or summarize what we have heard or read. A good summary maintains the structure of the original text and synthesizes its principal ideas and information. It concisely and accurately captures the central meaning of the original. Keep the following strategies in mind when you write a summary:

- Read the text carefully for the main ideas. Read it more than once.
- Write one or two sentences that summarize the main idea of each section you identify in the text.
- Try to use your own words.
- Do not inject your own opinion or add anything not in the original text.

**10-43 Preparación.** Lea una vez más el artículo "La fusión culinaria: una tendencia nueva con una historia larga" en la p. 355. Haga lo siguiente:

1. Identifique las secciones del artículo.
2. Pase su marcador (*highlighter*) por las ideas centrales de cada sección.

## Escribir

**10-44 Manos a la obra.** Escriba en sus propias palabras un resumen del artículo, usando las ideas principales que marcó en *Preparación*.

## Después de escribir

**10-45 Revisión.** Antes de compartir el resumen con un compañero editor/una compañera editora, léalo y verifique lo siguiente:

1. ¿Representa su resumen una síntesis del texto original? ¿El resumen refleja con precisión las ideas expresadas en el texto? ¿Hay detalles innecesarios?
2. ¿Sigue el resumen la estructura del texto original?
3. ¿Escribió transiciones claras que muestran las diversas secciones del texto original?
4. ¿Fluyen (*flow*) las ideas de una manera clara y natural? ¿Hay que aclarar algunos puntos?
5. ¿Usó el vocabulario y las estructuras correctas?
6. ¿Revisó la ortografía y la acentuación?

# ENFOQUE CULTURAL

## Ecuador: alimentación y salud pública

La diversidad geográfica del Ecuador le permite producir una gran variedad de alimentos. Y como es un país tropical, produce una cantidad suficiente de alimentos para satisfacer sus necesidades internas y para la exportación. En la región de la costa, se cultivan soya, café y aceite de palma, además de frutas tales como mango, cacao, banano, maracuyá y limón, entre otras. Por su parte, en la sierra, con sus diferentes niveles de clima, los campesinos producen una gran cantidad de comida, por ejemplo, papas, verduras (tomate, brócoli, cebolla) y frutas como manzanas y

Una plantación de banano en Ecuador

naranjas. La región amazónica produce principalmente carne de res, y algunos otros productos vegetales, como la yuca, que forman parte de la dieta ecuatoriana. Sin embargo, esta región tiene un déficit alimentario, porque sólo un porcentaje pequeño de su territorio está dedicado a la agricultura.

La industria del pescado en el Océano Pacífico

No hay que olvidar que la costa ecuatoriana es rica en pescado. Las aguas del Pacífico cercanas a las costas de Ecuador, Perú y Chile son rutas migratorias de grandes peces, y tradicionalmente los pescadores han aprovechado esas rutas para pescar. El puerto de Manta, por ejemplo, es conocido como la capital atunera del mundo. Además, en los últimos treinta años, se ha desarrollado en Ecuador una gran industria de cultivo de pescado o acuicultura. Uno de los productos más importantes de la acuicultura de Ecuador es el camarón. Gracias al camarón ecuatoriano, un producto que antes era de lujo, actualmente está al alcance de la clase media en Estados Unidos y Europa.

Los niños son las principales víctimas de la malnutrición, no sólo en Ecuador, sino en muchos países.

A pesar de que Ecuador es un país capaz de producir suficiente comida para su mercado interior y para la exportación, la salud de sus habitantes presenta varios problemas relacionados con la nutrición. En la actualidad aproximadamente una cuarta parte de la población ecuatoriana tiene problemas de desnutrición crónica. El sobrepeso y la obesidad afectan aproximadamente a un 10% de la población, mientras que la anemia es otra condición que afecta a amplios sectores, especialmente a los adolescentes, a las mujeres y a los infantes. Desafortunadamente, al igual que en otros países latinoamericanos, muchos de estos problemas son la consecuencia de la excesiva pobreza de muchos de sus habitantes. En efecto, más del 70% de los ecuatorianos viven en la pobreza.

Algunos datos sobre el consumo de alimentos en Ecuador son verdaderamente preocupantes. A causa de las crisis económicas, muchos ecuatorianos, principalmente de las clases más pobres, han perdido la capacidad de comprar alimentos básicos en los últimos diez años. Esas reducciones tienen un efecto desastroso sobre la alimentación y, por lo tanto, sobre la salud de los ecuatorianos. Según estadísticas del propio gobierno de Ecuador, en el año 2001 las tres comidas diarias se habían reducido a dos, especialmente en los sectores sociales más pobres. Desgraciadamente, los esfuerzos del gobierno de Ecuador y de muchas organizaciones internacionales de ayuda, no han tenido mucho éxito. Hoy día la pobreza parece relacionarse con los mayores problemas sanitarios del país: la malnutrición y el VIH/SIDA. Según un informe del gobierno ecuatoriano de 2004, se registraron más de mil casos nuevos de esta enfermedad en ese año.

---

## En otras palabras

**Expresiones ecuatorianas**

Mi **ñaña** se fue para Guayaquil.
*My sister left for Guayaquil.*

Tengo mucha sed, voy a tomar una **colita**.
*I am very thirsty; I'm going to drink a soda.*

Sí, sí, **te creo ocho veces**.
*Yeah, sure, I believe you.*
(said with disbelief)

**10-46 Comprensión.** PRIMERA FACE. **Reconocimiento de palabras clave.** Encuentre en el texto la palabra o expresión que mejor expresa el significado de las siguientes ideas.

1. enough        _____
2. beef        _____
3. close to/near      _____
4. aquaculture      _____
5. shrimp        _____
6. overweight      _____
7. poverty        _____

SEGUNDA FASE. **Oraciones importantes.** Subraye las afirmaciones que contienen ideas que se encuentran en el texto. Luego indique en qué parte del texto están.

1. All three of the geographical regions of Ecuador produce food in excess of their needs.
2. Many fisheries in Europe and the United States have gone out of business because of the industrial production of shrimp in Ecuador.
3. Manta, a port on the Pacific, was prohibited by the government of Ecuador from investing in the tuna fishing industry.
4. As a rule, Ecuador produces enough food to satisfy the needs of its internal markets, and even to export some of its crops.
5. Malnutrition is the cause of a number of health problems among Ecuadorians.
6. Women, infants, and adolescents are among the most common victims of health problems related to malnutrition.
7. Excessive poverty is at the root of malnutrition in Ecuador, as well as in other countries.
8. AIDS is still a problem in Ecuador, where over a thousand new cases were reported in 2004.

TERCERA FASE. **Ideas principales.** Escriba un párrafo breve en español resumiendo las ideas principales expresadas en el texto.

**10-47 Use la información.** Prepare un afiche sobre el tema de la pobreza y la malnutrición. Estas son algunas preguntas que usted puede tratar de responder en su afiche: ¿Cómo se comparan entre sí algunos países de América Latina en cuanto a la malnutrición? ¿Qué progresos o retrocesos han ocurrido recientemente en cuanto a la malnutrición en América Latina y otras regiones del mundo? ¿Qué papel juega la malnutrición en el desarrollo económico de los países? ¿Por qué es importante la buena nutrición materno-infantil? ¿Qué organizaciones están luchando contra la malnutrición a nivel global? Para preparar esta actividad, visite la página web de *Mosaicos* y siga los enlaces útiles.

# VOCABULARIO

CD 4
ks 34–41
r CD 5
ks 10–17

**Las especias y los condimentos** / *Spices and seasonings*

| | |
|---|---|
| el aceite | oil |
| el aderezo | salad dressing |
| el azúcar | sugar |
| las especias | spices |
| las hierbas | herbs |
| la mayonesa | mayonnaise |
| la mostaza | mustard |
| la pimienta | pepper |
| la sal | salt |
| la salsa de tomate | tomato sauce |
| la vainilla | vanilla |
| el vinagre | vinegar |

**Las frutas y las verduras** / *Fruits and vegetables*

| | |
|---|---|
| el aguacate | avocado |
| el ajo | garlic |
| la cebolla | onion |
| la cereza | cherry |
| las espinacas | spinach |
| la fresa | strawberry |
| el limón | lemon |
| el maíz | corn |
| la manzana | apple |
| el maracuyá | passion fruit |
| el melón | melon |
| la papaya | papaya |
| el pepino | cucumber |
| la pera | pear |
| el pimiento verde | green pepper |
| la piña | pineapple |
| el plátano/la banana | banana, plantain |
| la toronja/el pomelo | grapefruit |
| la uva | grape |
| la zanahoria | carrot |

**El pescado y la carne** / *Fish and meat*

| | |
|---|---|
| las aves | poultry, fowl |
| el camarón/la gamba | shrimp |
| la carne | meat |
| molida/picada | ground meat |
| de res | beef/steak |
| el cerdo | pork |
| la chuleta | chop |
| el cordero | lamb |
| la costilla | rib |
| la langosta | lobster |
| los mariscos | shellfish |
| la oveja | sheep |
| el pavo | turkey |

**Otros productos** / *Other products*

| | |
|---|---|
| los churros | fried dough |
| la crema | cream |
| el dulce | candy/sweets |
| la galleta | cookie |
| la harina | flour |
| la leche de coco | coconut milk |
| las legumbres | legumes |
| las lentejas | lentils |
| la manteca/la mantequilla | butter |
| la margarina | margarine |
| el pan dulce | bun, small cake |
| el pastel | pastry |
| el queso crema | cream cheese |
| el yogur | yogurt |

**En la mesa** / *On the table*

| | |
|---|---|
| la bandeja | tray |
| la botella | bottle |
| la copa | (stemmed) glass |
| la cuchara | spoon |
| la cucharita | teaspoon |
| el cuchillo | knife |
| el mantel | tablecloth |
| el plato | plate, dish |
| la servilleta | napkin |
| la taza | cup |
| el tenedor | fork |
| el vaso | glass |

**Verbos** / *Verbs*

| | |
|---|---|
| agregar/añadir | to add |
| batir | to beat |
| disfrutar | to enjoy |
| freír (i) | to fry |
| hervir (ie, i) | to boil |
| probar (ue) | to try, to taste |
| recomendar (ie) | to recommend |

**Las descripciones** / *Descriptions*

| | |
|---|---|
| agrio/a | sour |
| lácteo/a | dairy (product) |

**Palabras y expresiones útiles** / *Useful words and expressions*

| | |
|---|---|
| el campesino/la campesina | peasant |
| la receta | recipe |
| todavía | still, yet |
| ya | already |

See *Lengua* boxes on p. 329 and on p. 352 for additional food vocabulary.

# VOCABULARIO

| **La ciencia y la tecnología** | *Science and technology* |
|---|---|
| el acceso | *access* |
| el adelanto | *advance* |
| la biblioteca virtual | *virtual library* |
| el buscador | *search engine* |
| la cápsula | *capsule* |
| la clonación | *cloning* |
| el conocimiento | *knowledge* |
| el descubrimiento | *discovery* |
| la diseminación | *dispersal, dissemination* |
| el documento adjunto | *attachment, attached document* |
| la energía solar | *solar energy* |
| el enlace | *link* |
| la fuente | *source* |
| la infraestructura | *infrastructure* |
| el intercambio | *exchange* |
| el mensaje | *message* |
| el reto | *challenge* |
| el riel | *rail* |
| el robot | *robot* |
| el videojuego | *video game* |

| **El medio ambiente** | *Environment* |
|---|---|
| el banco de peces | *shoal; school of fish* |
| el bosque | *forest* |
| el bosque tropical | *rain forest* |
| el calentamiento | *warming* |
| la capa de ozono | *ozone layer* |
| la conservación | *preservation* |
| la cuenca | *(river) basin* |
| la deforestación | *deforestation* |
| la desaparición | *disappearance* |
| el deshielo | *thaw, thawing* |

| | |
|---|---|
| la extinción | *extinction* |
| la inundación | *flood* |
| la naturaleza | *nature* |
| la pérdida | *loss* |
| el planeta | *planet* |
| los recursos | *resources* |
| la reserva natural | *nature preserve* |
| la tierra | *land, soil* |

| **Las descripciones** | *Descriptions* |
|---|---|
| climatizado/a | *air-conditioned* |
| extinguido/a | *extinguished* |
| reciclado/a | *recycled* |
| volador/a | *flying* |

| **Verbos** | *Verbs* |
|---|---|
| aterrizar (c) | *to land* |
| bajar | *to download* |
| conectarse | *to connect* |
| construir (y) | *to build* |
| contribuir (y) | *to contribute* |
| despegar (u) | *to take off (airplane)* |
| difundir | *to spread, to disseminate* |
| encender (ie) | *to turn on* |
| enfocarse (qu) | *to focus* |
| meter | *to insert* |
| repoblar | *to reforest* |
| unificar (qu) | *to unify* |

| **Palabras y expresiones útiles** | *Useful words and expressions* |
|---|---|
| debido a | *due to* |
| en busca de | *in search of* |
| genéticamente | *genetically* |
| virtualmente | *virtually* |

# Expansión gramatical

This grammatical supplement includes structures often considered optional for the introductory level, because the functions and forms presented here are far beyond the performance level of most first-year students. Many instructors choose to present them for recognition only, if at all. The *vosotros* command forms are included in this section for the instructors who use them to address their students.

The explanation and activities in this section use the same format as the grammatical material throughout *Mosaicos* in order to facilitate their incorporation into the core lessons of the program or their addition as another chapter in the book.

## Funciones y formas

1. Giving informal orders or commands to two or more people (in Spain): *Vosotros* commands
2. Expressing an indirect wish that a third party do something: Indirect commands
3. Suggesting that someone and the speaker do something: The Spanish equivalents of English *let's*
4. Reacting to a past occurrence or event: The present perfect subjunctive
5. Hypothesizing about an occurrence or event in the past: The conditional perfect and the pluperfect subjunctive
6. Expressing contrary-to-fact conditions in the past: *If*-clauses (using the perfect tense)
7. Emphasizing a fact resulting from an action by someone or something: The passive voice

## 1. Giving informal orders or commands to two or more people (in Spain): *Vosotros* commands

| | AFFIRMATIVE | NEGATIVE |
|---|---|---|
| hablar | habla**d** | no **habléis** |
| comer | come**d** | no **comáis** |
| escribir | escribi**d** | no **escribáis** |

■ To use the affirmative **vosotros** command, change the final **-r** of the infinitive to **-d**.

■ Use the **vosotros** form of the present subjunctive for the **vosotros** negative command.

■ For the affirmative **vosotros** command of reflexive verbs, drop the final **-d** and add the pronoun **os: levantad + os = levantaos.** The verb **irse** is an exception: **idos.**

**EG-1 Buenos consejos.** Usted quiere que sus mejores amigos cambien sus hábitos y vivan una vida más sana. Dígales qué deben hacer.

**MODELO:** caminar dos kilómetros todos los días
*Caminad dos kilómetros todos los días.*

1. comer muchas frutas y vegetales
2. empezar un programa de ejercicios
3. no respirar por la boca
4. no cansarse mucho los primeros días
5. relajarse para evitar el estrés
6. dormir no menos de ocho horas

 **EG-2 Órdenes en grupo.** Cada uno/a de ustedes va a hacer el papel de profesor/a de educación física y le va a dar una orden a los otros estudiantes del grupo. Los estudiantes deben hacer lo que el/la profesor/a les indica.

**MODELO:** *Levantad los brazos y las piernas.*

## SITUACIONES

You and your partner have rented a cabin in the mountains for a month. Some of your friends are going to use the cabin part of the time and you would like to give them some rules to make sure they leave everything in order. Write the rules and then compare them with those of another couple.

## 2. Expressing an indirect wish that a third party do something: Indirect commands

You have used commands directly to tell others to do something: **Salga/Salgan ahora.** Now you are going to use indirect commands to say what someone else should do: **Que salga Berta.** Note that this indirect command is equivalent to saying **Quiero que Berta salga,** but without expressing the main verb **quiero.**

■  The word **que** introduces the indirect command. The subject, if stated, normally follows the verb.

| | |
|---|---|
| **Que cocine** Roberto. | *Let Roberto cook.* |
| **Que descanse** María. | *Let María rest.* |

■  Reflexive and object pronouns always precede the verb.

| | |
|---|---|
| Que **se siente** a la mesa. | *Let him sit at the table.* |
| Que **le sirvan** la cena. | *Let them serve him dinner.* |
| Que **se la sirvan** ahora. | *Let them serve it to him now.* |

**EG-3 Una clase de cocina.** Un chef muy conocido ha accedido a dar una clase de cocina con el fin de recaudar (*raise*) dinero para una obra social. Usted y su compañero/a forman parte del comité que organiza la clase. Su compañero/a tiene la lista de las personas que desean ayudar y usted tiene la lista de las tareas pendientes. Háganse preguntas y contéstense con la información que cada uno/a tiene.

**MODELO:**    *Eduardo, Alicia y Pedro preparar los anuncios, comprar los refrescos*
  E1:  *¿Quién va a preparar los anuncios?*
  E2:  *Que los preparen Alicia y Pedro. ¿Y qué va a hacer Eduardo?*
  E1:  *Que compre los refrescos.*

**Personas**

Beatriz
Alberto y Rubén
Miguel
Elena y Amanda
Ana María
Emilio
Un camarero

**Tareas**

traer los platos
tener los ingredientes listos
buscar las sillas
copiar las recetas
servir el vino
recibir a las personas
ayudar al chef

**EG-4 Una fiesta hispana.** PRIMERA FASE. Para celebrar el final de curso ustedes han decidido organizar una fiesta en el departamento de español. Hagan una lista de todo lo que necesitan y otra lista de todas las personas que van a invitar, además de sus compañeros/as de clase.

SEGUNDA FASE. Decidan qué otras personas de la clase pueden encargarse de cada sección y por qué. Su compañero/a, que está de acuerdo con usted, le dará algunas ideas.

MODELO:  E1: *Que se encargue Juan de comprar las invitaciones porque tiene que ir al supermercado esta tarde.*

E2: *Sí, pero que las escriban María y Pedro que escriben mejor.*

---

**En directo**

To negotiate politely:

**Esperamos que...**

**Es mejor que...**

**Proponemos que...**

To show agreement:

**¡Claro!**

**¡Por supuesto!**

**¡Cómo no!**

**¡Desde luego!**

---

## SITUACIONES

**Role A.** You are a new manager for the Student Union who wants to improve the food and the service at the cafeteria. In a meeting with the cafeteria manager, say a) that it is important that students receive a better service, b) inform the manager of the type of food you would like to find in the cafeteria and of the ways in which the service could be improved, and c) say that you hope the prices will not increase (**subir**) this semester.

**Role B.** You are the cafeteria manager. Agree with the Student Union manager and tell him/her a) that you have a good team and you want everyone to do a good job, b) that you will be happy to meet with a student committee and have students suggest (**sugerir**) menus, and c) that you will do your best (**hacer lo posible**) to convince your team to incorporate your suggestions.

### 3. Suggesting that someone and the speaker do something: The Spanish equivalents of English *let's*

In Spanish, you may suggest that two or more people, including yourself, do something together in the following ways.

- **Vamos + a +** *infinitive* is commonly used in Spanish to express English *let's +* *verb.*

    **Vamos a llamar** al doctor.                  *Let's call the doctor.*

- Use **vamos** by itself to mean *let's go.* The negative *let's not go* is **no vayamos.**

    **Vamos** al hospital.                          *Let's go to the hospital.*
    **No vayamos** al hospital.                     *Let's not go to the hospital.*

- Another equivalent for *let's + verb* is the **nosotros** form of the present subjunctive.

    **Hablemos** con el médico.                    *Let's talk to the doctor.*
    **No hablemos** con la enfermera.              *Let's not talk to the nurse.*

- The final **-s** of reflexive affirmative commands is dropped when the pronoun **nos** is attached. Note the additional written accent.

    **Levantemos + nos**        ➞        **Levantémonos.**
    **Sirvamos + nos**          ➞        **Sirvámonos.**

- Placement of object and reflexive pronouns is the same as with **usted(es)** commands.

    **Comprémosla.**                               *Let's buy it.*
    **No la compremos.**                           *Let's not buy it.*

 **EG-5 ¿Qué debemos hacer?** Usted y un/a compañero/a están estudiando y cuidando a su hermanito al mismo tiempo. El niño les dice que se siente mal. Cada uno/a de ustedes debe escoger tres de las siguientes opciones y decirle a su compañero/a lo que deben o no deben hacer.

**MODELO:**    llevarlo a su cuarto                     llamar a tus padres
               E1: *Llevémoslo a su cuarto.*            E2: *Llamemos a tus padres.*

1. darle agua
2. llevarlo al parque
3. comprarle juguetes
4. ponerle el termómetro
5. llamar al médico
6. preguntarle qué le duele
7. prepararle una hamburguesa
8. explicarle los síntomas al doctor
9. ponerle la televisión
10. acostarlo

**EG-6 Resoluciones.** Usted y su compañero/a deciden llevar una vida más sana. Túrnense para decir lo que piensan hacer. Su compañero/a va a decirle si está de acuerdo o no con su sugerencia.

**MODELO:**   comer más verduras
  E1: *Vamos a comer más verduras.*
  E2: *Sí, comamos más verduras./No, (no comamos más verduras,) comamos más frutas.*

1. tomar vitaminas y minerales
2. caminar tres kilómetros diariamente
3. beber ocho vasos de agua todos los días
4. acostarse más temprano
5. dormir ocho horas todas las noches
6. ...

 **EG-7 Los preparativos para un beneficio.** En pequeños grupos, decidan qué actividades van a hacer para recaudar (*collect*) fondos a beneficio de un hospital. Deben mencionar cinco actividades.

**MODELO:**   *Organicemos un partido del equipo de basquetbol.*

## SITUACIONES

You and your partner are planning to visit a classmate who is in the hospital. Decide a) when you will visit him/her, b) what you are going to take him/her, and c) what you can do for your classmate after he/she leaves the hospital. Then, exchange this information with another pair of students.

### 4. Reacting to a past occurrence or event: The present perfect subjunctive

Use the present perfect subjunctive to react to a past occurrence, event or condition. The present perfect subjunctive is formed with the present subjunctive of the verb **haber** + *past participle*.

| PRESENT SUBJUNCTIVE OF *HABER* + *PAST PARTICIPLE* | | |
|---|---|---|
| yo | **haya** | |
| yú | **hayas** | |
| Ud., él/ella | **haya** | **hablado** |
| nosotros/as | **hayamos** | **comido** |
| vosotros/as | **hayáis** | **vivido** |
| Uds., ellos/as | **hayan** | |

Note that the dependent clause using the present perfect subjunctive describes what has happened before the time expressed or implied in the main clause, which is the present. Its English equivalent is normally *has/have* + *past participle*, but it may vary according to the context.

| Your friend tells you: | Your reaction to this past event: |
|---|---|
| Mis hijos volvieron de sus vacaciones. → | Me alegro de que **hayan llegado**. *I'm glad they arrived early.* |

| Your secretary informs you: | Your reaction to this past news: |
|---|---|
| El gerente de ventas no vino a trabajar ayer. } → | Es posible que **haya estado** enfermo. *It's possible that he may have been sick.* |

 **EG-8 ¿Qué espera usted?** Escoja la oración que complete lógicamente las siguientes situaciones. Compare sus respuestas con las de su compañero/a.

1. Su computadora no estaba funcionando bien y usted se la dio a un técnico para que la reparara. Usted espera que...
   **a.** la haya vendido.
   **b.** haya destruido sus programas.
   **c.** haya encontrado el problema.
2. Su amigo acaba de regresar de Puerto Rico, donde fue a pasar sus vacaciones. Usted le dice: "Espero que...
   **a.** hayas visitado el Viejo San Juan".
   **b.** te hayas aburrido mucho".
   **c.** hayas perdido todo tu dinero".
3. Uno de sus compañeros ha estado muy grave en el hospital, pero ya está en la casa. Usted le habla y le dice: "Siento mucho que...
   **a.** hayas vendido la casa".
   **b.** hayas estado tan mal".
   **c.** hayas salido del hospital".

**4.** Usted llama por teléfono a un amigo para invitarlo a cenar, pero nadie contesta el teléfono. Es probable que su amigo...
   **a.** haya cenado ya.
   **b.** haya salido de su casa.
   **c.** haya cambiado su teléfono.

**5.** Uno de sus parientes dijo una mentira (*lie*). Como es natural, a usted le molesta mucho que no...
   **a.** haya dicho la verdad.
   **b.** haya dicho nada.
   **c.** haya hablado con sus parientes.

**EG-9 Un viaje.** Uno de sus amigos pasó un semestre en Los Ángeles. Túrnese con su compañero/a para decirle lo que esperan que haya hecho en su visita.

MODELO:      ir a Beverly Hills / visitar la Biblioteca Huntington
   E1:  *Espero que hayas ido a Beverly Hills.*
   E2:  *Y yo espero que hayas visitado la Biblioteca Huntington.*

**1.** ver las Torres de Watts
**2.** ir a los Estudios Universal
**3.** caminar por la calle Olvera
**4.** comer comida mexicana
**5.** manejar hasta el observatorio del Monte Wilson
**6.** asistir al Desfile de las Rosas

**EG-10 Los adelantos científicos.** Usted y su compañero/a trabajan con otros científicos en un laboratorio de ingeniería genética. Háganse preguntas para saber qué han logrado o no en sus investigaciones.

MODELO:      aislar el nuevo virus / es posible que
   E1:  *¿Han aislado el nuevo virus?*
   E2:  *Es posible que lo hayamos / hayan aislado.*

**1.** cambiar la estructura de la célula / dudar
**2.** no hacer implantes nuevos / es una lástima
**3.** duplicar órganos / no creer que
**4.** regular el ritmo del corazón / esperar
**5.** reactivar los músculos atrofiados / es probable que
**6.** modificar los genes / es importante que

> **En directo**
>
> To express that you remember or recognize someone in a photo:
>
> **Mira, mira, este/esta es...**
> *Look, this is . . .*
>
> **Te equivocas**
> *You are wrong.*
>
> **Pero, ¿no ves que es.../ Tiene/lleva...**
> *But, don't you see it is . . .*
> (a person's name)
>
> **¿Has visto a...?**

## SITUACIONES

You and your classmate graduated years ago and are remembering the times when you were at the university. You have found a group photo of your Spanish class. Talk about each of your classmates saying a) what you know they have done in their lives, b) what you hope they have done, and c) what you doubt they have done. Use your imagination and the expressions in the box to sound more natural.

## 5. Hypothesizing about an occurrence or event in the past: The conditional perfect and the pluperfect subjunctive

In this section you will study two new verb tenses: the conditional perfect and the pluperfect subjunctive. Use this tense to hypothesize about an occurrence or event in the past.

■ Use the conditional of **haber** + *past participle* to form the conditional perfect.

| CONDITIONAL PERFECT | | |
|---|---|---|
| yo | **habría** | |
| tú | **habrías** | |
| Ud., él, ella | **habría** | **hablado** |
| nosotros/as | **habríamos** | **comido** |
| vosotros/as | **habríais** | **vivido** |
| Uds., ellos/as | **habrían** | |

■ The conditional perfect usually corresponds to English *would have + past participle.*

| Sé que le **habría gustado** esta casa. | *I know you/he/she would have liked this house.* |
|---|---|

■ Use the past subjunctive of **haber** + *past participle* to form the pluperfect subjunctive.

| PLUPERFECT SUBJUNCTIVE | | |
|---|---|---|
| yo | **hubiera** | |
| tú | **hubieras** | |
| Ud., él, ella | **hubiera** | **hablado** |
| nosotros/as | **hubiéramos** | **comido** |
| vosotros/as | **hubierais** | **vivido** |
| Uds., ellos/as | **hubieran** | |

■ The pluperfect subjunctive corresponds to English *might have*, *would have*, or *had + past participle.* It is used in constructions where the subjunctive is normally required.

| Dudaba que **hubiera venido** temprano. | *I doubted that he had/would have come early.* |
|---|---|
| Esperaba que **hubieran comido** en casa. | *I was hoping that they would have eaten at home.* |
| Ojalá que **hubieran visto** ese letrero. | *I wish they had seen that sign.* |

**EG-11 ¿Qué habría hecho en estas situaciones?** PRIMERA FASE. Digan qué habría hecho cada uno/a de ustedes en las siguientes situaciones. Después escojan la respuesta que les parezca mejor para cada situación.

MODELO:  Usted recibió una invitación para una recepción en la Casa Blanca.
E1: *Se lo habría dicho a todos mis compañeros.*
E2: *Habría leído la invitación varias veces porque habría pensado que era una broma.*

1. En el aeropuerto le dijeron que podía viajar en primera clase todo el año sin pagar.
2. Le pidieron sugerencias para mejorar la situación de los vuelos y los aeropuertos.
3. La NASA lo/la llamó para ver si le interesaba vivir tres meses en una estación espacial.
4. Le dijeron que organizara la fiesta de fin de curso de su clase.
5. Le pidieron que revisara los programas en su universidad y sugiriera los cambios necesarios.

SEGUNDA FASE. Comparen las respuestas que escogieron con las de otra pareja y decidan cuál es la mejor. Después compartan sus respuestas con el resto de la clase.

 **EG-12 Nuestras esperanzas.** Usted y su compañero/a esperaban que el nuevo gobierno hiciera muchas cosas en beneficio de la sociedad. Se lograron algunas cosas, pero otras no. Túrnense para decir qué esperaban que el nuevo gobierno y su gabinete hubieran hecho y si lo han hecho o no.

MODELO:  subir el sueldo mínimo / mejorar el sistema de educación
E1: *Esperaba que hubieran subido el sueldo mínimo y (no) lo han hecho.*
E2: *Y yo esperaba que hubieran mejorado el sistema de educación y (no) lo han hecho.*

1. bajar los impuestos (*taxes*)
2. mejorar el transporte público
3. terminar con la corrupción
4. construir viviendas (*housing*) para familias pobres
5. ofrecer mejores planes de salud
6. proteger el medio ambiente
7. ...

## SITUACIONES

Role A. You had an argument (**pelea**) with your significant other. Explain to your best friend what happened and ask him/her what he/she would have done in your place. Then tell him/her what you intend to do.

Role B. Your best friend explains to you that he/she had an argument (**pelea**) with his/her significant other. Ask questions to obtain some details. Then a) tell him/her what you would have done in the same situation, b) ask him/her what he/she intends to do and c) give him/her your advice.

### 6. Expressing contrary-to-fact conditions in the past: *If*-clauses (using the perfect tenses)

The conditional perfect and pluperfect subjunctive are used in contrary-to-fact if-statements which refer to actions, events, experiences related to the past.

| | |
|---|---|
| Si **hubieras venido**, te **habría gustado** la conferencia. | *If you had come (which you did not), you would have liked the lecture.* |

 **EG-13 La vida sería diferente.** Con su compañero/a, diga cuáles habrían sido las consecuencias si...

**MODELO:** no se hubieran inventado los aviones
E1: *Habríamos viajado en barco, en tren o en autobús.*
E2: *Habríamos contaminado menos la atmósfera.*

1. no se hubiera inventado la bomba atómica
2. no se hubieran deforestado los bosques
3. los ingleses hubieran descubierto América
4. las mujeres hubieran tenido siempre las mismas oportunidades que los hombres
5. no se hubieran creado las vacunas (*vaccination*)
6. los jóvenes hubieran gobernado el mundo

 **EG-14 Unas excusas.** ¿Qué excusas darían ustedes en las siguientes situaciones?

**MODELO:** Un amigo le pidió que participara en un experimento.
E1: *Si mis padres me lo hubieran permitido, habría participado.*
E2: *Si hubiera tenido tiempo, habría participado.*

1. Una organización quería que usted donara botellas y papeles para reciclar.
2. Le pidieron su coche para llevar unas ratas al laboratorio.
3. Lo/La necesitaban de voluntario/a para probar una vacuna contra el catarro.
4. Un/a compañero/a quería venderle su computadora portátil.
5. Una compañía necesitaba probar unos paracaídas (*parachutes*) y buscaba personas interesadas en las pruebas.
6. Alquilaban un robot para que hiciera las tareas domésticas.

 **EG-15 Volver a vivir.** Piense en una experiencia negativa que usted haya tenido. Cuéntele a su compañero/a qué le pasó y dígale qué habría hecho si hubiera sabido en ese momento lo que sabe hoy. Después, su compañero/a debe hacer lo mismo.

## SITUACIONES

Role A. You attended a conference/lecture about the city of the future. Tell your classmate a) where and when the conference/lecture took place, b) that he/she would have found it very interesting, and c) the things that he/she would have learned if he/she had attended.

Role B. Your classmate has attended a conference/lecture about the city of the future. Ask him/her questions to find out more about the things he/she learned.

## 7. Emphasizing a fact resulting from an action by someone or something: The passive voice

The passive voice emphasizes a fact resulting from the action by someone or something.

■ The passive voice in Spanish is formed with the verb **ser** + *past participle*; the passive voice is most commonly used in the preterit, though at times you may see it used in other tenses.

| | |
|---|---|
| La planta nuclear **fue construida** en 1980. | *The nuclear plant was built in 1980.* |

■ Use the preposition **por** when indicating who or what performs the action.

| | |
|---|---|
| El bosque **fue destruido**. (Who or what did it is not expressed.) | *The forest was destroyed.* |
| El bosque **fue destruido por** el fuego. (The fire did it.) | *The forest was destroyed by the fire.* |

■ The past participle functions as an adjective and therefore agrees in gender and number with the subject.

| | |
|---|---|
| Los árboles fueron **destruidos** por la lluvia ácida. | *The trees were destroyed by acid rain.* |
| La cura fue **descubierta** el año pasado. | *The cure was discovered last year.* |

■ You'll most often find the passive voice in written Spanish, especially in newspapers and formal writing. However, in conversation, Spanish speakers normally use two different constructions that you have already studied—a third person plural verb or a **se** construction.

| | |
|---|---|
| **Vendieron** el laboratorio. | *They sold the laboratory.* |
| **Se vendió** el edificio. | *The building was sold.* |

 **EG-16 La comunicación oral.** Túrnense para decir lo que pasó en una reunión del presidente y los ministros. ¿Cómo lo dirían los periódicos? ¿Cómo lo dirían ustedes en una conversación?

MODELO: ministros / recibir / el presidente
E1: *Los ministros fueron recibidos por el presidente.*
E2: *El presidente recibió a los ministros.*

1. la agenda / preparar / el secretario
2. la agenda / aprobar / todos
3. el proyecto para disminuir la contaminación / escribir / el Sr. Sosa
4. el proyecto / presentar / la Ministra de Salud
5. unos comentarios / leer / el presidente
6. las preguntas / contestar / el ministro

**EG-17 Dos reporteros.** Túrnense para decir cómo escribirían las siguientes noticias para un periódico.

MODELO:   la lluvia ácida dañó las cosechas
*Las cosechas fueron dañadas por la lluvia ácida.*

1. La zona del Amazonas se conoce como el "pulmón" del planeta.
2. Los campesinos deforestaron la selva.
3. Los campesinos cultivaron la tierra.
4. Estos grupos cortaron muchos árboles.
5. La invasión de los seres humanos exterminó muchas especies de animales.
6. El gobierno plantará mil árboles para mejorar la situación.

## SITUACIONES

You and your classmate are TV newscasters. You must write and give a piece of news to your viewers on a great discovery. Inform them that a) some very secret plans have been discovered by the CIA, b) that important security measures have been taken, c) that politicians are now deliberating on how to respond to a possible threat (**peligro**) to the population, d) that public transport has been interrupted in major cities, e) that the situation is under control and f) that nobody should be afraid.

# Appendix 1

## Stress and Written Accents in Spanish

### Rules for Written Accents

The following rules are based on pronunciation.

1. If a word ends in *n*, *s*, or a vowel, the penultimate (second-to-last) syllable is usually stressed.

    Examples:  caminan
               **mu**chos
               silla

2. If a word ends in a consonant other than *n* or *s*, the last syllable is stressed.

    Example:  fa**tal**

3. Words that are exceptions to the preceding rules have an accent mark on the stressed vowel.

    Examples:  sar**tén**
               **lá**pices
               ma**má**
               **fá**cil

4. **Separation of diphthongs.** When *i* or *u* are combined with another vowel, they are pronounced as one sound (a diphthong). When each vowel sound is pronounced separately, a written accent mark is placed over the stressed vowel (either the *i* or the *u*).

    Example:  gracias  día

Because the written accents in the following examples are not determined by pronunciation, the accent mark must be memorized as part of the spelling of the words as they are learned.

5. **Homonyms.** When two words are spelled the same, but have different meanings, a written accent is used to distinguish and differentiate meaning.

    | Examples: | **de** | *of* | **dé** | *give* (formal command) |
    |---|---|---|---|---|
    | | **el** | *the* | **él** | *he* |
    | | **mas** | *but* | **más** | *more* |
    | | **mi** | my | **mí** | me |
    | | **se** | *him/herself,* *(to) him/her/them* | **sé** | *I know, be* (formal command) |
    | | **si** | *if* | **sí** | *yes* |
    | | **te** | *(to) you* | **té** | *tea* |
    | | **tu** | *your* | **tú** | *you* |

6. **Interrogatives and exclamations.** In questions (direct and indirect) and exclamations, a written accent is placed over the following words: **dónde, cómo, cuándo, cuál(es), quién(es), cuánto(s)/cuánta(s)**, and **qué**.

# Word Formation in Spanish

Recognizing certain patterns in Spanish word formation can be a big help in deciphering meaning. Use the following information about word formation to help you as you read.

■ **Prefixes.** Spanish and English share a number of prefixes that shade the meaning of the word to which they are attached: **inter-** (between, among); **intro/a-** (within); **ex-** (former, toward the outside); **en-/em-** (the state of becoming); **in-/a-** (not, without), among others.

| | |
|---|---|
| inter- | interdisciplinario, interacción |
| intro/a- | introvertido, introspección |
| ex- | exponer (*expose*) |
| en-/em- | enrojecer (*to turn red*), empobrecer (*to become poor*) |
| in-/a- | inmoral, incompleto, amoral, asexual |

■ **Suffixes.** Suffixes and, in general, word endings will help you identify various aspects of words such as part of speech, gender, meaning, degree, etc. Common Spanish suffixes are **-ría, -za, -miento, -dad/tad, -ura, -oso/a, -izo/a, -(c)ito/a,** and **-mente.**

| | |
|---|---|
| -ría | place where something is made and/or bought: **panadería, zapatería** (*shoe store*), **librería.** |
| -za | feminine, abstract noun: **pobreza** (*poverty*), **riqueza** (*wealth, richness*). |
| -miento | masculine, abstract noun: **empobrecimiento** (*impoverishment*), **entrenamiento** (*training*). |
| -dad/tad | feminine noun: **ciudad** (*city*), **libertad** (*liberty, freedom*) |
| -ura | feminine noun: **verdura, locura** (*craziness*). |
| -oso/a | adjective meaning having the characteristics of the noun to which it's attached: **montañoso, lluvioso** (*rainy*). |
| -izo/a | adjective meaning having the characteristics of the noun to which it's attached: **rojizo** (*reddish*), **enfermizo** (*sickly*). |
| -(c)ito/a | diminutive form of noun or adjective: **Juanito, mesita** (*little table*), **Carmencita.** |
| -mente | attached to the feminine form of adjective to form an adverb: **rápidamente, felizmente** (*happily*). |

■ **Compounds.** Compounds are made up of two words (e.g., *mailman*), each of which has meaning in and of itself: **altavoz** (*loudspeaker*) from **alto/a** and **voz**; **sacacorchos** (*corkscrew*) from **sacar** and **corcho**. Your knowledge of the root words will help you recognize the compound; and likewise, learning compounds can help you to learn the root words. What do you think **sacar** means?

■ **Spanish-English associations.** Learning to associate aspects of word formation in Spanish with aspects of word formation in English can be very helpful. Look at the associations below.

| SPANISH | ENGLISH |
|---|---|
| **es/ex +** consonant | *s +* consonant |
|   **esclerosis, extraño** |   *sclerosis, strange* |
| **gu-** | *w-* |
|   **guerra, Guillermo** |   *war, William* |
| **-tad/dad** | *-ty* |
|   **libertad, calidad** |   *liberty, quality* |
| **-sión/-ción** | *-sion/-tion* |
|   **tensión, emoción** |   *tension, emotion* |

## Verb Charts

### Regular Verbs: Simple Tenses

| Infinitive Present Participle Past Participle | Indicative | | | | | | Subjunctive | | Imperative |
| --- | --- | --- | --- | --- | --- | --- | --- | --- | --- |
| | Present | Imperfect | Preterit | Future | Conditional | Present | Imperfect | Commands |
| hablar hablando hablado | hablo hablas habla hablamos habláis hablan | hablaba hablabas hablaba hablábamos hablabais hablaban | hablé hablaste habló hablamos hablasteis hablaron | hablaré hablarás hablará hablaremos hablaréis hablarán | hablaría hablarías hablaría hablaríamos hablaríais hablarían | hable hables hable hablemos habléis hablen | hablara hablaras hablara habláramos hablarais hablaran | habla (tú), no hables hable (usted) hablemos hablad (vosotros), no habléis hablen (Uds.) |
| comer comiendo comido | como comes come comemos coméis comen | comía comías comía comíamos comíais comían | comí comiste comió comimos comisteis comieron | comeré comerás comerá comeremos comeréis comerán | comería comerías comería comeríamos comeríais comerían | coma comas coma comamos comáis coman | comiera comieras comiera comiéramos comierais comieran | come (tú), no comas coma (usted) comamos comed (vosotros), no comáis coman (Uds.) |
| vivir viviendo vivido | vivo vives vive vivimos vivís viven | vivía vivías vivía vivíamos vivíais vivían | viví viviste vivió vivimos vivisteis vivieron | viviré vivirás vivirá viviremos viviréis vivirán | viviría vivirías viviría viviríamos viviríais vivirían | viva vivas viva vivamos viváis vivan | viviera vivieras viviera viviéramos vivierais vivieran | vive (tú), no vivas viva (usted) vivamos vivid (vosotros), no viváis vivan (Uds.) |

**Perfect Tenses (Regular Verbs)**

| | Indicative | | | | | Subjunctive | |
|---|---|---|---|---|---|---|---|
| | **Present Perfect** | **Past Perfect** | **Preterit Perfect** | **Future Perfect** | **Conditional Perfect** | **Present Perfect** | **Past Perfect** |
| | he<br>has<br>ha<br>hemos<br>habéis<br>han | había<br>habías<br>había<br>habíamos<br>habíais<br>habían | hube<br>hubiste<br>hubo<br>hubimos<br>hubisteis<br>hubieron | habré<br>habrás<br>habrá<br>habremos<br>habréis<br>habrán | habría<br>habrías<br>habría<br>habríamos<br>habríais<br>habrían | haya<br>hayas<br>haya<br>hayamos<br>hayáis<br>hayan | hubiera<br>hubieras<br>hubiera<br>hubiéramos<br>hubierais<br>hubieran |
| hablado comido vivido | hablado comido vivido | hablado comido vivido | hablado comido vivido | hablado comido vivido | hablado comido vivido | hablado comido vivido | hablado comido vivido |

## Irregular Verbs

| Infinitive<br>Present Participle<br>Past Participle | Indicative | | | | | Subjunctive | | Imperative |
|---|---|---|---|---|---|---|---|---|
| | **Present** | **Imperfect** | **Preterit** | **Future** | **Conditional** | **Present** | **Imperfect** | **Commands** |
| andar<br>andando<br>andado | ando<br>andas<br>anda<br>andamos<br>andáis<br>andan | andaba<br>andabas<br>andaba<br>andábamos<br>andabais<br>andaban | anduve<br>anduviste<br>anduvo<br>anduvimos<br>anduvisteis<br>anduvieron | andaré<br>andarás<br>andará<br>andaremos<br>andaréis<br>andarán | andaría<br>andarías<br>andaría<br>andaríamos<br>andaríais<br>andarían | ande<br>andes<br>ande<br>andemos<br>andéis<br>anden | anduviera<br>anduvieras<br>anduviera<br>anduviéramos<br>anduvierais<br>anduvieran | anda (tú),<br>no andes<br>ande (usted)<br>andemos<br>andad (vosotros),<br>no andéis<br>anden (Uds.) |
| caer<br>cayendo<br>caído | caigo<br>caes<br>cae<br>caemos<br>caéis<br>caen | caía<br>caías<br>caía<br>caíamos<br>caíais<br>caían | caí<br>caíste<br>cayó<br>caímos<br>caísteis<br>cayeron | caeré<br>caerás<br>caerá<br>caeremos<br>caeréis<br>caerán | caería<br>caerías<br>caería<br>caeríamos<br>caeríais<br>caerían | caiga<br>caigas<br>caiga<br>caigamos<br>caigáis<br>caigan | cayera<br>cayeras<br>cayera<br>cayéramos<br>cayerais<br>cayeran | cae (tú),<br>no caigas<br>caiga (usted)<br>caigamos<br>caed (vosotros),<br>no caigáis<br>caigan (Uds.) |
| dar<br>dando<br>dado | doy<br>das<br>da<br>damos<br>dais<br>dan | daba<br>dabas<br>daba<br>dábamos<br>dabais<br>daban | di<br>diste<br>dio<br>dimos<br>disteis<br>dieron | daré<br>darás<br>dará<br>daremos<br>daréis<br>darán | daría<br>darías<br>daría<br>daríamos<br>daríais<br>darían | dé<br>des<br>dé<br>demos<br>deis<br>den | diera<br>dieras<br>diera<br>diéramos<br>dierais<br>dieran | da (tú),<br>no des<br>dé (usted)<br>demos<br>dad (vosotros),<br>no deis<br>den (Uds.) |
| decir<br>diciendo<br>dicho | digo<br>dices<br>dice<br>decimos<br>decís<br>dicen | decía<br>decías<br>decía<br>decíamos<br>decíais<br>decían | dije<br>dijiste<br>dijo<br>dijimos<br>dijisteis<br>dijeron | diré<br>dirás<br>dirá<br>diremos<br>diréis<br>dirán | diría<br>dirías<br>diría<br>diríamos<br>diríais<br>dirían | diga<br>digas<br>diga<br>digamos<br>digáis<br>digan | dijera<br>dijeras<br>dijera<br>dijéramos<br>dijerais<br>dijeran | di (tú),<br>no digas<br>diga (usted)<br>digamos<br>decid (vosotros),<br>no digáis<br>digan (Uds.) |

# Irregular Verbs (continued)

| Infinitive / Present Participle / Past Participle | Indicative | | | | | Subjunctive | | Imperative |
|---|---|---|---|---|---|---|---|---|
| | Present | Imperfect | Preterit | Future | Conditional | Present | Imperfect | Commands |
| estar<br>estando<br>estado | estoy<br>estás<br>está<br>estamos<br>estáis<br>están | estaba<br>estabas<br>estaba<br>estábamos<br>estabais<br>estaban | estuve<br>estuviste<br>estuvo<br>estuvimos<br>estuvisteis<br>estuvieron | estaré<br>estarás<br>estará<br>estaremos<br>estaréis<br>estarán | estaría<br>estarías<br>estaría<br>estaríamos<br>estaríais<br>estarían | esté<br>estés<br>esté<br>estemos<br>estéis<br>estén | estuviera<br>estuvieras<br>estuviera<br>estuviéramos<br>estuvierais<br>estuvieran | está (tú),<br>no estés<br>esté (usted)<br>estemos<br>estad (vosotros),<br>no estéis<br>estén (Uds.) |
| haber<br>habiendo<br>habido | he<br>has<br>ha<br>hemos<br>habéis<br>han | había<br>habías<br>había<br>habíamos<br>habíais<br>habían | hube<br>hubiste<br>hubo<br>hubimos<br>hubisteis<br>hubieron | habré<br>habrás<br>habrá<br>habremos<br>habréis<br>habrán | habría<br>habrías<br>habría<br>habríamos<br>habríais<br>habrían | haya<br>hayas<br>haya<br>hayamos<br>hayáis<br>hayan | hubiera<br>hubieras<br>hubiera<br>hubiéramos<br>hubierais<br>hubieran | |
| hacer<br>haciendo<br>hecho | hago<br>haces<br>hace<br>hacemos<br>hacéis<br>hacen | hacía<br>hacías<br>hacía<br>hacíamos<br>hacíais<br>hacían | hice<br>hiciste<br>hizo<br>hicimos<br>hicisteis<br>hicieron | haré<br>harás<br>hará<br>haremos<br>haréis<br>harán | haría<br>harías<br>haría<br>haríamos<br>haríais<br>harían | haga<br>hagas<br>haga<br>hagamos<br>hagáis<br>hagan | hiciera<br>hicieras<br>hiciera<br>hiciéramos<br>hicierais<br>hicieran | haz (tú),<br>no hagas<br>haga (usted)<br>hagamos<br>haced (vosotros),<br>no hagáis<br>hagan (Uds.) |
| ir<br>yendo<br>ido | voy<br>vas<br>va<br>vamos<br>vais<br>van | iba<br>ibas<br>iba<br>íbamos<br>ibais<br>iban | fui<br>fuiste<br>fue<br>fuimos<br>fuisteis<br>fueron | iré<br>irás<br>irá<br>iremos<br>iréis<br>irán | iría<br>irías<br>iría<br>iríamos<br>iríais<br>irían | vaya<br>vayas<br>vaya<br>vayamos<br>vayáis<br>vayan | fuera<br>fueras<br>fuera<br>fuéramos<br>fuerais<br>fueran | ve (tú),<br>no vayas<br>vaya (usted)<br>vamos,<br>no vayamos<br>id (vosotros),<br>no vayáis<br>vayan (Uds.) |
| oír<br>oyendo<br>oído | oigo<br>oyes<br>oye<br>oímos<br>oís<br>oyen | oía<br>oías<br>oía<br>oíamos<br>oíais<br>oían | oí<br>oíste<br>oyó<br>oímos<br>oísteis<br>oyeron | oiré<br>oirás<br>oirá<br>oiremos<br>oiréis<br>oirán | oiría<br>oirías<br>oiría<br>oiríamos<br>oiríais<br>oirían | oiga<br>oigas<br>oiga<br>oigamos<br>oigáis<br>oigan | oyera<br>oyeras<br>oyera<br>oyéramos<br>oyerais<br>oyeran | oye (tú),<br>no oigas<br>oiga (usted)<br>oigamos<br>oíd (vosotros),<br>no oigáis<br>oigan (Uds.) |

# Irregular Verbs (continued)

| Infinitive / Present Participle / Past Participle | Indicative | | | | | Subjunctive | | Imperative |
|---|---|---|---|---|---|---|---|---|
| | Present | Imperfect | Preterit | Future | Conditional | Present | Imperfect | Commands |
| poder / pudiendo / podido | puedo / puedes / puede / podemos / podéis / pueden | podía / podías / podía / podíamos / podíais / podían | pude / pudiste / pudo / pudimos / pudisteis / pudieron | podré / podrás / podrá / podremos / podréis / podrán | podría / podrías / podría / podríamos / podríais / podrían | pueda / puedas / pueda / podamos / podáis / puedan | pudiera / pudieras / pudiera / pudiéramos / pudierais / pudieran | |
| poner / poniendo / puesto | pongo / pones / pone / ponemos / ponéis / ponen | ponía / ponías / ponía / poníamos / poníais / ponían | puse / pusiste / puso / pusimos / pusisteis / pusieron | pondré / pondrás / pondrá / pondremos / pondréis / pondrán | pondría / pondrías / pondría / pondríamos / pondríais / pondrían | ponga / pongas / ponga / pongamos / pongáis / pongan | pusiera / pusieras / pusiera / pusiéramos / pusierais / pusieran | pon (tú), no pongas, ponga (usted), pongamos, poned (vosotros), no pongáis, pongan (Uds.) |
| querer / queriendo / querido | quiero / quieres / quiere / queremos / queréis / quieren | quería / querías / quería / queríamos / queríais / querían | quise / quisiste / quiso / quisimos / quisisteis / quisieron | querré / querrás / querrá / querremos / querréis / querrán | querría / querrías / querría / querríamos / querríais / querrían | quiera / quieras / quiera / queramos / queráis / quieran | quisiera / quisieras / quisiera / quisiéramos / quisierais / quisieran | quiere (tú), no quieras, quiera (usted), queramos, quered (vosotros), no queráis, quieran (Uds.) |
| saber / sabiendo / sabido | sé / sabes / sabe / sabemos / sabéis / saben | sabía / sabías / sabía / sabíamos / sabíais / sabían | supe / supiste / supo / supimos / supisteis / supieron | sabré / sabrás / sabrá / sabremos / sabréis / sabrán | sabría / sabrías / sabría / sabríamos / sabríais / sabrían | sepa / sepas / sepa / sepamos / sepáis / sepan | supiera / supieras / supiera / supiéramos / supierais / supieran | sabe (tú), no sepas, sepa (usted), sepamos, sabed (vosotros), no sepáis, sepan (Uds.) |
| salir / saliendo / salido | salgo / sales / sale / salimos / salís / salen | salía / salías / salía / salíamos / salíais / salían | salí / saliste / salió / salimos / salisteis / salieron | saldré / saldrás / saldrá / saldremos / saldréis / saldrán | saldría / saldrías / saldría / saldríamos / saldríais / saldrían | salga / salgas / salga / salgamos / salgáis / salgan | saliera / salieras / saliera / saliéramos / salierais / salieran | sal (tú), no salgas, salga (usted), salgamos, salid (vosotros), no salgáis, salgan (Uds.) |

# Irregular Verbs (continued)

| Infinitive / Present Participle / Past Participle | Indicative | | | | | Subjunctive | | Imperative |
|---|---|---|---|---|---|---|---|---|
| | Present | Imperfect | Preterit | Future | Conditional | Present | Imperfect | Commands |
| ser<br>siendo<br>sido | soy<br>eres<br>es<br>somos<br>sois<br>son | era<br>eras<br>era<br>éramos<br>erais<br>eran | fui<br>fuiste<br>fue<br>fuimos<br>fuisteis<br>fueron | seré<br>serás<br>será<br>seremos<br>seréis<br>serán | sería<br>serías<br>sería<br>seríamos<br>seríais<br>serían | sea<br>seas<br>sea<br>seamos<br>seáis<br>sean | fuera<br>fueras<br>fuera<br>fuéramos<br>fuerais<br>fueran | sé (tú),<br>no seas<br>sea (usted)<br>seamos<br>sed (vosotros),<br>no seáis<br>sean (Uds.) |
| tener<br>teniendo<br>tenido | tengo<br>tienes<br>tiene<br>tenemos<br>tenéis<br>tienen | tenía<br>tenías<br>tenía<br>teníamos<br>teníais<br>tenían | tuve<br>tuviste<br>tuvo<br>tuvimos<br>tuvisteis<br>tuvieron | tendré<br>tendrás<br>tendrá<br>tendremos<br>tendréis<br>tendrán | tendría<br>tendrías<br>tendría<br>tendríamos<br>tendríais<br>tendrían | tenga<br>tengas<br>tenga<br>tengamos<br>tengáis<br>tengan | tuviera<br>tuvieras<br>tuviera<br>tuviéramos<br>tuvierais<br>tuvieran | ten (tú),<br>no tengas<br>tenga (usted)<br>tengamos<br>tened (vosotros),<br>no tengáis<br>tengan (Uds.) |
| traer<br>trayendo<br>traído | traigo<br>traes<br>trae<br>traemos<br>traéis<br>traen | traía<br>traías<br>traía<br>traíamos<br>traíais<br>traían | traje<br>trajiste<br>trajo<br>trajimos<br>trajisteis<br>trajeron | traeré<br>traerás<br>traerá<br>traeremos<br>traeréis<br>traerán | traería<br>traerías<br>traería<br>traeríamos<br>traeríais<br>traerían | traiga<br>traigas<br>traiga<br>traigamos<br>traigáis<br>traigan | trajera<br>trajeras<br>trajera<br>trajéramos<br>trajerais<br>trajeran | trae (tú),<br>no traigas<br>traiga (usted)<br>traigamos<br>traed (vosotros),<br>no traigáis<br>traigan (Uds.) |
| venir<br>viniendo<br>venido | vengo<br>vienes<br>viene<br>venimos<br>venís<br>vienen | venía<br>venías<br>venía<br>veníamos<br>veníais<br>venían | vine<br>viniste<br>vino<br>vinimos<br>vinisteis<br>vinieron | vendré<br>vendrás<br>vendrá<br>vendremos<br>vendréis<br>vendrán | vendría<br>vendrías<br>vendría<br>vendríamos<br>vendríais<br>vendrían | venga<br>vengas<br>venga<br>vengamos<br>vengáis<br>vengan | viniera<br>vinieras<br>viniera<br>viniéramos<br>vinierais<br>vinieran | ven (tú),<br>no vengas<br>venga (usted)<br>vengamos<br>venid (vosotros),<br>no vengáis<br>vengan (Uds.) |
| ver<br>viendo<br>visto | veo<br>ves<br>ve<br>vemos<br>veis<br>ven | veía<br>veías<br>veía<br>veíamos<br>veíais<br>veían | vi<br>viste<br>vio<br>vimos<br>visteis<br>vieron | veré<br>verás<br>verá<br>veremos<br>veréis<br>verán | vería<br>verías<br>vería<br>veríamos<br>veríais<br>verían | vea<br>veas<br>vea<br>veamos<br>veáis<br>vean | viera<br>vieras<br>viera<br>viéramos<br>vierais<br>vieran | ve (tú),<br>no veas<br>vea (usted)<br>veamos<br>ved (vosotros),<br>no veáis<br>vean (Uds.) |

# Stem-Changing and Orthographic-Changing Verbs

| Infinitive / Present Participle / Past Participle | Indicative — Present | Imperfect | Preterit | Future | Conditional | Subjunctive — Present | Imperfect | Imperative — Commands |
|---|---|---|---|---|---|---|---|---|
| almorzar (z, c) almorzando almorzado | almuerzo almuerzas almuerza almorzamos almorzáis almuerzan | almorzaba almorzabas almorzaba almorzábamos almorzabais almorzaban | almorcé almorzaste almorzó almorzamos almorzasteis almorzaron | almorzaré almorzarás almorzará almorzaremos almorzaréis almorzarán | almorzaría almorzarías almorzaría almorzaríamos almorzaríais almorzarían | almuerce almuerces almuerce almorcemos almorcéis almuercen | almorzara almorzaras almorzara almorzáramos almorzarais almorzaran | almuerza (tú) no almuerces almuerce (usted) almorcemos almorzad (vosotros) no almorcéis almuercen (Uds.) |
| buscar (c, qu) buscando buscado | busco buscas busca buscamos buscáis buscan | buscaba buscabas buscaba buscábamos buscabais buscaban | busqué buscaste buscó buscamos buscasteis buscaron | buscaré buscarás buscará buscaremos buscaréis buscarán | buscaría buscarías buscaría buscaríamos buscaríais buscarían | busque busques busque busquemos busquéis busquen | buscara buscaras buscara buscáramos buscarais buscaran | busca (tú) no busques busque (usted) busquemos buscad (vosotros) no busquéis busquen (Uds.) |
| corregir (g, j) corrigiendo corregido | corrijo corriges corrige corregimos corregís corrigen | corregía corregías corregía corregíamos corregíais corregían | corregí corregiste corrigió corregimos corregisteis corrigieron | corregiré corregirás corregirá corregiremos corregiréis corregirán | corregiría corregirías corregiría corregiríamos corregiríais corregirían | corrija corrijas corrija corrijamos corrijáis corrijan | corrigiera corrigieras corrigiera corrigiéramos corrigierais corrigieran | corrige (tú) no corrijas corrija (usted) corrijamos corregid (vosotros) no corrijáis corrijan (Uds.) |
| dormir (ue, u) durmiendo dormido | duermo duermes duerme dormimos dormís duermen | dormía dormías dormía dormíamos dormíais dormían | dormí dormiste durmió dormimos dormisteis durmieron | dormiré dormirás dormirá dormiremos dormiréis dormirán | dormiría dormirías dormiría dormiríamos dormiríais dormirían | duerma duermas duerma durmamos durmáis duerman | durmiera durmieras durmiera durmiéramos durmierais durmieran | duerme (tú), no duermas duerma (usted) durmamos dormid (vosotros), no durmáis duerman (Uds.) |
| incluir (y) incluyendo incluido | incluyo incluyes incluye incluimos incluís incluyen | incluía incluías incluía incluíamos incluíais incluían | incluí incluiste incluyó incluimos incluisteis incluyeron | incluiré incluirás incluirá incluiremos incluiréis incluirán | incluiría incluirías incluiría incluiríamos incluiríais incluirían | incluya incluyas incluya incluyamos incluyáis incluyan | incluyera incluyeras incluyera incluyéramos incluyerais incluyeran | incluye (tú), no incluyas incluya (usted) incluyamos incluid (vosotros), no incluyáis incluyan (Uds.) |

# Stem-Changing and Orthographic-Changing Verbs (continued)

| Infinitive / Present Participle / Past Participle | Indicative | | | | | Subjunctive | | Imperative |
|---|---|---|---|---|---|---|---|---|
| | Present | Imperfect | Preterit | Future | Conditional | Present | Imperfect | Commands |
| llegar (g, gu) llegando llegado | llego llegas llega llegamos llegáis llegan | llegaba llegabas llegaba llegábamos llegabais llegaban | llegué llegaste llegó llegamos llegasteis llegaron | llegaré llegarás llegará llegaremos llegaréis llegarán | llegaría llegarías llegaría llegaríamos llegaríais llegarían | llegue llegues llegue lleguemos lleguéis lleguen | llegara llegaras llegara llegáramos llegarais llegaran | llega (tú), no llegues llegue (usted) lleguemos llegad (vosotros), no lleguéis lleguen (Uds.) |
| pedir (i, i) pidiendo pedido | pido pides pide pedimos pedís piden | pedía pedías pedía pedíamos pedíais pedían | pedí pediste pidió pedimos pedisteis pidieron | pediré pedirás pedirá pediremos pediréis pedirán | pediría pedirías pediría pediríamos pediríais pedirían | pida pidas pida pidamos pidáis pidan | pidiera pidieras pidiera pidiéramos pidierais pidieran | pide (tú), no pidas pida (usted) pidamos pedid (vosotros), no pidáis pidan (Uds.) |
| pensar (ie) pensando pensado | pienso piensas piensa pensamos pensáis piensan | pensaba pensabas pensaba pensábamos pensabais pensaban | pensé pensaste pensó pensamos pensasteis pensaron | pensaré pensarás pensará pensaremos pensaréis pensarán | pensaría pensarías pensaría pensaríamos pensaríais pensarían | piense pienses piense pensemos penséis piensen | pensara pensaras pensara pensáramos pensarais pensaran | piensa (tú), no pienses piense (usted) pensemos pensad (vosotros), no penséis piensen (Uds.) |
| producir (zc) produciendo producido | produzco produces produce producimos producís producen | producía producías producía producíamos producíais producían | produje produjiste produjo produjimos produjisteis produjeron | produciré producirás producirá produciremos produciréis producirán | produciría producirías produciría produciríamos produciríais producirían | produzca produzcas produzca produzcamos produzcáis produzcan | produjera produjeras produjera produjéramos produjerais produjeran | produce (tú), no produzcas produzca (usted) produzcamos pruducid (vosotros), no produzcáis produzcan (Uds.) |
| reír (i, i) riendo reído | río ríes ríe reímos reís ríen | reía reías reía reíamos reíais reían | reí reíste rio reímos reísteis rieron | reiré reirás reirá reiremos reiréis reirán | reiría reirías reiría reiríamos reiríais reirían | ría rías ría riamos riáis rían | riera rieras riera riéramos rierais rieran | ríe (tú), no rías ría (usted) riamos reíd (vosotros), no riáis rían (Uds.) |

## Stem-Changing and Orthographic-Changing Verbs (continued)

| Infinitive / Present Participle / Past Participle | Indicative | | | | | Subjunctive | | Imperative |
|---|---|---|---|---|---|---|---|---|
| | Present | Imperfect | Preterit | Future | Conditional | Present | Imperfect | Commands |
| seguir (i, i) (ga)<br>siguiendo<br>seguido | sigo<br>sigues<br>sigue<br>seguimos<br>seguís<br>siguen | seguía<br>seguías<br>seguía<br>seguíamos<br>seguíais<br>seguían | seguí<br>seguiste<br>siguió<br>seguimos<br>seguisteis<br>siguieron | seguiré<br>seguirás<br>seguirá<br>seguiremos<br>seguiréis<br>seguirán | seguiría<br>seguirías<br>seguiría<br>seguiríamos<br>seguiríais<br>seguirían | siga<br>sigas<br>siga<br>sigamos<br>sigáis<br>sigan | siguiera<br>siguieras<br>siguiera<br>siguiéramos<br>siguierais<br>siguieran | sigue (tú),<br>no sigas<br>siga (usted)<br>sigamos<br>seguid (vosotros),<br>no sigáis<br>sigan (Uds.) |
| sentir (ie, i)<br>sintiendo<br>sentido | siento<br>sientes<br>siente<br>sentimos<br>sentís<br>sienten | sentía<br>sentías<br>sentía<br>sentíamos<br>sentíais<br>sentían | sentí<br>sentiste<br>sintió<br>sentimos<br>sentisteis<br>sintieron | sentiré<br>sentirás<br>sentirá<br>sentiremos<br>sentiréis<br>sentirán | sentiría<br>sentirías<br>sentiría<br>sentiríamos<br>sentiríais<br>sentirían | sienta<br>sientas<br>sienta<br>sintamos<br>sintáis<br>sientan | sintiera<br>sintieras<br>sintiera<br>sintiéramos<br>sintierais<br>sintieran | siente (tú),<br>no sientas<br>sienta (usted)<br>sintamos<br>sentid (vosotros),<br>no sintáis<br>sientan (Uds.) |
| volver (ue)<br>volviendo<br>vuelto | vuelvo<br>vuelves<br>vuelve<br>volvemos<br>volvéis<br>vuelven | volvía<br>volvías<br>volvía<br>volvíamos<br>volvíais<br>volvían | volví<br>volviste<br>volvió<br>volvimos<br>volvisteis<br>volvieron | volveré<br>volverás<br>volverá<br>volveremos<br>volveréis<br>volverán | volvería<br>volverías<br>volvería<br>volveríamos<br>volveríais<br>volverían | vuelva<br>vuelvas<br>vuelva<br>volvamos<br>volváis<br>vuelvan | volviera<br>volvieras<br>volviera<br>volviéramos<br>volvierais<br>volvieran | vuelve (tú),<br>no vuelvas<br>vuelva (usted)<br>volvamos<br>volved (vosotros),<br>no volváis<br>vuelvan (Uds.) |

# Appendix 3

## Spanish to English Glossary

This vocabulary includes all words presented in the text, except for proper nouns spelled the same in English and Spanish, diminutives with a literal meaning, typical expressions of the Hispanic countries presented in the *Enfoque cultural*, and cardinal numbers (found on page 14). Other cognates and words easily recognized because of the context are not included either.

The number following each entry corresponds to the **capítulo** in which the word was first introduced. Numbers followed by "r" signal that the item was presented for recognition rather than as active vocabulary.

## A

a   *at, to* P
abajo   *below, under* 4r
el/la abogado/a   *lawyer* 9
abordar   *to board* 12r
abrazar(se) (c)   *to embrace* 13
el abrazo   *hug* 4r
el abrigo   *coat robe* 6
abril   *April* Pr
abrir   *to open* 12r
la abuela   *grandmother* 4
el abuelo   *grandfather* 4
abundar   *to abound* 13
aburrido/a   *bored* 6r; *boring* 1
acabar(se)   *to complete, to finish; to run out of* 9r
el acceso   *access* 15
el accesorio   *accessory* 5
el aceite   *oil* 10
la aceituna   *olive* 3r
el achiote   *paprika* 10r
acompañar   *to accompany* 8
aconsejable   *advisable* 11r
aconsejar   *to advise* 5r
el acontecimiento   *event* 13r
acostar(se) (ue)   *to put to bed; to go to bed* 4
la actividad   *activity* 1r
activo/a   *active* Pr
el actor/la actriz   *actor/actress* 9
actual   *present, current* 14
actualmente   *at the present time* 9
actuar   *to act* 13
la adaptación   *adjustment, adaptation* 14
adaptar   *to adapt* 11r

Adelante.   *Come in.* 5r
el adelanto   *advance* 15, 15r
adelgazar   *to lose weight* 10r
el ademán   *gesture* 15r
además   *besides* 11r
el aderezo   *salad dressing* 10
adinerado/a   *well-off* 8r
adiós   *good-bye* Pr
adivinar   *to guess* 6r
¿adónde?   *where (to)?* 3
adornado/a   *decorated* 8
la aduana   *customs* 12
la aerolínea/línea aérea el asiento   *airline seat* 12
el/la aeromozo   *flight attendant* 12r
el aeropuerto   *airport* 12
afeitar(se)   *to shave; to shave (oneself)* 4
el afiche   *poster* 4r
afirmar   *to affirm* 7r
afortunadamente   *fortunately* 4r
afuera   *outside* 4r
las afueras   *outskirts* 5
la agencia de viajes   *travel agency* 12
el/la agente de viajes   *travel agent* 12
agosto   *August* Pr
agradable   *agreeable* 11r; *nice* 2
agregar   *to add* 10
el/la agricultor/a   *farmer* 9
agrio/a   *sour* 10
el aguacate   *avocado* 10, 10r
agudo/a   *sharp, acute* 11r
el águila   *eagle* 14r
el/la ahijado/a   *godchild* 4
ahora   *now* 1
ahorrar   *to save* 6r
los ahorros   *savings* 9r

el aire acondicionado   *air conditioning* 5
el ají   *chile pepper* 10r
el ajo   *garlic* 10, 10r
al   *to the (contraction of a+el)* 3
la alacridad   *alacrity* 13r
al aire libre   *outdoors* 3
la alberca   *swimming pool* 5r
el albergue juvenil   *youth hostel* 13r
el alcalde   *mayor* 14r
la alcoba   *bedroom* 5r
al lado (de)   *next to* P
alegrarse (de)   *to be glad (about)* 11; *to be happy* 4r
alegre   *happy, glad* 2
alegremente   *happily* 4r
la alegría   *joy* 8
alemán/alemana   *German* 2
alérgico/a   *allergic* 11r
el alfiler   *pin* 15r
la alfombra   *carpet, rug* 5
al fondo   *at the back, in the rear* 13
la álgebra   *algebra* 11r
algo   *anything* 13r; *something* 1
alguien   *everyone* 13r; *someone* 13r
algún/alguno(s)/alguna(s)   *any* 13r; *any, some* Pr; *several* 13r
algunas veces   *sometimes* 13r
alguna vez   *ever* 13r; *sometime* 13r
aliviar   *to relieve* 12r
el alivio   *relief* 15r
allí   *there* 4r
el alma   *soul* 15r
el almacén   *department store; warehouse* 6
la almeja   *clam* 10r

**A24**

la almohada *pillow* 5

almorzar (ue) *to have lunch* 4

el almuerzo *lunch* 3, Pr

¿Aló? *Hello? (on the telephone)* 3r

el alojamiento *lodging* 11r, 12

el alquiler *rent* 5

alquilar *to rent* 3

alternativo/a *alternative* 1r

alto *loudly* Pr

alto/a *tall* 2

el/la alumno/a *student* 1

el ama/o de casa *housewife, homemaker* 9

amarillo/a *yellow* 2

ambicioso/a *ambitious* Pr

a menos que *unless* 14r

el/la amigo/a *friend* P

la amistad *friendship* 13, 13r

el amor *love* 13

amplio/a *ample* 14

añadir *to add* 10

el analfabetismo *illiteracy* 14

analfabeto/a *illiterate* 14

anaranjado/a *orange* 2

la anatomía *anatomy* 1r

ancho/a *wide* 6

andar *to go* 14r

el anillo *ring* 6

animado/a *lively* 8

el año *year* P

anoche *last night* 6r

el Año Nuevo *New Year's Day* 8r

el año pasado *last year* 6r

la ansiedad *anxiety* 12r

ante(a)noche *night before last* 6r

anteayer *day before yesterday* 6r

el antepasado *ancestor* 8

antes *before* 6r, 8

antes (de) que *before* 14r

el antibiótico *antibiotic* 11

antiguo/a *old* 1

antipático/a *unpleasant* 2

la antropología *anthropology* 1

el anuncio *ad, advertisement* 9

apagar *to extinguish, to turn off* 9

el apagón *blackout* 8r

el apartamento *apartment* 5

a petición *on demand* 5r

el apio *celery* 10r

la aplicación *application* 15r

apoyar *to support* 7r

aprender *to learn* 1

apropiado/a *appropriate* 6r

aprovechar *to take advantage* 7

el apunte *note* 1

aquel/aquella *that (over there)* 5r

el árbitro *umpire, referee* 7

el árbol *tree* 7

el arete *earring* 6

argentino/a *Argentinian* 2

el armario *cabinet* 5r; *closet, armoire* 5

el aro *earring* 6r

el arpa *harp* 13r

el/la arquitecto/a *architect* 9, 9r

la arquitectura *architecture* 1, 5

arrepentirse (ie) *to regret* 7r

arrogante *arrogant* Pr

el arroz *rice* 3

el arte *art* 1r

la artesanía *handicrafts* 6

el/la artesano/a *craftsman/woman* 9; *craftsperson* 9

los artes plásticas *plastic arts* 1r

el artículo de belleza *beauty item* 11

el/la artista *artist* 9r

asar *to roast* 10r

asegurar *to assure* 7r

el aserrín *sawdust* 8

el asiento *seat* 12

el asiento de pasillo *aisle seat* 12

el asiento de ventanilla *window seat* 12

asistir *to attend* 1

la aspiradora *vacuum cleaner* 5

el astronomía *astronomy* 1r

asumir *to assume* 12r

asustado/a *scared* 12r

atar *to bind* 13r

aterrizar (c) *to land* 15

el ático *attic* 5r

atlético/a *athletic* Pr

la atmósfera *atmosphere* 7

atractivo/a *attractive* Pr

atrás *back, behind, backwards* 6r

a través de *through* 13

atreverse *to dare* 7r

aun *event* 14r

aunque *although* 14r; *even if* 14r; *even though* 14r

el auto *car* 2

el autobús/bus *bus* 12

la autopista *freeway* 12

el autorretrato *self-portrait* 13

el/la auxiliar de vuelo *flight attendant* 12, 12r

avanzar *to advance* 15r

a veces *sometimes* 1r; *at times* 13r

la avenida *avenue* Pr

a la venta *for sale* 6r

averiguar *to find out* 5r

las aves *poultry, fowl* 10

el avión *plane* 12

ayer *yesterday* 6r

ayudar *to help* 5, 5r

la azafata *flight attendant* 12r

el azar *chance* 13r

el/la azúcar *sugar* 10

azul *blue* 2

# B

el bailarín/la bailarina *dancer* 13

bailar *to dance* 1

la bajada *slope* 7r

bajar *to download* 15

bajo/a *short (in stature)* 2

el balón *ball* 7r

el baloncesto/el básquetbol *basketball* 7

la bañadera *bathtub* 5r

la banana *banana, plantain* 10

el banano *banana, plantain* 10r

bañar(se) *to bathe; to take a bath* 4

el banco *bank* 9

el banco de peces *shoal; school of fish* 15

la banda ancha *broadband* 5r

la bandeja *tray* 10

la bañera *bathtub* 5, 5r

el baño *bathroom* 5

barato/a *inexpensive, cheap* 6

la barbacoa *barbecue pit; barbecue (event)* 5

el barco *ship/boat* 12

barrer *to sweep* 5

el barrio *neighborhood* 5

basar *to base* 13r

básicamente *basically* 4r

el básquetbol *basketball* 7

bastante *enough* Pr; *rather* P

la basura *garbage, trash* 5

la bata *robe* 6

el bate *bat* 7

el batido *milkshake, smoothie* 10r

batir *to beat* 10, 10r

el baúl *trunk* 12

el bautizo *baptism, christening* 4

beber *to drink* 1

la bebida *drink* 3

el béisbol *baseball* 7

las bellas artes *fine arts* 1r

beneficiar *to benefit* 6r

besar *to kiss* 11r

el beso  *kiss* 4r

la biblioteca  *library* 1; *library cafe, coffee shop cafeteria* 1

el/la bibliotecario/a  *librarian* 9, 9r

la biblioteca virtual  *virtual library* 15

la bicicleta  *bicycle* 3r

bien  *well* P

bienes raíces  *real estate* 5r

bien parecido  *good-looking* 2r

bilingüe  *bilingual* 2

el billete  *ticket (Spain)* 12r

la billetera  *wallet* 6

la bioquímica  *biochemistry* 1r

el bisonte  *bison* 13r

el bistec  *steak* 3

blando/a  *soft* 13

la blusa  *blouse* 6

blanco/a  *white* 2

la boca  *mouth* 11

la boda  *wedding* 3

la bodega  *wine cellar* 5

la bola  *bowling ball* 7r

el boleto  *ticket* 12r

el boliche  *bowling* 7r

el bolígrafo  *ballpoint pen* P

boliviano/a  *Bolivian* 2

el bolo  *bowling ball* 7r

la bolsa/el bolso  *purse* 6

el/la bombero/a  *firefighter* 9

bonito/a  *pretty* 2

el laboratorio  *laboratory* 1, Pr

el borrador  *eraser* P

el bosque  *forest* 15

el bosque tropical  *rain forest* 15

la bota  *boot* 6

la botella  *bottle* 10

el bowling  *bowling* 7r

el brazo  *arm* 6r, 11

la broma  *joke* 10r

brujo/a  *broke* 2r

el buceo  *snorkeling* 12r

buenas noches  *good evening* P

buenas tardes  *good afternoon* P

¡Buena suerte!  *Good luck!* 1

buen mozo  *good-looking guy* 2r

¡Bueno!  *Hello? (on the telephone)* 3r

bueno/a  *good* 1; *well (health); physically attractive* 6r

buenos días  *good morning* P

la bufanda  *scarf* 6, 6r

el burgués  *middle class* 13r

el bus  *bus (Puerto Rico, Cuba)* 12r

el buscador  *search engine* 15

buscar  *to look for* 1

la butaca  *armchair* 5, 7r

# C

el cabello  *hair* 11

la cabeza  *head* 6r, 11

la cabuya  *ammunition* 2r

cada  *each* 7

cada... horas  *every . . . hours* 11

la cadera  *hip* 11

caer  *to drop* 8r

caer bien  *to like* 6r

caer mal  *to dislike* 6r

caer(se)  *to fall* 11

café  *brown* 2r

el café  *cafe, coffee shop* 1; *coffee* 3

la cafetería  *cafeteria* 1

caigue  *lazy (Bolivia)* 13r

la caja  *box* 6r

la caja fuerte  *safe* 12

el/la cajero/a  *cashier* 9

el/la cajero/a  *cashier* 9r

el cajero automático  *ATM* 12

el calcetín  *sock* 6

el calcio  *calcium* 10r

la calculadora  *calculator* P

el cálculo  *calculus* 1r

callado/a  *quiet* 2

la calefacción  *heating* 5

el calendario  *calendar* Pr

el calentamiento  *warming* 15

la calidad  *quality* 6r, 13

caliente  *hot* 3

callarse  *to keep quiet* 14r

la calle  *street* 5, Pr

calmar  *to calm, alleviate* 11r

el calor  *heat* 5r

el calzado  *footwear* 6r

calzar  *to wear a shoe size* 6r

el calzoncillo  *boxer shorts* 6

la cama  *bed* 5

la cámara  *camera* 9r

el camarero/la camarera  *server, waiter/waitress* 3

el camarón  *shrimp* 10

cambiar  *to change, to exchange* 6

el cambio  *change* 4r, 14

el cambur  *banana, plantain* 10

caminar  *to walk* 1; *walk* 3r

el camino  *road; way* 8

el camión  *bus (Mexico)* 12r

la camioneta  *bus (Guatemala)* 9r

la camisa  *shirt* 6

la camisa de manga corta  *short-sleeved shirt* 6r

la camiseta  *T-shirt* 6

el camisón  *nightgown* 6

la campaña de publicidad  *publicity campaign* 15r

el campeonato  *championship* 7; *tournament* 7r

el campeón/la campeona  *champion* 7

el/la campesino/a  *peasant* 10

el campo  *countryside* 9

canadiense  *Canadian* 2

el canal  *channel* 7r

cancelar  *to cancel* 12

el cáncer  *cancer* 11

la canción  *song* 3

la canela  *cinnamon* 10r

el cangrejo  *crab* 10r

cansado/a  *tired* 2

cantar  *to sing* 3

la cantidad  *quantity* 9r

la capa de ozono  *ozone layer* 15

el capítan  *captain* 3r

la capitanía general  *administrative unit of the Spanish Empire* 3r

el capó  *hood* 12

la cápsula  *capsule* 15

la cara  *face* 4r, 11; *expression* 15r

el cargador de celular (del móvil)  *cell phone charger* 5r

cariños  *love (closing)* 3r

caritativo/a  *charitable* 13r

carmelita  *brown* 2r

el carnaval  *carnival* 8

la carne  *meat* 10

la carne de res  *beef/steak* 10

la carne molida/picada  *ground meat* 10

el carnet de conducir  *driver's license* 15r

caro/a  *expensive* 6, 6r

el/la carpintero/a  *carpenter* 9

la carrera  *major* 1r; *race* 7

la carreta  *cart, wagon* 8

la carretera  *highway* 12

el carro  *car* 2

la carroza  *float (in a parade)* 8

el cartero/la cartera  *mail carrier* 12

la casa  *house, home* 1

casado/a  *married* 2

la casa editorial  *editorial house* 13r

casar(se)  *to get married* 4

castaño/a  *brown* 2r

el catarro  *cold* 11

la cebolla  *onion* 10

la ceja *eyebrow* 11
la celebración *celebration* 3
celebrar *to celebrate* 3
el cementerio *cemetery* 8
la cena *dinner, supper* 3
cenar *to have dinner* 3
el centro *downtown, center* 5
el centro comercial *shopping center* 6
el centro de entrenamiento *training resort* 7r
el centro de salud *hospital* 11
el/la ceramista *potter* 9
cerca *near* 3r
cerca de *close to, near* 3
el cerdo *pork* 10
el cereal *cereal* 3
el cerebro *brain* 11
la cereza *cherry* 10
cerrar (ie) *to close* 4r
la certeza *certainty* 13r
la cerveza *beer* 1r, 3
el césped *lawn* 5
el cesto *wastebasket* P
el cesto/la cesta *basket, hoop* 7
el ceviche *dish of marinated raw fish* 3
las chanclas *flip-flops* 9r
la chancona *nerd (Peru)* 3r
chao *good-bye* Pr
la chaqueta *jacket* 6
chau *good-bye* Pr
el/la chef *chef* 9
el cheque *check* 9r
el/la chico/a *boy/girl* P
el chile *chile pepper* 10r
chileno/a *Chilean* 2
la chimenea *fireplace* 5
la chivita *bus* 1r; *bus (Colombia)* 12r
el choclo *corn* 10r
el/la chofer (chófer) *driver; chauffeur* 9
la chuleta *chop* 10
el chunche *thing (Costa Rica)* 12r
los churros *fried dough* 10
el ciclismo *cycling* 7
el/la ciclista *cyclist* 7, 7r
la ciencia *science* 1
las ciencias políticas *political science* 1
cien/ciento *hundred* 3r
el/la científico/a *scientist* 9, 9r
cierto/a *true* Pr
el cilantro *cilantro* 10r
el cine *cinema* 13r; *movies* 1r, 3

el/la cineasta *filmmaker* 13r
la cintura *waist* 11
el cinturón *belt* 6
el/la cirujano/a *surgeon* 11r
la cita *date* 6r
citar *to quote* 14r
la cita textual *quotation* 7r
la ciudad *city* 3
el ciudadano *citizen* 14r
clarear el día *dawn* 13r
¡claro! *of course!* 3
la clase turista *coach class* 12r; *tourist class* 12
el/la cliente/clienta *client* 6r, 9
climatizado/a *air-conditioned* 15
la clínica, el centro *clinic* 11
la clonación *cloning* 15
el clóset *closet* 5r
la cobija *blanket* 5r
el coche *car* 2
cocido/a *cooked* 3r
la cocina *kitchen* 5; *stove* 5r
la cocina fusión *fusion cuisine* 10r
cocinar *to cook* 5
el/la cocinero/a *cook* 5r
codiciado/a *sought after* 13r
el código *code* 15r
el codo *elbow* 11
el cognado *cognate* Pr
colapsar *to collapse* 9r
el colectivo *bus (Argentina)* 12r
el colesterol *cholesterol* 10r
colocar *to place* 5r
colombiano/a *Colombian* 2
los colores *colors* 2
el collar *necklace* 6
el comedor *dining room* 5, 5r
comenzar (ie) *to begin* 8
comer *to eat* 1
cómico/a *comic* Pr
la comida *food; meal; dinner, supper* 3
la comida chatarra *junk food* 10r
el comienzo *beginning* 7r, 8
el comino *cumin* 10r
¿cómo? *how/what?* 1r
la cómoda *dresser* 5
cómodo/a *comfortable* 9r
¿Cómo es? *What is he/she/it like?* P
¿Cómo está? *How are you (formal)?* P
¿Cómo estás? *How are you (informal)?* P

¡Cómo no! *Of course!* 9
¿Cómo se dice... ? *How do you say . . . ?* Pr
¿Cómo se escribe... ? *How do you spell . . . ?* Pr
¿Cómo se llama usted? *What's your name? (formal)* P
¿Cómo te llamas? *What's your name? (familiar)* P
¿Cómo te va? *How is it going?* 1
el/la compañero/a *partner, classmate* 1
la compañía de danza *dance company* 13
la compañía de teatro *theater company* 13
la compañía/empresa *company* 9
la comparsa *group dressed in similar costumes* 8
cómplice *complicit* 14r
el comportamiento *behavior* 9r
comprar *to buy* 1
comprender *to understand* 1
el compromiso *engagement* 8r
la computación *computer science* 1r
la computadora *computer* P
la computadora portátil *laptop* P
la comunicación *communication* 1r
comunicar *to communicate* 14r
comunicarse *to reach out to* 14r
con *with* 1
con cariño *affectionately* 4r
el concejo municipal *city council* 14r
la concha *shell* 8r
la conclusión *conclusion* 14r
la concordancia *agreement* 6r
el concurso *contest* 5r
el condimento *seasoning* 10
conducir *to drive* 15r
conectar *to connect* 15r
conectarse *to connect* 15
la conexión *connection* 12r
la confianza *trust* 14
el conflicto *conflict* 1r
congelar(se) *to freeze* 7
conmigo *with me* 7
conocer (zc) *to know* 3; *to meet* 13r
el conocimiento *knowledge* 15
con permiso *pardon me, excuse me* Pr
el/la consejero/a vocacional *career counselor* 9r
el consenso *consensus* 13r

la **conservación** *preservation* 15

**construir (y)** *to build* 15; *to construct* 12r

el **consultorio** *office (of doctor, dentist, etc.)* 9

**consumir** *to consume* 10r

la **contabilidad** *accounting* 1r

el/la **contable** *accountant* 9r

el/la **contador/a** *accountant* 9r

**con tal (de) que** *provided that* 14r

**contaminado/a** *polluted, contaminated* 7

**contar** *to count* 6r; *to tell* 7r

**contemporáneo/a** *contemporary* 1r

**contento/a** *happy, glad* 2

**contestar** *to answer* Pr

**contigo** *with you (familiar)* 7

**continuar** *to continue* 15r

**contraer** *to contract* 11r

**contrario/a** *opposing* 7, 7r

el **contraste** *contrast* 4r

el/la **contratista** *contractor* 9

**contribuir (y)** *to contribute* 15

**conversador/a** *talkative* 2

**conversar** *to talk, to converse* 1

la **copa** *(stemmed) glass* 10

la **Copa Mundial** *World Cup* 7r

el **corazón** *heart* 11, 11r

la **corbata** *tie* 6

el **cordero** *lamb* 10

el **coroto** *thing (Venezuela)* 6r

el **correo** *mail* 12

**correr** *to run* 1

la **correspondencia** *correspondence* 9r

la **corrida (de toros)** *bullfight* 8

**cortar** *to cut; to mow (lawn)* 5

la **cortina** *curtain* 5

**corto/a** *short (in length)* 2

la **cosa** *thing* 6

**cosechar** *to harvest* 9

**costarricense** *Costa Rican* 2

**costar (ue)** *to cost* 4

la **costilla** *rib* 10

la **costumbre** *custom* 8

**creativo/a** *creative* Pr

**creer** *to believe* 5

la **crema** *cream* 10

**claro** *of course* 4r

el **crucero** *cruise* 12

la **clase** *class* Pr

el **cuaderno** *notebook* P

la **cuadra** *city block* 12

el **cuadro** *picture, painting* 5

**¿cuál(es)?** *which?* 1r

**¿Cuál es la fecha?** *What is the date?* Pr

**cuando** *when* 14r

**¿cuándo?** *when?* 1r

**¿cuánto/a?** *how much?* 1r

**¿Cuánto cuesta?** *How much is it?* 1

**¿cuántos/as?** *how many?* 1r

el **cuarto** *bedroom* 5r; *room; bedroom* 5

el/la **cuate** *friend (Mexico)* 8r

**cubano/a** *Cuban* 2

**cubista** *cubist* 13

la **cuchara** *spoon* 10

la **cucharada** *spoonful* 10r

la **cucharita** *teaspoon* 10

el **cuello** *neck* 11

la **cuenca** *river basin* 15

la **cuenta corriente** *checking account* 9r

el **cuento** *story* 13

el **cuero** *leather* 6r

el **cuerpo** *body* 6r

el **cuidado** *care* 5r

**cuidadosamente** *carefully* 4r

**cuidar(se) (de)** *to take care of* 11

el **culantro** *cilantro* 10r

el **cumpleaños** *birthday* 3

**cumplir** *to fulfill* 7r

**curar** *to cure* 11

la **curiosidad** *curiosity* 12r

el **currículum** *résumé* 9

# D

**dañino/a** *harmful* 10r

la **danza** *dance* 13r

**dar** *to give, to hand* 6

**dar de comer** *to feed* 9r

**dar un paseo** *to take a walk* 8

los **datos** *data* 14

**de** *of, from* 2

**debajo (de)** *under* P

**deber** *should* 1

**debido a** *due to* 15

**débil** *weak* 2

**decepcionado/a** *disappointed* 6r

**decir (g, i)** *to say, to tell* 4

la **decisión** *decision* 13r

el **dedo** *finger* 11

**de estatura mediana** *average, medium (height)* 2

la **deforestación** *deforestation* 15

**de ida y vuelta** *round trip* 12

**dejar** *to leave* 9

**del** *of the (contraction of de + el)* 2

**delgado/a** *thin* 2

la **democracia** *democracy* 14

**de moda** *stylish* 6r

**de nada** *you're welcome* Pr

**denunciar** *to denounce* 13

el **departamento** *apartment* 5r

el **dependiente/la dependienta** *salesperson* 1

el **deporte** *sport* 7

el/la **deportista** *athlete* 7r

la **depresión** *depression* 1r

**deprimido/a** *depressed* 11

**¿de quién?** *whose?* 2

la **derecha** *right* 4

el **derecho** *right* 14

**derecho** *straight* 12r

**derretir** *to melt* 10r

**desamparado/a** *homeless* 14r

la **desaparición** *disappearence* 15

**desarmar** *to disassemble* 9r

**desarrollar(se)** *to develop* 8r

el **desarrollo** *development* 13

**desayunar** *to have breakfast* 4

el **desayuno** *breakfast* 3

**descansar** *to rest* 3

**descomponer(se)** *to break* 9r

**describir** *to describe* 6r

la **descripción** *description* 1

el **descubrimiento** *discovery* 15

**descuidado/a** *careless* 9r

**desde** *since* 13

**desear** *to desire* 5r; *to wish, to want* 2

**desechable** *disposable* 15r

el **desempleo** *unemployment* 14

el **desfile** *parade* 8

el **deshielo** *thaw, thawing* 15

**despacio** *slowly* Pr

la **despedida** *closing* 4r

**despedir (i)** *to fire* 9r

**despedir(se) (i)** *to say goodbye* 7r

**despegar (u)** *to take off (airplane)* 15

**despertar(se) (ie)** *to wake (someone up)* 4

la **despidida** *farewell* Pr

el **desplazamiento** *movement, displacement* 14

**después** *after, later* 3

**después (de) que** *after* 14r

**destacado/a** *outstanding* 13

**destacarse** *to stand out* 14

el **destino** *destination* 12r

la **desventaja** *disadvantage* 5

el detalle *detail* 12r
detener *to stop* 9r
detrás (de) *behind* P
devolver *to return* 6r, 15r
el día *day* P
diabético/a *diabetic* 11r
el Día del Amor y la Amistad
   *Valentine's Day* 8r
el Día de Acción de Gracias
   *Thanksgiving* 8r
el Día de la Independencia
   *Independence Day* 8r
el Día de la Independencia de México
   *Mexican Independence Day* 8r
el Día de las Brujas *Halloween* 8r
el Día de los Enamorados *Valentine's
   Day* 8r
el Día de los Muertos *Day of the
   Dead* 8r
el Día de la Madre *Mother's
   Day* 8r
el Día del Padre *Father's Day* 8r
el día feriado *legal holiday* 8
el día festivo *holiday* 8
dialogar *to talk* 14r
el diccionario *dictionary* 1
diciembre *December* Pr
dictatorial *dictatorial* 14
el diente *tooth* 10r, 11
el diente de ajo *clove of garlic* 10r
la dieta *diet* 3r
difícil *difficult* 1
difícilmente *difficultly* 4r
difundir *to spread, to disseminate* 15
difunto/a *dead* 8
¿Diga?, ¿Dígame? *Hello? (on the
   telephone)* 3r
digitalmente *digitally* 13r
dinámico/a *dynamic* Pr

la diversificación *diversification* 14
las diversiones *leisure activities* 3
divertido/a *fun, funny* 1r; *funny,
   amusing* 2
divertirse (ie, i) *to have a good
   time* 8
divorciado/a *divorced* 4
el lado *side* 4r
doblar *to turn* 12
doblar *to fold* 5, 5r
el documento adjunto *attached
   document* 15; *attachment* 15
el dólar *dollar* 3r
doler (ue) *to hurt, ache* 11
el dolor *pain* 11
doméstico/a *domestic* 5r
el domingo *Sunday* Pr
dominicano/a *Dominican* 2
dónde *where?* Pr
¿Dónde está... ? *Where is . . . ?* P
dorar *to brown* 10r
dormir(se) (ue) *to sleep; to fall
   asleep* 4
dormir (ue) la siesta *to take a nap* 4
el dormitorio *bedroom* 5r
el drama *drama* 1r
la droga *drug* 1r
la ducha *shower* 5
duchar(se) *to give a shower to;
   (to take a shower)* 4
la duda *doubt* 13r
dudoso/a *doubtful* 13r
el dulce *candy/sweets* 10
duplicar *to double* 10r
durante *during* 3; *for (time)* 3r
durar *to last* 7
el durazno *peach* 10r
el DVD *DVD; DVD player* P

…nía *economics* 1
…camente *economically* 5r
…no/a *Ecuadorian* 2
…o *building* 5
…fficient* 12r
…cia *efficiency* 14
…*efficient* Pr
…utivo/a *executive* 9
…io aeróbico *aerobic
   …ise* 11r

…*to produce* 9
…ón *election* 14r
…tricista *electrician* 9r
…doméstico *appliance* 5

elegante *elegant* Pr
elegir (i, i) *to choose, to
   elect* 14
ellos/ellas *they* 1
el elote *corn* 10r
el/la tenista *tennis player* 7
el embarque *departure* 12r
la emergencia *emergency* 9r
la emigración *emigration* 14
el/la emigrante *emigrant* 14
emigrar *to emigrate* 9
empezar (ie) *to begin, to start* 4
el/la empleado/a *employee* 9
en *in* P
en la actualidad *at the present
   time* 13
en busca de *in search of* 15
el encaje *lace* 13r
en cambio *on the other hand* 4r
encantado/a *pleased/nice to meet
   you* P
encantar *to delight, to
   love* 6
encargar *to order* 9r
encauzar *to channel* 7
encender (ie) *to turn on* 15
encerrar (ie) *to lock up* 8
encontrar (ue) *to find* 6
en contraste *in contraste* 4r
en cuanto *as soon as* 14r
la encuesta *Surveys/Polls* 14
la encuesta de opinión *opinion
   poll* 14r
la energía solar *solar
   energy* 15
enérgico/a *energetic* 14
enero *January* Pr
enfadarse *to get angry* 7
enfermarse *to become sick* 11
la enfermedad *illness* 11
el/la enfermero/a *nurse* 9
enfermo/a *sick* 11
enfocarse (qu) *to focus* 15
enfrente (de) *in front of* P
el enlace *link* 15
enojado/a *angry* 2
enojar(se) *to get angry* 7r
¿En qué puedo servirle(s)? *How may
   I help you?* 6
en realidad *in fact, really* 9
la ensalada *salad* 3
enseguida *immediately* 6
entender (ie) *to understand* 4
enterar *to find out* 7r
enterrar *to bury* 8r
entonces *then* 8

entrar (en)  *to go in, to enter* 6

entre  *between, among* P

entregar  *to deliver* 5r

el entrenador/la entrenadora  *coach* 7

el entrenamiento  *training* 7r

entretenerse  *to have fun* 5r

la entrevista  *interview* 9

entrevistar  *to interview* 7r

en vez de  *instead of* 14

enviar  *to send* 9

el equipaje  *luggage* 12

el equipo  *team; equipment* 7

el equipo deportivo  *sports equipment* 7

eres  *you are (familiar)* P

la ermita  *hermitage* 8r

es  *you are (formal), he/she is* P

la escala  *stopover* 12

la escalera  *stairs* 5

el escaparate  *store window* 6

la escena  *scene* 13

la escena retrospectiva  *flashback* 13r

escribir  *to write* 1, 6r, Pr

el escritorio  *desk* P

el escritor/la escritora  *writer* 13

escuchar  *to listen (to)* 1

la escuela  *school* 6r

el escultor/la escultora  *sculptor* 13

ese/a  *that (adjective)* P

el eslogan  *motto* 12r

eso  *that* 5r

los espaguetis  *spaghetti* 3

la espalda  *back* 11

el español  *Spanish* Pr

español/a  *Spanish* 2

la especialidad  *specialty* 9

el/la especialista  *specialist* 11r

las especias  *spices* 10

el espejo  *mirror* 5

el espejo retrovisor  *rearview mirror* 12

la esperanza de vida  *life expectancy* 14

esperar  *to wait for* 9

las espinacas  *spinach* 10

el espíritu  *spirit* 8r

la esposa  *wife* 4

el esposo  *husband* 4

el esquí  *skiing, ski* 7

esquiar  *to ski* 7

la esquina  *corner* 12, 12r

está  *he/she is, you are (formal)* P

está despejado  *it's clear* 7

el estadio  *stadium* 7r

la estadística  *statistics* 1

el estado de ánimo  *mood* 5r

Estados Unidos  *United States* 2r

estadounidense  *U.S. citizen* 2

esta noche  *tonight* 3r

está nublado  *it's cloudy* 7

estar  *to be* 1, Pr

estar de acuerdo  *to agree* 11r

estar de moda  *to be fashionable* 6

estar en forma  *to keep in shape* 7r

estás  *you are (familiar)* P

este/a  *this* 1

el estilo  *style* 5, 5r

Estimado/a  *Dear* 3r

esto  *this* 5r

el estómago  *stomach* 11

estornudar  *to sneeze* 11

estrecho/a  *narrow, tight* 6

la estrella  *star* 13

la estructura  *structure* 1r

el/la estudiante  *student* P

estudiar  *to study* 1

el estudio  *to show* 7r

estudioso/a  *studious* 1

la estufa  *stove* 5

estupendo/a  *fabulous* 3; *stupendous, marvelous* 10r

el evento  *event* 7

evidente  *evident* 12r

evitar  *to avoid* 10r

el examen  *test* 1

examinar  *to examine* 11

excelente  *excellent* 1

la excentricidad  *eccentricity* 15r

exigir  *to demand, exact, require* 14r

el éxito  *success* 10r, 13, Pr

la experiencia  *experience* 9

el experto  *expert* 7r

explicar  *to explain* 6r, 15r

exponer (g)  *to exhibit* 13

la exportación  *export* 14

la exposición  *exhibit* 12r

expresion  *expression* P

la extinción  *extinction* 15

extinguido/a  *extinct* 15r; *extinguished* 15

extrovertido/a  *extroverted* Pr

# F

fabuloso/a  *fabulous, great* 3

fácil  *easy* 1

fácilmente  *easily* 4r

facturar  *to check in (luggage)* 12

la facultad  *school, department* 1

la falda  *skirt* 6

falso/a  *false* Pr

la falta  *lack* 4r

la familia  *The family* 4

famoso/a  *famous* 10r

el/la farmacéutico/a  *pharmacist* 11

la farmacia  *pharmacy* 1r, 11

fascinar  *to fascinate, to be pleasing to* 6

favorito/a  *favorite* 1

febrero  *February* Pr

la fecha  *date* Pr

felicidades  *congratulations* 3

las felicitaciones  *congratulations* 11r

felicitar  *to congratulate* 11r

feo/a  *ugly* 2

el festival  *festival* 8

la festividad  *festivity; holiday* 8

la fibra  *fiber* 10r

la ficha  *note card* 7r

la fiebre  *fever* 11

la fiesta  *celebration* 8; *party* 3, 7r

la figura de autoridad  *authority figure* 6r

fijarse  *to check out* 3r; *to take note* 14r

¡Fíjate qué noticia!  *How about that!* 3r

la filología  *philology* 1r

la filosofía  *philosophy* 1r

finalmente  *finally, at last* 6r

el Fin de Año  *New Year's Eve* 8r

el fin de semana  *weekend* 1

firmar  *to sign* 9r

la física  *physics* Pr

la fisiología  *physiology* 1r

la flor  *flower* 2

fluir  *to flow* 10r

fomentar  *to encourage* 13r

el fondo  *background* 8r

el/la fontanero/a  *plumber* 9

la forma  *shape, form* 13

la foto(grafía)  *photo(graph)* 4

el fracaso  *failure* 13

fracturar(se)  *to fracture, to break* 11

francés/francesa  *French* 2

la frazada  *blanket* 5r

frecuentemente  *frequently* 4r

el fregadero  *kitchen sink* 5

freír (i)  *to fry* 10, 10r

la **frente**   *forehead* 11
la **fresa**   *strawberry* 10
el **frijol**   *bean* 3
el **frío**   *cold* 5r
**frío/a**   *cold* 3
**frito/a**   *fried* 3, 3r
la **fruta**   *fruit* 3, 10
el **fruto de pasión**   *passion fruit* 10r
la **fuente**   *bowl* 10r; *source* 15
**fuerte**   *strong* 2
**fumar**   *to smoke* 11
la **fundación**   *founding* 13
el **fútbol**   *soccer* 7
el **fútbol americano**   *football* 7r

## G

las **gafas**   *glasses* 13r
las **gafas de sol**   *sunglasses* 6r
la **galleta**   *cookie* 10
la **gamba**   *shrimp* 10
el **ganado**   *cattle* 10r
el **ganador**   *winner* 5r
**ganar**   *to win* 5r, 7
la **ganga**   *bargain* 6r
el **garaje**   *garage* 5
la **garganta**   *throat* 11
**gastar**   *to spend* 6
**gemelo/a**   *twin* 4, 4r
**generalmente**   *generally* 4r
**generoso/a**   *generous* Pr
**genéticamente**   *genetically* 15, 15r
la **gente**   *people* 8
la **geografía**   *geography* 1
el/la **gerente (de ventas)**   *(sales) manager* 9
el **gimnasio**   *gymnasium* 1
**globalizar**   *to globalize* 11r
la **gobernación**   *administrative unit of the Spanish Empire* 3r
el **gobernador**   *governor* 3r
**gobernar (ie)**   *to govern* 14
el **gobierno**   *government* 11
el **gol**   *goal* 7
el **golf**   *golf* 7
**golpear**   *to knock* 7r
**gordo/a**   *fat* 2
la **gorra**   *cap* 6, 6r
**grabar**   *to record* 13r
**gracias**   *thanks, thank you* Pr
**gracioso/a**   *funny* 15r
**gradualmente**   *gradually* 15r

**graduarse**   *to graduate* 14r
**gráfico/a**   *graphic* 15r
**grande**   *big* 1
la **grasa**   *fat* 10r
**grave**   *serious* 11; *seriously ill* 6r
la **gripe**   *flu* 11
**gris**   *gray* 2
el **grupo**   *group* 14r
la **guagua**   *bus (Puerto Rico, Cuba)* 12r
el **guajolote**   *turkey* 10r
el **guante**   *glove* 6
la **guantera**   *glove compartment* 12
**guapo/a**   *good-looking, handsome* 2
**guardar silencio**   *to keep silent* 14r
**guatemalteco/a**   *Guatemalan* 2
la **guía**   *guide* 6r
la **guitarra**   *guitar* 3, 8r
el/la **guitarrista**   *guitar player* 13
**gustar (le)**   *to be pleasing to, to like* 6; *to like* 2r

## H

la **habitación**   *bedroom, room* 5
la **habitación doble/sencilla**   *double/single room* 12
el/la **habitante**   *inhabitant* 14
**hablar**   *to speak* 1
**hace**   *ago* 4r; *since* 6r
**hace fresco**   *it's cool* 7
**hacer**   *to do, to make* 3r
**hacer cola**   *to stand in line* 12, 12r
**hacer la cama**   *to make the bed* 3
**hacerse**   *to become* 14r
**Hace sol.**   *It's sunny.* Pr
el **hacha**   *hachet* 13r
la **hambre**   *hunger* 5r
la **hamburguesa**   *hamburger* 3
la **harina**   *flour* 10
**hasta**   *including; until* 13
**Hasta luego.**   *See you later.* Pr
**Hasta mañana.**   *See you tomorrow.* Pr
**Hasta pronto.**   *See you soon.* Pr
**hasta que**   *until* 14r
**hay**   *there is, there are* P
el **hecho**   *fact* 6r
la **heladería**   *ice creamery* 6r
el **helado**   *ice cream* 3, 6r
**heredar**   *to inherit* 14r
el/la **herencia**   *inheritance* 14r

la **herida**   *wound* 11r
el/la **herido/a**   *injured person* 9r
**herido/a**   *wounded, injured* 9r
la **hermana**   *sister* 4
la **hermanastra**   *stepsister* 4
el **hermanastro**   *stepbrother* 4
el **hermano**   *brother* 4
el **herrero**   *blacksmith; ironworker* 9
**hervir (ie, i)**   *to boil* 10
el **hielo**   *ice* 7
la **hierba**   *herb* 10
el **higo**   *fig* 10r
la **hija**   *daughter* 4
el **hijo**   *son* 4
el **hijo único/ la hija única**   *only child* 4
**hinchar**   *to swell* 11r
la **hinchazón**   *swelling* 11r
la **hipótesis**   *hypothesis* 13r
**hispano/a**   *Hispanic* 2
la **historia**   *history* 1
**hola**   *hi, hello* P
el **hogar**   *home* 4r
la **hoja**   *leaf* 5
el **hombre**   *man* 3
el **hombre/la mujer de negocios**   *businessman/ woman* 9
el **hombro**   *shoulder* 11
**hondureño/a**   *Honduran* 2
la **honestidad**   *honesty* 14
la **hora**   *time; hour* Pr
el **horario**   *schedule* Pr
**hornear**   *to bake, to microwave* 10r
el **(horno) microondas**   *microwave (oven)* 5
**horrible**   *horrible* 15r
el **hospital**   *hospital* 11
el **hotel**   *hotel* 12
**hoy**   *today* P
**hoy en día**   *nowadays* 8
**Hoy es...**   *Today is . . .* Pr
el **hueso**   *bone* 11
el **huevo**   *egg* 3
las **humanidades**   *humanities* 1
**humano/a**   *human* 11

## I

la **idea**   *idea* 10r
**idealista**   *idealistic* Pr

la iglesia *church* 8
la igualdad *equality* 14
igualmente *likewise* P
imaginar *imagine* 3r
el imperfecto *imperfect* 6r
el impermeable *raincoat* 6
implementar *to implement* 14r
importante *important* Pr
imposible *impossible* 6r
la impresora *printer* 5r
impulsivo/a *impulsive* Pr
inapropiado/a *inappropriate* 6r
el incendio *fire* 9
increíble *incredible* 4r
independiente *independent* Pr
indicar *to indicate* 7r
la infancia *childhood* 6r
infantil *children's* 14
la infección *infection* 11
influir *to influence* 13r
la información *information* 7r
la informática *computer science* 1
la infraestructura *infrastructure* 15
el/la ingeniero/a *engineer* 9
el iniciado *apprentice* 13r
la inmigración *immigration* 14
el inodoro *toilet* 5
inolvidable *unforgettable* 13
el inspector *inspector* 12r
la instrucción *instruction* 14r
el instrumento *instrument* 3
inteligente *intelligent* Pr
el intercambio *exchange* 15
interesante *interesting* 1, Pr
interesar *to interest* 6
internacional *international* 7r
el/la intérprete *interpreter* 9; *performer, artist* 13
la intimidad *intimacy* 4r
introvertido/a *introverted* Pr
la inundación *flood* 15
la investigación *research* 7r
investigar *to study, research* 11r
el invierno *winter* 6r
la invitación *invitation* 3r, 8
invitar *to invite* 8
la inyección *injection* 11
el ipod *iPod* 5r
ir *to go* 3r, Pr
ir de compras *to go shopping* 6
ir de tapas *to go out for tapas* 1r

ir(se) *to go away, to leave* 7
la izquierda *left* 4

## J

el jabón *soap* 5
jamás *never* 13r; *(not) ever* 13r
el jamón *ham* 3
japonés/japonesa *Japanese* 2
el jardín *garden* 5
los jeans *jeans* 6
el jefe/la jefa *boss* 9
joven *young* 2, 8r
el/la joven *young man/woman* 3
la joya *piece of jewelry* 6
el/la joyero/a *jeweller* 9
jubilarse *to retire* 14r
el juego/partido *game* 7
el jueves *Thursday* Pr
el/la juez *judge* 9
el jugador/la jugadora *player* 7
jugar (ue) *to play (a game, sport)* 4
jugar (ue) a los bolos *to bowl* 7
el jugo *juice* 3
el juguete *toy* 5r, 6
julio *July* Pr
junio *June* Pr
la junta directiva *board of directors* 14r
juntos/as *together* 4
el juramento *oath* 13r

## L

ella *she* P
el labio *lip* 11
laboral *labor-related* 13r
la consola *game station* 5r
lácteo/a *dairy (product)* 10
el lago *lake* 7
lamentar *to be sorry* 11r
la lana *wool* 6r
la langosta *lobster* 10
lanzar *to throw* 7r
el lápiz *pencil* P
el lavabo *bathroom sink* 5
la lavadora *washer* 5
la lavandería *dry cleaner* 6r
lavar en seco *dry clean* 6r
la lección *lesson* 1r
la leche *milk* 3
la leche de coco *coconut milk* 10
la lechuga *lettuce* 3

la lectura *reading* Pr
leer *to read* 1, 7r, Pr
leer por encima *to skim* 15r
las legumbres *legumes* 10
lejano/a *distant* 14r
lejos (de) *far; (far from)* 3r, 5
la lengua *language* 1r; *tongue* 15r
lentamente *slowly* 4r
las lentejas *lentils* 10
los lentes de contacto *contact lenses* 2
levantar *to raise* Pr
levantar la mano *to raise one's hand* Pr
levantar(se) *to raise; to get up* 4
la librería *bookstore* 1
el libro *book* 1r, 6r, P
la licuadora *blender* 10r
ligero/a *lightweight* 15r
el limón *lemon* 10
el limpiaparabrisas *windshield wiper* 12
limpiar *to clean; to tidy up* 5
lindo/a *pretty, attractive* 2r
el lío *mess* 3r
la lista *list* 10r
listo/a *clever* 6r; *smart; ready* 2
la literatura *literature* 1, 13r
el living *living room* 5r
llamar *to call* 7r
la llanta *tire* 12
la llave *key* 12
la llegada *arrival* 12r
llegar *to arrive* 1
llenar *to fill (out)* 9
lleno/a *full* 12
llevar *to wear, to take* 6
llevarse bien *to get along well* 13r
llover (ue) *to rain* 7
la lluvia *rain* 7
la lluvia de ideas *brainstorming* 7r
loco/a *crazy* 11r
el/la locutor/a *radio announcer* 9
lógicamente *logically* 4r
lograr *to achieve* 4r
el logro *achievement* 4r
lo importante *the important thing* 9
Lo siento. *I'm sorry (to hear that).* Pr
lo siguiente *the following* 13r

los recursos   *resources* 15
**Lo vamos a pasar muy bien.**   *We are going to have a good time.* 3r
la lucha   *fight* 14
luchar   *to fight* 14r
el lucro   *non-profit* 14r
luego   *later* 3; *then* 4r
el lugar   *place* 1
el lujo   *luxury* 12r
el lunes   *Monday* Pr

## M

machacar   *to crush* 10r
la madera   *wood* 9
la madrastra   *stepmother* 4
la madre   *mother* 4
la madrina   *godmother* 4
magnífico/a   *great* 6
el maíz   *corn* 10
mal   *bad* P
la maleta   *suitcase* 12, 12r
el maletero   *trunk* 12
el maletín   *briefcase* 12r
malo/a   *bad* 1; *ill* 6r
la mamá   *mom* 4
la mañana   *morning* P, Pr
mañana   *tomorrow* P
mandar   *to send* 9
mandar saludos   *to say hello* 5r
el mandato   *command* 9r
manejar   *to drive* 12
la mano   *hand* 6r, 11, Pr
la manta   *blanket* 5, 5r
la manteca/la mantequilla   *butter* 10
el mantel   *tablecloth* 10
mantener (g, ie)   *to maintain* 8
mantenerse en contacto   *to stay in touch* 5r
la manzana   *apple* 10
la manzanilla   *chamomile* 11r
el mapa   *map* P
maquillar(se)   *to put makeup on (someone)*; 4
el mar   *sea* 3
el maracuyá   *passion fruit* 10
la maravilla   *marvel* 3r
maravilloso/a   *marvelous* 8
la marca   *brand* 7r
el marcador   *highlighter* 5r; *marker* P
la margarina   *margarine* 10
los mariscos   *shellfish* 10
marrón   *brown* 2, 2r
marroquí   *Moroccan* 2

el martes   *Tuesday* Pr
marzo   *March* Pr
más   *more* Pr
más o menos   *more or less* P
más tarde   *later* 3r; *much later* 4r
las matemáticas   *mathematics* Pr
el material   *material* 6r
mayo   *May* Pr
la mayonesa   *mayonnaise* 10
mayor   *old* 2
la mayoría   *majority* 14
el/la mecánico/a   *mechanic* 9r
el médano   *dune* 7r
el/la mediador   *mediator* 13r
la media hermana   *half-sister* 4
las medias   *stockings* 6r
la medicina   *medicine* 1, 11
el/la médico/a   *medical doctor* 9
la medida   *measure* 12r
el medio ambiente   *environment* 15
el medio hermano   *half-brother* 4
los medios de transporte   *means of transportation* 12
me gusta(n)   *I like* 2
Me gustaría...   *I would like . . .* 6
la mejilla   *cheek* 11
mejor   *better* 11r
mejorar   *to improve* 14
el melocotón   *peach* 10r
la melodía   *melody* 8, 13
el melón   *melon* 10
los menonitas   *Mennonites* 13r
el/la menor   *the youngest* 4
menos   *minus* Pr
el mensaje   *message* 14r, 15
mentir   *to lie* 11r
la mentira   *lie* 7r
el menú   *menu* 3r
el mercado   *market* 6
el mes   *month* P
la mesa   *table* 10, P
metal   *metal* 2r
meter   *to insert* 15
meter un gol   *to score a goal* 7
el metro   *subway* 12
el metro cuadrado   *square meter* 5r
mexicano/a   *Mexican* 2
mi amor   *my love (term of endearment)* 3r
mi cielo   *term of endearment* 3r
el micro   *bus (Chile)* 12r
el miedo   *fear* 5r
mientras   *while* 3, 8

el miércoles   *Wednesday* Pr
la migración   *migration* 14
migrar   *to migrate* 11r
mil   *thousand* 3r
mil gracias   *many thanks* 7r
el/la millionario/a   *millionaire* 15r
millón   *million* 3r
mirar   *to look (at)* 1
mi(s)   *my* P
mi vida   *my life (term of endearment)* 3r
la mochila   *backpack* P
moderno/a   *modern* 1r, Pr
módico/a   *moderate* 12r
molestar(le)   *to bother* 11
molido/a   *ground* 10
montar (en bicicleta)   *to ride (a bicycle)* 1
morado/a   *purple* 2
moreno/a   *brunette* 2
morir   *to die* 6r
la mortalidad   *mortality* 14
la mostaza   *mustard* 10
el mostrador   *counter* 12, 12r
mostrar (ue)   *to show* 6
el motor   *motor* 12
mover (ue)   *to move* 11r
muchas veces   *often* 1r
mucho   *much, a lot (adv.)* 2
mucho/a   *many (adj.)* 2
mucho gusto   *pleased/nice to meet you* P
mudarse   *to move* 5r
los muebles   *furniture* 5
muerto/a   *dead* 8; *dead (atmosphere); deceased* 6r
la mujer   *woman* 3
la mujer de negocios   *businesswoman* 9
la multa   *fine/ticket* 15r
mundial   *world, worldwide* 7
la muñeca   *wrist* 11
el mural   *mural* 13
el/la muralista   *muralist* 1r, 13
el músculo   *muscle* 11
el museo   *museum* 12r
la música   *music* 1r, 3; *Music* 8
muy   *very* P

## N

el nacimiento   *birth* 7r
nacional   *national* 7r
las nacionalidades   *Nationalities* 2

nada  *nothing* 13r
nadar  *to swim* 3
nadie  *nobody, no
   one* 13r
la naranja  *orange* 3
naranja  *orange (color)* 2r
la nariz  *nose* 11
natal  *native* 10r
la naturaleza  *nature* 15
la nave  *ship* 15r
la Navidad  *Christmas* 8r
necesario/a  *necessary* 11r
el negocio  *business* 1r
negrita  *bold* 4r
negro/a  *black* 2
el nervio  *nerve* 11
nervioso/a  *nervous* 2, Pr
nevar (ie)  *to snow* 7
la nevera  *refrigerator* 5r
ni... ni  *neither . . . nor* 13r
nicaragüense  *Nicaraguan* 2
la nieta  *granddaughter* 4
el nieto  *grandson* 4
la nieve  *snow* 6r, 7
nigeriano/a  *Nigerian* 2
ningún/ninguno/ninguna  *no; no one;
   not any* 13r
el niño/a  *child* 4
el nivel  *level* 14
no  *no* Pr
la noche  *night* Pr
la Nochebuena  *Christmas
   Eve* 8r
la Nochevieja  *New Year's
   Eve* 8r
No comprendo.  *I don't
   understand* Pr
¡No me digas!  *Really!* 4r
nominar  *to nominate* 13
no obstante  *however* 11r
normalmente  *normally* 4r
norteamericano/a  *North
   American* 1
No sé.  *I don't know* Pr
nosotros/nosotras  *we* 1
nostálgico  *nostalgic* 14r
la nota  *note* 1
la noticia  *news* 3r, 4
la novela  *novel* 13
el/la novelista  *novelist*
   13, 15r
la novia  *fiancée, girlfriend* 4
noviembre  *November* Pr
el novio  *fiancé,
   boyfriend* 4
nuevo/a  *new* 2

el número  *size* 6r
nunca  *never* 1r; *(not)
   ever* 13r

# O

o  *or* 13r
o... o  *either . . . or* 13r
el objeto  *object* 6r
la obra  *work* 13
el/la obrero/a  *worker,
   laborer* 9r
obtener  *to obtain* 10r
obvio/a  *obvious* 13r
el ocio  *free time* 11r
octubre  *October* Pr
la ocupación  *occupation* 9r
ocupado/a  *busy* 4
ocurrir  *to occur* 10r
odiar  *to hate* 8r
la oficina  *office* 1, Pr
ofrecer (zc)  *to offer* 9
el oído  *(inner) ear* 11
Oiga, por favor.  *Listen,
   please.* 1r
¡Oigo!  *Hello? (on the
   telephone)* 3r
oír  *to hear* 3r; *to listen* 1r
oír hablar  *to hear
   about* 7r
ojalá que...  *I/we hope
   that . . .* 11r
el ojo  *eye* 2
las Olimpiadas  *Olympics* 7r
olvidar  *to forget* 10r
el ómnibus  *bus (Peru)* 12r
la operación  *surgery* 11r
la opinión  *opinion* 14r
optimista  *optimistic* Pr
el ordenador  *computer* 1r
ordenar  *to clean* 5
la oreja  *ear* 6r; *(outer) ear* 11
la organización  *organization* 14r
organizar  *to organize* 7r
oro  *gold* 2r
la orquesta  *orchestra* 8
la oscuridad  *dark* 15r
oscuro/a  *dark* 2
el otoño  *fall, autumn* 6r
otra cosa  *something else* 6r
otra vez  *again* Pr
otro/a  *other* 4r; *other,
   another* 3
la oveja  *sheep* 10
el OVNI  *UFO* 15r
¡Oye!  *Listen!* 1r

# P

palabra  *word* P
el/la paciente  *patient* 11
paciente  *patient (adj.)* Pr
el padrastro  *stepfather* 4
el padre  *father* 4
los padres  *parents* 4
el padrino  *godfather* 4
pagar  *to pay (for)* 6
la página  *page* Pr
el país  *country, nation* 3
el paisaje  *landscape* 13
la palabra  *word* 6r
la palabra clave  *key
   word* 6r
el paladar  *palate* 13r
el palo  *golf club* 7
las palomitas de maíz  *popcorn* 10r
la palta  *avocado* 10r
el pan  *bread* 3
la panadería  *bakery* 6r
panameño/a  *Panamanian* 2
el pan dulce  *bun, small
   cake* 10
la pantalla  *screen* P
los pantalones  *pants* 6
los pantalones cortos  *shorts* 6
las pantimedias  *pantyhose* 6
el pan tostado  *toast* 3
el pañuelo  *handkerchief* 6
el papá  *dad* 4
la papa  *potato* 3
las papas fritas  *French
   Fries* 3
el penalti  *penalty* 7r
el pendiente  *earring* 6r
la pendiente  *slope* 7r
pensar de  *to think of/about
   (opinion)* 4r
pensar en  *to think of/about* 4r
pensar (ie)  *to plan to* 4; *to
   think* 4
el pepino  *cucumber* 10
pequeño/a  *small* 1
la pera  *pear* 10
perder (ie)  *to lose* 7
perderse (ie)  *to get lost* 12
la pérdida  *loss* 15
perdón  *pardon me, excuse
   me* Pr
el perejil  *parsley* 10r
perezoso/a  *lazy* 2
perfeccionista  *perfectionistic* Pr
perfectamente  *perfectly* 4r
perfecto/a  *perfect* 10r

el **periódico** *newspaper* 3; *periodical, newspaper* 1r
el/la **periodista** *journalist* 9, 9r
el **permiso de conducir** *driver's license* 15r
**pero** *but* 1
el **perro** *dog* 4, 11r
la **persona** *person* P
el **personaje principal** *main character* 13
la **perspectiva** *perspective* 11r
las **pertenencias** *belongings* 12r
**peruano/a** *Peruvian* 2
la **pesa** *weight* 10r
la **pesadilla** *nightmare* 12r
el **pescado** *fish* 3, 10
**pesimista** *pessimistic* Pr
la **pestaña** *eyelash* 11
el **petróleo** *petroleum* 15r
**picado/a** *chopped* 10r; *ground* 10
**picar** *to chop* 10r
**picar(se)** *to itch* 11r
el **pie** *foot* 2r, 5r, 11
la **piel** *skin* 10r
la **piel de gallina** *goosebumps* 15r
la **pierna** *leg* 2r, 6r, 11
el/la **piyama** *pajamas* 6
la **pileta** *swimming pool* 5r
el **pimentón** *paprika* 10r
la **pimienta** *pepper* 10
la **pimienta roja** *red pepper* 10r
el **pimiento (verde)** *(green) pepper* 10
la **piña** *pineapple* 10
el **pintor/la pintora** *painter* 13
la **pintura** *painting* 13
la **piscina** *swimming pool* 5, 5r
el **piso** *floor; apartment* 5
**pitar** *to whistle* 7
la **pizarra** *chalkboard* P
la **placa** *license plate* 12
el **placer** *pleasure* 7r
el **plan** *plan* 7r
el **planeta** *planet* 15
**plástico** *plastic* 2r
el **plátano** *banana, plantain* 10
el **plato** *plate, dish* 10
la **plaza** *city square* 13r
el/la **plomero/a** *plumber* 9
**planchar** *to iron* 5
la **planta baja** *first floor, ground floor* 5
la **población** *population* 14
**pobre** *poor* 2

la **pobreza** *poverty* 14
**poco** *few, little* 4r; *a little* 4r
**polaco/a** *Polish* 2
**poco a poco** *little by little* 4r
**poco después** *a little later* 4r
**poder (ue)** *to be able to, can* 4
el **poema** *poem* 13; *poema* 1r
la **poesía** *poetry* 13
el/la **poeta** *poet* 13
el/la **policía** *policeman/woman* 9
**políglota** *polyglot, multilingual* 14
el **pollo** *chicken* 3
el **pomelo** *grapefruit* 10
**poner** *to put* 3r
**poner la mesa** *to set the table* 3
**ponerse en marcha** *to go into effect* 15r
**ponerse (g)** *to become* 14r; *to put on (clothes)* 6r
**popular** *popular* Pr
la **popularidad** *popularity* 7r
**popularizar (c)** *to popularize* 13
**por** *by; for; along; through; in (time)* 3r
el **porcentaje** *percentage* 14
**por ciento** *percent* 3r
**por cierto** *by the way* 9
**por ejemplo** *for example* 3r
**por eso** *that is why* 3r
**por favor** *please* Pr
**por fin** *finally, at last* 3r, 15r
**por lo menos** *at least* 3r
**por la mañana** *in the morning* 3r
**por la noche** *in the evening* 3r
el **poroto** *bean* 10r
**por otro lado** *on the other hand* 4r
**porque** *because* 1r
**¿por qué?** *why?* 1r
**por supuesto** *of course* 3r
**por la tarde** *in the afternoon* 3r
**por teléfono** *by telephone* 3r
**portugués/portuguesa** *Portuguese* 2
**por último** *finally, at last* 4r
**por un lado** *on the one hand* 4r
**posible** *possible* 13r
la **posición** *position* P
**potente** *powerful* 15r
**practicar** *to practice* 1
**preceder** *to precede* 14
el **precio** *price* 6, 6r
**precioso/a** *beautiful* 6
**preferir (ie)** *to prefer* 4
la **pregunta** *question* Pr
**premiar** *to reward* 9r

el **premio** *award, prize* 13
**preocupar(se)** *to concern; to be concerned, worried* 11r
**preparar** *to prepare* 5
el **preparativo** *preparation* 8
la **presentación** *introduction* P
**presente** *here (present)* Pr
**presidencial** *presidential* 14r
el **presidente/la presidenta** *president* 14
**prestar** *to lend* 6r
el **pretérito** *preterit* 6r
**prever** *to foresee, to predict* 13r
la **primavera** *spring* 6r
la **primera clase** *first class* 12, 12r
**primero/a** *first* 4r
el **primo/a** *cousin* 4
la **prisa** *speed, haste* 5r
**probable** *probable* 13r
**probar** *to try* 10r
**probarse (ue)** *to try on* 6
el **problema** *problem* 1r, 13r
la **procesión** *procession* 8
**producir** *to produce* 15r
el **producto** *product* 10
el **profesor/la profesora** *professor, teacher* P
el **programa** *program* 1r
el **progreso** *progress* 14r
**prohibir** *to prohibit* 11r
el **promedio** *average* 8r, 14
**prometedor/a** *promising* 13
**promocionar** *to advertise* 6r
el **pronóstico del tiempo** *weather forecast* 7r
**propio/a** *own* 9
la **propuesta** *proposal* 7r
la **proteína** *protein* 10r
el **proveedor de comida** *caterer* 9r
el **proveedor de salud** *health care provider* 11
la **proximidad** *proximity* 14
**próximo/a** *next* 3r
la **(p)sicología** *psychology* 1, Pr
el/la **(p)sicólogo/a** *psychologist* 9
el/la **(p)siquiatra** *psychiatrist* 11r
el **plato** *dish, plate* 5
la **publicidad** *publicity* 6r
el **pueblo** *village* 5
la **puerta** *door* P
la **puerta (de salida)** *gate* 12
**puertorriqueño/a** *Puerto Rican* 2
el **puesto** *position* 9

**el pulmón** *lung* 11
**la pulsera** *bracelet* 6
**el punto culminante** *climax* 13r
**el punto de vista** *point of view* 11r
**el pupitre** *student desk* P
**la playa** *beach* 1
**la plaza** *plaza, square* 1

## Q

**¿qué?** *what?* 1r
**¡Qué bárbaro!** *Great!* 7r
**¡Qué bien/bueno!** *That's great!* 4r
**¡Qué casualidad!** *What a suprise/coincidence!* 1r
**quedar** *to arrange to meet* 8; *to fit; to be left over* 6
**¿Qué día es hoy?** *What day is it?* Pr
**¿Qué fecha es hoy?** *What is the date?* Pr
**¿Qué hay?** *Hello? (on the telephone)* 3r
**¿Qué hora es?** *What time is it?* Pr
**¡Qué increíble!** *How incredible!* 1r
**la queja** *complaint* 13r
**quejarse** *to complain* 7r
**¡Qué lástima!** *What a pity!* 1
**querer (ie)** *to want* 4
**querido/a** *dear* 3r
**Querido/a** *Dear* 3r
**el queso** *cheese* 3
**el queso crema** *cream cheese* 10
**¿Qué tal?** *What's up, What's new? (informal)* P
**¿Qué te/le(s) pasa?** *What's wrong (with you/them)?* 11
**¿Qué te parece?** *What do you think?* 3
**¿Qué tiempo hace?** *What is the weather like?* Pr
**¿Quién es... ?** *Who is . . . ?* P
**¿quién(es)?** *who?* 1r
**la quijada** *jawbone* 13r
**Quisiera...** *I would like . . .* 6
**quitar(se)** *to take away; to take off* 4

## R

**el radiador** *radiator* 12
**el/la radio** *radio* 5
**el/la radiólogo/a** *radiologist* 11r
**rallar** *to grate* 10r

**rápidamente** *quickly* 4r
**rápido/a** *fast* 3
**la raqueta** *racquet* 7
**el rasgo** *feature, trait* 12r
**la razón** *reason* 5r
**la realidad** *reality* 13r
**realizar (c)** *to carry out* 14
**realmente** *of course* 9; *in fact, really* 9; *really* 4r
**reaparecer** *to reappear* 11r
**la rebaja** *sale* 6
**rebajado/a** *marked down* 6
**la recámara** *bedroom* 5r
**la recepción** *front desk* 12
**la receta** *prescription* 11; *receipt* 10r; *recipe* 10
**recetar** *to prescribe* 11
**recibir** *to receive* 14r
**reciclado/a** *recycled* 15
**reclamar** *to claim* 12r
**recoger (j)** *to pick up* 5
**la recomendación** *recommendation* 15r
**recomendar (ie)** *to recommend* 10
**recopilar** *to compile* 14r
**recordar(se) (ue)** *to remember* 4r, 8
**recorrer** *to cover, to travel* 12; *to travel, to cover (distance)* 7
**el recuerdo** *memory* 13; *souvenir* 6r
**la red** *net* 7; *network* 5r
**reducir** *to reduce* 11r
**reflejar** *to reflect* 5r, 13
**el refrán** *proverb* 12r
**el refresco** *soda; soft drink* 3
**el refrigerador** *refrigerator* 5, 5r
**regalar** *to give (a present)* 6
**el regalo** *gift* 3r; *present* 6
**regar (ie)** *to water* 5
**regatear** *to haggle* 6r
**el régimen** *regime* 14
**la región** *region* 15r
**regular** *fair* Pr
**regularmente** *regularly* 4r
**reír (i)** *to laugh* 7r
**religioso/a** *religious* Pr
**el relleno** *filling* 10r
**relleno/a** *filled* 3r
**el reloj** *clock* P
**el remedio** *remedy, medicine* 11
**el renacimiento** *rebirth* 8r
**el rendimiento** *performance* 9r
**repetir (i)** *to repeat* 4r
**repoblar** *to reforest* 15; *to repopulate* 15r
**el reproductor de CDs** *CD player* 5r

**el reproductor de DVDs** *DVD player* 5r
**la reputación** *reputation* 7r
**la reseña** *review* 13r
**la reserva natural** *nature preserve* 15
**reservar** *to make a reservation* 12
**respetar** *to respect* 13r
**respirar** *to breathe* 11
**responder** *to respond* 15r
**responsable** *responsible* Pr
**el restaurante** *restaurant* 1r
**el resultado** *the result* 7r
**resumir** *to summarize* 4r
**relativamente** *relatively* 4r
**el reto** *challenge* 15
**retornar** *to return* 11r
**retratar** *to portray* 13
**la reunión** *meeting, gathering* 3
**reunirse** *to get together, to meet* 8
**revisar** *to inspect* 12
**la revista** *magazine* 3
**la revista de corazón** *gossip magazine* 13
**el rey/la reina** *king/queen* 8
**largo/a** *long* 2
**el riachuelo** *creek* 4r
**rico/a** *delicious (food)* 6r; *rich, wealthy* 2, 6r
**el riel** *rail* 15, 15r
**la risa** *laughter* 12r
**el robo** *robbery* 10r
**el robot** *robot* 15
**rociar** *to spray* 8r
**el rocoto** *pepper* 3r
**rodear** *to surround* 13
**la rodilla** *knee* 11
**rojo/a** *red* 2
**romántico/a** *romantic* Pr
**romper** *to break* 15r; *to tear* 15r
**la ropa** *clothes* 6
**la ropa de estar en casa** *loungewear* 6r
**la ropa deportiva** *sportswear* 6r
**la ropa formal** *formalwear* 6r
**la ropa informal** *casualwear* 6r
**la ropa interior** *underwear* 6, 6r
**rosa** *pink* 2
**rosado/a** *pink* 2
**el rotulador** *marker* P
**rubio/a** *blond* 2
**la ruda** *rue (herb)* 11r
**la rueda** *wheel* 12
**el ruido** *noise* 5r, 8

las ruinas *ruins* 5
la rutina *routine* 3r

# S

la sala *living room* 5, 5r
el sábado *Saturday* Pr
la sábana *sheet* 5
saber *to know* 3r, Pr
sacar *to take out* 5
sacar buenas/malas notas *to get good/bad grades* 1
el saco *blazer, jacket* 6
la sala de espera *waiting area* 12r
la sal *salt* 10
la salida *departure* 12r
la salida de emergencia *emergency exit* 12
la salida del sol *sunrise* 13r
salir *to go out* 3r
el salón *living room* 5r
el salón de clase *classroom* P
la salsa con queso *nacho cheese sauce* 10r
la salsa de tomate *tomato sauce* 10
saltear *to sauté* 10r
la salud *Health* 11
saludable *healthy* 10r
el saludo *greeting* 1
salvadoreño/a *Salvadorian* 2
la sandalia *sandal* 6
el sándwich *sandwich* 1r, 3
el sanatorio *hospital* 11r
las compras *shopping* 6
la secadora *dryer* 5
secar(se) *to dry (oneself)* 4
la sed *thirst* 5r
sedentario/a *sedentary* 11r
seguir (i) *to follow, to go on* 4
seguir (i) derecho *to go straight* 12
según *as* 14r; *according to* 14r
seguramente *surely, certainly* 4r
la seguridad *security* 13r
seguro/a *certain* 13r
la semana *week* P, Pr
la semilla *seed* 8
el seminario *seminar* 1r
la señal *signal* 9
el senderista *hiker* 4r
la señora (Sra.) *Ms., Mrs.* P
la señorita (Srta.) *Ms, Miss* P
el señor (Sr.) *Mr.* P

sentarse (ie) *to sit down* 4
sentimental *sentimental* Pr
sentir(se) (ie, i) *to be sorry* 11r; *to feel* 4, 11
septiembre *September* Pr
ser *to be* 2, Pr
serio/a *serious* 11, Pr
la servilleta *napkin* 10
servir (i) *to serve* 4
si *if* 3
sí *yes* P
siempre *always* 1r
sigilosamente *discreetly* 13r
el significado *meaning* 4r
siguiente *following* 14r
la silla *chair* P
el silencio *silence* 14r
silvestre *wild* 10r
el símbolo *symbol* 13
simpático/a *friendly* 14r; *nice, charming* 2
simplemente *simply* 4r
sin *without* 7r
sincero/a *sincere* Pr
sin embargo *nevertheless* 9, 9r
sin que *without* 14r
el síntoma *symptom* 11
las medias *stockings, socks* 6
sobre *on, above* P
sobrevivir *to survive* 9
la sobrina *niece* 4
el sobrino *nephew* 4
sobrio/a *sober* 14r
social *social* 1r
la sociedad *Society* 14
la sociología *sociology* 1
el sofá *sofa* 5
sofreír *to fry lightly* 10r
el sol *sun* Pr
solicitar *to apply (for)* 9
la solicitud *application* 9
sólo *only (adv.)* 1
soltero/a *single* 2
el sombrero *hat* 6, 6r
son *equals* Pr
sonar *to sound* 7r
la sopa *soup* 3
la sorpresa *surprise* 7r
sorprender *to surprise* 12r
el sostén *bra* 6
el sótano *basement* 5r
soy *I am* P
suave *soft* 8
subir *to get into* 15r; *to go up* 10r

subrayar *to underline* 4r
subvencionar *subsidize* 13r
la sucursal *branch (business)* 14
la sudadera *sweatshirt; jogging suit* 6
el sueldo *salary* 9
el sueño *dream* 5r; *sleep* 5r
la suerte *luck* 3r, 5r
el suéter *sweater* 6
sugerir *to suggest* 14r
el supermercado *supermarket* 6, 10r
surgir (j) *to emerge* 13
surrealista *surrealist* 13
su(s) *his/her/their* P
sustentar *to support* 12r
el susto *fear* 12r

# T

la talla *size (clothes)* 6
el taller *workshop* 9
el tamale *tamale* 3r
el tamaño *size* 6r
también *also, too* 1
tampoco *neither; not* 13r
tan pronto (como) *as soon as* 14r
tanto/a... como *as much . . . as* 8r
tapar *to cover* 10r
las tapas *tapas* 1r
la tarde *afternoon* Pr
tarde *late* 4
la tarea *chore, task* 5r; *homework* 1, Pr
la tarjeta de crédito *credit card* 6
la tarjeta de embarque *boarding pass* 12, 12r
la tarjeta magnética *key card* 12
la tarta *pie* 10r
la tasa *rate* 14
la tasa de cambio *exchange rate* 8r
la taza *cup* 10, 10r
la tela *fabric* 2r
el té *tea* 3
el teatro *theater* 8, 13r
el/la técnico/a *technician* 9
la tecnología *technology* 15
te gusta(n) *you (familiar) like* 2
el tejado *roof* 9r
el teléfono *telephone* 3
el teléfono celular/móvil *cell phone* 15r

la telenovela *soap opera* 11r
el televisor *television set* P
el tema *theme* 13
temer *to fear* 11
temprano *early* 4
tender (ie) *to hang (clothes)* 5
el tenedor *fork* 10
tener (g, ie) *to have* 4
tener... años *to be . . . old* 5r
tener calor *to be hot* 5r
tener cuidado *to be careful* 5r
tener dolor de... *to have a(n) . . . ache* 11
tener éxito *to be successful* 10r, 13
tener frío *to be cold* 5r
tener hambre *to be hungry* 5r
tener mala cara *to look terrible* 11
tener miedo *to be afraid* 5r
tener prisa *to be in a hurry, rush* 5r
tener que *to have to* 4r
tener razón *to be right, correct* 5r
tener sed *to be thirsty* 5r
tener sueño *to be sleepy* 5r
tener suerte *to be lucky* 5r
Tengo... años. *I am . . . years old.* 2
tengo/tienes *I have/you have* 1
el tenis *tennis* Pr
el/la tenista *tennis player* 7r
la tensión (arterial) *(blood) pressure* 11
la terapia *therapy* 13r
tercero/a *third* 5r
terminar *to finish* 14r
el termómetro *thermometer* 11
la terraza *deck* 9r; *terrace* 5
el terrorismo *terrorism* 14r
el testamento *will* 14r
la tía *aunt* 4
el tiempo *time; weather* Pr; *weather* 7
el tiempo libre *free time* 3
la tienda *store* 6
tiene *he/she has; you (formal) have* 2
la tierra *land, soil* 15
tímido/a *timid* Pr
la tina *bathtub* 5r
la tintorería *dry cleaner* 14r
el tío *uncle* 4
típico/a *typical* 3
titular(se) *to be called* 13
el título *motto* 12r; *title* 4r
la tiza *chalk* P
la toalla *towel* 5

el tobillo *ankle* 11
tocar (un instrumento) *to play (an instrument)* 3
todas las semanas *every week* 1r
todavía *still, yet* 10
todo *everything* 13r
todo/a *every* 1r
todos/as *all* 13r; *everybody* 2, 13r
todos los días *every day* 1r
todos los meses *every month* 1r
tomar *to take; to drink* 1
tomar apuntes/notas *to take notes* 1
tomar asiento *to take a seat* 9r
tomar el sol *sunbathe* 1r; *to sunbathe* 3
el tomate *tomato* 3
el tono *tone* 14r
tonto/a *silly, foolish* 2
torcer(se) (ue) *to twist* 11
el torneo *tournament* 7r
el toro *bull* 8
la toronja *grapefruit* 10
torpe *clumsy* 6r
la tos *cough* 11
toser *to cough* 11
tostar *to toast* 10r
la tostada *toast*
tóxico/a *toxic* 1r
trabajador/a *hardworking* 2
trabajar *to work* 1
el trabajo *work* 5, 9
el trabajo de campo *fieldwork* 13r
la tradición *tradition* 8
tradicional *traditional* Pr
tradicionalmente *traditionally* 4r
traducir (zc) *to translate* 7
traer *to bring* 3r
el tráfico *traffic* 15r
el tráfico de drogas *drug trafficking* 14
el traje *suit* 6
el traje de baño *bathing suit* 6
el traje de chaqueta *suit* 6
el traje pantalón *pantsuit* 6
tranquilo/a *tranquil* Pr
tranquilamente *tranquilly* 4r
transitar *to cross; to move back and forth* 12r
el tratamiento médico *medical treatment* 11
tratar *to treat* 11; *to be about* 13; *to try* 5r
el trayecto *route* 12
el tren *train* 12

triste *sad* 2, 14r
tropezarse *to stumble* 15r
tú *you (familiar)* P
tu(s) *your (familiar)* P
último/a *last* 8

# U

la uña de gata *cat's claw (herb)* 11r
una semana atrás *a week ago* 6r
una vez *once* 12, 13r
unificar (qu) *to unify* 15
la universidad *university* 1
un poco *a little* 4
un/una *a, an* P
urgente *urgent* 11r
uruguayo/a *Uruguayan* 2
usar *to use* 2
usted *you (formal)* P
ustedes *you (plural)* 1
útil *useful* P
la uva *grape* 10

# V

las vacaciones *vacation* 3
la vacante *opening* 9
vacío/a *empty* 12
la vainilla *vanilla* 10
valer *to be worth* 6
los vaqueros/jeans *jeans* 6
el vaso *glass* 10
Vaya. *Go.* Pr
la vecina *neighbor* 5r
el/la vecino/a *neighbor* 5r
el vegetal/la verdura *vegetable* 3
vegetariano/a *vegetarian* 12r
la velocidad *speed* 12
la vena *vein* 11
¡Ven/Anda, anímate! *Come on, cheer up!* 3r
el/la vendedor/a *salesperson,* 9; *seller* 6r
vender *to sell* 6, 6r
venezolano/a *Venezuelan* 2
venir (g, ie) *to come* 4
la venta *sale* 9r
la ventaja *advantage* 5
la ventana *window* 1r, P
la ventanilla *window* 12r
el ventilador *fan* 5
ver *to see* 1
el verano *summer* 6r
verbos *verbs* P

¿**verdad?** *right?* 1
**verdad** *true* 13r
**la verdad** *truth* 7r
**verde** *green; not ripe* 2
**la verdura** *vegetable* 10
**ver(se)** *to look, appear* 11r
**el vestido** *dress* 6
**el vestido de verano** *summer dress* 6r
**vestir(se) (i)** *to dress; to get dressed* 4
**el/la veterinario/a** *veterinarian* 9r
**viajar** *to travel* 12
**el viaje** *trips* 12
**el videojuego** *video game* 15, 15r
**el vidrio** *glass* 2r
**viejo/a** *old* 2, 8r
**el viento** *wind* 7
**el viernes** *Friday* Pr
**el vinagre** *vinegar* 10
**el vino** *wine* 3

**el virreinato** *administrative unit of the Spanish Empire* 3r
**virtualmente** *virtually* 15
**la viruela** *smallpox* 11r
**visitar** *to visit* 4
**la vista** *view* 5
**la vitamina** *vitamin* 11r
**la vivienda** *dwelling; apartment* 5r; *housing* 5
**vivir** *to live* 1
**vivo/a** *alive* 6r; *lively (personality)* 6r
**volador/a** *flying* 15, 15r
**el volante** *steering wheel* 12
**volar (ue)** *to fly* 12
**el vóleibol** *volleyball* 7
**el volibol** *volleyball* 7r
**volver (ue)** *to return* 4
**la voz** *voice* 13
**el vuelo** *flight* 12

# Y

**y** *and* P; *plus* Pr
**ya** *already* 10
**yo** *I* P
**el yogur** *yogurt* 10
**la yuca** *yucca* 3r

# Z

**la zanahoria** *carrot* 10
**las zapatillas de deporte** *tennis shoes* 6
**las zapatillas** *slippers* 6
**los zapatos** *shoes* 6
**los zapatos de tacón** *high-heeled shoe* 6
**el zarcillo** *earring* 6r
**la zona** *area* 5
**la zona peatonal** *pedestrian area* 10r

# Appendix 4

## English to Spanish Glossary

### A

a  un/una
a little later  poco después
a lot (of)  mucho/a (adj.); mucho (adv.)
to abound  abundar
above  sobre
access  el acceso
accessory  el accesorio
to accompany  acompañar
according to  según
accountant  el/la contador/a (contable)
accounting  la contabilidad
to ache  doler (ue)
to achieve  lograr
achievement  el logro
to act  actuar
active  activo/a
activity  la actividad
actor  el actor
actress  la actriz
ad, advertisement  el anuncio
to adapt  adaptar
adaptation  la adaptación
to add  agregar; añadir
to address  dirigirse
adjustment  la adaptación
advance  el adelanto
to advance  avanzar
advantage  la ventaja
to advertise  promocionar
advisable  aconsejable
to advise  aconsejar
aerobic exercise  el ejercicio aeróbico
affectionately  con cariño
to affirm  afirmar
after  después; después (de) que
afternoon  la tarde
again  otra vez
ago  hace
to agree  estar de acuerdo
agreeable  agradable
agreement  la concordancia
air-conditioned  climatizado/a
air conditioning  el aire acondicionado

airline  la aerolínea/línea aérea
airport  el aeropuerto
aisle seat  el asiento de pasillo
alacrity  la alacridad
algebra  la álgebra
alive  vivo/a
all  todos/as
allergic  alérgico/a
to alleviate  calmar
along  por
already  ya
also  también
alternative  alternativo/a
although  aunque
always  siempre
ambitious  ambicioso/a
ammunition  la cabuya
ample  amplio/a
amusing  divertido/a
anatomy  la anatomía
ancestor  el antepasado
and  y
angry  enojado/a
ankle  el tobillo
to answer  contestar
Antarctica  la Antártida
antes  before
antes (de) que  before
anthropology  la antropología
antibiotic  el antibiótico
anxiety  la ansiedad
any, some  algún/alguno/alguna
anything  algo
apartment  el apartamento; el departamento; el piso; la vivienda
to apologize  disculparse
apple  la manzana
appliance  el electrodoméstico
application  la aplicación; la solicitud
to apply (for)  solicitar
apprentice  el iniciado
appropriate  apropiado/a
April  abril
architect  el/la arquitecto/a
architecture  la arquitectura
area  la zona
Argentinian  argentino/a
to argue  discutir

arm  el brazo
armchair  la butaca
arrival  la llegada
to arrive  llegar
arrogant  arrogante
art  el arte
artist  el/la artista; el/la intérprete
as  según
as much . . . as  tanto ... como
as soon as  as en cuanto
to ask for  pedir (i)
to assist  ayudar
to assume  asumir
to assure  asegurar
astronomy  el astronomía
at  a
at times  a veces
athlete  el/la deportista
athletic  atlético/a
ATM  el cajero automático
atmosphere  la atmósfera
attached document  el documento adjunto
to attend  asistir
attic  el ático
attractive  atractivo/a; bonito/a; bueno/a; guapo/a; lindo/a
August  agosto
aunt  la tía
authority figure  la figura de autoridad
available  disponible
avenue  la avenida
average  el promedio
avocado  el aguacate; la palta
to avoid  evitar
award, prize  el premio

### B

back  al fondo, atrás; la espalda
background  el fondo
backpack  la mochila
backwards  atrás
bad  mal; malo/a
bakery  la panadería
ball  el balón/la pelota
ballpoint pen  el bolígrafo

**banana** el banano; el cambur; el plátano; la banana
**bank** el banco
**baptism, christening** el bautizo
**barbecue pit; barbecue (event)** la barbacoa
**bargain** la ganga
**to base** basar
**baseball** el béisbol
**basement** el sótano
**basically** básicamente
**basket (hoop)** el/la cesto/a
**basketball** el baloncesto/el básquetbol
**bat** el bate
**to bathe; to take a bath** bañar(se)
**bathing suit** el traje de baño
**bathroom** el baño
**bathroom sink** el lavabo
**bathtub** la bañera; la tina; la bañadera; la bañera
**to be** estar; ser
**to be able to, can** poder (ue)
**to be afraid** tener miedo
**to be called** titular(se)
**to be careful** tener cuidado
**to be cold** tener frío
**to be crazy (Cuba)** estar trocá
**to be fashionable** estar de moda
**to be glad (about)** alegrarse (de)
**to be happy** alegrarse
**to be hot** tener calor
**to be hungry** tener hambre
**to be in a hurry (Colombia)** estar de afán
**to be in a hurry, rush** tener prisa
**to be lucky** tener suerte
**to be . . . old** tener … años
**to be pleasing to, to like** gustar
**to be right, correct** tener razón
**to be sleepy** tener sueño
**to be sorry** lamentar; sentir(se) (ie, i)
**to be successful** tener éxito
**to be thirsty** tener sed
**to be worth** valer
**beach** la playa
**bead** la cuenta
**bean** el frijol; el poroto
**to beat** batir
**beautiful** precioso/a
**beauty item** el artículo de belleza
**beauty salon, barbershop** la peluquería
**because** porque
**to become** hacerse; poner(se)
**to become sick** enfermarse
**bed** la cama

**bedroom** el cuarto; el dormitorio; la habitación; la alcoba; la recámara
**beef/steak** la carne de res
**beer** la cerveza
**to begin** comenzar (ie)
**to begin, to start** empezar (ie)
**beginning** el comienzo
**behavior** el comportamiento
**behind** atrás; detrás (de)
**to believe** creer
**belongings** las pertenencias
**below** abajo
**belt** el cinturón
**to benefit** beneficiar
**besides** además
**better** mejor
**between, among** entre
**bicycle** la bicicleta
**big** grande
**bilingual** bilingüe
**to bind** atar
**biochemistry** la bioquímica
**birth** el nacimiento
**birthday** el cumpleaños
**bison** el bisonte
**black** negro/a
**blackout** el apagón
**blacksmith; ironworker** el herrero
**blanket** la manta; la cobija; la frazada
**blazer, jacket** el saco
**blender** la licuadora
**blond** rubio/a
**(blood) pressure** la tensión (arterial)
**blouse** la blusa
**blue** azul
**to board** abordar
**board of directors** la junta directiva
**boarding pass** la tarjeta de embarque;
**boat** el barco
**body** el cuerpo
**to boil** hervir (ie, i)
**bold** negrita
**Bolivian** boliviano/a
**bone** el hueso
**book** el libro
**bookstore** la librería
**boot** la bota
**bored** aburrido/a
**boring** aburrido/a
**boss** el jefe/la jefa
**to bother** molestar(le)
**bottle** la botella
**to bowl** jugar (ue) a los bolos
**bowl** la fuente
**bowling** el boliche; el bowling

**bowling ball** el bolo; la bola
**box** la caja
**boxer shorts** el calzoncillo
**boy** el chico
**boyfriend** el novio
**bra** el sostén
**bracelet** la pulsera
**brain** el cerebro
**brainstorming** la lluvia de ideas
**branch (business)** la sucursal
**brand** la marca
**bread** el pan
**to break** descomponer(se); fracturar(se); romper
**breakfast** el desayuno
**to breathe** respirar
**briefcase** el maletín
**to bring** traer
**broadband** la banda ancha
**broke** brujo/a
**brother** el hermano
**to brown** dorar
**brown** marrón
**brunette** moreno/a
**to build** construir (y)
**building** el edificio
**bull** el toro
**bullfight** la corrida (de toros)
**bumper** el parachoques
**bun, small cake** el pan dulce
**to bury** enterrar
**bus** el autobús, el bus
**business** el negocio
**businessman/woman** el hombre/la mujer de negocios
**busy** ocupado/a
**but** pero
**butter** la manteca/la mantequilla
**to buy** comprar
**by** por
**by telephone** por teléfono
**by the way** por cierto

# C

**cabinet** el armario
**cafe, coffee shop** el café
**cafeteria** la cafetería
**calcium** el calcio
**calculator** la calculadora
**calculus** el cálculo
**calendar** el calendario
**to call** llamar
**to calm, alleviate** calmar
**camera** la cámara
**Canadian** canadiense
**to cancel** cancelar

cancer   el cáncer
candy/sweets   el dulce
cap   la gorra
capsule   la cápsula
captain   el capítan
car   el auto; el carro; el coche
care   el cuidado
career counselor   el/la consejero/a
   vocacional
carefully   cuidadosamente
careless   descuidado/a
carnival   el carnaval
carpenter   el/la carpintero/a
carpet, rug   la alfombra
carrot   la zanahoria
to carry out   realizar (c)
cart, wagon   la carreta
cashier   el/la cajero/a
casualwear   la ropa informal
caterer   el/la proveedor/a de comida
cattle   el ganado
CD player   el reproductor de CDs
to celebrate   celebrar
celebration   la celebración; la fiesta
celery   el apio
cell phone   el teléfono celular; el
   teléfono móvil
cell phone charger   el cargador de
   celular; el cargador del móvil
cemetery   el cementerio
cereal   el cereal
certain   seguro/a
certainly   seguramente
certainty   la certeza
chair   la silla
chalk   la tiza
chalkboard   la pizarra
challenge   el reto
chamomile   la manzanilla
champion   el campeón/la campeona
championship   el campeonato
chance   el azar
to change   cambiar
change   el cambio
channel   el canal
charitable   caritativo/a
charming   simpático/a
chauffeur   el/la chofer (chófer)
cheap   barato/a
check   el cheque
to check in (luggage)   facturar
to check out   fijarse
checking account   la cuenta corriente
cheek   la mejilla
cheese   el queso
chef   el/la chef
cherry   la cereza

chest   el pecho
chicken   el pollo
chicken breast   la pechuga de pollo
child   el niño/ la niña
childhood   la infancia
children's   infantil
Chile   Chile
chile pepper   el ají; el chile
Chilean   chileno/a
cholesterol   el colesterol
to choose   elegir (i, i)
chop   la chuleta
to chop   picar
chopped   picado/a
chore   la tarea
Christmas   la Navidad
Christmas Eve   la Nochebuena
church   la iglesia
cilantro   el cilantro; el culantro
cinema   el cine
cinnamon   la canela
citizen   el ciudadano
city   la ciudad
city block   la cuadra
city council   el concejo municipal
city square   la plaza
to claim   reclamar
clam   la almeja
class   la clase
classmate   el/la compañero/a
classroom   el salón de clase
to clean   limpiar; ordenar
clever   listo/a
client   el/la cliente/clienta
climax   el punto culminante
clinic   la clínica, el centro
clock   el reloj
clone   la clonación
cloning   la clonación
to close   cerrar (ie)
close to, near   cerca de
closet   el armario; el clóset
closing   la despedida
clothes   la ropa
clove of garlic   el diente de ajo
clumsy   torpe
coach   el/la entrenador/a
coach class   la clase turista
coat   el abrigo
coconut milk   la leche de coco
code   el código
coffee   el café
cognate   el cognado
cold   el catarro; el frío; frío/a
to collapse   colapsar
Colombian   colombiano/a
colors   los colores

to comb (someone's hair)   peinar(se)
to come   venir (g, ie)
Come in.   Adelante.; Pase(n).
Come on, cheer up!   ¡Ven/Anda,
   anímate!
comfortable   cómodo/a
comic   cómico/a
command   el mandato
to communicate   comunicar
communication   la comunicación
company   la compañía/empresa
to compile   recopilar
to complain   quejarse
complaint   la queja
to complete, to finish; to run out of
   acabar(se)
complicit   cómplice
computer   la computadora; el
   ordenador
computer science   la informática; la
   computación
conclusion   la conclusión
conflict   el conflicto
to congratulate   felicitar
congratulations   las felicidades; las
   felicitaciones
to connect   conectar(se)
connection   la conexión
consensus   el consenso
to construct   construir
to consume   consumir
contact lenses   los lentes de
   contacto
contaminated   contaminado/a
contemporary   contemporáneo/a
contest   el concurso
to continue   continuar
to contract   contraer
contractor   el/la contratista
contrast   el contraste
to contribute   contribuir (y)
convenience store   la tienda de
   conveniencia
to converse   conversar
to cook   cocinar
cook   el/la cocinero/a
cooked   cocido/a
cookie   la galleta
corn   el choclo; el elote; el maíz
corner   la esquina
correspondence   la correspondencia
corridor, hall   el pasillo
to cost   costar (ue)
Costa Rican   costarricense
cough   la tos
to cough   toser
council   el concejo

**to count** contar
**counter** el mostrador
**country, nation** el país
**countryside** el campo
**cousin** el primo/la prima
**to cover** recorrer; tapar
**crab** el cangrejo
**craftsperson** el/la artesano/a
**crazy** loco/a
**cream** la crema
**cream cheese** el queso crema
**creative** creativo/a
**credit card** la tarjeta de crédito
**creek** el riachuelo
**to cross** cruzar; transitar
**cruise** el crucero
**to crush** machacar
**Cuban** cubano/a
**cubist** cubista
**cucumber** el pepino
**cumin** el comino
**cup** la taza
**to cure** curar
**curiosity** la curiosidad
**current** actual
**curtain** la cortina
**custom** la costumbre
**customs** la aduana
**to cut** cortar
**cycling** el ciclismo
**cyclist** el/la ciclista

## D

**dad** el papá
**dairy (product)** lácteo/a
**to dance** bailar
**dance** la danza
**dance club** la discoteca
**dance company** la compañía de
  danza
**dancer** el bailarín/la bailarina
**dangerous** peligroso/a
**to dare** atreverse
**dark** la oscuridad; oscuro/a
**data** los datos
**date** la fecha; la cita
**daughter** la hija
**dawn** clarear el día
**day** el día
**day after tomorrow** pasado mañana
**day before yesterday** anteayer
**Day of the Dead** el Día de los
  Muertos
**dead** difunto/a; muerto/a
**Dear** Estimado/a; Querido/a
**dear** querido/a

**December** diciembre
**decision** la decisión
**deck** la terraza
**decorated** adornado/a
**deforestation** la deforestación
**delicious** rico/a
**to delight** encantar
**to deliver** entregar
**to demand** exigir
**democracy** la democracia
**to denounce** denunciar
**department, school** la facultad
**department store** el almacén
**departure** la salida
**depressed** deprimido/a
**depression** la depresión
**to describe** describir
**description** a descripción
**design** el diseño
**designer** el diseñador
**to desire** desear
**desk** el escritorio
**destination** el destino
**detail** el detalle
**to develop** desarrollar(se)
**development** el desarrollo
**device** el dispositivo
**diabetic** diabético/a
**dictatorial** dictatorial
**dictionary** el diccionario
**to die** morir
**diet** la dieta
**difficult** difícil
**difficultly** dificilmente
**digitally** digitalmente
**dining room** el comedor
**dinner** la comida
**dinner, supper** la cena
**to direct** dirigir (j)
**disadvantage** la desventaja
**disappearence** la desaparición
**disappointed** decepcionado/a
**to disassemble** desarmar
**discovery** el descubrimiento
**discreetly** sigilosamente
**dish, plate** el plato
**dishwasher** el lavaplatos
**to dislike** caer mal
**dispersal, dissemination** la
  diseminación
**displacement** el desplazamiento
**disposable** desechable
**distant** lejano/a
**to distinguish** distinguir
**diversification** la diversificación
**divorced** divorciado/a
**to do** hacer

**dog** el perro
**dollar** el dólar
**domestic** doméstico/a
**Dominican** dominicano/a
**door** la puerta
**to double** duplicar
**double/single room** la habitación
  doble/sencilla
**doubt** la duda
**doubtful** dudoso/a
**to download** bajar
**downtown, center** el centro
**drama** el drama
**dream** el sueño
**dress** el vestido
**to dress; to get dressed** vestir(se) (i)
**dresser** la cómoda
**to drink** beber
**drink** la bebida
**to drink** tomar
**to drive** conducir; manejar
**driver** el/la chofer (chófer)
**driver's license** el carnet de conducir;
  el permiso de conducir
**to drop** caer
**drug** la droga
**drug trafficking** el tráfico de drogas
**dry clean** lavar en seco
**dry cleaner** la lavandería; la
  tintorería
**to dry (oneself)** secar(se)
**dryer** la secadora
**due to** debido a
**dune** el médano
**during** durante
**DVD** el DVD
**DVD player** el reproductor de DVDs
**dwelling** la vivienda
**dynamic** dinámico/a

## E

**each** cada
**eagle** el águila
**ear** el oído; la oreja; la oreja
**early** temprano
**earring** el arete
**easily** fácilmente
**Easter** la Pascua
**easy** fácil
**to eat** comer
**eccentricity** la excentricidad
**economically** económicamente
**economics** la economía
**Ecuadorian** ecuatoriano/a
**editorial house** la casa editorial
**efficiency** la eficiencia

**efficient** eficaz; eficiente
**egg** el huevo
**either . . . or** o . . . o
**elbow** el codo
**to elect** elegir (i, j)
**election** la elección
**electrician** el/la electricista
**elegant** elegante
**to embrace** abrazar(se) (c)
**to emerge** surgir (j)
**emergency** la emergencia
**emergency exit** la salida de emergencia
**emigrant** el/la emigrante
**to emigrate** emigrar
**emigration** la emigración
**employee** el/la empleado/a
**empty** vacío/a
**to encourage** fomentar
**energetic** enérgico/a
**engagement** el compromiso
**engineer** el/la ingeniero/a
**to enjoy** disfrutar
**enough** bastante
**to enter** entrar (en)
**entertainment** la diversión
**environment** el medio ambiente
**equality** la igualdad
**equals** son
**equipment** el equipo
**eraser** el borrador
**even if** aunque
**even though** aunque
**evening** por la noche
**event** el acontecimiento; aun; el evento
**ever** alguna vez
**every** todo/a
**every day** todos los días
**every . . . hours** cada ... horas
**every month** todos los meses
**every week** todas las semanas
**everybody** todos/as
**everyone** alguien
**everything** todo
**evident** evidente
**to exact** exigir
**to examine** examinar
**excellent** excelente
**to exchange** cambiar
**exchange** el intercambio
**exchange rate** la tasa de cambio
**excuse me** con permiso, perdón
**executive** el/la ejecutivo/a
**to exert effort** fajar(se)
**to exhibit** exponer (g)
**exhibit** la exposición

**expensive** caro/a
**experience** la experiencia
**expert** el experto
**to explain** explicar
**export** la exportación
**expression** la cara; expresion
**extinct** extinguido/a
**extinction** la extinción
**to extinguish, to turn off** apagar
**extinguished** extinguido/a
**extroverted** extrovertido/a
**eye** el ojo
**eyebrow** la ceja
**eyelash** la pestaña

# F

**fabric** la tela
**fabulous** fabuloso/a
**face** la cara
**fact** el hecho
**failure** el fracaso
**fair** regular
**to fall** caer(se)
**fall** el otoño
**false** falso/a
**family** la familia
**famous** famoso/a
**fan** el ventilador
**far (from)** lejos (de)
**farewell** la despedida
**farmer** el/la agricultor/a
**to fascinate** fascinar
**fast** rápido/a
**fat** gordo/a; la grasa
**father** el padre
**Father's Day** el Día del Padre
**favorite** favorito/a
**fear** el miedo; el susto
**to fear** temer
**feature, trait** el rasgo
**February** febrero
**to feed** dar de comer
**to feel** sentir (se) (ie)
**festival** el festival
**festivity; holiday** la festividad
**fever** la fiebre
**few** poco
**fiancé(e)** el/la novio/a
**fiber** la fibra
**fieldwork** el trabajo de campo
**fig** el higo
**fight** la lucha
**to fight** luchar
**to fill (out)** llenar
**filled** relleno/a
**filling** el relleno

**film** la película
**filmmaker** el/la cineasta
**finally, at last** finalmente; por fin; por último
**to find** encontrar (ue)
**to find out** averiguar; enterar(se)
**fine arts** las bellas artes
**fine/ticket** la multa
**finger** el dedo
**to finish** terminar
**to fire** despedir (i)
**fire** el incendio
**firefighter** el/la bombero/a
**fireplace** la chimenea
**first** primero/a
**first class** la primera clase
**first floor** la planta baja
**fish** el pescado
**flashback** la escena retrospectiva
**flight** el vuelo
**flight attendant** el/la auxiliar de vuelo; el/la aeromozo/a; la azafata
**flip-flops** las chanclas
**float (in a parade)** la carroza
**flood** la inundación
**floor** el piso; la planta
**flour** la harina
**to flow** fluir
**flower** la flor
**flu** la gripe
**to fly** volar (ue)
**flying** volador/a
**to focus** enfocarse (qu)
**to fold** doblar
**to follow** seguir (i)
**following** siguiente
**food** la comida
**foot** el pie
**football** el fútbol americano
**footwear** el calzado
**for** durante (time); para; por
**for example** por ejemplo
**for sale** a la venta
**forehead** la frente
**to foresee** prever
**forest** el bosque
**to forget** olvidar
**fork** el tenedor
**form** la forma
**formalwear** la ropa formal
**fortunately** afortunadamente
**to fracture** fracturar(se)
**free time** el ocio; el tiempo libre
**freeway** la autopista
**to freeze** congelar(se)
**French** francés/francesa

**French fries** las papas fritas
**frequently** frecuentemente
**Friday** el viernes
**fried** frito/a
**fried dough** los churros
**friend** el/la amigo/a
**friendly** simpático/a
**friendship** la amistad
**from** de
**front desk** la recepción
**fruit** la fruta
**to fry** freír (i)
**to fry lightly** sofreír
**to fulfill** cumplir
**full** lleno/a
**fun** divertido/a
**funny** divertido/a; gracioso/a
**furniture** los muebles
**furrier** el/la peletero/a
**fusion cuisine** la cocina fusión

# G

**game** el juego; el partido
**game station** la consola
**garage** el garaje
**garbage** la basura
**garden** el jardín
**garlic** el ajo
**gas station** la tienda de gasolina
**gate** la puerta (de salida)
**generally** generalmente
**generous** generoso/a
**genetically** genéticamente
**geography** la geografía
**German** alemán/alemana
**gesture** el ademán
**to get along well** llevarse bien
**to get angry** enfadarse; enojar(se)
**to get good/bad grades** sacar
   buenas/malas notas
**to get into** subir
**to get lost** perderse (ie)
**to get married** casar(se)
**to get together** reunirse
**to get up** levantar
**gift** el regalo
**girl** la chica; la chica
**girlfriend** la novia
**to give** dar
**to give (a present)** regalar
**glad** alegre; contento/a
**glass** la copa; el vaso; el vidrio
**glasses** las gafas
**to globalize** globalizar
**glove** el guante
**glove compartment** la guantera
**to go** andar; ir

**Go.** Vaya.
**to go away** ir(se)
**to go in** entrar (en)
**to go into effect** ponerse en marcha
**to go out** salir
**to go shopping** ir de compras
**to go straight** seguir (i) derecho
**to go to bed** acostarse
**to go up** subir
**goal** el gol
**godchild** el/la ahijado/a
**godfather** el padrino
**godmother** la madrina
**gold** oro
**golf** el golf
**golf club** el palo
**good** bueno/a
**good afternoon** buenas tardes
**good-bye** adiós; chao; chau
**good evening** buenas noches
**good-looking** bien parecido
**good-looking** guapo/a
**Good luck!** ¡Buena suerte!
**good morning** buenos días
**goosebumps** la piel de gallina
**gossip magazine** la revista de
   corazón
**to govern** gobernar (ie)
**government** el gobierno
**governor** el gobernador
**gradually** gradualmente
**to graduate** graduarse
**granddaughter** la nieta
**grandfather** el abuelo
**grandmother** la abuela
**grandson** el nieto
**grape** la uva
**grapefruit** el pomelo; la toronja
**graphic** gráfico/a
**graphic design** el diseño gráfico
**to grate** rallar
**gray** gris
**Great!** ¡Estupendo!
**great** fabuloso/a; magnífico/a
**green** verde
**green pepper** el pimiento verde
**greeting** el saludo
**grill** la parrilla
**ground** molido/a; picado/a
**ground floor** la planta baja
**ground meat** la carne molida/picada
**group** el grupo
**Guatemalan** guatemalteco/a
**to guess** adivinar
**guide** la guía
**guitar** la guitarra
**guitar player** el/la guitarrista
**gymnasium** el gimnasio

# H

**hachet** el hacha
**to haggle** regatear
**hair** el cabello; el pelo
**hairdresser** el/la peluquero/a
**half-brother** el medio hermano
**half-sister** la media hermana
**Halloween** el Día de las Brujas
**hallway** el pasillo
**ham** el jamón
**hamburger** la hamburguesa
**to hand** dar
**hand** la mano; la mano; la mano
**handicrafts** la artesanía
**handkerchief** el pañuelo
**handsome** guapo/a
**to hang (clothes)** tender (ie)
**to happen** pasar
**happily** alegremente
**happy** alegre; contento/a
**hardworking** trabajador/a
**harmful** dañino/a
**harp** el arpa
**to harvest** cosechar
**hat** el sombrero
**to hate** odiar
**to have** tener (g, ie)
**to have a good time** divertirse (ie, i);
   pasar bien
**to have a(n) . . . ache** tener dolor de...
**to have breakfast** desayunar
**to have dinner** cenar
**to have fun** divertirse (ie);
   entretenerse
**to have lunch** almorzar (ue)
**to have to** tener que
**he** él
**he/she is** es
**head** la cabeza
**health** la salud
**health care provider** el proveedor de
   salud
**health center** el centro de salud
**healthy** saludable
**to hear** oír
**to hear about** oír hablar
**heart** el corazón
**heat** el calor
**heating** la calefacción
**height** la estatura
**hello** hola
**Hello? (on the telephone)** ¿Aló?;
   ¡Bueno!; ¿Diga?; ¿Dígame?;
   ¡Oigo!; ¿Qué hay?
**to help** ayudar
**her** su(s)
**herb** la hierba

here (present)  presente
hi  hola
high-heeled shoe  el zapato de tacón
highlighter  el marcador
highway  la carretera
hiker  el senderista
hip  la cadera
his/her/their  su(s)
Hispanic  hispano/a
history  la historia
holiday  el día festivo
home  el hogar
homeless  desamparado/a
homemaker  el ama/o de casa
homework  la tarea
Honduran  hondureño/a
honesty  la honestidad
hood  el capó
horrible  horrible
hospital  el hospital; el sanitorio
hot  caliente
hotel  el hotel
hour  la hora
house, home  la casa
housewife  el ama/o de casa
housing  la vivienda
How about that!  ¡Fíjate qué noticia!
How are you (formal)?  ¿Cómo está?
How are you (informal)?  ¿Cómo estás?
How do you say . . . ?  ¿Cómo se dice … ?
How do you spell . . . ?  ¿Cómo se escribe … ?
How incredible!  ¡Qué increíble!
How is it going?  ¿Cómo te va?
how many?  ¿cuántos/as?
How may I help you?  ¿En qué puedo servirle(s)?
how much?  ¿cuánto/a?
How much is it?  ¿Cuánto cuesta?
how/what?  ¿cómo?
however  no obstante
hug  el abrazo
human  humano/a
humanities  las humanidades
hundred  cien/ciento
hunger  la hambre
to hurt  doler (ue)
husband  el esposo
hypothesis  la hipótesis

## I

I  yo
I am  soy
I am . . . years old.  Tengo … años.
I don't know  No sé.

I don't understand  No comprendo.
I have/you have  tengo/tienes
I like  me gusta(n)
I/we hope that . . .  ojalá que …
I would like . . .  Me gustaría …
I would like . . .  Quisiera …
ice  el hielo
ice cream  el helado
ice creamery  la heladería
idea  la idea
idealistic  idealista
if  si
ill  malo/a
ill person  el/la enfermo/a
illiteracy  al analfabetismo
illiterate  analfabeto/a
illness  la enfermedad
I'm sorry (to hear that)  lo siento
imagine  imaginar
immediately  enseguida
immigration  la inmigración
imperfect  el imperfecto
to implement  implementar
important  importante
impossible  imposible
to improve  mejorar
impulsive  impulsivo/a
in boldface  en negrita
in contrast  en contraste
in fact  in en realidad/realmente
in front of  enfrente (de)
in search of  en busca de
in (time)  por
inappropriate  inapropiado/a
including  hasta
incredible  increíble
Independence Day  el Día de la Independencia
independent  independiente
to indicate  indicar
inexpensive  barato/a
infection  la infección
to influence  influir
information  la información
infrastructure  la infraestructura
inhabitant  el/la habitante
to inherit  heredar
inheritance  el/la herencia
injection  la inyección
injured  herido/a
injured person  el/la herido/a
to insert  meter
to inspect  revisar
inspector  el inspector
instead of  en vez de
instruction  la instrucción
intelligent  inteligente
interesante  en

to interest  interesar
interesting  interesante
international  internacional
interpreter  el/la intérprete
interview  la entrevista
to interview  entrevistar
intimacy  la intimidad
introduction  la presentación
introverted  introvertido/a
invitation  la invitación
to invite  invitar
iPod  el ipod
to iron  to planchar
to itch  picar(se)
it's clear  está despejado
it's cloudy  está nublado
it's cool  hace fresco
It's sunny.  Hace sol.
it's sunny  hace sol

## J

jacket  la chaqueta
January  enero
Japanese  japonés/japonesa
jawbone  la quijada
jeans  los jeans; los vaqueros/ jeans
jeweller  el/la joyero/a
jewelry, piece of  la joya
job  el trabajo
jogging suit  la sudadera
joke  la broma
journalist  el/la periodista
joy  la alegría
judge  el/la juez
juice  el jugo
July  julio
June  junio
junk food  la comida chatarra

## K

to keep in shape  estar en forma
to keep quiet  callarse
to keep silent  guardar silencio
key  la llave
key card  la tarjeta magnética
key word  la palabra clave
king  el rey
to kiss  besar
kiss  el beso
kitchen  la cocina
kitchen sink  el fregadero
knee  la rodilla
to knock  golpear
to know  conocer; saber
knowledge  el conocimiento

# L

**labor-related** laboral
**laboratory** el laboratorio
**laborer** el/la obrero/a
**lace** el encaje
**lack** la falta
**lake** el lago
**lamb** el cordero
**to land** aterrizar (c)
**land** la tierra
**landscape** el paisaje
**language** la lengua
**laptop** la computadora portátil
**to last** durar
**last** último/a
**last night** anoche
**last year** el año pasado
**late** tarde
**later** después; luego; más tarde
**to laugh** reír (i)
**laughter** la risa
**laundry room** la lavandería
**lawn** el césped
**lawyer** el/la abogado/a
**layout** ladistribución
**lazy** perezoso/a
**leaf** la hoja
**to learn** aprender
**least** at por lo menos
**leather** el cuero
**to leave** dejar; ir(se)
**left** la izquierda
**leg** la pierna
**leg (animal)** la pata
**legal holiday** el día feriado
**legumes** las legumbres
**leisure activities** las diversiones
**lemon** el limón
**to lend** prestar
**lentils** las lentejas
**lesson** la lección
**lettuce** la lechuga
**level** el nivel
**librarian** el/la bibliotecario/a
**library** la biblioteca
**license plate** la placa
**to lie** mentir
**lie** la mentira
**life expectancy** la esperanza de vida
**lightweight** ligero/a
**to like** caer bien; gustar
**likewise** igualmente
**link** el enlace
**lip** el labio
**list** la lista
**to listen** oír

**Listen!** ¡Oye!
**Listen, please.** Oiga, por favor.
**to listen (to)** escuchar
**literature** la literatura
**little** a poco; poco; a un poco
**little by little** poco a poco
**to live** vivir
**lively** animado/a; vivo/a
**living room** el living; la sala; el salón
**lobster** la langosta
**to lock up** encerrar (ie)
**lodging** el alojamiento
**logically** lógicamente
**long** largo/a
**to look, appear** ver(se)
**to look (at)** mirar
**to look for** buscar
**to look terrible** to tener mala cara
**to lose** perder (ie)
**to lose weight** adelgazar
**loss** la pérdida
**loudly** alto
**loungewear** la ropa de estar en casa
**love** el amor
**Love (closing)** Cariños
**luck** lasuerte
**luggage** el equipaje
**lunch** el almuerzo
**lung** el pulmón
**luxury** el lujo

# M

**magazine** la revista
**mail** el correo
**mail carrier** el/la cartero/a
**main character** el personaje principal
**to maintain** mantener (g, ie)
**major** la carrera
**majority** la mayoría
**to make** hacer
**to make a reservation** reservar
**to make the bed** to hacer la cama
**man** el hombre
**manager** el/la gerente
**many** mucho/a (adj.)
**many . . . as** as tanto(s)/a(s) ... como
**map** el mapa
**March** marzo
**margarine** la margarina
**marked down** rebajado/a
**marker** el marcador; el rotulador
**market** el mercado
**married** casado/a
**marvel** la maravilla
**marvelous** estupendo/a;
     maravilloso/a

**material** el material
**mathematics** las matemáticas
**May** mayo
**mayonnaise** la mayonesa
**mayor** el alcalde
**meal** la comida
**meaning** el significado
**means of transportation** los medios de
     transporte
**measure** la medida
**meat** la carne
**mechanic** el/la mecánico/a
**mediator** el/la mediador
**medical doctor** el/la médico/a
**medical treatment** el tratamiento
     médico
**medicine** la medicina
**to meet** conocerse; reunir(se)
**meeting, gathering** la reunión
**melody** la melodía
**melon** el melón
**to melt** derretir
**memory** el recuerdo
**Mennonites** los menonitas
**menu** el menú
**mess** el lío; el majarete
**message** el mensaje
**metal** metal
**mexican** mexicano/a
**Mexican** mexicano/a
**Mexican Independence Day** el Día de
     la Independencia de México
**to microwave** hornear
**microwave (oven)** el (horno)
     microondas
**middle class** el burgués
**to migrate** migrar
**migration** la migración
**milk** la leche
**milkshake, smoothie** el batido
**million** millón
**millionaire** el/la millonario/a
**minus** menos
**mirror** el espejo
**moderate** módico/a
**modern** moderno/a
**mom** la mamá
**Monday** el lunes
**money in cash** el dinero en efectivo
**month** el mes
**mood** el estado de ánimo
**more** más
**more or less** más o menos
**morning** la mañana
**Moroccan** marroquí
**mortality** la mortalidad
**mother** la madre

**Mother's Day**  el Día de la Madre
**motor**  el motor
**motto**  el eslogan; el título
**mouth**  la boca
**to move**  mover; mudarse
**movement**  el desplazamiento
**movies**  el cine
**to mow (lawn)**  cortar
**Mr.**  el señor (Sr.)
**Ms, Miss**  la señorita (Srta.)
**Ms., Mrs.**  la señora (Sra.)
**much**  mucho/a (adj.); mucho (adv.)
**much later**  más tarde
**multilingual**  políglota
**mural**  el mural
**muralist**  el/la muralista
**muscle**  el músculo
**museum**  el museo
**music**  la música
**must**  tener que
**mustard**  la mostaza
**my**  mi(s)

# N

**napkin**  la servilleta
**narrow**  estrecho/a
**national**  nacional
**nationality**  las nacionalidad
**native**  natal
**nature**  la naturaleza
**nature preserve**  la reserva natural
**near**  cerca (de)
**necessary**  necesario/a
**neck**  el cuello
**necklace**  el collar
**neighbor**  el/la vecino/a
**neighborhood**  el barrio
**neither**  tampoco
**neither . . . nor**  ni ... ni
**nephew**  el sobrino
**nerve**  el nervio
**nervous**  nervioso/a
**net**  la red
**network**  la red
**never**  jamás; nunca
**nevertheless**  sin embargo
**new**  nuevo/a
**New Year's Day**  el Año Nuevo
**New Year's Eve**  el Fin de Año; la Nochevieja
**news**  la noticia
**newspaper**  el periódico
**next to**  al lado (de); próximo/a
**Nicaraguan**  nicaragüense
**nice**  agradable; majo/a; simpático/a
**niece**  la sobrina

**Nigerian**  nigeriano/a
**night**  la noche
**night before last**  ante(a)noche
**nightgown**  el camisón
**nightmare**  la pesadilla
**no**  ningún/ninguno/ninguna; no
**no one**  nadie
**nobody**  nadie
**noise**  el ruido
**to nominate**  nominar
**none**  ningún/ninguno/ninguna
**normally**  normalmente
**North American**  norteamericano/a
**nose**  la nariz
**nostalgic**  nostálgico
**not**  tampoco
**not any**  ningún/ninguno/ninguna
**(not) ever**  jamás; nunca
**note card**  la ficha
**notebook**  el cuaderno
**nothing**  nada
**novel**  la novela
**novelist**  el/la novelista
**November**  noviembre
**now**  ahora
**nowadays**  hoy en día
**nurse**  el/la enfermero/a

# O

**oath**  el juramento
**object**  el objeto
**to obtain**  obtener
**obvious**  obvio/a
**occupation**  la ocupación
**to occur**  ocurrir
**October**  octubre
**of**  de
**of course**  claro; por supuesto; realmente; cómo no
**to offer**  ofrecer (zc)
**office**  la oficina
**office (of doctor, dentist, etc.)**  el consultorio
**often**  muchas veces
**oil**  el aceite
**old**  antiguo/a; mayor; viejo/a
**olive**  la aceituna
**Olympics**  las Olimpiadas
**on, above**  sobre
**on demand**  a petición
**once**  una vez
**one hand**  por un lado
**onion**  la cebolla
**only (adv.)**  sólo
**only child**  el hijo único/la hija única
**to open**  abrir

**opening**  la vacante
**opinion**  la opinión
**opinion poll**  la encuesta de opinión
**opposing**  contrario/a
**optimistic**  optimista
**or**  o
**orange**  anaranjado/a, naranja (adj.); la naranja
**orchestra**  la orquesta
**to order**  encargar; pedir (i)
**organization**  la organización
**to organize**  organizar
**other**  otro/a
**other, another**  otro/a
**other hand**  en cambio; por otro lado
**outdoors**  al aire libre
**outside**  afuera
**outskirts**  las afueras
**outstanding**  destacado/a
**own**  propio/a
**ozone layer**  la capa de ozono

# P

**package**  el paquete
**page**  la página
**pain**  el dolor
**painter**  el/la pintor/a
**painting**  el cuadro; la pintura
**pajamas**  el/la piyama
**palate**  el paladar
**Panamanian**  panameño/a
**pants**  los pantalones
**pantsuit**  el traje pantalón
**pantyhose**  las pantimedias
**papaya**  la papaya
**paprika**  el achiote; el pimentón
**parade**  el desfile
**Paraguayan**  paraguayo/a
**pardon me**  con permiso, perdón
**parents**  los padres
**parsley**  el perejil
**to participate**  participar
**partner**  el/la compañero/a
**party**  la fiesta
**passenger**  el/la pasajero/a
**passion fruit**  el fruto de pasión
**passive**  pasivo/a
**passport**  el pasaporte
**past**  pasado/a
**pastry**  el pastel
**patient**  paciente; el/la paciente
**patriotic**  patriótico/a
**to pay (for)**  pagar
**peach**  el durazno; el melocotón
**pear**  la pera

**peasant** el/la campesino/a
**pedestrian area** la zona peatonal
**pediatrician** el/la pediatra
**pen** el bolígrafo
**penalty** el penalti
**pencil** el lápiz
**people** la gente
**pepper** la pimienta
**percent** por ciento
**percentage** el porcentaje
**perfect** perfecto/a
**perfectionistic** perfeccionista
**perfectly** perfectamente
**performance** el rendimiento
**performer** el/la intérprete
**periodical** el periódico
**person** la persona; la persona
**perspective** la perspectiva
**Peruvian** peruano/a
**pessimistic** pesimista
**petroleum** el petróleo
**pharmacist** el/la farmacéutico/a
**pharmacy** la farmacia
**philology** la filología
**philosophy** la filosofía
**photo(graph)** la foto(grafía)
**physics** la física
**physiology** la fisiología
**to pick up** recoger (j)
**picture** el cuadro
**pie** la tarta
**pill** la pastilla
**pillow** la almohada
**pin** el alfiler
**pineapple** la piña
**pink** rosado/a, rosa
**to place** colocar
**place** el lugar
**plan** el plan
**to plan to** pensar (ie) + infinitive
**plane** el avión
**planet** el planeta
**plastic** plástico
**plastic arts** los artes plásticas
**plate, dish** el plato
**to play (a game, sport)** jugar (ue)
**to play (an instrument)** tocar (un instrumento)
**player** el/la jugador/a
**plaza** la plaza
**please** por favor
**pleased/nice to meet you** encantado/a; mucho gusto
**pleasure** el placer
**plumber** el/la plomero/a; el/la fontanero/a
**plus** y

**poem** el poema
**poet** el/la poeta
**poetry** la poesía
**point of view** el punto de vista
**policeman/woman** el/la policía
**Polish** polaco/a
**political science** las ciencias políticas
**poll** la encuesta
**polluted** contaminado/a
**poor** pobre
**popcorn** las palomitas de maíz
**popular** popular
**popularity** la popularidad
**to popularize** popularizar (c)
**population** la población
**pork** el cerdo
**port** el deportes
**to portray** retratar
**Portuguese** portugués/ portuguesa
**position** el puesto
**possible** posible
**poster** el afiche
**potato** la papa
**potter** el/la ceramista
**poultry, fowl** las aves
**poverty** la pobreza
**powerful** potente
**position** la posición
**to practice** practicar
**to precede** preceder
**to predict** prever
**to prefer** preferir (ie)
**preparation** el preparativo
**to prepare** preparar
**to prescribe** recetar
**prescription** la receta
**present** actual; el regalo
**present time** actualmente; en la actualidad
**preservation** la conservación
**president** el presidente/la presidenta
**presidential** presidencial
**preterit** el pretérito
**pretty** bonito/a; lindo/a
**price** el precio
**printer** la impresora
**prize** el premio
**probable** probable
**problem** el problema
**procession** la procesión
**to produce** elaborar; producir
**product** el producto
**professor** el/la profesor/a
**program** el programa

**progress** el progreso
**to prohibit** prohibir
**promising** prometedor/a
**proposal** la propuesta
**protein** la proteína
**proverb** el refrán
**provided that** con tal (de) que
**proximity** la proximidad
**psychiatrist** el/la (p)siquiatra
**psychologist** el/la (p)sicólogo/a
**psychology** la (p)sicología
**publicity** la publicidad
**publicity campaign** la campaña de publicidad
**Puerto Rican** puertorriqueño/a
**purple** morado/a
**purse** la bolsa/el bolso
**to put** poner (g)
**to put to bed** acostar
**to put makeup on oneself** maquillar(se)
**to put one's clothes on** poner(se) (g) la ropa

# Q

**quality** la calidad
**quantity** la cantidad
**queen** la reina
**question** la pregunta
**quickly** rápidamente
**quiet** callado/a
**quotation** la cita textual
**to quote** citar

# R

**race** la carrera
**racquet** la raqueta
**radiator** el radiador
**radio** el/la radio
**radio announcer** el/la locutor/a
**radiologist** el/la radiólogo/a
**rail** el riel
**to rain** llover (ue)
**rain** la lluvia
**rain forest** el bosque tropical
**raincoat** el impermeable
**to raise one's hand** levantar la mano
**rate** la tasa
**rather** bastante
**to reach out to** comunicarse
**to read** leer
**reading** la lectura
**ready** listo/a
**real estate** bienes raíces
**reality** la realidad
**really** in en realidad/realmente

**Really!** ¡No me digas!
**to reappear** reaparecer
**rearview mirror** el espejo retrovisor
**reason** la razón
**rebirth** el renacimiento
**receipt** la receta
**to receive** recibir
**recipe** la receta
**to recommend** recomendar (ie)
**recommendation** la recomendación
**to record** grabar
**recycled** reciclado/a
**red** rojo/a
**red pepper** la pimienta roja
**redhead** pelirrojo/a
**to reduce** reducir
**to reflect** reflejar
**to reforest** repoblar
**refrigerator** el refrigerador; la nevera
**regime** el régimen
**region** la región
**to regret** arrepentirse (ie)
**regularly** regularmente
**relative** el pariente; el/la pariente
**relatively** relativamente
**relief** el alivio
**to relieve** aliviar
**religious** religioso/a
**remedy, medicine** el remedio
**to remember** recordar(se) (ue)
**to rent** alquilar
**rent** el alquiler
**to repeat** repetir (i)
**to repopulate** repoblar
**reputation** la reputación
**to require** exigir
**to research** investigar
**research** la investigación
**resources** los recursos
**to respect** respetar
**to respond** responder
**responsible** responsable
**to rest** descansar
**restaurant** el restaurante
**result** el resultado
**résumé** el currículum
**to retire** jubilarse
**to return** devolver; retornar; volver (ue)
**review** la reseña
**to reward** premiar
**rib** la costilla
**rice** el arroz
**rich, wealthy** rico/a
**to ride (a bicycle)** montar (en bicicleta)
**right** el derecho; la derecha

**right?** ¿verdad?
**ring** el anillo
**river basin** la cuenca
**road** el camino
**to roast** asar
**robbery** el robo
**robe** la bata
**robot** el robot
**romantic** romántico/a
**roof** el tejado
**room** la habitación
**room; bedroom** el cuarto
**round trip** de ida y vuelta
**route** el trayecto
**routine** la rutina
**rug** la alfombra
**ruins** las ruinas
**to run** correr

# S

**sad** triste
**safe** la caja fuerte
**salad** la ensalada
**salad dressing** el aderezo
**salary** el sueldo
**sale** la rebaja; la venta
**(sales) manager** el/la gerente (de ventas)
**salesman, saleswoman** el/la vendedor/a
**salesperson** el dependiente/la dependienta
**salt** la sal
**Salvadorian** salvadoreño/a
**sandal** la sandalia
**sandwich** el sándwich
**Saturday** el sábado
**to sauté** saltear
**to save** ahorrar
**savings** los ahorros
**sawdust** el aserrín
**to say** decir (g, i)
**to say goodbye** despedir(se) (i)
**to say hello** mandar saludos
**scared** asustado/a
**scarf** la bufanda
**scene** la escena
**schedule** el horario
**school** la escuela
**school, department** la facultad
**science** la ciencia
**scientist** el/la científico/a
**to score a goal** meter un gol
**screen** la pantalla
**sculptor** el escultor/la escultora
**sea** el mar

**search engine** el buscador
**seasoning** el condimento
**seat** el asiento
**security** la seguridad
**sedentary** sedentario/a
**to see** ver
**see you later** hasta luego
**see you soon** hasta pronto
**see you tomorrow** hasta mañana
**seed** la semilla
**to seem** parecer (zc)
**self-portrait** el autorretrato
**to sell** vender
**seller** el/la vendedor/a
**seminar** el seminario
**to send** enviar; mandar
**sentimental** sentimental
**September** septiembre
**serious** grave; serio/a
**to serve** servir (i)
**server** el/la camarero/a
**to set the table** poner la mesa
**several** algún/alguno(s)/alguna(s)
**shape** la forma
**sharp** agudo/a
**to shave (oneself)** afeitar(se)
**she** ella
**sheep** la oveja
**sheet** la sábana
**shell** la concha
**shellfish** los mariscos
**ship** la nave, el barco
**shirt** la camisa
**shoe** el zapato
**shopping** las compras
**shopping center** el centro comercial
**short (in length)** corto/a
**short (in stature)** bajo/a; chaparro/a
**short-sleeved shirt** la camisa de manga corta
**shorts** los pantalones cortos
**should** deber
**shoulder** el hombro
**to show** mostrar (ue)
**shower** la ducha
**shrimp** el camarón; la gamba
**sick** enfermo/a
**side** el lado
**to sign** firmar
**signal** la señal
**significant other** la pareja
**silence** el silencio
**silly, foolish** tonto/a
**simply** simplemente
**since** desde; hace
**sincere** sincero/a
**to sing** cantar

single   soltero/a
sister   la hermana
to sit down   sentarse (ie)
size   el número; la talla; el tamaño
to skate   patinar
ski   el esquí
to ski   esquiar
skiing   el esquí
to skim   leer por encima
skin   la piel
skirt   la falda
sleep   el sueño
to sleep (to fall asleep)   dormir(se) (ue)
slipper   la zapatilla
slope   la bajada; la pendiente
slowly   despacio; lentamente
small   pequeño/a
smallpox   la viruela
smart   listo/a
to smoke   fumar
snack   la merienda
to sneeze   estornudar
snorkeling   el buceo
to snow   nevar (ie)
snow   la nieve
so that   para que
soap   el jabón
soap opera   la telenovela
sober   sobrio/a
soccer   el fútbol
social   social
society   la sociedad
sociology   la sociología
sock   el calcetín
soda   el refresco
sofa   el sofá
soft   blando/a; suave
soft drink   el refresco
soil   la tierra
some   algún/alguno(s)/alguna(s)
someone   alguien
something   algo
something else   otra cosa
something foolish   la babada
sometime   alguna vez
sometimes   algunas veces; a veces
son   el hijo
song   la canción
to soon as   as tan pronto (como)
sorcerer   el brujo
soul   el alma
to sound   sonar
soup   la sopa
sour   agrio/a
source   la fuente
souvenir   el recuerdo

spaghetti   los espaguetis
Spanish   español/a; el español
to speak   hablar
specialist   el/la especialista
specialty   la especialidad
speed   la velocidad
speed, haste   la prisa
to spend   gastar
to spend (time)   pasar
spice   la especie
spinach   las espinacas
spirit   el espíritu
to sponsor   patrocinar
spoon   la cuchara
spoonful   la cucharada
sports equipment   el equipo deportivo
sportswear   la ropa deportiva
to spray   rociar
to spread, to disseminate   difundir
spring   la primavera
square   la plaza
square meter   el metro cuadrado
stadium   el estadio
stairs   la escalera
to stand in line   hacer cola
to stand out   destacarse
star   la estrella
to start   empezar
statistics   las estadísticas
to stay in touch   mantenerse en contacto
steak   el bistec
steering wheel   el volante
step   el paso
stepbrother   el hermanastro
stepfather   el padrastro
stepmother   la madrastra
stepsister   la hermanastra
still   todavía
stockings   las medias
stomach   el estómago
to stop   detener
stopover   la escala
store   la tienda
store window   el escaparate
story   el cuento
stove   la cocina; la estufa
straight   derecho
strawberry   la fresa
street   la calle
to stroll   pasear
strong   fuerte
structure   la estructura
student   el alumno/a; el/la estudiante
student desk   el pupitre
studious   estudioso/a

to study   estudiar; investigar
to stumble   tropezarse
stupendous   estupendo/a
style   el estilo
stylish   de moda
subsidize   subvencionar
subway   el metro
success   el éxito
sugar   el/la azúcar
to suggest   sugerir (ie, i)
suit   el traje; el traje de chaqueta
suitcase   la maleta
to summarize   resumir
summer   el verano
sun   el sol
to sunbathe   tomar el sol
Sunday   el domingo
sunglasses   las gafas de sol
sunrise   la salida del sol
supermarket   el supermercado
supper   la comida
to support   apoyar; sustentar
surely, certainly   seguramente
surgeon   el/la cirujano/a
surgery   la operación
to surprise   sorprender
surprise   la sorpresa
surrealist   surrealista
to surround   rodear
survey   la encuesta
to survive   sobrevivir
sweater   el suéter
sweatshirt; jogging suit   la sudadera
to sweep   barrer
to swell   hinchar
swelling   la hinchazón
to swim   nadar
swimming pool   la piscina; la alberca
symbol   el símbolo
symptom   el síntoma

# T

T-shirt   la camiseta
table   la mesa
tablecloth   el mantel
to take   llevar; tomar
to take a nap   to dormir (ue) la siesta
to take a seat   tomar asiento
to take a walk   dar un paseo; pasear
to take advantage   aprovechar
to take away   quitar(se)
to take care of   cuidar; cuidar(se) (de)
to take note   fijarse
to take notes   tomar apuntes/notas
to take off   quitar(se)
to take off (airplane)   despegar (u)

**to take out**  sacar (qu)
**to talk**  conversar; dialogar
**talkative**  conversador/a
**tall**  alto/a
**tamale**  el tamale
**tapas**  las tapas
**task**  la tarea
**tea**  el té
**teacher**  el/la profesor/a
**team; equipment**  el equipo
**to tear**  romper
**teaspoon**  la cucharita
**technician**  el/la técnico/a
**technology**  la tecnología
**telephone**  el teléfono
**television set**  el televisor
**to tell**  contar (ue); decir (g, i)
**tennis**  el tenis
**tennis player**  el/la tenista
**tennis shoe**  la zapatilla de deporte
**terrace**  la terraza
**terrorism**  el terrorismo
**test**  el examen
**thanks, thank you**  gracias
**Thanksgiving**  el Día de Acción de
  Gracias
**that**  ese/a (adj.); eso (pron.)
**that is why**  por eso
**that (over there)**  aquel/aquella
**That's great!**  ¡Qué bien/bueno!
**thaw, thawing**  el deshielo
**theater**  el teatro
**theater company**  la compañía de
  teatro
**their**  su(s)
**theme**  el tema
**then**  entonces; luego
**therapy**  la terapia
**there**  allí
**there is, there are**  hay
**thermometer**  el termómetro
**they**  ellos/ellas
**thin**  delgado/a
**thing**  la cosa
**to think**  pensar (ie)
**to think of/about**  pensar en
**to think of/about (opinion)**  pensar de
**third**  tercero/a
**thirst**  la sed
**this**  este/a; esto
**thousand**  mil
**throat**  la garganta
**through**  por; a través de
**to throw**  lanzar
**Thursday**  el jueves
**ticket**  el billete; el boleto, el pasaje
**tie**  la corbata

**tight**  estrecho/a
**time**  la hora; el tiempo
**timid**  tímido/a
**tire**  la llanta
**tired**  cansado/a
**title**  el título
**to**  a; para
**toast**  el pan tostado/la tostada
**to toast**  tostar
**today**  hoy
**Today is . . .**  Hoy es . . .
**together**  juntos/as
**toilet**  el inodoro
**tomato**  el tomate
**tomato sauce**  la salsa de tomate
**tomorrow**  mañana
**tone**  el tono
**tongue**  la lengua
**tonight**  esta noche
**too**  también
**tooth**  el diente
**toothpaste**  la pasta de dientes
**tourist class**  la clase turista
**tournament**  el campeonato; el torneo
**toward**  para
**towel**  la toalla
**toxic**  tóxico/a
**toy**  el juguete
**tradition**  la tradición
**traditional**  tradicional
**traditionally**  tradicionalmente
**traffic**  el tráfico
**train**  el tren
**trainer**  el/la entrenador/a
**training**  el entrenamiento
**training resort**  el centro de
  entrenamiento
**tranquil**  tranquilo/a
**tranquilly**  tranquilamente
**to translate**  traducir (zc)
**trash**  la basura
**to travel**  viajar
**travel agency**  la agencia de viajes
**travel agent**  el/la agente de viajes
**tray**  la bandeja
**to treat**  tratar
**to treat, to be about**  tratar
**tree**  el árbol
**trips**  el viaje
**true**  cierto/a; verdad
**trunk**  el baúl; el maletero
**trust**  la confianza
**truth**  la verdad
**to try**  probar; tratar
**to try on**  probarse (ue)
**Tuesday**  el martes
**turkey**  el pavo

**to turn**  doblar
**to turn on**  encender (ie)
**twin**  gemelo/a
**to twist**  torcer(se) (ue)
**typical**  típico/a

# U

**UFO**  el OVNI
**ugly**  feo/a
**umbrella**  el paraguas
**umpire, referee**  el árbitro
**uncle**  el tío
**under**  abajo; debajo (de)
**to underline**  subrayar
**to understand**  comprender;
  entender (ie)
**underwear**  la ropa interior
**unemployment**  el desempleo
**unforgettable**  inolvidable
**to unify**  unificar (qu)
**United States**  Estados Unidos
**university**  la universidad
**unless**  a menos que
**unpleasant**  antipático/a
**until**  hasta que
**urgent**  urgente
**Uruguayan**  uruguayo/a
**U.S. citizen**  estadounidense
**to use**  usar
**useful**  útil

# V

**vacation**  las vacaciones
**to vacuum**  pasar la aspiradora
**vacuum cleaner**  la aspiradora
**Valentine's Day**  el Día de los
  Enamorados; el Día del Amor y
  la Amistad
**vanilla**  la vainilla
**vegetable**  el vegetal, la verdura
**vegetarian**  vegetariano/a
**vein**  la vena
**Venezuelan**  venezolano/a
**verbs**  verbos
**very**  muy
**veterinarian**  el/la veterinario/a
**video game**  el videojuego
**view**  la vista
**village**  el pueblo
**vinegar**  el vinagre
**virtual library**  la biblioteca virtual
**virtually**  virtualmente
**to visit**  visitar
**vitamin**  la vitamina
**voice**  la voz
**volleyball**  el vóleibol; el volibol

# W

waist la cintura
to wait for esperar
waiter/waitress el/la camarero/a
waiting area la sala de espera
to wake (someone up); to despertar(se) (ie)
to wake up despertar(se)
to walk caminar
wallet la billetera
to want querer (ie)
warehouse el almacén
warming el calentamiento
to wash (oneself) lavar(se)
washer la lavadora
wastebasket el cesto
water el agua
to water regar (ie)
way el camino
we nosotros/nosotras
We are going to have a good time. Lo vamos a pasar muy bien.
weak débil
to wear llevar
to wear a costume disfrazarse
to wear a shoe size calzar
weather el tiempo; el tiempo
weather forecast el pronóstico del tiempo
wedding la boda
Wednesday el miércoles
week la semana
week ago a una semana atrás
weekend el fin de semana
weight la pesa
well bien; bueno/a
well-off adinerado/a
what? ¿qué?
What a pity! ¡Qué lástima!
What a suprise/coincidence! ¡Qué casualidad!
What day is it? ¿Qué día es hoy?
What do you think? ¿Qué te parece?

What for? ¿para qué?
What is he/she/it like? ¿Cómo es?
What is the date? ¿Cuál es la fecha?; ¿Qué fecha es hoy?
What is the weather like? ¿Qué tiempo hace?
What time is it? ¿Qué hora es?
What's new? ¿Qué tal?
What's up? ¿Qué tal?
What's wrong (with you/them)? ¿Qué te/le(s) pasa?
What's your name? (familiar) ¿Cómo te llamas?
What's your name? (formal) ¿Cómo se llama usted?
wheel la rueda
when cuando
when? ¿cuándo?
where? ¿dónde?
Where do we meet? ¿Dónde quedamos?
Where is . . . ? ¿Dónde está... ?
where (to)? ¿adónde?
wherever donde
which? ¿cuál(es)?
while mientras
to whistle pitar
white blanco/a
who? ¿quién(es)?
Who is . . . ? ¿Quién es... ?
whose? ¿de quién?
why? ¿para qué?; ¿por qué?
wide ancho/a
wife la esposa
wild silvestre
will el/la testamento
to win ganar
wind el viento
window la ventana; la ventanilla
window seat el asiento de ventanilla
windshield wiper el limpiaparabrisas
wine el vino
wine cellar la bodega

winner el ganador
winter el invierno
to wish, to want desear
with con
without sin; sin que
woman la mujer
wood la madera
wool la lana
word la palabra
work la obra
to work trabajar
work el trabajo
worker el/la obrero/a
workshop el taller
World Cup la Copa Mundial
world, worldwide mundial
to worry preocupar(se)
wound la herida
wounded herido/a
wrist la muñeca
to write escribir
writer el escritor/la escritora

# Y

year el año
yellow amarillo/a
yes sí
yesterday ayer
yet todavía
yogurt el yogur
you are (familiar) eres; estás
you are (formal) es; estás
you (familiar) tú (familiar); vos (Argentina)
you (formal) usted (formal)
you (plural) ustedes (plural)
young joven
young man/woman el/la joven
your (familiar) tu(s)
you're welcome de nada
youth hostel el albergue juvenil
yucca la yuca

# Credits

## Text Credits

**p. 48:** "Un buen repaso a la Universidad de Salamanca" reprinted with permission from Alberto López Nájera; **p. 73:** ® All Rights Reserved by World Editors, Inc.; **p. 434:** "Dame la mano" by Gabriela Minstral. La Orden Franciscana de Chile autoriza el uso de la obra de Gabriela Mistral. Lo equivalente a los derechos de autoría es entregado a la Orden Franciscana de Chile, para los niños de Monte-grande, de conformidad a la voluntad de Gabriela Minstral.; **p. 457:** El Entnógrafo by Jorge Luis Borges. ©1995 by Jorge Luis Borges, permission of The Wylie Agency Inc.; **p. 490:** Hombre pequenito by Alfonsina Storni. Editorial Losada S.A., Buenos Aires, 1997. Herederos de Alfonsina Storni. Used with permission; **p. 504:** Mafalda (#1126 and #104) por Joaquín S. Lavado, de QUINO. Ediciones de la Flor, 1997. Reprinted with permission of Caminito S.a.s.; **p. 520:** "Apocalipsis" © Denevi, Marco, Falsificaciones, Buenos Aires, Corregidor, 2007. Used with permission.

## Photo Credits

**Cover Image:** Ferran Traite Soler/ IStockphoto.com: p. 2 © Jeff Greenberg/Alamy; p. 5 (top) Ian O'Leary/ Getty Images Inc.—Stone Allstock; p. 5 (center) Getty Images—Stockbyte, Royalty Free; p. 5 (bottom) Christina Kennedy/ PhotoEdit Inc.; p. 22 Dagli Orti (A)/Picture Desk, Inc./Kobal Collection; p. 23 (lower bottom center) Matt Trommer/Shutterstock; p. 23 (right) Pilar Echevarria/Shutterstock; p. 23 (top) Jarno gonzalez Zarraonandia/ Shutterstock; p. 23 (bottom) Rafael Ramirez Lee/Shutterstock; p. 23 (lower upper left) © Robert Frerck/Odyssey/Chicago; p. 24 (top) Grimberg, Marc/Getty Images Inc.—Image Bank; p. 24 (bottom) Goncharov Roman/ Shutterstock; p. 25 Embassy of Peru; Robert Frerck/Odyssey Productions, Inc.; p. 35 Richard Nowitz/National Geographic Image Collection; p. 44 Spencer Grant/PhotoEdit Inc.; p. 50 © Robert Fried/robertfriedphotography.com; p. 51 (top) Robert Fried/robertfriedphotography.com; p. 51 (bottom) Denis Doyle/AP Widewrold Photo; p. 54 © Cristena Cardenas; p. 55 (bottom) Robin Holden, Sr./Shutterstock; p. 55 (center) Graca Victoria/Shutterstock; p. 55 (center) April Turner/Shutterstock; p. 55 (top right) Aaron D. Settipane/ Shutterstock; p. 55 (right) Photo by Rico Torres © 2003 Miramax/ Columbia Pictures, All Rights Reserved, Kobal Collection—The Picture Desk; p. 56 (top left) © Jimmy Dorantes/Latin Focus.com; p. 56 (bottom right) Andresr/Shutterstock; p. 56 (top right) digitalskillet/Shutterstock; p. 56 (bottom left) Mira.com/Artist Name; p. 57 EyeWire Collection/Getty Images—Photodisc; p. 60 (left) Wallenrock/Shutterstock; p. 60 (center left) Dallas Events Inc./Shutterstock; p. 60 (center right) Laurence Gough/ Shutterstock; p. 60 (right) Yuri Arcurs/Shutterstock; p. 66 (top left) © Michael Germana/SSI

Photo/Landov; p. 66 (top right) Jack Vartoogian/Front Row Photos; p. 66 (bottom right) © Steve Nesius/Reuters/ Landov; p. 66 (bottom left) © Ramon Espinosa/AP Wide World Photos; p. 67 Scott Harrison/Getty Images; p. 84 Courtesy of the Library of Congress; p. 84 Library of Congress; p. 85 (top) © 2008 Kendal Larson; p. 85 (bottom) Wikipedia, The Free Encyclopedia; Artist unknown. First wedding of Inca princess Nusta Beatriz to Spanish noble Martin de Loyola, 18th century; p. 88; © The Art Archive/Museo Pedro de Osma Lima/Mireille Vautier; p. 89 (center) Mike von Bergen/ Shutterstock; p. 89 (bottom) Marshall Bruce/Shutterstock; p. 89 (top left) Chris Howey/Shutterstock; p. 89 (bottom left) Paul Clarke/Shutterstock; p. 89 (top left) Nicholas Raymond/Shutterstock; p. 90 (top left) Todd B. Powell/Creative Eye/MIRA.com; p. 90 (top right) Nik Wheeler; p. 90 (center) Robert Frerck/Odyssey Productions, Inc.; p. 90 (bottom) © Bob Daemmrich/PhotoEdit; p. 94 Adalberto Rios Szalay/Sexto Sol/Getty Images, Inc.—Photodisc; p. 96 © John Van Hasselt/Sygma/ CORBIS; p. 103 (top) Getty Images, Inc.; p. 103 (top center) William Albert Allard/NGS Image Collection; p. 103 (bottom center) © Victor Englebert; p. 103 (bottom) Chad Ehlers/Stock Connection; p. 118 (top) © Scala/Art Resource; p. 118 (bottom) Dagli Orti/Picture Desk, Inc./Kobal Collection; p. 122 Fernando Botero, "En familia" (The Family). © Fernando Botero, courtesy of Marlborough Gallery, New York; p. 123 (center left) © Alejandro Velasquez; p. 123 (top) © Amra Pasic/Shutterstock; p. 123 (center right) © John Chang/Courtesy of www.istockphoto.com; p. 123 (bottom left) © Richard Gunion/Courtesy of www.istockphoto.com; p. 123 (bottom right) © Galyna Andrushko/Shutterstock; p. 124 (left) © Paloma Lapuerta; p. 124 (center) Tony Freeman/PhotoEdit Inc.; p. 124 (right) Michael Newman/PhotoEdit Inc.; p. 138 © Andre Schafer/Courtesy of www. istockphoto.com; p. 147 (top) Ellen Senisi; p. 147 (bottom) Bill Aron/PhotoEdit Inc.; p. 150 HERMANN BREHM/Nature Picture Library; p. 151 Colombia Information Service Tourist Office; p. 154 Mireille Vautier/ Woodfin Camp & Associates, Inc.; p. 155 (top) © Toon Possemiers/Courtesy of www.istockphoto. com; p. 155 (bottom left) Jeff Chevrier/Courtesy of www. istockphoto.com; p. 155 (bottom right) © Eli Coory/Fotolia; p. 155 (center right) Courtesy of www.istockphoto.com; p. 155 (center left) © Tatiana Popova/Shutterstock; p. 155 (center left) © Kmitu/Shutterstock; p. 155 (center left) © Valentyn Volkov/Shutterstock; p. 156 © Nik Wheeler/Alamy; p. 166 (top) Bruce Ayres/Getty Images Inc.—Stone Allstock; p. 166 (bottom) AP Wide World Photos; p. 166 (right) Robert Frerck/Odyssey Productions Inc.—Stone Allstock; p. 170 (left) Laura Dwight/PhotoEdit Inc.; p. 170 (center) Tony Freeman/PhotoEdit Inc.; p. 170 (right) Robert Fried/robertfriedphotography. com; p. 184 Brennan Linsley/AP Wide World

Photos; p. 185 (top) © Bettmann/CORBIS All Rights Reserved; p. 185 (bottom) Luis Romero/ AP Wide World Photos; p. 188 Simon Bolivar (1783–1830) (chromolitho) by Artist Unknown (pre 20th century). Private Collection/Archives Charmet/Bridgeman Art Library; p. 189 (center) Jos? Enrique Molina/ AGE Fotostock America, Inc.; p. 189 (bottom right) Mark Cosslett/National Geographic Image Collection; p. 189 (bottom left) Rhodes, Leonard L T/ Animals Animals/ Earth Scenes; p. 189 (top) © Kimberly White/Reuters/ CORBIS All Rights Reserved; p. 190 (top) Ulrike Welsch/PhotoEdit Inc.; p. 190 (center) Beryl Goldberg; p. 190 (bottom) Jeff Greenberg/PhotoEdit Inc.; p. 202 (left) David Welling/Nature Picture Library; p. 202 (center) © Patrick Keen/Courtesy of www.istockphoto. com; p. 202 (right) © Yann Arthus-Bertrand/Bettmann/ CORBIS; p. 202 (bottom) Silva, Juan/Getty Images Inc.— Image Bank; p. 208 (left) Getty Images, Inc.; p. 208 (center) AP Wide World Photos; p. 208 (right) AP Wide World Photos; p. 210 Gordon, Larry Dale/Getty Images Inc.—Image Bank; p. 211 (left) © Lluis Gene/AFP/ Getty; p. 211 (center) Getty Images; p. 211 (right) Courtesy of Marshall Field's; p. 218 © Michael Stokes/ Shutterstock; p. 219 (top) Joese Caruci/AP Wide World Photos; p. 219 (bottom) © Javier Galeano/AP Wide World; p. 222 Xul Solar (Argentina 1887–1963), "Jefa (Patroness)". 1923. Watercolor on paper, set on cardboard. 10"x 10" (25.4 x 25.4 cm); Framed: 21 3/4" x 21 3/4" (55.2 x 55.2 cm). The Museum of Fine Arts, Houston; Museum purchase with funds provided by the Latin American Experience Gala and Auction; p. 223 (center left) © Mariano Heluani/Shutterstock; p. 223 (bottom center) © Wolfgang Kaehler www.wkaehlerphoto.com; p. 223 (bottom) Ivonne Wierink-vanWetten/Courtesy of www.istockphoto.com; p. 223 (mid-center right) Daniel Rivademar/Odyssey Productions, Inc.; p. 223 (top) © Galina Barskaya/Shutter-stock; p. 224 (top) © Marcos Brindicci/ Reuters/CORBIS; p. 224 (center) Bill Bachmann/PhotoEdit Inc.; p. 224 (bottom) © Chen Wei Seng/Shutterstock; p. 226 (left) © James M. Phelps, Jr./Shutterstock; p. 226 (center) © Kanwarjit Singh Boparai/ Shutterstock; p. 226 (right) © Adrees Latif/ Reuters/CORBIS; p. 249 (left) CARL SCHNEIDER/ Getty Images, Inc.—Taxi; p. 249 (right) © Monique Rodriguez/Courtesy of www.istockphoto.com; p. 249 (bottom) Courtesy of www.istockphoto.com; p. 252 © Stuart Cohen/The Image Works; p. 253 (top) Geoff Brightling © Dorling Kindersley; p. 253 (bottom) Getty Images Inc.—Hulton Archive Photos; p. 256 Frida Kahlo, "Self-Portrait at the Border Between Mexico and the United States". 1932. Museo Nacional de Arte Moderno, © 2001 Banco de Mexico Diego Rivera & Frida Kahlo Museums Trust. Av. Cinco de Mayo No. 2, Col. Centro, Del. Cuauhtemoc 06059, Mexico, D.F. Reproduction authorized by the Instituto Nacional de Bellas Artes y Literatura. © Christie's Images/CORBIS All

**A54**

# Language Functions Index

# Subject Index

# The University of New Mexico

## Spanish as a Second Language Program
## Appendix Materials

1.)    Mission Statement

2.)    Course Descriptions

3.)    Grading Rubrics

   a. Compositions

   b. Oral Exam

4.)    Peer Editing Forms

# University of New Mexico
## Department of Spanish and Portuguese

### Our Mission

The mission of the Department of Spanish and Portuguese is to promote quality teaching and research that integrate the languages, literatures, linguistics and cultures of the Spanish-and-Portuguese-speaking worlds. We share our expertise with the university community, the city of Albuquerque, and the state of New Mexico. We are especially committed to revitalizing the Spanish language in New Mexico and to studying the interactions between cultures in the Southwest. Faculty and students work together in the classroom, in the community, and in study abroad to develop understanding, sensitive communication and critical thinking about our diverse and interconnected world. The Department prepares its' students with the skills, knowledge, and values necessary to lead productive and fulfilling lives as citizens and life-long learners.

### Nuestra misión

La misión del Departamento de Español y Portugués es promover la calidad de la enseñanza y de la investigación integrando las lenguas, literaturas, lingüística y culturas del mundo de habla española y portuguesa. Compartimos nuestra experiencia con la comunidad universitaria, con la ciudad de Albuquerque y con el Estado de Nuevo México. Estamos comprometidos especialmente con la revitalización de la lengua española en Nuevo México y con el estudio de las interacciones culturales en el Sudoeste de los Estados Unidos. Profesores y estudiantes trabajan juntos en las clases, en la comunidad y en los estudios internacionales para desarrollar la comunicación sensible, el pensamiento crítico y la comprensión de nuestro mundo diverso e interconectado. El Departamento prepara a sus estudiantes con la capacidad, el conocimiento y los valores necesarios para liderar sus vidas de forma productiva y satisfactoria como ciudadanos y como personas que nunca pierdan el interés de aprender.

### Nossa missão

A missão do departamento de espanhol e português é a de promover qualidade no campo do ensino e no da pesquisa que integrem as línguas, literaturas, lingüística e culturas do mundo hispano e luso-falante. Nós compartimos nosso conhecimento com a comunidade universitária, a cidade de Albuquerque e o estado de Novo México. Estamos especialmente dedicados a revitalizar a língua espanhola no Novo México e a investigar as interações entre as diferentes culturas do Sudoeste dos Estados Unidos. Professores e estudantes trabalham juntos na sala de aula, na comunidade e em programas de estudos no estrangeiro para desenvolver a comprensão, a comunicação respeituosa assim como o pensamento crítico sobre o nosso mundo diverso e, ao mesmo tempo, interconectado. O departamento prepara os/as seus/suas estudantes desenvolvendo suas habilidades, seus conhecimentos e os princípios necessários para que eles/elas possam ter vidas produtivas e realizadas tanto como cidadãos/ãs como contínuos alunos/as.

# Spanish as a Second Language
## Course Descriptions

## SPANISH 101

Spanish 101 is the first semester course in the four-semester Spanish as a Second Language Series. It is designed to introduce you to the Spanish language and the many facets of Hispanic culture. It also aims to develop basic second language skills for both oral (speaking and listening) and written (reading and writing) communication. In this course, you will develop your ability to communicate in Spanish in everyday situations.

Throughout the courses, you will:

> 1. Engage in conversations and written communication to describe daily activities, obtain information, express feelings and emotions, and give and ask directions.
>
> 2. Develop skills for understanding written and spoken language on the following topics: academic life, family, free time, and vacation.
>
> 3. Demonstrate understanding of the culture in the Americas and Spain.

## SPANISH 102

Spanish 102 is the second semester course in the four-semester Spanish as a Second Language Series. It is designed to continue to introduce you to the Spanish language and the many facets of Hispanic culture as well as review what you have learned in previous semesters. In doing so, it aims to develop basic second language skills for both oral (speaking and listening) and written (reading and writing) communication. In this course, you will develop your ability to communicate in Spanish in everyday situations.

Throughout the courses, you will:

> Engage in conversations and written communication related to a variety of topics.
>
> Develop skills for understanding written and spoken Spanish.
>
> Demonstrate understanding of the culture in the Americas and Spain.

# COMPOSITION GRADING RUBRIC: SPAN 101, 102, 275/276, 201, 202

| Category | Score | Rating | Description |
|---|---|---|---|
| **Focus/content** | 30- | Excellent-very good | Has fully anticipated reader questions in selecting information; topic well-thought-out and carefully developed with effective supporting detail; interesting to read. |
| | 24- | Good-Adequate | Has anticipated most reader questions in selecting information; topic may not be fully explored; development is adequate although some ideas may be incompletely supported or irrelevant; interesting ideas in places. |
| | 18- | Fair- Poor | Has anticipated few reader needs in selecting information; topic explored only superficially and inadequately developed with many ideas unsupported or irrelevant. |
| | 12-7 | Needs a lot of work | Shows no awareness of reader needs; ideas superficial and/or uninteresting with little development; OR not enough to evaluate. |
| | 6-0 | Not appropriate | Message is unclear or topic is inappropriate. No topic development or supported. Essay wanders from thesis statement. |
| **Organization** | 15- | Excellent-Very good | Has fully anticipated reader needs in organizing and presenting information; clear thesis; flow of ideas fluid and logical; a pleasure to read. |
| | 13- | Good-Adequate | Has anticipated most reader needs in organizing and presenting information; main ideas stand out, but sequencing of ideas somewhat choppy or disconnected; reader may sometimes have difficulty following flow of ideas. |
| | 11- | Fair-Poor | Has anticipated few reader needs in organizing and presenting information; ideas frequently confused and/or disconnected, with logical breakdowns apparent; reader frequently has difficulty 'getting the point' of message as communicated. |
| | 9-7 | Needs a lot of work | Shows no awareness of reader needs; logical organization absent; OR not enough to evaluate. |
| | 6-0 | Not appropriate | Writing is scattered. Lack of unity, cohesion and development. No evidence of planning in structure or paragraphs. |
| **Grammar** | 30- | Excellent-very good | Wide range of structures with few or no significant errors (e.g., sentence structure). |
| | 24- | Good-Adequate | Adequate range of structures, but little variety; tends to overuse simple constructions; both significant and minor errors (e.g., agreement) present, but meaning seldom obscured. |
| | 18- | Fair-Poor | Limited range of structures with control of grammar uncertain; errors frequent, especially when more complex constructions attempted; meaning often confused or obscured. |
| | 12-7 | Needs a lot of work | Frequent and persistent errors of basic grammar and sentence construction; meaning blocked as text dominated by errors; OR, not enough to evaluate. |
| | 6-0 | Not appropriate | No mastery of sentence construction. Errors obscure meaning. Text is dominated by grammatical inaccuracy. |

| Category | Points | Rating | Description |
|---|---|---|---|
| **Vocabulary** | 15- | **Excellent-very good** | Language choices appropriate for topic, purpose and reader; excellent use of idioms and precise, colorful vocabulary; little or no evidence of English interference. |
| | 13- | **Good-Adequate** | Language choices usually appropriate for topic, purpose and reader; vocabulary adequate but somewhat limited; some errors or interference may be present but meaning rarely obscured. |
| | 11- | **Fair-Poor** | Language choices sometimes inappropriate for topic, purpose and reader; vocabulary very limited, with overuse of imprecise or vague terms; English interference evident; particularly with respect to idioms; meaning often confused or obscured. |
| | 9-7 | **Needs a lot of work** | Language choices often inappropriate for topic, purpose and reader; range of vocabulary extremely limited; English interference frequent; OR not enough to evaluate. |
| | 6-0 | **Not appropriate** | Paper is essentially a translation from English. Little use of Spanish vocabulary, idioms, word forms. |
| **Conventions** | 10-9 | **Excellent-Very good** | Very few or no faults with respect to spelling/accentuation, punctuation or presentation (handwriting or typing). |
| | 8-7 | **Good-Adequate** | Occasional faults in spelling/accentuation, punctuation or presentation (handwriting or typing). |
| | 6-5 | **Fair-Poor** | Frequent errors in spelling/accentuation or punctuation; messy presentation that is sometimes illegible. |
| | 4-3 | **Needs a lot of work** | Persistent errors in spelling/accentuation and punctuation; handwriting often illegible; OR not enough to evaluate. |
| | 2-0 | **Not appropriate** | No mastery of conventions. Paper is dominated by errors of spelling, punctuation, capitalization and paragraphing. |
| **Total** | 100 | **Comments:** | |
| **Total** | | | |

**Oral Exam – Evaluation Sheet**

Nombre del estudiante: _____     Fecha: _____

| # of points | Content/information conveyed/interaction | Comprehensibility/ Pronunciation | Fluency | Vocabulary | Grammar | Student total |
|---|---|---|---|---|---|---|
| 18-20 A | Contributes relevant information. Develops ideas by speaking in multiple sentences. Consistent performance across entire activity. Is pivotal in maintaining interaction. Initiates interaction. Consistently responds to others' comments/ideas. | Stays all in Spanish and comprehensibility not affected by errors. | Speech natural and continuous; no unnatural pauses | Demonstrates extensive vocabulary. No use of English. Almost always uses appropriate word. Rarely if ever searches for words. | Uses appropriate syntax and morphological form. Controls most structures used (consistently high performance). Few error types. | |
| 16-17 B | Contributes relevant information. Some development of ideas but tends to use single sentences. Not so consistent performance across the entire activity. Helps maintain/initiates interaction. Often responds to others' ideas. | Stays all in Spanish but comprehensibility sometimes affected. | Speech generally natural and continuous; only slight stumbling or unnatural pauses | Demonstrates a large vocabulary. No use of English words. Almost always uses appropriate word. Seldom misses or searches for words. | Uses mostly appropriate syntax and morphological forms. Controls some structures used (some inconsistency in performance). Errors are infrequent | |
| 14-15 C | Contributes adequate information. Not much development of ideas. Almost always speaks in single sentences. Rarely helps maintain the interaction OR dominates the interaction. | Sometimes uses of English and/or comprehensibility is affected. | Some definite stumbling, but manages to rephrase or continue | Demonstrates moderate size vocabulary. Sometimes uses English or invents words. Frequently misses or searches for words. | Uses inappropriate syntax and morphological forms. Controls very few structures. Errors are frequent. | |
| 12-13 D | Contributes little information or information lacks substance, is superficial, inappropriate, or irrelevant. Speaks in single sentences or only in phrases. OR definitely dominates the interaction. | Overuse of English and/or comprehensibility is an issue. | Speech frequently hesitant and jerky; sentences may be left uncompleted | Demonstrates small vocabulary. Overuses English or overuses invented words. Vocabulary limits interaction. | Uses inappropriate syntax and morphological forms. Control of structures is an issue. Errors dominate. | |
| Total | | | | | | |

**Peer Editing – Capítulo 1 *En la Universidad* (A escribir, p. 49)**

Please read your partner's email all the way through before filling out this sheet. After reading all the way through, answer the following questions in order to help him/her with his/her composition.

Formatting:
Is the composition:    double spaced?_____

12 pt font?_____

1" Margins?_____

Look like an email?_____

Include a greeting and closing?_____

Are the accents included in the computer font and not written in?_____

Organization
Is the email organized into clear sections? _____

If not, give one suggestion as to how it could better be organized.

Is so, what do you like about it?

Does the writer use various transition words and vary sentence length?_____

Content
Does the writer address the following points?
- Introduction
- Tell how things are going
- Describe school, classes, and professors
- Describe his/her daily routine

If not, give two suggestions as to how it could be changed or added to.

Is so, what do you like about the content?

Are specific details from the pre-writing activities included? _____

Overall, what is one GREAT thing about the composition?

What is one thing that can be improved?

jms-peer editing;

## Peer Editing – Capítulo 2 *Mis amigos y yo* (A escribir, p. 82-83)

Please read your partner's email response all the way through before filling out this sheet. After reading all the way through, answer the following questions in order to help him/her with his/her composition.

Formatting:
Is the composition:    double spaced?_____

12 pt font?_____

1" Margins?_____

Look like an email?_____

Include a greeting and closing?_____

Are the accents included in the computer font and not written in?_____

Organization
Is the email organized into clear sections? _____

If not, give one suggestion as to how it could better be organized.



Is so, what do you like about it?



Does the writer use various transition words and vary sentence length?_____

Content
Does the writer address the following points?
- Introduction
- Your age
- Place of origin
- Physical description
- Personality description
- Daily routine

If not, give two suggestions as to how it could be changed or added to.

Is so, what do you like about the content?

Are specific details from the pre-writing activities included? _____



Overall, what is one GREAT thing about the composition?

What is one thing that can be improved?



jms-peer editing;

## Peer Editing – Capítulo 3 *El tiempo libre* (A escribir, p. 117)

Please read your partner's letter all the way through before filling out this sheet. After reading all the way through, answer the following questions in order to help him/her with his/her composition.

Formatting:
Is the composition:    double spaced?_____

12 pt font?_____

1" Margins?_____

Look like a letter?_____

Include a greeting and closing?_____

Are the accents included in the computer font and not written in?_____

Organization
Is the letter organized into clear sections? _____

If not, give one suggestion as to how it could better be organized.

Is so, what do you like about it?

Does the writer use various transition words and vary sentence length?_____

Content
Does the writer address the following points?
- Introduction
- A description of the place
- A description of the activities you can do there

If not, give two suggestions as to how it could be changed or added to.

Is so, what do you like about the content?

Are specific details from the pre-writing activities included? _____

Overall, what is one GREAT thing about the composition?

What is one thing that can be improved?

jms-peer editing;

| **Peer Editing – Capítulo 4 *En familia* (A escribir, p. 148-149)** |
|---|

Please read your partner's letter all the way through before filling out this sheet. After reading all the way through, answer the following questions in order to help him/her with his/her composition.

Formatting:
Is the composition:    double spaced?_____

                               12 pt font?_____

                               1" Margins?_____

                               Look like a formal letter?_____

                               Include a greeting and closing?_____

                               Are the accents included in the computer font and not written in?_____

Organization
Is the letter organized into clear sections? _____

If not, give one suggestion as to how it could better be organized.


Is so, what do you like about it?


Does the writer use various transition words and vary sentence length?_____

Content
Does the writer address the following points?
- Introduction
- An answer to all of the mother's questions
- A respectful response

If not, give two suggestions as to how it could be changed or added to.


Is so, what do you like about the content?

Are specific details from the pre-writing activities included? _____


Overall, what is one GREAT thing about the composition?

What is one thing that can be improved?


jms-peer editing;

| **Peer Editing – Capítulo 5** *Mi casa es su casa* **(A escribir, p. 183)** |
| --- |

Please read your partner's brochure all the way through before filling out this sheet. After reading all the way through, answer the following questions in order to help him/her with his/her composition.

Formatting:
Is the composition:    double spaced?_____

                          12 pt font?_____

                          1" Margins?_____

                          Look like a brochure?_____

                          Include proper formatting?_____

                          Are the accents included in the computer font and not written in?_____

Organization
Is the brochure organized into clear sections? _____

If not, give one suggestion as to how it could better be organized.

Is so, what do you like about it?

Does the writer use various transition words and vary sentence length?_____

Content
Does the writer address the following points?
- Personal information
- A description of house
- A drawing or photo of the house (or parts of the house)

If not, give two suggestions as to how it could be changed or added to.

Is so, what do you like about the content?

Are specific details from the pre-writing activities included? _____

Overall, what is one GREAT thing about the composition?

What is one thing that can be improved?

jms-peer editing;

Please read your partner's letter all the way through before filling out this sheet. After reading all the way through, answer the following questions in order to help him/her with his/her composition.

Formatting:
Is the composition:     double spaced?_____

                          12 pt font?_____

                          1" Margins?_____

                          Look like a letter?_____

                          Include a greeting and closing?_____

                          Are the accents included in the computer font and not written in?_____

Organization
Is the letter organized into clear sections? _____

If not, give one suggestion as to how it could better be organized.


Is so, what do you like about it?


Does the writer use various transition words and vary sentence length?_____

Content
Does the writer address the following points?
- Introduction
- The name of the store where you bought the item
- A description of the problem and the events that occured

If not, give two suggestions as to how it could be changed or added to.


Is so, what do you like about the content?

Are specific details from the pre-writing activities included? _____


Overall, what is one GREAT thing about the composition?

What is one thing that can be improved?

Please read your partner's article all the way through before filling out this sheet.  After reading all the way through, answer the following questions in order to help him/her with his/her composition.

<u>Formatting:</u>
Is the composition:     double spaced?_____

                            12 pt font?_____

                            1" Margins?_____

                            Look like an article?_____

                            Include an opening and closing?_____

                            Are the accents included in the computer font and not written in?_____

<u>Organization</u>
Is the article organized into clear sections? _____

If not, give one suggestion as to how it could better be organized.

Is so, what do you like about it?

Does the writer use various transition words and vary sentence length?_____

<u>Content</u>
Does the writer address the following points?
- The benefits of exercise
- A description of various types of physical activity
- A description of the frequency and amount of exercise one needs

If not, give two suggestions as to how it could be changed or added to.

Is so, what do you like about the content?

Are specific details from the pre-writing activities included? _____

Overall, what is one GREAT thing about the composition?

What is one thing that can be improved?

jms-peer editing;

Please read your partner's personal history all the way through before filling out this sheet. After reading all the way through, answer the following questions in order to help him/her with his/her composition.

<u>Formatting:</u>
Is the composition:    double spaced?_____

                                 12 pt font?_____

                                 1" Margins?_____

                                 Look like a personal history?_____

                                 Are the accents included in the computer font and not written in?_____

<u>Organization</u>
Is the story organized into clear sections? _____

If not, give one suggestion as to how it could better be organized.

Is so, what do you like about it?

Does the writer use various transition words and vary sentence length?_____

<u>Content</u>
Does the writer use a personal narration to describe his or her experience?

If not, give two suggestions as to how it could be changed or added to.

Is so, what do you like about the content?

Are specific details from the pre-writing activities included? _____

Overall, what is one GREAT thing about the composition?

What is one thing that can be improved?

| **Peer Editing – Capítulo 9** *Hay que trabajar* **(A escribir, p. 321)** |
|---|

Please read your partner's letter all the way through before filling out this sheet.  After reading all the way through, answer the following questions in order to help him/her with his/her composition.

Formatting:
Is the composition:  double spaced?_____

12 pt font?_____

1" Margins?_____

Look like a formal letter?_____

Include a greeting and closing?_____

Are the accents included in the computer font and not written in?_____

Organization
Is the letter organized into clear sections? _____

If not, give one suggestion as to how it could better be organized.

Is so, what do you like about it?

Does the writer use various transition words and vary sentence length?_____

Content
Does the writer address the following points?
- Introduction
- A description of his/her experience, knowledge, and talents
- A closing

If not, give two suggestions as to how it could be changed or added to.

Is so, what do you like about the content?

Are specific details from the pre-writing activities included? _____

Overall, what is one GREAT thing about the composition?

What is one thing that can be improved?

jms-peer editing;

**Peer Editing – Capítulo 10 *¡A comer!* (A escribir, p. 357)**

Please read your partner's article all the way through before filling out this sheet. After reading all the way through, answer the following questions in order to help him/her with his/her composition.

Formatting:
Is the composition:    double spaced?_____

                               12 pt font?_____

                               1" Margins?_____

                               Look like a summary?_____

                               Include an opening and closing?_____

                               Are the accents included in the computer font and not written in?_____

Organization
Is the article organized into clear sections? _____

If not, give one suggestion as to how it could better be organized.


Is so, what do you like about it?


Does the writer use various transition words and vary sentence length?_____

Content
Does the writer address the following points?
- The main ideas of the article **IN HIS OR HER OWN WORDS**
- A short opinion of the aricle

If not, give two suggestions as to how it could be changed or added to.


Is so, what do you like about the content?

Are specific details from the pre-writing activities included? _____


Overall, what is one GREAT thing about the composition?

What is one thing that can be improved?


jms-peer editing;

Mar Caribe

OCÉANO
ATLÁNTICO

Barranquilla
Cartagena
Maracaibo
Caracas
Barquisimeto
Río Orinoco
VENEZUELA
Georgetown
Paramaribo
Medellín
GUYANA
Cayenne
Manizales
Salto
Ángel
SURINAM
GUAYANA
FRANCESA
(Francia)
Cali
Bogotá
COLOMBIA
CORDILLERA DE LOS ANDES

Quito
ECUADOR
Ecuador
Guayaquil
Cuenca
Iquitos
Manaus
Río Amazonas
Belém

Islas
Galápagos
(Ec.)
Río Madeira
Fortaleza

Cajamarca

Trujillo
PERÚ
Río Branco
B R A S I L
Recife

Machu
Picchu
Lima
Ayacucho
Cuzco
BOLIVIA
Salvador

OCÉANO
PACÍFICO
I. Pinta
I. Fernandina
I. Marchena
I. San Salvador
I. Isabela
Santa Cruz
I. Santa Cruz
Puerto
Ayora
I. San
Cristóbal
Puerto
Villamil
Puerto
Baquerizo
Moreno
Arequipa
La Paz
Lago
Titicaca
Cochabamba
Santa Cruz
Brasília

Arica
Sucre
Potosí
Belo
Horizonte

Iquique
PARAGUAY

ISLAS GALÁPAGOS
(ECUADOR)
Antofagasta
Desierto de Atacama
Salta
Asunción
Salto
Iguazú
São Paulo
Santos
Río de Janeiro
Trópico de Capricornio

OCÉANO
PACÍFICO
CHILE
San Miguel
de Tucumán
ARGENTINA
Pôrto Alegre

Cabo Norte
Volcán
Katiki
Cabo
Cumming
Coquimbo
Córdoba
Rosario
Rivera
URUGUAY
Hanga Roa
Mataveri
Valparaíso
Santiago
Mendoza
Buenos Aires
La Plata
Montevideo
Río de la Plata

ISLA
Concepción
Bahía Blanca
OCÉANO
ATLÁNTICO

Puerto Montt

Estrecho de
Magallanes
Islas
Malvinas
(G.B.)

Punta Arenas
TIERRA DEL FUEGO
Cabo de Hornos